KT-529-606

Destination: Scotland

Like a fine single malt, Scotland is a connoisseur's delight – a land of salt-tanged sea air, peaty waters and a rich, multi-layered history that reveals its true depth and complex flavours only to those who savour it slowly.

It's a place where you can watch golden eagles soar over the bare, rock peaks of the Cuillin, play golf on some of the world's most hallowed courses, or ride a high-speed boat through the surging white water of the Corryvreckan whirlpool. It's a place where every corner of the landscape is steeped in the past: a deserted croft on an island shore, a moor that was once a battlefield, a beach where Vikings hauled their boats ashore, a cave where Bonnie Prince Charlie once sheltered.

And it's a place that changes with the seasons, offering something new each time you visit. Spring means a lilac haze of bluebells in the woods around Loch Lomond, and a frenzy of seabirds on the cliffs around the coast. In summer the Hebridean island beaches flaunt their golden sands and turquoise waters like Caribbean imposters, while boat-trip passengers 'ooh' and 'aah' at their first sight of a breaching minke whale.

In September the Loch Fyne oysters are at their juicy best, while October brings a riot of autumn colour to the Perthshire forests, and in the Highland hills you can hear the roaring of the red deer stags in rut. In winter a fresh layer of crisp snow lends grandeur to the mountains of Glen Coe. And what could be cosier than curling up in front of a log fire in a country-house hotel while the frost sparkles on the pine trees outside?

GRANT DIXON

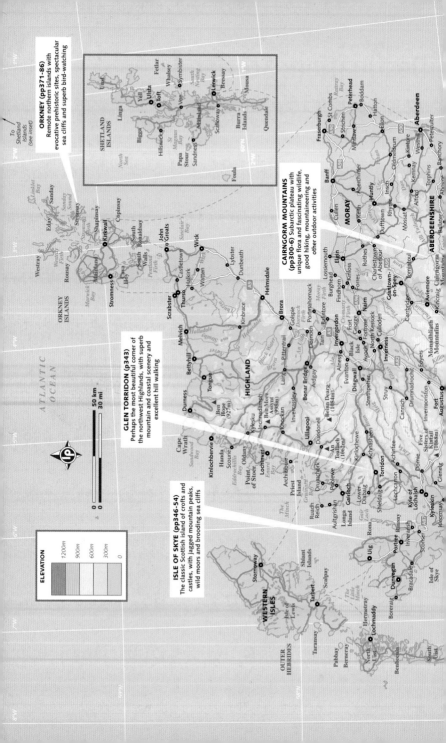

ORKNEY (pp371–86) Remote northern islands with evocative prehistoric sites, spectacular sea cliffs and superb bird-watching

CAIRNGORM MOUNTAINS (pp300–6) Subarctic plateau with unique flora and fascinating wildlife, good hiking, mountaineering and other outdoor activities

GLEN TORRIDON (p343) Perhaps the most beautiful corner of the northwest Highlands, with superb mountain and coastal scenery and excellent hill walking

ISLE OF SKYE (pp346–54) The classic Scottish island of crofts and castles, with jagged mountain peaks, wild moors and brooding sea cliffs

ELEVATION

1200m
900m
600m
300m
0

0   50 km
0   30 mi

To Shetland Islands (see inset)

SHETLAND ISLANDS

North Sea

Fetlar
Yell
Unst
Toft
Whalsay
Symbister
Lerwick
Bressay
Linga
Brae
Voe
Mainland
Bigton
Scalloway
Hillswick
Papa Stour
Sandness
Burra Islands
Mousa
Foula
Quendale

Atlantic Ocean

ORKNEY ISLANDS

Sanday
Eday
Westray
Shapinsay
Stromness
Kirkwall
Rousay
Hoy
Mainland
Copinsay
South Ronaldsay
South Walls
Flotta

John O'Groats
Castletown
Thurso
Scrabster
Halkirk
Wick
Lybster
Dunbeath

Durness
Bettyhill
Melvich
Tongue
Ben Hope (927m)
Helmsdale
Brora
Golspie
Dornoch
Portmahomack

Cape Wrath
Kinlochbervie
Scourie
Handa Island
Oldany
Lochinver
Point of Stoer

HIGHLAND

Kylesku
Inchnadamph
Ben More Assynt (998m)
Knockan
Ullapool
Ardgay
Bonar Bridge
Lairg
Invershin
Alness
Evanton
Dingwall
Strathpeffer
Contin

Ben Dearg (1084m)

An Teallach (1062m)
Aultbea
Poolewe
Gairloch
Kinlochewe
Lower Diabaig
Torridon
Shieldaig
Lochcarron
Achnasheen
Cannich
Drumnadrochit
Invermoriston
Fort Augustus

WESTERN ISLES
OUTER HEBRIDES

Isle of Lewis
Stornoway
Tarbert
Scalpay
Shiant Islands

Pabbay
Bernaray
North Uist
Lochmaddy
Benbecula
South Uist

Hermetray
Boreraig

Isle of Skye
Dunvegan
Portree
Raasay
Bracadale
Uig
Sconser

Rona
Longa Island
Ruadh Reidh
Gruinard Island
Priest Island
Summer Isles

Kyle of Lochalsh
Kyleakin
Glenelg
Dornie
Kintail
Five Sisters of Kintail (1068m)

Inverness
Nairn
Culloden
Black Isle
Avoch
Fortrose
North Kessock
Beauly

MORAY

Lossiemouth
Burghead
Elgin
Findhorn
Forres
Kinloss
Charlestown of Aberlour
Grantown-on-Spey
Aviemore
Kincraig
Kingussie
Monadhliath Mountains
Cairngorm Mountains

Banff
Cullen
Keith
Dufftown
Rhynie
Huntly
Insch

ABERDEENSHIRE

Fraserburgh
St Combs
Strichen
Peterhead
Boddam
Mintlaw
Hatton
Ellon
Oldmeldrum
Inverurie
Kemnay
Torphins
Banchory
Aboyne
Ballater

Fettercairn
Aberchirder
Alford
Mossat
Tomintoul

Aberdeen
Westhill
Peterculter

LP

N

Scotland

Neil Wilson
Alan Murphy

Contents

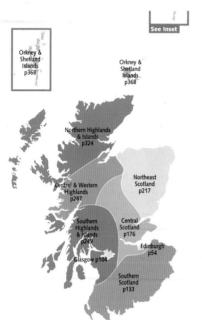

Orkney & Shetland Islands p368

See Inset

Orkney & Shetland Islands p368

Northern Highlands & Islands p324

Central & Western Highlands p287

Northeast Scotland p217

Southern Highlands & Islands p249

Central Scotland p176

Edinburgh p54

Glasgow p104

Southern Scotland p133

Lonely Planet books provide independent advice. Lonely Planet does not accept advertising in guidebooks, nor do we accept payment in exchange for listing or endorsing any place or business. Lonely Planet writers do not accept discounts or payments in exchange for positive coverage of any sort.

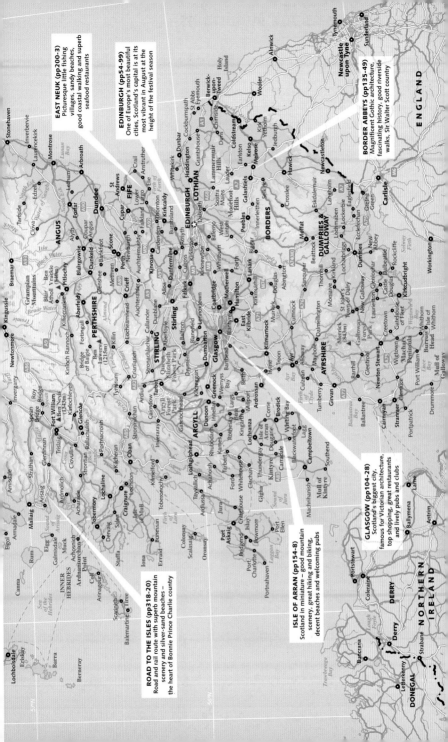

EAST NEUK (pp200-3)
Picturesque little fishing villages, sandy beaches, good coastal walking and superb seafood restaurants

EDINBURGH (pp54-99)
One of Europe's most beautiful cities, Scotland's capital is at its most vibrant in August at the height of the festival season

BORDER ABBEYS (pp135-49)
Magnificent Gothic architecture, fascinating history, good riverside walks, Sir Walter Scott country

ROAD TO THE ISLES (pp318-20)
Road and rail route with superb mountain scenery and silver-sand beaches – the heart of Bonnie Prince Charlie country

GLASGOW (pp104-28)
Scotland's biggest city, famous for Victorian architecture, top shopping, great restaurants and lively pubs and clubs

ISLE OF ARRAN (pp154-8)
Scotland in miniature – good mountain scenery, great hiking and biking, decent beaches and welcoming pubs

HIGHLIGHTS **Lochs and Mountains**

Scotland is famous for its magnificent scenery, whose charm lies in its mixture of mountain and loch. More than half the country is mountainous, stretching from the gentle, wooded hills of the **Trossachs** (p186) to the rugged wilderness of Sutherland around **Inverpolly** (p339).

Hike through the wild magnificence of **Glen Coe** (p308) or ride a **vintage steam train** (p312) across Glenfinnan Viaduct with its classic views along mountain-ringed Loch Shiel. Stroll along the shores of island-studded **Loch Maree** (p343), or take a boat trip to lonely **Loch Coruisk** (p349).

GRAEME CORNWALLIS

Take the ultimate challenge and climb UK's highest peak, **Ben Nevis** (p316)

CHRIS MELLOR

Cycle the road along the bonnie banks of **Loch Lomond** (p253)

Experience the remote beauty of the **Cairngorms** (p300)

GRAEME CORNWALL

GRANT DIXON

Wander off the beaten track beneath the wild hills of **Assynt** (p339)

Test your mountaineering skills on the jagged rock pinnacles of **Cuillin Hills** (p349)

GARETH MCCORMACK

GRAEME CORNWALLIS

Admire the beautiful mountain scenery near **Glen Torridon** (p343)

Scotland has some of Europe's finest hiking territory. The most popular trail is the **West Highland Way** (p253), which winds through magnificent scenery from Glasgow to Fort William. The less crowded **Southern Upland Way** (p135) is twice as long. Enjoy less strenuous walking close to Edinburgh on the Fife Coastal Path in the **East Neuk** (p200) and at **St Abb's Head** (p140).

Escape the mainland crowds on the **Isle of Eigg** (p322), or head for the wilds of **Knoydart** (p320). For sheer beauty, **Glen Affric** (p296) comes top.

Escape to the outlying islands of **Orkney** (p371)

Marvel at the beauty of Loch Shiel from historic **Glenfinnan** (p318)

For more challenging hiking, head to the **Isle of Jura** (p267)

GRAEME CORNWALLIS

Walk to the eerie Machrie Moor standing stones on the **Isle of Arran** (p154)

NEIL WILSON

Explore Jedburgh Abbey, one of the highlights of the **Borders Abbeys way** walk (p135)

Enjoy easy coastal walking around the Fife fishing village of **Crail** (p201)

GRAEME CORNWALLIS

Think of Scotland and you think of castles. Built by the aristocracy as expressions of their wealth and taste, they range from the elegant, neoclassical designs of Robert and William Adam, such as Culzean Castle and the refined **Hopetoun House** (p100), to the various manifestations of the Scottish Baronial style, including flamboyant Victorian-era revivals such as **Blair Castle** (p215) and **Torosay Castle** (p277).

JONATHAN SMITH

Explore the haunted crypt and chapel at **Glamis Castle** (p225)

Wallow in the neo-Gothic extravagance of **Mount Stuart** (p257)

GRAEME CORNWALLIS

Hunt for hidden rooms in rambling, romantic **Traquair House** (p148)

NEIL WILS

GRAEME CORNWALLIS

Marvel at the Edwardian eccentricity of **Kinloch Castle** (p321)

NICHOLAS REUSS

Admire the elegant, Robert Adams-designed **Culzean Castle** (p162)

Appreciate the original Scottish Baronial architecture of **Craigievar Castle** (p241)

STEPHEN SAKS

Scotland's cities offer inspiring architecture, great museums and galleries, and lively pubs and clubs. Edinburgh is famous for its castle, but don't miss the **Royal Yacht Britannia** (p72), the view from **Calton Hill** (p62) and the picture postcard village of **Cramond** (p72). Some of Glasgow's most memorable architecture and design includes the **Glasgow School of Art** (p112) and the **Willow Tea Rooms** (p112). There's more culture to soak up on the banks of the Tay at **Dundee Contemporary Arts Centre** (p222). Aberdeen's finest architecture includes the Gothic granite masterpiece of **Marischal College** (p233).

PAUL KENNEDY

Experience the vibrancy of Princes Street, **Edinburgh** (p69)

Explore the alleys and pubs along Edinburgh's famous **Royal Mile** (p63)

BETHUNE CARMICHAEL

Catch a rock concert at Glasgow's 'Armadillo', the **Clyde Auditorium** (p125)

MARTIN M

Getting Started

Scotland is the sort of place you can arrive in without a plan, and have a great time just wandering around and following your whims. But planning your trip is half the fun, and essential if your time is limited or if there is something in particular that you want to see or do.

WHEN TO GO

Any time is a good time to visit Scotland, but your choice of when to go will depend on what you want to do.

The main tourist period is April to September, and the height of the season is during the school holidays in July and August when accommodation, be it camping grounds, B&Bs or luxury hotels, is at a premium. Edinburgh in particular becomes impossibly crowded during the festival period in August so book well ahead if you plan to visit then (a year ahead is not too soon to start planning!).

See climate charts (p407) for more information.

In winter public transport is less frequent and travel to the islands can be a problem if high winds disrupt the ferries. Outside the main cities, some tourist attractions are closed from November to March.

Considering how far north it lies – Edinburgh is on the same latitude as Labrador in Canada – you might expect Scotland to have a colder climate, but the breezes from the Atlantic are warmed by the Gulf Stream, a warm ocean current that flows from the southeast coast of the USA and bathes the western shores of the British Isles. The southern Highlands (p249) are famous for their balmy climate, and palm trees and other subtropical plants grow outdoors here.

The east coast tends to be drier than the west – rainfall averages around 650mm – and it is often warmer in summer and colder in winter. Temperatures rarely drop below 0°C on the coast, although a wind blowing off the North Sea will make you shiver any time of year. The west coast is milder and wetter, with more than 1500mm of rain and average summer highs of 19°C. The western Highlands around Fort William are the wettest place in Britain, with annual rainfall as high as 3000mm.

Statistically, your best chances of fine weather are in May, June and September; July and August are usually warm, but may be wet too. In summer daylight hours are long; the midsummer sun sets around 11pm in the Shetland Islands and even Edinburgh evenings seem to last forever in June and July. Conversely, in December the sun doesn't show its face until after 9am, and it's dark again by 4pm.

In April and May Scotland's glorious scenery is set off by snow lingering on the mountains and colourful displays of wildflowers in the bluebell woods of southern Scotland and the machair of the Western Isles. June brings a pink haze of rhododendron blossoms to the Highland glens,

---

DON'T LEAVE HOME WITHOUT...

- a copy of your travel insurance policy details (p410)
- a pair of binoculars for whale- and dolphin-spotting
- insect repellent (p208)
- waterproofs, patience and a sense of adventure.

but it's not until August that the hillsides put on their famous show of purple heather.

October sees the forests of Perthshire and the Trossachs come alight with a blaze of glorious autumn colours. Midwinter can be *dreich* (a wonderfully descriptive Scots word meaning 'dull and miserable'), but if you get a clear spell of hard frost and sunshine the scenery can be every bit as stunning as in summer.

The many seabird colonies around the Scottish coast are at their most spectacular during the nesting season (April to July), while coastal nature reserves see huge flocks of migrating ducks, geese and waders in spring and autumn. You can see seals, dolphins and porpoises almost all year round, but the whale-watching season peaks in July and August. One seasonal species you should definitely be aware of is the dreaded midge (p208). They are usually around from June to September, but are at their worst in July and August.

HOW MUCH?

Cappuccino £1.80

Restaurant meal per head £15

Glass of wine £2.50

Bottle of malt whisky £25

Car hire per day £20 to £30

LONELY PLANET INDEX

Pint of beer £2.20

1.5L bottled water 65p

1L petrol 78p

Souvenir T-shirt £10

Street snack (fish & chips) £3 to £4

COSTS & MONEY

The strength of the pound sterling makes Scotland an expensive destination for non-Europeans. Food, accommodation and transport are all fairly pricey; the only real bargain is the many excellent museums and galleries that you can visit for free.

The price of food and fuel rises quite steeply in remote parts of the Highlands and islands where supplies depend on the ferries. Petrol can cost up to 15% more in the Outer Hebrides than in the Central Lowlands.

Surprisingly, Scotland is one of the most expensive places to buy Scotch whisky. If your travels will be taking you to continental Europe, you'll find you can buy whisky there for about 60% of the price charged in Scottish shops.

A realistic daily budget for two people sharing a double room, staying in B&Bs and guesthouses and eating in mid-range restaurants is around £30 to £40 per person per day. Backpackers using hostels and cooking their own meals can get by on £20 a day, not including transport.

If you're travelling in your own car you'll probably average a further £10 to £15 per day on petrol and parking; rental will add a minimum of £20 a day.

If you're travelling as a family, be aware that many hotels and guesthouses have family rooms, usually with a double bed and one or two singles, plus a folding bed, which can save a fair bit of money. Most tourist attractions with admission fees also offer discounted family tickets – a major saving at places such as Edinburgh Castle, which charges £8 for one adult.

Unless otherwise indicated, admission costs are given as adult/child throughout this book.

TRAVEL LITERATURE

Stone Voices: The Search for Scotland (2002) by respected Scots journalist Neal Ascherson is a highly readable and very personal exploration of Scottish history and culture, filled with fascinating insights and some contentious conclusions that will provide the starting point for some lively bar-room conversations.

For a look behind the tourism gloss, *Danziger's Britain* (1997) by Nick Danziger should be required reading. The picture it paints of modern Britain is thoroughly depressing, and includes descriptions of life for the marginalised in the Highlands and Glasgow. This guy has seen the world and if this is how he says it is, then it's hard to argue with him.

TOP TENS

FAVOURITE FESTIVALS & EVENTS

Scots always enjoy a good party, and will find some reason to celebrate at almost any time of the year. The following list is our Top 10, but for comprehensive listings of festivals and events see the Directory p400.

- Up-Helly-Aa
  (Shetland), January (p391)

- Melrose Sevens Rugby Match
  (Melrose), April (p144)

- Islay Festival
  (Isle of Islay), May (p266)

- Burns an' a' That
  (Ayr), May (p160)

- Royal Highland Show
  (Edinburgh), June (p80)

- Jethart Callant Festival
  (Jedburgh), July (p146)

- Edinburgh Festivals & Fringe
  (Edinburgh), August (p79)

- Edinburgh Military Tattoo
  (Edinburgh), August (p79)

- Braemar Gathering
  (Braemar), September (p240)

- Edinburgh's Hogmanay
  (Edinburgh), December (p80)

TOP READS

Scotland has produced many world-famous novelists. The following Top 10 novels provide insights into Scottish culture at various periods spanning the last two centuries. See the boxed text Essential Scottish Reads, p40.

- *Waverley* (1814)
  Sir Walter Scott

- *Kidnapped!* (1886)
  Robert Louis Stevenson

- *The Silver Darlings* (1941)
  Neil M Gunn

- *A Scot's Quair* (1946)
  Lewis Grassic Gibbon

- *Para Handy Tales* (1955)
  Neil Munro

- *The Prime of Miss Jean Brodie* (1962)
  Muriel Spark

- *Greenvoe* (1972)
  George Mackay Brown

- *Laidlaw* (1977)
  William McIlvanney

- *Trainspotting* (1993)
  Irvine Welsh

- *Black and Blue* (1997)
  Ian Rankin

MUST-SEE FILMS

Head down to the local video store or browse www.amazon.com to pick up our choice of Scotland's 10 best films. All are set in Scotland and many were directed by Scotsmen. See the Culture chapter, p41, for more information.

- *Whisky Galore!* (1949)
  Director: Alexander Mackendrick

- *Tunes of Glory* (1960)
  Director: Ronald Neame

- *Gregory's Girl* (1981)
  Director: Bill Forsyth

- *Local Hero* (1983)
  Director: Bill Forsyth

- *Braveheart* (1995)
  Director: Mel Gibson

- *Rob Roy* (1995) Director:
  Michael Caton-Jones

- *Trainspotting* (1996)
  Director: Danny Boyle

- *Small Faces* (1996)
  Director: Gillies Mackinnon

- *Mrs Brown* (1997)
  Director: John Madden

- *Sweet Sixteen* (2002)
  Director: Mike Loach

Anyone with an interest in the Scottish hills should seek out *Always A Little Further* (1939) by Alastair Borthwick and *Mountaineering in Scotland* (1947) by WH Murray. Both are classic accounts, beautifully written, of camping, hiking and rock-climbing in Scotland in the 1930s, when just getting to Glen Coe was an adventure in itself and the most advanced ice-climbing equipment was a slater's pick.

Two of the greatest Scottish travelogues date from the 18th century. *A Journey to the Western Isles of Scotland* (1759) and *Journal of a Tour to the Hebrides* (1785) by James Boswell are vivid accounts of two journeys made by the author in the company of the famous lexicographer Samuel Johnson. Boswell writes engagingly of their travails and encounters with the local people, from lairds to crofters, and paints a vivid picture of Highland life in the late 18th century.

A much more recent travelogue is *Native Stranger* (1995) by Alistair Scott, which recounts the efforts of a Scottish travel writer who 'knew more about the Sandinistas' than his native country but got to grips with the realities of modern Scotland by travelling the length and breadth of the land.

INTERNET RESOURCES

Internet Guide to Scotland (www.scotland-info.co.uk)
The best of several online tourist guides to Scotland.

ScotchWhisky.net (www.scotchwhisky.net)
Everything you wanted to know about Scotch whisky.

Scotland Online (www.scotlandonline.com)
An online directory of websites on all things Scottish.

Traveline (www.travelinescotland.com)
Public transport timetables and journey planner for all of Scotland.

Undiscovered Scotland (www.undiscoveredscotland.co.uk)
A guide to Scotland's towns, villages and visitor attractions.

VisitScotland (www.visitscotland.com)
The official Scottish Tourist Board site, with an online accommodation-booking service.

Itineraries
CLASSIC ROUTES

SKYE'S THE LIMIT   Two Weeks / Edinburgh to Inverness

This route is through the magnificent mountain scenery of the West Highlands. From **Edinburgh** (p54) head northwest to see Scotland's other great castle at **Stirling** (p179), then to the **Trossachs** (p186) for your first taste of Highland scenery. As you continue north, the mountain scenery becomes more impressive, culminating in the grandeur of **Glen Coe** (p308).

Keen hill walkers will pause at Fort William to climb **Ben Nevis** (p316), or you can view it from Corpach on the Road to the Isles. Head onto glorious **Glenfinnan** (p318) and the **Silver Sands of Morar** (p319), then **Mallaig** (p319); try to spend the night here and eat at one of its excellent seafood restaurants.

From Mallaig take the ferry to the **Isle of Skye** (p346); allow a day or two here to see the sights. Cross the Skye Bridge back to the mainland, and head north via the pretty village of **Plockton** (p344) to the magnificent mountain scenery of **Glen Torridon** (p343). Follow the A832 alongside lovely **Loch Maree** (p343) and continue north into the big-sky wilderness of western Sutherland, beneath the towering pinnacles of **An Teallach** (p342), before heading back east to the flesh-pots of **Inverness** (p289).

In theory you could cover this spectacular 475-mile (765km) route in two days, but allowing time to stop and enjoy the scenery and the seafood makes two weeks a more realistic estimate.

CASTLES & WHISKY   Two Weeks / Edinburgh to Inverness

From **Edinburgh** (p54) head north across the Forth Road Bridge to Fife, stopping at Queensferry first to visit stately **Hopetoun House** (p100). Then turn east along the coastal road through the delightful fishing villages of the **East Neuk** (p200) to the home of golf, **St Andrews** (p195). Continue north across the Tay Bridge to **Dundee** (p220) and **Glamis Castle** (p225) before heading into the Grampian Highlands to reach **Braemar** (p239).

A feast of castles lies ahead as you travel east along **Deeside** (p238), passing royal residence **Balmoral Castle** (p239) and fairy-tale **Crathes Castle** (p238) on your way to the granite city of **Aberdeen** (p231). Try to get a table at the Silver Darlings restaurant here.

Now strike west again along the A944, making small detours to visit Castle Fraser, **Craigievar Castle** (p241) and Kildrummy Castle before turning north to **Huntly** (p243) and west again to **Dufftown** (p245) in the heart of the Spey valley. Base yourself here for at least a day to explore the many whisky distilleries nearby.

Go northwest to **Elgin** (p243), then west on the A96, visiting **Brodie Castle** (p296), **Fort George** (p295), **Cawdor Castle** (p296) and **Culloden** (p295) on the way to **Inverness** (p289).

Whisky fans (see the boxed text on p246) can make the short trip north to the Glenmorangie Distillery at **Tain** (p326) before returning south on the A9, stopping off at **Blair Castle** (p215), **Dunkeld** (p212) and **Scone Palace** (p204).

This journey through the heart of Scotland is a 475-mile (765km) round-trip, starting and finishing in Edinburgh, with a total driving time of around 10 to 12 hours. Tain is an extra 50-mile (80km) round-trip north of Inverness.

ROADS LESS TRAVELLED

BORDER RAID   Eight Days / Edinburgh to Glasgow

From **Edinburgh** (p54) the majority of tourists head north, which is a very good reason to head south, into the Borders...

Your first objective should be a traipse around the beautiful Border abbeys of **Melrose** (p143) and **Jedburgh** (p146). Melrose is a charming place to stay. Then head southwest to **Selkirk** (p145) and along the A708 to **Moffat** (p174). Continue to **Dumfries** (p163) and make a short side-trip to see spectacular **Caerlaverock Castle** (p165).

Push on southwest around the Galloway coast to **Newton Stewart** (p169), and detour south to visit the bookshops of **Wigtown** (p170) and the holy site of **Whithorn** (p170). From Newton Stewart head back east along the A712 to **New Galloway** (p168), via the lovely Galloway Forest Park, and then north on the A713 towards **Ayr** (p158) and Burns Country.

At **Alloway** (p160) allow at least a day to visit Robert Burns' birthplace and other Burns-related sites, then go onto Ayr and head north to Ardrossan. Take the ferry here across to the lovely **Isle of Arran** (p154) for a spot of hill-walking, fishing or relaxing at one of the island's pubs.

Back on the mainland, head north to Wemyss Bay and take the ferry to Rothesay on the **Isle of Bute** (p257), where you can visit stunning Mount Stuart, one of Scotland's most impressive stately homes. Return to the mainland again and head east to **Glasgow** (p104).

You could cover this 430-mile (692km) loop through the southern uplands in two long days, or spin it out to two weeks, but eight days is comfortable.

ISLES AT THE EDGE OF THE SEA   Two Weeks / Oban to Inverness

This route can be done by car, but it also makes a brilliant cycle tour taking three to four weeks. Both start and finish are accessible by rail.

From **Oban** (p270) make the long ferry crossing to **Barra** (p366). After a look at romantic Kisimul Castle take the ferry across to **South Uist** (p365). If you've brought your fishing rod, look forward to a bit of sport on the island's many trout lochs. Keep your binoculars handy as you follow the road north through **Benbecula** (p365) and **North Uist** (p364), as this is prime bird-watching country; then take another ferry to **Harris** (p362).

Pray for sun, as the road along Harris' west coast has some of the most spectacular beaches in Scotland. The road continues north through the rugged Harris hills to Lewis.

Turn west to make a circuit past the **Callanish Standing Stones** (p361), **Dun Carloway** (p361) and **Arnol Blackhouse Museum** (p360) – the highlights of the Western Isles – and if you have time detour west to the beautiful beaches around **Miavaig** (p362).

From bustling **Stornoway** (p359) take the ferry to **Ullapool** (p340), where you have the choice of returning direct to Inverness, or continuing north around the mainland coast through the jaw-dropping wilderness scenery of **Inverpolly Nature Reserve** (p339), **Cape Wrath** (p338) and **Durness** (p337) to **Thurso** (p334), where the ferry to the **Orkney Islands** (p371) awaits.

CalMac's **Island Hopscotch** (p420) ticket No 8 includes all the ferries needed for this route.

This trip involves 290 miles (467km) between Oban and Thurso, plus a total of 10 hours of ferry crossings. You could drive it in four days at a push, but two weeks is more enjoyable. Touring Orkney would add another 60 or 70 miles, plus four hours on the ferry.

TAILORED TRIPS

ISLAND GARDENS

The southwestern Highlands is famed for its mild climate. Since the 18th century, estate owners have taken advantage of this to create some of Scotland's most beautiful gardens. Allow 10 days for the following trip.

From Glasgow, head west to Gourock and take the ferry to Dunoon. After visiting nearby **Benmore Botanic Garden** (p256), go west to Colintraive for the short crossing to the Isle of Bute, where you can visit the magnificent grounds of **Mount Stuart** (p257). Return to Colintraive and go west again on the ferry from Portavadie to **Tarbert** (p261), and drive south to the Isle of Gigha for a look at lovely **Achamore Gardens** (p262).

Go back north to Kennacraig for the ferries to Islay and Jura, where you'll find the walled garden of **Jura House** (p267), and out to Colonsay for a stroll around the **Woodland Garden** (p269). Catch a ferry from Colonsay to Oban, and then another to Mull to visit **Torosay Castle and Gardens** (p277) and make a tour of the island. Finally, take the ferry from Tobermory to Kilchoan in **Ardnamurchan** (p317) – where the road is lined with a spectacular display of rhododendrons in June – and drive back to Fort William via **Corran Ferry** (p317).

WILDLIFE-WATCHING

Begin in **Inverness** (p289) at the head of the Moray Firth, famous for its population of bottlenose dolphins. Boat trips depart from here. Head east along the southern shore of the firth to **Spey Bay** (p248), where there's an exhibit on the dolphins and the chance of seeing seals. Then follow the Spey Valley southwest to the Cairngorms, where you can see nesting ospreys at **Boat of Garten** (p306) and get close to some rare species at the **Highland Wildlife Park** (p305).

Continue southwest across the country to **Fort William** (p311) and follow the **Road to the Isles** (p318) to Mallaig. Take a day trip to the **Isle of Rum** (p321), a nature reserve famed for its rare white-tailed sea eagles and Manx shearwaters. Perhaps take another trip to the **Isle of Eigg** (p321), which has fine walking and there's a good chance of spotting porpoises and whales on the crossing.

Then take the ferry to the **Isle of Skye** (p346), one of the best wildlife destinations in Scotland and where there are lots of boats offering whale-watching trips.

Return to Inverness via the Skye Bridge and **Loch Ness** (p298). If you don't fancy monster-spotting, make a detour west to visit the beautiful nature reserve of **Glen Affric** (p296). Allow seven to 10 days.

The Authors

NEIL WILSON
Coordinating Author

Introductory chapters, Edinburgh, Northeast Scotland, Southern Highlands & Islands, Central & Western Highlands, Northern Highlands & Islands, Transport

Neil was born in Scotland and has lived here for most of his life. When he was 14 he relieved the boredom of a rainy school holiday by leafing through a book about the Scottish mountains, which inspired a lifelong enthusiasm for the great outdoors, and since then he has hiked, biked, climbed, sailed or snowboarded in almost every corner of the country. Neil has written around 40 guidebooks for various publishers including Lonely Planet's guide to Edinburgh.

My Favourite Trip

Spectacular sunsets, lonely beaches, smoky malt whiskies and an unforgettable hike around the northern end of Jura to the Corryvreckan whirlpool – these were the highlights of a memorable cycle tour of Argyll's islands during a two-week spell of glorious June sunshine. Having taken the train to Ardrossan, I bought a CalMac Island Rover ticket and caught the ferry to **Arran** (p154). After a circuit of Arran I crossed the water to Kintyre and cycled to Kennacraig for the ferry to **Islay** (p263). More ferries took me to **Jura** (p266) and **Colonsay** (p268), then on to **Oban** (p270), and finally out to **Coll** (p283) and **Tiree** (p283). As I headed home on the train I was thinking that if only I'd had more time, there's another ferry from Oban to Barra...

ALAN MURPHY
Glasgow, Southern Scotland, Central Scotland, Northern Highlands & Islands, The Orkney & Shetland Islands, Directory

Alan left his heart in Scotland sometime in the mid-1990s, when he lived and worked in Edinburgh for two years. Writing about the country has allowed him to return, first in 2002, when he contributed the Scotland chapters for the *Britain* guide, and again in 2003 for *Scotland*. With his journalistic background, Alan finds it a joy writing about Scotland because for him it's inspiring, *almost* indescribably beautiful and simply like coming home.

Snapshot

First thing to do when you arrive in Edinburgh is toddle down to the foot of the Royal Mile and look at the Scottish parliament building (p67). At the time of writing it was due to open at Easter 2004, with Scottish taxpayers footing the bill for around £400 million. It was originally scheduled to be ready in 2001 at a cost of only £40 million.

Scots are never happier than when they have something to moan about, and the ever-increasing cost of the new parliament building has been a subject of vociferous complaint for the last few years. Once the parliament – acclaimed as the most important new building project in Scotland for more than a hundred years – has finally opened, it will be interesting to see whether the people embrace it or continue to condemn it.

The MSPs' offices at the western end are adorned with unusually shaped windows, said to be based on the outline of the portrait *Reverend Robert Walker Skating on Duddingston Loch* (p44). These enclose a so-called 'contemplative space' in which the resident member can think over new policies. Having read the results of a forthcoming public inquiry into the spiralling costs of the project, no doubt many of them will be sitting there thinking 'Jings, these bloody windows cost £17,000 each!'

One of the subjects being debated in the new parliament is Scotland's 'secret shame' – the bitter religious hatred (sectarianism) that exists between sections of the country's Protestant and Catholic communities. At its worst in Glasgow, sectarianism's most public face appears in football matches between Rangers and Celtic. Since 1999 eight people have died in sectarian violence and thousands have had their lives blighted by religious bigotry. First Minister Jack McConnell has put forward proposals for a change in the law that would allow tougher sentences to be imposed for offences motivated by religious hatred.

If you're unfortunate enough to find yourself driving into one of Scotland's larger cities during the weekday rush hour, you'll soon find that traffic congestion is one of the country's curses. Edinburgh has led the way in trying to discourage car use with popular measures like cycle routes and dedicated bus lanes, and unpopular ones like increased parking charges and fines, and a small army of parking 'enforcers'. There are even plans to reintroduce trams to the city by 2009. But motorists are currently up in arms about a congestion-charging scheme that will require drivers to pay a £2 fee to enter the city centre; the scheme is set to be introduced in 2006.

One of the worst traffic bottlenecks in the country is the Forth Road Bridge and its approaches, with southbound tailbacks several miles long on weekday mornings. Ambitious plans have been proposed for a second road bridge across the Firth of Forth at Queensferry (p100), which would allow Edinburgh's proposed new tram network to be extended as far as Dunfermline.

Another transport issue that will be dominating the headlines for a while to come is a £130 million plan to reopen the Waverley Line, a railway link between Edinburgh and the Borders that was closed down in the 1960s. Supporters claim that reinstating the line between Edinburgh and Galashiels is crucial to the revival of the ailing Borders economy, but farmers and home-owners whose property lies next to – or in some cases on – the old railway line are understandably opposed to it. Present plans foresee construction taking place between 2005 and 2008.

FAST FACTS

Population: 5.06 million (Jun 2001)

Area: 78,722 sq km

Number of seats in Scottish parliament: 129

First Minister: Jack McConnell (Labour Party)

GDP (per head): £12,512 (1999)

Inflation: 2.9% (July 2003)

Unemployment: 5.5% (August 2003)

Amount of whisky exported annually: 1 billion bottles

Value of haggis sold for Burns Night: £1.2 million

Number of times Scotland has won the soccer World Cup: 0

For more information on the Scottish Outdoor Access Code, see www.snh.org.uk/soac.

The Land Reform (Scotland) Act, passed in 2003, introduced major changes relating to land ownership and access, the repercussions of which will no doubt rumble across the Scottish landscape for years to come. The headline-grabbing clause that allows crofting communities to buy out the land that they live on with the aid of taxpayers' money will probably see many more estates follow the likes of Eigg (p321), Knoydart (p320) and North Harris (p363) into community ownership.

The act also introduced a 'public right of access to and over land and inland water, exercised responsibly, for recreational purposes or for crossing land'. Invariably referred to in the press as the 'Right to Roam', this new legislation has been enthusiastically welcomed by ramblers and hill walkers, but received with consternation by a small group of private landowners.

With the soccer World Cup looming on the horizon in 2006, it's safe to say that bar-room debate will be swinging once again to the subject of Scotland's chances – or lack thereof – in the competition. Will the team qualify? (They failed in 2002.) Will they get beyond the second round for the first time in their history? Or will they, as is their wont, snatch defeat from the jaws of victory? But please, don't go mentioning that it will be the 40th anniversary of England's 1966 World Cup victory – unless you want a pint of McEwan's heavy emptied over your head.

History

PREHISTORIC & ROMAN TIMES

The standing stones at Callanish in Lewis (p358) are one of the most evocative prehistoric sites in Scotland, and testify to the advanced culture that had taken root in Scotland by 3000 BC. Little is known about these people, who were also responsible for Skara Brae in Orkney (p371), an entire Neolithic village dating from around 3100 BC, and the fascinating prehistoric landscape of Kilmartin Glen (p260).

The Roman invasion of Britain began in 55 BC, when Julius Caesar's legions first crossed the English Channel. However, the Roman onslaught ground to a halt in the north, not far beyond the present-day Scottish border.

By the 2nd century Emperor Hadrian, tired of fighting the wild tribes in the north, decided to cut his losses and built the wall (AD 122–28) that bears his name across northern England between Carlisle and Newcastle. Two decades later Hadrian's successor, Antoninus Pius, invaded Scotland again and built a turf rampart, the Antonine Wall, between the Firth of Forth and the River Clyde. The Roman fort at Cramond (p72) marked its eastern end.

A Traveller's History of Scotland by Andrew Fisher is a concise account of Scottish history that relates historical events to places you can visit.

FEUDING CELTIC TRIBES & CHRISTIANITY

When the Romans finally left Britain in the 4th century, there were at least two indigenous peoples in the northern region of the British isles: the Picts in the north and east, and the Celtic Britons in the south.

In the 6th century another Celtic tribe, the Scots, crossed the sea from northern Ireland and established a kingdom in Argyll called Dalriada (see Dunadd, p260). They were followed by the Irish missionary St Columba, who founded an important early-Christian centre on the tiny island of Iona (p282) in 563. By the late 8th century, most of the tribes in Scotland had converted to Christianity.

From the 780s onwards, Norsemen in longboats from Scandinavia began to pillage the Scottish coast and islands, eventually taking control of Orkney, Shetland and the Western Isles. Between 795 and 806, Norse raiders sacked the religious settlement at Iona three times, causing the monks to flee to Ireland with St Columba's bones. The Norsemen continued to control the entire western seaboard until Alexander III broke their power at the Battle of Largs in 1263.

The Sea Kingdoms by Alistair Moffat is an engaging narrative history of the Celtic fringes of Britain (Scotland, Wales and Cornwall), related in the context of a sea voyage around those regions.

MACALPIN & CANMORE DYNASTIES

The Picts and Scots were drawn together by the threat of a Norse invasion and by their common Christianity. In 843 Kenneth MacAlpin, the king of Dalriada (and son of a Pictish princess), took advantage of the Picts' custom of matrilineal succession to take over the Pictish throne, thus uniting Scotland north of the Firth of Forth into a single kingdom. He made Scone his capital, and brought to it the sacred Stone of Destiny used in the coronation of Scottish kings (see the Stone of Destiny boxed text, p63).

TIMELINE	**3000 BC**	**AD 142**
	Prehistoric sites testify to an advanced culture	Building of Antonine Wall marks northern limit of Roman Empire

Nearly 200 years later, Kenneth MacAlpin's great-great-great-grand-son, Malcolm II (reigned 1005–18), defeated the Northumbrian Angles led by King Canute at the Battle of Carham (1018) near Roxburgh on the River Tweed. This victory brought Edinburgh and Lothian under Scottish control and extended Scottish territory as far south as the Tweed.

With his Saxon queen, Margaret, Malcolm III Canmore (reigned 1058–93) – whose father Duncan was murdered by Macbeth (as described in Shakespeare's eponymous play) – founded a dynasty of able Scottish rulers. They introduced new Anglo-Norman systems of government and religious foundations.

Malcolm's son David I (reigned 1124–53) increased his power by adopting the Norman feudal system, granting land to noble Norman families in return for military service. By 1212 Walter of Coventry remarked that the Scottish court was 'French in race and manner of life, in speech and in culture'.

Stone of Destiny by Pat Gerber is an intriguing investigation into the history of Scotland's most famous lump of stone. Is the one in Edinburgh Castle a fake, with the real stone waiting to be rescued from its medieval hiding place?

But the Highland clans, inaccessible in their glens, remained a law unto themselves for another 600 years. A cultural and linguistic divide grew up between the Gaelic-speaking Highlanders and the Lowlanders who spoke the Scots tongue (p428).

WARS OF INDEPENDENCE

When Alexander III fell to his death over a coastal cliff at Kinghorn in Fife in 1286, there followed a dispute over the succession to the throne. There were no less than 13 claimants, but in the end it came down to a choice of two: Robert de Brus, lord of Annandale, and John Balliol, lord of Galloway. Edward I of England, as the greatest feudal lord in Britain, was asked to arbitrate. He chose Balliol, whom he thought he could manipulate more easily.

Seeking to tighten his feudal grip on Scotland, Edward – known as the 'Hammer of the Scots' – treated the Scots king as his vassal rather than his equal. The humiliated Balliol finally turned against him and allied Scotland with France in 1295, thus beginning the enduring 'Auld Alliance'.

Edward's response was bloody. In 1296 he marched on Scotland with an army of 30,000 men, razed the ports of Berwick and Dunbar and butchered the citizens, and captured the castles of Berwick, Edinburgh, Roxburgh and Stirling. Balliol was incarcerated in the Tower of London, oaths of allegiance were demanded from Scottish nobles and, in a final blow to Scottish pride, Edward I removed the Stone of Destiny from Scone and took it back to London.

Bands of rebels led by local warlords attacked and harried the English occupiers. One such band, led by William Wallace, defeated the English army at the Battle of Stirling Bridge in 1297, but Wallace was captured and executed in London in 1305. The Scots nobles, inspired by Wallace's example, looked around for a new leader and turned to Robert the Bruce, grandson of the lord of Annandale who had been rejected by Edward in 1292. Bruce murdered his rival, John Comyn, and had himself crowned king of Scotland at Scone in March 1306.

Bruce mounted a campaign to drive the English out of Scotland but suffered repeated defeats. According to legend, while Bruce was on the run he was inspired by a spider's persistence in spinning its web to renew

4th century	843
Romans leave Britain	Scotland united north of Firth of Forth

his own efforts. He went on to win a famous victory over the English at the Battle of Bannockburn in 1314. Continued raids on northern England forced Edward II to sue for peace and, in 1328, the Treaty of Northampton gave Scotland its independence, with Robert I, the Bruce, as its king.

THE STEWART DYNASTY & THE RENAISSANCE

Bannockburn and the Treaty of Northampton had no lasting effect. After the death of Robert I in 1329, the country was ravaged by civil disputes and continuing wars with England. Edinburgh was occupied several times by English armies, and in 1385 the Kirk of St Giles was burned to the ground.

Robert was succeeded by his five-year-old son, David II (reigned 1329–71), who returned from exile in France in 1341 and made Edinburgh his main residence. When David II died without a son in 1371, the crown passed to his nephew, Robert II (reigned 1371–90), the child of his sister Marjory and her husband, Walter the Steward. Thus was born the Stewart dynasty, which would rule Scotland and Britain for the next 300 years.

James IV (reigned 1488–1513) married the daughter of Henry VII of England, the first of the Tudor monarchs, thereby linking the two royal families through 'the Marriage of the Thistle and the Rose'. This didn't prevent the French from persuading James to go to war with his in-laws, and he was killed at the Battle of Flodden in 1513, along with 10,000 of his subjects.

Renaissance ideas flourished during James IV's reign. Scottish poetry thrived, created by 'makars' (makers of verses) such as William Dunbar, the court poet of James IV, and Gavin Douglas. The intellectual climate provided fertile ground for the rise of Protestantism, a reaction against the perceived wealth and corruption of the medieval Roman Catholic Church, that would eventually lead to the Reformation.

Much graceful Scottish architecture dates from this period, and examples of the Renaissance style can be seen in alterations made to the palaces at Holyrood (p66), Stirling (p179), Linlithgow (p102) and Falkland (p194).

The film *Braveheart*, starring Mel Gibson, is a romanticised Hollywood version of the life of William Wallace, though any relationship to actual historical events is pretty tenuous.

THE DECLARATION OF ARBROATH

During the Wars of Independence, a group of Scottish nobles sent a letter to Pope John XXII requesting support for the cause of Scottish independence. Bearing the seals of eight earls and 31 barons, and written in Latin by the abbot of Arbroath in 1320, it is the earliest document that seeks to place limits on the power of a king.

Having railed against the tyranny of Edward I of England and having sung the praises of Robert the Bruce, the declaration famously concludes:

Yet even the same Robert, should he turn aside from the task and yield Scotland or us to the English king or people, him we should cast out as the enemy of us all, and choose another king to defend our freedom; for so long as a hundred of us remain alive, we will yield in no least way to English dominion. For we fight, not for glory nor for riches nor for honour, but only and alone for freedom, which no good man surrenders but with his life.

1296	1314
King Edward 1 invades Scotland	Battle of Bannockburn

MARY QUEEN OF SCOTS & THE REFORMATION

In 1542 King James V lay on his deathbed in Falkland Palace in Fife, broken-hearted, it is said, after his defeat by the English at Solway Moss. His French wife, Mary of Guise, had borne him two sons, but both had died in infancy. On 8 December a messenger brought word that his wife had given birth to a baby girl at the Palace of Linlithgow. Fearing the end of the Stewart dynasty, and recalling its origin through Robert the Bruce's daughter, James sighed, 'It cam' wi' a lass, and it will gang wi' a lass.' He died a few days later, leaving his week-old daughter, Mary, to inherit the throne as queen of Scots.

Mary (reigned 1542–67) was sent to France, and Scotland was ruled by regents, who rejected overtures from Henry VIII of England urging them to wed the infant queen to his son. Henry was furious, and sent his armies to take vengeance on the Scots. Parts of Edinburgh were razed, Holyrood Abbey was sacked, and the great Border abbeys of Melrose (p143), Dryburgh and Jedburgh were burned down. The Rough Wooing, as it was called, failed to persuade the Scots of the error of their ways. In 1558, Mary was married to the French dauphin and became queen of France as well as Scotland.

Two books by TC Smout– *A History of the Scottish People 1560–1830* and *A Century of the Scottish People 1830–1950* provide a scholarly but readable account of Scots history from Reformation to WWII.

While Mary was in France, being raised as a Roman Catholic, the Reformation tore through Scotland. The wealthy Catholic Church was riddled with corruption, and the preachings of John Knox, a pupil of the Swiss reformer Calvin, found sympathetic ears. In 1560 the Scottish parliament created a Protestant Church that was independent of Rome and the monarchy. The Latin Mass was abolished and the pope's authority denied.

Following the death of her sickly husband, the 18-year-old Mary returned to Scotland, arriving at Leith on 19 August 1561. A week later she was formally welcomed to her capital city, dining in Edinburgh Castle before proceeding down the Royal Mile to the Palace of Holyroodhouse, where she held a famous audience with John Knox. The great reformer harangued the young queen and tried her Catholic faith; she later agreed to protect the Protestant Church in Scotland while continuing to hear Mass in private.

She married Henry Stewart, Lord Darnley, in the Chapel Royal at Holyrood and gave birth to a son (later James VI) in Edinburgh Castle in 1565. Any domestic bliss was short-lived and, in a scarcely believable train of events, Darnley was involved in the murder of Mary's Italian secretary Rizzio (rumoured to be her lover), before he himself was murdered, probably by Mary's new lover and second-husband-to-be, the earl of Bothwell.

Mary's enemies finally confronted her at Carberry Hill, just east of Edinburgh, and Mary was forced to abdicate in 1567. Her son, the infant James VI (reigned 1567–1625), was crowned at Stirling, and a series of regents ruled in his place. When Queen Elizabeth I of England died childless in 1603, James VI of Scotland inherited the English throne in the so-called Union of the Crowns, thus becoming James I of Great Britain (usually written as James VI/I). James moved his court to London and, for the most part, the Stewarts ignored Scotland from then on. Indeed, when Charles I (reigned 1625–49) succeeded James in 1625, he couldn't be bothered to travel north to Edinburgh to be formally crowned as king of Scotland until 1633.

1328	1371
Treaty of Northampton; Robert I, the Bruce, king of Scotland	Stewart dynasty born

COVENANTERS & CIVIL WAR

The 17th century was a time of civil war in Scotland and England. The arrogant attempts by Charles I to impose episcopacy (the rule of bishops) and an English liturgy on the Presbyterian Scottish Church set off public riots in Edinburgh. The Presbyterians believed in a personal bond with God that had no need of mediation through priests, popes and kings and, on 28 February 1638, hundreds of people gathered in Greyfriars Kirkyard (p68) to sign a National Covenant affirming their rights and beliefs. Scotland was divided between the Covenanters and those who supported the king.

In the 1640s civil war raged in England too, where the struggle was between the Royalists and Oliver Cromwell's Parliamentarians. Although the Scots opposed Charles I's religious beliefs and autocratic rule, they were appalled when the Parliamentarians executed the king in 1649. They offered his son the Scottish Crown provided he signed the Covenant, which he did. Charles II (reigned 1649–85) was crowned at Scone on 1 January 1651, but was soon forced into exile by Cromwell, who invaded Scotland and captured Edinburgh.

Following Charles II's restoration in 1660, he reneged on the Covenant; episcopacy was reinstated and hard-line Presbyterian ministers were deprived of their churches. Many clergymen rejected the bishops' authority and started holding outdoor services, or conventicles. Charles' brother and successor, the Catholic James VII/II (reigned 1685–89), made worshipping as a Covenanter a capital offence.

Mary Queen of Scots by Antonia Fraser is the classic biography of Scotland's ill-starred queen, digging deep behind the myths to discover the real woman caught up in the labyrinthine politics of the period.

UNION WITH ENGLAND IN 1707

The civil wars left the country and its economy ruined. During the 1690s famine killed up to a third of the population in some areas. Anti-English feeling ran high, exacerbated by the failure of an investment venture in Panama (the so-called Darien Scheme, set up by the Bank of England to boost the economy), which resulted in widespread bankruptcy in Scotland.

The failure of the Darien Scheme made it clear to the wealthy Scottish merchants and stockholders that the only way they could gain access to the lucrative markets of developing colonies was through union with England. The English parliament favoured union through fear of Jacobite sympathies in Scotland being exploited by its enemies the French. It threatened to end the Scots' right to English citizenship and ban the duty-free export of Scottish goods to England, and offered a financial incentive to investors who had lost money in the Darien Scheme. Despite popular opposition, the Act of Union, which brought England and Scotland under one parliament, one sovereign and one flag, took effect on 1 May 1707.

On receiving the Act of Union in Edinburgh, the chancellor of Scotland, Lord Seafield – leader of the parliament that the Act of Union abolished – is said to have murmured under his breath, 'Now there's an end to an auld sang.' Robert Burns later castigated the wealthy politicians who engineered the Union in characteristically stronger language: 'We're bought and sold for English gold – such a parcel of rogues in a nation!'

1488–1513	1560s
Renaissance; the rise of Protestantism	Reformation: Mary Queen of Scots abdicates

THE JACOBITES

The Jacobite rebellions of the 18th century sought to displace the Hanoverian monarchy (chosen by the English parliament in 1701 to succeed the house of Orange) and restore a Catholic Stuart king to the British throne.

James Edward Stuart, known as the Old Pretender, was the son of James VII/II. With French support he arrived in the Firth of Forth with a fleet of ships in 1708, causing panic in Edinburgh, but was seen off by English men-of-war. Another attempt in 1715 fizzled out after the inconclusive Battle of Sheriffmuir.

In 1745 the Old Pretender's son, Charles Edward Stuart, better known as Bonnie Prince Charlie (p318), landed in Scotland to claim the crown for his father. Supported by an army of Highlanders, he marched southwards and captured Edinburgh except for the castle in September 1745, holding court at Holyrood before defeating the Hanoverian forces of Sir John Cope at Prestonpans, 9 miles (14.5km) east of Edinburgh. He got as far south as Derby in England, but success was short-lived; a Hanoverian army led by the duke of Cumberland harried him all the way back to the Highlands, where Jacobite dreams were finally extinguished at the Battle of Culloden in 1746.

THE HIGHLAND CLEARANCES

In the aftermath of the Jacobite rebellions, the relationship of Highland chief to clansman changed from paternalistic to economic. Lands that had been confiscated after the '45 (as it became known) were returned to their owners in the 1780s, but by then the chiefs had tasted the aristocratic good life of the Lowlands, and were tempted by the easy profits to be made from sheep farming.

The clansmen, no longer of any use as soldiers and uneconomic as tenants, were evicted from their homes and farms to make way for the flocks – in Easter Ross the year 1792 was known for decades afterwards as the Year of the Sheep. A few stayed to work the sheep farms; many more were forced to seek work in the cities, or to eke a living from crofts (small holdings) on poor coastal land. And many thousands emigrated – some willingly, some under duress – to the developing colonies of North America, Australia and New Zealand.

If you do much walking in the Highlands and islands, you are almost certain to come across a ruckle of stones among the bracken, all that remains of a house or cottage. Look around and you'll find another, and another, and soon you'll realise that this was once a crofting settlement. It's one of the saddest sights you'll see in Scotland – this emptiness where once there was a thriving community. The Mull of Oa on the island of Islay, for example, once supported a population of 4000, but today there are barely 40 people living there.

THE SCOTTISH ENLIGHTENMENT

Following the loss of the Scottish parliament in 1707, Edinburgh declined in political importance, but its cultural and intellectual life flourished. During the period known as the Scottish Enlightenment (roughly 1740–1830), Edinburgh became known as 'a hotbed of genius'. The philosophers David Hume and Adam Smith and the sociologist Adam Ferguson emerged as

DID YOU KNOW?

The word Jacobite comes from *Jacobus*, the Latin form of the name James. The Jacobites were originally supporters of the exiled King James VII/II.

Bonnie Prince Charlie by Fitzroy Maclean is a very readable biography of the Young Pretender, including a detailed account of the battles in 1745 and the prince's escape to France after Culloden.

John Prebble's wonderfully written book *The Highland Clearances* tells the terrible story of how the Highlanders were driven out of their homes and forced into emigration.

1603	1707
Union of the Crowns	Act of Union passed

influential thinkers, nourished on generations of theological debate. Medic William Cullen produced the first modern pharmacopoeia, chemist Joseph Black advanced the science of thermodynamics, and geologist James Hutton challenged long-held beliefs about the age of the Earth.

After centuries of bloodshed and religious fanaticism, people applied themselves with the same energy and piety to the making of money and the enjoyment of leisure. There was a revival of interest in Scottish history and vernacular literature, reflected in Robert Fergusson's satires and Alexander MacDonald's Gaelic poetry. The poetry of Robert Burns, a true man of the people, achieved lasting popularity.

Capital of the Mind: How Edinburgh Changed the World by James Buchan is a vivid and engrossing account of the Scottish capital's transformation from a squalid slum into the Athens of the North.

THE INDUSTRIAL REVOLUTION

In the second half of the 18th century, the development of the steam engine ushered in the Industrial Revolution. The Carron Ironworks near Falkirk, established in 1759, became the largest ironworks and gun factory in Britain, and the growth of the textile industry saw the con-

RADICALS & REDS

Scotland, and especially Glasgow, has a long history of radical politics. These were founded on the emergence of a well-educated, literate and articulate working class in the late 18th century, and the long-held belief in self-improvement.

James Keir Hardie (1856–1915), the illegitimate son of a poor housemaid, was born in the Lanarkshire mining village of Holytown. He first went down the mines at the age of 10, but was an avid reader and self-improver. By the age of 22 he had become an active campaigner for better wages and working conditions, and was blacklisted by the mine owners. He founded the Scottish Labour Party in 1888 and its successor, the Independent Labour Party, in 1893, specifically to represent the interests of the working classes in parliament.

By the early years of the 20th century, Scotland had a fully fledged alternative political culture. The Independent Labour Party was joined by Marxist organisations such as the Social Democratic Federation and the Socialist Labour Party, who advocated class war and direct action. The Glasgow schoolteacher and socialist revolutionary John Maclean (1879–1923) delivered lectures on Marxist theory to audiences of thousands. Maclean was appointed 'Bolshevik consul in Scotland' by Lenin following the Russian Revolution of 1917, and was an outspoken critic of Britain's involvement in WWI; he was arrested for sedition on half-a-dozen occasions.

The most notorious event in the history of Scottish radicalism was the Bloody Friday Riot of 1919. Fearing mass unemployment after WWI, the Clyde Workers Committee called a strike in support of a shorter working week. Strikers demonstrating in Glasgow's George Square began a riot after they were repeatedly charged by police. Fearing a Bolshevik-style revolution, the government sent in tanks, a howitzer and machine-gunners; fortunately, no-one was hurt.

In the General Election of 1922, Scotland returned no less than 29 Labour MPs, one Communist and a left-wing Prohibitionist, most of them from Glasgow and the west of Scotland – the region's socialist sympathies earned it the nickname of 'Red Clydeside'. Backed by the influx of Clydeside Reds at Westminster, Lossiemouth-born James Ramsay Macdonald (1866–1937) was elected leader of the Labour Party and became Britain's first Labour prime minister in 1924.

Keir Hardie would barely recognise his party's present incarnation, the centre-left New Labour, which took power in Westminster in 1997. However, in that general election the Scots reinforced their left-wing credentials – of the 72 Scottish MPs returned to Westminster in 1997, not one was a Conservative.

1746	1740s–1830s
Battle of Culloden	Scottish Enlightenment

struction of huge weaving mills in Lanarkshire, Dundee (see Verdant Works p222), Angus and Aberdeenshire. The world's first steamboat, the *Charlotte Dundas*, sailed along the newly opened Forth and Clyde Canal in 1802, and the world's first sea-going steamship, the *Comet*, was launched on the Clyde in 1812.

DID YOU KNOW?

Between 1904 and 1931 around a million people emigrated from Scotland to begin new lives in North America and Australia.

Glasgow, deprived of its lucrative tobacco trade following the American War of Independence (1776–83), developed into an industrial powerhouse, the 'second city' of the British Empire (after London). Cotton mills, iron and steelworks, chemical works, shipbuilding yards and heavy-engineering works proliferated along the River Clyde in the 19th century, powered by the coal mines of Lanarkshire, Ayrshire, Fife and Midlothian.

By the start of the 20th century, Scotland was a world leader in the production of textiles, iron, steel and coal, and above all in shipbuilding and marine engineering. 'Clyde-built' was synonymous with engineering excellence, and Scottish-built ships plied the oceans the world over.

A well-presented and easily absorbed introduction to Scottish history is at: www.bbc.co.uk/history /scottishhistory.

WAR & PEACE

Although German bombers blitzed Clydebank in 1941, killing 1200 people, Scotland largely escaped the trauma and devastation wrought by WWII on the industrial cities of England. Indeed, the war brought a measure of renewed prosperity to Scotland as the shipyards and engineering works geared up to supply the war effort. But the postwar period saw the collapse of shipbuilding and heavy industry, on which Scotland had become overreliant.

The discovery of oil and gas in the North Sea in the 1970s brought new prosperity to Aberdeen and the surrounding area, and to the Shetland Islands. However, most of the oil revenue was siphoned off to England. This, along with takeovers of Scots companies by English ones (which then closed the Scots operation, asset-stripped and transferred jobs to England), fuelled increasing nationalist sentiment in Scotland. The Scottish Nationalist Party (SNP) developed into a third force in Scottish politics, taking 30% of the popular vote in the 1974 General Election.

DEVOLUTION

In 1967 the SNP won a landmark election victory when it took the Hamilton seat from Labour, and support for independence grew when oil – and the revenues it generated – began to flow from the Scottish sector of the North Sea in the 1970s. Both Labour and Conservative governments had toyed with offering Scotland devolution, or some degree of self-government, and in 1979 a referendum was held on whether to set up a directly elected Scottish Assembly. Fifty-two per cent of those who voted said 'yes' to devolution, but the Labour prime minister James Callaghan decided that everyone who didn't vote should be counted as a 'no'. By this devious reasoning, only 33% of the electorate had voted 'yes', so the Scottish Assembly was rejected.

From 1979 to 1997 Scotland was ruled by a Conservative government in London for which the majority of Scots hadn't voted. Separatist feelings, always present, grew stronger. Following the landslide victory of the Labour Party in May 1997, another referendum was held on the creation of a Scottish parliament. This time the result was overwhelmingly and unambiguously in favour.

Elections to the new parliament took place on 6 May 1999, and the Scottish parliament convened for the first time on 12 May in the Assembly Rooms of the Church of Scotland at the eastern end of the Royal Mile in Edinburgh; Donald Dewar (1937–2000), formerly the Secretary of State for Scotland, was nominated as first minister (the Scottish parliament's equivalent of prime minister). The parliament was officially opened by Queen Elizabeth II on 1 July 1999. A new parliament building is being constructed at Holyrood in Edinburgh, and is expected to open at Easter 2004.

The Scottish Parliament Project provides a fascinating online history of the Scottish parliament www.st-Andrews.ac.uk /~scotparl.

EXPLORING YOUR SCOTTISH ROOTS

Genealogy is a hugely popular pastime, and many visitors to Scotland take the opportunity to do some detective work on their Scottish ancestry.

The main records used in Scottish genealogical research – the Statutory Registers of births, marriages and deaths (1855–the present), the Old Parish Registers (1533–1854) and the 10-yearly census returns from 1841 to 1901 – are held at the General Register Office (GRO) at the east end of Princes Street in Edinburgh. The registration of births, marriages and deaths became compulsory in Scotland on 1 January 1855; before that date, the ministers of the Church of Scotland kept registers of baptisms and marriages. The oldest surviving parish registers date back to 1553, but these records are far from complete, and many births and marriages before 1855 went unrecorded. Next door to the GRO is the National Archives of Scotland (NAS), which holds records of wills, property transactions and many other items of interest to genealogists.

You can consult all these records yourself, but make sure to do some research before leaving home.

Gather as much information as possible from birth, marriage and death certificates and other family papers in your possession, and interview elderly relatives. You will need full names, dates and places of birth, marriage or death in Scotland. One of the best guides is the book *Tracing Your Scottish Ancestry* by Kathleen B Cory, and there are many useful websites: **GenUKI** (www.genuki.org.uk) is a good starting point.

At the **Scotland's People Website** (www.scotlandspeople.gov.uk) you can search the indexes to the Old Parish Registers and Statutory Registers up to 100 years ago (75 years ago for deaths), and the indexes to the 1881 and 1891 census returns, on a pay-per-view basis. The **International Genealogical Index** (www.familysearch.com), compiled by the Mormon Church, includes freely searchable records of Scottish baptisms and marriages from 1553 to 1875.

You can do your own research at the **General Register Office for Scotland** (☎ 0131-314 4433; www.gro-scotland.gov.uk; New Register House, 3 West Register St, Edinburgh EH1 3YT; admission £17/10 per full day/half day; ☻ 9am-4.30pm Mon-Fri).

On your first visit to the **National Archives of Scotland** (☎ 0131-535 1334; www.nas.gov.uk; Register House, 2 Princes St, Edinburgh EH1 3YY; admission free; ☻ 9am-4.45pm Mon-Fri) you will need to ask for a reader's ticket (free). Bring some form of ID bearing your name and signature (eg passport, driving licence, bank card). Use of the Historical Search Room is free, and is first-come, first-served – you can't book a seat here.

Another useful resource is the **Scottish Genealogy Society Library & Family History Centre** (☎ 0131-220 3677; www.scotsgenealogy.com; 15 Victoria Tce, Edinburgh EH1 2JL; ☻ 10.30am-5.30pm Tue-Thu, 10.30am-8.30pm Wed, 10am-5pm Sat), which maintains the world's largest library of Scottish gravestone inscriptions. Entry is free to society members, £5 to nonmembers.

The Culture

THE NATIONAL PSYCHE

Having lived next door to a large and powerful neighbour for so long, it is hardly surprising that a major part of the Scottish national identity lies in simply not being English. Throughout history England – still regularly referred to as 'the Auld Enemy' – was often seen as standing for power, greed, arrogance and oppression, and in reaction to that Scots have often seen themselves, collectively, as the plucky underdog, a freedom-loving David to England's imperialist Goliath.

DID YOU KNOW?

In June Shetland enjoys four hours more daylight each day than London.

Robert Louis Stevenson wrote that the mark of a Scot is that 'there burns alive in him a sense of identity with the dead even to the twentieth generation'. Scotland's unofficial national anthem – *Flower of Scotland,* written by the late Roy Williamson and sung with gusto at football and rugby matches – harks back to the Battle of Bannockburn in 1314 when the Scots, outnumbered 10 to one, defeated the English; in the words of the song, they 'stood against him, proud Edward's army, and sent him homewards to think again'.

This historical baggage weighs heavily on the Scots, and has led to a long-standing resentment against English cultural and political domination. This reached a peak during the Thatcher government (1979–90), when a Conservative administration used the Scots as guinea-pigs for the hugely unpopular poll tax, imposing it on Scotland a full year before it was extended to England and Wales – so much for a United Kingdom.

Although much of the resentment has dissipated since 1997, when a Labour government replaced the Conservatives, it still simmers under the surface. Just let a TV commentator once refer to a Scot as English – as happened with the British women's curling team (all Scots) when they won a gold medal at the 2002 Winter Olympics – and you can guarantee that a hundred hands will be reaching for the phone to complain to the BBC, while the next day's papers will be spluttering with outrage.

Today the Scotland-England rivalry is generally good-natured, and the field of conflict has long since moved from battlefield to sports stadium. A Scottish win over England at football or rugby is often seen as more important than winning an entire competition. There are few things Scots sports fans enjoy as much as an England team getting a good hiding, no matter who they are playing against. When a Scottish politician suggested that the Scots should lend their support to England during the 2002 soccer World Cup, he was drowned out in a wave of ridicule. On the contrary, there was a run on football shirts and flags belonging to all of England's forthcoming opponents.

But the rivalry runs both ways. Asked whether he would support the Scots in similar circumstances, an English fan replied: 'I have no problem at all in supporting the Scottish team. By doing so I am showing support for my fellow Britons and building on our common historical and cultural ties. Also, it really annoys them.'

LIFESTYLE

The Scottish lifestyle is pretty similar to that in any other northern European country. Unemployment is fairly low (5.5% in August 2003) and average income is reasonable (£22,200 a year, about 92% of the UK average).

However, Scotland shares in the UK's culture of long working hours: a third of people work more than 48 hours a week, and one in six works more than 60 hours. The EU average is 40.3 hours. This encourages a work hard, play hard culture.

Just as the Eskimos are supposed to have 40 different words for snow, it seems as if the Scots have 40 different words for drunk – bevvied, blootered, hammered, guttered, fleein', fou, steamin', stotious, paralytic, plaistered and just plain pished, to name but a few.

There's no denying that, like most northern Europeans, the Scots enjoy a drink. For the vast majority that means a few pints of beer down the pub or a few glasses of wine with a meal, but for a significant minority the attitude is: if a thing's worth doing, it's worth overdoing.

Although on average Scots consume less alcohol per head than the French, much of it is in the form of binge-drinking; that is, going out to the pub on Friday and Saturday night and getting, well, blootered. Around 33% of men and 15% of women drink more than the recommended 21 units of alcohol a week (one unit equals one glass of wine). This translates into problems with drunk and disorderly behaviour on the streets, and alcohol-related health problems.

On the positive side, however, Scotland consistently rates highly in quality of life surveys. It's an attractive place to live, with excellent social, cultural and leisure amenities. There is still a strong sense of community in rural areas, and even in parts of the big cities.

DID YOU KNOW?

There are an estimated 60 million people around the world who claim Scottish ancestry.

POPULATION

The popular image of Scotland abroad is of crofts and castles and wild mountain scenery, but the country's population is in fact overwhelmingly urban, with 80% living in the cities and towns of the Central Lowlands.

The Highland region is one of Europe's most sparsely populated areas, with an average of only nine people per sq km – 30 times fewer than the UK average. A major problem since WWII has been the depopulation of the rural Highlands and, especially, the Western Isles, as younger people leave to find jobs. This movement of people from rural to urban areas, which began in the 18th century, is still going on – the population of the Outer Hebrides fell by 10% between 1991 and 2002.

Scotland's total population is decreasing (by 0.2% a year) and getting older (more than half of Scots are aged 40 or over), mainly as a result of a decreasing birth-rate.

SPORT
Football

Football (soccer) in Scotland is not so much a sport as a religion, with thousands turning out to worship their local teams on Wednesdays and weekends throughout the season (August to May). Sacred rites include standing in the freezing cold of a February day, drinking hot Bovril and eating a Scotch pie as you watch your team getting gubbed.

Scotland's top 10 clubs play in the Scottish Premier League (www .scotprem.com), but two teams – Glasgow Rangers and Glasgow Celtic – dominate the competition. On only 18 occasions since 1890 have any team other than Rangers and Celtic won the league; the last time was when Aberdeen won in 1985. Celtic were Premier League champions in 2001 and 2002, but Rangers narrowly beat them in 2003.

Glasgow Celtic was the first British team to win the European Cup (1967) and, so far, the only Scottish club to have done so. The team that won back then was made up entirely of Scots players from the Glasgow area. Rangers made history in 2000 by fielding a team composed entirely of non-Scottish players, and today half the players in the Premier League are of non-Scottish origin, a situation that angers many grass-roots supporters and bodes ill for the future of the national team.

If supporting local teams is like a religion, supporting the Scottish national team is more like a penance. The beginning of each European Championship and World Cup is filled with hope, but usually ends in despair.

Despite their team's often poor results, Scotland fans – known as the Tartan Army – are famed for their friendliness and good behaviour abroad, to the extent that some English and French football fans have joined them. The non-Scottish contingent has been dubbed the 'Sporran Legion'.

Rugby Union

Traditionally, football was the sport of Scotland's urban working classes, while rugby union was the preserve of agricultural workers from the Borders and middle-class university graduates. Although this distinction is breaking down – rugby's popularity soared after the 1999 World Cup was staged in the UK, and the middle classes have invaded the football terraces – it still persists to some extent.

Each year, starting in January, Scotland takes part in the Six Nations Rugby Union Championship. The most important fixture is the clash against England for the Calcutta Cup – it's always an emotive event, though Scotland has only won once in the last 10 years.

At club level, the season runs from September to May, and among the better teams are those from the Borders such as Hawick, Kelso and Melrose. At the end of the season, teams play a Rugby Sevens (seven-a-side) variation of the 15-player competition.

For more information on shinty, see www.shinty.com.

For more information on curling, see www.rccc.org.uk.

Golf

Aberdonian Paul Lawrie shot into the golfing limelight in 1999 when he came from nowhere to win the Open Championship. However, he still hasn't caught up with Colin Montgomerie, who has been Scotland's top golfer for a decade, consistently finishing in the top five in international tournaments.

Shinty

Shinty (camanachd in Gaelic) is a fast and physical ball-and-stick sport similar to Ireland's hurling, with more than a little resemblance to clan warfare. It's an indigenous Scottish game played mainly in the Highlands, and the most prized trophy is the Camanachd Cup. The cup final, held on the first Saturday in June, is a great Gaelic get-together. The Kingussie team has dominated in recent times, winning the cup every year from 1997 to 2003.

Each year in October there's an international match between Scotland and Ireland, played under composite shinty/hurling rules, and held alternately in Ireland and Scotland.

Curling

Curling – basically lawn bowling on ice – got an enormous publicity boost when the British women's team (all Scots) won the gold medal in the 2002 Winter Olympics. The sport, which involves propelling a 42-lb granite stone along the ice towards a target, was probably invented in Scotland in medieval times.

Highland Games

Highland games are held in Scotland throughout the summer, and not just in the Highlands – the Edinburgh International Highland Games take place in July. Assorted sporting events with piping and dancing competitions attract locals and tourists alike.

Some events are peculiarly Scottish, particularly those that involve trials of strength: tossing the caber (heaving a tree trunk into the air), throwing the hammer and putting the stone.

Major Highland games are staged at Dunoon (p256), Oban (p272) and Braemar (p240).

MEDIA

Although London dominates the UK media industry, Scotland has a flourishing media sector of its own, the legacy of a long tradition of Scottish publishing. The *Herald* (formerly the *Glasgow Herald*), established in 1783, is one of the oldest English-language newspapers in the world.

BBC Scotland is the regional arm of the UK's public service TV and radio broadcaster, producing and broadcasting programmes that reflect Scotland's distinctive cultural identity. Funded by an annual TV licence, the BBC doesn't carry advertising.

There are two Scottish-based commercial TV broadcasters. Scottish Television (STV) covers southern Scotland and some of the western Highlands, while Grampian TV transmits to the Highlands from Perth to the Western Isles and Shetland. STV, Grampian and the BBC all provide some Gaelic-language programming.

There's a healthy newspaper sector too. Scotland's three main home-published broadsheets, the *Scotsman, Herald* and *Press & Journal* (total daily sales 300,000) easily outsell all five London-produced broadsheets combined (80,000).

RELIGION

Although the Christian church has played a hugely important role in Scottish history, religious observance in Scotland has been in decline for most of the 20th century. Today only 6.5% of the population regularly attend church on Sunday. Church attendance is highest in the Outer Hebrides (almost 40%) and lowest in the cities.

The two largest religious denominations are the Presbyterian Church of Scotland (47%) and the Roman Catholic Church (16%), with 28% claiming no religious affiliation at all. Non-Christian religions account for only 2% of the population, mostly small communities of Muslims, Hindus, Sikhs and Jews. See also the boxed text Wee Frees & Other Island Creeds p356.

ARTS
Literature

Scotland's best-loved and most famous literary figure is, of course, Robert Burns (1759–96). His works have been translated into dozens of languages and are known and admired the world over (see the boxed text p161).

In 1787 Burns was introduced to a 16-year-old boy at a social gathering in the house of an Edinburgh professor. The boy grew up to be Sir Walter Scott (1771–1832), Scotland's greatest and most prolific novelist. The son of an Edinburgh lawyer, Scott was born in Guthrie St (off Chambers St; the house no longer exists) and lived at various New Town addresses before moving to his country house at Abbotsford (p145). Scott's early works were rhyming ballads, such as *The Lady of the Lake*, and his first historical novels – Scott effectively invented the genre – were published anonymously. He almost single-handedly revived interest in Scottish history and legend in the early 19th century, and was largely responsible for

DID YOU KNOW?

The Falkirk Tartan is a piece of cream and brown cloth that was found with a hoard of Roman coins dating from around AD 320. It is now in the Museum of Scotland in Edinburgh.

You can search for your own clan tartan at www.scottish-tartans -society.com.

DID YOU KNOW?

It is illegal to import haggis into the USA, as the US government has declared that sheep lungs are unfit for human consumption.

TARTANALIA

Bagpipes

Highland soldiers were traditionally accompanied into battle by the skirl of the pipes, and the Scottish Highland bagpipe is unique in being the only musical instrument ever to be classed as a weapon. The playing of the pipes was banned – under pain of death – by the British government in 1747 as part of a scheme to suppress the Highlands after the Jacobite uprising. Officially described as a 'weapon of war', the pipes were revived when the Highland regiments were drafted into the British Army towards the end of the 18th century.

The bagpipe consists of a leather bag held under the arm, kept inflated by blowing through the blowstick; the piper forces air through the pipes by squeezing the bag with the forearm. Three of the pipes, known as drones, play a constant note (one bass, two tenor) in the background. The fourth pipe, the chanter, is the one on which the melody is played.

Queen Victoria did much to popularise the bagpipes with her patronage of all things Scottish. When staying at Balmoral she liked to be wakened by a piper playing outside her window.

Ceilidh

The Gaelic word *ceilidh* (pronounced *kay*-lay) means 'visit'. A *ceilidh* was originally a social gathering in the house after the day's work was over, enlivened with story-telling, music and song. These days, a *ceilidh* means an evening of traditional Scottish entertainment including music, song and dance.

Tartan

The oldest surviving piece of tartan – a patterned woollen textile now made into everything from kilts to key-fobs – dates back to the Roman period. Today tartan is popular the world over, and beyond – astronaut Al Bean took his MacBean tartan to the moon and back. Particular *setts* (tartan patterns) didn't come to be associated with particular clans until the 17th century, although today every clan, and indeed every Scottish football team, has one or more distinctive tartans.

The Kilt

The original Scottish Highland dress was not the kilt but the *plaid* – a long length of tartan cloth wrapped around the body and over the shoulder. The wearing of Highland dress was banned after the Jacobite rebellions but revived under royal patronage in the 19th century. George IV and his English courtiers donned kilts for their visit to Scotland in 1822. Sir Walter Scott, novelist, poet and dedicated patriot, did much to rekindle interest in Scottish ways. By then, however, many of the old *setts* (tartan patterns) had been forgotten – some tartans are actually Victorian creations. The modern kilt only appeared in the 18th century and was reputedly invented by Thomas Rawlinson, an Englishman!

The Scottish Flag

Scottish football and rugby supporters can never seem to make up their minds which flag to wave – the Saltire or the Lion Rampant. The Saltire or St Andrew's Cross – a diagonal white cross on a blue ground – is one of the oldest national flags in the world, dating from at least the 12th century. Originally a religious emblem – St Andrew was crucified on a diagonal cross – it became a national emblem in the 14th century. According to legend, white clouds in the form of a saltire appeared in a blue sky during the battle of Nechtansmere between Scots and Saxons, urging the Scots to victory. It was incorporated in the Union Flag of the United Kingdom following the Act of Union in 1707.

The Lion Rampant – a red lion on a golden-yellow ground – is the Royal Banner of Scotland. It is thought to derive from the arms of King William I the Lion (reigned 1143–1214), and strictly speaking should be used only by a Scottish monarch. It is incorporated in the British Royal Standard, quartered with the three lions of England and the harp of Ireland.

organising King George IV's visit to Scotland in 1822. Plagued by debt in later life, he wrote obsessively – to the detriment of his health – in order to make money, but will always be best remembered for classic tales such as *Waverley, The Antiquary, The Heart of Midlothian, Ivanhoe, Redgauntlet* and *Castle Dangerous*.

Along with Scott, Robert Louis Stevenson (1850–94) ranks as Scotland's best-known novelist. Born at 8 Howard Place in Edinburgh, into a family of famous lighthouse engineers, Stevenson studied law at Edinburgh University but was always intent on pursuing the life of a writer. An inveterate traveller, but dogged by ill-health, he finally settled in Samoa in 1889, where he was revered by the natives as 'Tusitala' – the teller of tales. Stevenson is known and loved around the world for those tales: *Kidnapped, Catriona, Treasure Island, The Master of Ballantrae* and *The Strange Case of Dr Jekyll and Mr Hyde*.

Sir Arthur Conan Doyle (1859–1930), the creator of Sherlock Holmes, was born in Edinburgh and studied medicine at Edinburgh University. He based the character of Holmes on one of his lecturers, the surgeon Dr Joseph Bell, who had employed his forensic skills and powers of deduction on several murder cases in Edinburgh.

Scotland's finest modern poet was Hugh MacDiarmid (born Christopher Murray Grieve; 1892–1978). Originally from Dumfriesshire, he moved to Edinburgh in 1908, where he trained as a teacher and later a journalist, but spent most of his life in Montrose, Shetland, Glasgow and Biggar. His masterpiece is *A Drunk Man Looks at the Thistle*, a 2685-line Joycean monologue.

Born in Edinburgh, Norman MacCaig (1910–96) is widely regarded as the greatest Scottish poet of his generation. A primary school teacher for almost 40 years, MacCaig wrote poetry that is witty, adventurous, moving and filled with sharp observation; poems such as *November Night, Edinburgh* vividly capture the atmosphere of his home city.

The poet and storyteller George Mackay Brown (1917–96) was born in Stromness in the Orkney Islands, and lived there almost all his life. Although his poems and novels are rooted in Orkney, his work, like that of Burns, transcends local and national boundaries. His novel *Greenvoe* is a warm, witty and poetic evocation of everyday life in an Orkney community.

Lewis Grassic Gibbon (born James Leslie Mitchell; 1901–35) is another Scots writer whose novels vividly capture a sense of place – in this case the

> **Robert Louis Stevenson, Scotland's best-known novelist, was always intent on pursuing the life of a writer**

AUTHOR PROFILE: IAIN BANKS

One of Scotland's most successful contemporary authors, Iain Banks (1954–) is also one of its most prolific. He has published 20 novels since 1984, nine of them science fiction written under 'the world's most penetrable pseudonym', Iain M Banks.

Hailed as one of the most imaginative writers of his generation, Banks burst on the Scottish literary scene with his dazzling debut novel *The Wasp Factory*, a macabre but utterly compelling exploration of the inner world of Frank, a strange and deeply disturbed teenager. Though violent and unsettling, its dark humour and sharp dialogue keep the pages turning right to the bitter (and twisted) end.

Banks' most enjoyable books are *Complicity* (1993), a gruesome and often hilarious thriller-cum-satire on the greed and corruption of the Thatcher years, and the immensely likeable *The Crow Road* (1992), a warm, witty and moving family saga based in the fictional Argyllshire town of Gallanach (a thinly disguised Oban transplanted to the shores of Loch Crinan). The latter provides one of Scottish fiction's most memorable opening sentences: 'It was the day my grandmother exploded.'

rural northeast of Kincardineshire and Aberdeenshire. His most famous work is the trilogy of novels called *A Scot's Quair*.

Dame Muriel Spark (1918–) was born in Edinburgh and educated at James Gillespie's High School for Girls, an experience that provided material for perhaps her best-known novel, *The Prime of Miss Jean Brodie*, a shrewd portrait of 1930s Edinburgh. Dame Muriel is a prolific writer; her 22nd novel, *The Finishing School*, is due out in 2004.

The most widely known Scots writers today include the award-winning James Kelman (1946–), Iain Banks (see the boxed text, p39) and Irvine Welsh (1961–). The grim realities of contemporary Glasgow are vividly conjured up in Kelman's short story collection *Not Not While the Giro*; his controversial novel *How Late It Was, How Late* won the 1994 Booker Prize.

The novels of Irvine Welsh, who grew up in Edinburgh's working-class district of Muirhouse, describe a very different world from that inhabited by

---

ESSENTIAL SCOTTISH READS

- *Waverley* (1814) by Sir Walter Scott was English Literature's first historical novel, a romantic account of a Scottish soldier caught up in the 1745 Jacobite Rebellion. Hard to get into but worth the effort.

- *Kidnapped!* (1886) by Robert Louis Stevenson is a rip-roaring adventure tale for all ages, following 16-year-old Davie Balfour as he escapes through the Highlands with Jacobite rebel Allan Breck Stuart.

- *The Silver Darlings* (1941) by Neil M Gunn is a moving and mystical novel set in 19th-century Caithness, following the attempts by Highlanders dispossessed by the Clearances to wrest a living from the herring fishery.

- *A Scot's Quair* (1946) by Lewis Grassic Gibbon is a trilogy set in rural northeast Scotland that follows heroine Chris Guthrie as she tries to resolve the conflict between her love of the land and her desire to escape a constricting peasant culture.

- *Para Handy Tales* (1955) by Neil Munro is a much-loved collection of humorous stories about the crew of a steam puffer as it cruises the sea lochs of Argyllshire and the Crinan Canal.

- *The Prime of Miss Jean Brodie* (1962) by Muriel Spark is the story of a charismatic teacher in a 1930s Edinburgh girls school who leads her chosen girls – her *creme de la creme* – in the pursuit of truth and beauty, with devastating consequences.

- *Greenvoe* (1972) by George Mackay Brown is a vivid evocation of life in an Orkney fishing village in the 1960s; it is warm, funny, poetic and ultimately very, very moving.

- *Laidlaw* (1977) by William McIlvanney is a gritty detective story set in the mean streets of 1970s Glasgow, following in the footsteps of unorthodox policeman-cum-philosopher Jack Laidlaw.

- *Trainspotting* (1993) by Irvine Welsh is a disturbing and darkly humorous journey through Edinburgh's junkie underworld, pulling no punches as it charts hero Renton's descent into heroin addiction.

- *Black and Blue* (1997) by Ian Rankin stars hard-drinking detective John Rebus, Edinburgh's answer to Laidlaw, as he re-examines the notorious Bible John murders of the late 1960s. Gripping noir-style writing.

- *The Trick Is to Keep Breathing* (1999) by Janice Galloway follows a young drama teacher, the ironically named Joy, as she slips over the edge into depression and madness. Fluent, witty writing and comic minor characters keep the pages turning.

- *Indelible Acts* (2003) by AL Kennedy is a collection of mesmerising short stories on the theme of love and longing written by a master (or rather mistress) of the form, writing at the very top of her game.

Miss Jean Brodie – the modern city's underworld of drugs, drink, despair and violence. Best known for his debut novel *Trainspotting*, Welsh's best work is probably *Marabou Stork Nightmares*, in which a soccer hooligan, paralysed and in a coma, reviews his violent and brutal life.

Cinema & Television

Scotland has never really had its own film industry, but in recent years the government-funded agency **Scottish Screen** (☎ 0141-302 1730; www.scottishscreen.com) has been created to nurture native talent and promote and develop all aspects of film and TV in Scotland.

Perthshire-born John Grierson (1898–1972) is acknowledged around the world as the father of the documentary film. His legacy includes the classic *Drifters* (about the Scottish herring fishery) and *Seaward the Great Ships* (about Clyde shipbuilding). Film-maker Bill Douglas (1934–91), the director of an award-winning trilogy of films documenting his childhood and early adult life, was born in the former mining village of Newcraighall just south of Edinburgh.

Glasgow-born writer-director Bill Forsyth (1946–) is best known for *Local Hero* (1983), a gentle comedy about an oil magnate seduced by the beauty of the Highlands, and *Gregory's Girl* (1980), about an awkward, teenage schoolboy's romantic exploits. The directing credits of Gillies MacKinnon (1948–), another Glasgow native, include *Small Faces* (1996), *Regeneration* (1997) and *Hideous Kinky* (1998). Michael Caton-Jones (1958–), director of *Memphis Belle* (1990) and *Rob Roy* (1995), was born in West Lothian and is a graduate of Edinburgh University.

In the 1990s the rise of the director-producer-writer team of Danny Boyle (English), Andrew Macdonald and John Hodge (both Scottish) – who wrote the scripts for *Shallow Grave* (1994), *Trainspotting* (1996) and *A Life Less Ordinary* (1997) – marked the beginnings of what might be described as a home-grown Scottish film industry. Other cinematic talents to emerge in this decade include actor and director Peter Mullan (*My Name is Joe*; 1998) and director Lynne Ramsay (*Ratcatcher*; 1999).

Scotland's most famous actor is, of course, Sir Sean Connery (1930–), the original and best James Bond, and star of dozens of other hit films including *Highlander* (1986), *The Name of the Rose* (1986), *Indiana Jones and the Last Crusade* (1989) and *The Hunt for Red October* (1990). Connery started life as 'Big Tam' Connery, sometime milkman and brickie, born in a tenement in Fountainbridge in Edinburgh.

Other Scottish actors who have achieved international recognition include Robert Carlyle, who starred in *Trainspotting* (1996), *The Full Monty* (1997) – the UK's most commercially successful film – and *The World Is Not Enough* (1999); and Ewan MacGregor, who appeared in *Trainspotting*, *Moulin Rouge* (2001) and the most recent Star Wars films.

It's less widely known that Scotland produced some of the stars of silent film, including Eric Campbell (the big, bearded villain in Charlie Chaplin's films) and Jimmy Finlayson (the cross-eyed character in Laurel and Hardy films); though born in England, Stan Laurel himself grew up and made his acting debut in Glasgow.

Music

FOLK MUSIC

Scotland has always had a strong folk tradition. In the 1960s and 1970s Robin Hall and Jimmy MacGregor, the Corries and the hugely talented Ewan McColl worked the pubs and clubs up and down the country. The Boys of the Lough, headed by Shetland fiddler Aly Bain, were one of

Despite dodgy Scottish accents from Liam Neeson and Jessica Lange, *Rob Roy* is a witty and moving cinematic version of Sir Walter Scott's tale of the outlaw MacGregor.

For a guide to Scottish film locations check out www.scotlandthemovie .com.

the first professional bands to promote the traditional Celtic music of Scotland and Ireland. They have been followed by the Battlefield Band, Runrig (who write songs in Gaelic), Alba, Capercaillie and others.

The Scots folk songs that you will often hear sung in pubs and at *ceilidhs* draw on Scotland's rich history. A huge number of them relate to the Jacobite rebellions of the early 18th century and, in particular, to Bonnie Prince Charlie – *Hey Johnnie Cope,* the *Skye Boat Song,* and *Will Ye No Come Back Again,* for example – while others relate to the Covenanters and the Highland Clearances.

ROCK & POP

The *Living Tradition* is a bi-monthly magazine covering the folk and traditional music of Scotland and the British Isles, and Celtic music with features and reviews of albums and live gigs. See also www.folkmusic.net.

Scottish artists who have been successful in rock and pop music include Gerry Rafferty, who wrote Baker Street, Fish (lead singer of Marillion) and Midge Ure, who helped organise the Band Aid famine relief in the 1980s. Iain Anderson, front man for Jethro Tull, was born in Edinburgh. Nazareth, Barbara Dickson, Big Country and The Rezillos all hailed from Fife. Aberdeen's greatest musical export is Annie Lennox. The Jesus & Mary Chain came from East Kilbride. Twin brothers Craig and Charlie Reid from Fife have enjoyed huge success, both at home and abroad, as The Proclaimers.

Glasgow has produced an amazing range of musical talent, including such performers as the BMX Bandits, Aztec Camera, Hue & Cry, Simple Minds, Wet Wet Wet, Primal Scream, Texas, Belle and Sebastian, Travis – and, of course, Lulu, who had her first hit as a teenager in 1964 and is still going strong. For more on Glasgow's music scene see the Glasgow Music Community boxed text, p126.

Edinburgh's contribution to the contemporary music scene includes the rock band Idlewild; reggae-soul-pop singer Finlay Quaye; Shirley Manson, lead singer of Garbage; and the red-hot jazz saxophonist Tommy Smith.

Architecture

There are interesting buildings all over Scotland, but Edinburgh has a particularly rich heritage of 18th- and early 19th-century architecture, and Glasgow is noted for its superb Victorian buildings.

ROMANESQUE (12TH CENTURY)

The Romanesque style – with its characteristic round arches and chevron decoration – was introduced to Scotland along with the monasteries that were founded during the reign of David I (1124–53). Good examples survive in Dunfermline Abbey (p193), St Magnus Cathedral in Kirkwall (p373) and the parish churches at Leuchars and Dalmeny.

GOTHIC (12TH TO 16TH CENTURIES)

The more elaborate Gothic style, with its tall, pointed arches, ornate window tracery and ribbed vaulting, was brought to Scotland and adapted by the monastic orders. Examples of Early Gothic architecture can be seen in the ruins of the great Border abbeys of Jedburgh (p146) and Dryburgh (p144), at Holyrood Abbey in Edinburgh (p67) and in Glasgow Cathedral (p112). The more decorative Middle and Late Gothic styles appear in Melrose Abbey (p143), the cathedrals of Dunkeld (p212) and Elgin (p244), and the parish churches of Haddington (St Mary's) and Stirling (Holy Rude).

POST-REFORMATION (16TH & 17TH CENTURIES)

After the Reformation many abbeys and cathedrals were damaged or destroyed, as the new religion frowned on ceremony and ornament.

During this period the old style of castle, with its central keep and curtain wall (eg Caerlaverock and Dirleton Castles), was superseded by the tower house. Good examples include Castle Campbell (p190), Loch Leven Castle (p203) and Neidpath Castle (p148). The Renaissance style was introduced in the royal palaces of Linlithgow (p103) and Falkland (p194), and in the remarkable Italianate courtyard at Crichton Castle.

GEORGIAN (18TH & EARLY 19TH CENTURIES)

The leading Scottish architects of the 18th century were William Adam (1684–1748) and his son Robert Adam (1728–92), whose revival of classical Greek and Roman forms influenced architects throughout Europe. Among the many neoclassical buildings they designed are Hopetoun House (p100), Culzean Castle (p162) and Edinburgh's Charlotte Square (p70), possibly the finest example of Georgian architecture anywhere.

The New Town of Edinburgh, and other planned towns such as Inveraray (Argyll) and Blair Atholl (Perthshire), are characterised by their elegant Georgian architecture.

VICTORIAN (MID- TO LATE 19TH CENTURY)

Alexander 'Greek' Thomson (1817–75) changed the face of 19th-century Glasgow with his neoclassical designs. Masterpieces such as the Egyptian Halls and Caledonia Road Church in Glasgow combine Egyptian and Hindu motifs with Greek and Roman forms.

In Edinburgh, William Henry Playfair (1790–1857) continued the neoclassical tradition of Robert Adam in the Greek temples of the National Monument on Calton Hill, the Royal Scottish Academy and the National Gallery of Scotland, before moving on to the neo-Gothic style in Edinburgh University's New College on The Mound.

The 19th-century boom in country-house building was led by architects William Burn (1789–1870) and David Bryce (1803–76). The resurgence of interest in Scottish history and identity, led by writers such as Sir Walter Scott, saw architects turn to the towers, pointed turrets and crow-stepped gables of the 16th century for inspiration. The Victorian revival of the Scottish Baronial style, which first appeared in 16th-century buildings such as Craigievar Castle (p241), produced many fanciful houses such as Balmoral Castle (p239), Scone Palace (p204) and Abbotsford (p145).

THE 20TH CENTURY

Scotland's most famous 20th-century architect and designer is Charles Rennie Mackintosh, one of the most influential exponents of the Art Nouveau style. The most acclaimed example of his work is Glasgow School of Art (p112), which still looks modern a century after it was built. The Art Deco style of the 1930s made little impact in Scotland, with only a few examples, such as St Andrews House in Edinburgh and the beautifully restored Luma Tower in Glasgow.

During the 1960s Scotland's larger towns and cities suffered badly under the onslaught of the motor car and the unsympathetic impact of large-scale, concrete building developments. However, modern architecture discovered a new confidence in the 1980s and 1990s, exemplified by the impressive gallery housing the Burrell Collection (p114) in Glasgow and the stunning modern buildings lining the banks of Glasgow's River Clyde (p109).

Scotland's most controversial new structure is the Scottish parliament building in Edinburgh (p67), currently nearing completion.

Scotland's Castles by Chris Tabraham is an excellent companion for anyone touring Scottish castles – a readable, illustrated history detailing how and why they were built.

Painting

If asked to think of a Scottish painting, most people probably picture *Monarch of the Glen,* a romanticised portrait of a magnificent Highland red deer stag by Sir Edwin Landseer (1802–73). Landseer was not a Scot but a Londoner, though he did spend a lot of time in Scotland, leasing a cottage in Glen Feshie and visiting the young Queen Victoria at Balmoral (p239) to tutor her in drawing and etching.

Perhaps the most famous Scottish painting is the portrait *Reverend Robert Walker Skating on Duddingston Loch* by Sir Henry Raeburn (1756–1823) in the National Gallery of Scotland (p69). This image of a Presbyterian minister at play beneath Arthur's Seat, with all the poise of a ballerina and the hint of a smile on his lips, is a symbol of Enlightenment Edinburgh, the triumph of reason over wild nature.

Scottish portraiture reached its peak during the Scottish Enlightenment the second half of the 18th century with the paintings of Raeburn and his contemporary Allan Ramsay (1713–84). You can see many fine examples of their work in the Scottish National Portrait Gallery (p70). At the same time, Alexander Nasmyth (1758–1840) emerged as an important landscape painter whose work had an immense influence on the 19th century. One of the greatest artists of the 19th century was Sir David Wilkie (1785–1841), whose genre paintings depicted rustic scenes of rural Highland life.

In the early 20th century the Scottish painters most widely acclaimed outside the country are the group known as the Scottish Colourists – SJ Peploe, Francis Cadell, Leslie Hunter and JD Ferguson – whose striking paintings drew on French post-impressionist and Fauvist influences. Peploe and Cadell, active in the 1920s and 1930s, often spent the summer painting together on the Isle of Iona (p282), and reproductions of their beautiful land- and sea-scapes appear on many a print and postcard. Aberdeen Art Gallery (p233), Kirkcaldy Art Gallery (p193) and the JD Ferguson Gallery in Perth (p205) all have good examples of their work.

The painters of the so-called Edinburgh School of the 1930s were modernist landscape artists. Chief among them were William Gillies (1898–1978), Sir William MacTaggart (1903–81) and Anne Redpath (1895–1965). Following WWII artists such as Alan Davie (1920–) and Sir Eduardo Paolozzi (1924–) gained international reputations in abstract expressionism and pop art. The Dean Gallery (p71) in Edinburgh has a large collection of Paolozzi's work.

Among contemporary Scottish artists the most famous – or rather notorious – are Peter Howson and Jack Vettriano. Howson (1958–), best known for his grim portraits of Glasgow down-and-outs and muscular workers, hit the headlines when he went to Bosnia as an official war artist in 1993 and produced some disturbing and controversial works. *Croatian and Muslim,* an uncompromising rape scene, sparked a debate about what was acceptable in a public exhibition of art. More recently his nude portraits of Madonna – the pop icon, not the religious one – garnered even more column inches in the press. His work is much sought after and collected by celebrities such as David Bowie and Madonna herself. You can see examples of Howson's work at Aberdeen Art Gallery (p233) and Glasgow's Museum of Modern Art (p111).

Jack Vettriano (1954–) was formerly a mining engineer, but now ranks as one of Scotland's most commercially successful artists. An entirely self-taught painter, his work – realistic, voyeuristic, occasionally sinister and often carrying a powerful erotic charge – has been compared to that of the American painters Edward Hopper and Walter Sickert. You can see reproductions of his work in coffee-table books and posters, but not in any Scottish art gallery. The Scottish art establishment looks down its nose at him, despite – or perhaps because of – the enormous popularity of his work.

Raeburn's image of a Presbyterian minister at play is a symbol of the triumph of reason over wild nature

SCOTTISH INVENTIONS & DISCOVERIES

The Scots have made a contribution to modern civilisation that is out of all proportion to the size of their country. Although Scotland accounts for only 10% of Britain's population, it has produced more than 20% of leading British scientists, philosophers, engineers and inventors. Scots established the modern disciplines of economics, sociology, geology, electromagnetic theory, anaesthesiology and antibiotics, and pioneered the steam engine, the pneumatic tyre, the telephone and the television.

Given the weather in Scotland perhaps it's not surprising that it was a Scot – the chemist Charles Macintosh (1766–1843) – who invented the waterproof material for the raincoat that still bears his name.

James Watt (1736–1819) didn't invent the steam engine (that was done by an Englishman, Thomas Newcomen) but it was Watt's modifications and improvements – notably the separate condenser – that led to its widespread usefulness in industry.

The chemical engineer James Young (1811–83), known as 'Paraffin' Young, developed the process of refining crude oil and established the world's first oil industry, based on extracting oil from the oil shales of West Lothian.

Not only did John Logie Baird (1888–1946) from Helensburgh invent television, but it was his own company that produced (with the BBC) the world's first TV broadcast, the first broadcast with sound and the first outside broadcast. He also developed the concept of colour TV and took out a patent on fibre optics.

Alexander Graham Bell (1847–1922) was born in Edinburgh and emigrated to Canada and the USA, where he made a series of inventions, the most famous being the telephone in 1876.

In 1996 a team of Scottish embryologists working at the Roslin Institute near Edinburgh scored a first when they successfully cloned a sheep, Dolly, from the breast cell of an adult sheep. They added to this success when Dolly was mated naturally with a Welsh ram; in April 1998 she gave birth to a healthy lamb, Bonnie.

The list of famous Scots goes on and on: James Gregory (1638–75), inventor of the reflecting telescope; John McAdam (1756–1836), who developed road-building and surfacing techniques; Thomas Telford (1757–1834), one of the greatest civil engineers of his time; Robert William Thomson (1822–73), who patented the pneumatic tyre in 1845; John Boyd Dunlop (1840–1921), who reinvented the pneumatic tyre in 1888; Sir Alexander Fleming (1881–1955), co-discoverer of penicillin; and Sir Robert Watson-Watt (1892–1973), a direct descendant of James Watt, who developed the radar system that helped Britain to victory in WWII.

Other Scottish inventions and discoveries:

antiseptics	grand pianos	morphine
breech-loading rifles	golf	postage stamp (adhesive)
bicycles	insulin	refrigeration
carbon dioxide	iron ploughs	speedometers
colour photography	iron and steel ships	steam-powered ships
decimal point	kaleidoscope	telescopes
electric light	lawnmowers	ultrasound
fire alarms	logarithms	vacuum flasks
gas-masks	marmalade	water softeners

Scotland has also produced a significant number of Nobel Prize winners. Sir William Ramsay (1852–1916), whose work helped in the development of the nuclear industry, received the chemistry prize in 1904. Physiologist John Macleod (1876–1935), whose work led to the discovery of insulin, received the prize for medicine in 1923. Sir Alexander Fleming (1881–1955), co-discoverer of penicillin, also received the prize for medicine (in 1945). Other prize winners include Charles Wilson, John Orr, Alexander Robertus Todd and Sir James Black.

Environment

THE LAND

The Scottish mainland can be neatly divided into three parts whose distinctive landscapes reflect their underlying geology – the Southern Uplands, the Central Lowlands and the Highlands.

The Southern Uplands, a range of rounded hills covered with grass and heather, bounded by fertile coastal plains, form the southern boundary to the Central Lowlands. The geological divide – the Southern Uplands Fault – runs in a straight line from Girvan in Ayrshire to Dunbar in East Lothian.

The Central Lowlands lie in a broad band stretching from Glasgow and Ayr in the west to Edinburgh and Dundee in the east. This area is underlaid by sedimentary rocks, including the beds of coal and oil shale that fuelled Scotland's industrial revolution. As a consequence, most of the country's industry, its two largest cities and 80% of the population are concentrated here.

Another great geological divide – the Highland Boundary Fault – runs from Helensburgh, through the southern part of Loch Lomond, to Stonehaven on the east coast, and marks the southern edge of the vast block of ancient metamorphic and igneous rocks that makes up the Scottish Highlands.

These Highland hills – most of their summits reach to around the 900m to 1000m mark – were deeply dissected by glaciers during the last Ice Age, creating a series of deep, U-shaped valleys. As the ice sheets melted and sea levels rose, the glacial valleys of the west coast were flooded, creating the long, narrow sea lochs that are such a distinctive feature of Highland scenery.

Among Scotland's biggest attractions are the wild, empty landscapes of the western and northern Highlands, but you should remember that, for all their pristine beauty, these are man-made wildernesses. Before the Highland Clearances many of these empty corners of Scotland supported sizeable populations until their human inhabitants were evicted in favour of the more profitable sheep.

New forests would spring up except for the fact that red deer – managed as a sporting asset on deer-stalking estates – eat the young trees before they have a chance to get established. And when you marvel at the August hillsides swathed in purple heather, remember that if gamekeepers didn't burn the heather moorland each year, it would revert to scrub – the burning promotes the growth of new shoots, which provide food and cover for grouse (another sporting asset) and keep the heather dominant.

WILDLIFE

Scotland's wildlife is one of its big attractions. Many species that have disappeared from, or are rare in, the rest of Britain survive among the hills and forests of the north, including red deer, golden eagles, otters, wildcats and ospreys.

Animals

Red deer are found in large numbers in Scotland, but the reindeer (apart from the herd of introduced domestic reindeer living in a semiwild state in the Cairngorms), beaver and auroch (wild ox) are all long extinct; the

DID YOU KNOW?

Scotland accounts for one third of the British mainland's surface area, but it has a massive 80% of Britain's coastline and only 10% of its population.

Woodland Trust Scotland is the Scottish arm of a UK charity dedicated to the conservation of native woodlands. See www.woodland-trust.org.uk.

last wolf was shot in Sutherland in 1700. There has been talk of reintroducing the beaver and, more controversially, the wolf. A small population of wildcats survives in parts of the Highlands but they are extremely shy and rarely seen in the wild.

Otters are found in most parts of Scotland, around the coast and along salmon and trout rivers. Their numbers are increasing and you stand a reasonable chance of spotting them in the wild if you are patient and observant. The best places are in the northwest, especially in Skye and the Outer Hebrides. The piers at Kyle of Lochalsh and Portree are otter 'hot spots', as the otters have learned to scavenge from fishing boats.

Bred for their quality beef, Highland cattle are Scotland's most distinctive bovine breed. They are fierce looking (with their horns) but docile-natured, with long reddish-brown coats.

Scotland has an immense variety of bird species. Large numbers of grouse graze the heather on the moors, and gamekeepers burn vast areas to encourage the new shoots that are the favourite food of this popular game bird. In heavily forested areas you may be lucky enough to see a capercaillie, a black, turkey-like bird, the largest member of the grouse family. Birds of prey, such as the golden eagle, osprey, peregrine falcon and hen harrier, are protected. Millions of greylag geese winter on the Lowland stubble fields.

> One of the best-loved pieces of Scottish wildlife writing is *Ring of Bright Water* by Gavin Maxwell, in which the author describes life in the remote Glenelg peninsula with his two pet otters in the 1950s.

The ptarmigan (a relative of the grouse) is a native of the hills, seldom seen below 700m, with the unusual feature of having feathered feet. It is the only British bird that plays the Arctic trick of changing its plumage from mottled brown in summer to dazzling white in winter, the better to blend in with the snowfields.

The blue mountain hare shares the ptarmigan's high mountain environment, and also its trait of swapping a grey-brown summer coat for a pure white winter one.

> Scottish Natural Heritage Government agency is responsible for the conservation of Scotland's wildlife, habitats and landscapes. See www.snh.org.uk.

Whale-watching has become very popular in recent years, and the waters off Scotland's west coast are rich in marine mammals. Dolphin and porpoise are fairly common, and in summer minke whales are regular visitors. Growing up to 10m long, they make an impressive sight when they breach through a shoal of herring fry. Killer whales are rarer, but they too are occasionally seen.

ENDANGERED SPECIES

Scotland is home to many animals and birds that are rare elsewhere in the UK, but they too are constantly threatened by the changing environment. The habitat of the once common corncrake, for example, was almost completely wiped out by modern farming methods. Farmers now receive a subsidy for mowing in a corncrake-friendly fashion and there are good prospects for its survival.

Wildlife species that were slaughtered to the point of extermination in the 19th century – golden eagles, buzzards, pine martens, polecats and wildcats among them – are now protected by law and are slowly starting to recover. Both the red kite and the white-tailed sea eagle, both absent from Scotland since the 19th century, have been successfully reintroduced.

You can see nesting ospreys at Loch Garten (p306), and white-tailed sea eagles (via CCTV cameras at a secret nesting site) at the Aros Centre on Skye (p350). Corncrakes are shy birds and rarely seen, but you can certainly hear them – their distinctive call sounds like a thumbnail drawn along the teeth of a comb – on Colonsay (p268) and at Loch Gruinart Nature Reserve on Islay (p265).

INTRODUCED SPECIES

The American grey squirrel is an alien invader, introduced at the end of the 19th century and now very common. You can see them scampering around city parks in Edinburgh and Glasgow. They took to the British environment so well that they have displaced the native red squirrel in most of England and Wales; Scotland is now home to 75% of Britain's surviving red squirrel population.

John Muir Trust is a charity that has purchased several properties, including Ben Nevis, and manages them in partnership with local communities. See www.jmt.org.

Scottish Wildlife Trust is a voluntary agency owning or managing more than 120 nature reserves. See www.swt.org.uk.

Park	Features	Activities to visit	Best time	Page
Balranald Nature Reserve	lochan (small lochs), moor and marsh: corncrake, red-necked phalarope	bird-watching	Apr-Aug	p364
Caenlochan National Nature Reserve	mountain and glen: rare alpine flora	hill walking	Jul-Aug	p228
Cairngorms National Park	subarctic mountain plateau, native pine forests: osprey, ptarmigan, pine marten	hill walking, climbing, skiing	Aug	p300
Craigellachie Nature Reserve	pine forest, crags: capercaillie, peregrine falcon	walking	May-Sep	p302
Galloway Forest Park	hills, forests, lochs: red deer, red kite	walking, mountain biking	Oct	p169
Glen Affric National Nature Reserve	mountain, loch, native pine forest: golden eagle, red deer, pine marten, wildcat	hill walking	Jul-Oct	p296
Hermaness Nature Reserve	coastal cliffs: puffins	bird-watching	Apr-Aug	p398
Inverpolly Nature Reserve	mountain, loch and moorland: red deer, wildcat, otter, golden eagle, peregrine falcon, red-throated diver	walking	Apr-Oct	p339
Isle of Rum National Nature Reserve	dramatic rocky mountains and coast: red deer, wild goat, golden eagle, white-tailed sea eagle, Manx shearwater	walking, hill walking, bird-watching	Apr-Oct	p321
Loch Druidibeg National Nature Reserve	freshwater loch, farmland, machair: dunlin, redshank, ringed plover, greylag goose, corncrake	bird-watching, walking	Apr-Oct	p365
Loch Gruinart Nature Reserve	farmland, tidal flats: corncrake, migrating geese and waders	bird-watching	Apr-Oct	p265
Loch Lomond & the Trossachs National Park	scenic lochs, forests, hills angling, watersports	hill walking,	Sep-Nov	p251
Noss National Nature Reserve	spectacular coastal cliffs: nesting seabirds	bird-watching	Apr-Aug	p392
St Abb's Head National Nature Reserve	coastal cliffs: nesting seabirds	walking, bird-watching	Apr-May	p140

Plants

Although the thistle is commonly associated with Scotland, the national flower is the Scottish bluebell (known in England as the harebell), which carpets the floor of native woodlands in spring. Heather, whose tiny pink and purple flowers emerge in August, covers much of the hills and moors. Other conspicuous flowering plants include vivid pink rhododendrons and bright yellow gorse (or whin), which both flower in May and June.

INTRODUCED SPECIES

Rhododendrons – flowering shrubs with beautiful pink, purple or red flowers – were introduced to Scotland from Southeast Asia and the Himalayas by plant collectors in the 19th century. Planted at first in private gardens, they thrived in Scotland's mild, damp climate and soon escaped the confines of estates to grow wild. Though beautiful to look at, they grow vigorously and tend to displace native trees and shrubs.

CONSERVATION AREAS

Since 2002 Scotland has gone from having no national parks to having two – Loch Lomond & the Trossachs National Park (www.lochlomond -trossachs.org) and the Cairngorms National Park (www.cairngorms.co.uk). The establishment of these parks was accompanied by much wailing and gnashing of teeth over how big an area the parks should encompass and what powers should be given to the park authorities. It's too early yet to tell what effect they will have on the regions they were set up to protect.

Friends of the Earth Scotland is a voluntary organisation campaigning on environmental issues. See www.foe-scotland .org.uk.

ENVIRONMENTAL ISSUES

Since the 1980s many sea lochs and sheltered inlets on the west coast have been disfigured by salmon cages. Salmon farming is worth £300 million a year to the Scottish economy, but the industry has been blamed for spreading disease and parasites in wild fish populations, and for causing pollution and toxic algal blooms.

So-called superquarries are another controversial development of recent decades. Plans for a vast, £70 million quarry on the island of Harris in the Outer Hebrides were finally blocked by the Scottish Executive in 2000, after a 10-year legal battle. A superquarry already scars the northwestern shore of Loch Linnhe at Glensanda, opposite the island of Lismore.

In Caithness the Dounreay nuclear-waste-reprocessing plant has had a poor safety record over several decades. Following a series of accidents and disclosures about errors and cover-ups – around 170kg of weapons-grade uranium remains unaccounted for – the British government decided to close it down in 1998. However, reprocessing will continue until about 2006 when the waste runs out; after that it'll take until 2095 to dismantle the plant safely, clean up the site and encase the remains in concrete.

The latest environmental issue to hit the headlines is the establishment of wind farms – concentrations of giant, electricity-generating windmills that are part of the government's commitment to reducing the electricity industry's dependence on fossil fuels and nuclear power. Although everyone agrees that wind power is clean and economical, there's a powerful 'nimby' (not in my back yard) element who don't want the windmills spoiling the view from their windows.

Food & Drink

Traditional Scottish cookery is all about basic comfort food: solid, nourishing fare, often high in fat, that would keep you warm on a winter's day spent in the fields or out fishing, and sweet treats to come home to in the evening.

STAPLES & SPECIALITIES

Haggis may be the national dish that Scotland is most famous for, but when it comes to what Scottish people actually cook and eat most often, the hands-down winner has to be mince and tatties (potatoes). Minced beef, browned in the pan and then stewed slowly with onion, carrot and gravy, served with mashed potatoes (with a splash of milk and a knob of butter added during the mashing) – it is tasty, warming and you don't even have to chew.

The classic work on traditional Scottish cooking is *The Scots Kitchen* by F Marian McNeill, first published in 1929 but still going strong in various reprints.

Breakfast

Surprisingly few Scots eat porridge for breakfast – these days a café latte and a croissant is just as likely – and even fewer eat it in the traditional way; that is, with salt to taste, but no sugar. The breakfast offered in a B&B or hotel usually consists of fruit juice and cereal or muesli, followed by a choice of bacon, sausage, black pudding (a type of sausage made from dried blood), grilled tomato, mushrooms, and a fried egg or two.

Fish for breakfast may sound strange, but was not unusual in crofting and fishing communities where seafood was a staple; many hotels still offer grilled kippers (smoked herrings) or smoked haddock (poached in milk and served with a poached egg) for breakfast – delicious with lots of buttered toast.

Soups

Scotch broth, made with mutton stock, barley, lentils and peas, is nutritious and tasty, while cock-a-leekie is a hearty soup made with chicken and leeks. Warming vegetable soups include leek and potato soup, and lentil soup (traditionally made using ham stock – vegetarians beware!).

Seafood soups include the delicious *Cullen skink*, made with smoked haddock, potato, onion and milk, and *partan bree* (crab soup).

HAGGIS – SCOTLAND'S NATIONAL DISH

Scotland's national dish is often ridiculed by foreigners because of its ingredients, which admittedly don't sound promising – the finely chopped lungs, heart and liver of a sheep, mixed with oatmeal and onion and stuffed into a sheep's stomach bag. However, it actually tastes surprisingly good.

Haggis should be served with *champit tatties* and *bashed neeps* (mashed potatoes and turnips), with a generous dollop of butter and a good sprinkling of black pepper.

Although it's eaten year-round, haggis is central to the celebrations of 25 January, in honour of Scotland's national poet, Robert Burns. Scots worldwide unite on Burns Night to revel in their Scottishness. A piper announces the arrival of the haggis and Burns' poem *Address to a Haggis* is recited to this 'Great chieftan o' the puddin-race'. The bulging haggis is then lanced with a *dirk* (dagger) to reveal the steaming offal within, 'warm, reekin, rich'.

Vegetarians (and quite a few carnivores, no doubt) will be relieved to know that veggie haggis is available in some restaurants.

Meat & Game

Steak eaters will enjoy a thick fillet of world-famous Aberdeen Angus beef, and beef from Highland cattle is much sought after. Venison, from the red deer, is leaner and appears on many menus. Both may be served with a wine-based or creamy whisky sauce. Then there's haggis, Scotland's much-maligned national dish...

Fish & Seafood

Scottish salmon is famous worldwide, but there's a big difference between farmed salmon and the leaner, more expensive, wild fish. Smoked salmon is traditionally dressed with a squeeze of lemon juice and eaten with fresh brown bread and butter. Trout, the salmon's smaller cousin – whether wild, rod-caught brown trout or farmed rainbow trout – is delicious fried in oatmeal.

As an alternative to kippers (smoked herrings) you may be offered Arbroath smokies (lightly smoked fresh haddock), traditionally eaten cold. Herring fillets fried in oatmeal are good, if you don't mind picking out a few bones. Mackerel pâté and smoked or peppered mackerel (both served cold) are also popular.

Juicy langoustines (also called Dublin Bay prawns), crabs, lobsters, oysters, mussels and scallops are also widely available in Scotland.

Popular Scottish TV chef Nick Nairn's book *Wild Harvest* contains over 100 recipes based on the use of fresh, seasonal Scottish produce.

Puddings

Traditional Scottish puddings are irresistibly creamy, high-calorie concoctions. *Cranachan* is whipped cream flavoured with whisky, and mixed with toasted oatmeal and raspberries. *Atholl brose* is a mixture of cream, whisky and honey, flavoured with oatmeal. *Clootie dumpling* is a rich steamed pudding filled with currants and raisins.

DRINKS

Scotland's most famous soft drink is Barr's Irn Bru: a sweet fizzy drink, radioactive orange in colour, that smells like bubble gum and almost strips the enamel from your teeth. Many Scots swear by its restorative effects as a cure for a hangover.

Scotch whisky (always spelt without an 'e' – whiskey *with* an 'e' is Irish or American) is Scotland's best-known product and biggest export. The spirit has been distilled in Scotland at least since the 15th century. See the boxed text on p52.

As well as whiskies, there are whisky-based liqueurs such as Drambuie. If you must mix your whisky with anything other than water try a whisky-mac (whisky with ginger wine). After a long walk in the rain there's nothing better to put a warm glow in your belly.

At a bar, older Scots may order a 'half' or 'nip' of whisky as a chaser to a pint or half-pint of beer (a 'hauf and a hauf'). Only tourists ask for 'Scotch' – what else would you be served in Scotland? The standard measure in pubs is either 25mL or 35mL.

Scottish breweries produce a wide range of beers. The market is dominated by the big brewers – Youngers, McEwans, Scottish & Newcastle and Tennent's – but smaller local breweries generally create tastier brews, some of them very strong. The aptly named Skullsplitter from Orkney is a good example, at 8.5% alcohol by volume.

Most Scottish brews are graded in shillings so you can tell their strength; the greater the number of shillings, the stronger the beer. The usual range is 60 to 80 shillings (written 80/-). What the English call bitter, Scots call heavy – Caledonian 80/-, Maclays 80/- and Belhaven 80/-

HOW TO BE A MALT WHISKY BUFF

'Love makes the world go round? Not at all! Whisky makes it go round twice as fast.'

From Whisky Galore *by Compton Mackenzie (1883–1972)*

Whisky-tasting today is almost as popular as wine-tasting was in the yuppie heyday of the late 1980s. Being able to tell your Ardbeg from your Edradour is *de rigueur* among the whisky-nosing set, so here are some pointers to help you impress your friends.

What's the difference between malt and grain whiskies?

Malts are distilled from malted barley – that is, barley that has been soaked in water, then allowed to germinate for around 10 days until the starch has turned into sugar – while grain whiskies are distilled from other cereals, usually wheat, corn or unmalted barley.

So what is a single malt?

A single malt is a whisky that has been distilled from malted barley and is the product of a single distillery. A pure (vatted) malt is a mixture of single malts from several distilleries, and a blended whisky is a mixture of various grain whiskies (about 60%) and malt whiskies (about 40%) from many different distilleries.

Why are single malts more desirable than blends?

A single malt, like a fine wine, somehow captures the essence of the place where it was made and matured – a combination of the water, the barley, the peat smoke, the oak barrels in which it was aged, and (in the case of certain coastal distilleries) the sea air and salt spray. Each distillation varies from the one before, like different vintages from the same vineyard.

How should a single malt be drunk?

Either neat, or preferably with a little water added. To appreciate the aroma and flavour to the utmost, a measure of malt whisky should be cut (diluted) with one-third to two-thirds as much spring water (still, bottled spring water will do). Ice, tap water and (God forbid) mixers are for philistines. Would you add lemonade or ice to a glass of Chablis?

Give me some tasting tips!

Go into a bar and order a Lagavulin (Islay) and a Glenfiddich (Speyside). Cut each one with half as much again of still, bottled spring water. Taking each one in turn, hold the glass up to the light to check the colour; stick your nose in the glass and take two or three short, sharp sniffs. By now, everyone in the pub will be giving you funny looks, but never mind.

For the Lagavulin you should be thinking: amber colour, peat-smoke, iodine, seaweed. For the Glenfiddich: pale white-wine colour, malt, pear drops, acetone, citrus. Then taste them. Then try some others. Either you'll be hooked, or you'll never touch whisky again.

Where's the cheapest place to buy Scotch whisky?

A French supermarket, unfortunately. In the UK, where a bottle of single malt typically costs £20 to £30, taxes account for around 72% of the price, making Scotland one of the most expensive places in Europe to enjoy its own national drink.

Where can I learn more?

If you're serious about spirits, the **Scotch Malt Whisky Society** (☎ 0131-554 3451; www.smws.com) in Edinburgh runs an intensive one-day Whisky School that covers the basics of whisky-tasting and evaluation. The cost is £210, including lunch, canapés and drinks. Membership of the society costs from £75 per year and includes use of members' rooms in Edinburgh and London.

are all worth trying, but Deuchar's IPA from Edinburgh's Caledonian Brewery is our favourite.

Draught beer is served in pints (from £1.50 to £2.50) or half-pints; alcoholic content ranges from 3.2% to 8.5%.

VEGETARIANS & VEGANS

Scotland has the same proportion of vegetarians as the rest of the UK – around 8% to 10% of the population – and vegetarianism has moved away from the hippie-student image of a few decades ago and is now firmly in the mainstream. Even the most remote Highland pub usually has at least one vegetarian dish on the menu, and there are many dedicated vegetarian restaurants in the cities. If you get stuck, there's almost always an Italian or Indian restaurant where you can get meat-free pizza, pasta or curry. Vegans, though, may find the options a bit limited outside of Edinburgh and Glasgow.

One thing to keep in mind is that lentil soup, a seemingly vegetarian staple of Scottish pub and restaurant menus, is traditionally made with ham stock.

FEEDING THE FAMILY

Sadly, the majority of Scotland's eating places make no effort to welcome children, and many are actively hostile. In a recent survey nine out of 10 families thought the majority of UK restaurants were not family friendly. There's no way of gauging restaurant attitudes other than by asking.

This situation is changing, albeit slowly, especially in the cities and more popular tourist towns where several restaurants and pubs now have family rooms and/or play areas, but in many smaller towns and country areas kids will still get a frosty reception.

Be aware that pubs without a restaurant licence are not allowed to serve those aged under 16, even if it's just food and soft drinks.

For a list of child-friendly restaurants in the Cairngorms–Inverness region (soon to be extended to the rest of Scotland), see www.kids-scotland.co.uk.

COOKING COURSES

There are two principal places that offer courses in Scottish cookery:
Kinloch Lodge Hotel (☎ 01471-833333; www.claire-macdonald.com; Kinloch Lodge, Isle of Skye IV43 8QY) Cookery demonstrations using fresh, seasonal Scottish produce given by Lady Claire Macdonald, author of Scottish Highland Hospitality.
Nairns Cook School (☎ 01877-385603; www.nairnscookschool.com; Port of Menteith, Stirling FK8 3JZ) Two-day courses in modern Scottish cooking at the school owned by Scotland's top TV chef Nick Nairn, author of Wild Harvest and Island Harvest.

Edinburgh

CONTENTS

The view as you walk out of Edinburgh's Waverley train station is probably the finest first impression of any city in the world – the castle battlements rising behind the Greek temple of the National Gallery, with the lush greenery of Princes Street Gardens in the foreground. To your left, the precipitous medieval tenements of the Old Town; to your right, the commercial bustle of Princes St. And almost all of the city's top sights, best restaurants and shopping streets are within 20 minutes' walk of where you're standing.

Not only is Edinburgh one of the most beautiful cities in Europe, it also enjoys one of Europe's most beautiful settings. There are unexpected vistas from almost every street corner – a glimpse of green sunlit hills, a blue flash of sea, silhouetted spires and rust-red crags. It's a city that begs to be explored on foot – narrow alleys, flights of stairs and hidden kirkyards tempt you off the main streets at every turn. Put the guidebook away for a bit, and just wander.

But there's more to Edinburgh than just sightseeing – there are top shops, world-class restaurants and a bacchanalia of bars to enjoy. This is a city of pub crawls and impromptu music sessions, mad-for-it clubbing and all-night parties, overindulgence, late nights and wandering home through cobbled streets at dawn.

All these superlatives come together in August at festival time, when it seems as if half the world descends on Edinburgh for one enormous party. If you can possibly manage it, join them.

HIGHLIGHTS

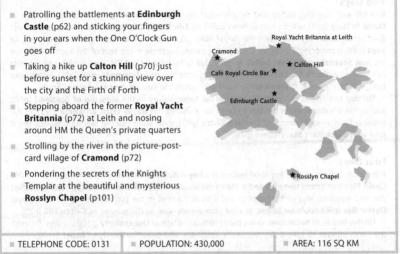

- Patrolling the battlements at **Edinburgh Castle** (p62) and sticking your fingers in your ears when the One O'Clock Gun goes off

- Taking a hike up **Calton Hill** (p70) just before sunset for a stunning view over the city and the Firth of Forth

- Stepping aboard the former **Royal Yacht Britannia** (p72) at Leith and nosing around HM the Queen's private quarters

- Strolling by the river in the picture-postcard village of **Cramond** (p72)

- Pondering the secrets of the Knights Templar at the beautiful and mysterious **Rosslyn Chapel** (p101)

Cramond
Café Royal Circle Bar ★
Edinburgh Castle
Royal Yacht Britannia at Leith
★ Calton Hill
★ Rosslyn Chapel

| ■ TELEPHONE CODE: 0131 | ■ POPULATION: 430,000 | ■ AREA: 116 SQ KM |

HISTORY

Back in the 7th century the Castle Rock was called Dun Eiden (meaning 'Fort on the Hill Slope'). When it was captured by invaders from the kingdom of Northumbria in northeastern England in 638, they took the existing Gaelic name 'Eiden' and tacked it onto their own Old English word for fort, 'burh', to create the name Edinburgh.

Originally a purely defensive site, Edinburgh began to expand in the 12th century when King David I held court at the castle and founded the abbey at Holyrood. The royal court came to prefer Edinburgh to Dunfermline and, as parliament followed the king, Edinburgh became Scotland's capital. The city's first effective town wall was constructed around 1450, enclosing the Old Town as far east as Netherbow and south to Grassmarket. This overcrowded area – by then the most populous town in Scotland – became a medieval Manhattan, forcing its densely packed inhabitants to build upwards instead of outwards, and creating tenements that in places soared to 12 storeys high.

The capital played an important role in the Reformation (1560–1690), led by the Calvinist firebrand John Knox. Mary, queen of Scots, held court in the Palace of Holyroodhouse for six brief years but, when her son James VI succeeded to the English throne in 1603, he moved his court to London. The Act of Union in 1707 further reduced Edinburgh's importance, but cultural and intellectual life continued to flourish.

In the second half of the 18th century a planned new town was created across the valley to the north of the Old Town. During the period known as the Scottish Enlightenment (roughly 1740–1830), Edinburgh became known as 'a hotbed of genius', inhabited by leading scientists and philosophers such as David Hume and Adam Smith.

In the 19th century Edinburgh's population quadrupled in size to 400,000, not much less than it is today, and the Old Town's tenements were taken over by refugees from the Irish famines. A new ring of crescents and circuses was built to the north of New Town, and grey Victorian terraces spread south of the Old Town.

Edinburgh entered a new era following the 1997 referendum vote in favour of a devolved Scottish parliament, which first convened in July 1999. The parliament is temporarily housed in the Church of Scotland Assembly Rooms, near the castle,

---

EDINBURGH IN...

Two Days

Kick off with morning coffee and people-watching in **Grassmarket** (p67) – an outside table at **Made In Italy** (p91) will do – then head uphill to **Edinburgh Castle** (p62) to do the touristy bit. Afterwards, begin strolling down the **Royal Mile** (p63) and think about where to have lunch; **Le Sept** (p88) is temptingly close by. Once you've eaten, continue to the foot of the Royal Mile to see the new **Scottish parliament building** (p64), due to be finished in 2004, then work up an appetite by climbing **Arthur's Seat** (p67), or ogling the designer shoes in **Harvey Nichols** (p98). Satisfy your hunger with dinner at **Oloroso** (p90), while you watch the sun set over the Firth of Forth.

On day two spend the morning soaking up some history in the **Museum of Scotland** (p68), and in the afternoon catch the bus to Leith for a visit to the **Royal Yacht Britannia** (p72). In the evening have an early dinner at **Daniel's Bistro** (p91), then scare yourself silly on a guided ghost tour with **Black Hart Storytellers** (p78).

Four Days

A third day calls for a morning stroll around the **Royal Botanic Garden** (p74) then lunch at the **Old Chain Pier** (see boxed text p87) and a trip to the seaside village of **Cramond** (p72). Take binoculars (for bird-watching and yacht-spotting) and a book (to read in the sun). Dinner at the **Café Royal Oyster Bar** (p90) could be before or after your sunset walk to the summit of **Calton Hill** (p70).

On day four head out of town to the pretty harbour village of **Queensferry** (p100), nestled beneath the Forth Bridges, or take a day trip to the enigmatic and beautiful **Rosslyn Chapel** (p100).

while a controversial new parliament building – a futuristic design that has gone way over budget – nears completion at Holyrood at the foot of the Royal Mile.

ORIENTATION

The city's most prominent landmarks are Edinburgh Castle, at the western end of the Old Town, and Arthur's Seat (251m), the rocky peak that rises above the eastern end of the Old Town. The Royal Mile (Lawnmarket, High St and Canongate) is the Old Town's main street and runs along the crest of a ridge from the castle to the Palace of Holyroodhouse at the foot of Arthur's Seat.

New Town lies to the north of the Old Town, separated by a dip containing Princes Street Gardens and Waverley train station. The city's main shopping street, Princes St, runs along the northern side of the gardens. At its eastern end rises Calton Hill, which is crowned by several monuments.

The Edinburgh & Scotland Information Centre (ESIC) lies between Waverley train station and Princes St, above Princes Mall shopping centre. The bus station is nearby in New Town at the northeastern corner of St Andrew Square, north of the eastern end of Princes St.

Bear in mind that long streets may be known by different names along their length. For example, the southern end of Leith Walk is variously called Union Pl and Antigua St on one side, Elm Row and Greenside Pl on the other.

Maps

Lonely Planet's fold-out *Edinburgh City Map* (£3.99) is handy for sightseeing. It is plastic-coated, virtually indestructible and indicates all the major landmarks, museums and shops. There's also a street index.

ESIC (p59) issues a free pocket map of the city centre. For coverage of the whole city, the most detailed maps are Nicolson's *Edinburgh Citymap* (£3.50) and the Ordnance Survey's (OS) *Edinburgh Street Atlas* (£5.99). You can buy these at the ESIC, and at many bookshops and newsagents.

The OS's 1:50,000 Landranger map *Edinburgh, Penicuik & North Berwick* (Sheet No 66; £5.99) covers the city and the surrounding region to the south and east at a scale of 1¼ inches to 1 mile (2cm to 1km);

it is useful for walking in the Pentland Hills and exploring East Lothian.

INFORMATION
Bookshops

Ottakar's (Map pp82-4; ☎ 225 4495; 57 George St; ☻ 9am-6pm Mon, Wed, Fri & Sat, 9.30am-6pm Tue, 9am-8pm Thu, 11.30am-5.30pm Sun) Has a coffee shop upstairs.

Stationery Office Bookshop (Map pp82-4; ☎ 606 5566; 71 Lothian Rd; ☻ 9am-5pm Mon-Fri, 10am-5pm Sat) Has a good selection of books on Scottish history and travel (including LP guides), and the widest range of OS maps in town.

Thin's Bookshop (Map pp82-4; ☎ 622 8222; 53-62 South Bridge; ☻ 9am-8pm Mon & Wed-Fri, 9.30am-8pm Tue, 9am-6pm Sat, 11am-5pm Sun) The city's principal home-grown bookstore, now owned by Blackwells.

Waterstone's West End (Map pp82-4; ☎ 226 2666; 128 Princes St; ☻ 8.30am-8pm Mon-Sat, 10.30am-7pm Sun); East End (☎ 556 3034; 13 Princes St; ☻ 9am-8pm Mon-Fri, 9am-7.30pm Sat, 10am-7pm Sun); George St (Map pp82-4; ☎ 225 3436; 83 George St; ☻ 9.30am-9pm Mon-Fri, 9.30am-8pm Sat, 11am-6pm Sun) The West End branch has a good in-store café.

Cultural Centres

Institut Français d'Écosse (Map pp60-1; ☎ 225 5366; www.ifecosse.org.uk; 13 Randolph Cres; ☻ 9.30am-1pm & 2-6.30pm Mon-Wed, 9.30am-6.30pm Thu, 2-6.30pm Fri; 9.30am-1pm 1st Sat of month) Runs courses in French and has a French language library.

Italian Cultural Institute (Map pp82-4; ☎ 668 2232; www.italcult.org.uk; 82 Nicolson St; ☻ 9am-1pm & 2-5pm Mon-Fri)

Emergency

In an emergency, dial ☎ 999 or ☎ 112 (no money needed at public phones) and ask for police, ambulance, fire brigade or coastguard.

Edinburgh Rape Crisis Centre (☎ 556 9437; edinirc@aol.com)

Lothian & Borders Police HQ (Map pp60-1; ☎ 311 3131; www.lbp.police.uk; Fettes Ave)

Lothian & Borders Police Information Centre (Map pp82-4; ☎ 226 6966; 188 High St, Royal Mile; ☻ 10am-10pm May-Aug; 10am-8pm Mar, Apr, Sep & Oct; 10am-6pm Nov-Feb) You can report a crime or make lost property enquiries here.

Internet Access

There are many Internet cafés spread around the city. Convenient ones include:

connect@edinburgh (Map pp82-4; ☎ 473 3800; ESIC, Princes Mall, 3 Princes St; £1 per 20 min; ☻ 9am-8pm

Mon-Sat, 10am-8pm Sun Jul & Aug; 9am-7pm Mon-Sat, 10am-7pm Sun May, Jun & Sep; 9am-5pm Mon-Wed, 9am-6pm Thu-Sat, 10am-5pm Sun Oct-Apr)

easyInternetcafé (Map pp82-4; ☎ 220 3580; www.easy-everything.com; 58 Rose St; £1.60 per hr, 50p minimum; ◷ 8am-11pm)

e-corner (Map pp82-4; ☎ 558 7858; www.e-corner.co.uk; Platform 1, Waverley station; £1 per 20 min; ◷ 7.30am-9pm Mon-Fri, 8am-9pm Sat & Sun)

That Internet Café (☎ 0870 770 41 21; www.that internetcafe.net) Tollcross (Map pp82-4; 1a Brougham Pl; £1 per 20 min; ◷ 8.30am-10pm) Haymarket (Map pp82-4; 18 West Maitland St; ◷ 8am-9pm)

Internet Café (Map pp82-4; ☎ 226 5400; 98 West Bow, Victoria St; £1 per 30 min; ◷ 10am-11pm)

Web (Map pp82-4; ☎ 229 8883; www.web13.co.uk; 13 Bread St; £1 per 20 min; ◷ 9am-10pm)

There are also several Internet-enabled telephone boxes (10p a minute, 50p minimum) scattered around the city centre.

Internet Resources

City of Edinburgh Council (www.edinburgh.gov.uk) The city council's official site, with a useful events guide.

City of Edinburgh Museums & Galleries (www.cac.org.uk) Details of events and exhibitions in the city council's museums and galleries.

Edinburgh Architecture (www.edinburgharchitecture .co.uk) Informative site dedicated to the city's modern architecture.

Edinburgh Guide (www.edinburghguide.com) Yahoo-style directory listing Edinburgh-related websites.

Edinburgh and Lothians Tourist Board (www.edinburgh.org) Official tourist board site, with listings of accommodation, sights, activities and events.

Laundry

Most of Edinburgh's backpacker hostels will wash and dry a load of laundry for you for around £3; some have self-service coin-operated washing machines where you can do the laundry yourself. There are self-service, coin-operated laundries all over the city – expect to pay around £4 for a wash and dry. Check the *Yellow Pages* under Launderettes to find the nearest.

Bendix Launderette & Dry Cleaners (Map p73; ☎ 554 2180; 342 Leith Walk)

Canonmills Dry Cleaners & Launderette (Map p73; ☎ 556 3199; 7 Huntly St)

Marchmont (Map pp60-1; ☎ 229 2137; 17 Roseneath St; ◷ 8am-7pm Mon-Fri, 8am-4pm Sat, 10am-2pm Sun)

Sundial Launderette (Map pp60-1; ☎ 556 2743; 7-9

East London St, New Town; ◷ 8am-7pm Mon-Fri, 8am-4pm Sat, 10am-2pm Sun) Has an excellent café next door called The Lost Sock Diner.

Left Luggage

Edinburgh airport left-luggage office (£3 per item per 24 hr; ◷ 5am-11pm) On the ground floor between check-in and international arrivals.

St Andrew Square bus & coach station lockers (Map pp82-4; small/medium/large locker £3/4/5 per 24 hr; ◷ 6am-midnight)

Waverley train station left-luggage office (Map pp82-4; £3.50 up to 6 hr, £4.50 6-24 hr, £4.50 per subsequent 24 hr; ◷ 7am-11pm) Beside platform 1.

Libraries

Central Library (Map pp82-4; ☎ 242 4800; George IV Bridge; ◷ 10am-8pm Mon-Thu, 10am-5pm Fri, 9am-1pm Sat) General lending library with a room devoted to Edinburgh (one floor down), another to all things Scottish (in the basement), and a reference room on the top floor.

National Library of Scotland (Map pp82-4; ☎ 226 4531; www.nls.uk; George IV Bridge; ◷ 9.30am-8.30pm Mon, Tue, Thu & Fri, 10am-8.30pm Wed, 9.30am-1pm Sat) Copyright library with a reference-only reading room; you'll need ID (passport or driving licence) to get admission.

Media

Edinburgh's home-grown daily newspapers include the *Scotsman* (www.scotsman.com), a broadsheet covering Scottish, UK and international news, sport and current affairs, and the *Edinburgh Evening News* (www.edinburghnews.com), covering news and entertainment in the city and its environs; *Scotland on Sunday* is the weekend broadsheet from the same publisher.

Medical Services

Edinburgh's main general hospital is the **Royal Infirmary of Edinburgh** (Map p73; ☎ 536 1000; 51 Little France Cres, Old Dalkeith Rd), which has a 24-hour accident and emergency department. There is another casualty department for children aged under 13 years at the **Royal Hospital for Sick Children** (Map pp60-1; ☎ 536 0000; 9 Sciennes Rd) in Marchmont.

For non-life-threatening injuries and ailments, you can attend the **Minor Injuries Unit** (Map p73; ☎ 537 1330; Western General Hospital, Crewe Rd South; ◷ 9am-9pm) without having to make an appointment. For emergency dental treatment, make an appointment at the

Edinburgh Dental Institute (Map pp82-4; ☎ 536 4958; Lauriston Bldg, Lauriston Pl; ☯ 9am-3pm Mon-Fri).

Chemists (pharmacists) can advise you on minor ailments. At least one local chemist remains open round the clock – its location will be displayed in the windows of other chemists. Alternatively look in the local newspaper or in the *Yellow Pages*. **Boots** (Map pp82-4; ☎ 225 6757; 48 Shandwick Pl; ☯ 8am-9pm Mon-Fri, 8am-6pm Sat, 10.30am-4.30pm Sun) opens longer hours than most.

Money

There are banks and ATMs all over the city. You can change currency and travellers cheques at private exchange counters (known by the French term 'bureau de change') scattered throughout the city centre, and in banks, post offices and travel agencies. Banks generally offer the best rates.

American Express (Map pp82-4; ☎ 718 2501; 139 Princes St; ☯ 9am-5.30pm Mon-Fri, 9am-4pm Sat) Charges no commission on Amex travellers cheques, 2% on cash, and generally offers a good rate of exchange.

Bank of Scotland (Map pp82-4; ☎ 465 3900; 38 St Andrew Sq; ☯ 9am-5pm Mon, Tue, Thu, Fri; 10am-5pm Wed)

Fexco (Map pp82-4; ☎ 557 3953; ESIC, Princes Mall, 3 Princes St; ☯ 9am-8pm Mon-Sat, 10am-8pm Sun Jul & Aug; 9am-7pm Mon-Sat, 10am-7pm Sun May, Jun & Sep; 9am-5pm Mon-Wed, 9am-6pm Thu-Sat, 10am-5pm Sun Oct-Apr) At ESIC; charges no commission on cash, but has a poor exchange rate.

Royal Bank of Scotland (Map pp82-4; ☎ 556 8555; 36 St Andrew Sq; ☯ 9.15am-4.45pm Mon, Tue, Thu & Fri, 10am-4.45pm Wed, 10am-2pm Sat)

Thomas Cook (Map pp82-4; ☎ 226 5500; 52 Hanover St; ☯ 9am-5.30pm Mon, Tue & Thu-Sat, 10am-5.30pm Wed) Charges 2% commission (minimum £3) on both cash and travellers cheques.

Post

Main post office (Map pp82-4; ☎ 0845 722 3344; St James Centre, Leith St; ☯ 8.30am-5.30pm Mon-Fri, 8.30am-6pm Sat) Items addressed to poste restante can be picked up here.

Branch post office (40 Frederick St, New Town; ☯ 9am-5.30pm Mon-Fri, 9am-12.30pm Sat)

Branch post office (46 St Mary's St, Old Town; ☯ 9am-5.30pm Mon-Fri, 9am-12.30pm Sat)

Telephone

There are telephone booths scattered all over the city; see also Telephone in the Directory chapter, p413.

Tourist Information

Edinburgh & Scotland Information Centre

(ESIC; Map pp82-4; ☎ 0845 22 55 121; info@visitscotland.com; Princes Mall, 3 Princes St; ☯ 9am-8pm Mon-Sat, 10am-8pm Sun Jul & Aug; 9am-7pm Mon-Sat, 10am-7pm Sun May, Jun & Sep; 9am-5pm Mon-Wed, 9am-6pm Thu-Sat, 10am-5pm Sun Oct-Apr) Includes an accommodation booking service, currency exchange, gift and bookshop, Internet access, and counters selling tickets for Edinburgh city tours and Citylink bus services.

Tourist & airport information desk (☎ 0845 22 55 121; Edinburgh airport)

Tourist Information Centre (TIC; ☎ 653 6172; Old Craighall Junction, A1) In a service area on the main A1 road, about 5 miles (8km) east of the city centre.

Travel Agencies

There are hundreds of travel agencies all over the city. Two agencies that specialise in budget and student travel are as follows:

Student Flights (Map pp82-4; ☎ 226 6868; www.studentflight.co.uk; 53 Forrest Rd; ☯ 9.30am-6pm Mon-Fri, 11am-5pm Sat)

STA Travel (Map pp82-4; ☎ 226 7747; www.statravel.co.uk; 27 Forrest Rd; ☯ 10am-6pm Mon-Wed & Fri, 10am-7pm Thu, 10am-5pm Sat)

Universities

Edinburgh has three universities. The oldest, biggest and most prestigious is the **University of Edinburgh**, with more than 15,000 undergraduates. Its **information centre** (Map pp82-4; ☎ 650 1000; www.ed.ac.uk; 7-11 Nicolson St; ☯ 9.15am-5pm Mon-Fri) provides details of short-term courses.

Heriot-Watt University (☎ 449 5111; www.hw.ac.uk) has its main campus southwest of the city at Riccarton, near Currie. **Napier University** (Map p73; ☎ 444 2266; www.napier.ac.uk) has its main campuses at 10 Colinton Rd in Merchiston and at 219 Colinton Rd in Craiglockhart.

DANGERS & ANNOYANCES

Edinburgh is safer than most cities of a similar size, but it has its share of crime so the normal big-city precautions apply.

Lothian Rd, Dalry Rd, Rose St and the western end of Princes St, at the junction with Shandwick Pl and Queensferry and Hope Sts, can get a bit rowdy on Friday and Saturday nights after the pubs close. Calton Hill offers good views during the day but is best avoided at night. Women on their own should avoid walking across the Meadows after dark.

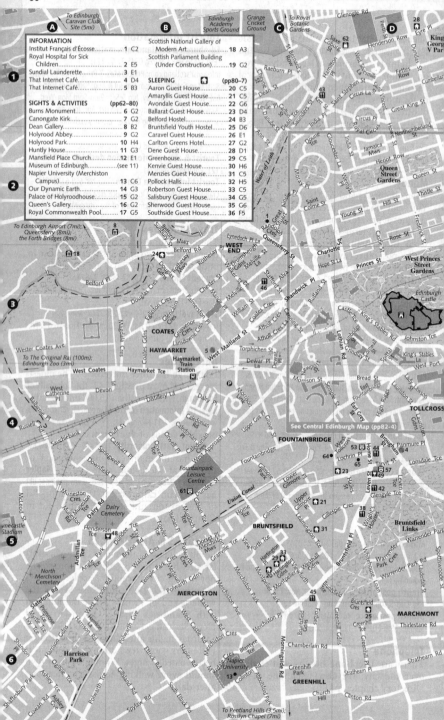

INFORMATION
Institut Français d'Écosse.................1 C2
Royal Hospital for Sick
  Children..2 E5
Sundial Launderette..........................3 E1
That Internet Café.............................4 D4
That Internet Café.............................5 B3

SIGHTS & ACTIVITIES (pp62–80)
Burns Monument................................6 G2
Canongate Kirk..................................7 G2
Dean Gallery......................................8 B2
Holyrood Abbey.................................9 G2
Holyrood Park..................................10 H4
Huntly House......................................11 G3
Mansfield Place Church...................12 E1
Museum of Edinburgh.............(see 11)
Napier University (Merchiston
  Campus)...13 C6
Our Dynamic Earth..........................14 G3
Palace of Holyroodhouse...............15 G2
Queen's Gallery.................................16 G2
Royal Commonwealth Pool............17 G5

Scottish National Gallery of
  Modern Art....................................18 A3
Scottish Parliament Building
  (Under Construction)...................19 G2

SLEEPING (pp80–7)
Aaron Guest House..........................20 C5
Amaryllis Guest House.....................21 C5
Avondale Guest House.....................22 G6
Ballarat Guest House........................23 D4
Belford Hostel...................................24 B3
Bruntsfield Youth Hostel..................25 D6
Caravel Guest House........................26 E1
Carlton Greens Hotel.......................27 G2
Dene Guest House............................28 D1
Greenhouse..29 C5
Kenvie Guest House.........................30 H6
Menzies Guest House.......................31 C5
Pollock Halls......................................32 H5
Robertson Guest House....................33 C5
Salisbury Guest House......................34 G5
Sherwood Guest House....................35 G6
Southside Guest House.....................36 F5

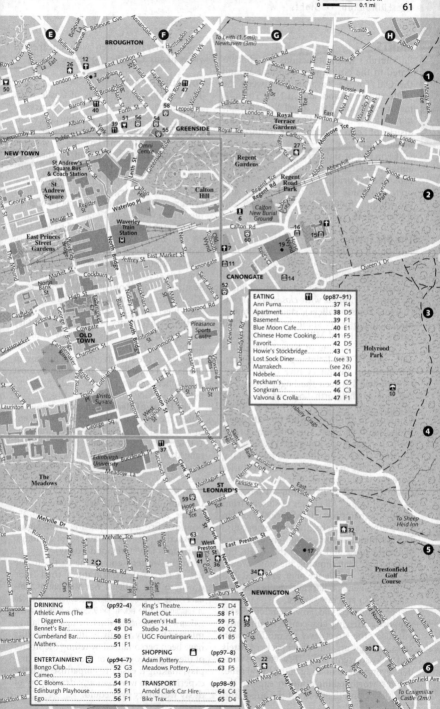

0 ———— 200 m
0 ———— 0.1 mi

BROADACRE / map labels:

To Leith (1.5mi);
Newhaven (3mi)

BROUGHTON

GREENSIDE

NEW TOWN

Royal Terrace Gardens

Regent Gardens

Calton Hill

St Andrew's Square Bus & Coach Station

St Andrew Square

Waverley Train Station

East Princes Street Gardens

Regent Road Park

Calton New Burial Ground

CANONGATE

OLD TOWN

Pleasance Sports Centre

Holyrood Park

Edinburgh University

The Meadows

ST LEONARD'S

NEWINGTON

Prestonfield Golf Course

To Sheep Heid Inn

To Craigmillar Castle (2mi)

Newington Cemetery

Carlton Cricket Ground

To Fairholme Guest House (50m);
32 Granby Road (150m)

EATING 🍴 (pp87–91)
Ann Purna.................................37 F4
Apartment................................38 D5
Basement..................................39 F1
Blue Moon Cafe.......................40 E1
Chinese Home Cooking...........41 F5
Favorit.....................................42 D5
Howie's Stockbridge................43 C1
Lost Sock Diner....................(see 3)
Marrakech.............................(see 26)
Ndebele....................................44 D4
Peckham's................................45 C5
Songkran..................................46 C3
Valvona & Crolla.....................47 F1

DRINKING 🍷 (pp92–4)
Athletic Arms (The
    Diggers)..............................48 B5
Bennet's Bar.............................49 D4
Cumberland Bar.......................50 E1
Mathers....................................51 F1

ENTERTAINMENT 🎭 (pp94–7)
Bongo Club...............................52 G3
Cameo......................................53 D4
CC Blooms................................54 F1
Edinburgh Playhouse...............55 F1
Ego...56 F1

King's Theatre..........................57 D4
Planet Out................................58 F1
Queen's Hall............................59 F5
Studio 24..................................60 G2
UGC Fountainpark....................61 B5

SHOPPING 🛍 (pp97–8)
Adam Pottery...........................62 D1
Meadows Pottery.....................63 F5

TRANSPORT (pp98–9)
Arnold Clark Car Hire..............64 C4
Bike Trax..................................65 D4

SIGHTS

Edinburgh's main attractions are concentrated in the city centre – on and around the Old Town's Royal Mile between the castle and Holyrood, and in New Town. A major exception is the Royal Yacht *Britannia*, which is in the redeveloped docklands district of Leith, two miles (3km) northeast of the centre.

If you tire of sightseeing, good areas for aimless wandering include the posh suburbs of Stockbridge and Morningside, the pretty riverside village of Cramond, and the winding footpaths of Calton Hill and Arthur's Seat.

The Old Town

Edinburgh's Old Town stretches along a ridge to the east of the castle, and tumbles down Victoria St to the broad expanse of Grassmarket. It's a jagged, jumbled maze of masonry riddled with *closes* and *wynds* (narrow lanes or alleys), stairs and vaults, and cleft along its spine by the cobbled ravine of the Royal Mile.

Until the founding of New Town in the 18th century, old Edinburgh was an overcrowded and insanitary hive of humanity. Constrained between the boggy ground of the Nor' Loch (North Loch, which is now drained and occupied by Princes Street Gardens) to the north and the city walls to the south and east, the only way for the town to expand was upwards. The five- and six-storey tenements that were raised along the Royal Mile in the 16th and 17th centuries were the skyscrapers of their day, remarked upon with wonder by visiting writers such as Daniel Defoe. All classes of society, from beggars to magistrates, lived cheek by jowl in these urban ants' nests, the wealthy occupying the middle floors – high enough to be above the noise and stink of the streets, but not so high that climbing the stairs would be too tiring – while the poor squeezed into attics, basements, cellars and vaults amid the rats, rubbish and raw sewage.

The renovated Old Town tenements still support a thriving city-centre community, but today the street level is crammed with cafés, restaurants, bars, backpacker hostels and tacky souvenir shops. Few visitors wander beyond the main drag of the Royal Mile, but it's worth taking time to explore the countless *closes* that lead off the street into quiet courtyards, often with unexpected views of cityscape, sea and hills.

EDINBURGH CASTLE

The brooding, black crags of Castle Rock rising above the western end of Princes St are the very reason for Edinburgh's existence. This rocky hill – the glacier-worn stump of an ancient volcano – was the most easily defended hilltop on the invasion route from England into central Scotland, a route followed by countless armies from the Roman legions of the 1st and 2nd centuries AD to the Jacobite troops of Bonnie Prince Charlie in 1745.

Edinburgh Castle (Map pp82-4; ☎ 225 9846; Castle Hill; adult/concession/child £8.50/6.25/2 including audioguide; ⊙ 9.30am-6pm Apr-Sep, 9.30am-5pm Oct-Mar; closed 25-26 Dec, but open 11am-5pm 1 Jan; last ticket sold 45 min before closing) has played a pivotal role in Scottish history, both as a royal residence – King Malcolm Canmore (reigned 1057–93) and Queen Margaret made their home here in the 11th century – and as a military stronghold. The castle last saw military action in 1745; from then until the 1920s it served as the British army's main base in Scotland. Today it is one of Scotland's most atmospheric, most popular – and most expensive – tourist attractions.

The **Entrance Gateway**, flanked by statues of Robert the Bruce and William Wallace, opens to a cobbled lane that leads up beneath the 16th-century **Portcullis Gate** to the cannon ranged along the Argyle and Mills Mount batteries. The battlements here have great views over New Town to the Firth of Forth.

At the far end of Mills Mount Battery is the famous **One O'Clock Gun**, where crowds gather to watch a gleaming WWII 25-pounder fire an ear-splitting time signal at exactly 1pm (every day except Sundays, Christmas Day and Good Friday).

At the western end of the castle, to the left of the castle restaurant, a road leads down to the **National War Museum of Scotland** (Map pp82-4; ☎ 225 7534; admission included in Edinburgh Castle ticket; ⊙ 9.45am-5.30pm Apr-Nov, 9.45am-4.30pm Dec-Mar), which brings Scotland's military history vividly to life. The exhibits have been personalised by telling the stories of the original owners of the objects on display, making it easier to empathise with the experiences of war than any dry display of dusty weaponry ever could.

South of Mills Mount, the road curls up leftwards through **Foog's Gate** to the highest part of Castle Rock, crowned by the tiny, Romanesque **St Margaret's Chapel**, the oldest surviving building in Edinburgh. It was probably built by David I or Alexander I in memory of their mother, Queen Margaret, sometime around 1130 (she was canonised in 1250). Beside the chapel stands **Mons Meg**, a giant 15th-century siege gun built at Mons (in what is now Belgium) in 1449.

The main group of buildings on the summit of Castle Rock are ranged around Crown Square, dominated by the shrine of the **Scottish National War Memorial**. Opposite is the **Great Hall**, built for James IV (reigned 1488–1513) as a ceremonial hall and used as a meeting place for the Scottish parliament until 1639. Its most remarkable feature is the original, 16th-century hammer-beam roof.

On the eastern side of the square is the **Royal Palace**, built during the 15th and 16th centuries, where a series of historical tableaux leads to the highlight of the castle – a strongroom housing the **Honours of Scotland** (the Scottish crown jewels), the oldest surviving crown jewels in Europe. Locked away in a chest following the Act of Union in 1707, the crown (made in 1540 from the gold of Robert the Bruce's 14th-century coronet), sword and sceptre lay forgotten until they were unearthed at the instigation of the novelist Sir Walter Scott in 1818. Also on display here is the **Stone of Destiny** (see the boxed text below).

Among the neighbouring **Royal Apartments** is the bedchamber where Mary, queen of Scots, gave birth to her son James VI, who was to unite the crowns of Scotland and England in 1603.

The **Castle Vaults** beneath the Great Hall (entrance at western end) were used variously as storerooms, bakeries and prisons – French prisoners carved the graffiti on the walls in the 18th century.

THE ROYAL MILE

This mile-long street earned its regal nickname in the 16th century when it was used by the king to travel between the castle and the Palace of Holyroodhouse. There are four sections – Castlehill, Lawnmarket, High St and Canongate – whose names reflect their historical origins. Allow at least half a day to wander down the Mile, taking time to visit the attractions.

A short distance downhill from the Castle Esplanade, a former school houses

---

THE STONE OF DESTINY

On St Andrew's Day 1996 a block of sandstone – 26½ inches by 16½ inches by 11 inches in size, with rusted iron hoops at either end – was installed with much pomp and ceremony in Edinburgh Castle. For the previous 700 years it had lain in London, beneath the Coronation Chair in Westminster Abbey. Almost all English, and later British, monarchs from Edward II in 1307 to Elizabeth II in 1953 have parked their backsides firmly over this stone during their coronation ceremony.

The legendary Stone of Destiny – said to have originated in the Holy Land, and on which Scottish kings placed their feet during their coronation (not their bums; the English got that bit wrong) – was stolen from Scone Abbey near Perth by King Edward I of England in 1296. It was taken to London and there it remained for seven centuries – except for a brief removal to Gloucester during WWII air raids, and a three-month sojourn in Scotland after it was stolen by Scottish Nationalist students at Christmas in 1950 – an enduring symbol of Scotland's subjugation by England.

The Stone of Destiny returned to the political limelight in 1996, when the then Scottish Secretary and Conservative Party MP, Michael Forsyth, arranged for the return of the sandstone block to Scotland. A blatant attempt to boost the flagging popularity of the Conservative Party in Scotland prior to a general election, Forsyth's publicity stunt failed miserably. The Scots said thanks very much for the stone and then, in May 1997, voted every Conservative MP in Scotland into oblivion.

Many people, however, believe that Edward I was fobbed off with a shoddy imitation in 1296 and that the true Stone of Destiny remains safely hidden somewhere in Scotland. This is not impossible – some descriptions of the original state that it was made of black marble and decorated with elaborate carvings. Interested parties should read *Stone of Destiny* (1997) by Pat Gerber, which details the history of Scotland's most famous lump of rock.

the **Scotch Whisky Heritage Centre** (Map pp82-4; ☎ 220 0441; 354 Castlehill; adult/child £7.50/3.95 including tour & tasting; ☺ 9.30am-6.30pm May-Sep, 10am-5pm Oct-Apr). The centre explains the making of whisky from barley to bottle, in a series of exhibits that combine sight, sound and smell.

The quaint building across the street is the **Outlook Tower and Camera Obscura** (Map pp82-4; ☎ 226 3709; Castlehill; adult/child £5.95/3.70; ☺ 9.30am-7.30pm Jul & Aug; 9.30am-6pm Apr-Jun, Sep & Oct; 10am-5pm Nov-Mar). The 'camera' itself is a curious 19th-century device that uses lenses and mirrors to throw a live image of the city onto a large horizontal screen. The accompanying commentary is entertaining, and the whole experience has a quirky charm. The Outlook Tower offers great views over the city.

With Edinburgh's tallest spire (71.7m), the **Highland Tolbooth Kirk** is a prominent feature of the Old Town's skyline. The interior has been refurbished and it now houses the **Hub** (Map pp82-4; ☎ 473 2000; www.eif.co.uk/thehub; Castlehill; admission free; ☺ ticket centre 10am-5pm Mon-Sat), the ticket office and information centre for the Edinburgh Festival. There's also a good café here.

Opposite the kirk are the Assembly Rooms of the Church of Scotland, which are the temporary home of the **Scottish parliament** (p67; the visitors' entrance is in Milne's Court, beside the Ensign Ewart pub).

Lawnmarket (a corruption of 'Landmarket', a market selling goods from the land outside the city) takes its name from the large cloth market that flourished here until the 18th century. This was the poshest part of the Old Town, where many of its most distinguished citizens made their homes.

One of these was the merchant Thomas Gledstanes, who in 1617 purchased the tenement later known as **Gladstone's Land** (Map pp82-4; ☎ 226 5856; 477 Lawnmarket; adult/child £3.50/2.60; ☺ 10am-5pm Mon-Sat, 2-5pm Sun Apr-Oct). It contains fine painted ceilings, walls and beams, and some splendid furniture from the 17th and 18th centuries. The volunteer guides provide a wealth of anecdotes and detailed history.

Tucked down a close just east of Gladstone's Land you'll find the **Writers' Museum** (Map pp82-4; ☎ 529 4901; Lady Stair's Close, Lawnmarket; admission free; ☺ 10am-5pm Mon-Sat year-round, plus 2-5pm Sun during Edinburgh Festival). Located in Lady Stair's House (built in 1622), the museum

contains manuscripts and memorabilia belonging to Robert Burns, Sir Walter Scott and Robert Louis Stevenson.

High St, which stretches from George IV Bridge down to the Netherbow at St Mary's St, is the heart and soul of the Old Town, home to the city's main church, the Law Courts, the city council and – until 1707 – the Scottish parliament.

On the corner of the Royal Mile and George IV Bridge is the **Scottish Parliament Visitor Centre** (Map pp82-4; ☎ 348 5000; www.scottish.parliament.uk; George IV Bridge; admission free; ☺ 10am-5pm Mon-Fri, earlier when parliament sitting). The centre explains the workings of the new parliament, which was officially opened on 1 July 1999 – the first Scottish parliament for almost 300 years. You can visit the debating chamber when parliament is not sitting (parliament usually sits from 10am to noon and 2pm to 4pm Monday and Friday), or you can phone ahead (☎ 348 5411, no more than a week in advance) to arrange free tickets for the public gallery while parliament is sitting.

Dominating High St is the great grey bulk of **St Giles Cathedral** (Map pp82-4; ☎ 225 9442; High St; admission free but donations welcome; ☺ 9am-7pm Mon-Fri, 9am-5pm Sat, 1-5pm Sun May-Sep; 9am-5pm Mon-Sat, 1-5pm Sun Oct-Apr). Properly called the High Kirk of Edinburgh (it was only a true cathedral – the seat of a bishop – from 1633 to 1638 and from 1661 to 1689), St Giles was named after the patron saint of cripples and beggars. A Norman-style church was built here in 1126 but was destroyed by English invaders in 1385; the only substantial remains are the central piers that support the tower.

The present church dates largely from the 15th century – the beautiful crown spire was completed in 1495 – but much of it was restored in the 19th century. The interior lacks grandeur but is rich in history: St Giles was at the heart of the Scottish Reformation, and John Knox served as minister here from 1559 to 1572. One of the most interesting corners of the kirk is the **Thistle Chapel**, built in 1911 for the Knights of the Most Ancient & Most Noble Order of the Thistle. The elaborately carved Gothic-style stalls have canopies topped with the helms and arms of the 16 knights – look out for the bagpipe-playing angel amid the vaulting.

By the side of the street, outside the western door of St Giles, is a cobblestone **Heart of Midlothian** (Map pp82–4) set into the paving. This marks the site of the Tolbooth. Built in the 15th century and demolished in the early 19th century, the Tolbooth served variously as a meeting place for parliament, the town council and the General Assembly of the Reformed Kirk, before becoming law courts and, finally, a notorious prison and place of execution. Passers-by traditionally spit on the heart for luck (don't stand downwind!).

At the other end of St Giles is the **Mercat Cross** (Map pp82–4), a 19th-century copy of the 1365 original, where merchants and traders met to transact business and Royal Proclamations were read.

Across the street from the Cross is the **City Chambers** (Map pp82–4), originally built by John Adam (brother of Robert) between 1753 and 1761 to serve as the Royal Exchange – a covered meeting place for city merchants. However, the merchants preferred their old stamping grounds in the street, and the building became the offices of the city council in 1811.

Part of the Royal Exchange was built over the sealed-off remains of Mary King's Close, and the lower levels of this medieval Old Town alley have survived almost unchanged in the foundations of the City Chambers for 250 years. Now open to the public as the **Real Mary King's Close** (Map pp82–4; ☎ 08702-430160; 2 Warriston's Close, Writers Court, High St; adult/child £7/5; ⏱ 10am-9pm Apr-Oct, 10am-4pm Nov-Mar; closed 25 Dec), this spooky, subterranean labyrinth gives a fascinating insight into the everyday life of 16th- and 17th-century Edinburgh. Costumed characters take you on a guided tour through a 16th-century town house and the plague-stricken home of a 17th-century gravedigger.

Halfway down the next block is 'the noisiest museum in the world' – the **Museum of Childhood** (Map pp82–4; ☎ 529 4142; 42 High St; admission free; ⏱ 10am-5pm Mon-Sat year-round, plus 2-5pm Sun Jul & Aug). Often filled with the chatter of excited children, it covers serious issues related to childhood – health, education, upbringing and so on – but also has an enormous collection of toys, dolls, games and books.

The Royal Mile narrows at the foot of High St beside the jutting façade of **John Knox House** (Map pp82–4; ☎ 556 9579; 43-45 High

St; adult/child £2.25/75p; ⏱ 10am-5pm Mon-Sat, plus noon-5pm Sun Jul & Aug). This is the oldest surviving tenement in Edinburgh, dating from around 1490; John Knox is thought to have lived here from 1561 to 1572. The labyrinthine interior has some beautiful painted timber ceilings and an interesting display on Knox's life and work.

Canongate – the stretch of the Royal Mile from Netherbow to Holyrood – takes its name from the Augustinian canons (monks) of Holyrood Abbey. From the 16th century it was home to aristocrats attracted to the Palace of Holyroodhouse. Originally governed by the monks, Canongate was an independent burgh separate from Edinburgh until 1856.

One of the surviving symbols of Canongate's former independence is the **Canongate Tolbooth** (Map pp60-1; ☎ 529 4057; 163 Canongate; admission free; ⏱ 10am-5pm Mon-Sat year-round, plus 2-5pm Sun during the Edinburgh Festival). Built in 1591, it served successively as a collection point for tolls (taxes), a council house, a courtroom and a jail. With its picturesque turrets and projecting clock, it's an interesting example of 16th-century architecture, and now houses a fascinating museum called the **People's Story**, which covers the life, work and pastimes of ordinary Edinburgh folk from the 18th century to the present day.

Across the street from the Tolbooth is **Huntly House**. Built in 1570, it now houses the **Museum of Edinburgh** (Map pp60-1; ☎ 529 4143; 142 Canongate; admission free; ⏱ 10am-5pm Mon-Sat year-round, plus 2-5pm Sun during the Edinburgh Festival). It covers the history of the city from prehistory to the present. Exhibits of national importance include an original copy of the National Covenant of 1638, but the big crowd-pleaser is the dog collar and feeding bowl that once belonged to Greyfriars Bobby, the city's most famous canine citizen.

Downhill on the left is the attractive curved gable of the **Canongate Kirk** (Map pp60-1), built in 1688. The kirkyard contains the graves of several famous people, including the economist Adam Smith (1723–1790), author of *The Wealth of Nations*, Mrs Agnes MacLehose (the 'Clarinda' of Robert Burns' love poems), and the 18th-century poet Robert Fergusson (1750–1774). Fergusson was much admired by Robert Burns, who paid for the gravestone and penned the epitaph – take a look at the inscription on the back.

UNDERGROUND EDINBURGH

As Edinburgh expanded in the late 18th and early 19th centuries, many old tenements were demolished and new bridges were built to link the Old Town to the newly built areas to its north and south. South Bridge (built between 1785 and 1788) and George IV Bridge (built between 1829 and 1834) lead southwards from the Royal Mile over the deep valley of Cowgate, but so many buildings have been built closely around them that you can hardly tell they are bridges – George IV Bridge has a total of nine arches but only two are visible; South Bridge has no less than 18 hidden arches.

These subterranean vaults were originally used as storerooms, workshops and drinking dens. But as early-19th-century Edinburgh's population was swelled by an influx of penniless Highlanders cleared from their lands, and Irish refugees from the potato famine, the dark, dripping chambers were given over to slum accommodation and abandoned to poverty, filth and crime.

The vaults were eventually cleared in the late 19th century, then lay forgotten until 1994 when the South Bridge vaults were opened to guided tours (p78). Certain chambers are said to be haunted and one particular vault was investigated by paranormal researchers in 2001.

Nevertheless, the most ghoulish aspect of Edinburgh's hidden history dates from much earlier – from the plague that struck the city in 1645. Legend has it that the disease-ridden inhabitants of Mary King's Close (a lane on the northern side of the Royal Mile on the site of the City Chambers – you can still see its blocked-off northern end from Cockburn St) were walled up in their houses and left to perish. When the lifeless bodies were eventually cleared from the houses, they were so stiff that workmen had to hack off limbs to get them through the small doorways and narrow, twisting stairs.

From that day on, the close was said to be haunted by the spirits of the plague victims. The few people who were prepared to live there reported seeing apparitions of severed heads and limbs, and the largely abandoned close fell into ruin. When the Royal Exchange (now the City Chambers) was constructed between 1753 and 1761, it was built over the lower levels of Mary King's Close, which were left intact and sealed off beneath the building.

Interest in the close revived in the 20th century when Edinburgh's city council began to allow occasional guided tours to enter. Visitors have reported many supernatural experiences – the most famous ghost is 'Sarah', a little girl whose sad tale has prompted people to leave gifts of dolls in a corner of one of the rooms. In 2003 the close was opened to the public as the Real Mary King's Close (see p65).

HOLYROOD

At the time of writing the district at the foot of the Royal Mile was undergoing a major upheaval during the construction of the new Scottish parliament building (due for completion in mid-2004).

The **Palace of Holyroodhouse** (Map pp60-1; ☎ 556 5100; Canongate; adult/child £7.50/4; 🕙 9.30am-6pm Apr-Oct, 9.30am-4.30pm Nov-Mar; closed 13-23 Oct, 25-26 Dec) is the royal family's official residence in Scotland, but is most famous as the 16th-century home of the ill-fated Mary, queen of Scots. The palace developed from a guesthouse attached to Holyrood Abbey, which was extended by King James IV in 1501. The oldest surviving part of the building, the northwestern tower, was built in 1529 as a royal apartment for James V and his wife, Mary of Guise. Mary, queen of Scots, spent six turbulent years here,

during which time she debated with John Knox, married both her first and second husbands, and witnessed the murder of her secretary Rizzio. The palace is closed to the public when the royal family is visiting and during state functions (usually in mid-May, and mid-June to early July).

The guided tour leads you through a series of impressive royal apartments, ending in the **Great Gallery**. The 89 portraits of Scottish kings were commissioned by Charles II and supposedly record his unbroken lineage from Scota, the Egyptian pharaoh's daughter who discovered the infant Moses in a reed basket on the banks of the Nile.

But the highlight of the tour is **Mary Queen of Scots' Bed Chamber**, home to the unfortunate Mary from 1561 to 1567, and connected by a secret stairway to her husband's bedchamber. It was here that her jealous first husband, Lord Darnley, restrained the pregnant queen while his henchmen murdered her secretary – and favourite – David Rizzio. A plaque in the neighbouring room marks the spot where he bled to death.

The exit from the palace leads into the ruins of **Holyrood Abbey** (Map pp60–1). King David I founded the abbey here in the shadow of Salisbury Crags in 1128. It was probably named after a fragment of the True Cross (*rood* is an old Scots word for cross), said to have been brought to Scotland by his mother St Margaret. Most of the surviving ruins date from the 12th and 13th centuries, although a doorway in the far southeastern corner has survived from the original Norman church.

The **Queen's Gallery** (Map pp60–1; adult/child £4/2, joint ticket incl admission to palace £10/5; as for palace), beside the palace ticket office, is a showcase for changing exhibitions of art from the Royal Collections.

The new **Scottish parliament building** (Map pp60–1) has been built on the site of a former brewery close to the Palace of Holyroodhouse and is due to open – three years late and more than £300 million over budget – in mid-2004. The competition to design the new parliament was won in July 1998 by the Catalan architect Enric Miralles, who envisaged a group of lenticular buildings with curved roofs inspired by upturned boats seen on a beach in northern Scotland.

The modernistic white marquee pitched beneath Salisbury Crags marks **Our Dynamic Earth** (Map pp60–1; 550 7800; Holyrood Rd; adult/child £7.95/5.45; 10am-6pm Apr-Oct, 10am-5pm Wed-Sun Nov-Mar, last admission 40 min before closing), billed as an interactive, multimedia journey of discovery through Earth's history from the Big Bang to the present day. Hugely popular with kids of all ages, it's a slick extravaganza of whizz-bang special effects cleverly designed to fire up young minds with curiosity about all things geological and environmental. Its true purpose, of course, is to disgorge you into a gift shop where you can buy model dinosaurs and souvenir T-shirts.

In **Holyrood Park**, Edinburgh is blessed in having a little bit of wilderness in the heart of the city. The former hunting ground of Scottish monarchs, the park covers 263 hectares of varied landscape, including crags, moorland and loch. The highest point is the 251m summit of **Arthur's Seat** (Map p73), the deeply eroded remnant of a long-extinct volcano. The park can be circumnavigated by car or bike along Queen's Drive (closed to motorised traffic on Sunday), and you can hike from Holyrood to the summit in 45 minutes.

NORTH OF THE ROYAL MILE

Cockburn St, lined with trendy fashion, jewellery and music shops, leads down from the Royal Mile to Waverley Bridge. A right turn into Market St leads to the **Fruitmarket Gallery** (Map pp82-4; 225 2383; www.fruitmarket.co.uk; 45 Market St; admission free; 11am-6pm Mon-Sat, noon-5pm Sun). One of Edinburgh's most innovative and popular galleries, the Fruitmarket showcases contemporary Scottish and international artists, and also has an excellent arts bookshop and café.

Across the street is the **City Art Centre** (Map pp82-4; 529 3993; 2 Market St; admission free except for temporary exhibitions; 10am-5pm Mon-Sat year-round, plus noon-5pm Sun Aug), comprising six floors of exhibitions with a variety of themes, including an extensive collection of Scottish art.

SOUTH OF THE ROYAL MILE

The site of a cattle market from the 15th century until the start of the 20th, **Grassmarket** has always been a focal point of the Old Town. It was also the city's main place of execution, and over 100 martyred Covenanters are commemorated by a monument at the eastern end, where the gallows used to stand. The notorious murderers Burke and Hare operated from a now-vanished close off the western end. In 1827 they enticed at least 18 victims to their boarding house, suffocated them and sold the bodies to Edinburgh's medical schools.

Nowadays the broad, open square, edged by tall tenements and dominated by the looming castle, has many lively pubs and restaurants, including the **White Hart Inn**, which was once patronised by Robert Burns. **Cowgate** – the long, dark ravine leading eastwards from Grassmarket – was once the road along which cattle were driven from the pastures around Arthur's Seat to the safety of the city walls. Today it is the heart of Edinburgh's nightlife, with around two dozen clubs and bars within five minutes' walk of each other.

Candlemaker Row leads from the eastern end of Grassmarket towards one of Edinburgh's most famous churches. **Greyfriars Kirk** (Map pp82–4) was built on the site of a Franciscan friary and opened for worship on Christmas Day 1620. In 1638 the National Covenant was signed here, rejecting Charles I's attempts to impose episcopacy and a new English prayer book, and affirming the independence of the Scottish Church. Many who signed were later executed at Grassmarket and, in 1679, 1200 Covenanters were held prisoner in terrible conditions in the southwestern corner of the kirkyard. There's a small exhibition inside the church.

Hemmed in by high walls and overlooked by the brooding presence of the castle, **Greyfriars Kirkyard** is one of Edinburgh's most evocative cemeteries, a peaceful green oasis dotted with elaborate monuments. Many famous Edinburgh names are buried here, including the poet Allan Ramsay (1686–1758), architect William Adam (1689–1748) and William Smellie (1740–95), the editor of the first edition of the *Encyclopedia Brittanica*. If you want to experience the graveyard at its scariest – inside a burial vault, in the dark, at night – go on one of Black Hart Storytellers guided tours (p78).

However, the memorial that draws the biggest crowds is the tiny statue of **Greyfriars Bobby**, in front of the pub beside the kirkyard gate. Bobby was a Skye terrier who, from 1858 to 1872, maintained a vigil over the grave of his master, an Edinburgh police officer. The story was immortalised (and romanticised) in a novel by Eleanor Atkinson in 1912, and in 1963 was made into a movie by – who else? – Walt Disney. Bobby's own grave – marked by a small, pink granite stone – is just inside the entrance to the kirkyard. You can see his original collar and bowl in the Museum of Edinburgh (p65).

CHAMBERS ST

The broad and elegant Chambers St stretches eastwards from Greyfriars Bobby, dominated by the long façade of the **Museum of Scotland and Royal Museum** (Map pp82–4; ☎ 247 4219; www.nms.ac.uk; Chambers St; admission free except for special exhibitions; ☒ 10am-5pm Mon & Wed-Sat, 10am-8pm Tue, noon-5pm Sun, closed 25 Dec). The golden stone and striking modern architecture of the Museum of Scotland – opened in 1998 – is one of the city's most distinctive landmarks. The five floors of the museum trace the history of Scotland from geological beginnings to the 1990s, with many imaginative and stimulating exhibits – audioguides are available in several languages. Highlights include the Monymusk Reliquary, a tiny silver casket dating from AD 750, which is said to have been carried into battle with Robert the Bruce at Bannockburn in 1314, and a set of charming, 12th-century chess pieces made from walrus ivory. Don't forget to take the lift to the Roof Terrace for a fantastic view of the castle.

The modern Museum of Scotland connects with the Victorian **Royal Museum**, dating from 1861, whose stolid, grey exterior gives way to a bright and airy, glass-roofed entrance hall. The museum houses an eclectic collection covering natural history, archaeology, scientific and industrial technology, and the decorative arts of ancient Egypt, Islam, China, Japan, Korea and the West.

New Town

Edinburgh's New Town lies north of the Old Town, on a ridge running parallel to the Royal Mile and separated from it by the valley of Princes Street Gardens. Its regular grid of elegant, Georgian terraces is a complete contrast to the chaotic tangle of tenements and *wynds* that characterise the Old Town.

Between the end of the 14th century and the start of the 18th, the population of Edinburgh – still confined within the walls of the Old Town – increased from 2000 to 50,000. The tottering tenements were unsafe and occasionally collapsed, fire was an ever-present danger, and the overcrowding and squalor became unbearable.

When the Act of Union in 1707 brought the prospect of long-term stability, the upper classes were keen to find healthier, more spacious living quarters, and in 1766 the lord provost of Edinburgh announced an architectural competition to design an extension to the city. It was won by an unknown 23-year-old, James Craig, a self-taught architect whose simple and elegant plan envisaged the main axis being George St, with grand squares at either end, and with building restricted to one side only of Princes and Queen Sts so that the houses enjoyed views over the Firth of Forth to the north and to the castle and Old Town to the south.

During the 18th and 19th centuries New Town continued to sprout squares, circuses, parks and terraces, with some of its finest neoclassical architecture designed by Robert Adam. Today Edinburgh's New Town remains the world's most complete and unspoilt example of Georgian architecture and town planning. Along with the Old Town, it was declared a Unesco World Heritage Site in 1995.

PRINCES ST   Map pp82–4

Princes St is one of the world's most spectacular shopping streets. Built up on the north side only, it catches the sun in summer and allows expansive views across Princes Street Gardens to the castle and the crowded skyline of the Old Town.

The western end of Princes St is dominated by the red-sandstone edifice of the Caledonian Hotel, and the tower of **St John's Church**, worth visiting for its fine Gothic Revival interior. It overlooks **St Cuthbert's Parish Church**, built in the 1890s on a site of great antiquity – there has been a church here since at least the 12th century, and perhaps since the 7th century. There is a circular **watch tower** in the graveyard – a reminder of the Burke and Hare days when graves had to be guarded against robbers.

At the eastern end is the prominent clock tower – traditionally three minutes fast so that you don't miss your train – of the **Balmoral Hotel**, and the beautiful **Register House** (1788), designed by Robert Adam, with a statue of the duke of Wellington on horseback in front. It houses the National Archives of Scotland.

Princes Street Gardens lie in a valley that was once occupied by the Nor' Loch, a boggy depression that was drained in the early 19th century. The gardens are split in the middle by **The Mound**, which was created by around two million cart-loads of earth excavated from the foundations of New Town being dumped here to provide a road link across the valley to the Old Town. It was completed in 1830.

The eastern half of the gardens is dominated by the massive Gothic spire of the **Scott Monument** (☎ 529 4068; East Princes St Gardens; admission £2.50; ☼ 9am-6pm Mon-Sat, 10am-6pm Sun Apr-Sep; 9am-3pm Mon-Sat, 10am-3pm Sun Oct-Mar), built by public subscription in memory of the novelist Sir Walter Scott after his death in 1832. You can climb the 287 steps to the top for a superb view of the city.

ROYAL SCOTTISH ACADEMY

The distinguished Greek Doric temple at the corner of The Mound and Princes St, its northern pediment crowned by a seated figure of Queen Victoria, is the home of the **Royal Scottish Academy** (RSA; Map pp82-4; ☎ 225 6671; The Mound; admission free, special exhibitions £2-5; ☼ 10am-5pm Mon-Sat, 2-5pm Sun). Designed by William Playfair and built between 1823 and 1836, it was originally called the Royal Institution; the RSA took over the building in 1910. The galleries display a collection of paintings, sculptures and architectural drawings by academy members dating from 1831, and they also host temporary exhibitions throughout the year.

NATIONAL GALLERY OF SCOTLAND

Immediately south of the RSA is the National Gallery of Scotland (Map pp82-4; ☎ 624 6200; The Mound; admission free, £1-5 for special exhibitions; ☼ 10am-5pm Fri-Wed, 10am-7pm Thu year-round; closed 25-26 Dec & 10am-noon 1 Jan). Also designed by William Playfair, this imposing classical building with its Ionic porticoes dates from the 1850s. It houses an important collection of European art from the Renaissance to postimpressionism, with works by Verrocchio (Leonardo da Vinci's teacher), Tintoretto, Titian, Holbein, Rubens, Van Dyck, Vermeer, El Greco, Poussin, Rembrandt, Gainsborough, Turner, Constable, Monet, Pissaro, Gauguin and Cezanne.

The USA is also represented by the works of Frederick Church, John Singer Sargent and Benjamin West. The section dedicated to Scottish art includes portraits by Allan Ramsay and Sir Henry Raeburn, rural scenes by Sir David Wilkie and impressionistic landscapes by William MacTaggart. Annually, in January, the gallery exhibits its collection of Turner watercolours, bequested by Henry Vaughan in 1900.

Antonio Canova's statue of the Three Graces (in Room 10) is owned jointly with London's Victoria & Albert Museum. In Greek mythology the Three Graces – Aglaia (Brightness), Euphrosyne (Joyfulness) and Thalia (Bloom) – were the daughters of Zeus and Euryonome, and embodied beauty, grace and youth.

At the time of writing, a major building project that will link the RSA and National Gallery via an underground mall, and increase their gallery space – giving them twice the temporary exhibition space of the Prado in Madrid, and three times that of the Royal Academy in London – was nearing completion.

GEORGE ST & CHARLOTTE SQUARE   Map pp82–4

Until recently George St – the major axis of New Town – was the centre of Edinburgh's financial industry, and Scotland's equivalent of Wall St. Now many of the big financial firms have moved to premises in the new Exchange office district west of Lothian Rd, and George St's former banks and offices house upmarket shops, pubs and restaurants.

At the western end of George St is **Charlotte Square**, the architectural jewel of New Town, designed by Robert Adam shortly before his death in 1791. The northern side of the square is Adam's masterpiece and one of the finest examples of Georgian architecture anywhere. **Bute House**, in the centre at No 6, is the official residence of Scotland's first minister.

Next door is the **Georgian House** (☎ 226 2160; 7 Charlotte Square; adult/child £5/3.75; ◯ 10am-5pm Apr-Oct, 11am-3pm Mar & 1 Nov-24 Dec), which has been beautifully restored and furnished to show how Edinburgh's wealthy elite lived at the end of the 18th century. The walls are decorated with paintings by Allan Ramsay, Sir Henry Raeburn and Sir Joshua Reynolds.

The headquarters of the **National Trust for Scotland** (☎ 243 9300; www.nts.org.uk; 28 Charlotte Square; admission free; ◯ 10am-5pm Mon-Sat) is on the southern side of the square. As well as a shop, café and information desk, the building contains a restored 1820s **drawing room** (◯ 11am-3pm Mon-Fri) with Regency furniture and a collection of 20th-century Scottish paintings.

ST ANDREW SQUARE   Map pp82–4

St Andrew Square is not as architecturally distinguished as its sister at the opposite end of George St. Dominating the square is the fluted column of the **Melville Monument**, commemorating Henry Dundas, 1st Viscount Melville (1742–1811), who was the most powerful Scottish politician of his time, often referred to when alive as 'Harry IX, the Uncrowned King of Scotland'. The impressive Palladian mansion of **Dundas House**, built between 1772 and 1774, on the eastern side of the square, was built for Sir Laurence Dundas (1712–81) – no relation to Viscount Melville. It has been the head office of the Royal Bank of Scotland since 1825 and has a spectacular domed banking hall dating from 1857 (you can nip inside for a look).

A short distance along George St is the **Church of St Andrew**, built in 1784 with an unusual oval nave. It was the scene of the Disruption of 1843, when 451 dissenting ministers left the Church of Scotland to form the Free Church.

Just north of the square at the junction with Queen St is the Venetian Gothic palace of the **Scottish National Portrait Gallery** (☎ 624 6200; 1 Queen St; admission free; open 10am-5pm Mon-Sat, noon-5pm Sun; hr extended during Edinburgh Festival). Its galleries illustrate Scottish history through portraits and sculptures of famous Scottish personalities, from Robert Burns and Bonnie Prince Charlie to Sean Connery and Billy Connolly.

Calton Hill

Calton Hill (100m), rising dramatically above the eastern end of Princes St, is Edinburgh's acropolis, its summit scattered with grandiose memorials mostly dating from the first half of the 19th century. It is also one of the best viewpoints in Edinburgh, with a panorama that takes in the castle, Holyrood, Arthur's Seat, the Firth of Forth, New Town and the full length of Princes St.

On the southern side of the hill, on Regent Rd, is the modernist façade of **St Andrew's House** (Map pp82–4), built between 1936 and 1939, which housed the civil servants of the Westminster government's Scottish Office until they were moved to the new Scottish Executive building in Leith in 1996.

Just beyond St Andrew's House and on the opposite side of the road is the imposing **Royal High School** (Map pp82–4) building, dating from 1829 and modelled on the Temple of Theseus in Athens. Former pupils include Robert Adam, Alexander Graham Bell and Sir Walter Scott. It now stands empty. To its east, on the other side of Regent Rd, is the **Burns Monument** (1830; Map pp60–1), a Greek-style memorial to Robert Burns.

You can reach the summit of Calton Hill via the road beside the Royal High School or by the stairs at the eastern end of Waterloo Pl. The largest structure on the summit is the **National Monument** (Map pp82–4), an over-ambitious attempt to replicate the Parthenon and intended to honour Scotland's dead in the Napoleonic Wars. Construction – paid for by public subscription – began in 1822, but funds ran dry when only 12 columns were complete.

Looking a bit like an upturned telescope – the similarity is intentional – and offering even better views, the **Nelson Monument** (Map pp82–4; ☎ 556 2716; Calton Hill; admission £2; ☑ 1-6pm Mon, 10am-6pm Tue-Sat Apr-Sep; 10am-3pm Mon-Sat Oct-Mar) was built to commemorate Admiral Lord Nelson's victory at Trafalgar in 1805.

The design of the **City Observatory** (Map pp82–4), built in 1818, was based on the ancient Greek Temple of the Winds in Athens. Its original function was to provide a precise, astronomical time-keeping service for marine navigators, but smoke from Waverley train station forced the astronomers to move to Blackford Hill in the south of Edinburgh in 1895.

Dean Village

If you follow Queensferry St northwards from the western end of Princes St, you come to **Dean Bridge** (Map pp60–1), designed by Thomas Telford and built between 1829 and 1832. Down in the valley just west of the bridge is Dean Village (*dene* is a Scots word for valley). It was founded as a milling community by the canons of Holyrood Abbey in the 12th century and by 1700 there were 11 water mills here operated by the Incorporation of Baxters (the bakers' trade guild). One of the old mill buildings has been converted into flats, and the village is now an attractive residential area.

SCOTTISH NATIONAL GALLERY OF MODERN ART & DEAN GALLERY

Set in an impressive neoclassical building surrounded by a sculpture park some 500m west of Dean Village is the **Scottish National Gallery of Modern Art** (Map pp60–1; ☎ 624 6200; 75 Belford Rd; admission free, £1-5 for special exhibitions; ☑ 10am-5pm Fri-Wed, 10am-7pm Thu). The collection concentrates on 20th-century art, with various European movements represented by the likes of Matisse, Picasso, Kirchner, Magritte, Miró, Mondrian and Giacometti. American and English artists are also represented, but most space is given to Scottish painters – from the Scottish colourists of the early 20th century to contemporary artists such as Peter Howson and Ken Currie. There's an excellent café downstairs, and the surrounding park features sculptures by Henry Moore, Sir Eduardo Paolozzi and Barbara Hepworth among others.

Directly across Belford Rd from the National Gallery of Modern Art, another neoclassical mansion houses its adjunct, the **Dean Gallery** (Map pp60–1; ☎ 624 6200; 73 Belford Rd; admission free except for special exhibitions; ☑ 10am-5pm Fri-Wed, 10am-7pm Thu). The Dean holds the Gallery of Modern Art's collection of Dada and surrealist art, including works by Dali, Giacometti and Picasso, and a large collection of sculpture and graphic art created by the Edinburgh-born sculptor Sir Eduardo Paolozzi.

Leith   Map p73

Leith – 2 miles (3km) northeast of the city centre – has been Edinburgh's seaport since the 14th century and remained an independent burgh with its own town council until it was incorporated by the city in the 1920s. Like many of Britain's dockland areas, it fell into decay in the decades following WWII but has been undergoing a revival since the late 1980s. Old warehouses have been turned into luxury flats, and a lush crop of trendy bars and restaurants has sprouted along the waterfront. The area was given an additional boost in the late 1990s when the Scottish Executive (a government department) moved to a new building on Leith docks. The city council has now formulated a major redevelopment plan for the entire Edinburgh waterfront from Leith to Granton, the first phase of which is **Ocean Terminal**, a shopping and leisure complex that includes the former Royal Yacht *Britannia* and a berth for visiting cruise liners. Parts of Leith are still a bit rough but it's a distinctive corner of the city and well worth exploring.

One of Scotland's biggest tourist attractions is the former **Royal Yacht Britannia** (☎ 555 5566; www.royalyachtbritannia.co.uk; Ocean Terminal, Leith; adult/child £8/4; 🕑 9.30am-6pm Apr-Sep, 10am-5pm Oct-Mar, 10am-4pm 24 & 31 Dec, last admission 1½ hr before closing; closed 1 Jan & 25 Dec). She was the British royal family's floating home during their foreign travels from the time of her launch in 1953 until her decommissioning in 1997, and is now moored permanently in front of Ocean Terminal.

The tour, which you take at your own pace with an audioguide (also available in French, German, Italian and Spanish), gives an intriguing insight into the Queen's private tastes – *Britannia* was one of the few places where the royal family could enjoy true privacy. The entire ship is a monument to 1950s décor and technology, and the accommodation reveals Her Majesty's preference for simple, unfussy surroundings – the Queen's own bed is surprisingly tiny and plain.

There was nothing simple or unfussy, however, about the running of the ship. When the Queen travelled, along with her went 45 members of the royal household, five tons of luggage and a Rolls-Royce that was carefully squeezed into a specially built garage on the deck. The ship's company consisted of an admiral, 20 officers and 220 yachtsmen. The decks (of Burmese teak) were scrubbed daily, but all work near the royal accommodation was carried out in complete silence and had to be finished by 8am. A thermometer was kept in the Queen's bathroom to make sure that the water was the correct temperature, and when in harbour one yachtsman was charged with ensuring that the angle of the gangway never exceeded 12 degrees. And note the mahogany windbreak that was added to the balcony deck in front of the bridge. It was put there to stop wayward breezes from blowing up skirts and inadvertently revealing the royal undies.

The *Britannia* Tour bus (see p78) runs from Waverley Bridge to *Britannia* during opening times. Alternatively, take Lothian Bus No 11, 22, 34, 35 or 36 to Ocean Terminal.

Greater Edinburgh   Map p73
CRAIGMILLAR CASTLE
If you want to explore a Scottish fortress away from the crowds that throng Edinburgh Castle, try **Craigmillar Castle** (☎ 661 4445; Craigmillar Castle Rd; adult/child £2.20/75p; 🕑 9.30am-6.30pm Apr-Sep; 9.30am-4.30pm Mon-Wed & Sat, 9.30am-1pm Thu, 2-4.30pm Sun Oct-Mar). Dating from the 15th century, the tower house rises above two sets of machicolated curtain walls. Mary, queen of Scots, took refuge here after the murder of Rizzio; it was here too that plans to murder her husband Darnley were laid. Look for the prison cell complete with built-in sanitation, something some 'modern' British prisons only finally managed in 1996.

The castle is 2½ miles (4km) southeast of the city centre. Take bus No 33 eastbound from Princes St to Old Dalkeith Rd and walk 500m up Craigmillar Castle Rd.

CRAMOND
With its moored yachts, stately swans and whitewashed houses spilling down a hillside at the mouth of the River Almond, Cramond is the most picturesque corner of Edinburgh. It is also rich in history. The Romans built a fort here in the 2nd century AD (the village's name comes from Caer Amon, 'the fort on the River Almond'), but recent archaeological excavations have revealed evidence of a Bronze-Age settlement dating from 8500 BC, the oldest known site in the whole of Scotland.

Cramond, which was originally a mill village, has a historic 17th-century church and a 15th-century tower house, as well as some rather unimpressive Roman remains, but most people come to enjoy the walks along the river to the ruined mills and to take the little rowing-boat ferry across the river to the Dalmeny Estate. A little downstream from the ferry landing is the **Maltings** (☎ 312 6034; Cramond Village; admission free; 🕑 2-5pm Sat & Sun Jun-Sep, daily during Edinburgh Festival), which hosts an interesting exhibition on Cramond's history.

Cramond is 5 miles (8km) northwest of the city centre; take bus No 41 from The Mound, Hanover St (northbound) or Charlotte Square to Cramond Glebe Rd, then walk north for 400m.

At the time of writing the **Cramond Ferry** (adult/child 50/10p; 🕑 9am-1pm & 2-7pm Sat-Thu Apr-Sep,

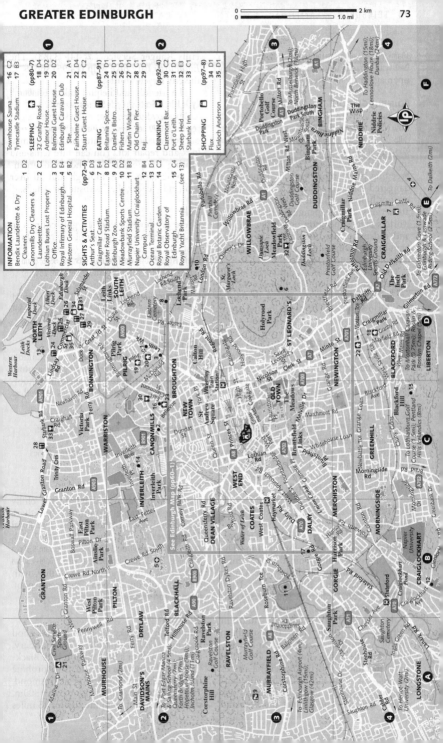

INFORMATION	
Bendix Launderette & Dry Cleaners	1 D2
Canonmills Dry Cleaners & Launderette	2 C2
Lothian Buses Lost Property Office	3 D2
Royal Infirmary of Edinburgh	4 E4
Western General Hospital	5 B2

SIGHTS & ACTIVITIES	(pp72–5)
Arthur's Seat	6 D3
Craigmillar Castle	7 E4
Easter Road Stadium	8 D2
Edinburgh Zoo	9 A3
Meadowbank Sports Centre	10 D2
Murrayfield Stadium	11 B3
Napier University (Craiglockhart Campus)	12 B4
Ocean Terminal	13 D1
Royal Botanic Garden	14 C2
Royal Observatory of Edinburgh	15 C4
Royal Yacht Britannia	(see 13)

SLEEPING	(pp80–7)
32 Granby Road	18 D4
Ardmor House	19 D2
Balmoral Guest House	20 D2
Edinburgh Caravan Club Site	21 A1
Fairholme Guest House	22 D4
Stuart Guest House	23 C2

EATING	(pp87–91)
Britannia Spice	24 D1
Daniel's Bistro	25 D1
Fishers	26 D1
Martin Wishart	27 D1
Old Chain Pier	28 C1
Raj	29 C2

DRINKING	(pp92–4)
Claremont Bar	30 C2
Port o'Leith	31 D1
Sheep Heid	32 E3
Starbank Inn	33 C1

Townhouse Sauna	16 C2
Tynecastle Stadium	17 B3

SHOPPING	(pp97–8)
Flux	34 D1
Kinloch Anderson	35 D1

10am-1pm & 2-4pm Sat-Thu Oct-Mar, closed 1 Jan & 25 Dec) was closed 'until further notice'; it may open again in summer 2004.

EDINBURGH ZOO

Opened in 1913, **Edinburgh Zoo** (☎ 334 9171; www.edinburghzoo.org.uk; 134 Corstorphine Rd; adult/child £8/5; ☺ 9am-6pm Apr-Sep, 9am-5pm Oct & Mar, 9am-4.30pm Nov-Feb) is one of the world's leading conservation zoos. Edinburgh's captive breeding programme has saved many endangered species, including Siberian tigers, pygmy hippos and red pandas. The main attractions are the penguins (kept in the world's biggest penguin pool), the sea lion and red panda feeding times, the animal handling sessions, and the Lifelinks 'hands on' zoology centre.

The zoo is 2½ miles (4km) west of the city centre; take Lothian Bus No 12, 26 or 31, First Bus No 16, 18, 80 or 86, or the Airlink Bus No 100 westbound from Princes St.

ROYAL BOTANIC GARDEN

Just north of Stockbridge is the lovely **Royal Botanic Garden** (☎ 552 7171; www.rbge.org.uk; 20a Inverleith Row; admission free; ☺ 10am-7pm Apr-Sep, 10am-6pm Mar & Oct, 10am-4pm Nov-Feb, closed 1 Jan & 25 Dec). Twenty-eight beautifully landscaped hectares include splendid Victorian palm houses, colourful swathes of rhododendron and azalea, and a world-famous rock garden. The Terrace Café offers good views towards the city centre. Take Lothian Bus No 8, 17, 23 or 27 to the East Gate, or the *Britannia* Tour bus (see p78).

ACTIVITIES
Cycling

Edinburgh and its surroundings offer many excellent opportunities for cycling. The main off-road routes from the city centre out to the countryside follow the Union Canal towpath and the Water of Leith Walkway from Tollcross southwestwards to Balerno (7½ miles; 12km) on the edge of the Pentland Hills, and the Innocent Railway Cycle Path from the southern side of Arthur's Seat eastwards to Musselburgh (5 miles; 8km) and on to Ormiston and Pencaitland. There are several routes through the Pentland Hills that are suitable for mountain bikes. For details ask at any bike shop or contact the Pentland

Hills Ranger Service (☎ 445 3383). The *Edinburgh City Bike Map* (£4.95) shows all the city's cycle routes.

The friendly and helpful folk at **Edinburgh Cycle Hire & Scottish Cycle Safaris** (Map pp82-4; ☎ 556 5560; www.cyclescotland.co.uk; 29 Blackfriars St; £10-15 per day, £50-70 per week; ☺ 10am-6pm Mon-Sat) rent out top-quality bikes; rates include helmet, lock and repair kit. You can hire tents and touring equipment too. They also organise cycle tours in Edinburgh and all over Scotland – check their website for details.

Golf

There are no less than 19 golf courses in Edinburgh and the following are two of the best city courses.

Braid Hills Public Golf Course (☎ 447 6666; Braid Hills Approach; green fees weekdays/weekends £14/16) A challenging course to the south of the city centre.

Lothianburn Golf Course (☎ 445 2206; 106a Biggar Rd, Fairmilehead; green fees weekdays/weekends £16.50/22.50) Enjoys a scenic setting at the foot of the Pentland Hills.

Horse Riding

There are many scenic bridle paths suitable for horse riding in the countryside around Edinburgh, and a number of riding schools offer two- and three-hour treks as well as tuition:

Pentland Hills Icelandics (☎ 01968-661095; www.phicelandics.co.uk; Windy Gowl Farm, Carlops, Midlothian)

Edinburgh & Lasswade Riding Centre (☎ 663 7676; Kevock Rd, Lasswade)

Swimming

The Firth of Forth is a bit on the chilly side for enjoyable swimming, but there are several indoor alternatives. The **Royal Commonwealth Pool** (Map pp60-1; ☎ 667 7211; 21 Dalkeith Rd; adult/child £3.10/1.80; ☺ 9am-9.30pm Mon, Tue, Thu & Fri, 10am-9.30pm Wed, 10am-4.30pm Sat & Sun) is Edinburgh's main facility, with a 50m pool, diving pool, children's pool, flumes and fitness centre.

Walking

Edinburgh is lucky to have several good walking areas within the city boundary, including Arthur's Seat, Calton Hill, Blackford Hill, Hermitage of Braid, Corstorphine Hill, and the coast and river at Cramond. The **Pentland Hills**, which rise to over 500m, stretch southwest from the city for 15 miles

EDINBURGH •• Walking Tour 75

(24km), offering excellent high- and low-level walking.

You can follow the **Water of Leith Walkway** from the city centre to Balerno (8 miles; 13km), and continue across the Pentlands to Silverburn (6½ miles; 10km) or Carlops (8 miles; 13km), and return to Edinburgh by bus. Another good option is to walk along the towpath of the **Union Canal**, which begins in Fountainbridge and runs all the way to Falkirk (31 miles; 50km). You can return to Edinburgh by bus at Ratho (8½ miles; 14km) or Broxburn (12 miles; 19km), and by bus or train from Linlithgow (21 miles; 34km).

Watersports

The sheltered waters of the Firth of Forth offer all kinds of watersports. **Port Edgar Marina & Sailing School** (☎ 331 3330; Shore Rd, Queensferry; ☺ boat rental 10am–noon & 2-4pm year-round, plus 7-9pm Mon-Fri Apr-Oct) rents out Topper/420/Wayfarer sailing dinghies at £9.80/18.20/25.40 for a two-hour session. It also offers a wide range of sailing, canoeing and power-boating tuition courses.

WALKING TOUR

Edinburgh's Old Town stretches along the Royal Mile to the east of the castle and south to Grassmarket and Cowgate. This walk explores a few of the many interesting nooks and crannies around the upper part of the Royal Mile, and involves a fair bit of climbing up and down steep stairs and *closes*. Allow one to two hours.

WALKING TOUR
■ Distance: ¾ mile
■ Duration: 1 hour

Begin on the Castle Esplanade, which provides a grandstand view to the south over Grassmarket. The prominent quadrangular building with all the turrets is **George Heriot's School (1)**. Head towards Castlehill and the start of the Royal Mile. The 17th-century house on the right, above the steps of North Castle Wynd, is known as **Cannonball House (2)** because of the iron ball lodged in the wall

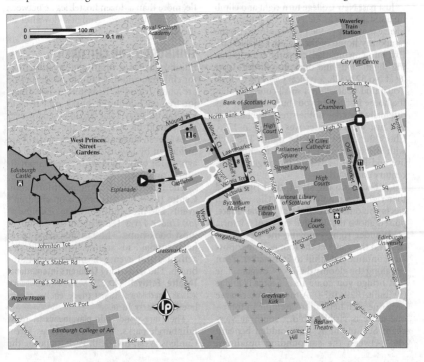

(look between, and slightly below, the two largest windows). It was not fired in anger, but instead marks the gravitation height to which water would flow naturally from the city's first piped water supply.

The low, rectangular building across the street (now a touristy tartan-weaving mill) was originally the reservoir that held Old Town's water supply. On its west wall is the **Witches Well (3)**, where a modern bronze fountain commemorates around 4000 people (mostly women) who were burned or strangled in Edinburgh between 1479 and 1722 for suspicion of witchcraft.

Go past the reservoir and turn left down Ramsay Lane, and take a look at **Ramsay Garden (4)** – one of the most desirable addresses in Edinburgh – where late 19th-century apartments were built around the nucleus of the octagonal Ramsay Lodge, once home to poet Allan Ramsay. The cobbled street continues around to the right below student residences, to the twin towers of the **New College (5)** – home to Edinburgh University's Faculty of Divinity. Nip into the courtyard to see the **statue of John Knox (6)**.

Just past New College turn right and climb up the stairs into Milne's Court, a student residence that houses the public entrance to the temporary home of the **Scottish parliament (7)**. Exit into Lawnmarket, cross the street (bearing slightly left) and duck into **Riddell's Court (8)** at No 322–328, a typical Old Town close. You'll find yourself in a small courtyard, but the house in front of you (built in 1590) was originally the edge of the street (the building you just walked under was added in 1726. Check the doorway on the right). The arch with the inscription *Vivendo discimus* (we live and learn) leads into the original 16th-century courtyard.

Go back into the street, turn right, and then right again down Fisher's Close, which ejects you onto the delightful **Victoria Terrace**, poised above the cobbled curve of Victoria St. Wander right, enjoying the view, then descend the stairs at the foot of Upper Bow and continue downhill to **Grassmarket**. Turn left along the gloomy defile of Cowgate. The first bridge you come to is **George IV Bridge (9)** (built 1829–1834). Although you can see only one arch here, there are nine in total – one more is visible a block south at Merchant St, but the rest are hidden beneath and between the surrounding buildings,

as are the haunted vaults of South Bridge, further west along Cowgate.

Pass under George IV Bridge. The buildings to your right are the new Law Courts, while high up to the left you can see the complex of buildings behind Parliament Square. Past the courts and on the right is **Tailors Hall (10)** (built 1621, extended 1757), now a hotel and bar, but formerly the meeting place of the 'Companie of Tailzeours' ('Tailors' Guild).

Turn left and climb up **Old Fishmarket Close**, and perhaps stop for lunch at the little brasserie **Le Sept (11)**. Emerge once more into the Royal Mile. Across the street and slightly downhill on the left is **Anchor Close**, named for a tavern that once stood there. It hosted the Crochallan Fencibles, an 18th-century drinking club that provided its patrons with an agreeable blend of intellectual debate and intoxicating liquor. The club was founded by William Smellie, editor of the first edition of the *Encyclopedia Brittanica*; its best known member was Robert Burns, the poet.

Should you wish to wet your own whistle, more than a dozen hostelries lie between here and Holyrood. And it's downhill all the way...

EDINBURGH FOR CHILDREN

Edinburgh has a multitude of attractions for children, and most things to see and do are child-friendly. Kids under five travel for free on Edinburgh buses, and five- to 15-year-olds pay a flat fare of 50p. However you should be aware that the majority of pubs – even those that sell bar meals – are forbidden by law to serve those under the age of 16; only pubs with a restaurant licence can do so.

The Edinburgh & Scotland Information Centre (p59) has lots of info on children's events, and the handy guidebook *Edinburgh for Under Fives* (£5.95) can be found in most bookshops. The *List* magazine (p94) has a special Kids section listing children's activities and events in and around Edinburgh. The week-long **Children's International Theatre Festival** (☎ 225 8050; www.edinburgh-festivals.com/childrens) takes place each year in late May/early June.

There are good, safe **playgrounds** in most Edinburgh parks, including Princes Street Gardens West, Inverleith Park (opposite the

Royal Botanic Garden), George V Park (New Town), the Meadows and Bruntsfield Links.

Ideas for outdoor activities include going to see the animals at **Edinburgh Zoo** (p74); exploring the **Royal Botanic Garden** (p74); visiting the statue of **Greyfriars Bobby** (p68); and feeding the swans and playing on the beach at **Cramond** (p72). During the Edinburgh and Fringe Festivals there's lots of **street theatre** for kids, especially on the High St and at the foot of The Mound, and in December there's an **open-air ice rink** and **fairground rides** in Princes Street Gardens.

If it's raining, you can visit the Discovery Centre, a hands-on activity zone on Level 3 of the **Museum of Scotland** (p68); play on the flumes at the **Royal Commonwealth Pool** (p74); try out the earthquake simulator at **Our Dynamic Earth** (p67); or take a tour of haunted **Real Mary King's Close** (p65).

Childminding Services

For full listings of government-approved childminding services, check out **Childcare Link** (www.childcarelink.gov.uk). The following are reliable Edinburgh agencies that charge around £4 an hour.

Emergency Mums (☎ 535 1106; mail@emergency mums.co.uk; 21 Lansdowne Cres, Haymarket)

Family Circle Recruitment (☎ 447 9162; www.familycircles.org; 37 Comiston Rd, Morningside)

Panda's Nanny Agency (☎ 663 3967; www.pandas nannyagency.co.uk; 22 Durham Pl, Bonnyrigg)

OFF-BEAT EDINBURGH

Edinburgh is full of unusual attractions and out-of-the-way corners that most visitors never see – even though they may be within a few metres of them. Here are a few of the city's less mainstream attractions.

In complete contrast to the austerity of most of Edinburgh's religious buildings, the 19th-century, neo-Romanesque **Mansfield Place Church** (Map pp60-1; ☎ 474 8033; www .mansfieldtraquair.org.uk; Mansfield Pl; 🕑 1-4pm 2nd Sun of month Jul-Dec, 10-11.45am Mon-Sat during Edinburgh Festival) at the foot of Broughton St contains a remarkable series of Renaissance-style frescoes painted in the 1890s by Irish-born artist Phoebe Anna Traquair (1852–1936). Now undergoing restoration, the murals are on view to the public at certain times (check the website for any changes).

The **Bank of Scotland Museum** (Map pp82-4; ☎ 529 1288; The Mound; admission free; 🕑 10am-

4.45pm Mon-Fri mid-Jun–Aug), housed in the bank's splendid Georgian HQ, is a treasure trove of gold coins, bullion chests, safes, banknotes, forgeries, cartoons and lots of fascinating old documents and photographs charting the history of Scotland's oldest bank.

Musicians will enjoy the **Edinburgh University Collection of Historic Musical Instruments** (Map pp82-4; ☎ 650 2423; Reid Concert Hall, Teviot Pl; admission free; 🕑 3-5pm Wed, 10am-1pm Sat year-round, 2-5pm Mon-Fri during Edinburgh Festival), which contains more than 1000 instruments ranging from a 400-year-old lute to a 1959 synthesiser.

Still further off the beaten track is the **Sir Jules Thorn Exhibition** (Map pp82-4; ☎ 527 1600; Surgeons Hall, Nicolson St; admission free; 🕑 2-4pm Mon-Fri), a fascinating exposition on the history of surgery, and the adjacent **Menzies Campbell Dental Museum**, with its wince-inducing collections of extraction tools. The more famous **Museum of Anatomy and Pathology** (in the same building), a gruesome 19th-century collection of diseased organs, massive tumours and deformed infants pickled in formaldehyde, can only be visited by groups of 12 to 24, by prior written arrangement. Its most famous exhibit is a wallet fashioned from the skin of the murderer William Burke, who was hanged in 1829.

While guided ghost tours of Edinburgh's underground vaults and haunted graveyards have become a mainstream attraction, few tourists have yet explored the recently opened **Gilmerton Cove** (☎ 557 6464; www.gilmertoncove.org.uk; 16 Drum St, Gilmerton; adult/ child £5/3; 🕑 tours 10am-5pm Sat, 7pm Wed, Sat & Sun). Hidden away in the southern suburbs, the mysterious Cove is a series of man-made subterranean caverns hacked out of the rock, their origin and function unknown.

Another refreshing alternative to mainstream walking tours is offered by **Celtic Trails** (☎ 477 5419; www.celtictrails.co.uk; tours £22-27), whose knowledgeable owner Jackie Queally leads guided tours of Edinburgh's ancient and sacred sites, covering subjects such as Celtic mythology, geomancy, sacred geometry and the Knights Templar.

And finally, if you're in Edinburgh on the first Friday of August, head west to the village of Queensferry (p100) to see the bizarre **Burry Man**. As part of the village gala day, a local man spends nine hours roaming the streets wearing a woolly suit, which has been laboriously covered from head to toe in big, green, prickly burrs. One glance at his costume – he looks like a child's drawing of a Martian, with added prickles – would make you think he's suffering a medieval punishment, but it's actually an honour to be selected as the Burry Man.

TOURS
Bus Tours
Open-topped buses leave from Waverley Bridge outside the main train station and offer hop-on/hop-off tours of the main sights, taking in New Town, Grassmarket and the Royal Mile. They're a good way of getting your bearings, although with a bus map and a Day Saver bus ticket (£2.50) you could do much the same thing but without the commentary. Tours run daily, year-round, except for 24 and 25 December.

Lothian Buses' bright red **Edinburgh Tour** (☎ 555 6363; adult/child £7.50/2.50) buses depart every 10 minutes from Waverley Bridge. **Mac Tours** (☎ 220 0770; adult/child £8.50/2.50) offer similar tours, but in a vintage bus. The **Britannia Tour** (☎ 220 0770 adult/child £8.50/2.50) runs every 30 minutes (every 15 minutes in July and August) from Waverley Bridge to the Royal Yacht *Britannia* at Ocean Terminal via the Royal Botanic Garden.

Walking Tours
There are lots of organised walks around Edinburgh, many of them related to ghosts, murders and witches. For starting times, phone or check the following websites:
Black Hart Storytellers (☎ 221 1249; www.black hart.uk.com; tours £6) Not suitable for children. The 'City of the Dead' tour of Greyfriars Kirkyard is probably the best of Edinburgh's 'ghost' tours. Many people have reported encounters with the 'McKenzie Poltergeist'.
Cadies & Witchery Tours (☎ 225 6745; www.witchery tours.com; adult/child £7/4) The becloaked and pasty-faced Adam Lyal (deceased) leads a 'Murder & Mystery' tour of the Old Town's darker corners. These tours are famous for their 'jumper-ooters' – costumed actors who 'jump oot' when you least expect it. Ooooh, scary.
Celtic Trails (☎ 477 5419; www.celtictrails.co.uk; tours £22-27) Guided tours of the city's ancient and sacred sites.
Edinburgh Literary Pub Tour (☎ 226 6665; www .scot-lit-tour.co.uk; adult/student £7/5) An enlightening two-hour trawl through Edinburgh's literary history – and its associated howffs – in the entertaining company of Messrs Clart and McBrain. One of the best of Edinburgh's walking tours.
Mercat Tours (☎ 557 6464; www.mercat-tours.co.uk; adult £6-7.50, child £4-5.50) Mercat offers a wide range of fascinating tours including history walks in the Old Town and Leith, 'Ghosts & Ghouls' tours, and visits to haunted underground vaults.

FESTIVALS & EVENTS
Edinburgh hosts an amazing number of festivals throughout the year, notably the Edinburgh International Festival, the Fringe Festival and the Military Tattoo, which are all held about the same time.

Edinburgh International Science Festival (☎ 220 1882; www.sciencefestival.co.uk; Roxburgh's Court, 323 High St, Edinburgh EH1 1PW) First held in 1987, it hosts a wide range of events, including talks, lectures, exhibitions, demonstrations, guided tours and interactive experiments designed to stimulate, inspire and challenge. From dinosaurs to ghosts to alien life forms, there's something to interest everyone. The Science Festival runs over 10 days in the first two weeks of April.

Scottish International Children's Festival (☎ 225 8050; www.imaginate.org.uk; 45a George St, Edinburgh EH2 2HT) This is Britain's biggest festival of performing arts for children, with events suitable for kids from three to 12. Groups from around the world perform classic tales like *Hansel and Gretel* as well as new material written specially for children. The Children's Festival takes place annually in the last week of May.

Caledonian Beer Festival (☎ 228 5688; www.caledonian-events.co.uk; Caledonian Brewery, 42 Slateford Rd, Edinburgh EH11 1PH) A celebration of all things fermented and yeasty, Scotland's biggest beer-fest is hosted by Edinburgh's leading brewer of cask-conditioned ales. You can also sample a wide range of traditionally brewed beers from around the world, while enjoying live jazz and blues and snacking on pies and barbecue. Froth-topped bliss. The Beer Festival is held on the first weekend in June.

Edinburgh International Jazz & Blues Festival (☎ 553 4000; www.jazzmusic.co.uk; Assembly Direct, 89 Giles St, Edinburgh EH6 6BZ) Held annually since 1978, the Jazz and Blues Festival pulls in the top talent from all over the world. The first weekend sees a Mardi Gras street parade on Saturday from the City Chambers, up the Royal Mile and down into Grassmarket, for an afternoon of free, open-air music. On the Sunday there's a series of free concerts at the Ross Bandstand in Princes Street Gardens. The Jazz Festival runs for nine days, beginning on the last Friday in July (the week before the Fringe and Tattoo begin).

Edinburgh Military Tattoo (☎ 08707 555 1188; www.edintattoo.co.uk; Tattoo Office, 32 Market St, Edinburgh EH1 1QB) The Military Tattoo is a spectacular display of military marching bands, massed pipes and drums, acrobats, cheerleaders and motorcycle display teams, all played out in front of the magnificent backdrop of the floodlit castle. Each show traditionally finishes with a lone piper, dramatically lit, playing a lament on the battlements. The Tattoo takes place over the first three weeks of August (from a Friday to a Saturday); there's one show at 9pm Monday to Friday, and two (at 7.30pm and 10.30pm) on Saturdays, but no performance on Sundays.

Edinburgh Festival Fringe (☎ 226 0026; www.edfringe.com; Fringe Office, 180 High St, Edinburgh EH1 1QS) When the first Edinburgh Festival was held in 1947, there were eight theatre companies who didn't make it onto the main programme. Undeterred, they grouped together and held their own mini-festival, on the fringe, and an Edinburgh institution was born. Today the Fringe is *the* biggest festival of the performing arts anywhere in the world.

Since 1990 the Fringe has been dominated by stand-up comedy, but the sheer variety of shows on offer is staggering – everything from chain-saw juggling to performance poetry to Tibetan yak-milk gargling. So how do you decide what to see? There are daily reviews in the *Scotsman* newspaper – one good *Scotsman* review and a show sells out in hours – but the best recommendation is word of mouth. If you have the time, go to at least one unknown show – it may be crap, but at least you'll have your obligatory 'worst show I ever saw' story to bandy about in the pub.

The big names play at the mega-venues like the Assembly Rooms and the Pleasance, and charge mega-prices (£8 a ticket and more), but there are plenty of good shows for under a fiver and, best of all, lots of free stuff. Fringe Sunday – usually the second Sunday – is a smorgasbord of free

performances, staged in the Meadows park to the south of the city centre.

The Fringe take place over three-and-a-half weeks in August, the last two weeks overlapping with the first two of the Edinburgh International Festival.

Edinburgh International Festival (☎ 473 2001; www.eif.co.uk; The Hub, Castlehill, Edinburgh EH1 2NE) First held in 1947 to mark a return to peace after the ordeal of WWII, the Edinburgh International Festival is festooned with superlatives – the oldest, the biggest, the most famous, the best in the world. The original was a modest affair, but today hundreds of the world's top musicians and performers from all over the world congregate in Edinburgh for three weeks of diverse and inspirational music, opera, theatre and dance.

Tickets for popular events – especially music and opera – sell out quickly, so it's best to book as far in advance as possible. You can buy tickets in person at The Hub, or by phone, fax or Internet.

Edinburgh's annual culture-fest takes place over the three weeks ending on the first Saturday in September; the programme is usually available from April.

Edinburgh International Book Festival (☎ 228 5444; www.edbookfest.co.uk; Scottish Book Centre, 137 Dundee St, Edinburgh EH11 1BG) Held in a little village of marquees in the middle of Charlotte Square, the Book Festival is a fun fortnight of talks, readings, debates, lectures, book signings and meet-the-author events, with a café and tented bookshop thrown in. The Book Festival lasts for two weeks in August (usually the first two weeks of the Edinburgh International Festival).

Edinburgh International Film Festival (☎ 229 2550; www.edfilmfest.org.uk; Filmhouse, 88 Lothian Rd, Edinburgh EH3 9BZ) The Film Festival is one of the original Edinburgh Festival trinity, having first been staged in 1947 along with the International Festival and the Fringe. It is a major international event, serving as a showcase for new British and European films, and staging the European premieres of one or two Hollywood blockbusters. The Film Festival lasts for two weeks in August (usually the first two weeks of the Edinburgh International Festival).

Edinburgh's Capital Christmas (☎ 529 4310; www.edinburghscapitalchristmas.org; City of Edinburgh Council, City Chambers, High St, Edinburgh EH1 1HQ) The newest of the Scottish capital's festivals, first held in 2000, the Christmas bash includes a big street parade, a fairground and ferris wheel, and an open-air ice rink in Princes Street Gardens. The celebrations are held over the three weeks before Christmas.

Edinburgh's Hogmanay (www.edinburghshogmanay .org) Traditionally, the New Year has always been a more important celebration for Scots than Christmas. In towns, cities and villages all over the country, people fill the streets at midnight on 31 December to wish each other a Guid New Year and, yes, to knock back a dram or six to keep the cold at bay.

In 1993 Edinburgh's city council had the excellent idea of spicing up Hogmanay by organising some events, laying on some live music in Princes St and issuing an open invitation to the rest of the world. Most of them turned up, or so it seemed, and had such a good time that they told all their pals and came back again the next year. Now Edinburgh's Hogmanay is the biggest winter festival in Europe, regularly pulling in more than 250,000 partying punters.

To get into the main party area in the city centre after 8pm on 31 December you'll need a ticket – book well in advance. New Year events run from 29 December to 1 January.

Royal Highland Show (☎ 335 6200; www.royal highlandshow.org; Royal Highland Centre, Ingliston, Edinburgh EH28 8NF) Scotland's hugely popular national agricultural show is a four-day feast of all things rural, with everything from show-jumping and tractor-driving to sheep-shearing and falconry. Countless pens are filled with coiffed show cattle and pedicured prize ewes. The show is held over the long weekend (Thursday to Sunday) in late June.

SLEEPING

A boom in hotel building has seen Edinburgh's tourist capacity swell significantly in recent years, but you can guarantee that the city will still be packed to the gills during the Festival and Fringe period (August) and over Hogmanay/New Year. If you want a room during these periods, book as far in advance as possible – a year ahead if possible. In general, it's best to book ahead for accommodation at Easter and from mid-May to mid-September.

Hotels and backpacker hostels are found throughout Old and New Towns, while mid-range B&Bs and guesthouses are concentrated outside the centre in the suburbs of Tollcross, Bruntsfield, Newington and Pilrig.

If you're driving, don't even think about staying in the city centre unless your hotel has its own private car park – parking in the centre is a nightmare. Instead look for somewhere in a suburb like Newington, where there's a chance of finding free, on-street parking (even then, don't bet on getting a parking space outside the front door). Alternatively stay outside the city and travel in by bus or train.

In the following sections the price breakdown is based on the cost per person for bed and breakfast (B&B), sharing a double room; Budget is less than £25, Mid-Range is £25 to £50, and Top End is more than £50.

Accommodation Agencies

If you arrive in Edinburgh without a room, the **ESIC** (p59) booking service will try to find a room to suit you and will charge a £5 fee if successful. If you have the time, get hold of its free brochure and ring around yourself.

You can also try the Scottish Tourist Board's **Booking Hotline** (☎ 0845 2255 121), which makes a £3 surcharge; or search for accommodation on the **Edinburgh & Lothians Tourist Board** (www.edinburgh.org/accommodation) website.

Budget

There's a growing number of independent backpackers' hostels in Edinburgh, many of them right in the centre of town. Most have 24-hour access and no curfew.

THE OLD TOWN & AROUND

Brodies Backpackers Hostel (Map pp82-4; ☎ 556 6770; www.brodieshostels.co.uk; 12 High St, Royal Mile; dm £10-16; 🖳) Brodies is a small (50 beds), friendly place with four dorms (three mixed and one women-only) and seriously comfy hotel-quality mattresses and duvets. It has a kitchen and a cosy lounge area with a fireplace. There is no TV, which makes for good socialising, though it can be a little cramped and smoky for some tastes. Top location bang in the middle of the Royal Mile.

Castle Rock Hostel (Map pp82-4; ☎ 225 9666; castlerock@scotlands-top-hostels.com; 15 Johnston Tce; dm £12-13; ⬚) With its bright, spacious, single-sex dorms, superb views and friendly staff, the 200-bed Castle Rock has prompted plenty of positive feedback from travellers. It has a great location only a minute's walk from the castle (but a fair uphill trek from train and bus stations), a games room, reading lounge, and big-screen video nights; shame the beds aren't as comfortable as those at Brodies.

Edinburgh Backpackers Hostel (Map pp82-4; ☎ 220 1717; www.hoppo.com; 65 Cockburn St; dm £13-15.50) Just a short walk from the train station, Edinburgh Backpackers is clean, bright and friendly. It's right in the heart of Edinburgh's pub culture, which makes it great for partying but not so good for a peaceful night's sleep.

St Christopher's Inn (Map pp82-4; ☎ 226 1446; www.st-christophers.co.uk; 9-13 Market St; dm £10-19; ⬚) The 108-bed St Christopher's is just across the street from the Market St entrance to Waverley train station, with accommodation in four- to 14-bed dorms, each with a toilet and power shower. It's a real party joint, with two bars (one chilled, one pumping) and a good-value restaurant, so don't come here to catch up on your beauty sleep.

Bruntsfield Youth Hostel (Map pp60-1; ☎ 0870 004 1114; 7 Bruntsfield Cres; dm £12-16; ✕ ⬚) Situated in an attractive location overlooking a park, this hostel has spick and span four- to 12-bed dorms, some with castle views, a canteen-style dining room, large-screen TV and resident cat. It's about 2½ miles (4km) from Waverley train station; take bus No 11 or 16 from Princes St (gardens side) and get off at Forbes Rd.

Also recommended:

High Street Hostel (Map pp82-4; ☎ 557 3984; high-street@scotlands-top-hostels.com; 8 Blackfriars St; dm £12-13) Party place.

Royal Mile Backpackers (Map pp82-4; ☎ 557 6120; royal-mile@scotlands-top-hostels.com; 105 High St; dm £12-13) Small, cosy and quaint.

Central Youth Hostel (Map pp82-4; ☎ 0870 004 1115; 11/2 Robertson's Close, Cowgate; s £17.50-20; ⌣ Jul & Aug) Summer only, all single rooms.

Pleasance Youth Hostel (Map pp82-4; ☎ 0870 004 1118; New Arthur Pl; s £20; ⌣ Aug) All single rooms.

NEW TOWN & AROUND

City Centre Tourist Hostel (Map pp82-4; ☎ 556 8070; www.edinburghhostels.com; 3rd fl, 5 West Register St; dm £12-20; ✕) The City Centre is a small (around 40 beds), clean and relatively quiet hostel, with pine-wood bunks and comfy mattresses in four-, six-, eight- and 10-bed dorms. There's a small kitchen and TV lounge, and a laundry. The location is great – just two minutes' walk from train and bus stations.

Belford Hostel (Map pp60-1; ☎ 225 6209; www.hoppo.com; 6/8 Douglas Gardens; dm £12-15.50; ⬚) An unusual hostel housed in a converted church, the Belford is under the same management as Edinburgh Backpackers. Although some people have complained of noise – there are only thin partitions between dorms, and no ceilings – it's cheerful and well run with good facilities. This hostel is about 20 minutes' walk west of Waverley train station. If you're arriving by train from Glasgow or the north, get off at Haymarket station, which is much closer.

OUTSIDE THE CENTRE

Edinburgh has two well-equipped camping grounds reasonably close to the city centre.

Edinburgh Caravan Club Site (Map p73; ☎ 312 6874; www.caravanclub.co.uk; Marine Drive; tent £3.50-5, each person £3.75) This site is 3 miles (5km) northwest of the city centre, overlooking the Firth of Forth. Take bus No 8A from North Bridge or Broughton St. Cars with tents are not admitted during August.

Mortonhall Caravan Park (Map p73; ☎ 664 1533; www.meadowhead.co.uk/mortonhall; 38 Mortonhall Gate, Frogston Rd East; tent site incl 1 car & 2 people £9.50-14.50, each extra person £1; ⌣ Mar-Oct) Located in attractive parkland 5 miles (8km) southeast of the centre, Mortonhall has an on-site shop, bar and restaurant. Take bus No 11 from Princes St (westbound).

Edinburgh has a large student population and during vacations universities and colleges offer accommodation in student halls of residence. Most are a fair way from the centre and cost as much as lower-end, more central B&Bs.

Pollock Halls of Residence (Map pp60-1; ☎ 0800 028 7118; www.edinburghfirst.com; 18 Holyrood Park Rd; s £27-30, with bathroom £42-46; ℗ ✕) This is a modern complex belonging to the University of Edinburgh, with 1200 rooms (500 with ensuite bathroom). It's busy and often noisy, but close to the city centre and with Arthur's Seat as a backdrop.

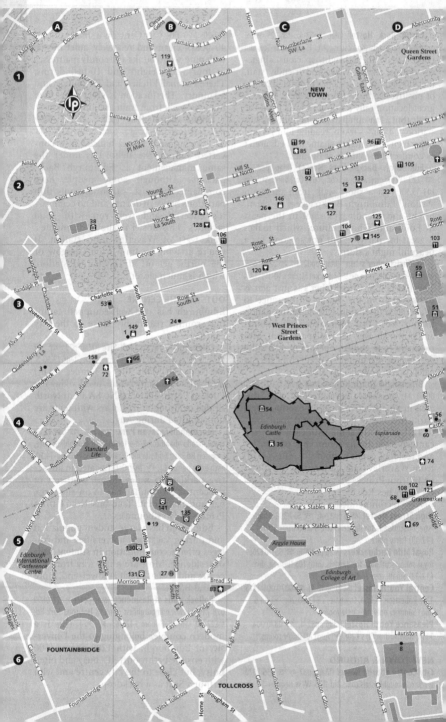

0 — 100 m
0 — 0.1 mi

E **F** **G** **H**

Dublin St La South

York Pl

St James Little King St

Greenside Row

143

Calton Hill

GREENSIDE

Omni Centre

110

138

62

Elder St East

Elder St

159

St James Shopping Centre

153

34

Calton Hill

St James St

Saint Andrew Sq

151

16

New Register House

139

124

81

52

55

46

2

93

76

58

Waterloo Pl

142

St Andrew Square

109

Register St

25

Calton Rd

63

Regent Rd

Royal High School

15

Meuse La

152

70

New St

Old Tolbooth Wynd

61

Princes Mall

5

6

12

156

Waverley Train Station

29

East Princes Street Gardens

Waverley Bridge

Canongate

East Market St

Jeffrey St

Cranston St

157

67

88

37

87

97

107

122

32

Cockburn St

78

86

150

44

148

71

Saint Boyd's

Market St

North Bank St

28

33

57

126

77

49

147

High St

48

9

144

Crowne Plaza

155

Blackfriars St

New

South Gray's Cl

94

Holyrood Rd

45

39

13

Hunter Sq

80

79

Skinner's Cl

Saint Mary's St

Bank St

Giles St

42

65

Old Fishmarket

South Bridge

Niddry St

Dickson's

30

Lawnmarket

117

101

100

Tron

Blair St

OLD TOWN

8

Victoria St

132

14

High Courts

Cowgate

Guthrie St

89

116

75

Robertson's Cl

High School Yards

Saint John's Hill

10

4

Sheriff Court

Chambers St

136

Infirmary St

21

Pleasance Sports Centre

134

George Heriot's school

95

154

40

114

Edinburgh University Old College

98

Drummond St

Roxburgh St

Roxburgh Pl

West Adam St

East Adam St

New Arthur Pl

Oldfield Pl

82

The Pleasance

50

South College St

23

111

47

Surgeons' Hall

Hill Pl

Richmond Pl

Richmond St

West Richmond St

Viewcraig Gdns

Briery

Holyrood Park

Brown St

41

137

18

20

Forrest Rd

Bristo Port

Brighton St

Lothian St

129

Nicolson Sq

11

Davie St

113

Gilmour St

Simon Sq

Carnegie St

Bristo Square

36

Marshall St

Crichton St

Charles St

Nicolson St

West Crosscauseway

Hardwell Cl

Boxmuir St

Edinburgh University

George Sq

91

112

123

Chapel St

West Crosscauseway

East Crosscauseway

Quarry Cl

Saint Patrick St

Haddon's Ct

Cowan's Cl

Napier University (Map p73; ☎ 455 4331; www.napier.ac.uk; 219 Colinton Rd; flats per week £340-490; **P**) Napier lets out self-catering flats for four to five people year-round. Some have disabled access and all have free car parking.

Mid-range

THE OLD TOWN   Map pp82–4
Ibis Hotel (☎ 240 7000; www.ibishotel.com; 6 Hunter Square; d £50-70) The Ibis is a spruce, modern, chain hotel, with a superb location just off the Royal Mile. The flat room rate includes a self-service breakfast buffet.

Premier Lodge (☎ 0870 990 6400; www.premier lodge.com; 94 Grassmarket; d £50; ✕) The Premier Lodge is a budget chain hotel with a great Old Town location. Rooms are small but comfy and can sleep up to two adults and two children. Breakfast is not included in the price.

NEW TOWN
Caravel Guest House (Map pp60-1; ☎ 556 4444; caravelguest@hotmail.com; 30 London St; s £20-30, d £40-60; ✕) The friendly, family-run Caravel is handy for New Town and for Broughton St nightlife. There's an excellent Moroccan restaurant in the basement (see p89).

Dene Guest House (Map pp60-1; ☎ 556 2700; deneguesthouse@yahoo.com; 7 Eyre Pl; s £20-35, d £40-70) The Dene is a friendly and informal guesthouse, set in a charming Georgian town house.

Stuart Guest House (Map pp60-1; ☎ 557 9030; 12 East Claremont St; june@stuartguesthouse.com; s £30-50, d £65-100; ✕) A readers' favourite, the Stuart is a welcoming late-Georgian town house with many period features, including staircase, fireplaces and cornices.

Castle Guest House (☎ 225 1975; info@castleguest house.com; 38 North Castle St; s £30-40, d £60-80, t £75-135; ✕) Lovely Georgian house with very central location.

TOLLCROSS   Map pp60–1
Tollcross is half a mile south of the western end of Princes St, along Lothian Rd.

Amaryllis Guest House (☎ 229 3293; ghamarylis@ aol.com; 21 Upper Gilmore Pl; s £25-40, d £36-70; **P**) The gay-friendly Amaryllis has five rooms, all with TV and some with bathroom. Princes St is 10 to 15 minutes' walk away.

Ballarat Guest House (☎ 229 7024; ballarat house@yahoo.com; 14 Gilmore Pl; s £20-35, d £40-70; ✕)

Named after a former gold-mining town in Australia, the Ballarat is a small (five rooms) and friendly family guesthouse, only a few minutes' walk from Tollcross' bars and restaurants.

BRUNTSFIELD   Map pp60–1
Another half-mile south from Tollcross is Bruntsfield.

Aaron Guest House (☎ 229 6459; www.aaron guesthouse.co.uk; 16 Hartington Gardens; s £40-60, d £60-120; **P** ✕) Located at the end of a quiet cul de sac, this large, 10-room guesthouse is comfortable and friendly, and caters for vegetarians.

Greenhouse (☎ 622 7634; greenhouse_edin@ hotmail.com; 14 Hartington Gardens; s £65-75, d £60-80; ✕) The award-winning Greenhouse is a wholly vegetarian and vegan guesthouse, which uses organic and GM-free foods as much as possible – even the soap and shampoo are free of animal products.

Robertson Guest House (☎ 229 2652; www .robertson-guesthouse.com; 5 Hartington Gardens; d £60-70; ✕) Tucked away in a quiet back street, this homely guesthouse offers a good range of healthy breakfast food, including yoghurt, fresh fruit and a cooked vegetarian breakfast.

Menzies Guest House (☎ 229 4629; www.menzies -guesthouse.co.uk; 33 Leamington Tce; s £15-30, d £30-60; **P**) This is a clean, friendly and well-run place, with seven rooms spread over three floors. The cheaper rooms, with shared bathroom, are small but offer excellent value.

NEWINGTON
There are lots of guesthouses on and around Minto St and Mayfield Gdns (the continuation of North Bridge and Nicolson St) in Newington. This is the main traffic artery from the south and a main bus route into the city centre.

32 Granby Road (Map p73; ☎ 667 9078; barbara .kellett@virgin.net; 32 Granby Rd; d from £75; ✕) This elegant Edwardian terraced house is located on a quiet back street and has three sumptuous bedrooms, beautifully decorated in different styles. Our favourite is the Drawing Room, with its original fireplace, mural-decorated bathroom and view of Arthur's Seat.

Southside Guest House (Map pp60-1; ☎ 668 4422; fionasouthside@aol.com; 8 Newington Rd; s £40-50, d £70-100; ✕) Forget traditional guesthouses – the

Southside is deeply trendy and has seven stylish rooms that just ooze interior design. It has a good café too.

Fairholme Guest House (Map p73; ☎ 667 8645; www.fairholme.co.uk; 13 Moston Tce; s £25-45, d £50-80; ✗) A pleasant, quiet Victorian villa with four rooms (three with ensuite bathroom), the gay- and vegetarian-friendly Fairholme has been recommended by several readers.

Other recommendations:

Kenvie Guest House (☎ 668 1964; dorothy@kenvie.co.uk; 16 Kilmaurs Rd, Newington; d £40-60; ✗) Situated in a quiet side street but close to a main bus route.

Salisbury Guest House (☎ 667 1264; www.salisburyguesthouse.co.uk; 45 Salisbury Rd, Newington; s £28-36, d £56-72; P ✗) Quiet, comfortable Georgian villa with large garden.

Avondale Guest House (☎ 667 6779; 10 South Gray St, Newington; s/d £25/45; ✗)

Sherwood Guest House (☎ 667 1200; www.sherwood-edinburgh.com; 42 Minto St, Newington; s £35-65, d £50-70; P ✗)

PILRIG   Map p73
Northeast of New Town and west of Leith Walk, Pilrig St has lots of guesthouses, all within about a mile of the centre. To get there, take bus No 11 from Princes St.

Ardmor House (☎ 554 4944; robin@ardmorhouse.com; 74 Pilrig St; s £45-60, d £60-100; ✗) The gay-friendly Ardmor is a stylishly renovated Victorian house with five ensuite bedrooms, and all those little touches that make a place special – an open fire, thick towels, crisp white bed linen and free newspapers at breakfast.

Balmoral Guest House (☎ 554 1857; bookings@balmoralguesthouse.co.uk; 32 Pilrig St; d £36-66; ✗) Travellers have written to recommend this comfortable B&B located in an elegant, flower-bedecked, Victorian terraced house.

Top End
THE OLD TOWN
Point Hotel (Map pp82-4; ☎ 221 5555; www.point-hotel.co.uk; 34 Bread St; s/d from £95/105; ✗) Housed in the beautiful former showrooms of the St Cuthbert Co-operative Association (built 1937), the Point is famous for its striking contemporary interior design. Some rooms have stunning castle views.

Apex International Hotel (Map pp82-4; ☎ 300 3456; www.apexhotels.co.uk; 31-35 Grassmarket; s & d £120-160; P ✗) Centrally located and with

SOMETHING SPECIAL...

The Scotsman Hotel (Map pp82-4; ☎ 556 5565; www.thescotsmanhotelgroup.co.uk; 20 North Bridge; s & d from £150; ☐ ✗ ♨) The former offices of the *Scotsman* newspaper – opened in 1904 and hailed as 'the most magnificent newspaper building in the world' – are now home to Edinburgh's newest luxury hotel. Standard rooms – those on the northern side enjoy superb views over New Town and Calton Hill – come with coffee machine, DVD player, wide-screen TV and computer with Internet access, while the Penthouse Suite (£950) has its own library and sauna.

good business facilities, the modern, 175-room Apex has a rooftop restaurant and great views towards the castle.

Crowne Plaza (Map pp82-4; ☎ 557 9797; www.crowneplazaed.co.uk; 80 High St; s/d from £155/180; ✗ ♨) This luxury hotel was built in the 1990s but blends in nicely with the Royal Mile's 17th-century architecture. The interior is, nonetheless, as modern as you would expect. Check the website for cheaper deals on rooms.

Tailors Hall Hotel (Map pp82-4; ☎ 622 6801; www.festival-inns.co.uk; 139 Cowgate; s/d/t £90/110/130) The Tailors Hall, with bright, modern rooms decorated in blue, pink and natural pine wood, is located bang in the middle of Edinburgh's clubland, and has three big bars of its own downstairs. Good for partying, but not a place for the quiet life.

NEW TOWN
Balmoral Hotel (Map pp82-4; ☎ 556 2414; www.thebalmoralhotel.com; 1 Princes St; s £190-230, d £220-280; ✗ ♨) The sumptuous Balmoral offers some of the best accommodation in Edinburgh, including suites with 18th-century décor and superb views of the city. All rooms have two phone lines, a modem point and satellite TV.

Caledonian Hilton Hotel (Map pp82-4; ☎ 222 8888; www.hilton.com; 4 Princes St; r £150-225; ✗ ♨) An Edinburgh institution, the 'Cally' is a vast, red-sandstone palace of Edwardian pomp and splendour, and one of two grandiose hotels built by competing railway companies at the turn of the 20th century (the other is the Balmoral, originally the

North British). It has a spa, swimming pool and gym, and full business and conference facilities.

Carlton Greens Hotel (Map pp60-1; ☎ 556 6570; carltongreens@british-trust-hotels.com; 2 Carlton Tce; s £60-90, d £80-180; ✗) Set at the leafy, eastern end of Calton Hill, the flower-bedecked Carlton Greens is a quiet, relaxing Georgian town house with views of Arthur's Seat.

Parliament House Hotel (Map pp82-4; ☎ 478 4000; phadams@aol.com; 15 Calton Hill; s/d from £90/130; ✗) Tucked away on a quiet corner of Calton Hill, the cosily traditional Parliament House is only five minutes' walk from Princes St.

rick's (Map pp82-4; ☎ 622 7800; www.ricks edinburgh.co.uk; 55a Frederick St; s & d £118) Describing itself as not a hotel, but a 'restaurant with rooms' (10 of them), rick's was voted one of the world's coolest places to stay by *Condé Nast Traveller* magazine. All walnut headboards and designer fabrics, the styling is sharp but the atmosphere laid-back.

EATING

In the last few years there has been a huge boom in the number of restaurants and cafés in Edinburgh, and there is a wide range of cuisines to choose from. Lunch is generally served from 12pm to 2.30pm, dinner from 7pm to 10pm, but many eating places are open all day.

In addition to restaurants and cafés, most pubs serve food, offering either bar meals or more formal dining, or both; here you generally have to order your food and drink at the bar. Be aware that pubs without a restaurant licence are not allowed to serve food to those aged under 16.

The Old Town & Around

BUDGET

Favorit (Map pp60-1; ☎ 220 6880; 19-20 Teviot Pl; sandwiches £4, salads £4-5; ✓ 8am-3am) A stylish café-bar with a slightly retro feel, Favorit caters for everyone: workers grabbing breakfast

---

LUNCH FOR LESS

Many restaurants in Edinburgh offer good-value lunches. Here are a few suggestions from various parts of the city.

Basement (Map pp60-1; ☎ 557 0097; 10a-12a Broughton St; mains £5-8; ✓ food served noon-10pm) The Basement is a pleasantly grungy bar with a separate restaurant area, offering a two-course lunch for only £5.95 (available noon to 3pm Monday to Friday). The grub is sort of international – bruschetta, nachos, spaghetti, chicken in orange and ginger sauce – but goes Thai on Wednesday and Mexican at the weekend.

Britannia Spice (Map p73; ☎ 555 2255; 150 Commercial St; Britannia Way; mains £8-11; ✓ noon-11.45pm) No, not Geri Halliwell's latest incarnation, but an award-winning curry house with ocean-liner décor, serving a wide range of dishes from northern India, Bangladesh, Nepal, Thailand and Sri Lanka. The waist-widening, all-you-can-eat buffet lunch costs £7.95.

Chinese Home Cooking (Map pp60-1; ☎ 668 4946; 34 West Preston St; mains £4-7; ✓ noon-2pm & 5-11pm Mon-Fri, 5-11pm Sat & Sun) You'll be hard pushed to find better value than the good, down-to-earth Chinese food served in this basic, no-nonsense restaurant, where the three-course set lunch costs only £4.50.

La P'tite Folie (Map pp82-4; ☎ 225 7983; 61 Frederick St; mains £8-10; ✓ noon-3pm & 6-11pm Mon-Sat, 6-11pm Sun) This is a delightful little restaurant with a Breton owner whose menu includes the French classics – onion soup, *moules marinières*, *Coquilles St Jacques* – steaks, seafood and a range of *plats du jour*. The two-/three-course lunch is a bargain at £5.90/6.90.

Old Chain Pier (Map p73; ☎ 552 1233; 1 Trinity Cres; mains £4-7.50; ✓ food served noon-8pm) The Old Chain Pier is a lovely little pub overlooking – nay, overhanging – the Firth of Forth on the waterfront near Granton Harbour. The excellent bar menu includes soup of the day, a creamy and filling mussel and smoked haddock stew, and a succulent steak and onion baguette with chips. The menu of real ales is no less enticing than the food.

Petit Paris (Map pp82-4; ☎ 226 2442; 38-40 Grassmarket; mains £6-10; ✓ noon-11pm daily Easter-Oct, noon-11pm Mon-Sat Oct-Easter) Like the name says, this is a little piece of Paris, complete with check tablecloths, friendly waiters and good-value grub – the *moules-frites* (mussels and chips) are excellent. There's a lunch and afternoon deal of the *plat du jour* and a coffee for £5, available noon to 5pm.

on the way to the office, coffee-slurping students skiving off afternoon lectures and late-night clubbers with an attack of the munchies. They also do the best bacon *butties* (sandwiches) in town. There's a second branch in Tollcross (30 Leven St).

Bar Italia (Map pp82-4; ☎ 228 6379; 100 Lothian Rd; mains £6-8; ☺ noon-midnight Mon-Thu, noon-1am Fri & Sat, 5pm-midnight Sun) A classic Italian restaurant of the old school, Bar Italia comes complete with red-and-white-check tablecloths, candles in Chianti bottles and smartly dressed, wise-cracking waiters who occasionally burst into song. Good-value Italian nosh and a lively atmosphere make it a popular venue for birthdays and office parties.

Khushi's (Map pp82-4; ☎ 556 8996; 16 Drummond St; mains £3-5; ☺ noon-3pm & 5-9pm Mon-Thu, noon-3pm & 5-9.30pm Fri & Sat) Established in 1947, Khushi's is an authentic Punjabi canteen and something of an Edinburgh institution. Its speciality is basic Indian dishes cooked in the traditional way, served with no frills at very low prices. It's not licensed, but you can bring your own booze (no corkage) or get a jug of beer from the pub next door.

MID-RANGE

Apartment (Map pp60-1; ☎ 228 6456; 7-13 Barclay Pl; mains £6-9; ☺ 5.45-11pm Mon-Fri, noon-3pm & 5.45-11pm Sat & Sun) Effortlessly cool, classy and almost always full, the Apartment is just too popular. Fantastic bistro food and a buzzy, busy atmosphere make it hard to get a table; book in advance – by at least three weeks, preferably – and don't be surprised if you still have to wait. But it's worth being patient for treats such as marinated lamb meatballs with merguez and basil-wrapped goat's cheese, roasted monkfish marinated in yoghurt with sweet red chilli, or deliciously sweet grilled scallops with smoked salmon and hazelnut butter.

Point Hotel (Map pp82-4; ☎ 221 5555; 34 Bread St; 2-course lunch £8.90, 3-course dinner £14.90; ☺ noon-2pm & 6-10pm Mon-Thu, noon-2pm & 6-11pm Fri & Sat, noon-2pm & 6-9pm Sun) The Point's now legendary lunch and dinner menus offer exceptional value – delicious Scottish/international cuisine served in an elegant room with crisp, white linen and attentive service. They must make their profit on the drinks, though the house wine costs only £10.95 per bottle. Reservations are strongly recommended.

Le Sept (Map pp82-4; ☎ 225 5428; 7 Fishmarket Close, High St; mains £7-13; ☺ noon-2pm & 6-10.30pm Mon-Thu, noon-11.30pm Fri, noon-11pm Sat, noon-10pm Sun) French bistro Le Sept is a hidden gem, stashed away down a steep cobbled alley off the Royal Mile, offering excellent crepes, daily seafood specials and a lovely little lunchtime sun-trap of a terrace.

blue bar café (Map pp82-4; ☎ 221 1222; 10 Cambridge St; mains £11-14; ☺ noon-3pm & 6-10.30pm Mon-Sat) Set above the foyer of the Traverse Theatre, this cool, white space is a lighter and less formal version of the Atrium (p89). The food is simple but perfectly cooked and presented, and the atmosphere loud and chatty, with all those luvvies from the theatre downstairs.

Buffalo Grill (Map pp82-4; ☎ 667 7427; 12-14 Chapel St; mains £7-13; ☺ noon-2.30pm & 6-10.30pm Mon-Fri, noon-4pm & 5-11pm Sat, noon-4pm & 5-10.30pm Sun) The Buffalo Grill is cramped, noisy, fun and always busy, so book ahead. An American-style menu offers burgers, steaks and side orders of fries and onion rings, along with fish and chicken dishes, prawn tempura and a vegetarian burger, but steaks are the main event. You can buy booze in the restaurant, or bring your own wine – £1 corkage per bottle.

Pancho Villa's (Map pp82-4; ☎ 557 4416; 240 Canongate, Royal Mile; mains £8-11; ☺ noon-2.30pm & 6-10.30pm Mon-Thu, noon-11pm Fri & Sat, 6-10pm Sun) With a Mexican manager and lots of Latin-American and Spanish staff, it's not surprising that Pancho's is one of the most authentic-feeling Mexican places in town. The dinner menu includes delicious steak *fajitas* and great vegetarian spinach *enchiladas*. It's often busy, so book ahead.

Suruchi (Map pp82-4; ☎ 556 6583; 14a Nicolson St; mains £7.50-11; ☺ noon-2pm & 5.30pm-11pm, closed Sun lunch) A laid-back Indian eatery with handmade turquoise tiles, lazy ceiling fans and chilled-out jazz guitar, Suruchi offers a range of exotic dishes as well as the traditional tandoori standards. Try *shakuti* from Goa (lamb or chicken with coconut, poppy seeds, nutmeg and chilli), or vegetarian *kumbhi narial* (mushrooms, coconut and coriander). An amusing touch is provided by the menu descriptions – they're translated into broad Scots ('a beezer o' a curry this...gey nippie oan the tongue').

TOP END

Tower (Map pp82-4; ☎ 225 3003; Museum of Scotland, Chambers St; mains £13-20; � noon-11pm) Chic and sleek, with a '*keek at the castle oot the windae*'. Set atop the new museum building, the Tower offers grand views of the Old Town and castle, and a menu of quality Scottish food, simply prepared – try half a dozen Loch Fyne oysters followed by an Aberdeen Angus steak. A two-course theatre supper menu (£12) is available from 4pm to 6.30pm.

Atrium (Map pp82-4; ☎ 228 8882; 10 Cambridge St; mains £16-20; � noon-2pm & 6-10pm Mon-Fri, 6-10pm Sat) Elegantly draped in cream linen and candlelight, the Atrium is one of Edinburgh's most fashionable restaurants, counting Mick Jagger and Jack Nicholson among its past guests. The cuisine is modern Scottish with a Mediterranean twist, with the emphasis on the finest of fresh, seasonal produce – fillet of sea bass with spinach and aubergine caviar, or wild mushroom risotto with truffle and tarragon.

Igg's (Map pp82-4; ☎ 557 8184; 15 Jeffrey St; mains £15-19; � noon-2.30pm & 6-10.30pm Mon-Sat) A sumptuous dining room with crisp white linen and rich, mustard-yellow walls help make Igg's a good choice for a special night out. The menu is mostly Spanish, with tapas-style starters and interesting main courses such as pan-fried fillet of barracuda on a spicy plum risotto with spinach and red pepper coulis. You can get a set two-/three-course lunch for £11.50/14.50.

New Town & Around

BUDGET

Blue Moon Café (Map pp60-1; ☎ 557 0911; 1 Barony St; mains £6-7; � 11am-10pm Mon-Fri, 9.30am-10pm Sat & Sun) The Blue Moon is the focus of Broughton Street's gay social life, always busy, always friendly, and serving up delicious nachos, salads, sandwiches and baked potatoes. It's famous for its brilliant, home-made hamburgers, which come plain or topped with cheese or chilli sauce, and delicious daily specials.

Marrakech (Map pp60-1; ☎ 556 4444; 30 London St; dinner £12; � 6-10pm Mon-Sat) A friendly and homely little Moroccan restaurant, in the basement of the Caravel Guest House (p85), the Marrakech dishes up delicious *tajines* (a slow-cooked casserole of lamb with almonds and dried fruit, usually prunes or apricots) accompanied by home-baked, caraway-scented bread. Round off the meal with a pot of mint tea.

MID-RANGE

Café Marlayne (Map pp82-4; ☎ 226 2230; 76 Thistle St; mains £12-14; � noon-2pm & 6-10pm Tue-Sat) All weathered-wood and warm-yellow walls, little Café Marlayne is a cosy nook offering French farmhouse cooking – *escargots* with garlic and parsley, oysters with lemon and tabasco, *boudin noir* (black pudding) with sautéed apples, peppered duck breast with balsamic vinegar – at very reasonable prices.

Nargile (Map pp82-4; ☎ 225 5755; 73 Hanover St; mains £9-12; � noon-3pm & 5.30-10.30pm Mon-Thu, noon-3pm & 5.30-11pm Fri & Sat) Throw away any preconceptions about kebabs – this glitzy Turkish restaurant is a class act. Enjoy a spread of delicious *mezeler* (think Turkish tapas) followed by meltingly sweet, marinaded lamb chargrilled to crispy perfection. Finish off with *baklava* (nut-filled pastry soaked in honey) and a Turkish coffee. If it wasn't for the prices, you could almost be in Turkey.

Mussel Inn (Map pp82-4; ☎ 225 5979; 61-65 Rose St; mains £6-15; � noon-10pm Mon-Sat, 1.30-10pm Sun) Owned by west-coast shellfish farmers, the Mussel Inn provides a direct outlet for fresh Scottish seafood. The busy restaurant, decorated with bright beech wood indoors, spills out onto the pavement in summer. A kilogram pot of mussels with a choice of sauces – try leek, bacon, white wine and cream – costs £9.70, while a smaller platter of queen scallops costs £6.30.

Songkran (Map pp60-1; ☎ 225 7889; 24a Stafford St; mains £8-10; � noon-2.30pm & 5.30-11pm Mon-Sat) You'd better book a table – and be prepared for a squeeze – to get in to this tiny New Town basement. The reason for the crush is some of the best Thai food in Edinburgh. Try the tender *yang* (marinated and barbecued beef, chicken or prawn), the crisp and tart orange chicken, or the chilli-loaded warm beef salad.

Howie's Stockbridge (Map pp60-1; ☎ 225 5553; 4-6 Glanville Pl; 3-course lunch/dinner £8/15.50; � noon-2.30pm & 6-10pm) This branch of Howie's – all chrome, blond wood and feng shui – is a trendier incarnation of their no-nonsense Bruntsfield restaurant, designed to pander to the fashionable New Town crowd. But the 'Scottish fusion' food is as tasty and as good value as ever. And who can resist a place with quaffable house wine at £7.90 a bottle?

Stac Polly (Map pp82-4; ☎ 556 2231; 29-33 Dublin St; mains £10-18; ☽ noon-2.30pm Mon-Fri, 6-11pm) Named after a mountain in northwestern Scotland, Stac Polly's kitchen adds sophisticated twists to fresh Highland produce. Meals such as garden pea and fresh mint soup with garlic cream and parmesan crouton, followed by pan-fried saddle of venison with orange, tarragon and green peppercorn sauce, keep the punters coming back for more. The restaurant's famous baked filo pastry parcels of haggis, served with plum sauce, are so popular they've almost become a national dish. What would Burns think?

TOP END

Café Royal Oyster Bar (Map pp82-4; ☎ 556 4124; 17a West Register St; mains £16-20; ☽ noon-2pm & 7-10pm) Pass through the revolving doors on the corner of West Register St and you're transported back to Victorian times – a palace of glinting mahogany, polished brass, marble floors, stained glass, Doulton tiles, gilded cornices and starched table linen so thick that it creaks when you fold it. The menu is mostly classic seafood, from oysters on

ice, to *Coquilles St Jacques Parisienne* and lobster thermidor, augmented by a handful of beef and game dishes.

Oloroso (Map pp82-4; ☎ 226 7614; 33 Castle St; mains £15-22, bar meals £5-9; ☽ restaurant noon-2.30pm & 6-10.30pm, bar 11am-1am) Oloroso is one of Edinburgh's newest and most stylish restaurants, perched on a glass-encased New Town rooftop with views across a Mary Poppins' chimneyscape to the Firth of Forth and the Fife hills. Swathed in sophisticated cream linen and charcoal upholstery enlivened with splashes of deep yellow, the dining room serves top-notch Scottish produce with Asian and Mediterranean touches. On a fine afternoon you can savour a snack and a drink on the outdoor roof terrace while soaking up the sun and a view of the castle.

Leith
MID-RANGE

Fishers (Map pp82-4; ☎ 554 5666; 1 The Shore; mains £12-19; ☽ noon-10.30pm) This cosy little bar-turned-restaurant, tucked beneath a 17th-century signal tower, is one of the city's best seafood places. Fishers' fishcakes are an Edinburgh institution, and the rest of the hand-written menu (you might need a calligrapher to decipher it) rarely disappoints.

VEGETARIAN EDINBURGH

Many Edinburgh restaurants offer vegetarian options on the menu, some good, some bad, some indifferent. The places listed here are all 100% veggie and all fall into the 'good' category.

David Bann (Map pp82-4; ☎ 556 5888; 56-58 St Mary's St; mains £9-11; ☽ 11am-1am) If you want to convince a carnivorous friend that cuisine á la veg can be as tasty and inventive as a meat-muncher's menu, take them to David Bann's stylish new restaurant. Dishes such as Shepherdless Pie, with vegetables in a rich, red-wine gravy and parmesan-crusted mashed potato, are guaranteed to win converts. They also do a tasty veggie brunch from 11am to 5pm at weekends.

Ann Purna (Map pp60-1; ☎ 662 1807; 45 St Patrick's Square; mains £5-8; ☽ noon-2pm & 5.30-11pm Mon-Fri, 5.30-11pm Sat & Sun) This little gem of an Indian restaurant serves exclusively vegetarian dishes from southern India. If you're new to this kind of food, opt for a *thali* – a self-contained platter that contains about half a dozen different dishes, including a dessert.

Susie's Diner (Map pp82-4; ☎ 667 8729; 51-53 West Nicolson St; mains £3-6; ☽ 9am-8pm Mon, 9am-9pm Tue-Sat) Susie's is a down-to-earth, self-service, vegetarian restaurant with scrubbed wood tables, rickety chairs and a friendly atmosphere. The menu changes daily but includes things such as tofu, aubergine and pepper casserole, stuffed roast tomatoes and Susie's famous falafel plates – reputedly 'the best falafel in the Western world'.

Henderson's (Map pp82-4; ☎ 225 2131; 94 Hanover St; mains £4.50-6; ☽ 7.30am-10.30pm Mon-Sat) Established in 1962, Henderson's is the grandmother of Edinburgh's vegetarian restaurants. The food is mostly organic and guaranteed GM-free, and special dietary requirements can be catered for. The self-service restaurant still has something of a 1970s cafeteria feel to it (but in a good way), and the daily salads (£1.50 a portion) and hot dishes are as popular as ever.

CAFÉS

Café culture has swept through Edinburgh in the last decade, and it is as easy to get your daily caffeine fix here as it is in New York or Paris. Most cafés offer some kind of food, from cakes and sandwiches to full-on meals.

Elephant House (Map pp82-4; ☎ 220 5355; 21 George IV Bridge; mains £4-6; ☽ 8am-11pm) Here you'll find counters at the front, tables and views of the castle at the back, and little effigies and images of elephants everywhere. Excellent cappuccino and tasty, home-made food – pizzas, quiches, pies, sandwiches and cakes – at reasonable prices make Elephant House deservedly popular with local students, shoppers and office workers.

Made In Italy (Map pp82-4; ☎ 622 7328; 42 Grassmarket; mains £3-5; ☽ 8am-11pm Mon-Thu, 8am-1.30am Fri & Sat, 10am-11pm Sun) Look out for this traditional-style café, where you can sit inside at the counters or outside at the pavement tables, and enjoy real Italian coffee and real Italian ice cream. If you're hungry, they do good pizzas and panini too.

Ndebele (Map pp60-1; ☎ 221 1141; 57 Home St; mains £6-7; ☽ 10am-10pm) This South African café is hidden deep in darkest Tollcross, but is worth seeking out for the changing menu of unusual African dishes (including at least one veggie option). Try a *boerewors* sandwich (sausage made with pork, beef and coriander). Downstairs is a gallery of African art.

Lower Aisle (Map pp82-4; ☎ 225 5147; St Giles Cathedral, High St, Royal Mile; snacks £2-4; ☽ 8.30am-4.30pm Mon-Fri, 9am-2pm Sun) Hidden in a vault beneath St Giles Cathedral (entrance on the side opposite the Royal Mile), the Lower Aisle is a good place to escape the Royal Mile crowds, except at lunchtime when it's packed with lawyers and secretaries from the nearby courts.

Booking is recommended – if you can't get a table here, try their New Town branch, **Fishers in the City** (☎ 225 5109; 58 Thistle St).

Daniel's Bistro (Map pp82-4; ☎ 553 5933; 88 Commercial St; mains £8-12; ☽ noon-10pm) The eponymous Daniel comes from Alsace, and his all-French kitchen staff combine top Scottish and French produce with Gallic know-how to create a wide range of delicious dishes. The fish soup is excellent, and main courses range from slow-cooked knuckle of pork to Alpine *tartiflette*. It's open from midday, so you can nip in for coffee and cake in the afternoon.

Raj (Map pp82-4; ☎ 553 3980; 91 Henderson St, The Shore; mains £7-11; ☽ noon-2.30pm & 5.30-11.30pm Sun-Thu, noon-2.30pm & 5.30pm-midnight Fri & Sat) Run by celebrity chef Tommy Miah (author of *True Taste of Asia*), the Raj is an atmospheric curry house overlooking the Water of Leith and serving Indian (including Goan) and Bangladeshi cuisine. Specialities include the tongue-tingling green Bengal chicken (marinated with lime juice, mint and chilli) and spicy Goan lamb garam fry.

TOP END

Martin Wishart (Map p73; ☎ 553 3557; 54 The Shore; mains £20-25; ☽ noon-2pm & 7-10pm Tue-Fri, 7-10pm Sat) In 2001 this restaurant became the only one in Edinburgh to win a Michelin star. The eponymous chef has worked with Albert Roux, Marco Pierre White and Nick Nairn, and brings a modern French approach to the best Scottish produce, from fillet of halibut to roast saddle of lamb. A set three-course lunch costs £18; book ahead as far as possible.

Self-Catering

There are grocery stores and food shops all over the city, many of them open 9am to 10pm daily. Many petrol stations also have late-opening shops that sell groceries.

There are several large supermarkets spread throughout the city such as **Sainsbury's** (Map pp82-4; ☎ 225 8400; 9-10 St Andrew Square; ☽ 7am-10pm Mon-Sat, 10am-8pm Sun) and **Tesco** (Map pp82-4; ☎ 456 2400; 94 Nicolson St; ☽ 7am-midnight Mon-Sat, 9am-10pm Sun). The food hall in **Marks & Spencer** (Map pp82-4; ☎ 225 2301; 54 Princes St; ☽ 9am-7pm Mon-Fri, 9am-8pm Thu, 8.30am-6pm Sat, 11am-5pm Sun) sells high-quality ready-cooked meals.

Good delis for buying picnic goodies include **Valvona & Crolla** (Map pp60-1; ☎ 556 6066; 19 Elm Row, Leith Walk; ☽ 8am-6.30pm Mon-Sat, 11am-5pm Sun), **Peckham's** (Map pp60-1; ☎ 229 7054; 155-159 Bruntsfield Pl; ☽ 8am-midnight Mon-Sat, 9am-11pm Sun) and the food hall in **Jenners** (Map pp82-4; ☎ 225 2442; 48 Princes St).

DRINKING

Edinburgh has more than 700 bars, which are as varied as the population – everything from Victorian palaces to rough-and-ready drinking dens, and from bearded, real-ale *howffs* to trendy cocktail bars.

ROYAL MILE & AROUND   Map pp82–4

Jolly Judge (☎ 225 2669; 7a James Court) A snug little *howff* tucked away down a close, the Judge exudes a cosy 17th-century atmosphere (low, painted ceilings), and has the added attraction of a cheering open fire in cold weather.

Malt Shovel (☎ 225 6843; 11-15 Cockburn St) A traditional-looking pub – all dark wood and subdued tartanry – offering a good range of real ales and more than 100 malt whiskies, the Malt Shovel is famed for its regular Tuesday night jazz.

Royal Mile Tavern (☎ 557 9681; 127 High St) An elegant, traditional bar lined with polished wood, mirrors and brass, Royal Mile serves real ale, good wines and fine food – *moules mariniéres* and crusty bread is a lunchtime speciality.

World's End (☎ 556 3628; 4 High St) So named because this part of High St once lay next to the Old Town's limit – part of the 16th-century Flodden Wall can still be seen in the basement – the World's End is an old local pub, with plenty of regulars as well as tourists. They do good bar food, including excellent fish and chips.

GRASSMARKET & AROUND   Map pp82–4

The pubs in Grassmarket have outdoor tables on sunny summer afternoons, but in the evenings are favoured by boozed-up lads on the pull, so steer clear if that's not your thing. Cowgate – Grassmarket's extension to the east – is Edinburgh's clubland.

Last Drop (☎ 225 4851; 74 Grassmarket) The name commemorates the gallows that used to stand nearby, but today's swingers are the pub's partying clientele, largely students and backpackers.

Bow Bar (☎ 226 7667; 80 West Bow) One of the city's best traditional-style pubs (it's not as old as it looks) serving a range of excellent real ales and a vast selection of malt whiskies, the Bow Bar often has standing room only on Friday and Saturday evenings.

Three Sisters (☎ 622 6800; 39 Cowgate) This huge pub is actually three bars – one American, one Irish and one Gothic – with a big cobbled courtyard for outdoor drinking in summer. It's a bit of a mad party place but you can come back the morning after and soothe your hangover with a big, fried breakfast – and a free Bloody Mary if you order before 11am.

Bannerman's (☎ 556 3254; 212 Cowgate) A long-established favourite, Bannerman's straggles through a warren of old vaults and pulls in crowds of students, locals and backpackers. The beer is good but their weekend breakfasts are best avoided.

Pear Tree House (☎ 667 7533; 38 West Nicolson St) The Pear Tree is another student favourite, with comfy sofas and board games inside, plus the city's biggest and most popular beer garden in summer.

ROSE ST & AROUND   Map pp82–4

Rose St was once a famous pub crawl, where generations of students, sailors and rugby fans would try to visit every pub on the street (around 17 of them) and down a pint of beer in each one.

Kenilworth (☎ 226 4385; 152-154 Rose St) A gorgeous, Edwardian drinking palace, complete with original fittings – from the tile floors, mahogany circle bar and gantry, to the ornate mirrors and gas lamps – the Kenilworth was Edinburgh's original gay bar back in the 1970s. Today it attracts a mixed crowd of all ages, and serves a good range of real ales and malt whiskies.

Robertsons 37 Bar (☎ 225 6185; 37 Rose St) No 37 is to malt whisky connoisseurs what the Diggers once was to real-ale fans. Its long gantry sports a choice of more than 100 single malts and the bar provides a quiet and elegant environment in which to sample them.

Guildford Arms (☎ 556 4312; 1 West Register St) Located next door to the Café Royal (see the Top Five Traditional Pubs boxed text, p93), the Guildford is another classic Victorian pub full of polished mahogany, brass and ornate cornices, with an unusual gallery bar from which you can look down into the main saloon.

Yo! Below (☎ 220 6040; 66 Rose St) Tucked away below the Yo! Sushi restaurant, this Japanese-themed bar has metered, serve-yourself beer taps on each table and offers free tarot readings and a range of oriental massages. DJs play house grooves on Friday and Saturday nights, Wednesday is karaoke night and Sunday is comedy night.

TOP FIVE TRADITIONAL PUBS

Edinburgh is blessed with a large number of traditional 19th- and early-20th-century pubs, which have preserved much of their original Victorian or Edwardian decoration and serve cask-conditioned real ales and a staggering range of malt whiskies. Here are our top five.

Athletic Arms (Diggers; Map pp60-1; ☎ 337 3822; 1-3 Angle Park Tce) Named after the cemetery across the street – the grave-diggers used to nip in and slake their thirst after a hard day's interring – the Diggers date from the 1890s. Its heyday as a real-ale drinker's mecca has passed· but it's still staunchly traditional – the décor has barely changed in 100 years – and it's packed to the gills with football and rugby fans on match days.

Abbotsford (Map pp82-4; ☎ 225 5276; 3 Rose St) One of the few pubs in Rose St that has retained its Edwardian splendour, the Abbotsford has long been a hang-out for writers, actors, journalists and media people, and has many loyal regulars. Dating from 1902, and named after Sir Walter Scott's country house, the pub's centrepiece is a splendid, mahogany island bar.

Bennet's Bar (Map pp60-1; ☎ 229 5143; 8 Leven St) Situated beside the King's Theatre, Bennet's has managed to hang on to almost all of its beautiful Victorian fittings, from the leaded, stained-glass windows and ornate mirrors to the wooden gantry and the brass water taps on the bar (for your whisky – there are over 100 malts to choose from).

Café Royal Circle Bar (Map pp82-4; ☎ 556 1884; 17 West Register St) Perhaps the classic Edinburgh bar, the Café Royal's main claims to fame are its magnificent oval bar and the series of Doulton tile portraits of famous Victorian inventors. Check out the bottles on the gantry – staff line them up to look like there's a mirror there, and many a drink-befuddled customer has been seen squinting and wondering why he can't see his reflection.

Sheep Heid (Map p73; ☎ 656 6951; 43-45 The Causeway, Duddingston) Possibly the oldest inn in Edinburgh – with a licence dating back to 1360 – the Sheep Heid feels more like a country pub than an Edinburgh bar. Set in the semi-rural shadow of Arthur's Seat, it's famous for its 19th-century skittles alley and the lovely little beer garden.

NEW TOWN & BROUGHTON ST

Cumberland Bar (Map pp60-1; ☎ 558 3134; 1-3 Cumberland St) Under the same management as the Bow Bar in Victoria St, the Cumberland pays similar attention to serving well-looked-after, cask-conditioned ales. The bar has an authentic, traditional wood-brass-and-mirrors look, and there's a nice little beer garden outside.

Opal Lounge (Map pp82-4; ☎ 226 2275; 51 George St; ☽ noon-3am) One of the city's newest style bars, the Opal is jammed at weekends with affluent twenty-somethings who've spent £200, and two hours in front of a mirror, to achieve that artlessly scruffy look. During the week, when the air-kissing, cocktail-sipping crowds thin out, it's a good place to relax with a fruit smoothie (or one of those expensive but excellent cocktails) and sample the tasty Asian food on offer. Expect to queue on weekend evenings.

Kay's Bar (Map pp82-4; ☎ 225 1858; 39 Jamaica St) Housed in a former wine-merchant's office, tiny Kay's Bar is a cosy haven with a coal fire and a fine range of real ales. Good food is served in the back room at lunchtime, but you'll have to book a table – Kay's is a popular spot.

Mathers (Map pp60-1; ☎ 556 6754; 25 Broughton St) Mathers is the 40-something generation's equivalent of the 20-something's the **Basement** (see the Lunch for Less boxed text, p87) across the street – a friendly, relaxed pub with Edwardian décor serving real ales and good pub grub.

Pivo Caffé (Map pp82-4; ☎ 557 2925; 2-6 Calton Rd) Aiming to add a little taste of Bohemia to Edinburgh's bar scene, Pivo (the Czech word for beer) serves goulash and dumplings, bottled and draught Czech beers, and two-pint cocktails – try a 'long absinthe' (absinthe with lemonade and lime).

Standing Order (Map pp82-4; ☎ 225 4460; 62-66 George St) One of several converted banks on George St, Standing Order is a cavernous beer hall with a fantastic vaulted ceiling and some cosy rooms off to the right – look for the one with the original 27-tonne safe. Despite its size, it can be standing-room only at weekends.

Tonic (Map pp82-4; ☎ 225 6431; 34a North Castle St) As cool and classy as a perfectly mixed martini, Tonic prides itself on the authenticity of its cocktails, of which there are many – the menu goes on forever. Check out the Phillipe Starck bar stools – do you sit on them, or use them as ashtrays?

LEITH & GRANTON   **Map p73**
Port O'Leith (☎ 554 3568; 58 Constitution St) This is a good, old-fashioned, friendly local boozer. The Port is swathed with flags and cap bands left behind by visiting sailors – the harbour is just down the road. Pop in for a pint and you'll probably stay till closing time.

Starbank Inn (☎ 552 4141; 64 Laverockbank Rd) Along with the Old Chain Pier (see boxed text 'Lunch for Less'), the Starbank is an oasis of fine ales and good, home-made food on Edinburgh's windswept waterfront. In summer there's a sunny conservatory, and in winter a blazing fire to toast your toes in front of.

ENTERTAINMENT

Edinburgh has a number of fine theatres and concert halls, and there are independent art-house cinemas as well as mainstream movie theatres. Many pubs offer entertainment ranging from live Scottish folk music to pop, rock and jazz as well as karaoke and quiz nights, while the new generation of style bars purvey house, dance and hip-hop to the pre-clubbing crowd.

The most comprehensive source of what's-on info is the *List* (£2.20; www.list.co.uk), an excellent listings magazine covering both Edinburgh and Glasgow. It's available from most newsagents, and is published fortnightly on a Thursday.

Cinema

Film buffs will find plenty to keep them happy in Edinburgh's art-house cinemas, while popcorn munchers can choose from a range of multiplexes.

Cameo (Map pp60-1; box office ☎ 228 4141; information ☎ 228 2800; 38 Home St; tickets £4.50-5.50) The three-screen, independently owned Cameo is a good, old-fashioned cinema showing an imaginative mix of mainstream and art-house movies. There's a good programme of midnight movies, late-night double bills and Sunday matinees, and the seats in Screen 1 are big enough to get lost in.

Filmhouse (Map pp82-4; ☎ 228 2688; 88 Lothian Rd; tickets £5.50) The Filmhouse is the main venue for the annual International Film Festival and screens a full programme of art-house, classic, foreign and second-run films, with lots of themes, retrospectives and 70mm screenings. It has wheelchair access to all screens.

UGC Fountainpark (Map pp60-1; ☎ 0870 902 0417; Fountainpark Complex, Dundee St; tickets £5.40) The UGC is a massive 12-screen multiplex complete with café-bar, movie-poster shop and frighteningly overpriced popcorn.

VUE Cinema (Map pp60-1; ☎ 0870 240 6020; Omni Centre, Greenside Pl; tickets £5.60) Another 12-screen multiplex, with three 'Gold Class' screens where you can watch from the comfort of a luxurious leather reclining seat complete with sidetable for your drink and complementary snacks.

Classical Music, Opera & Ballet

The following are the main venues for classical music.

Edinburgh Festival Theatre (Map pp82-4; ☎ 529 6000; www.eft.co.uk; 13-29 Nicolson St; ✆ box office 10am-6pm Mon-Sat, till 8pm on show nights) The modern Festival Theatre is the city's main venue for opera, dance and ballet, but also stages musicals, concerts, drama and children's shows.

Queen's Hall (Map pp60-1; ☎ 668 2019; www.queenshalledinburgh.co.uk; Clerk St; ✆ box office 10am-5.30pm, or till 15 min after show begins) The Queen's Hall is home to the Scottish Chamber Orchestra, but also stages jazz, blues, rock and comedy.

St Giles Cathedral (Map pp82-4; ☎ 225 9442; www.stgiles.net; High St, Royal Mile) The big kirk on the Royal Mile hosts a regular and varied programme of classical music, including popular lunch-time and evening concerts and organ recitals. The cathedral choir sings at the 10am and 11.30am Sunday services.

Usher Hall (Map pp82-4; ☎ 228 1155; www.usherhall.co.uk; Lothian Rd; ✆ box office 10.30am-5.30pm, till 8pm on show nights) The architecturally impressive Usher Hall hosts concerts by the Royal Scottish National Orchestra (RSNO) and performances of popular music.

Clubs

Edinburgh's club scene has some fine DJ talent and is well worth exploring; there are club night listings in the *List*. Most of the venues are concentrated in and around the twin sumps of Cowgate and Calton Rd – so it's downhill all the way...

Bongo Club (Map pp60-1; Moray House, Paterson's Land, 37 Holyrood Rd) The weird and wonderful Bongo Club has moved to new premises but is still famous for its hip-hop, funk and breakbeat club night **Headspin** (£7; 🕙 11pm-3am 2nd Sat of month). Also worth checking out is the booming bass of roots and dub reggae night **Messenger Sound System** (£7; 🕙 11pm-3am 1st & 3rd Sat of month).

Ego (Map pp60-1; ☎ 478 7434; 14 Picardy Pl) A glitzy two-floor venue in a former casino, Ego dishes up everything from the hard house, trance and techno of **NuklearPuppy** (£8;

🕙 11pm-5am 2nd & 4th Fri of month) to the glammy cheese-fest of **Disco Inferno** (£8; 🕙 10.30pm-3am 3rd Sat of month).

Liquid Room (Map pp82-4; ☎ 225 2564; www .liquidroom.com; 9c Victoria St) Set in a subterranean vault deep beneath Victoria St, the Liquid Room is a superb club venue with a thundering sound system. There are weekly club nights Wednesday to Friday and Sunday. The long-running **Evol** (£5; 10.30pm-3am Fri) caters to the indie-kid crowd, and is regularly voted as Scotland's top club night out.

Studio 24 (Map pp60-1; ☎ 558 3758; 24 Calton Rd) The programme at Studio 24 covers all bases, from house to goth to nu metal. The **Mission** (£5; 🕙 11pm-3am Sat) is the city's classic goth

---

GAY & LESBIAN EDINBURGH

Edinburgh has a small – but perfectly formed – gay and lesbian scene, centred on the area around Broughton St (known affectionately as the 'Pink Triangle') at the eastern end of New Town. **Blue Moon Café** (Map pp60-1; ☎ 556 2788; 1 Barony St; 🕙 11am-12.30am Mon-Fri, 9.30am-12.30am Sat & Sun) at the foot of Broughton St is a friendly, G&L caff offering good food and good company. It's also a good place to pick up on what's happening on the local scene.

Scotsgay (£2; www.scotsgay.co.uk) is the local monthly magazine covering gay and lesbian issues. Gay-friendly guesthouses include the Amaryllis, Ardmor House and Fairholme (see under Sleeping).

Useful contacts include the following:

Edinburgh LGB Community Centre (☎ 478 7069; 60 Broughton St; 🕙 11am-11pm Mon-Fri, 10am-11pm Sat & Sun)

Lothian Gay & Lesbian Switchboard (☎ 556 4049; www.lgls.co.uk; 🕙 7.30-10pm nightly)

Lothian Lesbian Line (☎ 557 0751; 🕙 7.30-10pm Mon & Thu)

PUBS, CLUBS & SAUNAS

CC Blooms (Map pp60-1; ☎ 556 9331; 23 Greenside Pl, Leith Walk; 🕙 6pm-3am Mon-Sat, 8pm-3am Sun) The raddled old queen of the Edinburgh gay scene, CC offers two floors of deafening dance and disco. It's a bit overpriced and overcrowded but worth a visit – if you can get past the bouncers and the crowds of drunks looking for a late drink.

Planet Out (Map pp60-1; ☎ 524 0061; 6 Baxter's Pl, Leith Walk; 🕙 4pm-1am Mon-Fri, 2pm-1am Sat & Sun) Planet Out pulls in a younger crowd than CC, and has a better party atmosphere at weekends. It's a bit quieter during the week, when you can chill out on the sofas and chat.

Claremont Bar (Map p73; ☎ 556 5662; 133-135 East Claremont St; 🕙 11am-midnight Mon-Thu, 11am-1am Fri & Sat, 12.30pm-midnight Sun) Scotland's only sci-fi theme pub (no, you have to see it), Claremont is a friendly, gay-owned bar and restaurant. The first and third Saturdays of the month are men-only nights, when leather, rubber, skinheads and bears are the order of the evening. If that's not your bag, Monday nights see the weekly meeting of the Edinburgh Doctor Who Appreciation Society (honest!).

Townhouse Sauna & Gym (Map p73; ☎ 556 6116; 53 East Claremont St; admission £4-9; 🕙 noon-11pm Sun-Thu, noon-midnight Fri & Sat) Gay-owned and operated, the Townhouse is Scotland's biggest gay sauna, spread over four floors of a Georgian town house. Facilities include two sauna cabins, steam room, spa, gym, video lounge and bar.

There are gay club nights at **Ego** (see above) on Tuesday and Sunday, but **Joy** (£10; 🕙 11pm-3am 3rd Sat of month) at the **Venue** (p96) is Edinburgh's gay club night par excellence.

and metal night, but the big session for serious clubbers is the hard house and techno of **Dogma** (£9; 10.30pm-3am 2nd Fri of month).

Venue (Map pp82-4; ☎ 557 3073; 17-23 Calton Rd) Spread over three floors and hosting live gigs as well as club nights, the Venue is one of Edinburgh's top nightspots. Try **Majestica** (£10; 10pm-3am 1st Sat of month), which offers three big-name clubs in one venue for one bargain cover charge.

Live Music

Check out the *List* and the *Gig Guide* (www.gigguide.co.uk), a free leaflet available in bars and music venues, to see who's playing where.

Henry's Jazz Cellar (Map pp82-4; ☎ 538 7385; 8a Morrison St) Edinburgh's hottest jazz joint, Henry's has something going on every night, from traditional and contemporary jazz to soul, funk, hip-hop and drum 'n' bass.

Henderson's vegetarian restaurant (Map pp82-4; ☎ 225 2131; 94 Hanover St) has live music, mainly jazz and classical guitar, at 7.30pm most evenings.

Liquid Room (Map pp82-4; ☎ 225 2564; www .liquidroom.com; 9c Victoria St; tickets £9-15) One of the city's top live-music venues, the Liquid Room stages all kinds of gigs from local bands to the Average White Band. Check the programme on their website.

Whistle Binkie's (Map pp82-4; ☎ 557 5114; www.whistlebinkies.com; 4-6 South Bridge; 7pm-3am) This crowded cellar bar just off the Royal Mile has live music every night, from rock and blues to folk and jazz. Open mic night, from 10pm on Monday, showcases new talent. Check the website for what's on.

The capital is a great place to hear traditional Scottish (and Irish) folk music, with a mix of regular spots and impromptu sessions.

Pleasance Cabaret Bar (Map pp82-4; ☎ 650 2349; 60 The Pleasance; admission £6) The Pleasance is home to the Edinburgh Folk Club, which runs a programme of visiting bands and singers at 8pm on Wednesday nights.

Royal Oak (Map pp82-4; ☎ 557 2976; 1 Infirmary St; admission free Mon-Sat, £3 Sun) The popular Wee Folk Club in the downstairs lounge, with a tiny bar and room for only 30 punters, is ticket only, so get there early (9pm start) if you want to be sure of a place. Saturday night is an open-session night – bring your own instruments (or a good singing voice).

Sandy Bell's (Map pp82-4; ☎ 225 2751; 25 Forrest Rd; admission free) This unassuming bar has been a stalwart of the traditional music scene since the Corrs were in nappies. There's music almost every evening at 9pm, and also from 2.30pm on Sunday afternoon.

Scottish Evenings

The **Thistle Hotel** (Map pp82-4; ☎ 333 9153; edinburgh@thistle.co.uk; 107 Leith St; show & dinner £43.50, show only £25; 6.45pm Apr-Oct) stages 'Jamie's Scottish Evening', a night of Scottish music, songs, dance and comedy accompanied by a four-course dinner (including the chance to try some haggis).

Sport

Edinburgh is home to two rival football teams playing in the Scottish Premier League – Heart of Midlothian (aka Hearts) and Hibernian (aka Hibs). The domestic football season lasts from August to May, and most matches are played at 3pm on Saturday or 7.30pm on Tuesday or Wednesday.

Hearts – winners of the Scottish Cup in 1998 – have their home ground at **Tynecastle Stadium** (Map p73; ☎ 200 7200; www.heartsfc.co.uk; Gorgie Rd) southwest of the city centre in Gorgie. Hibernian's home ground is northeast of the city centre at **Easter Road Stadium** (Map p73; ☎ 661 2159; www.hibs.co.uk; 12 Albion Pl).

Each year, from January to March, Scotland's national rugby team takes part in the Six Nations Rugby Union Championship. The most important fixture is the clash against England for the Calcutta Cup. At club level the season runs from September to May. **Murrayfield Stadium** (Map p73; ☎ 346 5000; www.sru.org.uk; 112 Roseburn St), about 1½ miles (2.5km) west of the city centre, is the venue for international rugby matches.

Most other spectator sports, including athletics and cycling, are held at **Meadowbank Sports Centre** (Map p73; ☎ 661 5351; 139 London Rd), Scotland's main sports arena.

Horse-racing enthusiasts should head 6 miles (10km) east to **Musselburgh Racecourse** (☎ 665 2859; www.musselburgh-racecourse.co.uk; Linkfield Rd, Musselburgh; admission £10-18), Scotland's oldest racecourse (founded 1816), where meetings are held throughout the year.

Theatre, Musicals & Comedy

Royal Lyceum Theatre (Map pp82-4; ☎ 248 4848; www.lyceum.org.uk; 30b Grindlay St; tickets £7-20; box office 10am-6pm Mon-Sat, till 8pm on show nights) A grand Victorian theatre located beside the Usher Hall, the Lyceum stages drama, concerts, musicals and ballet.

Traverse Theatre (Map pp82-4; ☎ 228 1404; www.traverse.co.uk; 10 Cambridge St; tickets £9-12; box office 10am-6pm Mon, 10am-8pm Tue-Sat, 4-8pm Sun) The Traverse is the main focus for new Scottish writing and stages an adventurous programme of contemporary drama and dance. The box office is open on Sunday only when there's a performance that day.

King's Theatre (Map pp60-1; ☎ 220 4349; 2 Leven St, Bruntsfield; tickets £7-18; box office open from one hour before show begins). King's is a traditional theatre with a programme of musicals, drama, comedy and its famous annual Christmas pantomime.

Edinburgh Playhouse (Map pp60-1; ☎ 524 3301; bookings ☎ 0870 606 3424; www.edinburgh -playhouse.co.uk; 18-22 Greenside Pl; tickets £7-26; box office 10am-6pm Mon-Sat, till 8pm on show nights) This restored theatre at the top of Leith Walk stages Broadway musicals, dance shows, opera and popular-music concerts.

The Stand Comedy Club (Map pp82-4; ☎ 558 7272; www.thestand.co.uk; 5 York Pl; tickets £1-8) The Stand, founded in 1995, is Edinburgh's main comedy venue. It's a cabaret bar with performances every night and a free Sunday lunch-time show.

SHOPPING

Princes St is Edinburgh's principal shopping street, lined with all the big high-street stores, with many smaller shops along pedestrianised Rose St. There are also two big shopping centres in New Town – **Princes Mall**, at the eastern end of Princes St, and the nearby **St James Centre** at the top of Leith St – but the huge **Ocean Terminal** in Leith is the biggest shopping centre in the city. A brand new shopping complex with a flagship Harvey Nichols (p98) store opened on the eastern side of St Andrew Square in 2002.

For more off-beat shopping – including fashion, music, crafts, gifts and jewellery – head for the cobbled lanes of Cockburn, Victoria and St Mary's Sts, all near the Royal Mile in the Old Town, and William St in the western part of New Town.

CASHMERE & WOOL

Woollen textiles and knitwear are one of Scotland's classic exports. Scottish cashmere –

a fine, soft wool from young goats and lambs – provides the most luxurious and expensive knitwear and has been seen gracing the torsos of pop-star Robbie Williams and England footballer David Beckham.

Designs On Cashmere (Map pp82-4; ☎ 556 6394; 28 High St, Royal Mile) and the **Cashmere Store** (Map pp82-4; ☎ 226 1577; 2 St Giles St, Royal Mile) are good places to start, with a wide range of traditional and modern knitwear, while the colourful designs at **Joyce Forsyth Designer Knitwear** (Map pp82-4; ☎ 220 4112; 42 Candlemaker Row; 11am-5.30pm Tue-Thu & Sat, 11am-4.45pm Fri) will drag your ideas about woollens firmly into the 21st century.

Edinburgh Woollen Mill (Map pp82-4; ☎ 226 3840; 139 Princes St) is an old stalwart of the tourist trade, with a good selection of traditional jerseys, cardigans, scarves, shawls and rugs.

CRAFTS & SOUVENIRS

During the Festival period, there's a good **Crafts Fair** in the churchyard at St John's Church, on the corner of Princes St and Lothian Rd, with a wide range of jewellery, ceramics and leather goods.

The **Meadows Pottery** (Map pp60-1; ☎ 662 4064; 11a Summerhall Pl; 10.30am-5.30pm Mon-Sat) sells colourful stoneware, all hand-thrown on the premises. The **Adam Pottery** (Map pp60-1; ☎ 557 3978; 76 Henderson Row; 10am-5.30pm Mon-Sat) also produces its own ceramics, mostly decorative, or in a wider range of styles.

Flux (Map p73; ☎ 554 4075; 55 Bernard St, Leith; 9am-5pm Mon & Tue, 9am-7pm Wed-Fri, 11am-7pm Sat & Sun) is an outlet for contemporary Scottish arts and crafts, including stained glass, metalware, jewellery and ceramics.

DEPARTMENT STORES

Founded in 1838, **Jenners** (Map pp82-4; ☎ 225 2442; 48 Princes St) is the *grande dame* of Scottish department stores. It stocks a wide range of quality goods, both classic and contemporary. **John Lewis** (Map pp82-4; ☎ 556 9121; St James Centre) is the place to go for good-value clothes and household goods.

Aitken & Niven (Map pp82-4; ☎ 225 1461; 77-79 George St), founded in 1905, is another independent Scottish store, with a good range of quality tartans and tweeds, and a wide selection of rugby shirts and accessories.

The newest addition to Edinburgh's shopping scene is the four floors of designer labels and eye-popping price tags that is **Harvey Nichols** (Map pp82-4; ☎ 524 8388; 30-34 St Andrew Sq; ◷ 10am-6pm Mon-Wed, 10am-8pm Thu, 10am-7pm Fri & Sat, noon-6pm Sun).

TARTAN & HIGHLAND DRESS

There are dozens of shops along the Royal Mile and Princes St where you can buy kilts and tartan goods. One of the best is **Kinloch Anderson** (Map p73; ☎ 555 1390; 4 Dock St, Leith), founded in 1868 and still family-run; they are a supplier of kilts and Highland dress to the royal family.

Geoffrey (Tailor) Inc (Map pp82-4; ☎ 557 0256; 57-59 High St, Royal Mile) can fit you out in traditional Highland dress, or run up a kilt in your own clan tartan. Their offshoot, 21st Century Kilts, offers modern fashion kilts in a variety of fabrics.

GETTING THERE & AWAY
Air

Edinburgh airport (☎ 333 1000), 8 miles (13km) west of the city, has numerous services to other parts of Scotland, the UK, Ireland and Europe. See the Transport chapter (p416) for details of flights to Edinburgh from outside Scotland. **British Airways** (☎ 08457 77 333 77) operates daily flights to Inverness, Orkney, Shetland and Stornoway.

Bus

Edinburgh's brand new St Andrew Square bus & coach station (Map pp82-4) is at the northeast corner of the square, with pedestrian entrances from the square and from Elder St. For timetable information, call **Traveline** (☎ 0870 608 2 608; www.travelinescotland.com).

Citylink (☎ 08705 50 50 50; www.citylink.co.uk) buses connect Edinburgh with all Scotland's cities and major towns. The following are sample fares from Edinburgh.

Destination	Single fare	Duration (hrs)	Frequency
Aberdeen	£15.40	3¼	hourly
Dundee	£8.40	1¾	30 min
Fort William	£18	4	3 a day
Glasgow	£4	1¼	20 min
Inverness	£15	4	hourly
Portree	£25	8	2 a day
Stirling	£6.20	1¼	hourly

Motorvator (☎ 01698-870768, 01501-821782) operates a competing bus service between Edinburgh and Glasgow (£3.50, 1¼ hours, every 30 minutes).

Car & Motorcycle

Arriving in or leaving Edinburgh by car during the morning and evening rush hours (7.30am to 9.30am and 4.30pm to 6.30pm Monday to Friday) is an experience you can live without. Try to time your journey to avoid these periods. In particular, there can be huge tailbacks on the A90 between Edinburgh and the Forth Road Bridge.

Train

The main terminus in Edinburgh is Waverley train station, located in the heart of the city. Trains arriving from, and departing for, the west also stop at Haymarket station, which is more convenient for the West End. You can buy tickets, make reservations and get travel information at the **Edinburgh Rail Travel Centre** (Map pp82-4; ◷ 4.45am-12.30am Mon-Sat, 7am-12.30am Sun) in Waverley station. For fare and timetable enquiries, phone the **National Rail Enquiry Service** (☎ 08457 48 49 50) or check the timetable on the Railtrack website (www.railtrack.co.uk).

ScotRail operates a regular shuttle service between Edinburgh and Glasgow (£8.60, 50 minutes, every 15 minutes), and frequent daily services to all Scottish cities including Aberdeen (£24.50, 2½ hours), Dundee (£15.70, 1½ hours) and Inverness (£31.60, 3¼ hours).

See the Transport chapter, p418, for details of trains to Edinburgh from London.

GETTING AROUND
To/From the Airport

The Lothian Buses Airlink service No 100 runs from Waverley Bridge, just outside the train station, to the airport (£3.30/5 one-way/return, 30 minutes, every 10–15 minutes) via the West End and Haymarket. The Airsaver ticket (adult/child £4.20/2.50) can be purchased on the bus and gives a one-way trip on the Airlink bus plus unlimited travel for one day on all Lothian Bus services in the city.

An airport taxi to the city centre costs around £13 and takes about 20 minutes. Both buses and taxis depart from just outside the arrivals hall.

Bicycle

Thanks to the efforts of local cycling campaign group Spokes and a bike-friendly city council, Edinburgh is well-equipped with bike lanes and dedicated cycle tracks. You can buy a map of the city's cycle routes from most bike shops.

Biketrax (Map pp60-1; ☎ 228 6633; 11 Lochrin Pl; ☺ 9.30am-6pm Mon-Fri, 9.30am-5.30pm Sat, noon-5pm Sun) rents out a wide range of cycles and equipment, including kids' bikes, tandems, recumbents, pannier bags, child seats – even unicycles! A mountain bike costs £15 for 24 hours, £10 for extra days, and £60 for one week. You'll need a £100 cash or credit-card deposit and some form of ID.

See also Cycling in the Activities chapter (p74).

Car & Motorcycle

Though useful for day trips beyond the city, a car in central Edinburgh is more of a liability than a convenience. There is restricted access on Princes St, George St and Charlotte Square, many streets are one-way and finding a parking place in the city centre is like striking gold. Queen's Drive around Holyrood Park is closed to motorised traffic on Sunday.

PARKING

There's no parking on main roads into the city from 7.30am to 6.30pm Monday to Saturday. On-street parking in the city centre is controlled by self-service ticket machines from 8.30am to 6.30pm Monday to Saturday, and costs £1.20 per hour, with a two-hour maximum. If you break the rules, you'll get a parking fine, often within minutes of your ticket expiring – Edinburgh's parking wardens are both numerous and notorious. The fine is £60, reduced to £30 if you pay up within 14 days. Cars parked illegally will be towed away. There are large, long-stay car parks at the St James Centre, Greenside Pl, New St, Castle Tce and Morrison St. Motorcycles can be parked for free at designated areas in the city centre.

CAR RENTAL

All the big, international car rental agencies have offices in Edinburgh (see p420).

There are many smaller, local agencies that offer better rates. One of the best is **Arnold Clark** (Map pp60-1; ☎ 228 4747; 1-13 Lochrin Pl)

in Tollcross, which charges from £20 a day, or £100 a week for a small car, including VAT and insurance. The daily rate includes 250 miles (400km) a day; excess is charged at 4p a mile. For periods of four days and more, mileage is unlimited.

Public Transport

Edinburgh's public transport system consists entirely of buses; the main operators are **Lothian Buses** (www.lothianbuses.co.uk) and **First Edinburgh** (www.firstedinburgh.co.uk): for timetable information contact **Traveline** (☎ 0870 608 2 608; www.travelinescotland.com).

Bus timetables, route maps and fare guides are posted at all main bus stops, and you can pick up the free *Lothian Buses Route Map* from the **Lothian Buses office** (Map pp82-4; ☎ 555 6363; Waverley Bridge; ☺ 8.30am-6pm Mon-Sat, 9.30am-5pm Sun). There's also a second **Lothian Buses** office (Map pp82-4; ☎ 555 6363; 7-9 Shandwick Pl; ☺ 8.30am-6pm Mon-Sat).

Adult fares range from 60p to £1; children aged under five travel free and those aged five to 15 pay a flat fare of 50p. On Lothian Buses you must pay the driver the exact fare, but First Edinburgh buses will give change. Lothian Buses drivers also sell a Daysaver ticket (£2.50, or £1.80 if purchased after 9.30am Monday to Friday or all day Saturday and Sunday) that gives unlimited travel on Lothian Buses for a day. Night-service buses, which run hourly between midnight and 5am, charge a flat fare of £2.

The Lothian Buses bus company has its own **lost property office** (Map p73; ☎ 554 4494; 4 Shrub Pl, Leith Walk; ☺ 10am-1.30pm Mon-Fri).

Taxi

Edinburgh's black taxis can be hailed in the street, ordered by phone (extra 60p charge), or picked up at one of the many central ranks. Taxis are fairly expensive – the minimum charge is £1.40 for the first 340 yards, then 22p for every subsequent 240 yards – a typical 2-mile trip across the city centre will cost around £4 to £5. Tipping is up to you – because of the high fares local people rarely tip on short journeys, but occasionally round up to the nearest 50p on longer ones.

Capital Taxis (☎ 228 2555)
Central Radio Taxis (☎ 229 2468)
City Cabs (☎ 228 1211)
Radiocabs (☎ 225 9000)

EDINBURGH

AROUND EDINBURGH

Edinburgh is small enough that, when you need a break from the city, the beautiful surrounding countryside isn't far away and is easily accessible by public transport. The old counties around Edinburgh are called Midlothian, West Lothian and East Lothian, often referred to collectively as 'the Lothians'.

MIDLOTHIAN

☎ 0131

Queensferry

Queensferry is located at the narrowest part of the Firth of Forth, where ferries have sailed across the water to Fife from the earliest times – the village takes its name from Queen Margaret (1046–93), who gave pilgrims free passage across the firth on their way to St Andrews. Ferries continued to operate until 1964 when the graceful **Forth Road Bridge** – now the fifth longest in Europe – was opened.

Predating the road bridge by 74 years, the magnificent **Forth Bridge** – only outsiders ever call it the Forth Rail Bridge – is one of the finest engineering achievements of the 19th century. Completed in 1890 after seven years' work, its three huge cantilevers span 1447m and took 59,000 tonnes of steel, 8 million rivets and the lives of 58 men to build.

In the pretty, terraced High St in Queensferry is the small **Queensferry Museum** (☎ 331 5545; 53 High St; admission free; 🕑 10am-1pm & 2.15-5pm Mon & Thu-Sat, noon-5pm Sun). It contains some interesting background information on the bridges, and a fascinating exhibit on the 'Burry Man', part of the village's summer gala festivities (see p77).

There are several good pubs along High St. The atmospheric **Hawes Inn** (☎ 331 1990; Newhalls Rd; mains £4-8; 🕑 food served noon to 10pm), famously mentioned in Robert Louis Stevenson's novel *Kidnapped*, serves excellent pub grub; it's opposite the Inchcolm ferry, right beside the railway bridge.

GETTING THERE & AWAY

Queensferry lies on the southern bank of the Firth of Forth, 8 miles (13km) west of Edinburgh city centre. To get there, take First Edinburgh bus No 43 (£1.80,

30 minutes, three an hour) westbound from St Andrew Square. It's a 10-minute walk from the bus stop to the Hawes Inn and the Inchcolm ferry.

There are also frequent trains from Edinburgh Waverley and Haymarket stations to Dalmeny station (£2.90, 15 minutes, two to four an hour). From the station exit, the Hawes Inn is only a five-minute walk along a footpath (across the road, behind the bus stop) that leads north beside the railway and then under the bridge.

Inchcolm

The island of Inchcolm lies east of the Forth bridges, less than a mile off the coast of Fife. Only 800m long, it is home to the ruins of **Inchcolm Abbey** (☎ 01383-823332; Inchcolm, Fife; adult/child £3/1; 🕑 9.30am-6.30pm Apr-Oct), one of Scotland's best-preserved medieval abbeys, founded by Augustinian priors in 1123.

The ferry boat **Maid of the Forth** (☎ 331 4857) sails to Inchcolm from Hawes Pier in Queensferry. There are two or three sailings daily in July and August, and at weekends only from April to June and in September and October. The return fare is £11/4.50 for adults/children, including admission to Inchcolm Abbey. It's a half-hour sail to Inchcolm and you get 1½ hours ashore. As well as the abbey, the trip gives you the chance to see the island's grey seals, puffins and other seabirds.

Hopetoun House

Hopetoun House (☎ 331 2451; adult/child £6/3; 🕑 10am-5.30pm Apr-Sep, last admission 4.30pm) is one of Scotland's finest stately homes, with a superb location in lovely grounds beside the Firth of Forth. There are two parts – the older built to Sir William Bruce's plans between 1699 and 1702 and dominated by a splendid stairwell with (modern) trompe l'oeil paintings; and the newer designed between 1720 and 1750 by three members of the Adam family, William and sons Robert and John. The highlights are the red and yellow Adam drawing rooms, lined in silk damask, and the view from the roof terrace.

Britain's most elegant equine accommodation – where the marquis once housed his pampered racehorses – is now the stylish **Stables Tearoom** (mains £4-7; 🕑 same as house), a delightful spot for lunch.

Hopetoun House is 2 miles (3km) west of Queensferry along the coast road. Driving from Edinburgh, turn off the A90 onto the A904 just before the Forth Bridge and follow the signs.

Rosslyn Chapel

Scotland's most beautiful and enigmatic church – **Rosslyn Chapel** (Collegiate Church of St Matthew; ☎ 440 2159; www.rosslyn-chapel.com; Roslin; adult/child £4/1; ⏰ 10am-5pm Mon-Sat, noon-4.45pm Sun) – was built in the mid-15th century for William St Clair, third earl of Orkney. The ornately carved interior – at odds with the architectural fashion of its time – is a monument to the mason's art, and rich in symbolic imagery. As well as flowers, vines, angels and biblical figures, the carved stones include many examples of the pagan 'Green Man'; other figures are associated with Freemasonry and the Knights Templar. Intriguingly, there are also carvings of plants from the Americas that predate Columbus' voyage of discovery. The symbolism of these images has led some researchers to conclude that Rosslyn is some kind of secret Templar repository, and it has been claimed that hidden vaults beneath the chapel could conceal anything from the Holy Grail or the head of John the Baptist to the body of Christ himself. The chapel is owned by the Episcopal Church of Scotland and services are still held here on Sunday mornings.

The chapel is on the eastern edge of the village of Roslin, 7 miles (11km) south of Edinburgh city centre. Lothian Bus No 15A runs from St Andrew Square in Edinburgh to Roslin (£1, 30 minutes) hourly on weekdays, every two hours on Saturday, and twice a day on Sundays.

Pentland Hills

Rising on the southern edge of Edinburgh, the Pentland Hills stretch 16 miles (26km) southwest to near Carnwath in Lanarkshire. The hills rise to 579m at their highest point and offer excellent, not-too-strenuous walking with great views. There are several access points along the A702 road on the southern side of the hills. MacEwan's bus No 100 runs four times daily along the A702 from Princes St in Edinburgh to Biggar.

EAST LOTHIAN

Beyond the former coalfields of Dalkeith and Musselburgh, the fertile farmland of East Lothian stretches eastwards along the coast to the seaside resort of North Berwick and the fishing harbour of Dunbar. In the middle lies the prosperous market town of Haddington.

Haddington & Around

☎ 01620 / pop 8850

Haddington, straddling the River Tyne 18 miles (29km) east of Edinburgh, was made a royal burgh by David I in the 12th century. Most of the modern town, however, dates from the 17th to 19th centuries during the period of prosperity that followed the Agricultural Revolution. The prettiest part of town is the tree-lined Court St, with its wide pavement and grand 18th- and 19th-century buildings.

Church St leads from the eastern end of High St to **St Mary's Parish Church** (☎ 823109; Sidegate; admission free; ⏰ 11am-4pm Mon-Sat, 2-4.30pm Sun Apr-Sep). Built in 1462, it's the largest parish church in Scotland and one of the finest pre-Reformation churches in the country.

A mile south of Haddington is **Lennoxlove House** (☎ 823720; Lennoxlove Estate; adult/child £4/2; ⏰ guided tours 2-4.30pm Wed, Thu & Sun Easter-Oct), a hidden gem of a country house dating originally from around 1345, with major extensions and renovations from the 17th to the early 20th centuries. It contains fine furniture and paintings, and memorabilia relating to Mary, queen of Scots. Chief among these are her death mask and a silver casket given to her by Francis II of France, her first husband. The house has been the seat of the duke of Hamilton since 1947.

With a lovely location overlooking the River Tyne, the **Waterside Bistro & Restaurant** (☎ 825764; 1-5 Waterside, Nungate, Haddington; mains bistro £7-9, restaurant £15-18) is a great place to have lunch on a summer's day, watching the swans and ducks go by. The bistro does good-quality light meals, while the upstairs restaurant is more formal.

First Edinburgh bus Nos X6 and X8 run between Edinburgh and Haddington every 30 minutes. The nearest train station is at Drem, 3 miles (5km) to the north.

North Berwick

☎ 01620 / pop 6220

North Berwick is an attractive Victorian seaside resort with long sandy beaches, three golf courses and a small harbour. The **TIC** (☎ 892197; Quality St; 9am-6pm Mon-Sat, 11am-4pm Sun) is two blocks inland from the harbour.

SIGHTS & ACTIVITIES

Top marks to the bright spark who came up with the idea for the **Scottish Seabird Centre** (☎ 890202; www.seabird.org; The Harbour; adult/child £4.95/3.50; 10am-6pm daily Apr-Sep; 10am-4pm Mon-Fri, 10am-5.30pm Sat & Sun Oct-Mar), an ornithologist's paradise that uses remote-control video cameras sited on the Bass Rock and other islands to relay live images of nesting gannets and other seabirds – you can control the cameras yourself, and zoom in on scenes of gannet domesticity.

Off High St, a short steep path climbs up **North Berwick Law** (184m), a conical hill that dominates the town. When the weather's fine there are great views to the spectacular **Bass Rock**, iced white in spring and summer with the guano from thousands of nesting gannets. **Fred Marr** (☎ 892838) runs boat trips (adult/child £5/3, 1¼ hours, daily April to September) around Bass Rock and Fidra Island, departing from North Berwick's harbour.

Two miles (3km) west of North Berwick is **Dirleton Castle** (☎ 850330; Dirleton; adult/child £3/1; 9.30am-6.30pm daily Apr-Sep; 9.30am-4.30pm Mon-Sat & 2.30-4.30pm Sun Oct-Mar), an impressive medieval fortress with massive round towers, a drawbridge and a horrific pit dungeon, surrounded rather incongruously by beautiful, manicured gardens.

Perched on a cliff 3 miles (5km) east of North Berwick is the spectacular ruin of **Tantallon Castle** (☎ 892727; adult/child £3/1; 9.30am-6.30pm daily Apr-Sep, 9.30am-4.30pm Sat-Wed, 9.30am-1pm Thu Oct-Mar). Built around 1350, it was the fortress residence of the Douglas Earls of Angus (the 'Red Douglases'), defended on one side by a series of ditches and on the other by an almost sheer drop into the sea.

SLEEPING & EATING

North Berwick has plenty of places to stay, though they can fill up quickly at weekends when golfers are in town. Recommended B&Bs include the central **Palmerston** (☎ 892884; 28b St Andrew St; r per person £25; P) with spacious rooms (all with ensuite), and homely **Beach Lodge** (☎ 892257; 5 Beach Rd; r per person £25), which offers sea views and vegetarian breakfasts.

The top eating places in the area are the **Grange** (☎ 893344; 35 High St; 3-course lunch/dinner £8/16) in the centre of town, and the delightful **Deveau's Brasserie** (☎ 850241; Open Arms Hotel, Dirleton; mains £9-11) in the village of Dirleton.

GETTING THERE & AWAY

North Berwick is 24 miles (39km) east of Edinburgh. First Edinburgh bus No 124 runs between Edinburgh and North Berwick (£4.20, 1¼ hours, every 20 minutes). There are frequent trains between North Berwick and Edinburgh (£3.80, 35 minutes, hourly).

Dunbar
☎ 01368 / pop 6350

Dunbar was an important Scottish fortress town in the Middle Ages, but little remains of its past save for the tottering ruins of **Dunbar Castle** overlooking the harbour. Today the town survives as a fishing port and seaside resort, famed in the USA as the birthplace of John Muir (1838–1914), pioneer conservationist and father of the US national park system.

The **TIC** (☎ 863353; 143 High St; 9am-6pm Mon-Sat, 11am-4pm Sun Jun-Aug; 9am-5pm Mon-Sat Apr, May & Sep; 9am-5pm Mon-Fri Oct-Mar) is near the town hall.

The slightly down-at-heel town centre is home to **John Muir House** (☎ 862595; 128 High St; admission free; 11am-1pm & 2-5pm Mon-Sat, 2-5pm Sun Jun-Sep), the birthplace and childhood home of the great man (closed for renovation at time of writing, due to re-open in late 2003). The nearby **Dunbar Town House Museum** (☎ 863734; High St; admission free; 12.30-4.30pm Apr-Oct) provides an introduction to local history and archaeology.

From the castle, a scenic, 2-mile (3km) cliff-top trail follows the coastline west to the sands of Belhaven Bay and **John Muir Country Park**.

Perrymans (☎ 01289-308719) bus No 253/254 (50 minutes, every two hours) and First Edinburgh bus No X6 (one hour, hourly) run between Edinburgh and Dunbar. Trains from Edinburgh's Waverley train station serve Dunbar (£6.70, 20 minutes) every hour or so.

WEST LOTHIAN
Linlithgow
☎ 01506 / pop 13,370

This ancient royal burgh is one of Scotland's oldest towns, though much of it 'only' dates from the 15th to 17th centuries. Its centre retains a certain charm, despite some ugly modern buildings and occasional traffic congestion, and the town makes an excellent day trip from Edinburgh.

The **TIC** (☎ 844600), in the Burgh Halls at the Cross, opens 10am to 5pm daily April to October.

SIGHTS & ACTIVITIES

The town's main attraction is the magnificent ruin of **Linlithgow Palace** (☎ 842896; Church Peel; adult/child £3/1; 🕙 9.30am-6.30pm daily Apr-Sep; 9.30am-4.30pm Mon-Sat, 2-4.30pm Sun Oct-Mar). Begun by James I in 1425, the building of the palace continued for over a century. It was a favourite royal residence – James V was born here in 1512, as was his daughter Mary (later Queen of Scots) in 1542. Cromwell billeted his troops here in the 1650s and Bonnie Prince Charlie briefly visited in 1745 – legend has it that a cooking fire left by retreating Jacobite soldiers caused the blaze that gutted the palace in 1746.

Beside the palace is the Gothic **St Michael's Church** (☎ 842188; Church Peel; admission free; 🕙 10am-4.30pm Mon-Sat, 12.30-4.30pm Sun May-Sep; 10am-3pm Mon-Fri Oct-Apr). Built between the 1420s and 1530s, it is topped by a controversial aluminium spire that was added in 1964. The church is said to be haunted by a ghost that foretold King James IV of his impending defeat at Flodden in 1513.

The **Linlithgow Story** (☎ 670677; Annet House, 143 High St; adult/child £1/60p; admission free Sun; 🕙 10am-5pm Mon-Sat, 1-4pm Sun Easter-Oct) is a small museum that tells the story of the Stewart monarchy and the history of the town.

Just 150m south of the town centre lies the Union Canal and the pretty **Linlithgow Canal Centre** (☎ 671215; www.lucs.org.uk; Manse Rd Canal Basin; admission free; 🕙 2-5pm Sat & Sun Easter-Sep, plus 2-5pm Mon-Fri Jul & Aug), where a little museum records the history of the canal.

The centre runs three-hour **canal boat trips** west to the Avon Aqueduct (adult/child £6/3) departing at 2pm Saturday and Sunday, Easter to September, and to the **Falkirk Wheel** (see p192) on weekdays in July and August. Shorter, 20-minute cruises (adult/child £2.50/1.50) leave every half-hour during the centre's opening times.

EATING & DRINKING

Linlithgow has several good pubs and restaurants. The **Four Marys** (☎ 842171; 65-76 High St; mains £4-8; 🕙 food served noon-3pm & 5-9pm Mon-Fri, noon-9pm Sat & Sun) is an attractive traditional pub (opposite the palace entrance) that serves real ales and excellent pub grub, including haggis, neeps and tatties. A few doors along the street is **Marynka** (☎ 840123; 57 High St; lunch mains £6-8, 2-course dinner £19.50; 🕙 noon-2pm & 6-11.30pm Tue-Sat), a pleasant little gourmet restaurant.

The rustic **Champany Inn** (☎ 834532; Champany; mains £10-20; 🕙 12.30-2pm & 7-10pm Mon-Fri, 7-10pm Sat) is a trencherman's delight, famous for its excellent Aberdeen Angus steaks and Scottish lobsters. The neighbouring **Chop and Ale House** (mains £6-13) is a less expensive alternative to the main dining room, offering delicious home-made burgers and steaks. The inn is 2 miles (3km) northeast of Linlithgow on the A803/A904 road towards Bo'ness and Queensferry.

GETTING THERE & AWAY

Linlithgow is 15 miles (24km) west of Edinburgh, and is served by frequent trains from the capital (£3.20, 20 minutes, four an hour); the train station is 250m east of the town centre.

You can also cycle from Edinburgh to Linlithgow along the Union Canal towpath; allow 1½ to two hours.

Glasgow

CONTENTS

Enigmatic Glasgow is slowly muscling in on Edinburgh's tourism crown, and deservedly so – you shouldn't leave Scotland without a visit. Don't expect prim and proper Edinburgh here – Glasgow is raw and energetic with a gritty honesty. You don't have to scratch far under the surface to find a beguiling magnetism that combines affability, urban mayhem, wry humour and…oomph. If you don't have fun in Glasgow, we'd suggest therapy.

Architecturally superb streets lie side by side with concrete monoliths, but that's Glasgow – what you see here is what you get and it wears its scars with style.

There's a lot of rivalry between Scotland's two foremost cities – don't start a conversation with a Glaswegian expounding the virtues of that other city, or it will be a short conversation. Glasgow is a refreshing alternative from any other urban centre in Scotland though, and the friendliness of its inhabitants can even be unnerving. Glasgow has a spirit and a character that embodies much of this country: hardship, opportunity, rejuvenation and tourism.

Rejuvenation is the buzz word in Glasgow, with the city going through a major period of transformation that is turning the riverfront into a prime tourist-puller. It's a canny city that came up with the idea: the Clyde built Glasgow and now Glasgow is building the Clyde. The diversity of pubs and clubs is astounding; only in this unique city could unpretentious style bars materialise. Try to catch a gig while you're here – the city is the heart of Scotland's live music scene, and there's a smorgasbord of raw, fresh Scottish bands and loads of thumping venues.

HIGHLIGHTS

- Meandering along the reinvigorated **Clyde River** (p109), and discovering the city's fascinating heritage
- Marvelling at the architectural genius of **Charles Rennie Mackintosh** (p111)
- Catching the hottest tunes from Glasgow's local artists in the seething **live music scene** (p124)
- Visiting **Glasgow Cathedral** (p112), the only cathedral on the Scottish mainland to have survived the turbulent Reformation
- Sniffing out the **perfect watering hole** among the countless bars, pubs and clubs (p122)

Glasgow School of Art, Willow Tea Rooms ★
Clyde River ★
Glasgow Science Centre ★
Burrell Collection ★

| ■ TELEPHONE CODE: 0141 | ■ POPULATION: 629,501 | ■ AREA: 176 SQ KM |

GLASGOW

HISTORY

Glasgow grew up around the cathedral founded by St Mungo in the 6th century, and in 1451 the city became the site of the University of Glasgow, the second university to be founded in Scotland

In the 18th century, much of the tobacco trade between Europe and the USA was routed through Glasgow and provided a great source of wealth. Even after the tobacco trade declined in the 19th century, the city continued to prosper as a centre of textile manufacturing, shipbuilding and the coal and steel industries.

The new industries created a huge demand for labour, and peasants poured in from Ireland and the Highlands to crowd the city's tenements. The outward appearance of prosperity, however, was tempered by the dire working conditions in the factories, particularly for women and children.

In the second half of the 19th century life expectancy was a mere 30 years.

While the workers suffered, the textile barons and shipping magnates prospered, and Glasgow could justifiably call itself the second city of the empire. In the first half of the 20th century, Glasgow was the centre of Britain's munitions industry, supplying arms and ships for the two world wars. After those boom years, however, the port and heavy industries began to decline and, by the early 1970s, the city looked doomed. Glasgow has always been proud of its predominantly working-class nature but, unlike middle-class Edinburgh with its varied service industries, it had few alternatives when recession hit and unemployment spiralled.

In the late 20th and early 21st centuries there has been increasing confidence in the city. Glasgow won the 1990 European City of Culture award, and followed this up by

GLASGOW IN...

Two Days

Start your day with breakfast and a spot of people-watching in the trendy **Merchant City**. Take a stroll around the leafy cathedral precinct in the East End, popping your head into **Glasgow Cathedral** (p112) and **St Mungo's Museum of Religious Life & Art** (p113). Treat yourself to fine dining at the elegant, Victorian-era **The Buttery** (p122), followed by a night at **The Arches** (p123), one of Glasgow's premier pubs/clubs.

A visit to the wonderful **Burrell Collection** (p114) is a must on your second day and while you're in the area check out the **Scottish Football Museum** (p114). If you're here on the weekend don't miss **The Barras** (p115), Glasgow's flea market and some would say, its heart and soul. At night head to **Sauchiehall St** to eat and drink along the city centre's funkiest strip. Drop into **King Tut's Wah Wah Hut** (p124) to hear some of Glasgow's freshest live music talent.

Four Days

Follow the two-day itinerary, then on your third day add a trip over to the bohemian **West End** (p121); some of the city's best **cafés** and **restaurants** are here. Be sure to check out the **Hunterian Museum** (p113) and **Hunterian Art Gallery** (p113). On the fourth day have a stroll along the **Clyde Walkway** (p109) and discover the rejuvenation along Glasgow's waterfront. Learn about the city's unique heritage by taking a boat trip down the **River Clyde** (p110), visiting the **Clydebuilt** (p110) museum and **Tall Ship** (p110) en route – then catch a 3D flick at the **Glasgow Science Centre** (p110).

One Week

Follow the four-day itinerary and then spend a day discovering what all the **Mackintoshania** (p111) fuss is about. Drop into the **Glasgow School of Art** (p112), **Willow Tea Rooms** (p112) and **Queens Cross Church** (p115). Finish up with a couple of day trips out of the city: head to **Paisley** (p129) and marvel at its magnificent abbey and take a wander around the revitalised waterfront at **Greenock** (p131), popping into the **HM Customs & Excise Museum** (p131).

serving as the UK's City of Architecture & Design in 1999. But, behind all the optimism, the general standard of living remains relatively low, and life is tough for those affected by the comparatively high unemployment, inadequate housing and generally poor diet.

ORIENTATION

The city centre is built on a grid system on the northern side of the River Clyde. The two train stations (Central and Queen St), the Buchanan bus station and the Tourist Information Centre (TIC) are all on or within a couple of blocks of George Sq, the main city square. Merchant City is the city's main commercial district, east of George Sq.

Motorways bore through the suburbs and the M8 sweeps round the northern and western edges of the centre, passing the airport 10 miles (16km) west. There are buses every 10 or 15 minutes from Glasgow International Airport to Buchanan bus station (£3.30).

Maps

Philip's *Glasgow Street Atlas* (£3.99) is a handy, easy to read street guide, available in bookshops. Glasgow City Council publishes the excellent *Fit for Life* map (free from the TIC) showing cycle and walking routes around the city.

INFORMATION

The *List* (www.list.co.uk), available from newsagents (£2.20), is Glasgow and Edinburgh's invaluable fortnightly guide to films, theatre, cabaret, music, clubs – the works. The 136-page *Eating & Drinking Guide*, published by the *List* every April, covers Glasgow and Edinburgh and costs £4.95.

Bookshops

Borders (Map pp108-9; ☎ 222 7700; 98 Buchanan St) A browsing bonanza, also sells CDs and international newspapers and magazines.
Waterstone's (Map pp108-9; ☎ 332 9105; 153 Sauchiehall St) Five floors of just about anything you might want to read, including street maps of Glasgow.

Emergency

In an emergency call ☎ 999 or ☎ 112 for police, fire, ambulance, mountain rescue or coastguard.

Internet Access

EasyInternet café (Map pp108-9; ☎ 222 2364; www.easy-everything.com; 57 St Vincent St; £1.30 per hr)
Gallery of Modern Art (Map pp108-9; ☎ 229 1996; Queen St; free; ☯ 10am-8pm Mon, Tue & Thu, 10am-5pm Wed & Sat, 11am-5pm Fri & Sun) In basement library at the gallery; booking recommended.
Mitchell Library (Map pp108-9; ☎ 287 2999; North St; free) Booking recommended.

Internet Resources

Glasgow City Council (www.glasgow.gov.uk) A particularly good daily 'What's On' section.
Glasgow Disability Access Guide (www.glasgowaccesspanel.org.uk) An online guide for the disabled.
Glasgow Museums (www.glasgowmuseums.com) A very useful guide to the city's superb museums.
Search Engine & Directory (www.scotfind.com) A search engine for all things Glaswegian and Scottish.
The Guide (wwww.glasgowlife.com) An online city guide particularly good for eating and entertainment.

Left Luggage

Buchanan bus station (Map pp108-9; ☎ 333 3708; Killermont St; per 2 hr/day £2/3; ☯ 6.30am-10.30pm)
Central station (Map pp108-9; ☎ 0845 748 4950; Gordon St; sm/med/lge piece of luggage per 24 hr £3/4/5)

Medical Services

To see a doctor, visit the out-patients department at any general hospital.
Glasgow Dental Hospital (Map pp108-9; ☎ 211 9600; 378 Sauchiehall St)
Glasgow Royal Infirmary (Map pp108-9; ☎ 211 4000; 84 Castle St)
Southern General Hospital (Map pp108-9; ☎ 201 1100; Govan Rd)

Money

The post office and the TIC have a bureau de change.
American Express (Map pp108-9; Amex; 115 Hope St; ☯ 8.30am-5.30pm Mon, Tue, Thu & Fri, 9.30am-5.30pm Wed, 9am-noon Sat)
Clydesdale Bank (Map pp108-9; 7 St Enoch Sq; ☯ 9.15am-4pm Mon-Wed, Fri, 9.15am-5.30pm Thu, 10am-3pm Sat) Four 24-hour ATMs.

Post

There are post offices in some supermarkets in Glasgow; the larger ones are open on Sunday.
Branch post office (Map pp108-9; 228 Hope St; ☯ 8.30am-5.30pm Mon-Thu, 9am-5.30pm Fri , 9am-1pm Sat)

GLASGOW

GLASGOW

CENTRAL GLASGOW

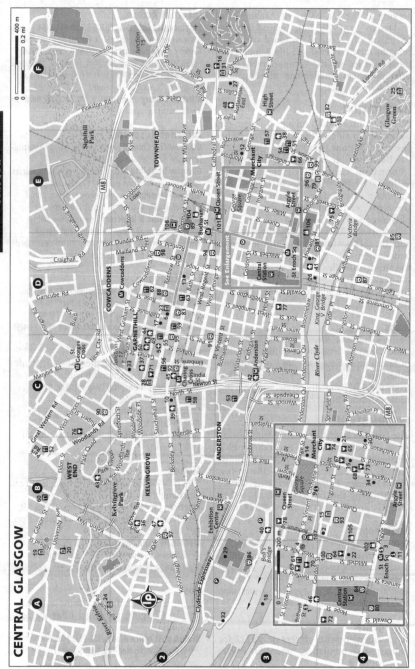

INFORMATION
American Express.....................................1 A3
Borders...2 B4
Clydesdale Bank.....................................3 A4
EasyInternet Cafe...................................4 A3
Glasgow Dental Hospital......................5 C2
Glasgow Flight Centre...........................6 D2
Glasgow LGBT Centre............................7 D3
Glasgow Royal Infirmary......................8 F2
Glasgow TIC...9 B3
Mitchell Library....................................10 C2
Spa 19..(see 7)
St Enoch Square Travel Centre...........11 A4
USIT..12 E3
Waterstone's Bookshop......................13 D2

SIGHTS & ACTIVITIES   (pp109–18)
City Chambers.......................................14 B3
Gallery of Modern Art.........................15 B4
Glasgow Cathedral...............................16 F3
Glasgow School of Art.........................17 D2
Glasgow Science Centre.......................18 A3
Hunterian Art Gallery..........................19 A1
Hunterian Museum...............................20 A1
Hutchesons' Hall...................................21 B4
Lighthouse...22 A4
McLellan Galleries................................23 D2
Museum of Transport...........................24 A1
People's Palace......................................25 F4
Pride o'the Clyde..................................26 D3
Provand's Lordship...............................27 F3
Royal Highland Fusiliers Museum......28 C2
Seaforce...(see 32)
SECC..29 A3
Sheriff Court House..............................30 B4
St Mungo's Museum of Religious Life &
    Art..31 F3
Tall Ship & Pumphouse........................32 A3
Tenement House...................................33 C2
Tobacco Exchange................................34 B4
Trades Hall..35 B4

SLEEPING   (pp118–20)
Alamo Guest House...............................36 B2

Atlantic Hotel.......................................37 C2
Babbity Bowster...................................38 E3
Blue Sky Backpackers...........................39 C2
City Inn..40 B3
Euro Hostel...41 D3
Glasgow Marriott..................................42 C3
Glasgow Youth Hostel..........................43 B1
Old School House..................................44 D2
Premier Lodge.......................................45 C2
Quality Hotel..46 A3
Smith's Hotel...47 B2
University of Strathclyde Campus Village
    Office..48 F3
Victorian House.....................................49 C2
Willow Hotel..50 C2

EATING   (pp120–22)
Artà...51 E3
Bay Tree Café..52 B1
Belfry...53 C3
Buttery...(see 53)
Café Gandolfi..54 E3
Centre for Contemporary Arts.............55 C2
Loon Fung...56 C2
Loop...57 E3
Mitchell's...58 C2
Paperino's..59 D2
Stravaigin..60 B1
Vancouver Muffin Co...........................61 A3
Wee Curry Shop....................................62 D2
Willow Tea Rooms.................................63 D2

DRINKING   (pp122–4)
Bar 10..64 A4
Bennet's...65 B4
Blackfriars..66 E3
Corinthian...67 B4
Delmonica's..68 B4
Drum & Monkey....................................69 A3
Horse Shoe..70 B4
Moda..(see 68)
Nice 'n' Sleazy.......................................71 C2
Pivo Pivo...72 A4
Polo Lounge..73 B4

Revolver...74 B4
Scotia...75 E4
Uisge Beatha..76 C1
Waterloo Bar..77 D3
Waxy O'Connors....................................78 B3

ENTERTAINMENT   (pp124–7)
13th Note Cafe......................................79 E3
Arches..80 A4
Barfly...81 D3
Barrowlands..82 F4
Brunswick Cellars.................................83 D2
Cathouse..84 A4
Citizens' Theatre...................................85 D4
Clyde Auditorium (Armadillo).............86 A3
Glasgow Academy.................................87 D4
Glasgow Film Theatre...........................88 D2
Glasgow Royal Concert Hall................89 E2
Halt Bar...90 C1
King Tut's Wah Wah Hut......................91 C2
King's Theatre.......................................92 C2
MAS..93 B4
Odeon Renfield St.................................94 D2
Shack...95 C2
Sharmanka Kinetic Gallery &
    Theatre...96 E3
Stereo..97 B2
Theatre Royal..98 D2
Tron Theatre..99 E3
Tunnel...100 A4

SHOPPING   (p127)
Adventure 1..101 E3
Argyll Arcade..102 A4
Barras..103 F4
Buchanan Galleries...............................104 E2
Catherine Shaw.............................(see 102)
Italian Centre.................................(see 74)
Princes Square......................................105 B4
St Enoch Shopping Centre...................106 E3
Tiso's...107 B3

TRANSPORT   (pp127–9)
Buchanan Bus Station..........................108 E2

Main post office (Map pp108-9; 47 St Vincent St, 8.30am-5.45pm Mon-Fri, 9am -5.30pm Sat) Passport photos available here for £3.50.

Tourist Information

Glasgow TIC (Map pp108-9; ☎ 204 4400; www.seeglasgow.com; 11 George Sq; 9am-6pm Mon-Sat Oct-May, to 7pm June & Sep, to 8pm July & Aug; 10am-6pm Sun Easter-Sept) Charges £2/3 for local/national accommodation bookings.

St Enoch Square Travel Centre (Map pp108-9; ☎ 226 4826; St Enoch Sq; 8.30am-5.30pm Mon-Sat) Travel information only.

TIC branch (☎ 848 4440; Glasgow International Airport; 7.30am-5pm daily Easter-Sep; 7.30am-5pm Mon-Sat, 8am-3.30pm Sun Jan-Easter & Oct-Dec)

Travel Agencies

Glasgow Flight Centre (Map pp108-9; ☎ 353 1351; 280 Sauchiehall St)

USIT (Map pp108-9; ☎ 553 1818; 122 George St)

DANGERS & ANNOYANCES

Keep clear of Orange marches, which are exhibitions of solidarity with the Protes-tant Northern Irish cause; violence can result when Catholics try to 'break the ranks'. These events aren't for tourists. See also Dangers and Annoyances (p407) and Women Travellers (p415) in the Directory chapter.

SIGHTS

Glasgow's major sights are fairly evenly dispersed around the city with the most important found along the **Clyde** – the focus of a major regeneration programme – the leafy cathedral precinct in the **East End** and the museum-rich **South Side**. The **City Centre** itself also contains a variety of attractions, particularly Mackintoshiana. The trendy **West End** swarms with students during term time, but it's quieter during the holidays.

The Clyde

The tide is definitely turning for the Clyde. In the last few years Glasgow has been re-turning to its roots with a major campaign to rejuvenate the riverfront and celebrate the city's unique industrial heritage. Included in this strategy is a long term redevelopment of Glasgow Harbour, converting former docklands into shops and public areas and rebuilding seven art nouveau Mackintosh-designed tearooms.

GLASGOW SCIENCE CENTRE

Scotland's flagship millennium project, the superb, ultra-modern **Glasgow Science Centre** (Map pp130-1; ☎ 420 5000; 50 Pacific Quay; Science Mall adult/child £6.95/4.95, IMAX £5.95/4.45; combined ticket £9.95/7.45; ☷ 10am-6pm, IMAX 11am-6pm Sun-Wed, 11am-8pm Thu-Sat) will keep the kids entertained for hours (that's middle-aged kids too!). It brings science and technology alive through hundreds of interactive exhibits on four floors. Look out for the illusions (like rearranging your features through a 3D head scan) and the cloud chamber, showing tracks of natural radiation. It consists of an egg-shaped titanium-covered **IMAX** theatre (call for current screenings) and an interactive **Science Mall** with floor to ceiling windows – a bounty of discovery for young, inquisitive minds. There's also a rotating **observation tower** 127m high. Two recent additions to the science centre are a planetarium, **Scottish Power Space Theatre**, bringing the night sky to life and a **Virtual Science Theatre**, treating visitors to a 3D molecular journey. Take Arriva bus No 24 from Renfield St or First Glasgow Bus No 89 or 90 from Union St.

TALL SHIP & PUMPHOUSE

Just across the Clyde from the Science Centre, via Bells Bridge, is the magnificent **Tall Ship** (*Glenlee*; Map pp130-1; ☎ 339 0631; 100 Stobcross Rd, Glasgow Harbour; adult/child £4.50/3.25, 1 child free; ☷ 10am-5pm Mar-Oct, 11am-4pm Nov-Feb), one of five sailing ships built on the Clyde still afloat. The *Glenlee* was launched in December 1896. The sheer size of this three-masted ship is impressive and there are displays about her history, restoration and life on board in the early 20th century.

Inside the nearby old **Pumphouse** (Map pp130-1), now a visitor centre, a captivating exhibit unfurls the interwoven stories of Glasgow and the Clyde, including the amazing dredging work carried out to enable the big ships to sail into Glasgow.

CLYDEBUILT

If immersing yourself in a city's heritage floats your boat, a visit to **Clydebuilt** (☎ 886 1013; Kings Inch Rd, Braehead; adult/child £3.50/1.75;

GETTING AROUND ON THE CLYDE

Pride o' the Clyde (Map pp108-9; ☎ 778 6635; Central Station Bridge; single/return £3/5; four to six sailings daily) is a waterbus linking Glasgow city centre with the Braehead shopping centre, home of the Clydebuilt museum. It's a terrific way to witness the progress of the Clyde's regeneration and to avoid city congestion.

Seaforce (Map pp130-1; ☎ 221 1070; at Tall Ship,100 Stobcross Rd, Glasgow Harbour; tickets £5-30) offer speedy powerboat jaunts along the Clyde. You can do a variety of trips including a half-hour ride around central Glasgow, an hour trip to the Erskine Bridge or four-hour rides to local wildlife hotspots.

The Waverley (☎ 0845 130 4647; www .waverleyexcursions.co.uk; Anderston Quay; tickets £6-30), the world's last ocean-going paddle steamer (built in 1947), cruises the Firth of Clyde from April to September; the website details days of departure. It serves several towns and the islands of Bute, Great Cumbrae and Arran.

☷ 10am-6pm Mon-Thu & Sat, 11am-5pm Sun) will get you paddlin'. It's a superb collection of model ships, industrial displays and narrative, vividly painting the history of the Clyde, the fate of which has been inextricably linked with Glasgow and its people. It's a cleverly designed museum with twists and turns that offer something new around every corner. Getting here via the *Pride o' the Clyde* waterbus (see above) is half the fun. Outside you can board *Kyles*, a typical 1872 vessel. Moored on the empty shores of the Clyde, with only the crying gulls above breaking the silence, it's a perfect place to contemplate the defunct shipyards that formed the cornerstone of Glasgow's industrial heritage.

City Centre   Map pp108–9

The grid layout of the city centre makes it easy to get around and there are many cafés and pubs that make a good pit stop between attractions.

CITY CHAMBERS

The grand **City Chambers** (☎ 287 4018; George Sq; admission free; guided tours 10.30am & 2.30pm Mon-Fri), the seat of local government, were built in the 1880s at the high point of the city's wealth. Their interior is even more extravagant than their exterior, and locals highly recommend a visit.

GALLERY OF MODERN ART

Scotland's most popular contemporary art gallery, the **Gallery of Modern Art** (☎ 229 1996; Queen St; admission free; ⏰ 10am-5pm Mon-Thu & Sat, 11am-5pm Fri & Sun), features modern works from artists worldwide, in a graceful neoclassical building. The original interior is used superbly to make a daring, inventive art display. Social issues are a focal point of the museum and if you're interested in seeing some thought-provoking artistic interpretations of the more marginalised people in today's society, then you should definitely swing by this museum.

MCLELLAN GALLERIES

Built in 1856, the **McLellan Galleries** (☎ 565 4100; 270 Sauchiehall St; admission free; ⏰ 10am-5pm Mon-Thu & Sat, 11am-5pm Fri & Sun) is displaying an exhibition entitled, 'Art Treasures of Kelvingrove'. It is a selection of some of the finest treasures from Kelvingrove Museum, which is currently being refurbished (closed until 2006). You can view more than 200 pieces from the picture galleries including Thomas Faed's *The Last of the Clan* and Rembrandt's *A Man in Armour*. There

are also displays covering Charles Rennie Mackintosh.

THE TENEMENT HOUSE

For an extraordinary time-capsule experience, visit the small apartment in the **Tenement House** (☎ 333 0183; 145 Buccleuch St; adult/child £3.50/2.60; ⏰ 1-5pm Mar-Oct). It gives a vivid insight into middle-class city life at the turn of the 20th century, with box-beds, the original kitchen range and all the fixtures and fittings of the family who lived here for more than 50 years.

It's an interesting place, but surely the Toward family wouldn't have kept it quite so squeaky clean and orderly as the National Trust of Scotland (NTS) manages now. Despite the additional exhibition area in the ground-floor flat, it can get crowded.

THE ROYAL HIGHLAND FUSILIERS MUSEUM

Visitors with an interest in Scotland's proud military history should duck into the commendable **Royal Highland Fusiliers Museum** (☎ 332 5639; 518 Sauchiehall St; admission free; ⏰ 9am-4pm Mon-Fri, weekends by appointment only). It charts the history of this and previous regiments from 1678 to the present. The walls are dripping with exhibits including uniforms, medals, pictures and other militaria. Wrought ironwork within the museum was designed by Mackintosh (see below).

THE GENIUS OF CHARLES RENNIE MACKINTOSH

Great cities have great artists, designers and architects contributing to the cultural and historical roots of their urban environment while expressing its soul and individuality. Charles Rennie Mackintosh was all of these. The quirky, linear and geometric designs of this famous Scottish architect and designer have had almost as much influence on the city as have Gaudi's on Barcelona. Many of the buildings Mackintosh designed in Glasgow are open to the public, and you'll see his tall, thin, Art Nouveau typeface repeatedly reproduced.

Born in 1868, Mackintosh studied at the Glasgow School of Art. In 1896, when he was aged only 27 he won a competition for his design of the School of Art's new building. The first section was opened in 1899 and is considered to be the earliest example of Art Nouveau in Britain, as well as Mackintosh's supreme architectural achievement. This building demonstrates his skill in combining function and style.

Although Mackintosh's genius was quickly recognised on the Continent, he did not receive the same encouragement in Scotland. His architectural career here lasted only until 1914 when he moved to England to concentrate on furniture design. He died in 1928, and it was only in the last decades of the 20th century that Mackintosh's genius has been widely recognised. If you want to know more about the man and his work, contact the **Charles Rennie Mackintosh Society** (☎ 946 6600; www.crmsociety.com; Queen's Cross Church, 870 Garscube Rd, Glasgow G20 7EL). From April to October the Society runs weekend tours of his buildings (once or twice a month); the cost is £270/452 for one/two people, including DB&B for two nights, lunches, coach, guide and admission.

GLASGOW

GLASGOW SCHOOL OF ART

Widely recognised as Mackintosh's greatest building, the **Glasgow School of Art** (☎ 353 4526; 167 Renfrew St; adult/child £5/4; ☽ guided tours only – times vary, usually 11am & 2pm Mon-Fri, 10.30am & 11.30am Sat, 1pm Sat & Sun June-Aug) still houses the educational institution. It's hard not to be impressed by the thoroughness of the design; the architect's pencil seems to have shaped everything inside and outside the building. The interior design is strikingly austere, with simple colour combinations (often just black and cream) and those uncomfortable-looking high-backed chairs for which Mackintosh is famous. The library, designed as an addition in 1907, is a masterpiece.

WILLOW TEA ROOMS

Admirers of the great Mackintosh are going to love the **Willow Tea Rooms** (☎ 332 0521; 217 Sauchiehall St; admission free; ☽ 9am-5pm Mon-Sat, 11-5pm Sun), an authentic reconstruction of the tearoom Mackintosh designed and furnished in 1904 for restaurateur Kate Cranston. Relive the original splendour of this unique tearoom and admire the architect's touch in just about everything. He had a free rein and even the teaspoons were given his distinctive touch. Reconstruction took two years and the Willow opened as a tearoom again in 1980 (having been closed since 1926). The street name Sauchiehall means 'lane of willows', hence the choice of a stylised willow motif.

THE LIGHTHOUSE

If you've been admiring Glasgow's architecture, make sure you check out the **Lighthouse** (☎ 221 6362; 11 Mitchell Lane; adult/child £3/80p; ☽ 10.30am-5pm Mon & Wed-Sat, 11am-5pm Tue, 12-5pm Sun), one of Glasgow's hidden treasures. Tucked away in a small lane, in the former Glasgow Herald building, it now serves as **Scotland's Centre for Architecture & Design**, giving an insight into modern architectural feats. It was designed by Charles Rennie Mackintosh in 1893 and also features the **Mackintosh Interpretation Centre**. You can learn more about this extraordinary man, see exhibitions of avant-garde furniture and drink in great rooftop views from the former water tower.

East End   Map pp108–9

The oldest part of the city, given a facelift in the 1990s, is concentrated around Glasgow Cathedral, to the east of the modern centre. The crumbling tombs of the city's rich and famous, crowd the necropolis, behind the cathedral.

It takes about 15 to 20 minutes to walk from George Sq, but numerous buses pass nearby, including Nos 11, 12, 36, 37, 38 and 42.

GLASGOW CATHEDRAL

An attraction that shouldn't be missed, **Glasgow Cathedral** (☎ 552 6891; Cathedral Sq; admission free; ☽ 9.30am-6pm Mon-Sat, 1-5pm Sun Apr-Sep; 9.30am-4pm Mon-Sat, 1-4pm Sun Oct-Mar) has a rare timelessness. The dark and imposing interior conjures up medieval might and can send a shiver down the spine. It's a shining example of pre-Reformation Gothic architecture, and the only mainland Scottish cathedral to have survived the Reformation. Most of the current building dates from the 15th century, and only the western towers were destroyed in the turmoil.

The entry is through a side door into the **nave**, which is hung with some regimental colours. The wooden roof above has been restored many times since its original construction, but some of the timber dates from the 14th century; note the impressive shields. Many of the cathedral's stunning, narrow windows of stained glass are modern and, to your left, you'll see Francis Spear's 1958 work *The Creation*, which fills the west window.

The cathedral is divided by a late 15th-century stone choir screen, decorated with seven pairs of figures to represent the Seven Deadly Sins. Beyond is the **choir**. The four stained-glass panels of the east window, depicting the apostles and also by Francis Spear, are particularly effective. At the northeastern corner is the entrance to the 15th-century **upper chapter house**, where Glasgow University was founded. It's now used as a sacristy.

The most interesting part of the cathedral, the **lower church**, is reached by a stairway. Its forest of pillars creates a powerful atmosphere around St Mungo's tomb (St Mungo founded a monastic community here in the 5th century), the focus of a famous medieval pilgrimage that was believed to be as meritorious as a visit to Rome.

Sunday services are at 11am and 6.30pm.

ST MUNGO'S MUSEUM OF RELIGIOUS LIFE & ART

A startling achievement, **St Mungo's Museum** (☎ 553 2557; 2 Castle St; admission free; ☯ 10am-5pm Mon-Thu & Sat, 11am-5pm Fri & Sun) is an audacious attempt to capture the world's major religions in an artistic nutshell. The result, of what must have been an overwhelming task, is commendable. The attraction is twofold: firstly, impressive art that blurs the lines between religion and culture; and secondly the opportunity to delve into different faiths, an experience that can be as deep or shallow as you wish.

There are three galleries, representing religion as art, religious life and, on the top floor, religion in Scotland. In the main gallery Dali's *Christ of St John of the Cross* hangs beside statues of the Buddha and Hindu deities. Outside, you'll find Britain's only Zen garden.

PROVAND'S LORDSHIP

Across the road from St Mungo's Museum is **Provand's Lordship** (☎ 552 8819; 3 Castle St; admission free; ☯ 10am-5pm Mon-Thu & Sat, 11am-5pm Fri & Sun), the oldest house in Glasgow. A rare example of 15th-century domestic Scottish architecture, it was built in 1471 as a manse for the chaplain of St Nicholas Hospital. The ceilings and doorways are low and the rooms are sparsely furnished with period artefacts, except for an upstairs room, which has been furnished to reflect the living space of an early 16th-century chaplain. The building's best feature is its authentic feel – if you ignore the tacky imitation-stone linoleum covering the ground floor.

West End

With its expectant buzz, trendy bars and cafés, and nonchalant swagger, the West End is probably the most engaging area of Glasgow – it's especially good for people-watching, and is as close as Glasgow gets to bohemian.

HUNTERIAN MUSEUM & ART GALLERY

Part of the university and housed in two separate buildings on either side of University Ave, the Hunterian contains the collection of William Hunter (1718–83), famous physician, medical teacher and one-time student of the university.

Don't forget to drag your eyes down to the exhibits in the **Hunterian Museum** (Map pp108-9; ☎ 330 4221; University Ave; admission free; ☯ 9.30am-5pm Mon-Sat), which can be difficult as the university building itself is quite breathtaking. The museum comprises a disparate collection of artefacts including a notable coin collection, fossils and minerals, dinosaur eggs, Romano-British stone slabs and carvings, and some of Captain Cook's curios from his voyages to the South Seas. The West African carvings incorporating the arrival of Europeans are fascinating.

Across the road, the Scottish Colourists – Samuel Peploe, JD Fergusson, Francis Cadell – are well represented in the **Hunterian Art Gallery** (Map pp108-9; ☎ 330 5431; 82 Hillhead St; admission free; ☯ 9.30am-5pm Mon-Sat). There are also McTaggart's impressionistic Scottish landscapes, and a gem by Thomas Millie Dow. There's a special collection of James McNeill Whistler's limpid prints, drawings and paintings. The **Mackintosh House** (☎ 330 5431; Hillhead St; admission free; ☯ 9.30am-12.30pm & 1.30-5pm Mon-Sat) is the final section in the gallery. Set up as a reconstruction of architect Charles Rennie Mackintosh's Glasgow home (which had to be demolished), the style of the Mackintosh House is quite startling even today. You ascend from the gallery's sombre ground floor into the cool, white, austere drawing room. There's something other-worldly about the very mannered style of the beaten silver panels, the long-backed chairs, and the surface decorations echoing Celtic manuscript illuminations. Bus Nos 11 and 44 pass this way from the city centre (Hope St).

KELVINGROVE ART GALLERY & MUSEUM

Note this magnificent museum is closed until 2006 for a major refurbishment – most of the pieces are going to the McLellan Galleries (p111) in Sauchiehall St.

MUSEUM OF TRANSPORT

Across Argyle St from the Hunterian Museum & Art Gallery is the surprisingly interesting and very comprehensive **Museum of Transport** (Map pp108-9; ☎ 287 2720; 1 Bunhouse Rd; admission free; ☯ 10am-5pm Mon-Thu & Sat, 11am-5pm Fri & Sun). Not convinced? This is actually a very fine museum with exhibits including an excellent reproduction of a 1938 Glasgow street scene, a display of cars made in

GLASGOW

Scotland, plus assorted railway locos, trams, bikes (including the world's first pedal-powered bicycle from 1847) and model ships. There's also a room dedicated to the Clyde shipyards. It's like peeping through a porthole at the not too distant past.

FOSSIL GROVE
With sections of 350-million-year-old fossilised trees lying as they were found, **Fossil Grove** (Map pp130-1; ☎ 287 2000; Victoria Park, Dumbarton Rd; admission free; ☼ noon-5pm Apr-Sep) is an intriguing sight. This site of special scientific interest feels quite spooky and makes visitors realise they are but a blimp on the earth's timeline. To get here, take bus No 44 from the city centre to Victoria Park Drive North or bus No 9 or 62 to Dumbarton Rd.

South Side
The south side is a tangled web of busy roads with a few oases giving relief from the urban congestion. It does, however, contain some of Glasgow's best museums.

BURRELL COLLECTION
One of Glasgow's top attractions is the **Burrell Collection** (Map pp130-1; ☎ 287 2550; Pollok Country Park; admission free, parking £1.50; ☼ 10am-5pm Mon-Thu & Sat, 11am-5pm Fri & Sun). Amassed by wealthy industrialist Sir William Burrell before being donated to the city, it is housed in an outstanding museum, 3 miles (5km) south of the city centre. This idiosyncratic collection of treasure includes everything from Chinese porcelain and medieval furniture to paintings by Renoir and Cézanne. It's not so big as to be overwhelming, and the stamp of the collector lends an intriguing coherence.

Most visitors will find their own favourite part of this museum, but the exquisite tapestry galleries are outstanding. Intricate stories capturing life in Europe are woven into staggering, wall-size pieces dating from the 13th-century. The massive *Triumph of the Virgin* exemplifies the complexity in nature and theme of this medium, while posing the serious question, 'How long must this have taken?'

Within the truly spectacular interior, carved-stone Romanesque doorways are incorporated into the structure so you actually walk through them. It feels as though

THE GLASGOW BOYS

The great rivalry between Glasgow and Edinburgh goes back a long way. In the late 19th century a group of Glaswegian painters challenged the domineering artistic establishment in Edinburgh. Up to this point paintings were largely confined to historical scenes and sentimental visions of the Highlands. These painters – including Sir James Guthrie, EA Hornel, George Henry and Joseph Crawhall – experimented with colour and themes of rural life, shocking Edinburgh's artistic society. Like Charles Rennie Mackintosh, the Glasgow Boys achieved success on the Continent, where their work met with admiration and artistic recognition.

The Glasgow Boys had an enormous influence on the Scottish art world, inspiring the next generation of Scottish painters – the Colourists. The works of the Glasgow Boys can be seen in various Scottish collections, including the Burrell Collection (see left) above and Broughton House, Kirkcudbright (p167).

you are wandering around a huge tranquil greenhouse. Floor-to-ceiling windows admit a flood of natural light and enable the trees and surrounding landscape outside to enhance the effect created by the exhibits.

There are occasional guided tours. Numerous buses pass the park gates (including Nos 45, 47, 48 and 57 from the centre), and there's a twice-hourly bus service between the gallery and the gates (a pleasant 10-minute walk). Alternatively catch a train to Pollokshaws West from Central station (four per hour; you want the second station on the line for East Kilbride or Kilmarnock).

SCOTTISH FOOTBALL MUSEUM
Football fans will just love the **Scottish Football Museum** (Map pp130-1; ☎ 616 6106; Hampden Park; adult/child £5/2.50; ☼ 10am-5pm Mon-Sat, 11am-5pm Sun), which features exhibits on the history of the game in Scotland and the influence of Scots on the world game. Football inspires an incredible passion in Scotland and the museum is crammed full of impressive memorabilia, including a cap and match ticket from the very first international football

game (which took place in 1872 between Scotland and England, and ended with a score of 0 – 0). The museum's engrossing exhibits give insight into the players, the fans, the media and the way the game has changed over the last 130 years. The museum's location is at Hampden Park, off Aikenhead Rd. To get there, you can take a train to Mount Florida station or take bus No 5, 31, 37 or 75 from Stockwell St.

THE BARRAS
Glasgow's flea market, the **Barras on Gallowgate** (Map pp108-9; ☎ 552 4601; London Rd; ☼ 10am-5pm Sat & Sun), has almost a thousand stalls and people come here just for a wander as much as for shopping, which gives the place a holiday air. The Barras is notorious for designer frauds, so be cautious. Watch your wallet too.

THE PEOPLE'S PALACE
On Glasgow Green is the city's oldest park, the **People's Palace** (Map pp108-9; ☎ 554 0223; Glasgow Green; admission free; ☼ 10am-5pm Mon-Thu & Sat, 11am-5pm Fri & Sun). It is an impressive museum of social history, telling the story of the city from 1750 to the present. It has creative, inventive displays, which are great for families – the kids will love the re-creation of a WWII air raid. The Palace was built in the late 19th century as a cultural centre for Glasgow's East End. Drop into the Winter Gardens next door for a coffee.

SCOTLAND STREET SCHOOL MUSEUM
An impressive Mackintosh building, the **Scotland Street School Museum** (Map pp130-1; ☎ 287 0500; 225 Scotland St; admission free; ☼ 10am-5pm Mon-Thu & Sat, 11am-5pm Fri & Sun) is dominated by two glass towers. It's a fascinating museum of education with reconstructions of classrooms from Victorian times, and the 1940s, through to the 1960s. The place evokes childhood memories for just about everyone – don't be surprised if you hear a few titters from elderly visitors as they pass the headmaster's office.

HOUSE FOR AN ART LOVER
Although designed in 1901 as an entry to a competition run by a German magazine, the **House for an Art Lover** (Map pp130-1; ☎ 353 4770; Bellahouston Park, 10 Dumbreck Rd; adult/child £3.50/ 2.50; ☼ 10am-4pm Sun-Thu, 10am-3pm Sat) was not

completed until 1996. Mackintosh worked closely with his wife on the design and her influence is evident, especially in the rose motif. The overall result of this brilliant architect's design is one of space and light. Bus Nos 3, 9, 54, 55 and 56 all run here from the city centre.

HOLMWOOD HOUSE
An interesting building designed by Alexander 'Greek' Thomson, **Holmwood House** (☎ 637 2129; 61-63 Netherlee Rd, Cathcart; adult/child £3.50/2.50; ☼ noon-5pm Apr-Oct) dates from 1857. Despite ongoing renovations, it's well worth a visit. Look out for sun symbols downstairs and stars upstairs in this attractive house with its adaptation of classical Greek architecture. To get to Cathcart train station, take a 'Cathcart Circle' train via Queen's Park or a train to Neilston. Otherwise, take bus No 44, 44A, 44D or 66 from the city centre. Then you should follow Rhannan Rd for about half a mile (1km) to Holmwood House.

North Side
QUEEN'S CROSS CHURCH
Now the headquarters of the Charles Rennie Mackintosh Society, **Queen's Cross Church** (Map pp130-1; ☎ 946 6600; 870 Garscube Rd; adult/child £2/free; ☼ 10am-5pm Mon-Fri, plus 2-5pm Sun Mar-Oct) is the only one of Mackintosh's church designs to be built. It has excellent stained glass and relief carvings, and the wonderful simplicity and grace of the barrel-shaped design is particularly inspiring.

HILL HOUSE
See Helensburgh, p255, for information on Hill House.

ACTIVITIES
There are numerous green spaces within the city. **Pollok Country Park** surrounds the Burrell Collection and has numerous woodland trails. Nearer the centre of the city, the **Kelvin Walkway** follows the River Kelvin through Kelvingrove Park, the Botanic Gardens and on to Dawsholm Park.

The TIC has a range of maps and leaflets detailing these jaunts, and the long distance routes described below, most of which start from Bell's Bridge (by the Scottish Entertainment and Conference Centre - SECC). They also stock the *Fit for Life* map.

GLASGOW

Walking & Cycling

It's possible to walk 9 miles (14.5km) of the Clyde through Glasgow. An outstanding section lies between the Victoria Bridge and the SECC, taking in 150 years of bridge engineering and a chunk of Glasgow's shipbuilding heritage. The **Clyde Walkway** is in the process of being continued through to the Falls of Clyde in Lanark (p150) and should be about 40 miles (64km) long when completed.

The well-trodden, long-distance footpath known as the **West Highland Way** begins in Milngavie, 8 miles (13km) north of Glasgow, and runs for 95 spectacular miles (153km) to Fort William.

There are several long-distance pedestrian/cycle routes that originate in Glasgow and follow off-road routes for most of the way.

The **Glasgow–Loch Lomond** route traverses residential and industrial areas, following a disused railway to Clydebank, the Forth and Clyde canal towpath to Bowling, then a disused railway to Dumbarton, reaching Loch Lomond via the towpath by the River Leven. This route continues all the way to Inverness, from Balloch via Aberfoyle, Loch Vennachar, Callander and Strathyre to link with the Glen Ogle Trail, Killin, Pitlochry and Aviemore.

The **Glasgow–Greenock/Gourock** route runs via Paisley, the first section partly on roads. From Johnstone to Greenock the route follows a disused railway line, and the final section to Gourock has also been built.

Sculpture from the Sustrans public arts project brightens parts of the way.

The **Glasgow–Irvine**, **Ardrossan** and **West Kilbride Cycle Way** runs via Paisley, then off-road as far as Glengarnock. From here to Kilwinning it follows minor roads, then the route is partly off-road. Ferries to the Isle of Arran, popular with cyclists, leave from Ardrossan. An extension via Ayr, Maybole and Glentrool leads to the Solway coast and Carlisle.

The **Glasgow–Edinburgh Cycle Way** partly follows the Clyde Walkway and a disused railway line. It skirts south Lanarkshire and continues through Uddingston, Airdrie, Bathgate and onto Edinburgh.

To hire a bike drop into **West End Cycles** (Map pp130-1; ☎ 357 1344, 0800 072 8015; 16 Chancellor St) at the southern end of Byres Rd. They hire out 24-speed mountain bikes for £15/70 per day/week. You'll need two forms of ID, or a credit card and a £50 deposit.

WALKING TOUR

This absorbing stroll will take you from George Sq to Glasgow Cathedral through the trendy **Merchant City**, a planned 18th-century civic development and home to many fine pubs and restaurants.

The TIC on **George Square** (1) is a good starting point for exploring the city. The square is surrounded by imposing Victorian architecture, including the old post office, the Bank of Scotland and the grandiose **City Chambers** (2). There are statues of Robert

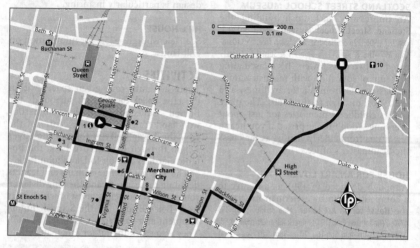

Burns, James Watt, Lord Clyde and, atop a 24m-high Doric column, Sir Walter Scott.

Once you've ogled the City Chambers, cross George Sq and walk one block south down Queen St to the **Gallery of Modern Art** (**3**). This striking four-floor colonnaded building, built in 1827, was once the Royal Exchange. Pop in for a look at some of the best contemporary art displays in the country.

WALKING TOUR

■ Distance: just over 2km

■ Duration: approximately 1½ hours

The gallery faces Ingram St, which you should cross and then follow east for four blocks to **Hutchesons' Hall** (**4**). Built in 1805 to a design by David Hamilton, this elegant building is now maintained by the National Trust for Scotland (NTS). On your way, duck into the former Court House cells now housing the ornate, dazzling **Corinthian** (**5**) pub/club for a glimpse of the extravagant interior (and perhaps a cheeky half!). Retrace your steps one block and continue south down Glassford St past **Trades Hall** (**6**), designed by Robert Adam in 1791 to house the trades guild. This is the only surviving building in Glasgow by this famous Scottish architect; the exterior is best viewed from Garth St. Turn right into Wilson St and first left along Virginia St, which is lined with the old warehouses of the Tobacco Lords; many of these have now been converted into flats for the upwardly mobile. The **Tobacco Exchange** (**7**) became the Sugar Exchange in 1820 but it's now in poor condition.

Back on Wilson St, the bulky **Sheriff Court House** (**8**) fills a whole block. This arresting building was originally Glasgow's town hall, but is currently being developed as a new home for the Scottish Youth Orchestra. Continue east on Wilson St into Bell St and take a break at the excellent **Blackfriars pub** (**9**) where you can do some fine people-watching while sipping a cask ale. Turn left into Albion St, then first right into Black-friars St. Emerging onto High St, turn left and follow High St up to the **Cathedral** (**10**) – you can't miss it!

GLASGOW FOR CHILDREN

Although Glasgow is a bigger, busier city that Edinburgh, it is an easy city to travel around with children due to its extensive public transport system and friendly locals. The city boasts excellent family attractions including the **Glasgow Science Centre** (p110)and **Sharmanka Kinetic Gallery & Theatre** (see below), which both vie for Glasgow's top child-friendly attraction. The **People's Palace** (p115) and **Museum of Transport** (p113) are also recommended. A boat trip along the Clyde can be a lot of fun for kids. For more ideas pick up a copy of the *Glasgow Guide for Under 6's* (£5.99) from the TIC.

For suggestions of short-term child-care agencies, get in touch with the council-run **Childcare Information Service** (☎ 287 8307; www.childcarelink.gov.uk/glasgowcity).

Parks in Glasgow often have playground facilities for children, call ☎ 287 5064 for information. We recommend two indoor playgrounds (far more practical). The crèche at **Buchanan Galleries** (☎ 333 9898; www.buchanangalleries.co.uk) shopping centre is available for two- to eight-year olds and staffed by qualified nursery assistants. The **Jelly Club** (Map pp8-9; ☎ 248 6800; www.jellyclub.co.uk; St Enoch shopping centre; child £2.50; ☒ 10am-6pm Mon-Wed & Fri-Sat 10am-8pm Thu, 10.30am-5.30pm Sun) encourages physical activity by providing imaginative exercises to stimulate the mind and body (children under 13).

QUIRKY GLASGOW

For those up to their eyeballs in museums and galleries, check out a show at the extraordinary **Sharmanka Kinetic Gallery & Theatre** (Map pp108-9; ☎ 552 7080; 14 King St; adult/child £3/free; ☒ 9.30am-5.30pm, shows 7pm Thu, 3 & 6pm Sun). Originally from St Petersburg this unique mechanical theatre brings inanimate objects to life; sculptured pieces of old scrap and tiny carved figures perform humorous and tragic stories of the human spirit to haunting music. It's joyful, ironic theatre, inspirational one moment and macabre the next, but always colourful, clever and thought-provoking. It's art for reflection – and lots of fun!

TOURS

Walkabout Glasgow Tours (☎ 243 2437) provide an entertaining half-hour audio commentary for a 1½- to 3½-hour walking route through the city. Headphones cost £5 per day from the TIC.

From April to November **City Sightseeing** (☎ 204 0444) runs tourist buses every 15 minutes (9.30am to 4.15pm) along the main sightseeing routes, starting at George Sq. You get on and off as you wish. A day ticket for adults/children costs £8/3; if you buy a day ticket you get the next day's travel for free (buy from the driver or the TIC). All buses have wheelchair access. **Guide Friday** (☎ 248 7644) is similar with a slightly longer route.

FESTIVALS & EVENTS

Not to be outdone by Edinburgh, Glasgow has initiated several festivals of its own, starting each January with the two-week **Celtic Connections** music festival (☎ 353 8000; www.grch.com).

If you're in the city with a loved one in February, don't miss the **City of Love** (☎ 331 2668), a festival celebrating St Valentine, whose partial remains lie in a city church.

The **West End Festival** of music and the arts (☎ 341 0844; www.westendfestival.co.uk) runs for two weeks in June and is Glasgow's biggest festival. The excellent **Glasgow Jazz Festival** (☎ 552 3552; www.jazzfest.co.uk) is held in July.

Other festivals include the classical **RSNO Proms** (☎ 353 8000; www.grch.com) in June and the **World Pipe Band Championships** (☎ 221 5414) with around 200 pipe bands in mid-August.

SLEEPING

Finding somewhere decent in July and August can be difficult. Finding accommodation in Glasgow on weekends can be dicey at any time of year – it's wise to book ahead.

Budget

Craigendmuir Park (☎ 779 4159; www.craigendmuir .co.uk; Campsie View, Stepps; tent sites from £7.50) The nearest camping ground to town, this is about half a mile from Stepps station. It has sites for caravans and tents, and also has a few chalets.

CITY CENTRE   **Map pp108–9**
Euro Hostel (☎ 222 2828; www.euro-hostels.com; 318 Clyde St; B&B per person £13.75-29; 🖳) This bustling 380-bed hostel right in the heart of the city has 24-hour reception, ensuite rooms and there's a microwave facility (but

no kitchen). Confirm your booking as the admin can be a little sloppy. Internet access costs around £1.50 to £3 per hour. The more people to a room the cheaper it gets.

Glasgow Youth Hostel (☎ 0870 004 1119; 7-8 Park Tce; dm adult/child £13/11) In a clean, bright townhouse on a hill overlooking the city, this hostel was closed due to fire damage in 2003 – it should re-open in 2004, but call before showing up.

Blue Sky Backpackers (☎ 221 1710; 65 Berkeley St; dm £8-10, d £25; 🖳) This place has tidy dorms and offers a free breakfast. It's a little scruffy and improvised, but has loads of personality and is friendly, comfortable and close to the city centre.

University of Strathclyde (☎ 548 3560; Cathedral St; 🕑 mid-Jun–Sep) The uni opens its halls of residence to tourists over summer. Its **Campus Village** (☎ 548 4381; 6-bed flats per person weekly £54, B&B s/d £25/35.50, bed only £15.50; 🕑 24hr), opposite Glasgow Cathedral, offers accommodation in shared, single-sex, self-catering flats on a weekly basis or good-value bed and breakfast.

EAST END

Alison Guest House (Map pp130-1; ☎ /fax 556 1431; 26 Circus Dr; s/d with shared bathroom from £15/30) This is an informal guesthouse where you're made to feel right at home by the chatty hosts – some people just enjoy their work. There's a great room for singles in the attic, as long as you don't mind a climb up a ladder; once there, you'll have plenty of room to yourself. The communal dining table encourages breakfast conversation.

WEST END

Bunkum Backpackers (Map pp130-1; ☎ /fax 581 4481; www.bunkumglasgow.co.uk; 26 Hillhead St; dm/tw £11/30) This is a hostel with a great vibe in a terrific house with kitchen facilities, a common lounge area, spotless bathrooms and no curfew. The massive dorms have loads of space and the twins are also good. It's very close to Glasgow University and the hotspots on Byres Rd, but book ahead.

Mid-Range
CITY CENTRE   **Map pp108–9**
There are several similarly priced places along and around Renfrew St. All are relatively expensive due to their central location.

The **Old School House** (☎ 332 7600; oschoolh@hotmail.com; 194 Renfrew St; s/d £35/52; ✗) The contemporary rooms in this beautiful, heritage-listed building have been pleasingly restored and are fresh, clean and well-furnished. The family room is a good size and all rooms have an ensuite except one. It's very friendly and the sun-soaked dining area (for breakfast) will lure you out of bed.

Atlantic Hotel (☎ 332 0000; fax 333 0100; 232 Renfrew St; s/d £27/42) The Atlantic is fairly basic but the most likely place along the Renfrew St strip that will bargain if things are quiet. It's especially good for solo travellers as there is no outrageous surcharge.

Babbity Bowster (☎ 552 5055; 16-18 Blackfriars St; s/d £35/50) Smack-bang in the heart of the trendy Merchant City, this lively bar also has six bedrooms with bathroom. It is the only bar (p123) with a beer garden in the city centre. The building's design is attributed to Robert Adam. It's a great place to stay, but forget turning in early with a cup of cocoa.

Other recommendations:

Willow Hotel (☎ 332 2332; fax 353 0961; 228 Renfrew St; s/d from £30/48) Worn, but well kept and clean rooms with bathroom.

Victorian House (☎ 332 0129; www.thevictorian.co.uk; 212 Renfrew St; s without/with bathroom £30/44, d £38/54; ✗) Large and tidy, dripping with pine and decadent red carpet.

EAST END   Map pp130–1
The rooms in the following guesthouses have shared bathrooms.

Craigpark Guest House (☎ 554 4160; www.craig parkguesthouse.com; 33 Circus Dr; s £25, d £36-52; ✗) The meticulously kept interior reflects the owner's quiet efficiency. This is a sedate place suitable for families, couples or solo travellers. Country furnishings complement the bright, light rooms (particularly No 3).

Seton Guest House (☎ 556 7654; passway@seton .prestel.co.uk; 6 Seton Tce; s/d £20/36) A big, jovial owner, rooms cleaned like clockwork and a location across from a small park makes Seton deservedly popular – book ahead or you'll miss out.

WEST END
Belhaven Hotel (Map pp130–1; ☎ 339 3222; www .belhavenhotel.com; 15 Belhaven Tce; s £35-45, d £40-60; ✗) Amicable Belhaven is a favourite with

LP readers. It has spacious art nouveau-meets-renaissance rooms and one has been modified for disabled access. The small bar serves the delicious Kingfisher lager on tap. It's just off Great Western Rd.

Alamo Guest House (Map pp108–9; ☎ 339 2395; www.alamoguesthouse.com; 46 Gray St; s/d from £23/42; ✗) The Alamo may sound forbidding, but that couldn't be further from the truth. It's a great place to stay in a leafy spot overlooking Kelvingrove Park, and oozes warmth and sumptuous living.

Chez Nous Guest House (Map pp130–1; ☎ 334 2977; enquiries@cheznousguesthouse.co.uk; 33 Hillhead St; s £20-25, d £40-50; **P**) There's nothing flash about this 31-room place, but it's decent value and is brilliantly located in the West End on the fringe of the nightlife action on Byres Rd. If the city centre is busy and accommodation difficult to find, this place may be your best bet.

Smith's Hotel (Map pp108–9; ☎ 339 7674; info@smiths-hotel.com; 963 Sauchiehall St; s/d from £21/40, with bathroom £36/52) Established in 1928, this pleasant family-run hotel is an amiable rabbit warren with a large variety of rooms. There is a slight whiff of disinfectant in the narrow corridors, and what you see is what you get, but rooms are well-presented. This is a good inner-city option; it won't blow your socks off – but most folk leave satisfied.

SOUTH SIDE   Map pp130–1
Reidholme Guest House (☎ 423 1855; 36 Regent Park Sq; r with shared bathroom per person £20) Homely accommodation here is followed up by a cracking breakfast in the morning. Reidholme is informal, and familiar with an old-worldly air about it. It's also in a tranquil, tree-lined street.

Holly House (☎ 427 5609; www.hollyhouse.net43 .co.uk; 54 Ibrox Tce; r per person £24) If you're seeing a football game at Ibrox this friendly place is very handy. The great rooms are large enough to have a table and couch, and the family room is like a small flat.

Top End
THE CLYDE
City Inn (Map pp108–9; ☎ 240 1002; glasgow@ cityinn.com; Finnieston Quay; r weekend/weekday £65/89; ✗ **P**) Reflecting the rejuvenation occurring along the River Clyde, the City Inn is a brand-spanking new hotel with

clinically clean rooms that come with views, CD player and cable TV. Service is top notch and there's also a decent restaurant with an excellent outdoor terrace overlooking the river. Call in advance for the best rate.

CITY CENTRE   Map pp108–9

Quality Hotel (☎ 221 9680; admin@gb627.u-net.com; 99 Gordon St; s/d from £95/105; ✗ P) The Quality Hotel is down-to-earth, couldn't be more central and will do deals, particularly for groups and bookings of more than one night. Recommended by readers, it's a huge old-style place in a perennial state of renovation. Rooms are large and some overlook the inside of the train station – a must for all our trainspotting aficionados!

Premier Lodge (☎ 0870 700 1394; www.premier lodge.com; 10 Elmbank Gardens; r £50; ✗) This hotel is located in the tower above Charing Cross train station, and is interested primarily in business clientele. However, its price, location and creature comforts make it excellent for couples and families; there are cots available for no extra charge. Rooms have satellite TV, modem points and desks.

Glasgow Marriott (☎ 226 5577; www.marriott hotels.com; 500 Argyle St; r from £109; ✗ P ▯) If you like having doors opened for you at every turn, the plush Marriott is for you. It attracts conferences, business people on expense accounts and Europeans living in the way to which they've become accustomed. Service comes with a smile, which gets wider on receiving an appropriate tip.

WEST END   Map pp130–1

One Devonshire Gardens (☎ 339 2001; www.one devonshiregardens.com; 1 Devonshire Gardens; s/d £100/ 225; ✗ P) A five-star hotel and reputedly the best hotel in Glasgow, this place is sumptuously decorated and comes with the atmosphere of a luxurious country house. It occupies four classical terrace houses and the individually designed rooms are very well appointed. There is also an excellent restaurant.

Kirklee Hotel (☎ 334 5555; fax 339 3828; 11 Kensington Gate; s/d £52/68; ✗) Kirklee Hotel combines the luxury of a classy hotel with the warmth of staying in someone's home. You'll probably be treated as well as the

---

THE GLESCA PATOIS

Glasgow enjoys a rich local dialect (read: bloody hard to understand) and a knowledge of the vernacular will help you know when to stand and chat and when to run.

Unusually, for Scotland, the pub is the focal point of social life and there may be some football supporters in the crowd. The 'Bhoys' (Celtic football club) wear green colours and are traditionally supported by the 'Tims' (Catholics). The 'Gers' (Rangers football club) wear blue and are the 'Huns' (Protestant) team. Football is a touchy subject in Glasgow. Tell anyone who asks that you're a 'Jags' (Partick Thistle) supporter and you're on neutral ground. Billy Connolly, the comedian, who grew up in Partick, claims that he always thought the full team name was 'Partick Thistle Nil'.

When males spot a *wee stoater* (good-looking young woman) in the bar, they might be inclined to try their 'patter' (witty chat) on her. Should her boyfriend, 'the Big Yin', arrive unexpectedly, and offer to *mollocate*, *wanner* or *stiffen* the would-be Lothario, or alternatively to give him his *heid in your hauns* (head in your hands), then violence is probably imminent.

At that point it's best to *shoot the crow* (go) before a *stooshie* (brawl) develops and, in future, to give that particular pub the *body swerve* (a wide berth).

However Glaswegians are very friendly to travellers. If you refer to their city as *Glesca*, and never *Glasgie*, they may even mistake you for a local.

John McKenna

---

plants in the window boxes – which are very well treated indeed. For families there is an excellent downstairs room with enormous ensuite.

EATING

Glasgow is the best place to eat in Scotland with an excellent range of eateries. The West End is the culinary centre of the city. Many Glasgow restaurants post offers on the Internet (changing daily) at www.5pm.co.uk. Note also that pubs (p122) are always a good lunchtime option.

City Centre
Map pp108–9

BUDGET

Vancouver Muffin Co (☎ 221 9253; 73 St Vincent St; meals £3.80; ⏰ 8am-6pm Mon-Fri, 9am-6pm Sat, 10am-5pm Sun) This proudly Canadian establishment makes a great pit stop when you're strolling around town. There's also a good range of sandwiches, baguettes and paninis; look out for the great value meal deals. Grab an espresso, sit near the window and watch Glasgow tick over.

Centre for Contemporary Arts (☎ 332 7521; 350 Sauchiehall St; light meals £2-9) The lovely, open café at the Centre for Contemporary Arts is a trendy dining experience and a popular meeting spot. The skylight-roof makes you feel as though you're dining outdoors. This is also the place to head for delectable fish dishes.

Willow Tea Rooms (☎ 332 0521; 217 Sauchiehall St; light meals £4-6; ⏰ 9am-5pm Mon-Sat, 11am-4.30pm Sun) Designed by Charles Rennie Mackintosh in 1903, these tearooms are located above a jewellery shop. At lunch- and tea-time the queues can extend into the shop downstairs. Avoid them by arriving when it opens and splash out on a cracking breakfast of smoked salmon, scrambled eggs and toast. There's also another **branch** (☎ 204 5242; 97 Buchanan St).

Wee Curry Shop (☎ 353 0777; 7 Buccleuch St; lunch £4.75, dinner mains £5.50-7; closed Sun) Some of the best home-cooked curries you're likely to taste outside India can be found here. You'd be wise to book – it's a snug place with a big reputation, a limited menu and a sensational value three-course lunch.

MID-RANGE

Paperino's (☎ 332 3800; 283 Sauchiehall St; pizza & pasta £6.50-8) This is a great little Italian diner with efficient service, booth seating ideal for couples and simple delicious Italian creations. It's a cheerful spot with a perpetual buzz. Enough Italian is spoken to make you believe the recipes may just be from Mama.

Loon Fung (☎ 332 1240; 417 Sauchiehall St; mains £8.50-11.50, 3-course lunch £7.95) One of the best Chinese restaurants in town, it does seafood dishes particularly well. Elaborately furnished, dining is an upmarket experience.

Café Gandolfi (☎ 552 6813; 64 Albion St; mains £5.50-12) In the fashionable Merchant City, near the City Halls, this café was once part of the old cheese market. It's been pulling in the punters for more than 20 years, and packs an interesting clientele: die-hard Gandolfers, upwardly mobile city-dwellers and tourists. It's an excellent, friendly bistro and upmarket coffee shop – very much the place to be seen. Book a medieval-inspired, designer table in advance.

Artà (☎ 552 2101; 13 Walls St; tapas £3-6, mains £7.50-16; ⏰ closed Mon & Tue) If only every city had an Artà. Very much a favourite, this extraordinary hacienda-style place has to be seen to be believed. Eat on the mock-baroque, Spanish-style ground floor among the drinking crowd, or the elegant upstairs restaurant. Vegetarian options are available. See p000 for details of what else Artà has to offer. All dishes are half price, 5pm to 9pm Sunday, Wednesday and Thursday.

Loop (☎ 572 1472; 64 Ingram St; starters £4.24-5.50, mains £8.50-14.50) Loop is a bright and modern bistro-style place with an excellent Scottish and international menu. Its minimalist furnishings create a sense of space. The food is delicious and, from 11am to 7pm, Loop offers substantial mains and a drink for £7.95 – great value!

West End

Just off Byres Rd, on the east side, Ashton Lane is packed with places to eat, including some of Glasgow's best restaurants.

BUDGET

Grosvenor Café (Map pp130-1; ☎ 339 1848; 35 Ashton Lane) The small, intimate Grosvenor Café serves simple fare during the day, when you can get burgers and sandwiches, but in the evening, particularly weekends, they get tarted up, candles are lit and classier scran is served. It's cosy and popular with families. All mains are £5 Thursday evening and dinner on Friday and Saturday is £9.95 for two courses and £12.50 for three.

Wee Curry Shop (Map pp130-1; ☎ 357 5280; upstairs at Jinty McGintys, 23-29 Ashton Lane; 2-course lunch £5.90, dinner mains £6.25-8.50) A bit classier and more expensive than its city-centre cousin, Wee Curry is very big on quality home-cooked Indian food.

MID-RANGE

On the west side of Byres Rd, directly across from Ashton Lane, is Ruthven Lane. Here and nearby are a number of fine places to eat. Those staying in the vicinity of

GLASGOW

Kelvingrove Park will find a scattering of good restaurants on or around Gibson St and Great Western Rd. There are also several other places scattered around the West End, just west of the M8.

Stravaigin II (Map pp130-1; ☎ 334 7165; 8 Ruthven Lane; starters £5, mains £9.50-13) Clinking wine glasses and cracking mussel shells greet patrons at this classy eatery. The restaurant challenges patrons to 'get off the eaten track' and it boasts the best scotch beef burgers (they also do ostrich burgers) on a chargrilled menu that also features cumin scented swordfish souvalaki. Two-course, pre-theatre meals are great value at £10.95.

Di Maggio's (Map pp130-1; ☎ 334 8560; 61 Ruthven Lane; pizza & pasta £5-11) Di Maggio's is a cramped, vibrant Italian restaurant with tempting aromas wafting down Ruthven Lane. There's quick service, reliable food and good meal deals Monday to Wednesday.

Bay Tree Café (Map pp130-1; ☎ 334 5898; 403 Great Western Rd; mains £7.50-8.50; 🕑 9am-9pm) The mostly vegetarian Bay Tree Café is excellent value. It has smiling staff, filling mains (mostly Middle Eastern and Greek), generous salads and there's a good range of hot drinks. The *baba ganoush* is compulsory for aubergine fans. The café is famous for its all-day Sunday brunch, including vegetarian burger, tattie scone, mushrooms, beans and tomato. It also serves a vegan breakfast.

Belfry (Map pp108-9; ☎ 221 8188; 652 Argyle St; starters £5, mains £14-18; 🕑 6-9pm Fri & Sat) Downstairs from the Buttery (see right) is this cheaper, more relaxed bistro, featuring wild produce. It's run by the same people as the Buttery so the food is superb. Try the Angus beef with a truffled wild mushroom fricasse and wild garlic mustard potato swirl.

Mitchell's (Map pp108-9; ☎ 204 4312; 157 North St; mains £11-18, 3-course pre-theatre meals £11.95; 🕑 noon-2.30pm, 5-10pm Tue-Thu, noon-2.30pm, 5-10.30pm Fri, 5-10.30pm Sat) Near the Mitchell Library this place is an excellent, laid-back bistro with a Scottish and international menu. Occasionally there's piano playing, but the warmth and cheery ambience are a constant. The roar of the M8 outside seems miles away.

TOP END

Ubiquitous Chip (Map pp130-1; ☎ 334 5007; 12 Ashton Lane; 2/3 course dinner £32.50/37.50) This restaurant has won a plethora of awards for its excellent Scottish cuisine, fresh seafood and game dishes (which are accompanied by wild vegetables), and for its lengthy wine list. Set among potted plants of arboreal proportions this is an excellent place for a night out. There's a cheaper restaurant here, **Upstairs at the Chip** (starters £3.45-5.75, mains £7.65-11.45), where the menu follows in the tradition of creativity and top-notch ingredients.

The Buttery (Map pp108-9; ☎ 221 8188; 652 Argyle St; 2/3-course dinner £32/36; 🕑 closed Sun & Mon) This elegant place is just west of the M8. Although it's surrounded by grim, grey, tower-block flats, it's a top, Victorian-era restaurant offering fine dining with a classy clientele to match. The menu is a combination of seasonal Scottish and British organic produce.

Stravaigin (Map pp108-9; ☎ 334 2665; 28 Gibson St; 2-course dinner £21.95) Stravaigin is a serious foodie's delight with a menu constantly pushing the boundaries of originality and offering serious creative culinary excellence. There's a buzzing bar upstairs and a cool contemporary dining space in the basement with booth seating, and helpful, laid-back waiting-staff to assist in deciphering the audacious menu.

DRINKING

Some of Scotland's best nightlife is found in the din and sometimes roar of Glasgow's pubs and bars. There are as many different styles of bar as there are punters to guzzle in them; a month of solid drinking wouldn't get you past the halfway mark.

City Centre — Map pp108–9

TRADITIONAL PUBS

Glasgow is simply laden with traditional pubs exuding an old-world character.

Drum & Monkey (☎ 221 6636; 93-95 Vincent St) Jazz fans can get their fix on Sunday afternoons; the rest of the week, jazz records accompany the dark wood and marble columns of this attractive drinking emporium, peppered with church pews and leather lounge chairs. Its cosy and relaxing vibe makes you want to curl up in an armchair with a pint for the afternoon.

Horse Shoe (☎ 221 3051; 17 Drury St) This is a legendary city pub and popular meeting place, dating from the late 19th century and remains largely unchanged. It has the longest continuous bar in the UK, but its main attraction is what's served over it – real ale and good food offers. Upstairs in the lounge are the best value three-course lunches (£2.95) in town.

Scotia (☎ 552 8681; 112 Stockwell St) Drinks have been poured down throats at Scotia, Glasgow's oldest pub, since 1792. And while the last good airing feels like it happened back in the mid-1850s, Scotia's cheery charm outweighs the grungy atmosphere. There's an open session on Saturdays, musos welcome, and a singalong on Monday.

Blackfriars (☎ 552 5924; 36 Bell St) Merchant City's most relaxed and atmospheric pub, Blackfriars' friendly staff and chilled-out house make it special. Importantly you don't have to ask – it's a cask! There's a seating area with large windows great for people watching.

Babbity Bowster (☎ 552 5055; 16-18 Blackfriars St) Babbity Bowster is perfect for a quiet daytime drink, particularly in the adjoining beer garden. The interior has a classy diner vibe with a suit crowd to match on weekday evenings. There's music on Saturday night, usually of the folky-fiddler variety.

MODERN BARS

Artà (☎ 552 2101; 13-19 Walls St) As its door slides open, Artà's opulent, cavernous candlelit interior is exposed. Floor-to-ceiling velvet, red curtains reveal a staircase to the tapas bar and restaurant above (p121) in a show of decadence that the Romans would have appreciated. This mock baroque-cum-Mediterranean showpiece is a must-see, but you're better off staying for at least one drink as it's a relaxed, chilled place with a mixed crowd. There's live music on weekends.

Corinthian (☎ 552 1101; 191 Ingram St) A breathtaking domed ceiling and majestic chandeliers makes Corinthian an awesome venue, though the lavish bill might also leave you awe-struck. Originally a bank and later Glasgow's High Court, this regal building also houses two plush clubs, downstairs in old court cells, which pump out funk, R'n'B, house and garage. There is a strict dress code. Don't miss the half-price cocktails Friday and Saturday in the cocktail lounge. It also has Glasgow's only late-night piano bar, open till 3am nightly.

Bar 10 (☎ 572 1448; 10 Mitchell Lane) A little city treasure that will cause the canny Glasgow drinker to give you a knowing glance if you mention its name. As laid back as you could ask in a hip city bar, the friendly, tuned-in staff complete the happy picture. It transforms from a quiet daytime bar to a happening weekend pub on Friday and Saturday nights.

Nice 'N' Sleazy (☎ 333 0900; 421 Sauchiehall St) Close to the Glasgow School of Art, students come here to discuss primers, Duchamp and Nietzche over Glasgow's cheapest drinks. With its 1970s retro décor, relaxed atmosphere and great menu for under a fiver, it makes an excellent spot to kick back and relish the tunes of the city's freshest live music acts.

Pivo Pivo (☎ 564 8100; 15 Waterloo St) A cavernous downstairs beer-hall with a chilled atmosphere and beers a plenty – 100 from 32 different countries to be exact. Add to that an impressive array of vodka and schnapps, and it may be a while before you see daylight.

Arches (☎ 565 1023; 253 Argyle St) A one-stop culture fix this place doubles as a theatre showing contemporary, avant-garde productions and there's also a club (p124). The hotel-like entrance belies the deep interior, which make you feel as though you've discovered Hades' bohemian underworld. The crowd is mixed – hiking boots are as welcome as Versace.

Waxy O'Connors (☎ 354 5154; 46 West George St) If you've been trying to avoid those acid flashbacks, steer clear of Waxy O'Connors. This labyrinthine maze of six bars on three levels, including the inspiringly named Murphy's Bar, is an Escher drawing brought to life. Sadly, it's also an Irish-themed bar, but even that doesn't ruin the surreal fun.

West End
TRADITIONAL PUBS
Uisge Beatha (Map pp108-9; ☎ 564 1596; 232-246 Woodlands Rd) If you enjoy a drink among dead things, you'll love Uisge Beatha (Gaelic for whisky, literally 'water of life'). This mishmash of church pews, stuffed animal heads and portraits of depressed nobility (the Maggie mannequin is our favourite) is patrolled by Andy Capp-like characters during the day and students at night. With 100 whiskies and four quirky

rooms to choose from, this unique pub is one of Glasgow's best – an antidote to style bars.

Aragon Bar (Map pp130-1; 131 Byers Rd) A traditional bar in this trendy part of town, with changing guest ales and board games behind the bar for those lazy afternoons.

MODERN BARS

Jinty McGuinty's (Map pp130-1; ☎ 339 0747; 23-29 Ashton Lane) This is a popular Irish theme pub with unusual booth seating and a literary hall of fame, with a spacious and popular beer garden that often spills into secluded Ashton Lane in summer.

Vodka Wodka (Map pp130-1; ☎ 341 0669; 31 Ashton Lane; cocktails £3.50) This watering hole is every vodka drinker's dream with more varieties of the stealthy poison than you could possibly conquer in one sitting. It attracts the type of crowd trying to do just that!

ENTERTAINMENT

Glasgow is Scotland's entertainment city, from classical music, fine theatres and ballet to cracking nightclubs pumping out cheesy chart tunes or the latest dance music phenomenon, and contemporary Scottish bands at the cutting edge of modern music.

To tap into your scene, check out the *List* (www.list.co.uk), an invaluable fortnightly events guide available at newsagents and bookshops. If you plan to spend any time in the city, pick up a copy of *Itchy* (£3.50), a handy pocket-sized entertainment guide, available at bookshops. The *Herald* and *Evening Times* newspapers list events happening around the city. Pick up a copy of the *Gig Guide* (www.gigguide.co.uk), published monthly and available free in most pubs and venues for the latest on music gigs.

For theatre tickets book directly with the venue. For concerts a useful booking centre is **Tickets Scotland** (☎ 204 5151; www.tickets-scotland.com; 239 Argyle St).

Clubs

Glasgow has one of Britain's biggest clubbing scenes attracting style-cats from afar. Glaswegians usually hit the clubs after the pubs have closed, so many clubs offer discounted admission and cheaper drinks if you go before 11pm. Entry to most clubs

is between £3 to £5 (up to £10 for bigger venues), although bars often hand out free passes. Most clubs close around 3am.

Arches (Map pp108-9; ☎ 565 1035; Argyle St, off Jamaica St) With a capacity of 2000 people and a design based around hundreds of arches slammed together, this venue is a must for funk and hip-hop freaks. It is one of the city's biggest clubs pulling top DJs, and you'll also hear some of the UK's up-and-coming turntable spinners.

Cathouse (Map pp108-9; ☎ 248 6606; 15 Union St) Don the ghostly warpaint, dust off the steelcaps and rejoin your Goth brethren at the three-level Cathouse, Glasgow's top indie and alternative venue. It has two dance floors: upstairs is pretty intense with lots of metal and hard rock, downstairs is a little less scary if you're not keen on moshing.

MAS (Map pp108-9; ☎ 204 7080; 29 Royal Exchange Sq) Run by the same folk as the achingly cool **Republic Biere Halle** (☎ 204 0706; 9 Gordon St), with its long room, mood lighting and mirrors, MAS is less style-obsessed and instead puts together Glasgow's best hard house. It has a reputation for a party vibe, quality DJs and thumping weekend nights with plenty of beautiful people.

Shack (Map pp108-9; ☎ 332 7322; 193 Pitt St) In a converted church and renowned as Glasgow's top student pick-up joint, The Shack plays current chart-topping horrors and the odd indie classic.

Tunnel (Map pp108-9; ☎ 204 1000; 88 Mitchell St) This is the venue to hear big-name DJs such as Paul Oakenfold and Judge Jules; resident mixers pump out trance and hard house at other times. It's a venue that perhaps takes itself a bit seriously. Don't show up in trainers – you'll need to dolly yourself up to get in here.

Cleopatra's (Map pp130-1; ☎ 334 0560; cnr Great Western Rd & Bank St) Clatty Pats seems to have a monopoly in the West End and therefore gets packed. It's pretty grungy but a lot of fun, and best enjoyed in a crowd. And no, that's not chewing gum making your shoes stick to the floor!

Live Music

Glasgow has long been regarded as the centre of Scotland's live music scene (see boxed text p126).

One of the city's premier live music pub venues is the excellent **King Tut's Wah Wah Hut**

TOM SMALLMAN

One of Edinburgh's popular shopping streets, **Victoria Street** (p97)

The battlements at **Edinburgh Castle** (p62)
BETHUNE CARMICHAEL

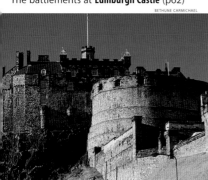

PAT YALE

The box office for the **Edinburgh International Festival** (p79)

Looking towards St Cuthberts Church from Edinburgh's **Princes Street Gardens** (p69)
JONATHAN SMITH

Glasgow's main train station, **Central Station** (p128)

A busker in **Edinburgh** (p96)

Many Glasgow walking tours start at **Bell's Bridge** (p116)

View from Edinburgh's **Calton Hill** (p62)

GAY & LESBIAN GLASGOW

Glasgow has a vibrant gay scene, with the gay quarter found in and around the Merchant City (particularly Virginia, Wilson and Glassford Sts). The city's gay community has a reputation for being very friendly.

To get the lowdown the best contact for gay and lesbian travellers is the **Glasgow LGBT Centre** (Map pp108-9; ☎ 0141-221 7203; www.glgbt.org.uk; 11 Dixon St, ☽ 10am-midnight) at the back of St Enoch Sq. It has a bulletin board with information about activities and events as well as personal ads; there's also a bar here. For confidential advice or help try the **Gay & Lesbian switchboard** (☎ 332 8372). See also the Gay & Lesbian section in the Directory chapter, p410.

Spa 19 (Map pp108-9; ☎ 572 0347; 2nd floor, 19 Dixon St; admission £9; ☽ noon-10pm Sun-Fri, noon-4am Sat) is an excellent gay health centre with small gym, sauna and Jacuzzi, TV lounge, café and cyber centre for firing off emails.

Many straight clubs and bars have gay and lesbian nights, such as the glittery **Fruitfly@The Arches** (Map pp108-9; ☎ 221 4001; Midland St) on the 3rd Saturday of the month. Check out the List, the free Scots Gay magazine, and the websites at www.gayscotland.com/glasgow/glasgow_index.htm, and www.glasgow-gay.info.

The following are just a selection of gay and lesbian pubs and clubs in the city.

- **Waterloo Bar** (Map pp108-9; ☎ 229 5891; 306 Argyle St) This is a traditional place and Scotland's oldest gay bar. Recently refurbished, it attracts punters of all ages. It's very friendly and, with a large group of regulars, a good place to meet people.

- **Polo Lounge** (Map pp108-9; ☎ 553 1221; 84 Wilson St) Staff claim 'the city's best talent' is found here; a quick glance at the many glamour pusses – male and female – proves their claim. The downstairs club is packed at weekends; just the main bars open on other nights.

- **Moda** (Map pp108-9; ☎ 553 1221; cnr Virginia & Wilson Sts) Blonde wood and fake tan are the chief attributes of Moda, a place where beautiful folk strike a pose over daytime drinks, or recuperate before returning to the Polo Lounge next door or going downmarket at Delmonica's.

- **Delmonica's** (Map pp108-9; ☎ 552 4803; 68 Virginia St) Metres from the Polo Lounge, Delmonica's is a world away, with its predatorial feeling of people on the pull. It's packed on weekday evenings. Friday night is glam night with chart tunes and Sunday is a karaoke free-for-all.

- **Revolver** (Map pp108-9; ☎ 553 2456; 5a John St) Hip little Revolver, downstairs on cosmopolitan John St, sports a relaxed crowd and, crucially, a free jukebox.

- **Bennet's** (Map pp108-9; ☎ 552 5761; www.bennets.co.uk; 90 Glassford St) Glasgow's longest-running gay club, Bennet's has three bars over two levels and cranks out tunes from hard house to cheesy chart favourites from Wednesday to Sunday.

If you're in Glasgow in autumn check out **Glasgay** (%334 7126; www.glasgay.co.uk), a gay performing arts festival, held around October/November each year.

(Map pp108-9; ☎ 221 5279; www.kingtuts.co.uk; 272a St Vincent St), which hosts bands every night of the week. Oasis made Britpop history by debuting here.

Two bars to see the best, and worst, of Glasgow's newest bands are **Brunswick Cellars** (Map pp108-9; ☎ 572 0016; 239 Sauchiehall St) and the **Halt Bar** (Map pp108-9; ☎ 564 1527; 160 Woodlands Rd), which is a popular university pub that hasn't been tarted up.

Other recommendations:

13th Note Cafe (Map pp108-9; ☎ 553 1638; 50-60 King St)
Barfly (Map pp108-9; ☎ 0870 907 0999; www.barflyclub.com/listings/glasgow; 260 Clyde St)
Barrowlands (Map pp108-9; ☎ 552 4601; www.glasgow-barrowland.com; 244 Gallowgate) An exceptional old dancehall catering for some of the larger acts that visit the city.
Clyde Auditorium (Map pp108-9; ☎ 0870 040 4000) Also known as the Armadillo because of its bizzare shape, adjoins SECC and caters for big national and international acts playing in Glasgow.

Glasgow Academy (Map pp108-9; ☎ 418 3000; www.glasgow-academy.co.uk; 121 Eglinton St)

Nice 'n' Sleazy (Map pp108-9; ☎ 333 9637; 421 Sauchiehall) Nurturing much of Glasgow's alternative music scene

SECC (Map pp108-9; ☎ 0870 040 4000; www.secc.co.uk; Finnieston Quay) Adjoins Clyde Auditorium and hosts major national and international acts.

Stereo (Map pp108-9; ☎ 576 5018; 12-14 Kelvinhaugh St)

Cinemas

Glasgow Film Theatre (Map pp108-9; ☎ 332 8128; 12 Rose St; www.gft.org.uk; adults £3.90-£4.90, concessions £2.50-3.50) The two-screen Glasgow Film

Theatre, off Sauchiehall St, screens arthouse cinema and classics.

Odeon Renfield Street (Map pp108-9; ☎ 0870 5050 007; 56 Renfield St; adult/concession £4.95/3) The nine-screen Odeon Renfield Street shows mainstream films.

Theatres & Concert Halls

Theatre Royal (Map pp108-9; ☎ 332 3321; www .theatreroyalglasgow.com; 282 Hope St) This is the home of Scottish Opera, and the Scottish Ballet often performs here. Ask about standby tickets if you're going to be in town for a few days.

GLASGOW'S MUSIC COMMUNITY

Year after year, touring artists and travellers alike name Glasgow as one of their favourite cities in the world to enjoy live music.

As much of Glasgow's character is encapsulated within the soul and humour of its inhabitants, the main reason for the city's musical success lies within its audience and the musical community it has bred and nurtured for years. Glaswegians laugh together, cry together and sing together, and it is their passion and intensity, coupled with an almost intrinsic understanding and love of music, that makes the live music experience in Glasgow unique.

With such a strong musical heritage it is inevitable that Glasgow and its surrounding communities consistently introduce a string of potent acts to an enthusiastic audience.

Originally from Ireland but now adopted Glaswegians, **Snow Patrol** bring a subtle, poetic beauty to their barb-wire and cotton-wool alternative guitar pop. In a similar vein **Odeon Beatclub**, the latest pretenders to Glasgow's live music crown, are currently cresting on their wave of guitar-propelled melodic snapshots on modern day life. In the process they are building a persuasive live reputation and considerable fan base, as are other new-comers **Sneak Attack Tigers**. Intertwining lush arrangements, delicate instrumentation and battered guitars, **The Delgados** bounce between male and female vocal leads as they generate an encompassing sonic landscape full of cinematic swells and tainted prose. **El Hombre Trajeado, Sputnik's Down** and **Mogwai** all offer diverse, dizzying soundscapes with their guitar-led instrumental experimentalism, while **Biffy Clyro** and **Aereogramme** serve up their own distinct slices of Glaswegian rock. Radiant in an altogether more acoustic manner are **The Reindeer Section**, a Glaswegian indie super-group, who'll bring a rapturous smile to your face as they slowly break your heart with their tales of love and loss.

Of course not all of the best bands in Scotland rise out of Glasgow. Elsewhere, **Ballboy** are plying a fine line in intelligently crafted *paeans* wrapped in a strong pop sensibility, while **X-Tigers** take a harder approach, combining melody with a surging intensity and charisma. **Sam's Hot Car Lot**, with their take on the three-piece aesthetic, and **Degrassi** leak angularity and melody with a hardcore subtlety that comes enjoyably close to implosion. Combining break beats and dirty blues, **Mystery Juice** are a stunning live band as are **Huckleberry** with their modernised take on 1960s garage, while **Babacool** emanate from a dance rock origin. Both consuming and hypnotic, **James Yorkston** and **The Athletes** peddle a beautifully restrained nu-folk vibe, while **Polly Phillips** takes the singer-songwriter track with her acerbic, witty observations and powerful, stunning voice.

On any given night you may find your breath taken by a wave of voices as the audience spontaneously harmonises with an artist on a chorus, a song or even, at times, an entire show. Maybe it's the spine-tingling, hear-a-pin-drop silence that the audience respectfully affords an artist as they perform a quiet, acoustic or delicate piece. Whatever the occasion, the band or venue, Glasgow is, by proxy of its inhabitants, a music city, an intricate web of emotions and poetry, passion and melody, and most of all honesty and soul.

Bryan McRitchie (Edinburgh songwriter)

Glasgow Royal Concert Hall (Map pp108-9; ☎ 353 8000; www.grch.com; 2 Sauchiehall St) A feast of classical music is showcased here, the modern home of the Royal Scottish National Orchestra.

King's Theatre (☎ 0845 330 3511; 294 Bath St; tickets £5-28.50) The King's Theatre hosts mainly musicals; on rare occasions there are variety shows, pantomimes and comedies.

Citizens' Theatre (Map pp108-9; ☎ 429 0022; www.citz.co.uk; 119 Gorbals St; tickets £6-12) This is one of the top theatres in Scotland and it's well worth trying to catch a performance here.

Tron Theatre (Map pp108-9; ☎ 552 3748; www.tron.co.uk; 63 Trongate; ticket sales 10am-6pm Mon-Sat) Tron Theatre stages contemporary Scottish and international performances. There's also a good café.

Centre for Contemporary Arts (Map pp108-9; ☎ 332 7521; www.cca-glasgow.com; 350 Sauchiehall St) After a £10-million facelift, this is a smick venue making terrific use of space and light. It showcases the visual and performing arts, including movies, talks and galleries.

Tramway (Map p130-1; ☎ 422 2023; 25 Albert Dr) The Tramway theatre and exhibition space attracts cutting-edge theatrical groups, visual and performing arts and varied artistic exhibitions.

Sport

Two football clubs dominate sport in Scotland, having vastly more resources than other clubs and a long history (and rivalry). This rivalry is also along partisan lines, with Rangers representing Protestant supporters, and Celtic, of course, Catholic.

Celtic Football Club (☎ 551 8653; www.celticfc.co.uk; Celtic Park, Parkhead; adult/child £24/14) Has a 60,832-seat stadium.

Rangers Football Club (☎ 0870 600 1972; www.rangers.co.uk; Ibrox Stadium, 150 Edmiston Dr; tickets £10-£22) Tours of the stadium and trophy room run three times daily Monday and Friday, once on Saturday (tour tickets £6/5). Rangers' stadium holds 50,500.

SHOPPING

Boasting the UK's largest retail contingency outside London, Glasgow is a shopaholic's paradise.

Fashion junkies can procure relief at **Versace** (☎ 552 6510) and **Armani** (☎ 552 2277) in the stylish **Italian Centre** (Map pp108-9; John St). Alternatively **Designer Exchange** (☎ 221 6898;

3 Royal Exchange Ct) stocks cheaper samples and re-sale designer labels. Trendy traders litter the pedestrian malls of Sauchiehall and Buchanan Sts. Try **Buchanan Galleries** (Royal Exchange Sq) and the exquisite **Princes Square** (Map pp108–9), which is set in a magnificent 1841 renovated square.

Munro-baggers and other outdoor enthusiasts can go berserk at **Tiso's** (Map pp108-9; ☎ 248 4877; 129 Buchanan St) and **Adventure 1** (Map pp108-9; ☎ 353 3788; 38 Dundas St), which is an excellent place to buy hiking boots.

Institutions include Buchanan St's splendid, jewellery-laden **Argyll Arcade** (Map pp108–9); try **Catherine Shaw** (Map pp108-9; ☎ 221 9038) for distinct pieces transcending mass-production, and the **Barras** (Map pp108-9; ☎ 552 4601; London Rd), Glasgow's burgeoning flea market, open every weekend.

GETTING THERE & AWAY

Glasgow is 42 miles (68km) from Edinburgh and 166 miles (267km) from Inverness.

Air

Glasgow International Airport (☎ 887 1111; www.baa.co.uk/glasgow), 10 miles (16km) west of the city, handles domestic traffic and international flights. Glasgow Prestwick airport, 30 miles (48km) southwest of Glasgow handles some of the cheap, no-frills airlines. **Ryanair** (☎ 0871 246 0000; www.ryanair.com) flies to Glasgow Prestwick airport from London Stansted airport (1¼ hours, frequent) for ridiculously low prices – from £3 excluding taxes.

Bus

All long-distance buses arrive and depart from **Buchanan bus station** (Map pp108-9; ☎ 333 3708; Killermont St).

Buses from London are very competitive. **Silver Choice** (☎ 01355-230403; www.silverchoicetravel .co.uk) is currently the best deal (apex return ticket £24, 8½ hours). It departs at 10pm daily from both London Victoria coach station and Buchanan bus station in Glasgow. The service is very popular so you'll need to book well in advance.

National Express (☎ 0870 580 8080; www .nationalexpress.com) leaves from the same stations (single £28.50, nine hours, at least five daily). There's a daily direct overnight bus from Heathrow Airport, usually departing at 11.05pm.

GLASGOW

National Express also has numerous links with other English cities. Services and single tickets include: three daily buses from Birmingham (£38.50, 5¾ hours); up to three from Cambridge (£44, 9¾ hours); at least five from Carlisle (£14, two hours); one from Newcastle (£23.50, four hours); and one from York (£27.50, 7½ hours).

Scottish Citylink (☎ 08705 505050; www.citylink.co.uk) has buses to most major towns in Scotland. There are very frequent services to Edinburgh (single/return £4/6, 1¼ hours, every 15 to 20 minutes during the day). Frequent buses also run to Stirling (£4/6.80, 40 minutes), Inverness (£15.50/26.40, from 3½ hours) and Aberdeen (£17.80/27.30, 3¼ to four hours). Regular long distance services to/from Glasgow include Oban (£12.20/20.70, three hours, four daily), Fort William (£13/22, three hours, four daily) and Portree on Skye (£22/36, 6¼ to seven hours, three daily).

There's a twice-daily summer service (late-May to early-October) to Stranraer, connecting with the ferry to Belfast in Northern Ireland (£20/35, six hours).

Stagecoach Express (☎ 01592-261461; www .stagecoachbus.com) operates services to Anstruther (three hours, hourly), St Andrews (2¼ hours, hourly) and Dundee (2¼ hours, half-hourly); the return fare to all costs £9.

Walkers should check out **First Glasgow** (☎ 423 6600), which runs buses every hour or two to Milngavie (30 minutes), the start of the West Highland Way.

Car

There are numerous car-rental companies; the big names have offices at Glasgow international airport.

Arnold Clark (☎ 0845 607 4500, 423 9559; www.arnoldclark.co.uk; 43 Allison St) Rates from £18/90 per day/week.

Avis (☎ 0870 606 0100, 221 2827; www.avis.co.uk; 70 Lancefield St)

Train

As a general rule, Glasgow Central serves southern Scotland, England and Wales, and Queen St serves the north and east. There are buses every 10 minutes between them. There are direct trains from London's King's Cross and Euston stations; they're much quicker (from £25, five hours, 10 direct daily) and more comfortable than the bus.

ScotRail (☎ 0845 748 4950; www.scotrail.co.uk) has the West Highland line heading north to Oban and Fort William, and other direct links to Dundee (£20.70), Aberdeen (£31.60) and Inverness (£31.60). There are trains every 15 minutes to/from Edinburgh (£8.60, 50 minutes).

GETTING AROUND
To/From the Airport

There are buses every 10 or 15 minutes from Glasgow International Airport to Buchanan bus station (single £3.30). Buses continue to Edinburgh (£6.30 from the airport). A taxi costs about £18.

Car & Motorcycle

The most difficult thing about driving in Glasgow, as with most Scottish urban centres, is the confusing one-way system. If you miss a turn-off, you can end up a long way from your destination. For short-term parking (30 minutes to an hour) you've a decent chance of finding something on the street, especially away from the city centre. Otherwise multi-storey car parks are probably your best bet – the St Enoch Centre in the city has free parking. Note that the West End generally, and Great Western Rd in particular, are very busy during the day and bumper to bumper during peak hour (8am to 10am and 4pm to 6pm).

Public Transport

Glasgow has an excellent public transport system, especially the rail network. The Roundabout Glasgow ticket (adult/child £3.50/1.75) covers all underground and train transport in the city for a day. **First Glasgow** (☎ 423 6600; www.firstglasgow.com) has a FirstDay ticket that allows hop-on/off travel on all its buses; it can be bought from drivers for £2.50/2.10 before/after 9.30am and is valid until midnight. If you're going further afield, get the FirstTourist ticket for £3, which allows unlimited travel in Greater Glasgow after 9.30am.

BUS

City bus services are frequent. You can buy tickets when you board buses, but on most you must have the exact change. **First Glasgow** publishes the complicated but useful *Glasgow Mapmate* (£1), which shows all local First bus routes. Trips around the city cost from 57p to £1.27 and up to £2.47 in the Greater Glasgow area. Pick up a copy of the First Glasgow *Night Network* brochure to find out about services running through until the wee hours.

TAXI

There's no shortage of taxis, and if you want to know anything about Glasgow, striking up a conversation with a cabbie is a good place to start. Here's a good line to break the ice: 'So, Glasgow's not really as much fun as Edinburgh is it?'

If you order by phone from **Glasgow Wide Taxis** (☎ 429 7070) you can pay by credit card (£1 surcharge); most of their taxis are wheelchair accessible.

TRAIN

There's an extensive suburban network of trains in and around Glasgow; tickets should be bought before travel if the station is staffed, or from the conductor if it isn't.

There's also an underground line that serves 15 stations in the centre, west and south of the city (90p). The rail network connects with the Underground at Buchanan St station. The Discovery Ticket (£1.70) gives unlimited travel after 9.30am on the Underground system for a day.

AROUND GLASGOW

There are some wonderful sights in the urban centres around Glasgow, although it's best to visit this grim hinterland of post-industrial communities via a day trip. It's like finding diamonds in a coal mine – well worth looking at, but you wouldn't want to spend the night there. Paisley's abbey should head your itinerary – it's a stupendous sight and a marvellous architectural achievement. If you're interested in Clyde shipbuilding and its spectacular fall from economic grace, then Greenock is a must.

PAISLEY

☎ 0141 / pop 74,170

Effectively a suburb west of Glasgow, the reason for visiting Paisley is to see its timeless abbey – one of the finest in southern Scotland. The town with its boarded-up shops possesses an air of neglect, but this is the place that gave its name to the well-known

fabric design of swirling stylised teardrops or pinecones called the Paisley Pattern.

The helpful **TIC** (Map pp108-9; ☎ 889 0711; 9a Gilmour St;) has leaflets on local attractions.

Sights

Overlooking the river like a giant sentinel, **Paisley Abbey** (☎ 889 7654; Abbey Close; admission free; ☽ 10am-3.30pm Mon-Sat) is an awesome sight. Inside, the stonework gives a chilly embrace and you feel as though you've passed through a portal to another age – the scruffy town outside seems a world away.

The abbey was founded in 1163 by Walter Fitzallan, the first high steward of Scotland and ancestor of the Stuart dynasty. It was badly damaged by fire during the Wars of Independence in 1306, but rebuilt soon after. Most of the nave is 14th or 15th century. The building was a ruin from the 16th century until the 19th-century restoration, not completed until 1928. There are two royal tombs in the abbey, excellent stained-glass windows and the 10th-century Celtic **Barochan Cross**.

At the western end of the High St, there's the **University of Paisley** and the **Museum and Art Gallery** (☎ 889 3151; High St; admission free; ☽ 10am-5pm Tue-Sat, 2-5pm Sun), which features Paisley psychedelia! There are some marvellous exhibits, including contemporary displays of children in the modern world – it's worth at least a couple of hours. It also has collections of local and natural history, ceramics and 19th-century Scottish art.

Sleeping

There's not much point in staying overnight in Paisley, being so close to Glasgow, and there are few guesthouses. However if you get stuck, try the following.

Watermill Hotel (☎ 889 3201; Lonend; s/d £50/60) On the site of a 17th-century flour mill, this is a good central spot to stay as it gives relief from Paisley's urban chaos – a tranquil place by the river rapids. Rooms are dignified, business-like and some have great river views. These folks will negotiate price, particularly if they're quiet, so have a go!

Getting There & Away

There are frequent buses from Central Rd. Trains leave Glasgow's Central station for Paisley's Gilmour St Station (£2.60/3.40 off peak/day return, 15 minutes, eight per hour).

GLASGOW

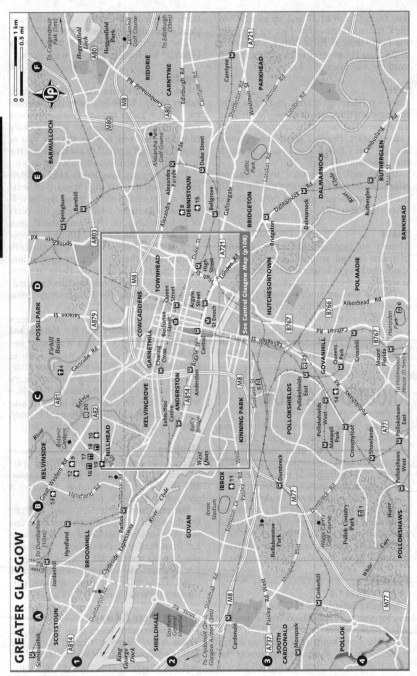

GREATER GLASGOW

0 ___ 1 km
0 ___ 0.5 mi

INVERCLYDE

The ghostly remains of once-great ship-yards still line the banks of the Clyde west of Glasgow.

The only place worth stopping along the coast west of the city is Greenock, although there are a couple of items of interest in the otherwise unprepossessing town of **Port Glasgow**, including the fine 16th-century **Newark Castle** (☎ 01475 741858; adult/child £2.20/75p; ☘ 9.30am-6pm Mon-Sun Apr-Sep), which is still largely intact.

Greenock

☎ 01475 / pop 45,467

Greenock has a lovely, revitalised water-front area by the James Watt College, which is very pleasant to wander around. Other parts of town are a little scrappy and can be confusing to navigate.

An enjoyable walk up to Lyle Hill, above Gourock Bay, leads to the Free French memorial, commemorating sailors who lost their lives in the Battle of the Atlantic during WWII, and a great view over the Firth of Clyde.

The **Inverclyde Information Office** (☎ 712555; 7 Clyde Sq) near the High St and behind the

Town Hall, stocks tourist information and is open year-round.

SIGHTS

McLean Museum and Art Gallery (☎ 715624; 15 Kelly St; admission free; ☘ 10am-5pm Mon-Sat) is well worth checking out. It's quite an extensive collection with displays charting the history of steam power and Clyde shipping. There's also a pictorial history of Greenock through the ages, while upstairs there are very good temporary exhibitions and small displays from China, Japan and Egypt. The natural history section highlights the sad reality of species extinction in the modern world.

HM Customs & Excise Museum (☎ 881300; Custom House Quay; admission free; ☘ 10am-4pm Mon-Fri) is intriguing in parts, and good for killing an hour or so. You can also learn a thing or two about searches and smuggling techniques. You have to feel sorry for the customs officers who searched an Airbus from the West Indies and found more than five kilos of grass in the aircraft toilet tanks! The search took 4½ hours.

SLEEPING & EATING

James Watt College (☎ 731360; ahurrell@jameswatt.ac.uk; Ardmore Hall, Custom House Way; r per person £20-25) Fairly central and down on the waterfront, this hall of residence has 168 single rooms, many with ensuite. It's good value and the management only ask that you leave the place as you found it. Fair enough.

Tontine Hotel (☎ /fax 723316; 6 Ardgowan Sq; r from £55) This grand hotel, with well-appointed rooms, each with private bath, is genteel and surprisingly good value. The premier rooms in the old wing are more luxurious and spacious. Book early for stays over summer.

Port & Harbour (☎ 73 0370; Custom House Pl; mains £8.50-15.50) Right on the waterfront next to the Customs & Excise Museum, this fine restaurant offers candlelit dinner, special-ising in local seafood, lamb and venison dishes. The surroundings are suitably dark and cosy, perfect for those blustery nights.

GETTING THERE & AWAY

Greenock is 27 miles (43km) west of Glasgow. The Glasgow–Greenock pedestrian/cycle route (p116) follows an old railway track for 10 miles (16km). There are trains from Glasgow Central (£4.60 off-peak return, 45 minutes, three per hour) and hourly buses.

SHIPBUILDING ON THE CLYDE

One of the earliest permanent Lower Clyde shipyards was established in 1711 by John Scott at Greenock. Initial construction was for small-scale local trade but, by the end of the 18th century, large ocean-going vessels were being built. As the market expanded, shipyards also opened at Dumbarton and Port Glasgow.

The *Comet*, Europe's first steamship, was launched at Port Glasgow in 1812. By the 1830s and 1840s, the Clyde had secured its position as world-leader in shipbuilding. Steel hulls came into use by the 1880s, allowing construction of larger ships with the latest and best engines.

In 1899 John Brown & Co, a Sheffield steelmaker, took over a Clydebank yard and by 1907 had become part of the world's largest shipbuilding conglomerate, producing ocean-going liners. Output from the Clyde shipyards steadily increased up to WWI and, with the advent of the war, there was huge demand for new shipping from both the Royal Navy and Merchant Navy.

During and after the war, many small companies disappeared and shipbuilding giants such as Lithgows Ltd took their place. The depression years of the 1920s and 1930s saw many yards moth-balled or closed. Another boom followed during WWII but these were to be the twilight years.

Many yards went into liquidation in the 1960s, and in 1972 Upper Clyde Shipbuilders was liquidated, causing complete chaos, a sit-in and a bad headache for Ted Heath's government.

Now the great shipyards of the Clyde are mostly derelict and empty. The remains of a once mighty industry include just a handful of companies still operating along the Clyde.

Gourock

☎ 01475 / pop 11,511

Gourock is a seaside resort 3 miles (5km) west of Greenock. Although the small central area is run-down, the town's location is wonderful and it's an important transport hub.

For accommodation, you'd be best to head for Glasgow or Dunoon, though there are options in Gourock.

Spinnaker Hotel (☎ 633107; www.spinnakerhotel .co.uk; 121 Albert Rd; s/d from £25/45; mains £5) is an excellent pub. Rooms (with either ensuite or shared bathroom) have country-pine décor, are clean and spacious and have large screen TVs. Downstairs the comfy bar is laid-back and has guest ales on tap. Pretty basic pub grub is also on offer.

CalMac (☎ 650100) ferries leave every day for Dunoon (passenger/car £2.95/7.25, 20 minutes, hourly) on Argyll's Cowal peninsula. CalMac also runs a passenger-only service to Kilcreggan (£1.90, 12 minutes,

three to 12 daily) and Helensburgh (£1.90, 30 minutes, three or four daily).

Western Ferries (☎ 01369-704452) has a service to Dunoon (passenger/car £3/8.50, 20 minutes, two to three hourly) from McInroy's Point, 2 miles (3km) from the train station; Citylink buses run to here.

Gourock train station is next to the CalMac terminal; there are trains to/from Glasgow Central (£4.20, 45 minutes, three per hour).

Wemyss Bay

☎ 01475 / pop 2466

Eight miles (13km) south of Gourock is Wemyss Bay (pronounced weemz), where you can jump off a train and onto a ferry for Rothesay on the Isle of Bute (p258). There are trains from Glasgow (£4.40, 50 minutes, hourly). **CalMac ferries** (☎ 520521) to Rothesay connect with most trains and cost £3.45 per passenger and £13.85 for a car.

Southern Scotland

CONTENTS

Southern
Scotland

SOUTHERN SCOTLAND

Southern Scotland is a stunning area often skipped on itineraries – the perfect reason to include it on yours. Among the fertile landscape of undulating hills and lush valleys, grand stately homes, superb castles and enchanting villages pepper the countryside. The one thing you will see down here is domestic tourists – they've been onto this magical corner of the country for years. But it's easy to escape the tourist hordes in summer and most visitors will stumble across a pocket of country that they'll have all to themselves. And that's one of Southern Scotland's most alluring aspects – crowd-free castles to ramble around, miles of open countryside and small traffic-free roads along which to explore it all.

The landscape is simply glorious – gentle, flat, open fields and beautiful wooded hills flank the River Tweed to the east, and the high, remote Glenken and Galloway hills dominate the west. The countryside is well suited to walking and cycling – especially the area around the ruins of the great Border abbeys, which themselves encapsulate the turmoil of centuries of conflict with England.

Southern Scotland is an area that ignites the imagination – Sir Walter Scott and Robert Burns, Scotland's two great literary sons, romanticised the region. After a short time here it's easy to see why.

HIGHLIGHTS

- Peeping through a portal to the past at the World Heritage site of **New Lanark** (p149)
- Poking around the ruins of the great **Border abbeys** (p143)
- Hiking the challenging **Southern Upland Way** (p135) a unique way to experience the beauty of the countryside
- Discovering the concealed room in the musty grandeur of **Traquair House** (p148)
- Relishing the great outdoors at **St Abb's Head** (p140)
- Exploring the stunning **Isle of Arran** (p154), a walking and cycling paradise
- Watching **Culzean Castle** (p162) float into view like a mirage
- Coming face to face with red deer in the vast wilderness of **Galloway Forest Park** (p169)

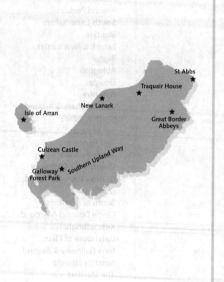

St Abbs ★

Traquair House ★

New Lanark ★

Isle of Arran ★

Great Border Abbeys ★

Culzean Castle ★

Galloway Forest Park ★ Southern Upland Way

- POPULATION: 1,245,911
- AREA: 16,769 SQ KM

HISTORY

Historically, Southern Scotland was the buffer between the rambunctious, imperialist English and the equally unruly Scots.

The Wars of Scottish independence fought at the end of the 13th century and the beginning of the 14th, took a terrible toll on southern Scotland. The Debatable Lands, as they were known, were virtually ungoverned and ungovernable from the late 13th to the mid-17th centuries. It's been argued that this continuous state of guerrilla warfare had an indelible effect on the region and its people.

Following the 1707 union, peace allowed a new surge of development and during the 19th century the knitting and weaving industries that survive today were created.

GETTING AROUND

Bus transport is excellent around Ayrshire (p152) the Borders (p136) and Lothians, and reasonable on the main north–south routes and the A75 to Stranraer, but limited elsewhere in Dumfries and Galloway. Various explorer tickets, which can be bought from bus drivers or bus stations, are usually your best-value option.

Train services are limited. There are stations at Berwick-upon-Tweed (in Northumberland on the English side of the border, but the natural jumping-off point for the Tweed Valley) on the main east-coast line; at Dumfries on the main west-coast line; and at Stranraer and Ayr, which are linked to Glasgow. For timetables and fares call the **National Rail Enquiry Service** (☎ 0845 748 4950; www.railtrack.co.uk).

BORDERS REGION

The Borders country has a quality distinct from anywhere else in Scotland. The link to the country's medieval past somehow seems closer here. Centuries of war and plunder have left their mark on a region that, strangely, appears relatively undiscovered by foreign visitors. The hills, glens and stately homes of the Borders are captivating, and the concentration of great ruined abbeys is unique. Areas to the west are wild and empty but the Tweed Valley has been a source of wealth for centuries.

The countryside is lush with an artist's palette of innumerable shades of green. Glens with winding burns and balding hills, occasionally sporting mohawk-like tree growth, make travelling around the area delightful – it's fine walking and cycling country.

WALKING & CYCLING

The region's most famous walk is the challenging 212-mile (341km) **Southern Upland Way**. If you want a sample, one of the best bits is the two-day section from St John's Town of Dalry to Beattock. Another long-distance walk is the 100-mile (161km) **St Cuthbert's Way**, inspired by the travels of St Cuthbert (a 7th century saint who worked in Melrose Abbey), which crosses some superb scenery between Melrose and Lindisfarne (in England). In Galloway the **Pilgrims Way** follows a 25-mile (40km) trail from Glenluce Abbey to the Isle of Whithorn.

The recently created **Borders Abbeys Way** will eventually link all the great Border abbeys in a 65-mile (105km) circuit. Currently only the Kelso to Jedburgh to Hawick link is open. For shorter walks and especially circular loops in the hills, the towns of Melrose, Jedburgh and Kelso all make ideal bases.

With the exception of the main north–south A roads and the A75 to Stranraer, traffic is sparse, which, along with the beauty of the countryside, makes this ideal cycling country.

The **Tweed Cycle Way** is a waymarked route running 62 miles (along the beautiful Tweed Valley following minor roads from Biggar to Peebles (13 miles), Melrose (16 miles), Coldstream (19 miles) and Berwick-upon-Tweed (14 miles). Jedburgh Tourist Information Centre (TIC) has details.

For an island tour, the **Isle of Arran** offers excellent cycling opportunities. The 50-mile (80km) coast-road circuit is stunning and is worth splitting into two or three days.

The Scottish Borders Tourist Board produces useful free booklets called *Walking in the Scottish Borders* and *Cycling in the Scottish Borders*.

SOUTHERN SCOTLAND

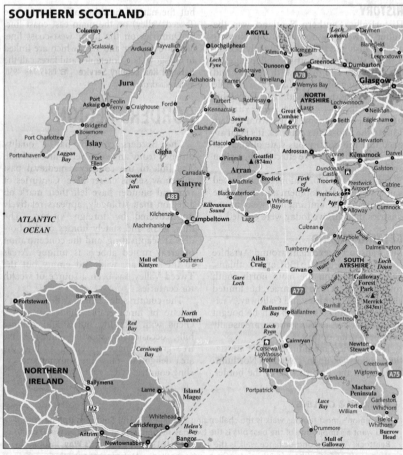

SOUTHERN SCOTLAND

Small burghs supported large, wealthy monastic communities from the 12th century. They provided an irresistible magnet during the Border wars and were destroyed and rebuilt numerous times. The monasteries met their final fiery end in the mid-16th century and were never rebuilt; today their ruins are one of the highlights of the area.

GETTING AROUND

There's a good network of local buses. **First** (☎ 01896-752237) operates between most of the border towns and connects the larger towns with Edinburgh. Their Rover ticket, allowing a day of unlimited travel around the Scottish Borders (£6.45/4.50 adult/child), is great value.

Swan's Coaches (☎ 01289-306436) is a useful service linking Kelso with Berwick-upon-Tweed. Local bus companies serving border towns include **Munro's of Jedburgh** (☎ 01835-862253) and **Buskers** (☎ 01896-755808).

TICs stock excellent public transport booklets to local areas.

COLDSTREAM

☎ 01890 / pop 1813

On a sweeping bend of the River Tweed, which forms the border with England, Coldstream is small and relatively hidden from the well-trodden Borders tourist beat. It can be a handy base when nearby Kelso is overflowing with visitors and accommodation options are sparse.

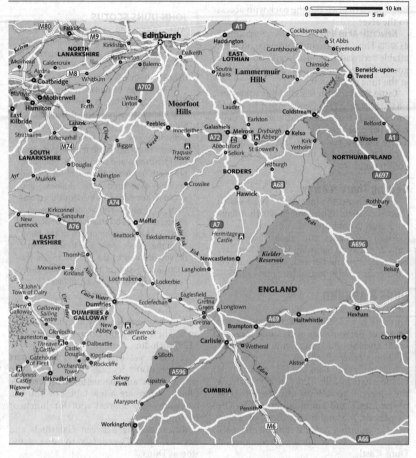

SOUTHERN SCOTLAND

The proud history of the Coldstream Guards is covered in the **Coldstream Museum** (☎ 882630; 12 Market Sq; admission free; ☯ 10am-4pm Mon-Sat, 2-4pm Sun Apr-Sep; 1-4pm Mon-Sat Oct), including recent missions in the 1990s. The Coldstream Guards were formed in 1650 in Berwick-upon-Tweed for duty in Scotland as part of Oliver Cromwell's New Model Army. The regiment took its present name from the town where it was stationed in 1659. The regiment played a significant part in the restoration of the monarchy in 1660. It saw service at Waterloo against Napoleon, at Sebastopol during the Crimean War, in the Boer War, at the Somme and Ypres in WWI, and at Dunkirk and Tobruk in WWII. It remains the oldest regiment in continuous existence in the British army and is the only one directly descended from the New Model Army.

Sleeping & Eating

Coldstream Caravan & Camping Site (☎ 882333; tent sites 1/2 people £6/7; ☯ Apr-Sep) This beautiful grassy site is 100m southwest of Market Sq, beside Leet Water, a small tributary of the River Tweed. Follow the signs from Market Sq.

Eastbraes B&B (☎ 883949; godfrey.bryson@talk21 .com; 100C High St; r per person £25) Eastbraes is full of personality and good vibes. There's a twin and a double room, but it's the twin you want as it has stupendous views through its bay windows. There's also a huge patch of grass out the back with access to the river.

Newcastle Arms Hotel (☎ 882376; 50 High St; s £20, d £20-30) This child-friendly hotel has a warm, affable feel and the tidy, largish rooms are good value. A number were being renovated at the time of research.

Castle Hotel (☎ /fax 882830; 11 High St; r per person £25; lunch mains £5-7) Castle Hotel has good rooms with bathroom and also does delicious bar meals (try the wild boar sausages). There's also a restaurant and on Saturday nights the hotel has both types of music – country and western.

Getting There & Away

The town is on the busy A697 road which links Newcastle upon Tyne in Northumberland with Edinburgh.

Swan's Coaches run about five buses daily Monday to Saturday (two on Sunday) between Kelso and Berwick-upon-Tweed via Coldstream. Kelso to Coldstream is £1.95.

DUNS & AROUND

☎ 01361 / pop 2308

Duns is a peaceful market town in the centre of Berwickshire with some pleasant walks and the odd attraction in town to kill time on a rainy afternoon.

You can get to **Duns Law** (218m) in Duns Castle Estate by following Castle St up from the square. The summit offers great views of the Merse and Lammermuir Hills. The Covenanter's Stone marks the spot where the Covenanting armies camped in 1639; a copy of the Covenant was later signed at Duns Castle.

The **Jim Clark Room** (☎ 883960; 44 Newtown St; adult/child £1.30/free; ☺ 10.30am-1pm & 2-4.30pm Mon-Sat, 2-4pm Sun Apr-Sep; 1-4pm Mon-Sat Oct) is a museum dedicated to the amazing life of Jim Clark (1936–68), who lived (and is buried) at nearby Chirnside. A farmer by trade, he was twice world motor-racing champion in the 1960s before being killed in a crash while practising.

On the northern side of the main square, **White Swan Hotel** (☎ 883338; 31-32 Market Sq; s/d £35/60) is a solid old place with decent-sized rooms and is due for an imminent refurbishment. With its lively bar it's worth checking out.

Barniken House Hotel (☎ 882466; 18 Murray St; r per person £27; ✗) is a grand Georgian villa

SOUTHERN SCOTLAND

JOHN DUNS SCOTUS

While wandering around the tranquil market town of Duns, curious minds might ask – does this town have any relation to the word 'dunce'? Deeerrrrrr, of course it dunce…ah, that is does.

Duns is the birthplace of John Duns Scotus (1266–1308), a renowned medieval Franciscan scholar and theologian. He argued in favour of the primacy of the individual and that faith could come through an act of will. His teachings divided the Franciscans and Dominicans. Following his death, his ideas fell out of favour and became associated with dullness and stupidity. And hence the modern 'dunce' was born. So if you're ever accused of being a dunce, perhaps you could ask your accuser if they're aware of the origins of the term.

In the public park is a bronze statue of him, donated by the Franciscans on the 300th anniversary of his birth. Near Duns Castle, a cairn marks his birthplace.

with a beer garden and a children's play area. There are good three-night deals for £120, including dinner.

A classy yet brash eatery, the **Orchard** (☎ 884800; Market Sq; meals £1.10-4) serves up panini, rolls and baguettes with creative fillings. There are a few tables or you can take away. It's a great spot for lunch or morning tea.

Buses running between Galashiels and Berwick-upon-Tweed (six to nine daily) stop at Duns.

LAMMERMUIR HILLS

North of Duns, the low-lying Lammermuir Hills, with their extensive grouse moors, rolling farmland and wooded valleys, run east-west along the border with East Lothian. The hills are popular with walkers and there are numerous trails, including a section of the **Southern Upland Way**.

To the west the Way can be accessed at **Lauder**, where it passes through the grounds of **Thirlestane Castle** (☎ 01578-722430; castle & grounds adult/child £5.50/3, grounds only £2/1; ☺ 10.30am-4.30pm daily except Sat May-early Oct). The narcissism and folly of the aristocracy is evident here perhaps more than in most 'great homes'. Notice how many of the family portraits adorning the walls look similar. The extensive assemblage here is the result of the common practice of mass production used at the time. Many of the family have almost identical features as the same bodies were used for their portraits with different clothes, faces and hands superimposed.

Thirlestane is also home to some of the finest plasterwork ceilings in Europe, and don't miss Henry the Ram (a snuff box) in the dining room – kitsch beyond kitsch!

Thirlestane is just outside town, off the A68, beside Leader Water. Munro's bus Nos 29 and 30, running between Kelso and Edinburgh, pass by.

You can also get onto the Southern Upland Way from the tiny village of Abbey St Bathan's in the secluded, bucolic Whitead-der Valley, off the B6355. From here, the final 10-mile (12km) section of the trail heads northeast to Cockburnspath beside the coast.

EYEMOUTH

☎ 018907 / pop 3383

Eyemouth is a busy fishing port and popular domestic holiday destination. Visitors approaching from Coldingham will spot the evidence: a clutch of caravans perched on the edge of the town's cliffs.

The community here suffered its greatest catastrophe in October 1881, when a storm destroyed the coastal fishing fleet, killing 189 fishermen, 129 of whom were locals.

Information

The Bank of Scotland and the Royal Bank of Scotland have ATMs.

Laundrette (Church St; 🕑 9am-12.30pm & 2-4pm Mon-Fri, 9am-12.30pm Sat)

TIC (☎ 50678; Manse Rd; 🕑 daily Apr-Sep, Mon-Sat Oct) It's in Eyemouth Museum near the harbour.

Sights & Activities

Captivating **Eyemouth Museum** (☎ 50678; Auld Kirk, Manse Rd; adult/child £2/1.50; 🕑 10am-5pm Mon-Sat, noon-3pm Sun Apr-Jun, Sep; 10am-5pm Mon-Sat, noon-4pm Sun Jul-Aug; 10am-4pm Mon-Sat Oct) has displays on local history, particularly relating to the town's fishing heritage. The centrepiece is the large tapestry commemorating the 1881 fishing disaster.

If you feel like clearing the lungs, get a copy of the brochure *Walks in & Around*

Eyemouth (50p), available from the TIC, which describes a number of short walks. One of the most scenic is the 4-mile (6km) cliff-top path south to Burnmouth.

Sleeping & Eating

Hillcrest (☎ 50463; Coldingham Rd; r per person £19) The central Hillcrest is a traditional family home and has three rooms with shared bathroom. There's also a shared sitting room packed with hot drinks for guests. It's very handy for the harbour.

Churches Hotel (☎ 50401; www.churcheshotel.co.uk; Albert Rd; s £60-80, d £80-110; mains £11.50-16.50) This classy hotel has stylish and contemporary rooms, all kitted out slightly differently. A speck of dirt would be lonely in the bathrooms. The menu at its renowned seafood restaurant changes frequently according to the local catch, and the service is friendly and efficient.

Cafe Rialto (☎ 50278; 33 High St; snacks & light meals £1.50-4.50) A bright, modern tearoom on the main drag, Cafe Rialto serves baked potatoes, sandwiches, pastas and salads and does a full Scottish breakfast. There are also good options for vegetarians.

The pubs along the quay have suitably nautical names – the **Contented Sole** (☎ 50268; 3 Old Quay, Harbour Rd) and the **Ship Hotel** (☎ 750224; Harbour Rd) – and serve freshly caught seafood.

Getting There & Away

Eyemouth is 5 miles (8km) north of the Scotland–England border. Bus No C4 runs to/from Kelso via Duns (£3.75, 1½ hours, once daily Monday to Friday); bus Nos 34, 235, 236 and 253 go south to Berwick-upon-Tweed (15 minutes, every 30 minutes), which has the nearest train station. Bus No 253 from Berwick to Edinburgh (£4, 1¾ hours, six daily Monday to Saturday, three Sunday) passes through Eyemouth.

SOUTH OF EYEMOUTH

Further south, beyond the village of Foulden and about 3 miles (5km) west of the A1 along the B6461, is **Paxton House** (☎ 01289-386291; adult/child £6/3; 🕑 11am-5pm Apr-Oct, grounds open 10am-sunset Apr-Oct). It's beside the River Tweed and surrounded by over 32 hectares of parkland and gardens. It was built in 1758 by Patrick Home for his intended

RIDING OF THE MARCHES

The Riding of the Marches, or Common Riding, takes place in early summer in the major Border towns. Like many Scottish festivals it has ancient traditions, dating back to the Middle Ages when riders would be sent to the town boundary to check on the common lands. The colourful event normally involves extravagant convoys of horse riders following the town flag or standard, or as it's taken on a well-worn route. Festivities vary between towns, but usually involve lots of singing, sports, pageants, concerts and a screaming good time! If you want to zero in on the oldest and largest of the Ridings, head to Selkirk.

wife, the daughter of Prussia's Frederick the Great. Unfortunately she stood him up, but it was her loss; designed by the Adam family – brothers John, James and Robert – it's acknowledged as one of the finest 18th-century Palladian houses in Britain. It contains a large collection of Thomas Chippendale and Regency furniture, and its picture gallery houses paintings from the national galleries of Scotland.

In the grounds there are walking trails and a riverside museum on salmon fishing.

COLDINGHAM BAY & ST ABB'S HEAD

About 3 miles (5km) north of Eyemouth, this picturesque area is fantastic for those who love the great outdoors – there's loads to do as evidenced by the anglers, scuba divers, bird-watchers and walkers who flock here.

From the village of Coldingham, with its twisting, winding streets, take the B6438 road downhill to the small fishing village of St Abbs, a gorgeous, peaceful little village with a picture-perfect harbour nestled below the cliffs.

The clear, clean waters around St Abbs form part of **St Abbs & Eyemouth Voluntary Marine Reserve** (☎ 018907-71443; www.marine-reserve.org.uk; Rangers Cottage, Northfield, St Abbs), one of the best cold-water diving sites in Europe. The reserve is home to a wide variety of marine life, including grey seals and porpoises. Visibility is about 7m to 8m but has been recorded at 24m.

Drop by the **St Abbs Dive Centre** (☎ 018907-71237) at the post office; these folk provide plenty of advice on diving in the area and also sell and repair equipment. Divers can charter boats from **Dive St Abbs** (☎ 018907-71412) or **Donny** (☎ 018907-71377).

North of the village, the 78-hectare **St Abb's Head National Nature Reserve** (☎ 018907-71443; Rangers Cottage, Northfield St, St Abbs; £2 donation encouraged) is an ornithologist's wonderland, with large colonies of guillemots, kittiwakes, herring gulls, fulmars, razorbills and some puffins. You get to the reserve by following the trail that begins beside the Northfield Farm car park and Head Start café, on the road just west of St Abbs.

Sleeping

Mrs Wilson (☎ 018907-71468; 7 Murrayfield St, St Abbs; r per person £17.50-25) If you're staying in town, try this place which provides homely accommodation in clean and tidy facilities. Not the place to be throwing parties, it's popular with divers who are tuckered out after a day's exploration of the marine reserve's underwater treasures.

Back in Coldingham a signposted turn-off to the east leads three-quarters of a mile down to quiet, away-from-it-all Coldingham Bay, which has a sandy beach and a cliff-top walking trail to Eyemouth (3 miles/5km).

Coldingham Youth Hostel (SYHA; ☎ 0870 004 1111; The Mount; dm £10/8.50; Apr-Sep) This hostel is on the cliff above the southern side of the bay and is a grand old property with a slightly school-holiday camp feel. But you can't fault the excellent location set amid lush greenery with sweeping sea views. Facilities include a rather small kitchen and a pool table.

St Veda's Hotel (☎ 018907-71679; www.stvedas.co.uk; Coldingham Bay; r per person £25-30; mains £5-8;) Just opposite the path down to the beach, St Veda's is a cheery, British-beach-resort-style hotel. Make sure you get a sea-facing room, as the views can be magnificent. It's well kept, with a touch of faded grandeur, and is very popular on weekends over summer.

Getting There & Away

Bus No 253 between Edinburgh and Berwick-upon-Tweed (six daily Monday to Saturday, three Sunday) stops in Coldingham and St Abbs, as does bus No 235, which runs at least hourly from Eyemouth.

COCKBURNSPATH

The 16th-century Mercat Cross in Cockburnspath village square, about a mile inland from the coast, is the official eastern-end start of the Southern Upland Way.

KELSO

☎ 01573 / pop 5116

Kelso is a prosperous market town with a broad, cobbled square, flanked by Georgian buildings, at the hub of narrow streets. During the day it's a busy little place, but after 8pm you'll have the streets to yourself. The town has a lovely site at the junction of the Rivers Tweed and Teviot, and is one of the most enjoyable in the Borders.

Information

TIC (☎ 0870 608 0404; Town House, The Square; ⏰ daily Apr-Oct, Mon-Sat Nov-Mar)

Kelso Library (☎ 223171; Bowmont St; ⏰ 10am-1pm & 2-5pm Mon, Tue, Thu & Fri, plus 5.30-7pm Tue & Thu; 10am-1pm Wed; 9.30am-12.30pm Sat; 🖳) Internet access is free.

Sights & Activities

KELSO ABBEY

Once one of the richest abbeys in southern Scotland, **Kelso Abbey** (admission free; ⏰ 9.30am-6pm Mon-Sat, 2-6pm Sun Apr-Sep; 9.30am-4pm Mon-Sat, 2-4pm Sun Oct-Mar) was built by the Tironensians, an order founded at Tiron in Picardy and brought to the Borders around 1113 by David I. English raids in the 16th century reduced it to ruins, though what remains today is some of the finest surviving Romanesque architecture in Scotland.

Nearby, the rare, octagonal **Kelso Old Parish Church** (⏰ 10am-4pm Mon-Fri, May-Sep), built in 1773, is intriguing.

FLOORS CASTLE

Grandiose **Floors Castle** (☎ 223333; adult/child £5.75/3.25; ⏰ 10am-4.30pm Easter-Oct) is Scotland's largest inhabited mansion and overlooks the Tweed about a mile west of Kelso. Built by William Adam in the 1720s, the original Georgian simplicity was 'improved' during

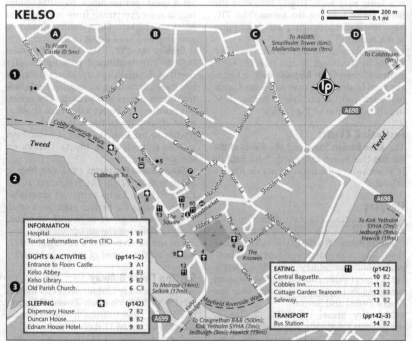

KELSO

INFORMATION	
Hospital	1 B1
Tourist Information Centre (TIC)	2 B2

SIGHTS & ACTIVITIES	(pp141–2)
Entrance to Floors Castle	3 A1
Kelso Abbey	4 B3
Kelso Library	5 B2
Old Parish Church	6 C3

SLEEPING	(p142)
Dispensary House	7 B2
Duncan House	8 B2
Ednam House Hotel	9 B3

EATING	(p142)
Central Baguette	10 B2
Cobbles Inn	11 B2
Cottage Garden Tearoom	12 B3
Safeway	13 B2

TRANSPORT	(pp142–3)
Bus Station	14 B2

SOUTHERN SCOTLAND

the 1840s with the addition of rather ridiculous battlements and turrets. Inside, keep an eye out for the vivid colours of the 17th-century Brussel tapestries in the drawing room and the intricate oak carvings in the ornate ballroom. Palatial windows reveal a ribbon of green countryside extending well beyond the estate. Unfortunately there is also a rather questionable collection of stuffed birds, easily interpreted as bad taste. Floors is unashamedly in the tourism business – you walk past the restaurant to enter and past the gift shop to leave.

WALKING

The **Pennine Way**, which starts its long journey at Edale in the Peat district, ends at Kirk Yetholm Youth Hostel, about 6 miles (10km) southeast of Kelso on the B6352.

The new **Borders Abbeys Way** walk will eventually link the great abbeys of Kelso, Jedburgh, Melrose and Dryburgh in a 65-mile (105km) circuit. At the time of writing only the Kelso–Jedburgh and Jedburgh–Hawick links were open; the Kelso–Jedburgh section (12 miles/19km) is a fairly easy walk, largely following the River Teviot between the towns. The TIC has a free leaflet with a map and description of the route.

Less ambitious walkers should leave The Square by Roxburgh St and take the signposted alley to **Cobby Riverside Walk**, a pleasant ramble along the river to Floors Castle (although you have to rejoin Roxburgh St to gain admission to the castle).

Festivals & Events

The **Kelso Borders Show** and the **Riding of the Marches** (see boxed text p140), both held in July, are two of the main events on Kelso's calendar.

Sleeping

Accommodation can be difficult to find during local festivals and over summer.

Duncan House (☎ 225682; Chalkheugh Tce; s £25, d £36-40) This is an elderly resident in the hospitality industry. Musty rooms lack sparkle but it's great value considering the location near the town centre, with a view over the Rivers Tweed and Teviot.

Dispensary House (☎ 228738; 106 Roxburgh St; r per person £28-30; ✗) A guesthouse with wonderful views, sumptuous rooms (one

with a four-poster bed) and clipped accents, it's a very refined place. The doubles have huge bathrooms and the single comes with a shared bathroom that has an enormous Victorian bathtub.

Ednam House Hotel (☎ 224168; contact@ednamhouse.com; Bridge St; s/d from £60/90; ✗) The genteel, Georgian Ednam House is the top place in town, with fine gardens overlooking the river and an excellent restaurant (see below). They organise salmon fishing on the Tweed River for £30 a day.

Craignethan B&B (☎ 224818; Jedburgh Rd; s/d £22/40) This is a welcoming, laid-back family home with stupendous views.

Eating

Cottage Garden Tea Room (☎ 225889; 7 Abbey Crt; light meals £1.50-4.50) This cosy tearoom, tucked away in a delightful sunny corner near the museum, also has a touch of al fresco dining. It serves fresh salads, home-baked snacks and light lunches, including a nut roast at lunchtime.

Central Baguette (52 The Square; large baguette £1.80; ☉ 8.30am-2.30pm Mon-Thu, 8.30am-3pm Fri & Sat) A great spot for lunch, baguette fillings here feature everything from hot haggis to Mexican chicken. On a sunny afternoon, grab one and head down to the river.

Cobbles Inn (☎ 223548; 7 Bowmont St; mains £6.50-10) This traditional pub, up an alley north of the main square, serves delicious bar meals, including an excellent rainbow trout with capers and prawns. The generous portions are better value than those of most other pubs in town. It unashamedly pitches to the tourist crowd, so you'll get a cross-section of the town's visitors on any given day.

Ednam House Restaurant (☎ 224168; Bridge St; 2-/3-course dinner £17/22) The restaurant at the Ednam House Hotel turns out delectable dinners and is the perfect place for a treat. Try a breast of goose or haunch of rabbit; there's a daily vegetarian option too.

For self-caterers there's a Safeway supermarket on the corner of the main square.

Getting There & Away

See Coldstream (p136) for details on the bus service to Berwick-upon-Tweed. Munro's bus No 20 runs to/from Jedburgh (£1.50, 25 minutes, up to 11 daily Monday to Saturday, five Sunday) and Hawick (£2.50, one hour, seven daily Monday to Saturday, four Sunday). There are also frequent services to Galashiels (£2.80, 55 minutes), and from there to Edinburgh.

AROUND KELSO
Smailholm Tower
Perched on a rocky knoll above a small lake, the narrow stone **Smailholm Tower** (☎ 01573-460365; Sandyknowe Farm, Smailholm; adult/child £2.20 /75p; ☺ 9.30am-6.30pm Apr-Sep; 9.30am-4.30pm Sat, 2-4.30pm Sun Oct-Mar) provides one of the most evocative sights in the Borders and keeps the bloody uncertainties of its history alive. Although the displays inside are sparse, the panoramic view from the top is worth the climb.

The nearby farm, **Sandyknowe**, was owned by Sir Walter Scott's grandfather. As Scott himself recognised, his imagination was fired by the ballads and stories he heard as a child at Sandyknowe, and by the ruined tower a stone's throw away.

The tower is 6 miles (9.5km) west of Kelso, a mile south of Smailholm village on the B6397. You pass through the farmyard to get to the tower. Munro's bus No 65 between Melrose and Kelso stops in Smailholm village.

Mellerstain House
Completed in 1778, **Mellerstain House** (☎ 01573-410225; Gordon; adult/child £5.50/3; ☺ 12.30-5pm Wed-Mon May-Sep, Easter, plus Sat & Sun Oct) is considered Scotland's finest Robert Adam-designed mansion. It is famous for its classic elegance, ornate interiors and plaster ceilings; the library in particular is outstanding. Give the garish upstairs bedrooms a miss, but have a peek at the bizarre puppet and doll collection in the gallery.

It's about 10 miles (16km) northwest of Kelso near Gordon. Take the A698 north from Kelso, then turn left onto the A6089. Munro's bus No 65 between Melrose and Kelso passes about a mile from Mellerstain House.

Town Yetholm & Kirk Yetholm
The twin villages of Town Yetholm and Kirk Yetholm, separated by Bowmont Water, are close to the English border, about 6 miles (10km) southeast of Kelso. Hill-walking centres, they lie at the northern end of the **Pennine Way** and on **St Cuthbert's Way** between Melrose and Lindisfarne (Holy Island) in Northumberland.

As the last stop on the Pennine Way, **Kirk Yetholm Youth Hostel** (SYHA; ☎ 0870 004 1132; Kirk Yetholm, Kelso; dm adult/child £9.50/8; ☺ Apr-Sep) is often busy – there's a twin room and two dorms (six and eight beds); book well in advance. Bus No 81 from Kelso runs up to seven times a day Monday to Saturday (three Sunday).

MELROSE
☎ 01896 / pop 1656
Tiny, charming Melrose is a polished village running on the well-greased wheels of tourism. This little enclave is a complete contrast with overbearing Galashiels, whose urban sprawl laps at its western edges. Sitting at the feet of the three heather-covered Eildon Hills, Melrose entices walkers and cyclists. It has a classic market square, some attractive parks and its most famous resident, one of the great abbey ruins.

Information
Melrose Library (☎ 823052; 18 Market Sq; ☺ 10am-1pm & 2.30-5pm Mon & Wed, 2.30-5pm & 5.30-7pm Fri)
Post office (Buccleuch St)
TIC (☎ 0870 608 0404; Abbey House, Abbey St; ☺ daily Apr-Oct, Mon-Sat Nov-Mar)

Sights
MELROSE ABBEY
Perhaps the most interesting of all the great Border abbeys, the red sandstone **Melrose Abbey** (☎ 822562; adult/child £3.30/1.20; ☺ 9.30am-6.30pm Apr-Sep; 9.30am-4.30pm Mon-Sat, 2-4.30pm Sun Oct-Mar) was repeatedly destroyed by the English in the 14th century. The remaining broken shell is pure Gothic and the ruins are famous for their decorative stonework – see if you can glimpse the pig gargoyle playing the bagpipes on the roof. You can climb to the top for tremendous views. The abbey was founded by David I in 1136 for Cistercian monks from Rievaulx in Yorkshire. It was rebuilt by Robert the Bruce, whose heart is buried here. The ruins date from the 14th and 15th centuries and were repaired by Sir Walter Scott in the 19th century.

The adjoining **museum** (free for abbey ticket holders) has many fine examples of 12th- to 15th-century stonework and pottery found in the area. Note the impressive remains of the 'great drain' outside – a medieval sewerage system.

TRIMONTIUM EXHIBITION

The small but absorbing **Trimontium Exhibition** (☎ 822651; The Ormiston, Market Sq; adult/child £1.50/1; ☟ 10.30am-4pm Apr-Oct) tells the story of the Roman fort of Trimontium (literally 'three hills') at nearby Newstead, and of life on the Scottish–Roman frontier. You can also join a 3½-hour guided **Trimontium Walk** to the Roman sites around Melrose; walks start at 1.30pm Thursday (and Tuesday July and August) and cost £2.80.

Activities

There are many attractive walks in the **Eildon Hills**, accessible via a footpath off Dingleton Rd (the B6359) south of the town, or via the trail along the River Tweed.

The **St Cuthbert's Way** long-distance path starts in Melrose, while the coast-to-coast **Southern Upland Way** passes through town. You can do a day's walk along St Cuthbert's Way as far as Harestanes (16 miles/26km), on the A68 near Jedburgh, and return to Melrose on the hourly Jedburgh–Galashiels bus. The **Tweed Cycle Way** also passes through Melrose.

Festivals & Events

In mid-April rugby followers fill the town to see the week-long **Melrose Rugby Sevens** competition.

Sleeping

Melrose B&Bs and hotels aren't cheap by Scottish standards but they are of a high standard; this would make a great place to treat yourself.

Melrose Youth Hostel (SYHA; ☎ 0870 004 1141; Priorwood; dm adult/child £12/10; ☟ late Mar-Oct; ▣) Housed in a large, Georgian mansion on the edge of town, these spick and span dorms are complemented by a big garden and BBQ area. Not a party place, this hostel is mainly used by walkers looking to turn in early. From the market square, follow the signposts to the A68.

Braidwood (☎ 822488; Buccleuch St; r per person £23-25) Mr Graham's popular town house near the abbey is an excellent place with high-quality facilities and a warm welcome. The small sparkling rooms are finely decorated, and there's home-baking too.

Little Fordel (☎ 822206; little.fordel@virgin.net; Abbey St; s/d £30/48) A top B&B, this little gem of a place is in a nook off Abbey St. There's

a ritzy double and a twin; both are large, brightly decorated and have polished wood furnishings.

Millars Hotel (☎ 822645; www.millarshotel.co.uk; Market Sq; s/d £50/85) The classy Millars, exuding warmth and professionalism, has some of the best rooms in town – tastefully furnished with attention to detail. The ones at the back are particularly cosy and quiet, and there's a good restaurant (see below).

Burts Hotel (☎ 822285; www.burtshotel.co.uk; Market Sq; s/d £52/94) Set in an early-18th-century house, and with an enviable reputation, Burts retains much of its period charm and has been run by the same couple for over 30 years. It would suit older visitors or families. Room No 5 is the best.

Eating

Marmion's Brasserie (☎ 822245; Buccleuch St; snacks £3-5, mains £13.50-15.50) This atmospheric, oak-panelled niche serves snacks all day, but the lunch and dinner menus include gastronomic delights such as roast quail, braised lamb and sweetbreads. For lunch the focaccias with creative fillings are a good choice.

Millars Hotel (☎ 822645; www.millarshotel.co.uk; Market Sq; lunch mains £7.50-9, dinner £15) The gourmet cuisine here is the best in town, as evidenced by the strong local contingent patronising the place. Millar's is happy to doctor their dishes to your culinary wishes.

Russell's Restaurant (☎ 822335; Market Sq; dishes £3.50-7.50; ☟ 9.30am-4.30pm Mon-Thu, 9.30am-5pm Fri, noon-5pm Sun) Russell's is a stylish little tearoom/restaurant with a large range of snacks and more substantial offerings such as a ploughman's lunch. They also brew an excellent mug of coffee.

Getting There & Away

There are First buses to/from Galashiels (£1.40, 20 minutes, frequent), Jedburgh (£2.40, 30 minutes, five daily Monday to Saturday), Peebles (£3.75, 1¼ hours, eight daily Monday to Saturday) and Edinburgh (£4.55, 2¼ hours, eight daily Monday to Saturday).

AROUND MELROSE
Dryburgh Abbey

The most beautiful and complete Border abbey is **Dryburgh Abbey** (☎ 01835-822381; adult/child £3/1; ☟ 9.30am-6.30pm Apr-Sep, 9.30am-4.30pm Mon-Sat, 2-4.30pm Sun Oct-Mar), partly because the

---

SIR WALTER SCOTT (1771–1832)

Sir Walter Scott is one of Scotland's greatest literary figures. It was here, rambling around the Borders countryside as a child, that he developed a passion for historical ballads and Scottish heroes.

Scott wrote a number of successful ballads. *The Lay of the Last Minstrel* (1805) was an early critical success; further works earning him an international reputation included *The Lady of the Lake* (1810), set around Loch Katrine and the Trossachs. He later turned his hand to novels and virtually invented the historical genre. *Waverley* (1814), which dealt with the 1745 Jacobite rebellion, set the classical pattern of the historical novel. Other works included *Guy Mannering* (1815) and *Rob Roy* (1817). In *Guy Mannering*, he wrote about the Border farmer Dandie Dinmont and his pack of dogs, which became so popular that they became known as Dandie Dinmont Terriers, the only breed of dog named after a literary character.

Later in life Scott wrote obsessively to stave off bankruptcy. His works virtually single-handedly revived interest in Scottish history and legend in the early 19th century. TICs stock a *Sir Walter Scott Trail* booklet, guiding you to many places associated with his life in the Borders.

---

neighbouring town of Dryburgh no longer exists (another victim of the wars), partly because it has a lovely site in a sheltered valley by the River Tweed, accompanied only by a symphony of birds. The abbey conjures up images of 12th-century monastic life more successfully than its counterparts in nearby towns. Dating from about 1150, it belonged to the Premonstratensians, a religious order founded in France. The pink-hued stone ruins were chosen as the burial place for Sir Walter Scott.

The abbey is 5 miles (8km) southeast of Melrose on the B6404 which passes famous **Scott's View** overlooking the valley. You can hike there along the southern bank of the River Tweed, or take a bus to the nearby village of Newtown St Boswells.

Abbotsford

Fans of Sir Walter Scott should visit his former residence, **Abbotsford** (☎ 01896-752043; adult/child £4/2; ❍ 9.30am-5pm Mon-Sat late Mar-Oct, 2-5pm Sun Mar-May & Oct, 9.30am-5pm Sun Jun-Sep). Probably drawing inspiration from the surrounding 'wild' countryside, he created an extraordinary collection of works. These are on display, as are many other personal possessions.

The mansion is about 2 miles (5km) west of Melrose between the River Tweed and the B6360. Frequent buses run between Galashiels and Melrose; alight at the Tweedbank roundabout and follow the signposts (it's a 15-minute walk). You can also walk from Melrose to Abbotsford in an hour along the southern bank of the Tweed.

GALASHIELS

☎ 01896 / pop 14,361

Galashiels has little to recommend it, during the day it's uninviting and in the evening it carries an air of menace, but it's an important transport hub for the Scottish Borders. Fortunately the charming town of Melrose is just 3 miles (5km) east.

The unmanned TIC is in the **Lochcarron Cashmere & Wool Centre** (☎ 751100; Waverley Mill, Huddersfield St; tours £2.50/free for adult/child; ❍ Mon-Sat year-round, plus Sun Jun-Sep). Tours of the woollen factory leave at 10am, 11.30am, 1.30pm and 2.30pm daily except Friday afternoon. The centre also houses a museum on Galashiels' history.

There are frequent buses to/from Edinburgh, Melrose, Hawick, Kelso and Peebles.

SELKIRK

☎ 01750 / pop 5742

Selkirk is a serene little town that climbs a steep ridge above the Ettrick Water, a tributary of the Tweed. Mills came to the area in the early 1800s, but today it's a quiet place with a couple of great attractions.

The helpful **TIC** (☎ 20054; Halliwell's Close; ❍ Apr-Oct) is tucked away off Market Sq. Inside is **Halliwell's House Museum** (☎ 20096; Halliwell's Close; admission free; ❍ 10am-5pm Mon-Sat, 2-4pm Sun late Mar-Jun, Sep & Oct; 10am-5pm Mon-Sat, 2-5pm Sun Jul & Aug), the oldest building in Selkirk (1712). The museum charts local history with an engrossing exhibition. Drop into **Sir Walter Scott's Court Room** (☎ 20096; Market Sq; admission free; ❍ 10am-4pm Mon-Sat Apr-Oct, plus 2-4pm Sun Jun-Aug), where the great man served as sheriff of Selkirk County. It houses an exhibition on his life and writings. There is also a fascinating account of the courageous explorer Mungo Park (born near Selkirk) and his search for the River Niger.

You're better off staying overnight in Melrose or Jedburgh, or try the **County Hotel** (☎ 21233; Market Sq; s/d £32.50/55; bar meals £6), which has comfortable rooms with small couches and is popular with golfers. It also serves good bar meals.

First bus No 95 and express bus X95 run hourly between Hawick, Selkirk, Galashiels and Edinburgh. From Selkirk to Edinburgh costs £4 (two hours).

JEDBURGH
☎ 01835 / pop 4090

The most popular of the Border towns, attractive Jedburgh is a lush, compact oasis, where many old buildings and *wynds* (narrow alleys) have been intelligently restored, inviting exploration by foot. It's constantly busy with domestic tourists, but wander into some of the pretty side streets and you won't hear a pin drop.

Information
Library (Castlegate; ❤ 10am-1pm & 2-5pm Mon-Fri, 5.30-7pm Mon & Fri) Free Internet access.

Post office (High St)

TIC (☎ 863170; Murray's Green; ❤ 9.30am-5pm Mon-Sat, 10am-5pm Sun Apr, May & Oct; 9am-6pm Mon-Sat, 10am-5pm Sun Jun & Sep; 9am-7pm Mon-Sat, 10am-6pm Sun Jul & Aug; 9.30am-4.30pm Mon-Sat Nov-Mar)

Sights
JEDBURGH ABBEY
Dominating the town skyline, **Jedburgh Abbey** (☎ 863925; Abbey Bridge End; adult/child £3.50/1.20; ❤ 9.30am-6.30pm Apr-Sep; 9.30am-4.30pm Mon-Sat, 2-4.30pm Sun Oct-Mar) was the first great Border abbey to be passed into state care, and it shows – numerous audio and visual presentations telling the abbey's story are scattered throughout the carefully preserved ruins. The red sandstone ruins are roofless but relatively intact and the ingenuity of the master mason can be seen in some of the rich (if somewhat faded) stone carvings in the nave (be careful of the staircase in the nave – it's slippery when wet). The abbey was founded in 1138 by David I as a priory for Augustinian canons.

MARY QUEEN OF SCOTS HOUSE
Mary stayed at this beautiful 16th-century **tower house** (☎ 863331; Queen St; adult/child £3/free; ❤ 10am-4.30pm Mon-Sat, 11am-4.30pm Sun Mar-Nov) in 1566 after her famous ride to visit the injured earl of Bothwell, her future husband, at Hermitage Castle (p147). The interesting displays evoke the sad saga of Mary's life.

Activities
A **town trail** takes you past all the interesting sites, while for those really wanting to stretch their legs, there are one- to three-hour walks around Jedburgh; leaflets are available from the TIC. See Kelso, p142, for information about the **Borders Abbeys Way**.

Festivals & Events
For two weeks in late June/early July the **Jethart Callant Festival** commemorates the perilous time when people rode out on horseback checking for English incursions (p140).

Sleeping
Jedburgh Camping & Caravanning Club Site (☎ 863393; Elliot Park, A68; tent sites £5.15-6.55) About a mile north of the town centre, opposite Jedburgh Woollen Mill, this site is set on the banks of Jed Water and is quiet and convenient, particularly if you're interested in fishing.

Craigowen (☎ 862604; suzy@foster21.fslife.co.uk; 30 High St; r per person £16-20; ✗) Craigowen is a terrific place close to everything in town. It has huge rooms that have been tastefully furnished and there are large windows overlooking the main drag. It's recommended for solo and female travellers.

Reiver's Rest (☎ 864977; relax@reiversrest.co.uk; 91 Bongate St; r £20) Travellers have recommended this friendly place, on the main A68 road about half a mile north of the town centre. There is only one room and it's fairly small (most of it taken up by an enormous double bed), but it's very private and there's even a built-in sauna!

Glenfriars Hotel (☎ 862000; glenfriars@edenroad.demon.co.uk; Friarsgate; s/d £30/50) The very comfortable Glenfriars Hotel, in a Georgian mansion, is classy in a run-down kind of way. Stupendous views, four-poster beds and plenty of space make this stylish, ramshackle hotel a favourite.

Eating

Cookie Jar (37 High St; breakfast £4.25, other meals £2-5)
This is a top café, with a bright little dining
area just perfect for a coffee and a snack.
The freshly prepared sandwiches, rolls
and sweet treats are too tempting for most
mortals. Grab a window seat for a bout of
people watching.

Simply Scottish (☎ 864696; 6-8 High St; dinner
mains £7-12, 3-course dinner £11.95) This buzzing bistro-style place serves good-value
snacks all day, plus an interesting á la
carte menu in the evenings, including
dishes such as venison casserole with red
wine and mushrooms. The bright décor,
cheery ambience, clinking glasses and
constant hum make for a relaxed dining
experience.

Forresters Restaurant (☎ 862380; 23 Castlegate;
mains £6-10) Recommended by locals, the Forresters has tasty options for carnivores and
an extensive wine list; it's a good spot for a
nightcap – there are 40 drams of whisky to
choose from.

Getting There & Away

Jedburgh has good bus connections to Hawick (£1.60, 25 minutes, at least hourly),
Melrose (£2.40, 30 minutes, five daily
Monday to Saturday) and Kelso (£1.50, 25
minutes, up to 11 daily Monday to Saturday, five Sunday). Munro's bus No 29 runs
from Edinburgh to Jedburgh (£5.30, two
hours, up to eight daily Monday to Saturday, five Sunday).

HAWICK

☎ 01450 / pop 14,573

Straddling the River Teviot, Hawick is
the largest town in the Borders and has
long been a major production centre for
knitwear. Most people come to Hawick to
shop: it's a bargain hunter's paradise with
numerous factory outlets including **Pringle**
(☎ 377644; Commercial Rd) and **Eric Hope Knitwear**
(☎ 370549; 58 High St). A full list is available
from the TIC.

The **TIC** (☎ 372547; 1 Tower Knowe; ☯ daily
Apr-Sep, Mon-Sat Oct, call for winter hours) is at the
western end of High St. In the same building (and with the same opening hours) is
Drumlanrig's Tower Visitor Centre (☎ 377615;
1 Tower Knowe; adult/child £2.50/free), which tells
the story of cross-border warfare from the
16th century.

Across the river, **Hawick Museum & Scott Art
Gallery** (☎ 373457; Wilton Lodge Park; admission free;
☯ 10am-noon & 1-4.45pm Mon-Fri, 2-4.45pm Sat & Sun
Apr-Sep; 1-4pm Mon-Fri, 2-4pm Sun Oct-Mar) has an interesting collection of mostly 19th-century
manufacturing and domestic memorabilia.

You'll be met with a cheery welcome
at the amiable **Bridgehouse B&B** (☎ 370094;
sergioshawick@aol.com; Sandbed; d/f £40/70). Rooms,
in a former stables dating back to 1760,
are neat as a pin and there's a café, bar and
great courtyard.

First bus No 72 runs to Melrose (£1.40,
50 minutes, roughly hourly) and Galashiels,
while the hourly bus No 95 and X95 connects Hawick with Galashiels, Selkirk and
Edinburgh (£4.25, two hours).

HERMITAGE CASTLE

A massive collection of stone, with a heavy
cubist beauty, **Hermitage Castle** (☎ 01387-
376222; adult/child £2/75p; ☯ 9.30am-6.30pm Apr-Sep,
call for possible Oct opening) sits isolated beside a
rushing stream surrounded by bleak, empty
moorland. Dating from the 13th century,
but substantially rebuilt in the 15th, it
embodies the brutal history of the Borders;
the stones themselves almost speak of the
past. Sir Walter Scott's favourite castle, it
is probably best known as the home of the
earl of Bothwell and the place to which
Mary, Queen of Scots, rode in 1566 to
see him after he had been wounded in a
border raid.

It's also where, in 1338, Sir William
Douglas imprisoned his enemy Sir Alexander Ramsay in a pit and deliberately starved
him to death. Ramsay survived for 17 days
by eating grain that trickled into his pit
(which can still be seen) from the granary
above. The castle is said to be haunted and
it certainly has a slightly spooky feel, especially when dark clouds gather.

The castle is about 12 miles (19km) south
of Hawick on the B6357.

PEEBLES

☎ 01721 / pop 8065

Although Peebles is lacking in stand-out
attractions, it's agreeable and picturesque
ambience will entice you to happily linger
for a couple of days. It's a good base for
exploring the area and is in a delightful
spot, set among rolling, wooded hills on
the banks of the River Tweed.

SOUTHERN SCOTLAND

The extremely helpful **TIC** (☎ 720138; High St; ☻ daily Apr-Dec, Mon-Sat Jan-Mar) will chase down accommodation for you.

Sights & Activities

Have a quick look at **Tweedale Museum & Gallery** (☎ 724820; High St; admission free; ☻ 10am-noon & 2-5pm year-round, plus 10am-1pm & 2-4pm Sat Easter-Oct) in the Chambers Institute. It's mainly given over to famous border sons such as Sir Walter Scott. There is also a 'museum' of a Victorian museum.

If it's sunny, the **riverside walk** along the River Tweed has plenty of grassed areas ideal for a picnic and there's a children's playground (near the main road bridge). You could even walk to **Neidpath Castle** (☎ 720333; adult/child £3/1; ☻ 10.30am-4.30pm Mon-Sat, 12.30-4.30pm Sun mid-Jun–early Sep, also limited days in May), a tower house perched on a bluff above the River Tweed. It's in a lovely spot, a mile west of the centre, with good views from the parapets.

Sleeping & Eating

Rosetta Caravan & Camping Park (☎ 720770; www.rosettacaravanpark.com; Rosetta Rd; tent site & 2 people £11; ☻ Apr-Oct) This award-winning camping ground, about half a mile north of the centre, has an exquisite green setting just minutes from town. There are plenty of amusements for the kids, such as a bowling green and a games room.

MacIver B&B (☎ 721073; 5 Innerleithen Rd; s/d £25/36; ✗) MacIver is not flash or luxurious, but rather dishevelled and a little eccentric, and that's why we like it. Always welcoming, informal and very friendly, it's a short walk from High St.

Cross Keys Hotel (☎ 724222; fax 724333; Northgate; s/d £32/56) The Cross Keys is a renovated 17th-century coaching inn and the current owners have maintained the tradition of fine hospitality. Some rooms are very large, though all are neat and well presented. There's a restaurant, and a recently renovated bar with real ales and live music at weekends.

Cringletie House Hotel & Restaurant (☎ 730233; www.cringletie.com; r per person from £75; lunch £7.95-19.50, 3-course dinner £34) This elegant baronial mansion 2 miles (3km) north of Peebles on the A703, calls itself a house, but that's being coy – it's a mansion. A very comfortable, baronial mansion, in fact, set in lovely grounds with an excellent restaurant.

Sunflower Restaurant (☎ 722420; 4 Bridgegate; mains lunch £7.50, dinner £9.95-14.95; ☻ 10am-5pm Sun-Wed, 10am-9pm Thu-Sat) The Sunflower, with its warm, yellow dining room, is in a quiet spot off the main drag. It serves good salads for lunch (such as warm chicken pea salad with melted goat's cheese) and has an admirable menu in the evenings, with dishes such as Thai fishcakes, and venison with cranberry sauce and lentil mash.

Getting There & Around

The bus stop is beside the post office on Eastgate. First bus No 62 runs hourly to Edinburgh (£3.75, 1¼ hours), Galashiels (£3.50, 45 minutes) and Melrose (£3.75, 1¼ hours).

The Bicycle Works (☎ 723423; www.thebicycleworks.co.uk; 3 High St; ☻ 10am-6pm) hires good mountain bikes with all-round disc brakes for £10/16 for a half/full day. They also do repairs.

AROUND PEEBLES
Traquair House

One of Scotland's great country houses, **Traquair House** (☎ 01896-830323; www.traquair.co.uk; Innerleithen; adult/child £5.60/3.10; ☻ 10.30am-5.30pm Jun-Aug, noon-5pm mid-Apr–May & Sep, 11am-4pm Oct) has a powerful ethereal beauty and an exploration here is like time travel. Odd, sloping floors and a musty smell bestow a genuine feel, and parts of the building are believed to have been constructed long before the first official record of its existence in 1107. The massive tower house was gradually expanded over the next 500 years, but has remained virtually unchanged since 1642.

Since the 15th century, the house has belonged to various branches of the Stuart family, and the family's unwavering Catholicism and loyalty to the Stuart cause is largely why development ceased when it did. The family's estate, wealth and influence were gradually whittled down after the Reformation and there was neither the opportunity nor, one suspects, the will to make any changes.

One of its most interesting places is the concealed room where priests secretly lived and performed Mass – up until 1829 when the Catholic Emancipation Act was finally passed. Other beautiful, time-worn rooms hold fascinating relics, including the cradle used by Mary for her son, James VI of Scotland (who also became James I of England),

and many letters written by the Stuart pretenders to their supporters.

In addition to the house, there's a **garden maze**, an **art gallery**, a small **brewery** producing the tasty Bear Ale, and an active craft community. The **Scottish Beer Festival** takes place here in late May and there's the Traquair Fair in early August.

Traquair is 1½ miles south of Innerleithen, about 6 miles (9.5km) southeast of Peebles. Bus C1 departs from Peebles at 10.15am for Traquair daily and returns at 3.05pm.

SOUTH LANARKSHIRE

South Lanarkshire combines a highly urbanised area with scenically gorgeous country around the old milling area of New Lanark, which is by far the biggest drawcard of the region. If you're coming up to Scotland on the M74 there are some excellent places to break your journey.

South and east of Glasgow are the large satellite towns of **East Kilbride**, **Hamilton**, **Motherwell** and **Coatbridge**. These are, for the most part, urban nightmares, and day trips only from Glasgow are recommended. Note also that you're far better off on public transport, given the plethora of roundabouts and one-way streets in these towns.

BLANTYRE

Blantyre's most famous son is David Livingstone, the epitome of the Victorian missionary-explorer, who opened up central Africa to European religion. Visitors with an interest in Africa shouldn't miss the absorbing **David Livingstone Centre** (☎ 01698-823140; 165 Station Rd; adult/child £3.50/2.60; ☑ 10am-5pm Mon-Sat, 12.30-5pm Sun), which tells the story of his life. In 30 years it's estimated he travelled 29,000 miles (46,000km), mostly on foot – the sheer tenacity of the man was incredible! The centre is just downhill from Blantyre train station.

It's a 30-minute walk along the river to **Bothwell Castle** (☎ 01698-816894; adult/child £2.20/75p; ☑ 9.30am-6.30pm Apr-Sep; 9.30am-4.30pm Mon-Wed & Sat, 9.30am-12.30pm Thu, 2-4.30pm Sun Oct-Mar), regarded as the finest 13th-century castle in Scotland. The stark, roofless, red sandstone ruins are substantial and, largely due to their beautiful green setting,

romantic. The castle is very popular with wedding parties.

Trains run from Glasgow Central to Blantyre (£2.70/3.60 peak/off-peak return, 20 minutes, twice hourly).

LANARK & NEW LANARK
☎ 01555 / pop 8253

Below the market town of Lanark, in an attractive gorge by the River Clyde, is the World Heritage site of **New Lanark** – an intriguing collection of restored mill buildings and warehouses.

Once the largest cotton-spinning complex in Britain, it was better known for the pioneering social experiments of Robert Owen, who managed the mill from 1800. New Lanark is really a memorial to this enlightened capitalist. He provided his workers with housing, a cooperative store (the inspiration for the modern cooperative movement), the world's first nursery school for children, a school with adult education classes, a sick-pay fund for workers and a social centre he called the New Institute for the Formation of Character. You'll need at least half a day to explore this large site as there's plenty to see.

Information
There are two banks with ATMs on High St.
Lanark Health Centre (☎ 665522)
Post office (St Leonards St)
TIC (☎ 661661; Horsemarket, Ladyacre Rd, Lanark; ☑ 10am-5pm daily Apr-Oct, 10am-5pm Mon-Sat Nov-Mar) Close to the bus and train stations.

Sights & Activities
NEW LANARK
The best way to get the feel of New Lanark is to wander round the outside of this impressive place. What must once have been a thriving, noisy, grimy industrial village, pumping out enough cotton to wrap the planet, is now a peaceful oasis with only the swishing of trees and the rushing of the River Clyde to be heard.

At the **New Lanark Visitor Centre** (☎ 661345; www.newlanark.org; New Lanark Mills; adult/child/family £5.95/3.95/16.95; ☑ 11am-5pm) you need to purchase a ticket to enter the main attractions. These include the **New Millennium Experience**, an innovative high-tech ride to New Lanark's past and possible future. The kids will love it as it's reminiscent of a fun-park ride, although the 'do good for all mankind' theme is a little overbearing.

Also included in your admission is a **millworker's house**, Robert Owen's **home** and his **school**, where you can see exhibitions on 'saving New Lanark' as well as the **Annie McLeod Experience** – an audiovisual in which the spirit of a 10-year-old mill girl describes life here in 1820. There's also a 1920s-style **village store**.

FALLS OF CLYDE

After you've seen New Lanark you can then walk up to the **Falls of Clyde** (one hour) through the beautiful nature reserve managed by the Scottish Wildlife Trust. But before you go, drop into the **Falls of Clyde Wildlife Centre** (☎ 665262; admission free; ☿ 11am-5pm Mar-Dec, noon-4pm Jan & Feb) by the river in New Lanark. There are exhibitions on peregrine falcons, woodlands and peatland conservation.

OTHER WALKS

You can organise bat walks (£2.50) or badger watching (£5) at the Falls of Clyde Wildlife Centre (see above). There's also a walk for 2½ miles (4km) to the beautiful **Cora Linn** (waterfalls that inspired both Turner and Wordsworth) and beyond them, **Bonnington Linn**.

CRAIGNETHAN CASTLE

Craignethan Castle (☎ 860364; Tillietudlem; adult/child £2.20/75p; ☿ 9.30am-6.30pm Apr-Sep, 9.30am-4.30pm Mon-Sat, 2-4.30pm Sun Oct-Mar; closed Thu afternoon & Fri Oct) has a very authentic feel – it hasn't been restored beyond recognition – and is in a stunning, tranquil spot too. You'll feel miles from anywhere, so bring a picnic and make a day of it.

With a commanding position above the River Nethan, this extensive ruin includes a virtually intact tower house and a **caponier** (unique in the UK) – a small gun emplacement with holes in the wall so men with handguns could pick off attackers. The chilly chambers under the tower house are quite eerie.

Craignethan is 5 miles (8km) northwest of Lanark. If you don't have your own transport, take an hourly Lanark–Hamilton bus to Crossford, then follow the footpath along the northern bank of the River Nethan (20 minutes).

Sleeping

New Lanark Youth Hostel (SYHA; ☎ 0870 004 1143; Wee Row, Rosedale St, New Lanark; dm adult/child £11/9, tw £22; ☿ Mar-Oct; ▣) This hostel has a great location in an old mill building by the River Clyde. There are four-bed dorms with attached bathroom and one twin room. It makes a great base for exploring this fascinating World Heritage site.

Summerlea (☎ 664889; 32 Hyndford Rd; s/d £25/40; ☒) Just up from the TIC, this modern guesthouse is one of the more central choices available. It has all the comforts of home, including a breakfast that enables a 24-hour fast afterwards.

Mrs Berkley (☎ 665487; mary@martinberkley.com; 159 Hyndford Rd; r per person £18-25; ☒) A green oasis next to the thumping A73, Mrs Berkley provides simple, traditional accommodation on a lovely property.

Clarkston Farmhouse (☎ 663751; B7018, Kirkfieldbank; s/d £26/44; ☒) If you fancy a stay on a farm with panoramic views of the countryside and a hearty breakfast, this place is a good choice. There are two twins and one double room. You'll receive a hearty welcome and an even heartier breakfast. It's on the A72 to Hamilton.

New Lanark Mill Hotel (☎ 667200; hotel@newlanark.org; Mill One, New Lanark; s/d from £60/80, cottages from £45; ☒) Cleverly converted from an 18th-century mill, this hotel is full of character and a stone's throw from the major attractions. It has luxury rooms or self-catering accommodation in cottages. The hotel also serves meals, see Eating (p151).

Eating

Prego (☎ 666300; 3 High St; mains £6.50-12) This perpetually busy Italian restaurant manages to create a modern ambience in a traditional setting. It dishes out excellent pasta, pizza and fillet steak at very reasonable prices, and the service matches the cuisine. Try the goat's cheese and tomato bruschetta.

Crown Tavern (☎ 664639; 17 Hope St; mains £6-12) Off the main street, the Crowny is a local secret…oh, was a local secret. It's a highly regarded place that does good bar meals and even better food (pasta, seafood and vegetarian dishes) in the evenings in its restaurant.

Cafe Espresso (Bannatyne St; light meals from £2.50) For a strong coffee after tramping around New Lanark all day, drop into this café, pull up a pew by the window and watch Lanark life tick by.

Mill Pantry (snacks £1.80-3.50; 10am-5pm) In the New Lanark Visitor Centre, the pantry is good for pick-me-ups.

New Lanark Mill Hotel (667200; hotel@new lanark.org; Mill One, New Lanark; bar meals £7, 2-course dinner £15) The Mill has creative and tasty bar meals.

Self-caterers can stock up at the large Somerfield supermarket, conveniently situated by the TIC.

Getting There & Around

Lanark is 25 miles southeast of Glasgow. Express buses from Glasgow, run by Irvine's Coaches, make the hourly run from Monday to Saturday (£4, one hour). Trains also run daily between Glasgow Central and Lanark (£4.20, 55 minutes, every 30 minutes).

There's an hourly bus service from the train station (daily) to/from New Lanark. If you need a taxi, call **Clydewide** (663221).

BIGGAR

01899 / pop 2098

Biggar is a pleasant town in a rural setting dominated by Tinto Hill (712m). The town is well worth a visit – it probably has more museums and attractions per inhabitant than anywhere else its size.

Information

Health Centre (220383; South Croft Rd)
Post office (High St)
Royal Bank ATM (High St)
TIC (221066; 155 High St; Mon-Sat year-round, plus Sun Jun-Aug)

Sights

The **Biggar Museums Trust** (221050) looks after four major museums in the town.

Moat Park Heritage Centre (221050; Kirkstyle; adult/child £2/1; 11am-4.30pm Mon-Sat, 2-4.30pm Sun Easter–mid-Oct), in a renovated church, covers the history of the area with geological and archaeological displays.

Greenhill Covenanter's House (221050; Burnbrae; adult/child £1/50p; 2-4.30pm Sat & Sun May-Sep) is an intelligently reconstructed farmhouse, with 17th-century furnishings and artefacts relating to the fascinating story of the local Covenanters, who valiantly defied their king to protect their religious beliefs.

Gladstone Court (221050; North Back Rd; adult/child £2/1; 11am-4.30pm Mon-Sat, 2-4.30pm Sun Easter–mid-Oct) is an indoor street museum with historic nook-and-cranny shops that you can pop into to steal a glimpse of the past. Don't miss the old printing press and the Albion A2 Dogcart, one of the oldest British cars still around.

Gasworks Museum (221050; Gasworks Lane; adult/child £1/50p; 2-5pm Jun-Sep) is the only coal-fired gasworks left in Scotland. The gasworks were originally opened in 1839. There's a video to explain its operation.

Biggar Puppet Theatre (220631; Broughton Rd; all seats £5, guided tours adult/child £2.50/2; 10am-4.30pm Tue-Sat) has miniature Victorian puppets and bizarre modern ones over 1m high that glow in the dark. There are several ultraviolet displays but you shouldn't need your sunglasses.

Tinto Hill dominates the town. The hill is a straightforward ascent by its northern ridge from Thankerton.

Sleeping & Eating

School Green Cottage (220388; iburness@talk21 .com; 1 Kirkstyle; r per person £20;) This cottage has a couple of decent rooms and is close to the Gasworks, but be warned – there's no puffin' on the premises.

Cornhill House (220001; www.cornhillhousehotel .com; Coulter; s/d £50/70; mains £6-18) This is a well-appointed place, complete with turrets, and is in a peaceful setting 2 miles (3km) southwest of Biggar. The rooms are good value, particularly those that have been refurbished, and a three-course breakfast is included. Its excellent restaurant opens for lunch and dinner.

La Capannina Restaurant (221032; 55 High St; pasta £5.75-8, grills £11-15) This intimate Italian restaurant, around the corner from School Green Cottage, dishes up pasta with panache. It's good for a glass of wine too.

Townhead Cafe (220159; 185 High St; snacks & light meals under £5) is popular with families and has outdoor seating for when the sun pokes through the clouds.

Getting There & Away

Biggar is 33 miles (53km) southeast of Glasgow. McEwan's bus No 100 runs to/from Edinburgh (£3.30, 1¼ hours, six daily). HAD Coaches bus No 191 runs hourly to/from Lanark (£1.80, 30 minutes).

ABINGTON

☎ 01864

Abington, 35 miles (56km) south of Glasgow, has a 24-hour motorway service station with a **TIC** (☎ 502436; 🕐 10am-5pm). In Abington village, you'll find a general store, post office, tearoom and Royal Bank (no ATM). If you need to stay overnight, try the peaceful **Holmlands Country House** ☎ www.holmlandsscotland.co.uk; 22 Carlisle Rd, Crawford s/d £25/45), which is in a pleasant spot, sheltered from the motorway.

DOUGLAS

☎ 01555 / pop 1676

Douglas has close ties to Scottish history, which began during the Wars of Independence when the Good Sir James Douglas fought alongside Robert the Bruce. Historically it's very interesting but it's also very rundown, so visit on a day trip only and bring a packed lunch (there's nowhere to buy food).

The excellent **St Bride's Church** (☎ 851657; Main St; admission free) brings to life these historical links. The 14th-century choir stalls and nave contain three Douglas family wall-tombs, including one for the Good Sir James, who was killed in Spain in 1330 while taking Robert the Bruce's heart to the Holy Land. Look out for the lead-encased hearts of James and Archibald, 5th earl of Angus (also known as 'Bell-the-Cat', one of the most colourful figures in Scottish history), on the floor of the chapel. The superb 16th-century clock tower has the oldest working clock in Scotland (1565). **Mrs Cowan** (☎ 851657; 2 Clyde Rd) behind the Crosskeys Inn, holds the key for the church.

Douglas is about 7 miles (11km) northwest of Abington.

AYRSHIRE

Faded, retro holiday towns by the seaside give Ayrshire a unique flavour. The region has both rich farmland and spectacular coastal scenery, which inspired Robert Adams to build Culzean Castle here, one of the finest stately homes in the country.

It's also the birthplace of the famous poet Robert Burns and there's enough Burns memorabilia to satisfy his most fanatic admirers. Most attractions are Burns or golf related. It was at Prestwick Golf Club that the major golf tournament, the British Open Championship, was initiated in 1860. The region's main drawcard, however, is the delightful Isle of Arran, the most varied and scenic of the southern Hebridean islands and easily accessible.

GETTING THERE & AROUND

Stagecoach Western (☎ 01292-613500) is the main bus operator on the mainland. On Arran **Western** (☎ 01770-302000) and **Royal Mail** (☎ 01463-256200) buses whizz you around the island, while **CalMac** (☎ 01770-302166) ferries will get you there from the mainland (p158).

NORTH AYRSHIRE
Largs

☎ 01475 / pop 11,241

Largs has a kitsch, buried-in-the-past, resort-style waterfront that is loads of fun. You need to approach the amusements, old-fashioned eateries and bouncing castle with the right attitude – on a sunny day buy an ice cream and go for a stroll to check out this slice of retro Scotland.

There's a **TIC** (☎ 01292-678100; 🕐 Easter-Oct) at the train station. The **post office** (Aitken St) is just off Main St.

Largs hosts a **Viking festival** during the first week in September. The festival celebrates the battle of Largs (1263) and the end of Viking political domination in Scotland.

The main attraction in Largs is the award-winning **Vikingar!** (☎ 689777; Greenock Rd; adult/child £4/3; 🕐 10.30am-5.30pm Sun-Fri, 12.30-3.30pm Sat Apr-Sep; 10.30am-3.30pm Mon-Fri & Sun, 12.30-3.30pm Sat Oct & Mar; 12.30-3.30pm Sat, 10.30am-3.30pm Sun Nov & Feb) This multimedia exhibition describes Viking influence in Scotland until its demise at the Battle of Largs in 1263. Tours with staff in Viking outfits run every half-hour. There's also a theatre, cinema, café, shop, swimming pool and leisure centre. To get here, follow the A78 coast road north from the TIC. You can't miss it, it's the only place with a longship outside.

SLEEPING & EATING

Glenroy Guest House (☎ 674220; 3 Charles St; r per person £17; ✗) They don't bother locking the doors at Glenroy – always a good sign. Typical of the friendliness of this town, Glenroy is the last B&B in a street full of 'em. It's a stone's throw from the water and a short walk into town. Rooms upstairs share a bathroom, but are comfortable, clean and all a good size.

Glendarroch (☎ 676305; 24 Irvine Rd; r per person £20; ✕) This B&B typifies Scottish hospitality – the rooms are well kept and the owner is friendly without being intrusive. If it's full they'll probably ring around to try and find you something else.

Brisbane House Hotel (☎ 687200; www.maksu -group.co.uk; The Esplanade, Greenock Rd; s/d from £75/ 85) A genteel place standing proudly on the foreshore, Brisbane House is set in lovely gardens and has luxury rooms, some with spas and sea views. Children under five stay for free and there are cots available.

Toby's Bar (☎ 687183; 68 Gallowgate; mains £5) Squeezed in among the amusements on the foreshore, Toby's (with the Blues Brothers standing guard out front) offers good, reliable pub food. Try the Indian tika masala or a chilli beef burrito.

There's a large Safeway supermarket beyond the southern end of Main St.

GETTING THERE & AWAY
Largs is 32 miles (51km) west of Glasgow by road. Buses run to Greenock (£2.80, 45 minutes, half-hourly) and at least half-hourly to Ardrossan (£2.30, 30 minutes), Irvine (£2.70, 50 minutes) and Ayr (£4.05, 1¼ hours). There are trains to Largs from Glasgow Central (£5, one hour, hourly).

Isle of Great Cumbrae
☎ 01475/pop 1200
Walking or cycling is the best way to explore this accessible, hilly island, ideal for a day trip from Largs. It's only 4 miles (6km) long, but it's called 'great' because it's bigger than privately owned Little Cumbrae island, just to the south.

Millport is the only town, and on its main street around the bay you'll find a post office, supermarket, bank (with ATM), two fish and chip shops and a couple of cafés.

The town boasts Europe's smallest cathedral, the lovely **Cathedral of the Isles** (☎ 530353; College St; admission free; ☽ daylight hours), which was completed in 1851. Just east of town is the interesting **Robertson Museum & Aquarium** (☎ 530581; adult/child £1.50/1; ☽ 9.30am-12.15pm & 2-4.30pm Mon-Fri year-round, plus Sat Jun-Sep). A short way along the coast from the aquarium is a remarkable rock feature, the **Lion**.

The **Museum of the Cumbraes** (☎ 01294-464174; Garrison Grounds; admission free; ☽ 10am-1pm & 2-5pm Thu-Tue Apr-Sep) presents the unique life of Cumbrae Island through an excellent collection of photographs and local regalia.

Rural parts of the island are very pleasant for cycling; the narrow Inner Circle Rd is a particularly good cycle route. There are several bike-hire places in Millport, including **Mapes** (☎ 530444; 3-5 Guildford St; 1/6 hr £1.80/4).

If you're staying overnight on the island, try the unusual **College of the Holy Spirit** (☎ 530353, fax 530204; College St; r per person £18-24), right next to the cathedral; there's a refectory-style dining room and a library.

A frequent 15-minute CalMac ferry ride links Largs with Great Cumbrae (passenger/car £3.80/16.55). Buses meet the ferries for the 3½-mile journey to Millport (£2 return).

Irvine
☎ 01294 / pop 33090
You have to admire the attractive redevelopment of **Irvine Harbourside** – it typifies the regeneration of old port areas in Scotland, and has turned into a healthy tourist puller. The cobbled street **Linthouse Vennel** is lined with impressive buildings.

Boat-lovers should check out the **Scottish Maritime Museum** (☎ 278283; Gottries Rd, Harbourside; family/adult/child £5/2.50/1.75; ☽ 10am-5pm), which has various ships you can clamber about on, and visitors can also see a shipyard-worker's restored flat.

You're better off staying in Ayr or Largs, but you could try the seafront **Harbour Guest House** (☎ 276212, 07787-565817; 1 Harbour St; s/d with continental breakfast £22/30) in the heart of the impressive redeveloped area. It's in a handy spot to most attractions and the best pubs.

If you're feeling peckish, drop into the wonderful **Ship Inn** (☎ 279722; 120 Harbour St; mains £6.50-8.50). It's the oldest pub in Irvine, built in 1597, serves tasty bar meals and has bucket loads of character.

GETTING THERE & AWAY
Irvine is 26 miles (42km) from Glasgow. Buses depart from High St (Irvine Cross) for Ayr (£2.50, 30 minutes, every 20 minutes Monday to Saturday, every two hours Sunday), and Largs (£2.70, 45 minutes, every 30 minutes Monday to Saturday, every two hours Sunday). Trains run to/from Glasgow

Central (£4.50, half-hourly, 35 minutes); in the other direction they go to Ayr.

Ardrossan

☎ 01294 / pop 11,000

The main reason – OK the *only* reason – for coming here, is to catch a CalMac ferry to Arran. Trains leave Glasgow Central (£4.70, one hour, four or five daily) to connect with ferries.

Ardrossan is very rundown and if you're hungry you're better off saving your appetite for more palatable surrounds, which beckon just across the bay.

If you need a B&B, **Edenmore Guest House** (☎ 462306, fax 604016; 47 Parkhouse Rd; r per person £18-25) is the saving grace of this ramshackle town. It's very friendly and offers small, spotless rooms and a hearty welcome – nothing seems too much trouble for the owner. Room No 4 is the best double. It's just off the main A78 and offers evening meals (thank goodness!).

ISLE OF ARRAN

☎ 01770 / pop 4800

Enchanting Arran is often bypassed by international visitors in favour of its better known neighbours. What a mistake! This island is a visual feast and has some top-class attractions. Short-term visitors to Scotland, in particular, should scribble Arran into their quick-fire itinerary – the variations in Scotland's dramatic landscape can all be experienced on this one small island.

To join the real trend-setting crowd, leave the Gucci at home and don walking gear or jump on a bicycle. Arran offers some challenging walks in the mountainous north, often compared to the Highlands, while the island's circular road is very popular with cyclists. In the south the land rises and falls more gently (although it's no less spectacular), similar to the rest of southern Scotland.

The island's many watering holes are legendary and over summer most have regular live music sessions.

Orientation & Information

The ferry from Ardrossan docks at Brodick, the island's main town. To the south, Lamlash is actually the capital and, like nearby Whiting Bay, a popular seaside resort. From the village of Lochranza in the

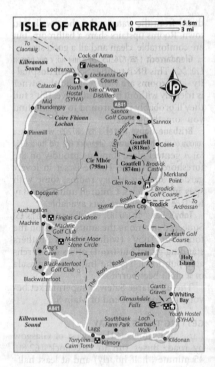

ISLE OF ARRAN

north there's a ferry link to Claonaig on the Kintyre peninsula.

Near Brodick pier you'll find the helpful **TIC** (☎ 303774). Also in Brodick are banks with ATMs. Free Internet access is available in Blackwaterfoot at the **Blackwaterfoot Lodge** (☎ 860202) and in Kildonan at the **Kildonan Hotel** (☎ 820207). The **hospital** (☎ 600777) is in Lamlash. There's a laundry by the Collins Good Food Shop (next to the River Cloy) in Brodick.

For more information about Arran, check out the websites at www.ayrshire-arran.com or www.arrantourism.com.

Sights

BRODICK

Most visitors arrive in Brodick, the heartbeat of the island, and congregate along the coastal road to admire the town's long curving bay.

Brodick Castle & Park (☎ 302202; adult/child castle & park £7/5.25, park only £3.50/2.60; ☼ castle 11am-4.30pm Apr-Oct, park 9.30am-sunset) is 2½ miles (4km) north of Brodick. The first impression is that of an animal morgue as you enter via the hunting gallery, wallpapered with prized deer heads. On your way to the formal dining room (with its peculiar table furnishings) note the intricacy of the fireplace in the library. The castle has rather more of a lived-in feel than some National Trust for Scotland (NTS) properties. Only a small portion is open to visitors. The extensive grounds, now a country park with various trails among the rhododendrons, justify the steep entry fee.

As you follow the coast along Brodick Bay, look out for **seals**, often seen on the rocks around Merkland Point. Two types live in these waters, the Atlantic grey and the common seal. They're actually quite easy to tell apart – the common seal has a face like a dog; the Atlantic grey seal has a Roman nose.

CORRIE

The coast road continues to the small, pretty village of Corrie, where there's a shop and hotel, and one of the tracks up **Goatfell** (the island's tallest peak) starts here. Corrie Village Shop sells wonderful sculptures by local artist Marvin Elliot. After **Sannox**, with a sandy beach and great views of the mountains, the road cuts inland. Heading to the very north, on the island's main road, visitors weave through lush glens flanked by Arran's towering mountain splendour.

LOCHRANZA

Lochranza is a village in a small bay at the north of the island. On a promontory stand the ruins of the 13th-century **Lochranza Castle** (admission free; key available from the Lochranza shop), said to be the inspiration for the castle in *The Black Island*, Hergé's Tintin adventure. Also in Lochranza is **Isle of Arran Distillers** (☎ 830264; tours adult/child £3.50/free; ☺ 10am-5pm), which conducts innovative tours of its facilities including an obligatory dram. Just under the Cock of Arran is **Lochranza Studio Gallery**, where painter Ian Buchanan, a self-confessed island addict, recreates Hebridean magic in vivid watercolours.

WEST COAST

On the western side of the island, reached by the String Rd across the centre (or the coast road), is the **Machrie Moor Stone Circle**, upright sandstone slabs erected around 6000 years ago. It's an eerie place, and these are the most impressive of the six stone circles on the island. There's another group at nearby Auchagallon, surrounding a Bronze Age burial cairn.

Blackwaterfoot is the largest village on the west coast; it has a shop/post office and two hotels. You can walk to King's Cave from here, via Drumadoon Farm – Arran is one of several islands that lay claim to a cave where Robert the Bruce had his famous arachnid encounter (p26). This walk could be combined with a visit to the Machrie stones.

SOUTH COAST

The landscape in the southern part of the island is much gentler; the road drops into little wooded valleys, and it's particularly lovely around **Lagg**. There's a 10-minute walk from Lagg post office to **Torrylin Cairn**, a chambered tomb over 4000 years old where at least eight bodies were found. By the roadside at East Bennan, there's **Southbank Farm Park** (☎ 820206; adult/child £3.50/2.50; ☺ 10am-5.30pm Sun-Fri Easter-Oct), with lots of beasts, including pygmy goats, Shetland ponies and those wonderful hairy Highland cattle. It's a great spot to take the kids. **Kildonan** has pleasant sandy beaches, two hotels, a campground and an ivy-clad ruined castle.

In **Whiting Bay** you'll find small sandy beaches, a village shop, post office and craft shops.

LAMLASH

Lamlash is an upmarket town (even the streets feel wider here) in a gorgeous setting, strung out along the beachfront. The bay was used as a safe anchorage by the Navy during WWI and WWII.

Just off the coast is **Holy Island**, owned by the Samye Ling Tibetan Centre and used as a retreat, but day visits are allowed. The **ferry** (☎ 600998) makes eight trips a day (£8, 15 minutes) from Lamlash and runs between May and September. No dogs, alcohol or fires are allowed on the island. There's a good walk to the top of the hill (314m), taking two or three hours return.

Activities

Drop into the TIC for plenty of walking and cycling suggestions around the island.

The walk up and down **Goatfell** takes up to eight hours return, starting in Brodick and finishing in the grounds of Brodick Castle. If the weather's fine, there are superb views to Ben Lomond and the coast of Northern Ireland. It can, however, be very cold and windy up there; take the appropriate maps (available at the TIC), waterproof gear and a compass.

Another good walk on a marked path goes up to **Coire Fhionn Lochan** from Mid Thundergay; it takes about an hour to reach the loch. You can continue up to the top of **Beinn Bhreac** (711m), taking another 1½ hours from the loch.

More moderate walks include the trail through Glen Sannox, which goes from the village of Sannox up the burn, a two-hour return trip. From Whiting Bay Youth Hostel there are easy one-hour walks through the forest to the **Giant's Graves** and **Glenashdale Falls**, and back – keep an eye out for Golden Eagles and other birds of prey.

The 50-mile (60km) circuit on the coastal road is popular with cyclists and has few serious hills – more in the south than the north.

Festivals & Events

The week-long **Arran Folk Festival** (☎ 302623; www.arranfolkfestival.org) takes place in early June. There are also local village festivals from June to September.

Sleeping

BUDGET

Camping isn't allowed without permission from the landowner but there are several camping grounds (open April to October).

Glen Rosa Farm (☎ 302380; sites per person £2.50) In a lush glen by a river, 2 miles (3km) from Brodick, the large Glen Rosa has plenty of nooks and crannies to pitch a tent. It's remote camping with basic facilities (cold water and toilets only). To get there from Brodick head north, take the String Rd and then turn right almost immediately on the single-track road signed to Glen Rosa. After about 400m, on the left is a white house where you book in; the campground is a bit further down the road.

Seal Shore Camping Site (☎ 820320; Kildonan; sites per person/tent £4/50p) This campground is by the sea, and the breeze keeps the midges away. It has a decent grassed area and is right next to the Kildonan Hotel.

Lochranza Youth Hostel (SYHA; ☎ 0870 004 1140; Lochranza; dm adult/child £10.50/8.75; ☺ Mar-Oct) In the north of the island, this hostel has clean, spacious dorms, helpful owners and buckets of information about Arran.

Whiting Bay Youth Hostel (SYHA ☎ 0871 3308 558; Shore Rd, Whiting Bay; dm adult/child £10.50/8.75; ☺ Apr-Oct) In a rather austere building, this is plainer and smaller than its cousin in the north. Dorms range from three to eight beds and it's popular with cyclists and walkers.

Lighthouse Tearoom & Bunkhouse (☎ 850240; Pirnmill; bunks with bedding £10) The clean, eight-bed bunkhouse has no self-catering facilities, but there's an excellent restaurant next door (see Eating, p158).

MID-RANGE

Brodick

Glenfloral (☎ /fax 302707; Shore Rd; s/d £18/40) This B&B claims a prime spot overlooking the bay and you'll need to book early to claim a space. The spacious double upstairs with a bay view is recommended, although unlike its counterpart at the rear of the house it doesn't have an attached bathroom.

McAlpine Hotel (☎ 302155; Shore Rd; s/d £20/40, with bathroom £30/60) An enormous, ageing hotel, just up from the pier, McAlpine is the epitome of faded glory – in its heyday it must have been a stunner. It's now undergoing extensive redevelopment at the hands of new owners. The signs are good and with gloriously large rooms, many with sweeping views, it's great value. Check out the views from the guest lounge upstairs – wonderful!

Rosaburn Lodge (☎ /fax 302383; r per person £25; ☒) Half a mile from the centre of Brodick, by the River Rosa, this lodge has heaps of natural light. The Rosa suite is closer to an apartment than a bedroom.

Corrie

Corrie Hotel (☎ 810273; corriehotel@btinternet.com; s/d from £21/42) The traditional stone Corrie Hotel offers well-kept, loft-style rooms – No 6 is a good option for three people. There are good bar meals (see Eating, p158), and a beer garden scrapes the water's edge.

Blackrock Guest House (☎ 810282; r per person £22-26; ☒) A tidy little seafront guesthouse, in a tranquil spot a half a mile north of the Corrie Hotel, it has smallish but presentable rooms –

PAUL BIGLAND

Bar scene at a local inn, **Borders region**
(p135)

TOM SMALLMAN

The ruins of Kelso Abbey, **Kelso** (p141)

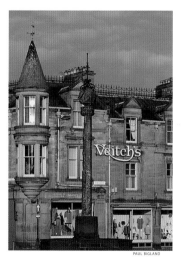

PAUL BIGLAND

The Mercat Cross in the village square,
Cockburnspath (p141)

Crofting on the **Isle of Arran** (p154)

NICOLA WELLS

JONATHAN SMITH

The rhineland style country-side around **Perth and Kinross** (p203)

GARETH MCCOR

Female red deer, **Upper Strathearn** (p209)

MANFRED GOTTSCHALK

A stately mansion in the Tay River Valley near **Dunkeld and Birnam** (p212)

Old stone bridge, **Stirling** (p179)

MARTIN

try to get one upstairs. The guest lounge is very cosy and has smashing views.

Lochranza
Castlekirk (☎ 830202; r per person £20-22.50) In a converted 19th-century church (a little creepy), Castlekirk has congenial staff, comfortable rooms, and a fine collection of local Scottish art in its in-house art gallery.

Lochranza Hotel (☎ /fax 830223; hotel@lochranza .co.uk; s/d £40/66) The Lochranza, an old bastion of Arran hospitality, has some rooms with outrageous pink floral décor, but they're a good size, sort of homely, and the double and twin at the front (room Nos 1 and 10) have views you can't buy.

Whiting Bay
Viewbank House (☎ 700326; pebar@btinternet.com; r per person from £21.50) Appropriately named, it does indeed have tremendous views from its vantage point above Whiting Bay. Rooms are comfortable, tastefully furnished and well kept.

Royal Hotel (☎ 700286; www.royalarran.co.uk; r per person from £26) An excellent, small hotel with an elegant interior, amicable staff, and faithful clientele; there's no surcharge for single travellers at the Royal.

TOP END
Kilmichael Country House Hotel (☎ 302219; www .kilmichael.com; Glen Cloy; s/d from £95/140; ✗) The island's best hotel the Kilmichael is also the oldest building – it has a glass window dating from 1650. The hotel is a luxurious, tastefully decorated hideaway, a mile outside Brodick, with eight rooms and an excellent restaurant.

Lagg Inn (☎ 870255; thelagginn@connectfree.co.uk; Lagg; B&B per person £25-55) An 18th century coach house, this inn has a beautiful location and is the perfect place for a romantic weekend. Grab a superior room with garden views. The package deals (from £160 per person including ferry tickets, car and dinner and B&B for three nights) are terrific value. There's also a cracking beer garden and a fine restaurant (see Eating, p158).

Apple Lodge (☎ /fax 830229; Lochranza; d £62-74) Lavish Apple Lodge, the finest place to stay in Lochranza, has beautifully furnished rooms, one with a four-poster bed, and a guest lounge perfect for curling up with a good book.

Kildonan Hotel (☎ 820207; www.kildonanhotel .com; Kildonan; r per person £75) The Kildonan has had an extensive makeover and now offers stylish, upmarket B&B in light and airy rooms with a minimalist bent. Bar meals are available all day and the restaurant specialises in fresh, local seafood – the menu changes daily depending on the catch.

Eating
Creelers Seafood Restaurant (☎ 302810; Duchess Ct; mains £9-16; ☺ lunch & dinner Tue-Sun) This award-winning restaurant, 1½ miles north of Brodick, is religious about seafood and sources all of its delicacies from Arran and the Western Isles. It's a bistro-style place with some outside seating. The **Smokehouse** next door sells seafood over the counter.

Anyone with a fetish for cheese should stop by the **Island Cheese Co** (Home Farm), where you can stock up on local cheeses and watch the masters at work. Opposite, you can have a snack in the pleasant **Home Farm Kitchen** (☎ 302731; Duchess Court; light meals £1.50-4.50), where you'll find tasty bagels, baguettes and panini.

Brodick Bar & Brasserie (☎ 302169; Alma Rd; mains £8-14) By the post office, this is a good choice for an upmarket bar meal – fresh fish is the specialty. It's popular with families (high chairs available) and groups.

Ormidale Hotel (☎ 302293; Glen Cloy; mains £5.25-7.75) This hotel has decent bar food and a barn-like conservatory that makes dining on a sunny day particularly pleasurable. Live music cranks out on some nights and there's a good atmosphere. Vegetarians should try the mushroom stuffed aubergines while others can dig into Arran clams in Arran cheese sauce.

Isle of Arran Distillers Restaurant (☎ 830264; Lochranza; light meals £5, mains £8-12; ☺ 10am-6.30pm) Arran's specialities, including salmon, game and cheese, are used in inventive and elegant ways at this fine restaurant. The dining area is modern and sun-drenched. Skip the baguettes and go straight to dishes such as oak-smoked salmon with a whisky and Arran mustard dressing.

Catacol Bay Hotel (☎ 830231; Catacol; bar mains £5.50-8) Two miles from Lochranza, the bar here does great food. The Sunday buffet for £7.50 is famous and the cheery service makes you feel like a local. In summer there are ceilidhs (Tuesday) and live music (once a week).

Breadalbane Hotel (☎ 820284; Kildonan; mains £7-8) Good home-cooked food is served here, and you can dine by the fire on blustery nights. If you want to drown out the sound of your chomping, give the jukebox a whirl.

Pantry (☎ 700489; Shore Rd, Whiting Bay; mains £6-10; ☺ 10.30am-9pm Mon-Sat, 10.30am-4pm Sun) This bubbly eatery, with great views, friendly service and tasty tucker, is a fine place to spend an evening (or a lunchtime). There are some good vegetarian choices and the seafood enchiladas are very tempting.

Glenisle Hotel (☎ 600559; Shore Rd, Lamlash; lunch mains £6, 2-/3-course dinners £16/19) The Glenisle Hotel dishes up delectable and innovative meals from an extensive menu and the set dinners are very good value. There's nothing 'packaged' about the food here – it's bursting with freshness and innovation. Try the Scottish beef medallions with Dijon sauce.

Drift Inn (☎ 600656; Shore Rd, Lamlash; mains £6.50) There are few better places to be on the island on a sunny day than the beer garden at this child-friendly hotel ploughing your way through an excellent bar meal while gazing over to the Holy Isle.

Lighthouse Tearoom & Bunkhouse (☎ 850240; Pirnmill; mains £5-9) Calling itself a tearoom is being coy! The restaurant here has an extensive menu, great desserts and outdoor seating.

Other recommendations:

Corrie Hotel (☎ 810273; corriehotel@btinternet.com; mains £6.50-9) There are substantial bar meals, including excellent options for vegetarians.

Lagg Inn (☎ 870255; thelagginn@connectfree.co.uk; Lagg; 2-/3-course dinners £16.95/19.95)

Getting There & Away

CalMac runs a car ferry between Ardrossan and Brodick (passenger/car £4.70/33.50, 55 minutes, four to six daily) and from late March to late October runs services between Claonaig and Lochranza (passenger/car £4.25/19, 30 minutes, seven to nine daily).

Getting Around

There are frequent bus services on the island. There are five or six buses daily from Brodick Pier to Lochranza (£2, 45 minutes, Monday to Saturday), and four to 13 daily from Brodick to Lamlash and Whiting Bay (£1.85, 30 minutes). An Arran Rural Rover ticket costs £3.50 and permits travel any-

where on the island for a day. For a taxi, call ☎ 302274 in Brodick or ☎ 600903 in Lamlash.

There are several places that rent bicycles in Brodick, including **Mini Golf Cycle Hire** (☎ 07968-024040; Shore Rd; day/week £10/33). Other bike rental places around the island include **Blackwaterfoot Garage** (☎ 860277; Blackwaterfoot; £8 per day) and the **Coffee Pot** (☎ 700382; Whiting Bay; £9 per day), which can organise 18-speed mountain bikes.

EAST AYRSHIRE

In **Kilmarnock**, where Johnnie Walker whisky has been blended since 1820, is **Dean Castle** (☎ 01563-522702; www.deancastle.com; Dean Rd; admission & guided tour free; ☺ noon-5pm Apr-Oct, noon-4pm Sat & Sun Nov-Mar), a 15-minute walk from the bus and train stations. The castle, restored in the first half of the 20th century, has a virtually windowless keep (from 1350) and an adjacent palace (from 1468) with a superb collection of medieval arms, armour, tapestries and musical instruments. The grounds, an 81-hectare park, are a good place for a picnic, or you can eat at the visitor centre's **tearoom**, where snacks and light meals cost under £4.

From Irvine there are frequent buses (£1.05, every 10 minutes) throughout the day.

SOUTH AYRSHIRE

Ayr

☎ 01292 / pop 46,431

Ayr is a large, bustling town and a convenient base for a tour of Burns territory. The town's long sandy beach has made it a popular family seaside resort since Victorian times. There are many fine Georgian and Victorian buildings, although some areas of town are showing signs of neglect.

INFORMATION

There are banks with ATMs on High St and Sandgate. The post office is also on Sandgate.

Ayr Hospital (☎ 610555) South of town, by the Dalmellington road.

Carnegie Library (☎ 618492; 12 Main St; ☺ 10am-7.30pm Mon, Tue, Thu & Fri, 10am-5pm Wed & Sat) Offers fast, free Internet access.

TIC (☎ 678100; 22 Sandgate; ☺ 9am-5pm Mon-Sat Apr-Jun & Sep-Mar; 9am-6pm Mon-Sat, 10am-5pm Sun Jul & Aug)

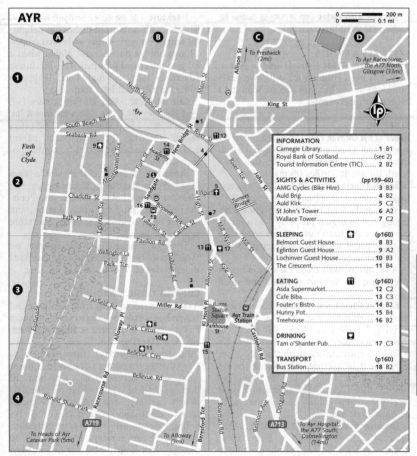

AYR

INFORMATION	
Carnegie Library	1 B1
Royal Bank of Scotland	(see 2)
Tourist Information Centre (TIC)	2 B2

SIGHTS & ACTIVITIES	(pp159–60)
AMG Cycles (Bike Hire)	3 B3
Auld Brig	4 B2
Auld Kirk	5 C2
St John's Tower	6 A2
Wallace Tower	7 C2

SLEEPING	(p160)
Belmont Guest House	8 B3
Eglinton Guest House	9 A2
Lochinver Guest House	10 B3
The Crescent	11 B4

EATING	(p160)
Asda Supermarket	12 C2
Cafe Biba	13 C3
Fouter's Bistro	14 B2
Hunny Pot	15 B4
Treehouse	16 B2

DRINKING	
Tam o'Shanter Pub	17 C3

TRANSPORT	(p160)
Bus Station	18 B2

SIGHTS

Most things to see in Ayr are Burns-related. The bard was baptised in the **Auld Kirk** (Old Church; ☎ 262938; Sun Mass 11am) off High St. Several of his poems are set here in Ayr; in *Twa Brigs* Ayr's old and new bridges argue with one another. The **Auld Brig** (Old Bridge) was built in 1491 and spans the river just north of the church. In Burns' poem *Tam o'Shanter*, Tam spends a boozy evening in the pub that now bears his name, at 230 High St.

St John's Tower (☎ 286385; Eglinton Tce; admission free; ☽ by arrangement) is the only remnant of a church where a parliament was held in 1315, the year after the celebrated victory at Bannockburn. John Knox's son-in-law was

the minister here, and Mary Queen of Scots stayed overnight in 1563.

The **Wallace Tower** is a neo-Gothic structure, 34m high, and includes a statue of William Wallace (p181).

CYCLING

With only a few steep hills, the area is well suited to cyclists. See the Glasgow chapter (p116) for details on the cycle way from that city.

From Ayr, you could cycle to Alloway and spend a couple of hours seeing the Burns sights before continuing to Culzean via Maybole. You could either camp here, after seeing Culzean Castle, or cycle back along the coast road to Ayr, a round trip of about 22 miles (35km).

SOUTHERN SCOTLAND

In Ayr **AMG Cycles** (☎ 287580; 55 Dalblair Rd; day/week £12.50/35) hires out bikes.

FESTIVALS & EVENTS
The **Burns an' a' That** festival, held in Ayr in May, has been running for only two years but looks set to become one of Scotland's biggest cultural events.

SLEEPING
Heads of Ayr Caravan Park (☎ 442269; tent site & 2 people £11.50) This caravan park is in a great, quiet location. From Ayr take the A719 south for about 5 miles (8km).

Eglinton Guest House (☎/fax 264623; www.eglintonguesthouse.co.uk; 23 Eglinton Tce; r per person £18-25) A short walk west of the bus station, this family-run Georgian property is in a lovely cul-de-sac and has a range of tidy rooms. Be warned: you'll also find the scariest coffee/tea maker in Scotland here.

A 10-minute walk from the station brings you to a quiet crescent of B&Bs and small hotels.

Belmont Guest House (☎ 265588; www.belmontguesthouse.co.uk; 15 Park Circus; s/d £25/44) There's a relaxing lounge and library for guests in this comfortable Victorian town house. It's a little deceptive inside, with the '70s décor punctuated by pictures of wildlife staring hungrily down at diners, but the rooms are well-furnished, clean and mostly of a good size. Note that over busy periods they don't accommodate singles.

Lochinver Guest House (☎/fax 265086; 32 Park Circus; s/d £22.50/40) Though a little faded, Lochinver is a solid old guesthouse that is particularly good value for singles.

Crescent (☎ 287329, fax 286779; 26 Bellevue Cres; s/d £40/52; ✗) If you want to move up a couple of rungs on the luxury and comfort scale, consider this outstanding small hotel. There are five opulent, individually furnished rooms, including a four-poster suite and a room with French doors opening on to the garden.

EATING
Fouter's Bistro (☎ 261391; 2a Academy St; dinner mains £7.50-12.50, lunch mains £6-8, 2-course set dinner £9.50) The best place to eat in town, in a former bank vault opposite the town hall, is a class act. Fouters is an ideal place to splash out on a top-class dinner without breaking the budget. It specialises in Ayrshire produce and Mediterranean-style seafood.

Treehouse (☎ 288500; 67 Sandgate; mains £4-8) This big pub-restaurant dishes out delightful fajitas, burgers, salads and filled crepes. Things hot up on weekend nights when a DJ gets the crowd pumped. The Treehouse advertises 'Start your night here!' It appears some may finish it here too!

Cafe Biba (☎ 288666; 231 High St; mains £5-7; ⏲ 8.30am-6pm Mon & Tue, 8.30am-9pm Wed & Thu, 8.30am-10pm Fri & Sat, 9.30am-6pm Sun) Biba offers mouth-watering Tex Mex, pasta, panini and filled pancakes in comfy, contemporary surrounds.

Hunny Pot (☎ 263239; 35-37 Beresford Tce; mains £3.50-5; ⏲ 9am-10pm Mon-Sat, 10.30am-9pm Sun) The pleasant Hunny Pot is a Winnie-the-Pooh-themed coffee shop and licensed restaurant, serving open sandwiches, salads and more substantial meals.

There is a huge Tesco supermarket on Whitletts Rd by Ayr Racecourse, and an Asda supermarket on Wallace St near the river.

GETTING THERE & AROUND
Ayr is 33 miles (55km) from Glasgow and is Ayrshire's major transport hub. The main bus operator in the area is **Stagecoach Western** (☎ 01292-613500) – its hourly X77 service (Monday to Saturday) from Glasgow to Ayr costs £4 (one hour). It also runs buses from Ayr to Girvan (£3.60, one hour 10 minutes, half-hourly Monday to Saturday, hourly Sunday), Stranraer (£6, 1¾ hours, four to eight daily), Greenock (£5.95, 1¾ hours, twice hourly Monday to Saturday, every two hours Sunday), Irvine (£2.50, 30 minutes, half-hourly Monday to Saturday, every two hours Sunday), Largs (£4.05, 1¼ hours, half-hourly Monday to Saturday, every two hours Sunday) and Dumfries (£4.60, 2¼ hours, five to seven daily).

There are at least two trains an hour from Glasgow Central to Ayr (£5.30, 50 minutes), and some trains continue south from Ayr to Stranraer (£10, 1½ hours).

The Ayr Dayrider (£3) allows one day's unlimited travel in and around Ayr, including Alloway, from 9am.

For a taxi, call **Central Taxis** (☎ 267655).

Alloway
☎ 01292
The pretty, lush town of Alloway (3 miles/5km south of Ayr) should be on the itinerary of every Robert Burns fan – he was

ROBERT BURNS (1759–96)

Best remembered for penning the words of *Auld Lang Syne*, Robert Burns is Scotland's most famous poet and a popular hero whose birthday (25 January) is celebrated as Burns Night by Scots around the world. Plans are afoot to turn Burns Night into a national celebration to rival Ireland's St Patrick's Day. The Scottish executive intends to spend about £1 million around the globe promoting the event to help reinvigorate the Scottish tourism industry.

Burns was born in 1759 in Alloway. At school he soon showed an aptitude for literature and a fondness for the folk song. He began to write his own songs and satires. When the problems of his arduous farming life were compounded by the threat of prosecution from the father of Jean Armour, with whom he'd had an affair, he decided to emigrate to Jamaica. He gave up his share of the family farm and published his poems to raise money for the journey.

The poems were so well reviewed in Edinburgh that Burns decided to remain in Scotland and devote himself to writing. He went to Edinburgh in 1787 to publish a second edition, but the financial rewards were not enough to live on and he had to take a job as a customs officer in Dumfriesshire. He contributed many songs to collections published by Johnson and Thomson in Edinburgh, and a third edition of his poems was published in 1793. To give an idea of the prodigious writings of the man, Robert Burns composed more than 28,000 lines of verse over 22 years. Burns died of rheumatic fever in Dumfries in 1796, aged 37.

Burns wrote in Lallans, the Scottish Lowland dialect of English that is not very accessible to the Sassenach (Englishman), or foreigner; perhaps this is part of his appeal. He was also very much a man of the people, satirising the upper classes and the church for their hypocrisy.

Many of the local landmarks mentioned in the verse-tale *Tam o'Shanter* can still be visited. Farmer Tam, riding home after a hard night's drinking in a pub in Ayr, sees witches dancing in Alloway churchyard. He calls out to the one pretty witch, but is pursued by them all and has to reach the other side of the River Doon to be safe. He just manages to cross the Brig o'Doon, but his mare loses her tail to the witches.

The Burns connection in southern Scotland is milked for all it's worth and TICs have a *Burns Heritage Trail* leaflet leading you to every place that can claim some link with the bard. Burns fans should have a look at www.robertburns.org.

born here on 25 January 1759. Even if you haven't been seduced by Burns mania, it's still well worth a visit since the Burns-related exhibitions give a good impression of life in Ayrshire in the late 18th century. The sights are within easy walking distance of each other and come under the umbrella title **Burns National Heritage Park** (www.burnsheritagepark.com).

The **Burns Cottage & Museum** (☎ 441215; adult/child £3/1.50, incl Tam o' Shanter Experience & Burns Monument & Gardens £5/2.50; ☒ 9.30am-5.30pm Apr-Oct, 10am-5pm Nov-Mar) stands by the main road from Ayr. A 10-minute video introduces you to Burns, his family and the cottage. Born in the little box bed in this cramped thatched dwelling, the poet spent the first seven years of his life here. A fascinating museum of Burnsiana next to the cottage exhibits some fabulous artwork as well as many of his songs and letters.

From here, you can visit the ruins of **Alloway Auld Kirk**, the setting for part of *Tam*

o'Shanter. Burns' father, William Burnes (his son dropped the 'e' from his name) is buried in the kirkyard.

The nearby **Tam o'Shanter Experience** (☎ 443700; Murdoch's Lane; adult/child £1.50/75p; ☒ 9.30am-5.30pm Apr-Oct, 10am-5pm Nov-Mar) has a clever audiovisual display of the famous poem, although an understanding of Burns' 18th-century lowland Scots dialect would greatly enhance appreciation.

The **Burns Monument & Gardens** (☒ 9am-5pm) are adjacent to the Tam o'Shanter. The monument was built in 1823 and affords a view of the 13th-century **Brig o'Doon** (see boxed text above). There are also statues of Burns' drinking cronies in the gardens.

GETTING THERE & AWAY

Stagecoach Western bus No 57 runs hourly between Alloway and Ayr from 8.45am to 5.50pm Monday to Saturday (£1.40). Otherwise, rent a bike and cycle here.

Troon

☎ 01292 / pop 14,766

Troon, a major sailing centre on the coast 7 miles (11km) north of Ayr, has excellent sandy beaches and six golf courses. The demanding championship course **Royal Troon** (☎ 311555; www.royaltroon.co.uk; Craigend Rd) offers two rounds of golf for £170, including lunch in the clubhouse (caddie hire is £30 extra).

Dundonald Castle (☎ 01563-850201; Dundonald; adult/child £2.20/1.10; ☉ 10am-5pm Apr-Oct) commands impressive views and has one of the finest barrell-vaulted ceilings in Scotland. The compulsory guided tour can be tiresome, but inside you can still see the original mason's signature on the stones. It was the first home of the Stuart kings, built by Robert II in 1371, and reckoned to be the third most important castle in Scotland, after Edinburgh and Stirling. The visitor centre has a useful timeline of settlements here starting from 1500 BC. There are also models of the castle's development starting with a Dark Age Fort at about 500AD.

GETTING THERE & AWAY

Dundonald Castle is 4 miles (6km) northeast of Troon. Stagecoach Western runs hourly buses (Monday to Saturday) between Troon and Kilmarnock, via Dundonald village.

There are half-hourly trains to Ayr (£1.95, 11 minutes) and Glasgow (£4.80, 45 minutes).

Seacat (☎ 0870 552 3523; www.seacat.co.uk) sails two to three times daily to Belfast (£15 to £20 for passengers, £70 to £145 for a car and driver, 2½ hours).

Culzean Castle & Country Park

The Scottish National Trust's flagship property, magnificent **Culzean** (cull-ane; ☎ 01655-884400; adult/child/family £9/6.50/23, park only adult/child £5/3.75; ☉ castle 10.30am-5pm daily Apr-Oct, 11am-4pm Sat & Sun Nov-Mar; park 9.30am-sunset) is one of the most impressive of Scotland's great stately homes. The entrance to the castle is a converted viaduct, and on approach the castle appears like a mirage, floating into view. Designed by Robert Adam, who was encouraged to exercise his romantic genius in its design, this 18th-century mansion is perched dramatically on the edge of the cliffs. Robert Adam was

the most influential architect of his time, renowned for his meticulous attention to detail and the elegant classical embellishments with which he decorated his ceilings and fireplaces.

The beautiful oval staircase here is regarded as one of his finest achievments. On the 1st floor, the opulence of the circular saloon contrasts violently with the views of the wild sea below. Lord Cassillis' bedroom is said to be haunted by a lady in green, mourning for a lost baby. Even the bathrooms are palatial, the dressing room beside the state bedroom being equipped with a Victorian state-of-the-art shower.

There's also a visitor centre, two ice houses, a swan pond, a pagoda, a recreation of a Victorian vinery, an orangery, a deer park and an aviary. Wildlife in the area includes otters.

If you really want to experience the magic of this place, it's possible to stay in the **castle** (culzean@nts.org.uk; s/d £140/200, Eisenhower ste £265-375; available Apr-Oct). If you're not in that league there's a **Camping & Caravanning Club** (☎ 01655-760627; tent sites members/nonmembers £5.50/10) with good facilities in the park.

GETTING THERE & AWAY

Culzean is 12 miles (19km) south of Ayr; Maybole is the nearest train station, but since it's 4 miles (6km) away it's best to come by bus from Ayr (£2.50, 30 minutes, 11 daily, Monday to Saturday). Buses pass the park gates, from where it's a 20-minute walk through the grounds to the castle.

Turnberry

☎ 01655 / pop 192

Visitors playing the world-famous golf course here usually stay at the luxurious **Turnberry Hotel** (☎ 01655-331000; turnberry@westin.com; s/d from £175/220), where they're able to land their private aircraft or helicopter. If you can afford the price of accommodation, a four-course dinner in the award-winning restaurant is a snip at £49.

Kirkoswald

☎ 01655 / pop 500

Two miles east of Kirkoswald, by the A77, **Crossraguel Abbey** (☎ 883113; adult/child £2.20/75p; ☉ 9.30am-6.30pm Apr-Sep) is a substantial ruin dating back to the 13th century that is good fun to explore. The recently renovated

SOUTHERN SCOTLAND

16th-century gatehouse is the best part of the ruin – you'll find decorative stonework and superb views from the top. Inside, if you have the place to yourself, you'll hear only the whistling wind – an apt reflection upon the abbey's long-deceased monastic tradition. Don't miss the echo in the chilly sacristy.

Stagecoach Western runs Ayr to Girvan buses via Crossraguel and Kirkoswald (£2.50, 37 minutes, twice hourly Monday to Saturday, hourly Sunday).

Ailsa Craig

Curiously shaped Ailsa Craig can be seen from much of southern Ayrshire. While its unusual blue-tinted granite has been used by geologists to trace the movements of the great Ice Age ice sheet, bird-watchers know Ailsa Craig as the world's second largest gannet colony – around 10,000 pairs breed annually on the island's sheer cliffs.

To see the island close up you can take a cruise from Girvan on the **MV Glorious** (☎ 01465-713219; bookings at 7 Harbour St). It's possible to land if the sea is reasonably calm; a four-hour trip costs £12/8 per adult/child. A minimum of eight people and one week's notice is required. Trains to Girvan run approximately hourly (with only three trains Sunday) from Ayr (£3.40, 30 minutes).

DUMFRIES & GALLOWAY

Scotland's southwest country is one of the forgotten corners of Britain – forgotten by tourists that is – which is exactly why it's so good to explore. A string of southern Scotland's most idyllic, appealing towns off the usual tourist eat, and remote forests where the bellow of the mighty red deer can be heard are just a taste of this enticing region. Although devoid of the tourist crush, domestic day-trippers flood towns like pretty Castle Douglas when the sun shines. And shine it does. Warmed by the Gulf Stream, this is also the mildest region in Scotland, a phenomenon that has allowed the development of some famous gardens. Off the major routes, even public transport seems to have passed the region by, so it's better to explore the mountains, forests, castles and

dramatic coastline with your own wheels – motorised or pedal powered.

GETTING THERE & AROUND

Eurolines/National Express (☎ 08705 143 219) operates buses between London and Belfast, via Birmingham, Manchester, Carlisle, the towns along the A75 (including Dumfries and Newton Stewart) and Stranraer.

Local bus operators frequently change routes, although the end destinations (and bus Nos) rarely change. The main operators are **Stagecoach Western** (☎ 01387-260383, 01776-704484) and **MacEwan's** (☎ 01387-256533). The Day Discoverer (£5/2 adult/child) is a useful day ticket valid on most buses in the region and on Stagecoach Cumberland in Cumbria.

Two train lines from Carlisle to Glasgow cross the region, via Dumfries and Moffat respectively. The line from Glasgow to Stranraer runs via Ayr.

DUMFRIES

☎ 01387 / pop 31,146

Despite having several important Burns-related museums, Dumfries has escaped mass tourism. Lovely, red-hued sandstone bridges connect the sprawling town, which is bisected by the wide River Nith, and there are pleasant grassed areas along the riverbank.

Historically, Dumfries held a strategic position smack in the path of vengeful English armies. Consequently, although it has existed since Roman times, the oldest standing building dates from the 17th century.

Orientation

Most of the attractions and facilities are on the eastern side of the river. The bus station is situated by the main bridge; the train station is a 10-minute walk northeast.

Information

There's a bank with ATMs near the TIC.
Dumfries library (☎ 253820; Catherine St;
⊗ 9.15am-7.30pm Mon-Wed & Fri, 9.15am-5pm Thu & Sat) Free Internet access is available at the excellent cybercentre.
TIC (☎ 253862; 64 Whitesands; ⊗ 9.30am-5pm Mon-Sat Apr-Jun; 9.30am-6pm Mon-Sat, noon-5pm Sun Jul–mid-Sep; 9.30am-5pm Mon-Sat, noon-4pm Sun mid-Sep–mid-Oct; 9.30am-5pm Mon-Fri, 9.30am-4pm Sat

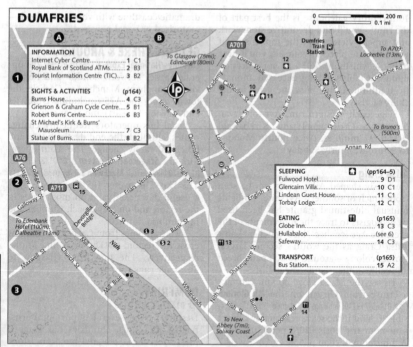

DUMFRIES

INFORMATION	
Internet Cyber Centre...................	1 C1
Royal Bank of Scotland ATMs.......	2 B3
Tourist Information Centre (TIC).....	3 B2
SIGHTS & ACTIVITIES	(p164)
Burns House....................................	4 C3
Grierson & Graham Cycle Centre...	5 B1
Robert Burns Centre......................	6 B3
St Michael's Kirk & Burns'	
Mausoleum.................................	7 C3
Statue of Burns.............................	8 B2

SLEEPING	(pp164–5)
Fulwood Hotel................................	9 D1
Glencairn Villa...............................	10 C1
Lindean Guest House.....................	11 C1
Torbay Lodge................................	12 C1
EATING	(p165)
Globe Inn......................................	13 C3
Hullabaloo...................................	(see 6)
Safeway..	14 C3
TRANSPORT	(p165)
Bus Station....................................	15 A2

mid–Oct-Mar) Opposite the car park by the river, this is the best TIC in Southern Scotland. You can book Eurolines and Scottish Citylink buses here. Pick up a copy of the town *pub guide* if you're planning a boozy stay.

Sights

Burns House (☎ 255297; Burns St; admission free; ⏱ 10am-5pm Mon-Sat, 2-5pm Sun Apr-Sep; 10am-1pm & 2-5pm Tue-Sat Oct-Mar) is a place of pilgrimage for Burns enthusiasts; it's here that the poet spent the last years of his life and there are some interesting relics, original letters and manuscripts.

Robert Burns Centre (☎ 264808; Mill Rd; admission free, audiovisual presentation £1.50/75p; ⏱ 10am-8pm Mon-Sat, 2-5pm Sun Apr-Sep; 10am-1pm & 2-5pm Tue-Sat Oct-Mar) is an award-winning museum in an old mill on the banks of the River Nith. It tells the story of Burns and Dumfries in the 1790s. The audiovisual replicates the exhibition's content. There's also a restaurant, Hullabaloo, here (see Eating, p165).

Burns' **mausoleum** is in the graveyard at St Michael's Kirk. At the top of High St is a statue of the bard; take a close look at the sheepdog at his feet.

Sleeping

Glencairn Villa (☎ /fax 262467; info@glencairnvilla.co.uk; 45 Rae St; s/d from £18/40) Glencairn Villa excels in the B&B trade, offering spacious double rooms (with bathrooms), thoughtful hosts and a couple of small but good single rooms.

Torbay Lodge (☎ 253922; www.torbaylodge.co.uk; 31 Lovers Walk; r per person £20-30) This place offers fine hospitality and elegant, well-appointed rooms.

Fulwood Hotel (☎ 252262; 30 Lovers Walk; s £28-35, d £38-48) A Victorian villa, opposite the train station, Fulwood has rooms with lots of natural light and modern furnishings, and the friendly owner is particularly partial to Antipodean guests. Solo travellers should make a beeline for it.

Edenbank Hotel (☎ 252759; www.edenbankhotel .co.uk; 17 Lauriknowe; s/d £40/60) The refurbished, family-run Edenbank is a very good small hotel – friendly and down to earth. The squarish, functional rooms vary and some doubles are larger than others, but they're all well presented. There's a large bar area and occasionally live music on the weekends.

Lindean Guest House (☎ 251888; 50 Rae St; s/d £18/42) An efficiently run place with decent rooms, Lindean is a popular guesthouse so try to book ahead.

Eating

Hullabaloo (☎ 259679; Mill Rd; lunch mains £3.25-4.75, dinner mains £7.50-12; ✈ 11am-4pm & 6-10pm Tue-Sat, 11am-4pm Mon, 11am-3pm Sun) This contemporary restaurant, at the Robert Burns Centre, is the best in town for creative cooking. Locals flock here on weekends. At lunch you'll get melts and ciabattas, but for dinner they come up with inventive angles on traditional creations – try the monkfish, pancetta and rosemary kebab.

Bruno's (☎ 255757; 3 Balmoral Rd; mains £6.50-15, 3-course dinner £18.95) A velvet-red Italian restaurant, Bruno's has a hint of decadence as evidenced by the glass cabinet of mouthwatering desserts. It serves succulent steaks, al dente pastas, superb thin-crust pizzas and there's a good selection of red wines. The bench seats with small table lamps are perfect for couples.

Globe Inn (☎ 252335; 56 High St; bar mains £4-5) This traditional, rickety old nook-and-cranny pub, said to be Burns' favourite watering hole, serves great home-cooked bar meals. It's atmospheric, warm and welcoming.

For self-caterers, you can buy all you need at the huge Safeway supermarket on Brooms Rd.

Getting There & Away

Dumfries is 80 miles (129km) northwest of Edinburgh on the A76. Stranraer is 68 miles (109km) west on the A75, via Castle Douglas and Newton Stewart.

BUS

Eurolines and National Express run bus Nos 920 and 921 twice daily between London and Belfast, via Carlisle, Dumfries, towns along the A75 and Stranraer; London to Dumfries is £26. Scottish Citylink has a service to/from Glasgow (£7.20, two hours, two or three daily).

Local buses run regularly to Kirkcudbright (£2.50, 1¼ hours, at least hourly Monday to Saturday, six on Sunday) and towns along the A75 to Stranraer (£5.20, 2¼ hours, eight daily Monday to Saturday, three on Sunday). Bus No 100 runs to/from Edinburgh (£5, 2¾ hours, five daily Monday to Saturday, three on Sunday), via Moffat and Biggar.

TRAIN

There are trains between Carlisle and Dumfries (£3.40/6.50 off-peak/peak, 35 minutes, every hour or two Monday to Saturday), and direct trains between Dumfries and Glasgow (£9.90, 1¾ hours, eight daily Monday to Saturday); there's a reduced service on Sunday.

Getting Around

Grierson & Graham (☎ 259483; 10 Academy St; 24 hr £10, 8hr weekday £7) rents bikes. For a taxi call **Dixon's Taxis** (☎ 720900).

SOUTH OF DUMFRIES

Caerlaverock

The ruins of **Caerlaverock Castle** (☎ 01387-770244; by Glencaple; adult/child £3/1; ✈ 9.30am-6.30pm Apr-Sep; 9.30am-4.30pm Mon-Sat, 2-4.30pm Sun Oct-Mar), on a beautiful stretch of the Solway coast, are among the loveliest in Britain. Surrounded by a moat, lawns and stands of trees, the unusual pink-stoned triangular castle looks impregnable – in fact, it fell several times. The current castle dates from the late 13th century. Inside, there's an extraordinary Scottish Renaissance façade to apartments that were built in 1634.

It's worth combining a visit to the castle with one to **Caerlaverock Wildlife & Wetlands Centre** (☎ 01387-770200; by Glencaple; adult/child £4/2.50; ✈ 10am-5pm), a mile east. It protects 546 hectares of salt marsh and mud flats, the habitat for numerous birds, including barnacle geese. There's a coffeeshop here that serves organic food.

New Abbey

The small, picturesque village of New Abbey lies 7 miles (11km) south of Dumfries and contains the remains of the 13th-century Cistercian **Sweetheart Abbey** (☎ 01387-850397; adult/child £1.80/1; ✈ 9.30am-6.30pm Apr-Sep; 9.30am-4.30pm Mon-Wed & Sat, 2-4.30pm Sun Oct-Mar). The shattered, red sandstone remnants of the abbey are impressive and stand in stark contrast to the manicured lawns surrounding them. The abbey was founded by Devorgilla de Balliol in honour of her dead husband (with whom she had founded Balliol College, Oxford). On his death, she had his heart embalmed and carried it with her until she died 22 years later. She and the heart are buried in the presbytery – hence the name.

SOUTHERN SCOTLAND

Kirkbean

About a mile southeast of Kirkbean, there's a cottage on a hillside overlooking the Solway Firth that was the birthplace of John Paul Jones (1747–92), a former pirate who became father of the US navy. **John Paul Jones Cottage** (☎ 01387-880613; adult/child £2/1.50; ☺ 10am-5pm Tue-Sun Apr-Sep, daily Jul & Aug) is a museum that provides a glimpse of the man's remarkable life. It includes a small exhibition, an audiovisual display and a video.

Dalbeattie

Off the B794, 2 miles (3km) north of Dalbeattie, the **Motte of Urr** (admission free) is one of Scotland's largest 12th-century Norman motte-and-bailey castles. About 4 miles (6km) south, is the 15th-century **Orchardton Tower** (Palnackie; admission free; ☺ 9.30am-6.30pm Apr-Sep; 9.30am-4.30pm Mon-Sat, 2-4.30pm Sun Oct-Mar), the only circular tower house in Scotland; the keyholder lives in the nearby cottage.

From **Dalbeattie**, you can either follow the scenic coast road to Kirkcudbright or head inland on the A745 to Castle Douglas.

Getting There & Away

From Dumfries, Stagecoach Western bus No 371 runs nine times a day Monday to Saturday (twice Sunday) to Caerlaverock Castle. By car take the B725 south.

McEwan's bus No 372 from Dumfries stops in New Abbey, Kirkbean, Rockcliffe, Kippford and Dalbeattie; from there bus No 505 continues to Kirkcudbright (but not on Sunday).

CASTLE DOUGLAS & AROUND

☎ 01556 / pop 3671

Castle Douglas attracts a lot of day-trippers, but hasn't been 'spruced up' for tourism. It's an open, attractive, well-cared for town. There are some remarkably beautiful areas close to the centre, such as the small **Carlingwark Loch**. The town was laid out in the 18th century by Sir William Douglas, who had made a fortune in the Americas.

The **TIC** (☎ 502611; ☺ Mon-Sat Apr-Jun, daily Jul-Oct) is in a small park on King St.

Sights & Activities
SULWATH BREWERY

You can see traditional brewing processes at **Sulwath Brewery** (☎ 504525; 209 King St; adult/ child £3.50/free; ☺ 10am-4pm Mon-Sat, closes 1pm Sat Nov-Mar). Admission includes a half-pint of Galloway real ale (tea or coffee is also available). Recommended is the Criffel, an original pale ale, and Knockendoch, a dark brew with a delicious taste of roasted malt.

THREAVE GARDEN

Threave Garden (☎ 502575; Threave House; adult/ child £5/3.75; ☺ visitor centre 9.30am-5.30pm Apr-Oct, 10am-4pm Feb-Mar & Nov-23 Dec; garden 9.30am-sunset year-round), a mile west off the A75, houses the NTS horticultural school, and is noted for its spectacular spring daffodil display from mid-March to mid-May, though it is colourful from mid-May to October too.

THREAVE CASTLE

Two miles (3km) farther west, **Threave Castle** (☎ 07711 223101; adult/child including ferry £2.20/75p; ☺ 9.30am-6.30pm Apr-Sep) is an impressive tower on a small island in the River Dee. Built in the late 14th century, it became a principal stronghold of the Black Douglases. It's now basically a shell, having been badly damaged by the Covenanters in the 1640s, but it's a romantic ruin nonetheless.

It's a 10-minute walk from the car park to the ferry landing where you ring a bell for the custodian to take you across to the island in a small boat.

LOCH KEN

Stretching for 9 miles (14km) northwest of Castle Douglas beside the A713, Loch Ken is a popular outdoor recreational area. The range of watersports includes windsurfing (£27 per day), sailing, canoeing (£13.50 per half-day), power-boating and fishing. **Galloway Sailing Centre** (☎ 01644-420626; www.lochken.co.uk), on the eastern bank north of Parton village, provides equipment, training and accommodation. There are also walking trails and a rich variety of bird life. The Royal Society for the Protection of Birds (RSPB) has a **nature reserve** (☎ 01671-402861) on the western bank, north of Glenlochar.

CYCLING

Castle Douglas Cycle Centre (☎ 504542; Church St; ☺ 9am-5pm Mon-Wed, Fri & Sat; 24 hr £10) hires out touring and mountain bikes.

Sleeping & Eating

Lochside Caravan & Camping Site (☎ /fax 502949; Lochside Park; tent sites £8.45-10.15; ☼ Easter-Oct) This is an attractive spot beside Carlingwark Loch; there's plenty of grass and fine trees providing shade.

Galloway Sailing Centre (☎ /fax 01644-420626; Loch Ken; dm £12) Six miles (10km) north of Castle Douglas, this sailing centre offers year-round backpacker accommodation in four-bed dorms, which are small but clean and well-kept. There's also a kitchen and guest lounge.

Woodlea (☎ 502247; 37 Ernespie Rd; r per person £18-19; ☒) Woodlea is a welcoming stone-built villa and a warm reception is guaranteed. The spacious rooms are tastefully furnished and share a huge bathroom. The family room is particularly good.

Douglas Arms Hotel (☎ 502231, fax 504000; King St; s/d £39/70; bar meals £4.50-13) This place, smack bang in the middle of town, was originally a coaching inn, but these days all the mod cons comfort the weary traveller. There's a range of decent rooms, some with large-screen TVs (good if the football is on), and an attractive, upstairs sitting room for guests. The lively bar serves scrummy food.

Simply Delicious (134 King St; lunch £2-6) Simply delicious is simply that, and satisfies those snacking and lunchtime cravings with a range of fresh sandwiches and rolls. If you've worked up an appetite try the New York steak sandwich.

Getting There & Away

McEwan's bus Nos 501 and 502 pass through Castle Douglas roughly hourly Monday to Saturday (six times Sunday) en route to Dumfries (£2, 45 minutes) and Kirkcudbright (£1.30, 20 minutes). Bus Nos 520 and S2 along the A713 connect Castle Douglas with New Galloway (£1.35, 30 minutes, six daily Monday to Saturday, one Sunday) and Ayr (£5, 2¼ hours, three daily Monday to Saturday, one Sunday).

KIRKCUDBRIGHT

☎ 01557 / pop 3447

Kirkcudbright (kirk-*coo*-bree), with its dignified streets of 17th- and 18th-century merchants' houses and its appealing harbour, is the ideal base to explore the south coast. This delightful town has one of the most beautifully restored high streets in Dumfries & Galloway. Look out for the nook-and-cranny wynds in the elbow of the High St. With its architecture and setting, it's not hard to see why Kirkcudbright has been something of an artists' colony since the late 19th century.

Orientation & Information

The town is on the eastern bank of the River Dee, at the northern end of Kirkcudbright Bay. Everything in town is within easy walking distance. There's a handy **TIC** (☎ 330494; Harbour Sq; ☼ Mon-Sat Apr-Jun, daily Jul-Oct) with some useful brochures detailing walks and road tours in the surrounding district. You'll find a bank with an ATM on St Mary St.

Sights & Activities

Kirkcudbright is a great town for a wander and it won't be long before you stumble across its charming sights.

MacLellan's Castle (☎ 331856; Castle St; adult/child £2/75p; ☼ 9.30am-6.30pm daily Apr-Sep, call for Oct opening times), near the harbour, is a large, atmospheric ruin built in 1577 by Thomas MacLellan, then provost of Kirkcudbright, as his town residence. Inside look for the 'lairds' lug', a 16th century hidey hole designed for the laird to eavesdrop on his guests.

Tolbooth Arts Centre (☎ 331556; High St; adult/child £1.50/free; ☼ 10am-6pm Mon-Sat, 2-5pm Sun May-Sep; 11am-4pm Mon-Sat Oct-Apr), as well as catering for today's local artists, has an exhibition on the history of the town's artistic development.

Nearby, the 18th-century **Broughton House** (☎ 330437; 12 High St) displays paintings by EA Hornel, one of the 'Glasgow Boys' group of painters (p114). Behind the house is a lovely Japanese-style garden. Broughton House was closed (except for the garden) for major renovations in 2003 – ask the TIC when it will reopen.

Stewartry Museum (☎ 331643; St Mary St; admission free; ☼ 10am-6pm Mon-Sat, 2-5pm Sun May-Sep; 11am-4pm Mon-Sat Oct-Apr) is definitely worth nosing around. It's an interesting local museum in a beautiful old building and has an eclectic collection of exhibits reflecting the history of the town and the Solway region.

River trips, taking in both scenery and wildlife, aboard the *Lovely Nellie*, leave from Kirkcudbright marina and cost £5/2.50 per adult/child; there are five daily over summer.

Sleeping & Eating

Silvercraigs Caravan & Camping Site (☎/fax 330123; Silvercraigs Rd; car & tent £8.45-10.15) There are brilliant views from this campground; you feel like you're sleeping on top of the town. The campground has good facilities, including showers, toilets and laundry.

Toadhall (☎ 330204; toadh16@aol.com; 16 Castle St; d £40; ✗) This excellent B&B is possibly the best value in town, considering its central location, and has cracking rooms (it was an old bank), welcoming hosts and stonking breakfasts.

Parkview (☎ 330056; kathmac@talk21.com; 22 Millburn St; s/d £19/34) This is a small blue-painted, traditional guesthouse off St Cuthbert St. Be careful if you scale the steep staircase 'under the influence.

Mrs McGeoch (☎ 331885; 109 St Mary St; s £20; ✗) Reasonably priced single rooms can be extremely hard to find in Kirkcudbright, especially over summer. Try this homely place just before the town centre, coming in from Castle Douglas. Rooms are small, but neat as a pin, and there's an immaculate shared bathroom.

Gordon House Hotel (☎/fax 330670; gordonhousehotel@yahoo.co.uk; 116 High St; s/d £40/70; mains £7-10) This small, laid-back Italian-run hotel has lavish rooms and serves excellent meals. You can dine in the restaurant or the lounge bar (which really does feel like a lounge!). The home-made lasagna is recommended, and there's a beer garden for sunny afternoons.

Selkirk Arms Hotel (☎ 330402; www.selkirkarmshotel.co.uk; High St; s/d £65/95; 3-course dinner £25; ✗) The 'superior' rooms at the sophisticated Selkirk Arms Hotel are the best, but the rooms in the nearby cottage are more spacious and have king-size beds. There are good bar meals too.

Auld Alliance (☎ 330569; 5 Castle St; starters £5-7, mains £10-16; ☒ daily for dinner, plus Sun lunch) The Auld Alliance is the best place to eat in town. The name refers to the former political alliance between Scotland and France, but here it also means a combination of local fresh Scots produce (such as small scallops known as queenies) with French cooking and wine. Booking is advised. They have an excellent value three-course Sunday lunch for £10.50.

There's a decent fish and chip shop opposite the Safeway supermarket on St Cuthbert St.

Getting There & Away

Kirkcudbright is 28 miles (45km) west of Dumfries. Bus Nos 501 and 505 run hourly to Dumfries (£2.50, one hour) via Castle Douglas and Dalbeattie respectively. To get to Stranraer (about £5), take bus No 501 to Gatehouse of Fleet (two to five daily) and change to bus No 500 or X75.

GATEHOUSE OF FLEET
☎ 01557 / pop 892

Gatehouse of Fleet is an attractive little town stretched along a sloping, main street, in the middle of which sits an unusual castellated clock tower. The town lies on the banks of the Water of Fleet, completely off the beaten track, and is surrounded by partly wooded hills. There's a **TIC** (☎ 814212; High St; ☒ Mon-Sat Apr-Jun, daily Jul-Oct).

One mile southwest on the A75, the well-preserved **Cardoness Castle** (☎ 814427; adult/child £2.20/75p; ☒ 9.30am-6.30pm Apr-Sep; 9.30am-4.30pm Mon-Sat, 2-4.30pm Sun Oct-Mar; closed Thu afternoon & Fri Oct) was the home of the McCulloch clan. It's a classic 15th-century tower house with great views from the top. **Mill on the Fleet Museum** (☎ 814099; High St; adult/child £1.50/50p; ☒ 10.30am-5pm Apr-Oct), in a converted 18th-century cotton mill with a working water wheel, traces the history of the local industry. The town was originally planned as workers' accommodation.

Bobbin Guest House (☎ 814229; 36 High St; s/d £35/48), right in the middle of town, is a homely, child-friendly place with well-appointed rooms.

The friendly **Bank O' Fleet Hotel** (☎ 814302; www.bankofleethotel.co.uk; 47 High St; s/d from £28/60; mains £6-14) has refurbished rooms with a blue décor that gives them a cool, contemporary feel. Live entertainment and good bar meals are also on offer.

Bus Nos X75 and 500 between Dumfries (£2.75, one hour) and Stranraer (£3, one hour 10 minutes) stop here three to eight times daily. Bus No 501 from Dumfries (£2.50, one hour, eight daily), via Castle Douglas, terminates in the village.

NEW GALLOWAY & AROUND
☎ 01644 /pop 290

New Galloway lies in the Glenkens district, north of Loch Ken. The unremarkable village is surrounded by some magnificent countryside in which you feel as if you're on a high plateau, surrounded by tumbling, short-pitched hills. This great swathe of wooded landscape is unique in Southern Scotland.

GALLOWAY FOREST PARK

South and west of town is the 300-sq-mile Galloway Forest Park, with numerous lochs and great whale-backed, heather- and pine-covered mountains. The highest point is **Merrick** (843m). The park is crisscrossed by some superb signposted walking trails, from gentle strolls to long-distance paths, including the **Southern Upland Way** (p135).

The 19-mile (30km) A712 (Queen's Way) between New Galloway and Newton Stewart slices through the southern section of the park.

On the shore of Clatteringshaws Loch, 6 miles (9.5km) west of New Galloway, is **Clatteringshaws Visitor Centre** (☎ 420285; admission free, parking £1; 🕒 10.30am-5pm Apr-Aug, 10.30am-4.30pm Sep-Oct), with an exhibition on the area's flora and fauna, including information on the endangered red kite. There's also a coffee shop here with snacks for about £2.75. From the visitor centre, you can walk to a replica of a Romano-British homestead, and to Bruce's Stone, where Robert the Bruce is said to have rested after defeating the English at the Battle of Rapploch Moss (1307).

Near the loch there are ranger-guided walks of the **Galloway Red Deer Range** (☎ 07771-748400; adult/child £3/1; walks at 11am & 2pm Tue & Thu, 2.30pm Sun, mid–Jun-mid–Sep). During rutting season in autumn it's a bit like watching a bullfight as snorting, charging stags compete for the harem.

Walkers and cyclists head for **Glen Trool** in the park's west, accessed by the forest road east from Bargrennan off the A714, north of Newton Stewart. Just over a mile from Bargrennan, there's the **Glen Trool Visitor Centre** (☎ 01671-402420; admission free; 🕒 10.30am-5pm Apr-Aug, 10.30am-4.30pm Sep-Oct), which stocks information on activities in the area. There is also a coffee shop with snacks to replenish those weary legs. The road then winds and climbs up to Loch Trool, where there are magnificent views.

ST JOHN'S TOWN OF DALRY

St John's Town of Dalry is a charming village, distinctly more pleasant than New Galloway, hugging the hillside about 3 miles (5km) north on the A713. It's on the Water of Ken and gives access to the Southern Upland Way.

Sleeping

Kendoon Youth Hostel (SYHA; ☎ 0870 004 1130; St John's Town of Dalry; dm adult/child £9.50/8; 🕒 Apr-Sep) This hostel, popular with walkers, is about 5 miles (8km) north of St John's on the B7000. Bus No 520 stops about a mile away.

Lochinvar Hotel (☎ 430210; St John's Town of Dalry; s/d from £20/40) The vine-engulfed Lochinvar, with its stately interior, is a fine place to stay. Splash out another 10 quid and and get a room with bathroom – they're beautifully furnished and very roomy.

Leamington House Hotel (☎ 420327; High St, New Galloway; s/d £23.50/50; ✗) The Leamington has a range of rooms, with and without bathroom. The congenial owner prides herself on her guests' comfort and wouldn't let a fly in the bedrooms. The split-level family room would suit three people.

Newfield B&B (☎ 430227; Newfield Farm, St John's Town of Dalry; r per person £20) This comfortable B&B has a gorgeous landscaped garden and neat rooms.

Getting There & Away

Bus No 521 runs once or twice daily (except Sunday) to Dumfries (£2.20, 55 minutes). Bus No 520/S2 connects New Galloway with Castle Douglas (£1.35, 30 minutes, six daily Monday to Saturday, one Sunday); one to three continue north to Ayr (£3.50, 1¼ to 1¾ hours).

NEWTON STEWART

☎ 01672 / pop 3573

On the banks of the sparkling River Cree, Newton Stewart is at the heart of some beautiful countryside and is popular with hikers and anglers. On the eastern bank, across the bridge, is the older and smaller settlement of Minnigaff. It's worth dropping into the **TIC** (☎ 402431; Dashwood Sq; 🕒 Mon-Sat Apr-Jun, daily Jul-Oct).

Many hikers head for Galloway Forest Park (see left). Creebridge House Hotel (p170) rents fishing gear and arranges permits.

Sleeping & Eating

Minnigaff Youth Hostel (SYHA; ☎ 0870 004 1142; Minnigaff; dm adult/child £9.50/8; 🕒 Apr-Sep) This converted school is a well-equipped hostel in a tranquil spot a half-mile north of the bridge on the eastern bank. Although it's popular with outdoor enthusiasts, you may just about have the place to yourself.

Flowerbank Guest House (☎ 402629; www
.flowerbankgh.com; Millcroft Rd, Minnigaff; s/d from £23/
38) Flowerbank is a dignified 18th-century house set in a magnificent landscaped garden on the banks of the River Cree. The two elegantly furnished rooms at the front of the house are slightly more expensive, but are spacious and have lovely garden views.

Creebridge House Hotel (☎ 402121; www
.creebridge.co.uk; Minnigaff; s/d £64/108) This is a magnificent, refurbished, 18th-century mansion built for the earl of Galloway. A maze inside, the tastefully decorated rooms have modern furnishings and loads of character. Try to get a room overlooking the garden (No 7 is a good one).

Bruce Hotel (☎ 402294; 88 Queen St; mains £6-7) The filling bar meals here include local seafood, venison, salmon and lamb. Its a good place to try Galloway beef and it's situated in the quieter part of town.

Kilwarlin (☎ 403047; hazelkilwarlin@bushinternet
.com; 4 Corvisel Rd; r per person £19) Just uphill from the TIC, this friendly B&B has good, solid rooms with shared bathrooms. The double room is the best.

Getting There & Away

Buses stop in Newton Stewart (Dashwood Sq) on their way to Stranraer (£2.15, 45 minutes) and Dumfries (£3, 1½ hours), including bus Nos 920 and 921 (Eurolines/National Express) and bus Nos X75 and 500 (various operators, three to eight daily).

Bus No 359 runs to Girvan (£3.55, 1¼ hours, two to five daily) via Glentrool. Frequent buses also run south to the Isle of Whithorn.

THE MACHARS

South of Newton Stewart, the Galloway Hills give way to the softly rolling pastures of the triangular peninsula known as The Machars. The south has many early Christian sites and the loping 25-mile/40km **Pilgrims Way**.

Bus No 415 runs every hour or two between Newton Stewart and the Isle of Whithorn (£2, one hour) via Wigtown (£1.20, 15 minutes).

Wigtown
☎ 01988 / pop 987

Wigtown is a huge success story. Economically run down for many years, the town's revival began in 1998 when it became Scotland's 'National Book Town'. Today 24 bookshops offer the widest selection of books in Scotland and give book enthusiasts the opportunity to get lost here for days (check out www.wigtown
-booktown.co.uk).

Book Shop (☎ 402499; 17 North Main St; ⏰ 9am-
5pm Mon-Sat) Claims to be Scotland's largest second-hand bookshop and is worth a browse.

Corner Bookshop (☎ 402010; 2 High St; ⏰ 10am-
5pm Mon, Tue, Thu-Sat, 1-5pm Sun) Also a good place if you're serious about book hunting

Readinglasses Bookshop Cafe (☎ 403266; 17 South Main St; ⏰ 10am-5pm Mon-Sat) Provides caffeine to prolong your reading time. There are sometimes local musicians here to keep your ears as well as your eyes entertained.

Four miles west of Wigtown, off the B733, the well-preserved recumbent **Torhouse Stone Circle** dates from the 2nd millennium BC.

Glaisnock House (☎ 402249; www.glaisnockhouse
.co.uk; 20 South Main St; r per person £20.50), in the town centre, has a range of nicely furnished rooms (most with bathroom). It has a licensed restaurant open for lunch and dinner Tuesday to Sunday.

Also worth trying for the home-spun vibe is **Mora House** (☎ 403410; morabooktown@aol.com; Bank St; r £20).

Garlieston

You can't get more off the beaten track than Garlieston, which has a neat little harbour with a ring of 18th-century cottages behind a bowling green. A coastal path leads south to the ruins of **Cruggleton Castle**.

Drop into the **Harbour Inn** (☎ 01988-600685; 18 South Cres; mains £4-10) for great views and tasty pub grub.

Whithorn
☎ 01988 / pop 867

Whithorn has a broad, attractive High St virtually closed at both ends – designed to enclose a medieval market. There are few facilities in town, but it's worth visiting because of its fascinating history.

In 397, while the Romans were still in Britain, St Ninian established the first

Christian mission beyond Hadrian's Wall in Whithorn (predating St Columba on Iona by 166 years). After his death, Whithorn Priory was built to house his remains, and Whithorn became the focus of an important medieval pilgrimage.

Today, the priory's substantial ruins are the centre-point of the **Whithorn Trust Discovery Centre** (☎ 500508; 45 George St; adult/child £2.70/1.50; ☺ 10.30am-5pm Apr-Oct), with absorbing exhibitions and an audiovisual display. The considerable remains of the old monastic settlement are being excavated and you'll see some important finds. There's also a museum with early-Christian stone sculptures, including the Latinus Stone (c. 450), reputedly Scotland's oldest Christian artefact.

Isle of Whithorn
☎ 01988 / pop 400

The Isle of Whithorn, once an island but now linked to the mainland by a causeway, is a curious place with an attractive natural harbour and colourful houses. The roofless 13th-century **St Ninian's Chapel**, probably built for pilgrims who landed nearby, is on the windswept, evocative, rocky headland. Around Burrow Head, to the southwest but accessed from a path off the A747 before you enter the Isle of Whithorn, is **St Ninian's Cave**, where the saint went to pray.

The 300-year-old **Dunbar House** (☎ 500336; Tonderghie Rd; s/d £18/30) overlooking the harbour has large, bright rooms. You can admire the view while you tuck into your breakfast in the dining room.

The quayside **Steam Packet Inn** (☎ 500334; fax 500627; Harbour Row; r per person £25-35; mains £4-6) is a popular pub with real ales, scrumptious bar meals and comfortable lodgings.

STRANRAER
☎ 01776 / pop 10,851

Stranraer is more pleasant than the average ferry port, though it's a little on the scrappy side. There's no reason to stay unless you're catching or coming off a ferry, or you need a base to explore some of the beautiful Galloway peninsula.

Orientation & Information
The bus stops, train station, accommodation and TIC are close to the Stena Sealink terminal.

Clydesdale Bank (Bridge St) Has an ATM.

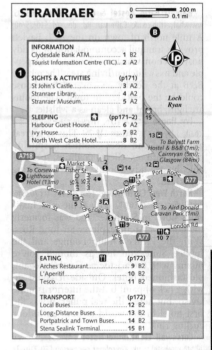

STRANRAER

INFORMATION		
Clydesdale Bank ATM	1	B2
Tourist Information Centre (TIC)	2	A2

SIGHTS & ACTIVITIES	(p171)	
St John's Castle	3	A2
Stranraer Library	4	A2
Stranraer Museum	5	A2

SLEEPING	(pp171-2)	
Harbour Guest House	6	A2
Ivy House	7	B2
North West Castle Hotel	8	B2

EATING	(p172)	
Arches Restaurant	9	B2
L'Aperitif	10	B2
Tesco	11	B2

TRANSPORT	(p172)	
Local Buses	12	B2
Long-Distance Buses	13	B2
Portpatrick and Town Buses	14	B2
Stena Sealink Terminal	15	B1

Stranraer library (☎ 707400; North Strand St; ☺ 9.15am-7.30pm Mon-Wed & Fri, 9.15am-5pm Thu & Sat) Has free Internet access.

TIC (☎ 702595; stranraer@dgtb.ossian.net; 28 Harbour St; ☺ Mon-Sat late Oct-Jun, daily Jul–mid-Oct) Can organise day trips to Ireland, including the Giant's Causeway, for £18/26 per child/adult.

Sights
Worth a quick visit, **St John's Castle** (☎ 705544; George St; admission free; ☺ 10am-1pm & 2-5pm Mon-Sat Easter to mid-Sep) was built in 1510 by the Adairs of Kihilt, a powerful local family. The old stone cells carry a distinctly musty smell. There are displays and a couple of videos that trace its history and, from the top of the castle, superb views of Loch Ryan and the ferries chugging out to Ireland.

Sleeping
Aird Donald Caravan Park (☎ 702025; aird@ mimmanu-net.com; London Rd; tent site for 2 from £6.50) The nearest tent-friendly camping ground is one mile east of the centre. It has manicured lawns, plenty of trees and countless bunnies.

SOUTHERN SCOTLAND

Balyett Farm Hostel & B&B (☎/fax 703395; www.balyettbb.co.uk; Cairnryan Rd; dm/s/d £10/25/40) A mile north of town on the A77, Baylett provides tranquil accommodation in its tidy hostel section, which accommodates six people and has a kitchen/living area. The relaxed B&B at the nearby ivy-covered farmhouse could be the best deal in town. The rooms are light, bright and clean as a whistle.

Ivy House (☎ 704176; www.ivyplace.worldonline .co.uk; 3 Ivy Pl; r per person £18-25) This is a great guesthouse and does Scottish hospitality proud, with excellent facilities, personable hosts, tidy rooms and a smashing breakfast.

North West Castle Hotel (☎ 704413, fax 702646; Port Rodie; s/d from £61/92) This is the most luxurious hotel in Stranraer and was formerly the home of Arctic explorer Sir John Ross. With the Prince Phillip Lounge and the Jubilee Suite you feel as though you're mixing with the aristocracy in this elegant, old-fashioned hotel. Outside it could do with a lick of paint but the interior is quite lavish. But here's the real puller: it was the first hotel in the world to have an indoor curling rink!

Corsewall Lighthouse Hotel (☎ 853220; www .lighthousehotel.co.uk; Kirkcolm; r per person £80-210) If you fancy a night in a lighthouse, this remarkable place to stay is 13 miles (21km) northwest of Stranraer at Corsewall Point. The rooms have great views (one has its own conservatory right on the rocks). It also has a highly regarded restaurant. One room is specially equipped for disabled travellers.

Eating

L'Aperitif (☎ 702991; London Rd; mains from £6, set 3-course dinner £11, available 5.30-7pm) With its extensive menu, fine wines and delectable food, this is the best restaurant in town.

Arches Restaurant (☎ 702196; 77 Hanover St; snacks £2-4, mains £5) Arches is a bright, perpetually busy café with huge windows – great for people-watching.

If you're after a supermarket for self-catering, there's a Tesco on Charlotte St.

Getting There & Away

BOAT

See the Transport chapter (p419) for full details on services to Northern Ireland. From Stranraer there are two alternatives:

P&O (☎ 0870 242 4777; www.poirishsea.com) ferries from Cairnryan to Larne, and **Stena Line** (☎ 0870 570 7070; www.stenaline.co.uk) HSS and Superferries from Stranraer to Belfast.

The Cairnryan to Larne service is used mainly by motorists and hauliers. Cairnryan is 5 miles (8km) north of Stranraer on the eastern side of Loch Ryan. Bus No 358 runs frequently to Cairnryan (terminating at the post office). For a taxi to Cairnryan (around £5), contact **McLean's Taxis** (☎ 703343, 24 hr), just up from the TIC. Stena Line ferries for Belfast connect directly with rail and bus services. The train station is on the ferry pier.

BUS

Eurolines and National Express bus Nos 920 and 921 run twice daily between London and Belfast, via the towns along the A75 and Stranraer. Stagecoach Western buses run to Glasgow, change at Ayr (£8.25, three hours, four to six daily). There are also several daily local buses to Kirkcudbright and the towns along the A75, such as Newton Stewart (£2.15, 45 minutes, three to eight daily) and Dumfries (£5.20, 2¼ hours, eight daily Monday to Saturday, three on Sunday).

TRAIN

Scotrail runs to/from Glasgow (£15, 2½ hours, two to seven trains daily); it may be necessary to change at Ayr.

AROUND STRANRAER

Magnificent **Castle Kennedy Gardens** (☎ 01776-702024; www.castlekennedygardens.co.uk; Rephad; adult/child £3/1; ⏰ 10am-5pm Apr-Sep), 3 miles (5km) east of Stranraer, are among the most famous in Scotland. They cover 30 hectares and are set on an isthmus between two lochs and two castles (Castle Kennedy, burned in 1716, and Lochinch Castle, built in 1864). The landscaping was undertaken in 1730 by the earl of Stair, who used unoccupied soldiers to do the work. Bus Nos 430 (hourly) and 500 from Stranraer stop here.

PORTPATRICK

☎ 01776 /pop 585

Portpatrick is a charming port on the rugged west coast of the Rhinns (or Rhins) of the Galloway peninsula. Until the mid-19th century it was the main port for Northern

Ireland, so it's quite substantial. It's now a coastguard station and a quiet holiday resort.

It is also a good base from which to explore the south of the peninsula, and it's the starting point for the Southern Upland Way. You can follow part of the Way to Stranraer (9 miles/14km). It's a cliff-top walk, followed by sections of farmland and heather moor. Start at the Way's information shelter at the northern end of the harbour. The walk is waymarked until half a mile south of Stranraer, where you get the first good views of the village.

Good, old-fashioned hospitality starts with a handshake and a smile at **Melvin Lodge** (☎ 810238; South Cres; r per person £20-23). Room Nos 2 or 4 will give you cracking views of this pretty village strung around the bay.

Harbour House Hotel (☎ 810456; www.harbour house.co.uk; 53 Main St; s/d from £30/60; bar meals from £6.50) was formerly the customs house, but is now a popular, solid old pub. Some of the tastefully furnished rooms have brilliant views over the harbour. The tariff is an extra £5 if you bring your pooch. The hotel is also a warm nook for a traditional bar meal. You may have trouble dragging yourself outside again.

McCulloch's and King's run bus Nos 358 and 367 to Stranraer (£1.20, 20 minutes, roughly hourly, three Sunday).

SOUTH OF PORTPATRICK

From Portpatrick, the road south to the Mull of Galloway passes coastal scenery that includes rugged cliffs, tiny harbours and sandy beaches. The warm waters of the Gulf Stream give the peninsula the mildest climate in Scotland.

This mildness is demonstrated at **Logan Botanic Garden** (☎ 01776-860231; adult/child £3/1; ☺ 10am-5pm Mar & Oct, 10am-6pm Apr-Sep), a mile north of Port Logan, where an array of subtropical flora includes tree ferns and cabbage palms. The garden is an outpost of the Royal Botanic Garden in Edinburgh.

Farther south, **Drummore** is a fishing village on the east coast. From here it's another 5 miles (8km) to the **Mull of Galloway**, Scotland's most southerly point. It's a rocky, bleak and windy headland. The 26m-high lighthouse here was built by Robert Stevenson in 1826. The Mull of Galloway

RSPB nature reserve, home to thousands of seabirds, has a **visitor centre** (☎ 01671-402861; admission free; ☺ 10am-4pm Apr-Oct).

ANNANDALE & ESKDALE

These valleys, in Dumfries & Galloway's east, form part of two major routes that cut across Scotland's south. Most people rush through but, away from the highways, the roads are quiet and there are some interesting places to visit, especially if you're looking to break a road trip.

Gretna & Gretna Green
☎ 01461 / pop 2705

This is one eccentric place, and it's worth dropping in just to experience the tourist hoards. Many people are drawn to Gretna and Gretna Green by its romantic associations – differences in Scottish and English law once meant that it was easier to marry in Scotland and many young runaway couples from the south came here to wed.

Today's Gretna Green, on the northwestern edge of Gretna, is very touristy, giving the place a real buzz. Such is the power of the name that about 5000 weddings are performed here annually.

The very helpful **TIC** (☎ 337834; Old Headless Cross, Gretna Green; ☺ Apr-late Oct) can assist with most enquiries.

Opposite the TIC, the commercialised **Old Blacksmith's Shop** (☎ 338441; Gretna Green; adult/child £2.50/2; ☺ 9am-5pm Nov-Mar, 9am-6pm Apr-May & Oct, 9am-7pm Jun & Sep, 9am-8pm Jul & Aug) has an exhibition on Gretna Green's history, a sculpture park and an arts centre.

Hazeldene Hotel (☎ 338292; www.hotels -gretnagreen.co.uk; Gretna Green; s/d from £35/55, honeymoon ste £100), a small hotel near the Old Blacksmith's Shop, has eight modern, comfortable rooms. The honeymoon suite has a four-poster bed, sauna and a complimentary bottle of champagne.

Bus No 79 runs between Gretna and Dumfries (£2.50, one hour, hourly Monday to Saturday, every two hours Sunday). Trains run from Gretna Green to Dumfries (£5.30, 25 minutes, every hour or two, five Sunday) and Carlisle (£3, 11 minutes).

Ecclefechan
☎ 01576 / pop 880

Nearly 10 miles (16km) north of Gretna Green, Ecclefechan – a quiet village despite its proximity to the M74 – was the birthplace of Thomas Carlyle (1795–1881), writer, historian, social reformer and one of the great thinkers of Victorian Britain. **Thomas Carlyle's Birthplace** (☎ 300666; adult/child £2.50/1.90; ☿ 1-5pm Thu-Mon May-Sep) is set up to reflect 19th-century domestic life and contains a collection of portraits and Carlyle memorabilia.

The sandstone **Cressfield Country House Hotel** (☎ 300281, fax 204218; Townfoot; s/d £45/55; mains £7; ✗) has a stately interior, spacious rooms with Victorian furnishings and drop-dead gorgeous views. It also does good, substantial meals, including vegetarian fare.

Ecclefechan is served by bus No 382 from Carlisle to Moffat (via Gretna Green and Lockerbie).

Lockerbie
☎ 01576 / pop 4009

Red sandstone buildings line the main street of this small country town. Its peace was shattered in 1988 when pieces from a Pan-Am passenger jet fell on the town after a bomb blew up the aircraft; 207 people were killed, including 11 townsfolk. In 2001 a Libyan intelligence agent was convicted of the bombing and sentenced to life imprisonment. A second Libyan was acquitted. In 2003 Libya agreed to set up a $2.7 billion fund for the families of people killed in the bombing, admitting 'civil responsibility' for the tragedy. Little evidence of the event remains, but the townspeople have created a small garden of remembrance in **Dryfesdale Cemetery**, about a mile west on the Dumfries road. Bus No 382 runs to/from Moffat (£1.50, 30 minutes, hourly).

Moffat
☎ 01683 pop 2135

Moffat lies in wild, hilly country near the upper reaches of Annandale. The former spa town is now a centre for the local woollen industry, symbolised by the bronze ram statue on High St. If you have your own transport, it's a good base from which to explore the **Lowther Hills** and the western Borders.

The **TIC** (☎ 220620; Ladyknowe; ☿ Mon-Sat Easter-Oct, 11am-5pm Sun Jul-late Sep) is well-organised.

At **Moffat Woollen Mill** (☎ 220134; Ladyknowe; admission free; ☿ 9am-5pm), near the TIC, you can see a working weaving exhibition, and trace your Scottish ancestry. Nearby, **Moffat Museum** (☎ 220868; Church Gate; adult/child £1/20p;

TYING THE KNOT IN GRETNA GREEN

From the mid-18th-century, eloping couples south of the border realised that under Scottish law, people could (and still can) tie the knot at the age of 16 without parental consent (in England and Wales the legal age was 21). Gretna Green's location, close to the border, made it the most popular venue.

At one time anyone could perform a legal marriage ceremony, but in Gretna Green it was usually the local blacksmith, who became known as the 'Anvil Priest'. Scandals associated with tiny Gretna Green were frequent, and church pressure led to a law being passed in 1857, which stated that couples had to be resident in Scotland for 21 days before they could get married. In 1940 the 'anvil weddings' were outlawed, but eloping couples still got married in the church or registry office.

Nowadays, many people make or reaffirm their marriage vows in the village. If you want to get married over the famous anvil in the Old Blacksmith's Shop at Gretna Green, check out the website at www.gretnaweddings.com.

☿ 10.30am-4.30pm Mon, Tue, Thu-Sat year-round, plus 2.30-5pm Sun Jun-Sep), in a former bakery, tells the town's history.

Arden House (☎ 220220; High St; s/d from £22.50/42), a former bank, is a large B&B with an air of faded grandeur. One of the highlights is the ornate sitting room with its imposing view over the High St.

The flower-decked **Buchan Guest House** (☎ 220378; www.buchanguesthouse.co.uk; Beechgrove; s/d £25/46; ✗) is in a quiet street just a short walk north of the centre.It has a very happy vibe about it, emanating from its smiling owner Room No 5 is a good choice as it has a lovely outlook over nearby fields.

There are several daily buses to Edinburgh (bus Nos 100 and X100), Glasgow (Scottish Citylink bus No 974) and Dumfries (bus Nos 100 and 114). Bus No 382 runs regularly to Gretna Green and Carlisle, via Lockerbie.

Langholm
☎ 013873 / pop 2311

The waters of three rivers – the Esk, Ewes and Wauchope – meet at Langholm, a gracious old town at the centre of Scotland's tweed industry. Most people come for **fishing** and low-key **walking** (see the website at www.langholmwalks.co.uk) in the surrounding moors and woodlands.

Reivers Rest Hotel (☎ 81343; www.reivers -rest.demon.co.uk; 81 High St; s/d £38/64) has tidy, well-furnished rooms which are good value. Toast the toes by the open fireplace in the Lounge Bar while you sample a pint of Clipper Ale or a glass of wine.

Bus Nos A1 and 112 have up to five daily connections with Eskdalemuir (no Sunday service).

Eskdalemuir

Surrounded by wooded hills, Eskdalemuir is a remote settlement 14 miles (22km) north-west of Langholm. About 1½ miles farther north is the **Samye Ling Tibetan Centre** (☎ 013873-73232), the first Tibetan Buddhist monastery built in the West (1968). The colourful prayer flags and the red and gold of the temple itself are a striking contrast to the stark grey and green landscape. The centre offers meditation courses, including weekend workshops (£45) for which basic food and board is available (dorm beds £16.50, breakfast £2 and lunch £4).

Those staying here are asked to give two hours a day to help in the kitchen, garden and farm. The temple opens to casual visitors (9am to 5pm daily), for whom there's also a small café.

Bus Nos A1 and 112 from Langholm/ Lockerbie stop at the centre.

SOUTHERN SCOTLAND

Central Scotland

CONTENTS

CENTRAL SCOTLAND

Thriving with life, Central Scotland is a good catalogue of the country's library of attractions. It's home to big tree country, has superb walking and cycling opportunities and is dotted with delightful towns chronicling the country's charismatic history. It's an ideal destination for visitors as it's easy to reach from Edinburgh and Glasgow but feels a world away.

It's an area of enormous beauty and variation, possibly the most scenically diverse territory in Britain. The Highland line, a massive geological fault, snakes across part of this region. You can dine at trendy cafés in cosmopolitan Stirling or Perth and then spend the afternoon rambling around the wild, soaring peaks of the Highlands and cavernous glens for which Scotland is famous.

West Perthshire is one of Scotland's hidden gems, whose remote location and lack of public transport keeps it off many itineraries – it shouldn't. It's the type of area many people come to Scotland for, offering a wilderness experience on the back doorstep of urban living.

Central Scotland is not so much a defined region, but a buffer between the Lowlands and the Highlands, and the 'kingdom of Fife' demonstrates its diversity. Fife has a unique lowland identity that differentiates it from the rest of the country and an exploration of its prime tourist puller – medieval St Andrews – peels away the layer of yet another alluring corner of Central Scotland's multilayered skin.

HIGHLIGHTS

- Poking around one of Scotland's grandest medieval castles at **Stirling** (p179)
- Getting back to nature in **The Trossachs** (p186), an area of outstanding natural beauty
- Belting a golf ball down the hallowed fairways of **St Andrews Old Course** (p197)
- Basking in the majesty of **Glen Lyon** (p210), one of Perthshire's scenic treasures
- Discovering the traditional fishing villages dotted along the beautiful coastline of **East Neuk** (p200)
- Jumping into the time capsule of **Scotland's Secret Bunker** (p202) and immersing yourself in the cold war era
- Picnicking on the grassy banks of the River Tay in the shadow of breathtaking **Dunkeld Cathedral** (p212)

Glen Lyon ★
★ Dunkeld Cathedral
St Andrews ★
Scotland's Secret Bunker ★
East Neuk ★
Stirling ★
The Trossachs ★

CENTRAL SCOTLAND

- POPULATION: 763,858
- AREA: 9254 SQ KM

GETTING AROUND

Scottish Citylink (☎ 0870 550 5050) connects the main towns in the area, and Perth is a major hub for its services. **Royal Mail postbuses** (☎ 01246-546329) serve many remote communities, such as those in West Perthshire, charging on average £2 to £5 for single journeys.

Central Scotland's rail Rover ticket (£29), valid for three days out of seven, allows train travel between Edinburgh, Glasgow, Falkirk and Stirling.

STIRLING REGION

History buffs will adore the Stirling region, which has played a pivotal role in Scotland's historical development. The capital, also named Stirling, controlled the main route into the Highlands and its strategic location meant it was the stage for some of Scotland's crucial battles of independence against the repressive English. It has one of the finest castles in Scotland and a wonderfully atmospheric old town.

WALKING & CYCLING

One of Scotland's finest long-distance walks, the **West Highland Way**, covers 95 miles (153km) of paths and track through mountains and glens via Rannoch Moor and Central Scotland; most trekkers do it in a week.

The northern part of the Stirling region and most of Perth & Kinross are mountainous areas that boast munros and superb hill walking.

The **Fife Coastal Path** runs for 80 miles (129km) between the Forth and Tay Bridges. TICs provide leaflets on sections of the walk.

Aside from the busy A9, which roars up the middle of Scotland, the side roads are refreshingly free of traffic and excellent for cycling. The long-distance (214 miles/344km) **Lochs & Glens Cycle route** runs from Glasgow to Pitlochry via The Trossachs, Callander and Killin, following forest trails, small roads and disused rail routes. **Fife** takes cycling very seriously and TICs have detailed routes on the area – with few steep hills, quiet country roads and tumbling, lush countryside, it's ideal cycling country.

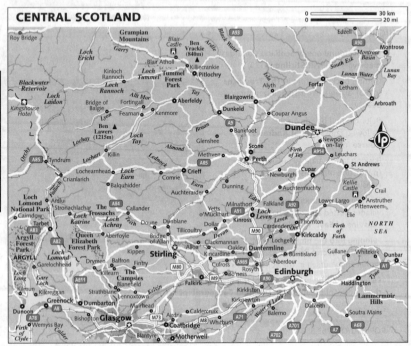

The Stirling region is also blessed with outstanding natural beauty that has lured walkers and climbers since Victorian times. The forests and wildlife in this unique environment are protected as part of the Loch Lomond & the Trossachs National Park (p251).

GETTING AROUND

For local transport information in the Stirling region, phone ☎ 01786-442707 or contact the nearest TIC. The main bus operator is **First** (☎ 01324-613777). Its FirstDay ticket (£4.25) gives one day's travel on all its services in the Central Scotland region.

From late May to early October the vintage **Trossachs Trundler** (☎ 01786-442707) is a useful bus service circling Aberfoyle, Callander and Trossachs Pier on Loch Katrine. Call for details of its reduced winter timetable. Alternatively, **Royal Mail postbus** (☎ 01246-546329) No 24 does the same circuit twice daily Monday to Friday (once on Saturday) via Port of Mentieth and Brig o'Turk.

Stirling town is the rail hub, but the lines only skirt the rest of the region.

STIRLING

☎ 01786 / pop 45,115

Stirling is Scotland's newest city – it was also declared the Queen's Jubilee City of 2002. A bustling place at one of Scotland's most strategic sites (there has been a fortress here since prehistoric times), Stirling has been at the heart of many conflicts. The castle, which was wrestled over countless times, is perched high on a rocky outcrop and dominates Stirling and its tourist industry. Enthusiasts of medieval castles will enjoy exploring this, one of Scotland's best. With its winding cobblestone streets, the atmospheric old town clings to the slopes beneath the castle and the fascinating remnants divulge tales of Stirling's historical development, stretching over a 500-year period.

There's a real energy and vitality in this city, making it one of Central Scotland's most appealing urban areas.

Orientation

The old town slopes up from the train and bus stations to the castle, which sits 75m above the plain atop the plug of an extinct volcano.

Information

The main post office, and banks with ATMs, can be found on Barnton St and Murray Pl respectively.

Stirling library (Corn Exchange Rd; ☒ 9.30am-5.30pm Mon, Wed & Fri, 9.30am-7pm Tue & Thu, 9.30am-5pm Sat) Provides free Internet access.

Stirling Royal Infirmary (☎ 434000; Livilands Rd) South of the town centre.

TIC (☎ 08707-200620; stirlingtic@aillst.ossian.net; 41 Dumbarton Rd; ☒ Mon-Sat year-round, plus Sun Jun-Sep) Ask about the popular ghost walks (adult/child £6/4) that take place at 8.30pm daily, except Monday and Sunday, in July and August. Also pick up a flyer about the visitor attraction 10% discount scheme.

Sights
STIRLING CASTLE & ARGYLL'S LODGING

Hold Stirling and you control the country. This simple strategy has ensured that a **castle** (☎ 450000; adult/child incl Argyll's Lodging £7.50/2; ☒ 9.30am-6pm Apr-Oct, 9.30am-5pm Nov-Mar) has existed here since prehistoric times. Commanding superb views, you cannot help drawing parallels with Edinburgh Castle – but Stirling is better. The location, architecture and historical significance combine to make it one of the grandest of all Scottish castles. This means it also attracts visitors, like bees to honey, so we'd advise you visit in the afternoon; most of the tour buses have buzzed off by 4pm and you may have the castle to yourself.

There has been a fortress of some kind here for several thousand years, but the current building dates from the late 14th to the 16th centuries, when it was a residence of the Stuart monarchs. James II murdered the earl of Douglas in the castle and threw his body from a window (1452). The Great Hall and Gatehouse were built by James IV. The spectacular palace was constructed in the reign of James V (1540–42). French masons were responsible for the stonework. James VI remodelled the Chapel Royal and was the last king of Scots to live here. In the Great Kitchens, there is an excellent depiction of 16th-century food preparation and apparently only men used to work in the kitchen.

In the King's Old Building is the museum of the **Argyll & Sutherland Highlanders** (admission free but donations encouraged), which traces the history of this famous regiment from 1794 to the present day. It has a great collection of ornately decorated dirks.

CENTRAL SCOTLAND

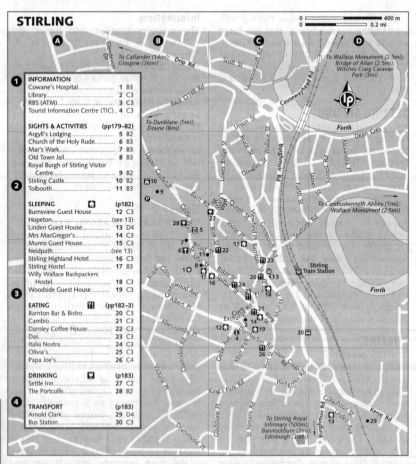

STIRLING

0 — 400 m
0 — 0.2 mi

The **Royal Burgh of Stirling Visitor Centre** (☎ 479901; Castle Esplanade; admission free; ⏰ 9.30am-6pm Apr-Oct, 9.30am-5pm Nov-Mar) has an audiovisual presentation and exhibition about Stirling, including the history and architecture of the castle.

There's a car park next to the castle (£2 for two hours). Visitors in wheelchairs should contact **Historic Scotland** (☎ 0131 668 8600; www.historic-scotland.gov.uk; Longmore House, Salisbury Pl Edinburgh) for a courtesy vehicle to assist their entry into the castle.

Complete with turrets, spectacular **Argyll's Lodging** is the most impressive 17th-century town house in Scotland and you'll find it by the castle, at the top of Castle Wynd. It's the former home of

William Alexander, an earl of Stirling and noted literary figure. It has been tastefully restored and gives an insight into lavish, 17th-century aristocratic life.

OLD TOWN

Below the castle, the old town has a remarkably different feel to modern Stirling, its cobblestone streets packed with fine examples of 15th- to 17th-century architectural gems. Its growth began when Stirling became a royal burgh, around 1124, and in the 15th and 16th centuries rich merchants built their houses here. The steep slopes ensure visitors will enjoy recuperation in a nearby coffee shop or pub after exploring for a couple of hours.

Stirling has the best surviving town wall in Scotland and it can be followed on the **Back Walk**. It was built around 1547 when Henry VIII of England began the 'Rough Wooing' – attacking the town in order to force Mary Queen of Scots to marry his son so that the two kingdoms could be united (p28). The walk follows the line of the wall from Dumbarton Rd (near the TIC) to the castle, continuing around Castle Rock and back to the old town.

Mar's Wark, on Castle Wynd at the head of the old town, is the ornate façade of what was once a Renaissance-style town house commissioned in 1569 by the wealthy earl of Mar, regent of Scotland during James VI's minority.

The **Church of the Holy Rude** (St John St; admission free; 🕙 10am-5pm May-Sep) has been the town's parish church for 500 years and James VI was crowned here in 1567. The nave and tower date from 1456 and the church features one of the few surviving medieval, open-timber roofs. Behind the church is **Cowane's hospital** (☎ 472247; 49 St John St; admission free, donations welcome; 🕙 10am-5pm). Built as an almshouse in 1637 by the merchant John Cowane, its medicinal methods now include hosting *ceilidhs*, banquets and concerts. The curator is extremely knowledgeable about tartan, local genealogy and history.

The **Mercat Cross**, in Broad St, is topped with a unicorn and was once surrounded by a bustling market. Nearby is the **Tolbooth**, built in 1705 as the town's administrative centre. A courthouse and jail were added in the following century and it was renovated in 2001 as a performing arts centre.

WALLACE MONUMENT

Two miles (3km) north of Stirling is Scotland's impressive Victorian monument to **Sir William Wallace** (☎ 472140; Abbey Craig, Causewayhead; adult/child/family £5/3.25/13.25; 🕙 10am-5pm Mar-May & Oct, 10am-6pm Jun, 9.30am-6.30pm Jul & Aug, 9.30am-5pm Sep, 10.30am-4pm Nov-Feb), who was hung, drawn and quartered by the English in 1305. The view from the top, of no less than seven battlegrounds, is as breathtaking as the 67m climb up to it, and the monument contains interesting displays including a parade of other Scottish heroes and Wallace's mighty two-handed sword. Clearly the man was no weakling.

WILLIAM WALLACE, SCOTTISH PATRIOT

William Wallace is one of Scotland's most endearing heroes and a patriot whose exploits helped revive interest in Scottish history. Born in 1270, he was catapulted into fame and a place in history as a highly successful guerrilla commander who harassed the English invaders for many years.

Wallace was knighted by Robert the Bruce and proclaimed Guardian of Scotland in March 1298. However, it was only a matter of time before English military superiority and the fickle nature of the nobility's loyalties would turn the tide against the defender of Scottish independence.

Disaster struck in July of that year when Edward's force defeated the Scots at the Battle of Falkirk. Wallace resigned as guardian, went into hiding, and travelled throughout Europe to drum-up support for the Scottish cause. Many of the Scots nobility were prepared to side with Edward, and Wallace was betrayed after his return to Scotland in 1305.

Sir William Wallace was tried for treason at Westminster, and he was hanged, beheaded and disembowelled at Smithfield, London.

BANNOCKBURN

On 24 June 1314, the greatest victory in the history of Scotland's struggle to remain independent took place at the Battle of Bannockburn. Robert the Bruce overcame superior numbers and sent Edward II's English force running for their lives. In the long and bitter struggle against the threat of English domination, this victory turned the tide of fortune sufficiently in favour of the Scots for the following 400 years.

The **Bannockburn Heritage Centre** (☎ 812664; Glasgow Rd; adult/child £3.50/2.60; 🕙 10am-5.30pm Apr-Oct, 10.30am-4pm Feb-Mar, Nov, Dec) tells the story of the battle in a simple and eloquent exhibition, including a 12-minute audiovisual display. There are also interesting dioramas about medieval Scotland and the Battle of Stirling Bridge. Outside is the eerie Borestone site, said to have been Robert the Bruce's command post before the battle. Check out his grim-looking statue, dressed in full battle gear and mounted on a charger. The battle site itself never closes.

CENTRAL SCOTLAND

Activities

The best way to reach the Wallace Monument is on foot or by bike; it takes about 45 minutes to walk there. Cross the railway line on Seaforth Pl, continue straight ahead onto Shore Rd and Abbey Rd. There's a footbridge over the River Forth where you can visit the ruins of **Cambuskenneth**, an Augustinian abbey. The Wallace Monument is a mile north of here; follow Ladysneuk Rd and turn left at the junction with Alloa Rd.

Tours

From April to October, City Sightseeing runs an open-top, hop-on hop-off bus tour every 30 minutes, daily, between the castle and the Wallace Monument via Bridge of Allan. A day ticket costs £7.50/6/2.50 for an adult/student/child.

Sleeping

BUDGET

Witches Craig Caravan Park (☎ 474947; Blairlogie; tent site £10-12; ☼ Apr-Oct) In a brilliant spot right at the foot of the Ochil Hills, which are begging to be walked, Witches Craig is 3 miles (5km) east of Stirling by the A91.

Stirling Hostel (SYHA; ☎ 0870 004 1149; St John St; dm £12.75/11; ☐) The façade of an 18th-century church conceals this place, which is in a perfect location in the old part of town. It's a superb, modern hostel with 126 beds in small dorms. The less-attractive annexe in Union St opens in summer only.

Willy Wallace Backpackers Hostel (☎ 446773; manager@willywallace.f9.co.uk; 77 Murray Pl; dm/t/d £11/12/13) This is an excellent, clean and friendly hostel in the middle of town. There are mixed, male and female dorms generally accommodating six to eight beds. The lounge area has comfy chairs and great views.

MID-RANGE & TOP END

Mrs MacGregor's (☎ /fax 471082; jennifer@sruighlea .com; 27 King St; d £40; ☒) This place feels like a secret hideaway but it's conveniently located smack-bang in the centre of town. There are beds you sink into and smile, and it's a B&B that welcomes guests with the kind of warmth that keeps them returning.

Munro Guest House (☎ 472685; www.munroguest house.co.uk; 14 Princes St; s £26-30, d £30-44; ☒) A family-run guesthouse, 10 minutes walk from the castle, the traditional breakfast here is simply cracking and a great way to start the day. The five rooms with bathrooms are all bordering on luxurious and feel like a home away from home.

Burnsview Guest House (☎ 451002; m.watt@ totalise.co.uk; 1 Albert Pl; d per person £18-22; ☒) Burnsview has three rooms with private facilities and is monastic in its sobriety. Not for party animals, the thoughtful owners enjoy hosting discerning guests.

Woodside Guest House (☎ 475470; 4 Back Walk; s/d with shower £20/36) Woodside is extremely convenient and surprisingly peaceful; it's on the hill right across from the TIC. It's efficiently run, clean and home to a labyrinth of small, well-furnished rooms, all of which are a good deal.

Stirling Highland Hotel (☎ 272727; stirling@ paramount-hotels.co.uk; Spittal St; r per person £49-59; ☎ ; ☒) Stirling Highland Hotel, the smartest hotel in town, is a sympathetic refurbishment of the old high school. It's very convenient for the castle and old town and the rooms are deluxe, although staying in an old school may not generate good memories for everyone!

Other recommendations:

Hopeton (☎ 473418; 28 Linden Ave; s/d £17.50/36) Good-value, old-fashioned hospitality.

Linden Guest House (☎ /fax 448850; www.lindeng uesthouse.co.uk; 22 Linden Ave; d & t per person £20-25; ☒) No singles, but three well-furnished rooms.

Neidpath (☎ 469017; 24 Linden Ave; s/d £30/40) Spotless rooms and a filling breakfast.

Eating

Cambio (☎ 461041; 1 Corn Exchange; mains £5; ☼ 11am-8pm) Attracting the town's style-cats, this trendy, nouveau bar-restaurant serves amazingly cheap food that has a definite Mexican twist. The décor and furnishings are minimalist and it's a definite cut above the usual pub menus in town. The Mexican caesar salad with chillies is inventive to say the least!

Papa Joe's (☎ 446414; 21 Dumbarton Rd; starters £4, mains £7-13) At Papa Joe's the decades are shamelessly glorified. The walls are cluttered with an amazingly varied and eclectic collection of antiques, musical instruments, sporting paraphernalia – and junk. It's a barn of a place serving excellent seafood, vegetarian, pasta, pizzas and some Tex-Mex.

Olivia's (☎ 446277; 5 Baker St; mains £12-17, 2-/3-course pre-theatre menu £12.95/14.95) Olivia's is the place to spoil that someone special and tuck into a guinea fowl casserole or a cut of Angus beef in candlelight. It's a crisp white linen kind of place boasting an excellent menu.

Das (☎ 472137; 16-18 Barnton St; starters £3.45, mains £7-10; ☺ lunch & dinner Mon-Sat, 3-11pm Sun) Classy Das epitomises good Scottish curry houses and is the best Indian/Punjabi restaurant in Stirling. Try one of the masala or Karahi dishes. The evening buffets (£9.95 Sunday to Thursday; £11.95 Friday and Saturday) are terrific value.

Barnton Bar & Bistro (☎ 461698; 312 Barnton St; soup & snacks £1.65-4.95; ☺ daily until late) Opposite the post office, this is a very popular, grungy student and hosteller hang-out serving excellent, all-day breakfasts. It's a great place to eat or drink, with large servings of good food, but it can get rather smoky.

Italia Nostra (☎ 473208; 25 Baker St; antipasti £5-6, pizza & pasta £7-9; ☺ lunch & dinner) The Nostra is a busy Italian place popular with families. It has a warm, friendly atmosphere and is good for women or solo travellers. There's a large menu, including delicious gelati, and it does takeaways.

Darnley Coffee House (☎ 474468; 18 Bow St; snacks £3.50-5) Just down the hill from the castle, beyond the end of Broad St, Darnley Coffee House is a good pit stop for home baking and speciality coffees on a walk around the old town.

Drinking

Portcullis (☎ 472290; Castle Wynd) With a friendly atmosphere and great location just below the castle, this is the best pub in Stirling. Excellent bar meals are served all day and there's a large range of malt whiskies too.

Settle Inn (☎ 474609; 91 St Mary's Wynd) Established in 1733, the Settle Inn is the oldest pub in Stirling and is a good place to rest weary legs and enjoy a cosy drink, especially when the rain is lashing outside.

Barnton Bar & Bistro (see above) is another popular place for a drink.

Getting There & Away

Stirling is 26 miles (42km) northeast of Glasgow and 35 miles (56km) from Edinburgh.

BUS

Scottish Citylink runs hourly buses to/from Glasgow (£4, 45 minutes). Some buses continue to Aberdeen (£14.70, 3½ hours) via Perth (£4.60) and Dundee (£7.40); others go to Inverness. For buses to Inverness (£12.40, 3¾ hours) you'll usually have to change at Perth. A three-times daily service from Edinburgh to Fort William goes via Stirling once a day (with connections to Oban or Skye); fares to Edinburgh, Oban, Fort William, and Portree are £6.20, £13.70, £14.20 and £24 respectively.

First runs local buses (to Callander, Aberfoyle, and so on) and operates an express service to Edinburgh (£4, one hour, hourly Monday to Saturday).

TRAIN

ScotRail runs services to/from Edinburgh (£5.30, 55 minutes, at least twice hourly Monday to Saturday, hourly Sunday). Services also run at least twice an hour from Glasgow (£5.50, 40 minutes, every two hours or so on Sunday) and regular services to Perth (£8, 35 minutes), Dundee (£12.20, 55 minutes) and Aberdeen (£30, 2¼ hours).

Getting Around

It's easy enough to walk around the central part of the town.

If you want to drive, you can hire a car from **Arnold Clark** (☎ 478686; Kerse Rd). The cheapest deal is for a Daewoo at £18 per day (or £90 for a week).

AROUND STIRLING
Bridge of Allan
☎ 01786 / pop 4607

This former spa town, just 2½ miles (4km) north of Stirling, has an open street plan giving a sense of space and making it very pleasant to mooch around, particularly along the banks of the river. Although its attractions justify a visit, it could also make a good base for Stirling.

SIGHTS

Village Glass (☎ 832137; 14 Henderson St; admission free; ☺ 9am-5pm Mon-Sat) sells unusual glassware gifts costing from £2 to £50; there are even solid-glass writing pens. You can also watch the glassblowers at work – wear a T-Shirt though as it gets hot!

At the **Bridge of Allan Brewery** (☎ 834555; Queen's Lane; admission free; ✆ noon-5pm Apr-Sep, noon-5pm Sat & Sun Oct-Mar), just off Henderson St, you can learn about the micro-brewing techniques behind traditional Scottish ales. And yes, free tasting is offered!

SLEEPING & EATING

Inverallan Lodge (☎ 832791; david.thursby@tesco.net; 116 Henderson St; s/d £22/40, f £55) This is possibly the best guesthouse in town and a travellers' favourite. Down to earth, friendly and good value, the rooms here are fantastic – an excellent size and some have huge bay windows drawing in plenty of light.

Queen's Hotel (☎ 833268; www.queenshotel scotland.com; 24 Henderson St; s/d £85/130) A stylish hotel and a superb example of modern design, the Queen's has very plush rooms – check out the penthouse suite. If you're not staying, drop in and taste the contemporary cooking in the **Longbar** (main dishes £7.50), or if you're a serious foodie try the attached **Jekyll's Restaurant** (mains £10-15) with its impressive Mediterranean-inspired menu. The three-course pre-theatre meal for £13.95 is a great deal.

Clive Ramsay Cafe (☎ 831616; Henderson St; mains £9-12) This little number is the main drag's attention grabber, proudly flaunting undercover outdoor tables where you can eat even when it's raining – a concept that should take off in Scotland. It has a very trendy vibe and somehow seems the centre of the town's universe.

GETTING THERE & AWAY

You can walk to Bridge of Allan from Stirling in just over an hour. Frequent local buses from Stirling stop in Henderson St. Trains to Dunblane, Stirling, Glasgow and Edinburgh depart frequently from the station at the western end of Henderson St.

Dunblane

☎ 01786 / pop 7911

Dunblane is a very enjoyable town to wander around – the screwed-up one-way traffic system means you're better off walking than driving anyway. The name Dunblane will always be associated with the horrific massacre that took place in the primary school in March 1996.

There's a friendly, seasonal **TIC** (☎ 824428; Stirling Rd; ✆ 10am-5pm Mon-Sat May-Sep, 11am-4pm Sun Jul & Aug).

SIGHTS

The main attraction is the fabulous **Dunblane Cathedral** (☎ 823388; Cathedral Sq; admission free; ✆ 9.30am-6.30pm Mon-Sat, 1-6.30pm Sun Apr-Sep; 9.30am-4.30pm Mon-Sat, 2-4.30pm Sun Oct-Mar), which is well worth a detour. It's a superb, elegant, sandstone building – a fine example of Gothic style. The lower parts of the walls date from Norman times, the rest is mainly 13th to 15th century. The cathedral was saved from ruin by a major restoration project in the 1890s. There is a sculptured Pictish stone (p229) on display (found on the site), suggesting that it was used as a centre of worship well before the current structure existed.

The fine **Dunblane Museum** (☎ 823440; Cathedral Sq; admission free; ✆ 10.30am-4.30pm Mon-Sat early May-early Oct) includes barrel-vaulted rooms dating from 1624 and relates the history of both cathedral and town.

The musty old **Leighton Library** (☎ 822296, 01786 822 296; 61 High St; admission free; ✆ call for hrs), dating from 1684, is the oldest private library in Scotland. There are 4500 books in 90 languages.

SLEEPING & EATING

Stirling Arms (☎ 822156; www.theindependents.co.uk; Stirling Rd; s/d from £42.50/65; mains £5-15; ✗) The rooms at the bustling Stirling Arms vary a lot so ask to see a few – some of the doubles are huge while the twins tend to be more cramped, especially the bathrooms. Its excellent, oak-panelled restaurant has a Scottish and international menu and serves the best food in town.

Westlands Hotel (☎ 822118; Doune Rd; tw/f £58/70; ✗) This hotel is a fine place to stay, representing both elegance and character. Most rooms overlook the gardens and there's a good play area for kids on the front lawn.

SHOPPING

Ian McNab Gallery (☎ 0141-638 3072; 62 High St; ✆ 10.30am-5pm, closed Wed & Sun) This talented Scottish landscape artist sells paintings from £200 to £1200, but cheaper framed prints are available for £15 to £125.

GETTING THERE & AWAY

You can walk to Bridge of Allan from Dunblane along Darn Rd, an ancient path used by monks, in about an hour. Alternatively, there are local buses from

Stirling. Citylink buses run to Stirling, Glasgow and Perth, once every hour or two. Trains to Stirling (£2.10) and Glasgow or Edinburgh, are more frequent – roughly three per hour, fewer on Sunday.

Doune
☎ 01786 / pop 1635

Doune is a picturesque, rural town with some gorgeous façades and a small central square with a mercat cross.

Doune Castle (☎ 841742; Castle Rd; adult/child £2.80/1; ⊙ 9.30am-6.30pm Apr-Sep; 9.30am-4.30pm Mon-Wed & Sat, 9.30am-12.30pm Thu, 2-4.30pm Sun Oct-Mar) is one of the best-preserved 14th-century castles in Scotland, having remained largely unchanged since it was built for the duke of Albany. It was a favourite royal hunting lodge, but was also of great strategic importance because it controlled the route between the Lowlands and Highlands, and Mary Queen of Scots stayed here. The inner hall was restored in 1883. There are great views from the castle walls, and the lofty gatehouse is very impressive, rising nearly 30m. If you're a Monty Python fan you may recognise the castle from the *Holy Grail.*

Sleep and eat under the same roof at the **Red Lion Hotel** (☎ 842066; Balkerach St; r per person £18-20), which dates from 1692 and has three rooms that are in excellent condition. For such a wee pub the rooms are a good size, but watch the step into them and note that in places the roof is *really* low. When it's chucking it down outside, it's harder to find a cosier spot in town.

Doune is 7 miles (11km) northwest of Stirling. First buses run every hour or two to Doune from Stirling (£2.40, 27 minutes), less frequently on Sunday.

THE CAMPSIES & STRATHBLANE

The beautiful Campsie Fells, commonly called the Campsies, reach nearly 600m and lie about 10 miles (16km) north of Glasgow. The plain of the River Forth lies to the north; Strathblane and Loch Lomond lie to the west.

One of several villages around the Campsies, attractive **Killearn** is known for its 31m-high obelisk, raised in honour of George Buchanan, James VI's tutor. Eight miles (13km) to the east, **Fintry** is another pretty village, on the banks of the Endrick Water, which has an impressive

28m waterfall, the **Loup of Fintry**. Six miles (10km) north of Fintry, **Kippen** has a very attractive **parish church** (admission free; ⊙ 9.30am-5pm). In the west (on the West Highland Way) is **Drymen**, a pretty village with lots of character, which is popular due to its close proximity to Loch Lomond. There's a **TIC** (☎ 08707-200611; The Square; ⊙ Mon, Tue, Thu-Sat, May-Sep) in Drymen Library.

Walking

One of the best walks in the area is the ascent of spectacular Dumgoyne hill (427m) from Glengoyne distillery, about 2 miles (3km) south of Killearn. Allow at least one hour for the ascent of Dumgoyne. It will take another hour to Earl's Seat, and 1½ hours to return from there to the distillery. The TIC in Drymen, and other local TIC offices, have detailed route information.

Sleeping & Eating

Fintry Inn (☎ 01360-860224; rrr.fintryinn@barbox .net; 23 Main St, Fintry; self-catering per person £25) Above the inn is a self-catering flat sleeping up to six. It's light, bright and well furnished and is an excellent place to stay. The fridge is stocked daily with breakfast for the following morning – you just have to cook it!

Lander B&B (☎ 01360-660273; 17 Stirling Rd, Drymen; s/d £23/36; ✗) Mrs Landers provides simple B&B lodgings consisting of rooms with bunk beds sharing a cramped bathroom. There is, however, private access to guest rooms, and the common dining table makes it all very homely.

Clachan Inn (☎ 01360-660824; The Square, Drymen; mains £5-15; ✗) The best place to eat in the area is the cosy Clachan Inn, perhaps Scotland's oldest registered inn (opened in 1734), although a few places lay claim to that title. The extensive menu includes steaks, burgers, salads and vegetarian choices. Try the fillet steak stuffed with haggis.

Getting There & Away

First runs up to five buses daily from Glasgow to Drymen (£3.20) via Queen's View (The Whangie). The No 10 bus from Glasgow to Stirling goes via Dumgoyne and Balfron every hour or two; change at Balfron for Aberfoyle (£3.70 from

CENTRAL SCOTLAND

ROB ROY

As all the tourist literature repeatedly informs you, this is Rob Roy country. Rob Roy Macgregor (1671–1734) was the wild leader of one of the wildest of Scotland's clans, Clan Gregor. Although he claimed direct descent from a 10th-century king of Scots and rights to the lands the clan occupied, these Macgregor lands stood between powerful neighbours. Rob Roy became notorious for his daring raids into the Lowlands to carry off cattle and sheep – hence the clan's sobriquet, 'Children of the Mist' – and led to the outlawing of the clan. He also achieved a reputation as a champion of the poor. Rob Roy is buried in the churchyard at Balquhidder, by Loch Voil.

Glasgow). A Royal Mail postbus runs twice on weekdays between Balfron and Fintry, once on Saturday.

THE TROSSACHS

The Trossachs has been a major tourist draw card since the early 19th century when Sir Walter Scott's historical novel *Rob Roy* brought eager visitors to the region. In the 21st century its outstanding natural beauty, variety of wildlife and fragile environment has been recognised with the establishment of the Loch Lomond & Trossachs National park.

The narrow glen between Loch Katrine and Loch Achray is actually named the Trossachs, but it's now used to describe a wider scenic area around the southern border of the Highlands.

Aberfoyle & Around

☎ 01877 / pop 576

Crawling with visitors most weekends and dominated by a huge car park, Aberfoyle is a hit with domestic tourists and best avoided by everyone else, unless you're using it as a base to explore the beautiful Trossachs.

The **TIC** (☎ 382352; Main St; ☼ 10am-5pm Apr-Jun, Sep-Oct, 9.30am-6pm Jul & Aug, 10am-4pm Sat & Sun Nov-Mar) is in the Trossachs Discovery Centre, which details a history of the Trossachs and provides a soft play area for kids.

Three miles (5km) east is one of Scotland's two lakes, the Lake of Menteith.

A ferry takes visitors from Port of Menteith village (on the lake) to the substantial ruins of **Inchmahome Priory** (☎ 385294; Inchmahome Island; adult/child £3.50/1.20, including ferry; ☼ 9.30am-5.15pm Apr-Sep). Mary Queen of Scots was kept safe here as a child during Henry VIII's 'Rough Wooing' (p181).

About half a mile north of Aberfoyle, on the A821, is the **Queen Elizabeth Forest Park Visitor Centre** (☎ 382258; admission free, car park fee £1; ☼ 10am-6pm Mar-24 Dec), which has audiovisual displays, exhibitions and information about the numerous walks and cycle routes in and around the park. It's worth visiting solely for the views.

WALKING & CYCLING

Waymarked trails start from the visitor centre on the hills above the town; the TIC has a booklet for £1.

There's an excellent 20-mile (32km) circular cycle route that links with the **ferry** (☎ 376316) along Loch Katrine. Following the southern shore of Loch Achray, you reach the pier on Loch Katrine; departures are at 11am Thursday to Tuesday, April to October. The ferry should drop you at Stronachlachar (adult/child single £4.50/2.80) at the western end (note that afternoon sailings do not stop here). From Stronachlachar, follow the B829 via Loch Ard to Aberfoyle.

SLEEPING & EATING

Crannaig House (☎ 382276; crannaighouse@aol.com; s/d from £35/48; ☒) An opulent Victorian house, Crannaig provides excellent B&B in large rooms that have great views and are big enough to include a small couch. Each room can accommodate three guests and the property is set back from the road, behind Main St, making for a peaceful night's sleep. There are facilities for guests with wheelchairs.

Forth Inn (☎ 382372; www.forthinn.com; Main St; s/d £40/56; bar meals £5.50, evening mains £12) In the middle of the village, the solid Forth Inn provides food, shelter and beer. The tasty bar meals are the best in town – try the canon of pork with apple chutney and cider sauce.

Mayfield Guest House (☎ 382962; randmhooks@btopenworld.com; Main St; s/d £28/45) Nothing is too much trouble for the friendly hosts at this guesthouse.

GETTING THERE & AWAY

First has up to four daily buses from Stirling (£3.40) and connecting services from Glasgow (£3.70) via Balfron.

A postbus does a round trip, Monday to Saturday, from Aberfoyle to Inversnaid Hotel on Loch Lomond, giving access to the West Highland Way.

The Trossachs Trundler does a circuit starting from Stirling, which includes, Aberfoyle, Port of Mentieth, Trossachs Pier on Loch Katrine and Callander; a day ticket per adult/child is £7.50/6.

GETTING AROUND

Bicycles can be hired from **Trossachs Cycle Hire** (☎ 382614; Trossachs Holiday Park; half/full day £9/15).

Callander
☎ 01877 / pop 3000

Callander has been pulling in the tourists for over 150 years, especially domestic day-trippers from Glasgow and Stirling who flock to the town on weekends. It's a far better place than Aberfoyle to spend time in, quickly lulling visitors into lazy pottering. There's also an excellent array of accommodation options from budget to luxury. Callander is on the eastern edge of the Loch Lomond & Trossachs National Park.

INFORMATION

You'll find two banks near the TIC.

DOT Computers (50 Main St; ⏰ 10am-9pm Mon-Sat, 1-9pm Sun) Internet access costs £1 per 15 minutes.

Health Clinic (☎ 331001; 4 Bracklinn Rd) Off the east end of Main St.

Rob Roy & Trossachs Visitor Centre (☎ 08707 200 628; Ancaster Sq; audiovisual Rob Roy show adult/child £3.25/2.25; ⏰ 10am-5pm Mar-May & Oct-Dec, 9.30am-6pm Jun, 9am-8pm Jul & Aug, 10am-6pm Sep, 11am-4pm Sat & Sun Jan-Feb), in an old church, contains the helpful TIC and runs an audiovisual about the great man.

WALKING

The impressive Bracklinn Falls are reached by track and footpath from Bracklinn Rd (30 minutes each way from the car park). Also off Bracklinn Rd, a woodland trail leads up to Callander Crags, with great views over the surroundings; a round trip takes 1½ hours.

SLEEPING & EATING

Trossachs Backpackers (☎ /fax 331200; mark@ scottish-hostel.co.uk; Invertrossachs Rd; dm/t £12.50/35) The backpackers is in a beautifully isolated spot; take Bridge St off Main St, then turn right onto Invertrossachs Rd and follow the road, which runs on the southern side of the river draining Loch Vennachar, for a mile. The dorms are excellent, very spacious with four or six beds and have their own bathroom. Rates include sheets and breakfast.

Callander Meadows (☎ 330181; meadows@callander inn.fsnet.co.uk; 24 Main St; r per person £18-26; mains £8-10; ⊠) Rooms have been tastefully redecorated

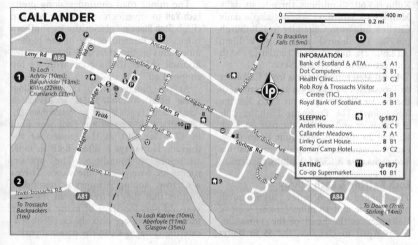

CALLANDER

here and have the best of modern convenience in Victorian elegance. The Callander Meadows also has the best food in town. The chef is from the Gleneagles and the beautifully presented food is delectable. It's small and personal but provides so-phisticated dining with faultless service.

Linley Guest House (☎ 330087; www.linleyguest house.co.uk; 139 Main St; r per person £17-20; ✗) Linley is a spic-and-span B&B. The dirtiest thing you'll find in this house is the grime you tramp in on your shoes. Rooms are light and bright and the owners are helpful.

Arden House (☎ /fax 330235; www.ardenhouse .org.uk; Bracklinn Rd; r per person £27.50-30; ✗) Just north of Main St, this is a wonderful place for grown-ups (no kids allowed) and was used as the setting for the TV series *Doctor Finlay's Casebook*.

Roman Camp Hotel (☎ 330003; www.roman -camp-hotel.co.uk; r £110-180; 5-course dinner £35, á la carte mains £20) Indulgent Roman Camp is the spot to spoil yourself. It's magnificently located by the River Teith and dates from 1625. There is complimentary sherry upon arrival, a first-class restaurant (reservations required) and even a tiny chapel for weddings.

Along Main St, you'll find a Co-op supermarket and lots of places offering meals and snacks for under £5.

GETTING THERE & AWAY

First operates buses from Stirling (£3.50, 45 minutes, hourly Monday to Saturday) and Killin (£3.60, 45 minutes, three to six daily Monday to Saturday). There's also a daily Citylink bus from Callander to Edinburgh (£8.70, 1¾ hours) and Fort William (£12.60, 2½ hours) via Crianlarich, with connections to Oban and Skye.

Royal Mail runs a postbus from Callander to Trossachs Pier linking with the sailing of the SS *Sir Walter Scott* on Loch Katrine (see below). The Trossachs Trundler calls at Callander and reaches the pier on Loch Katrine 26 minutes later four times daily, except Wednesday. A trip covering just the Trossachs area is £5/4 for adults/children.

Loch Katrine & Loch Achray

This rugged area, 6 miles (10km) north of Aberfoyle and 10 miles (16km) west of Callander, is the heart of the Trossachs. From April to October, the **SS Sir Walter**

Scott (☎ 01877-376316; www.lochkatrine.com; adult/ child return from £5.80/4.30) chugs along Loch Katrine from Trossachs Pier at the eastern tip of the loch.

There are two good **walks** starting from Loch Achray. The path to the rocky cone called **Ben A'an** (460m) begins at a car park near the old Trossachs Hotel. It's easy to follow, but you'll need over an hour to get to the top.

On the other side of the Trossachs lies rugged **Ben Venue** (727m); there's a path all the way to the summit. Start walking from Loch Achray Hotel, follow the Achray Water westwards to Loch Katrine, then turn left and ascend the steep flanks of Ben Venue. There are great views of both the Highlands and the Lowlands from the top. Allow four to five hours for the round trip.

BALQUHIDDER & AROUND

Steeped in clan history, this mountainous and sparsely populated area is in the northern part of the Stirling administrative region. There are a few villages and lots of good hill walks.

Balquhidder

☎ 01567 / pop 50

In this small village (pronounced 'balwhidder'), 2 miles (3km) off the A84, there's a churchyard with **Rob Roy's grave**. His wife and two of his sons are also interred here. In the church there's the 8th-century **St Angus' stone** and a 17th-century church bell.

The minor road continues along pretty **Loch Voil** to Inverlochlarig, where you can climb **Stob Binnein** (1165m) by its southern ridge. Stob Binnein is one of the highest mountains in the area, and it has a most unusual shape: like a cone with its top chopped off.

At the junction with the A84, **Kings House Hotel** (☎ 01877-384646; www.kingshouse -scotland.co.uk; Balquhidder; r per person from £25; self-catering cottages per wk from £165) was built in 1779 for £40, at the request of the drovers. Nowadays it offers B&B in more salubrious surroundings. The upstairs rooms are lovely with fine views. There's a narrow, sloping passageway reminding visitors that they're treading in the 200-year-old-plus footsteps of many a passing traveller. There are also six excellent self-catering cottages set in the national park –

cots and children's beds are available. The **Rob Roy Bar** (mains £2-6.50) at the hotel is a tiny, rickety, wood-and-stone affair providing food and shelter from the elements. There's everything from sandwiches to curries to local venison sausages. It also serves an outstanding pint of Guinness – best drunk by the open fire.

GETTING THERE & AWAY

Buses between Callander and Killin stop at the Kings House Hotel. On weekdays a postbus operates from Killin to Callander; it also stops at the Kings House Hotel. The daily Citylink bus from Edinburgh to Fort William also stops here at 11.20am.

Crianlarich & Tyndrum

☎ 01838 / combined pop 350

In good tramping country, and on the West Highland Way, these villages are little more than service junctions on the main A82 road, just north of the Loch Lomond & Trossachs National Park. At Crianlarich, there's a train station. Tiny Tyndrum, just 5 miles (8km) along the road, is blessed with two stations and a very flash **TIC** (☎ 400246; info@tyndrum.visitscotland.co.uk; ☼ daily Apr-early Sep, 11.30am-3pm late Dec-early Jan), which has piles of information and a bureau de change. Ask here about day walks along the West Highland Way and ascents of popular An Caisteal (995m), Ben More (1174m) and magnificent Ben Lui (1130m). It stocks OS maps and has detailed route information.

I & L Slaven supermarket (Station Rd) is also home to Crianlarich's post office. In Tyndrum, Brodie's is the local grocer and post office.

SLEEPING & EATING

Crianlarich Youth Hostel (SYHA; ☎ 0870 004 1112; Station Rd; dm adult/child £9.75/8.50; ☼ mid–Feb-Oct; ▦) This hostel is a modern bungalow with six-bed dorms. It has a good Highland setup – a large kitchen, clean dining area and warm comfy lounge. There's bike hire (£12 per day) and it's the best budget option (B&Bs tend to be expensive in Crianlarich).

Riverside Guest House (☎ 300235; Crianlarich; r per person from £20; ✄) Off the A82, just outside Crianlarich toward Tyndrum, Riverside is a peaceful spot away from the hum of the main drag. It makes the cottage-style rooms here worth hunting out – the family room has great views.

Auchtertyre Farm (Strathfillan Wigwams; ☎ 400251; www.sac.ac.uk/wigwams; Tyndrum; wigwam per person £10, campsite per person £5) This charismatic place, 3 miles (5km) from Crianlarich (and 2 miles/3km from Tyndrum), is off the A82 and has 16 heated wigwams – essentially A-framed wooden cabins. They're a little squashy (each has five beds) but great value. It also has camping with access to all facilities.

Invervey Hotel (☎ 400219; Tyndrum; r per person adult/child £25/12.50; bar meals £5) In Tyndrum, try this solid, old hotel, which has live music on weekends. There are good family facilities – baby cots, for example, are £2.50.

Self-caterers can stock-up at Brodie's, Tyndrum's grocers and post office.

GETTING THERE & AWAY

Citylink runs several buses daily to Glasgow, Oban and Skye from both villages. A postbus service links Crianlarich, Tyndrum and Killin twice on each weekday (with connections to Callander) and once on Saturday.

ScotRail runs train services from Tyndrum and Crianlarich to Fort William (£12.50, 1¾ hours, four daily Monday to Saturday, two on Sunday), Oban (£7.40, one hour, three daily Monday to Saturday) and Glasgow (£11.40, 1¾ hours, three or four daily).

Killin

☎ 01567 / pop 700

Roaring through the centre of this charming little village are the frothy **Falls of Dochart**. The canny locals have made the best of their unusual water feature, pulling in many a passing tourist coach. Killin is in the northeastern corner of the region and is a handy base for exploring the mighty mountains and glens that surround it.

INFORMATION

The village has a post office and a Bank of Scotland ATM, both on Main St.

Outdoor Centre (☎ 820652; Main St) Hires out all sorts of equipment, including canoes (£40 per day) and mountain bikes (£15/11 per day/half day). Note that a child's seat is complimentary when two bikes are hired.

TIC (☎ 0870 720 0627; ☼ Mar-Nov) is in the Breadalbane Folklore Centre (see below), by the River Dochart.

SIGHTS

Bringing ancient magic and miracles to life is the **Breadalbane Folklore Centre** (☎ 820254; adult/child £2/1.25; ☼ 10am-5pm Mar-May & Oct,

10am-6pm Jun & Sep, 9.30am-6.30pm Jul & Aug), in an old watermill overlooking the falls. There is an audiovisual about St Fillan, a local saint whose religious teachings are said to have helped unite the ancient kingdoms of the Scots and the Picts in the 8th century. Robert the Bruce carried a relic of the saint into battle at Bannockburn some 600 years later, which he used to inspire his followers. There are also displays about local and clan history, including the MacGregors and MacNabs.

ACTIVITIES

Killin is at the northern end of the National Cycle Network route from Glasgow, which follows forest trails, small roads and disused rail routes (see p178 for more information).

Seven miles (11km) northeast of Killin, **Ben Lawers** (1214m) rises above Loch Tay. There's an NTS visitor centre here and trails lead to the summit (see under West Perthshire, p210).

Glen Lochay runs westwards from Killin into the hills of Mamlorn. You can take a **mountain bike** for about 11 miles (18km) up the glen to just beyond Batavaime. The scenery is impressive and the hills aren't too difficult to climb. It's possible, on a nice summer day, to climb over the top of **Ben Challum** (1025m) and descend to Crianlarich, but it's very hard work.

For more information, pick up a copy of the *Walks Around Killin* leaflet (30p) from the TIC.

SLEEPING & EATING

Shieling Accommodation (☎ /fax 820334; Aberfeldy Rd; campsite per adult/child £3.50/1.75; ☺ Apr-Oct) This is one of the best camping spots in the region, with loads of grassy areas set among wooded slopes, just outside Killin.

Killin Youth Hostel (SYHA; ☎ 0870 004 1131; dm adult/child from £9.50/8; ☺ Mar-Oct) At the northern end of the village, this hostel has large, well-kept dorms in a lovely Victorian mansion. It's well equipped, popular with walkers and is about a mile north of the centre on the A827.

Drumfin Guest House (☎ 820900; drumfinnhouse@ beeb.net; Manse Rd; r per person £20-25; ✗) This impressive place is under new management and the hosts provide those little extras, such as a dressing gown in your room,

and even offer wine by the glass or bottle. They seem eager to make their guests as comfortable as possible. The rooms are a great size and some have terrific views over surrounding mountains.

Coach House (☎ 820349; Lochay Rd; r per person £23-30; ✗) There are some good-value rooms in this grand old house. It becomes very festive when Scottish folk bands play downstairs on weekends over summer – if you want to turn in early, take one of the cheaper rooms on the top floor.

Falls of Dochart Inn (☎ 820270; Falls of Dochart; s/d £30/55; mains £7-10) Overlooking the falls, the Dochart Inn has creaky upstairs rooms that have recently been renovated. It's very friendly and the bar downstairs has a roaring fire and plenty of chatty locals. There are two intimate dining rooms open all day for bistro-style meals. In the evening a few more dishes are added to the menu, including steaks. Try the local salmon rolled in oatmeal and coated in whisky sauce.

You'll find supermarkets along Main St, including Costcutter and Co-op.

GETTING THERE & AWAY

First operates a service from Stirling (£4.75, 1¾ hours, two daily Monday to Friday, one on Saturday) via Callander. There's a postbus between Killin and Callander (50 minutes, daily Monday to Friday). There's also a postbus to Crianlarich and Tyndrum, twice on weekdays and once on Saturday. There's a postbus service between Aberfeldy and Killin (1¾ hours to Aberfeldy) Monday to Saturday. A Citylink bus leaves for Oban once a day (Friday, Saturday and Monday) and stops at Lix Toll Garage.

CLACKMANNANSHIRE

Inviting Clackmannanshire has some excellent attractions that are well worth a detour if you're in the Stirling region. The tiny district makes a great spot for day trips from the city of Stirling.

DOLLAR
☎ 01259 / pop 2877

About 11 miles (18km) east of Stirling, in the foothills of the Ochil Hills, is the charming town of Dollar. **Castle Campbell** (☎ 742408;

Dollar Glen; adult/child £3/1; 9.30am-6.30pm Apr-Sep; 9.30am-4.30pm Mon-Wed & Sat, 9.30am-12.30pm Thu, 2-4.30pm Sun Oct-Mar) is a 20-minute walk up **Dollar Glen**, into the wooded hills above the town. It's a spooky, old stronghold of the dukes of Argyll and stands between two ravines; you can clearly see why it was known as Castle Gloom. There's been a fortress of some kind on this site from the 11th century, but the present structure dates from the 15th century. The castle was sacked by Cromwell in 1654, but the tower is well preserved. There's a great ramble with sweeping views over Castle Campbell and the surrounding country, from the little car park near the castle. Note it can get boggy if it's been raining.

There are regular First buses to Dollar from Stirling; other services run from Alloa (£1.30, every two hours Monday to Friday).

ALLOA
☎ 01259 / pop 18,989

Alloa is a large town 6 miles (10km) east of Stirling. **Alloa Tower** (☎ 211701; Alloa Park; adult/child £3.50/2.60; 1-5pm Apr-Oct) is a short, clearly signposted walk from the town centre. The 24m-high tower dates from before 1497 and it's one of the most interesting NTS properties in the region. The Italianate staircase and dome are superb. There is also a well, a pit dungeon, and furnishings and paintings belonging to the Mar family. Views from the parapet walk are spectacular.

First runs buses to Clackmannan, Dollar, Stirling (£1.90, 30 minutes, every 20 minutes) and Glasgow.

CLACKMANNAN
☎ 01259 / pop 3450

This village lies 2 miles (3km) southeast of Alloa and has several interesting sights. **Clackmannan Stone** (Main St) sits on top of a large shaft – it's sacred to the pagan deity Mannan and predates Christian times.

The adjacent 17th-century **Cross** is engraved with the Bruce coat of arms; the lower part is heavily worn due to prisoners' chains. Also adjacent is the **Tolbooth**, built in 1592 for £284, which served as a court and prison. **Clackmannan Tower**, uphill from the church and about 450m from Main St, was a residence of the Bruce family

from 1365 to 1772. The widow of the last laird knighted Robert Burns in the tower, with the sword of Robert the Bruce, in 1787. The five-storey tower has structural problems due to subsidence and it isn't open to the public, but the exterior is well worth a look.

First buses run roughly every hour to/from Stirling (£2.15, 40 minutes, every 20 minutes) and frequently to Alloa.

FALKIRK REGION

The little administrative district of Falkirk contains one of Scotland's modern marvels of engineering – The Falkirk Wheel, which, more than anything else in the district, is encouraging a new wave of tourism. The region also covers some interesting areas to the east, including Bo'ness.

FALKIRK
☎ 01324 / pop 32,379

Falkirk, a large town about 10 miles (16km) southeast of Stirling, is home to the famous Falkirk Wheel – an astounding, modern, engineering achievement. Watching it spin its boat-bound occupants around is becoming a major tourist attraction. Drop into the **TIC** (☎ 0870 720 0614; 2 Glebe St) for more information and see the Modern Marvels boxed text (p192).

First runs regular buses to Stirling (£2.50) and Edinburgh (£3.40). Trains go to Stirling, Dunblane, Perth, Glasgow (£4.40) and Edinburgh (£3.90) from Falkirk Grahamston station. Glasgow–Edinburgh express trains stop at Falkirk High every 15 minutes.

BO'NESS & KINNEIL RAILWAY

The town of Bo'ness on the Firth of Forth is best known for the steam train that shuttles to and fro on the **Bo'ness & Kinneil Railway** (☎ 01506-822298; Bo'ness Station, Union St; adult/child return £4.50/2; 4 departures weekends only Apr-Oct & Tue-Sun Jul & Aug). Tickets costing £7/4 include admission to the **Birkhill Fireclay Mine**, 130 steps down in the Avon gorge; guided tours run in conjunction with train arrivals. There's also a free **railway exhibition** at the station in Bo'ness.

Direct buses to Bo'ness from Glasgow, Edinburgh, Falkirk and Stirling are run by First.

MODERN MARVELS

A £78-million Millennium Link Project has restored the Forth & Clyde and Union canals to full working order, linking Edinburgh with west and central Scotland. The expansion of the railways in the mid-19th century rendered the canals, built in 1822, obsolete and they had fallen into disuse.

The centrepiece is the **Falkirk Wheel**, a unique engineering structure designed to replace the flight of locks that once linked the two canals at Falkirk. It is the world's first rotating boat lift, raising vessels (plus almost 300 tonnes of water) 35m in one steel caisson, while descending boats are carried down in the second caisson on the opposite side of the wheel.

Visitors can take boat trips on the **Falkirk Wheel** (☎ 0870 050 0208; www.thefalkirkwheel.co.uk; child/adult/family £4/8/21, car park fee £2; ☼ 9.30am-5pm), spinning around on its giant gondolas. Boats leave every half hour and travel from the visitor centre into the wheel, getting delivered to the Union Canal, high above. Boats then go through Roughcastle Tunnel before the descent on the wheel and return trip to the visitor centre. Anyone with an interest in engineering marvels should not miss this boat ride – it's great for kids too! The nearby visitor centre explains the workings of the mighty wheel – it only takes the power of about eight toasters for a full rotation!!

FIFE

A chubby finger of land jutting out into the icy North Sea, Fife or 'the kingdom of Fife', as it likes to be known, is a treasure trove of attractions. It was home to the early Scottish faith and to Scottish kings for 500 years. Despite integration with the rest of Scotland, Fife has held onto its unique Lowland identity. Many people enter 'the kingdom' via the Forth Road or Tay Bridges – perhaps traversing these enormous gateways adds to the sense of entering a new realm. Certainly the laid-back and serene nature of the region is immediately apparent; rolling, lush farmland dominates the countryside. Apart from the Lomond Hills in the west, the terrain is generally flat, which makes it ideal cycling territory.

GETTING AROUND

Fife Council produces a useful transport map, *Getting Around Fife*, available from TICs and has a **Public Transport Information Line** (☎ 01592-416060). The main bus operator is **Stagecoach Fife** (☎ 01334-474238). For £5 you can buy a Fifedayrider ticket which gives unlimited travel around Fife on Stagecoach buses.

If you're driving from the Forth Road Bridge to St Andrews, a slower but much more scenic route than the M90/A91 is along the signposted **Fife Coastal Tourist Route**.

CULROSS

☎ 01383 / pop 460

An enchanting little town, Culross (pronounced coo-*ross*) is Scotland's best-preserved example of a 17th-century Scottish burgh, and the NTS owns 20 of the buildings, including the palace. Small, red-tiled, whitewashed buildings line the cobbled streets and the winding Back Causeway to the Abbey is embellished with whimsical, street-front, stone cottages.

Sights

You can visit **Culross Palace** (☎ 880359; admission to palace, town house & study adult/child £5/3.75; ☼ 10am-5pm Easter-Sep), more a large house than a palace, which features extraordinary decorative, painted woodwork, barrel-vaulted ceilings, and an interior largely unchanged since the early 17th century. It's dark and spooky inside on an overcast day. The **town house** and the **study**, also completed in the early 17th century, are open to the public but the other NTS properties can only be viewed from the outside. The **visitors centre** (☎ 880359; admission free), in the lower part of the town house, has an exhibition on the long history of the town.

Ruined **Culross Abbey** (admission free; ☼ 9am-7pm Easter-Aug, other times by arrangement), founded by the Cistercians in 1217, is on the hill in a lovely peaceful spot with vistas of the Firth; the choir of the abbey church is now the parish church. In the northeastern corner of the north transept there's an unusual sight – statues of eight children kneeling in front of their parents' memorial.

Sleeping

Burnbank Cottage (☎ 880240; Blairburn, Low Causeway; r per person £18) This cottage has one double and one twin, both with shared bathroom. It's very homely and guests have use of a private lounge with one stipulation – you must invite the owners if you decide to have a party!

Getting There & Away

Culross is 12 miles (19km) west of the Forth Road Bridge. Stagecoach Fife bus Nos 14 and 14A run between Stirling (£2.60, one hour, hourly) and Dunfermline (£1.60, 20 minutes, hourly), via Culross.

DUNFERMLINE

☎ 01383 / pop 39,229

Dunfermline is reminiscent of Stirling although smaller and with a green, leafy centre, especially near the abbey. It's a large regional hub surrounded by suburbs that aren't particularly attractive, however this belies its historical importance as the former capital of the country.

The **TIC** (☎ 720999; kftb@dunfermlinetic.fsnet.co.uk; 1 High St; ☼ 10am-5pm Mon-Sat) is close to the abbey.

There are **banks** (High St) with ATMs, and a **post office** (Pilmuir St).

Sights

Queen Margaret founded a Benedictine priory on the hill here in the 11th century, and later her son King David I built **Dunfermline Abbey** (☎ 739026; St Margaret St; adult/child £2.20/75p; ☼ 9.30am-6.30pm Apr-Sep; 9.30am-4.30pm Mon-Wed & Sat, 9.30am-12.30pm Thu, 2-4.30pm Sun Oct-Mar) in a commanding but sheltered position on the site. Six Scottish kings are buried at Dunfermline Abbey. You can explore the wonderful Norman nave with its ornate columns and superb stained-glass windows. Note the picture of Robert the Bruce standing over the devil (England perhaps?). The Bruce is buried under the pulpit.

Next to the abbey are the ruins of **Dunfermline Palace** (☎ 739026), rebuilt from the abbey guesthouse in the 16th century for James VI. If it's quiet you'll get a guided tour from staff, which is well worthwhile as their commentary brings a previously wealthy and thriving royal court to life.

The award-winning **Abbot House Heritage Centre** (☎ 733266; Maygate; adult/child £3/free; ☼ 10am-5pm), near the abbey, dates from the 15th century. History buffs could get lost for hours among the absorbing displays about the history of Scotland, the abbey and Dunfermline.

Sleeping

Davaar House Hotel (☎ 721886; fax 623633; 126 Grieve St; s/d £55/90; ☒) Davaar is a Victorian villa, around 500m northwest of the abbey. A personable, well-established hotel with 10 excellent rooms, the standard of hospitality here is very high. Rooms are a good size with large bay windows and are beautifully furnished and immaculately presented. The restaurant (closed Sunday) has good Scottish cuisine (a three-course meal costs around £17).

Learig (☎ 729676; learig@bushinternet.com; 2A Victoria St; r per person £20) For something a bit simpler try the Learig, a solid Victorian town house with two well-presented twin rooms and a family room.

Getting There & Away

Dunfermline is a major transport hub, with frequent buses to Edinburgh (£2.85, 40 minutes), Stirling (£2.85, 1¼ hours) and Dundee. There are express buses to Kirkcaldy (£2.65, 30 minutes, hourly). There are trains with Scotrail to/from Edinburgh (£3.30, 30 minutes, at least hourly Monday to Saturday, less frequently Sunday).

KIRKCALDY

☎ 01592 / pop 46,912

Kirkcaldy (kir-kod-ay) sprawls along the edge of the sea for several miles and has a rather shabby promenade with spectacular pounding surf on windy days. It's worth stopping in town to visit the excellent museum.

The **TIC** (☎ 267775; 19 Whytecauseway; ☼ 10am-5pm Mon-Sat) is just off High St. The pedestrianised part of High St has the Mercat Cross shopping centre and banks with ATMs.

Sights

Just a short walk east from the train and bus stations, in the War Memorial Gardens, you'll find the **Kirkcaldy Museum & Art Gallery** (☎ 412860; admission free; ☼ 10.30am-5pm Mon-Sat, 2-5pm Sun), which combines historical accounts and contemporary exhibits. The kids will have a ball as there is stuffed wildlife, and plenty of hands-on exhibits. The museum has an innovative, quirky display on decades of the 20th century in its upstairs gallery. The exhibit representing 2001 is a micro-scooter and there is an anonymously donated shell-suit in the 1990s room! There's also an impressive collection of Scottish paintings from the 18th to 20th centuries.

Two miles (3km) north of Kirkcaldy is the **John McDouall Stuart Museum** (☎ 260732; Rectory Lane, Dysart; admission free; ☼ 2-5pm Jun-Aug), the birthplace of the explorer who, in 1862, became the first person to cross Australia from south to north.

Sleeping

Close to the train station, the **Bennochy Bank Guest House** (☎ 200733; 26 Carlyle Rd; tr without/with bathroom £35/40) has loft-style rooms and is clean and comfortable. Note that breakfast is not offered. Or try **Cherrydene** (☎ 202147; 44 Bennochy Rd; s/d £25/45), with large, tastefully furnished rooms close to the bus and train stations.

Getting There & Away

Frequent buses run from Hill St bus station, two blocks inland from the Esplanade. Destinations include St Andrews (£4.20, one hour), Anstruther (£4, one hour 10 minutes), Dunfermline (£2.65, 30 minutes) and Edinburgh (£4.20, one hour). Kirkcaldy is on the main railway line between Edinburgh (£4.80, 30 minutes) and Dundee (£8, 40 minutes); there are two to four trains an hour.

FALKLAND

☎ 01337 / pop 1183

Below the soft ridges of the Lomond Hills in the centre of Fife, is the charming village of Falkland. This is one of the most captivating inland towns in the region and there are many heritage-listed conservation buildings here. It's a top spot to soak up central Scotland's historical roots.

Sights

Rising majestically out of the town centre and dominating the skyline is the outstanding 16th-century **Falkland Palace** (☎ 857397; adult/child £7/5.25; ☼ 10am-6pm Mon-Sat

& 1-5pm Sun Mar-Oct), a country residence of the Stuart monarchs. Mary Queen of Scots is said to have spent the happiest days of her life 'playing the country girl in the woods and parks' at Falkland. Built between 1501 and 1541 to replace a castle dating from the 12th century, French and Scottish craftspeople were employed to create a masterpiece of Scottish Gothic architecture. The king's bedchamber and the chapel, with its beautiful painted ceiling, have both been restored. Don't miss the prodigious 17th-century Flemish hunting tapestries in the hall. One feature of the royal leisure centre still exists: the oldest royal tennis court in Britain, built in 1539 for James V. It's in the grounds and still in use.

If you're curious about the town's history, drop into the **Royal Burgh of Falkland Exhibition** (Old Town Hall, Back Wynd; ☼ 11am-4pm Sat, 1-4pm Sun). It's a small developing museum that has fascinating displays on Falkland's historical development. Better yet is the curator – a very knowledgeable guide and storyteller, happy to impart some of his extensive archival knowledge to visitors.

Sleeping & Eating

Burgh Lodge (☎ 857710; www.burghlodge.co.uk; Back Wynd; dm £9-10; ☐) This is one of the best budget accommodation options in Fife. It's good for backpackers or families and the facilities have been adapted for travellers with disabilities and are very well kept. The dorms range in size from two to eight modern bunks and there are two family rooms. It's luxury budget accommodation, extremely friendly and would make a great base for exploring the area.

Hunting Lodge (☎ 857226; timlees@huntinglodge .fsbusiness.co.uk; High St; s/d from £25/40) Opposite the palace, this very cosy little inn dates back to 1607. The homely rooms, exuding warmth and character, are upstairs, while pints and chattering locals furnish the downstairs area.

Covenanter Hotel (☎ 857224; www.covenanter hotel.com; The Square; s/d £45/58; mains £4.50-14.50) This 18th-century coaching inn, on the square opposite the palace, is a snug, classy little abode with fine rooms that are often discounted when things are quiet (it's worth asking!). The three-person family room is the best. The bistro meals here are delicious (try the Scottish catfish) and there's a four-course carvery lunch on Sunday for £9.95.

Getting There & Away

Falkland is 11 miles (18km) north of Kirkcaldy. There are Stagecoach Fife buses roughly every two hours Monday to Saturday to/from Perth (£3.50, one hour) and Cupar (£2.20, 30 minutes).

CUPAR & CERES

☎ 01334 / pop 7610

Cupar is a bustling market town, and a busy transport centre, while Ceres, 3 miles (5km) southeast of Cupar, is a pretty village with pantiled roofs, a Georgian church and the shortest High St in Scotland.

Fife Folk Museum (☎ 828180; High St, Ceres; adult/child £2.50/free; ☼ 2-5pm Easter & mid–May-Sep), in the historic 17th-century weigh-house, is well worth a visit. There's a wide-ranging collection of folk history exhibits, agricultural tools and a heritage trail. This place is child-friendly, making it good for the family.

Arisaig (☎ /fax 654529; Westfield Rd, Cupar; r per person £24-28; ✗) is a spacious modern bungalow a few minutes' walk from Cupar town centre in a pocket of tranquility. Vegetarians are catered for, and the breakfast porridge here won a Fife Tourist Board award.

There are direct Stagecoach Fife bus services hourly to St Andrews (£2.30, 30 minutes), Dundee (£3.40, one hour) and Edinburgh (£6, 1½ hours). Cupar is also on the rail line between Edinburgh (£7.70, one hour, at least hourly) and Dundee.

ST ANDREWS

☎ 01334 / pop 14,209

The reverence in which golf is held in St Andrews, a unique and prosperous seaside town, is a fascinating eccentricity of this part of Scotland. St Andrews is the headquarters of golf's governing body, the Royal & Ancient Golf Club. It's also the location of the world's most famous golf course, the Old Course.

Even if belting little white balls with sticks isn't your thing, it's definitely still worth making tracks here. St Andrews boasts an impressive concoction of medieval ruins, and has some idyllic coastal scenery. Covering the streets on foot is easy and very rewarding as it's one of the most pleasant towns in Scotland to explore.

You'll hear just as many English accents around town as you will Scottish; it's home to an ancient university where wealthy English undergraduates (including Prince William) rub shoulders with Scottish theology students.

History

St Andrews is said to have been founded by St Regulus, who arrived from Greece in the 4th century bringing the bones of St Andrew – Scotland's patron saint. The town soon grew into a major pilgrimage centre and St Andrews developed into the ecclesiastical capital of the country. The university was founded in 1410, the first in Scotland. By the mid-16th century there were three colleges: St Salvator's, St Leonard's and St Mary's.

The British Open Championship has taken place regularly at St Andrews since 1873.

Orientation

St Andrews preserves its medieval plan of parallel streets with small closes leading off them. The most important parts of the old town, lying to the east of the bus station, are easily explored on foot. Like Cambridge and Oxford, St Andrews has no campus – most university buildings are integrated into the central part of the town. There's a small harbour near the cathedral, and two sandy beaches: East Sands extends south from the harbour and the wider West Sands is north of the town.

Information

You'll find the post office, and banks with ATMs on South St. Parking in the central area requires a voucher (80p for two hours), which is on sale in many shops.

Costa Coffee (Market St; ☼ 8am-6pm Mon-Sat, 10am-1pm Sun) Internet access £1 per 20 minutes.

St Andrews Memorial Hospital (☎ 472327; Abbey Walk) South of Abbey St.

TIC (☎ 472021; www.visit-standrews.co.uk; 70 Market St; ☼ Mon-Sat Oct-Mar; daily Apr-Sep) Makes bookings for the theatre and the Scotland–Belgium ferry.

Sights

ST ANDREWS CATHEDRAL

At the eastern end of North St is the ruined west end of **St Andrews Cathedral** (☎ 472563; The Pends; adult/child £2.50/75p, including St Andrews Castle £4/1.25; ☼ 9.30am-6.30pm Apr-Sep, 9.30am-4.30pm Oct-Mar), once the largest and one of the most magnificent cathedrals in Britain; the striking ruins convey a sense

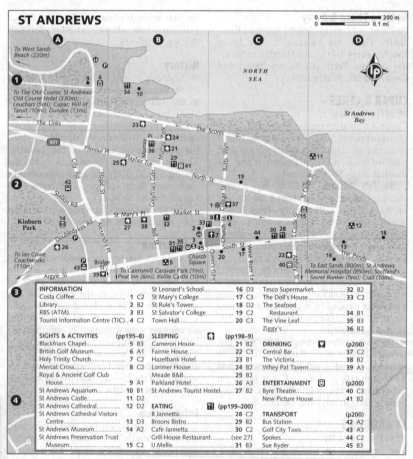

ST ANDREWS

To West Sands Beach (220m)

To The Old Course; St Andrews Old Course Hotel (330m); Leuchars (5mi); Cupar; Hill of Tarvit (10mi); Dundee (13mi)

The Links

A91

NORTH SEA

St Andrews Bay

The Scores

North St

Market St

Kinburn Park

St Mary's Pl

To Ian Cowe Coachworks (110m)

To Cairnsmill Caravan Park (1mi); Peat Inn (6mi); Kellie Castle (10mi)

Church Square

South St

The Pends

To East Sands (800m); St Andrews Memorial Hospital (850m); Scotland's Secret Bunker (5mi); Crail (10mi)

Argyle St

INFORMATION		St Leonard's School..............	16 D3	Tesco Supermarket..............	32 B2
Costa Coffee.................	1 C2	St Mary's College................	17 C3	The Doll's House..............	33 C2
Library......................	2 B2	St Rule's Tower..................	18 D2	The Seafood	
RBS (ATM)...................	3 B3	St Salvator's College............	19 C2	Restaurant..................	34 B1
Tourist Information Centre (TIC)..	4 C2	Town Hall......................	20 C3	The Vine Leaf.................	35 B3
				Ziggy's......................	36 B2
SIGHTS & ACTIVITIES	(pp195–8)	SLEEPING	(pp198–9)		
Blackfriars Chapel.............	5 B3	Cameron House..................	21 B2	DRINKING	(p200)
British Golf Museum...........	6 A1	Fairnie House..................	22 C3	Central Bar...................	37 C2
Holy Trinity Church...........	7 C2	Hazelbank Hotel................	23 B1	The Victoria..................	38 B2
Mercat Cross.................	8 C2	Lorimer House.................	24 B2	Whey Pat Tavern..............	39 A3
Royal & Ancient Golf Club		Meade B&B...................	25 B2		
House.....................	9 A1	Parkland Hotel.................	26 A3	ENTERTAINMENT	(p200)
St Andrews Aquarium..........	10 B1	St Andrews Tourist Hostel.......	27 B2	Byre Theatre.................	40 C3
St Andrews Castle.............	11 D2			New Picture House............	41 B2
St Andrews Cathedral..........	12 D2	EATING	(pp199–200)		
St Andrews Cathedral Visitors		B Jannetta....................	28 C2	TRANSPORT	(p200)
Centre....................	13 D3	Broons Bistro.................	29 B2	Bus Station..................	42 A2
St Andrews Museum...........	14 A2	Cafe Jannetta.................	30 C2	Golf City Taxis...............	43 A3
St Andrews Preservation Trust		Grill House Restaurant.........	(see 27)	Spokes.....................	44 C2
Museum...................	15 C2	IJ Mellis.....................	31 B3	Sue Ryder...................	45 B3

of its immensity. Although it was founded in 1160, it wasn't consecrated until 1318. It was a focus of pilgrimage until the Reformation, when it was pillaged in 1559.

St Andrew's bones lay under the high altar. Until the cathedral was built, they had been enshrined in the nearby **Church of St Rule**. All that remains is the church tower – well worth the climb for the view across St Andrews and a great place for taking photographs. In the same area are parts of the ruined 13th-century priory. The visitor centre includes the **calefactory**, the only room where the monks could warm themselves by a fire; masons' marks on the red sandstone blocks, identifying who shaped each block, can still be clearly seen.

There's also a collection of Celtic crosses and gravestones found on the site.

ST ANDREWS CASTLE

Not far from the cathedral and with dramatic coastline views, **St Andrews Castle** (☎ 477196; The Scores; adult/child £4/1.25; ⏰ 9.30am-6.30pm Apr-Sep, 9.30am-4.30pm Oct-Mar) is mainly in ruins, but the site itself is evocative. The most intriguing feature is the complex of siege tunnels, said to be the best surviving example of siege engineering in Europe. You can walk along the damp, mossy tunnels, now lit by electric light – but be warned, it helps if you're short! The castle was founded around 1200 as the fortified home of the bishop. A visitor centre gives a good audiovisual introduction and also has a small collection of Pictish stones.

In 1654, part of the castle was pulled down to provide materials for rebuilding the harbour wall and pier. Enough survives to give you an idea of what each of the chambers was used for. After the execution of Protestant reformers in 1545, other reformers retaliated by murdering Cardinal Beaton and taking over the castle. The cardinal's body was hung from a window in the Fore Tower before being tossed into the bottle-shaped dungeon. The reformers then spent almost a year besieged in the castle.

ST ANDREWS MUSEUM
Near the bus station, **St Andrews Museum** (☎ 412690; Kinburn Park, Doubledykes Rd; admission free; ☺ 10am-5pm Apr-Sep; 10.30am-4pm Mon-Fri, 12.30-5pm Sat & Sun Oct-Mar) has interesting displays that chart the history of the town from its founding by St Regulus to its growth as an ecclesiastical, academic and sporting centre. Local preservation work is a focal point of the museum.

BRITISH GOLF MUSEUM
Golfers shouldn't miss the **British Golf Museum** (☎ 460046; Bruce Embankment; adult/child £4/2; ☺ 9.30am-5.30pm Easter–mid-Oct, 11am-3pm Thu-Mon mid-October–Easter), an interesting (even for non-golfers), modern museum charting the history of the game and its intimate association with St Andrews. It's equipped with audiovisual displays and touch screens, as well as golf memorabilia.

Opposite the museum is the clubhouse of the **Royal & Ancient Golf Club**. Outside the club is the **Old Course**, and beside it stretch the West Sands, the beach made famous by the film *Chariots of Fire*.

Activities
The TIC has a list of local walks and sells OS maps. The **Fife Coastal Path** stretching from the Forth Bridge to the Tay Bridge – a distance of 80 miles (129km) – was completed in 2003; note that improvements and upgrading of sections of the walk are ongoing, so check with the TIC before heading off. You can walk from St Andrews to Crail along the coast (15 miles/24km) or toward the Tay Bridge in the other direction. A good shorter walk follows the coast east to Boarhills (4 miles/6km), from where you can return by bus or by retracing your steps.

Kellie Castle (p202) is within easy cycling distance. You can also cycle north to the forest, beach and nature trail at Tentsmuirs

---

PLAY THE OLD COURSE BUT DON'T FORGET YOUR WATERPROOFS
Golf has been played at St Andrews since the 15th century and by 1457 was apparently so popular that James II had to ban it because it was interfering with his troops' archery practice. Few people realise that anyone can play the Old Course, the world's most famous golf course. Although it lies beside the exclusive, all-male Royal & Ancient Golf Club, the Old Course is a public course, and is not owned by the club.

It's worth getting a round in soonish as it's possible the Old Course could acquire some new water features. With the rising sea levels in St Andrews Bay due to global warming, golfers may soon require waders! St Andrews Links Trust take the threat of rising sea levels seriously, closely monitoring the effects on the Old Course. Flood barriers currently keep the sea at bay, but if levels continue to rise other measures will need to be taken to keep the hallowed grounds safe.

Getting a tee-off time is – literally – something of a lottery. Unless you book months in advance, the only chance you have of playing here is by entering a ballot before 2pm on the day before you wish to play. Be warned that applications by ballot are normally heavily oversubscribed, and green fees are a mere £90. There's no play on Sunday.

If your number doesn't come up, there are five other public courses in the area, none with quite the cachet of the Old Course, but all of them significantly cheaper. Their fees are: New £45, Jubilee £40, Eden £30, Strathtyrum £20 and Balgove £10.

Advance bookings for the Old Course can be made online or by letter, phone, fax or email to the **Reservations Office, St Andrews Links Trust** (☎ 01334-466666; fax 479555; reservations@standrews.org.uk; www.standrews.org.uk; Pilmour House, St Andrews, Fife KY16 9SF). You must present a handicap certificate or letter of introduction from your club.

Sands (8 miles/13km). It's not advisable to cycle the narrow and busy coast road from St Andrews to Crail as it has dangerous bends and no verges in places.

Walking Tour

The best place to start a walking tour is **St Andrews Museum**. Turn left out of the museum driveway and follow Doubledykes Rd back to the roundabout on City Rd. Turn right, then left onto South St. You'll pass through **West Port**, formerly Southgait Port, the main entrance to the old town. It was built in 1589 and based on Netherbow Port in Edinburgh. Walking east along South St, you pass **Louden's Close** on the right, a good example of the closes built according to the city's medieval street plan. Continuing along South St, the apse of the 16th-century **Blackfriars Chapel** stands in front of Madras College.

Opposite the Victorian town hall is **Holy Trinity**, the town's parish church, built in 1410. On the same side of the street as the town hall is **St Mary's College**, founded in 1537; beside it is the university library. The oak tree in the courtyard is over 250 years old.

Go left along Church St to cobbled Market St. Street markets are held around the **Mercat Cross**, although the cross is now a fountain. The TIC is nearby, at No 70.

Tours

St Andrews Walkabout Tours (☎ 472021; TIC; audio tours £5) are self-guided audio tours of the town, which relate stories of historical St Andrews. There's an option to hire overnight and tours last for one to three hours. Tours include discounted entry to other attractions.

Witches Tour (☎ 655057; adult/child £6/4) recounts the history and folklore of the town in an unusual fashion, with tales of ghosts and witches enlivened by theatrical stunts. It starts at 8pm on Tuesday, Friday and Sunday in June and July and Friday only the rest of the year (starts 7.30pm October to April). Meet outside the Tudor Inn on North St.

Festivals & Events

The Royal & Ancient Golf Club is the body that organises the annual **Open Golf Championship**, which takes place in July.

However, the tournament venue changes from year to year, and the Open only comes to St Andrews itself every five or six years – the venue for future championships can be found on the Open's official website (www.opengolf.com).

St Andrews Highland Games (☎ 476305) are held on the North Haugh on the last Sunday in July.

During the **Lammas Fair**, held over four days preceding the second Tuesday in August, South St and part of Market St are taken over by carnival rides, craft stalls and street theatre.

St Andrews Week is five days of festivities held around St Andrews Day (30 November), the feast day of Scotland's patron saint. The celebrations include a festival of Scottish food and drink, and various arts events.

Sleeping

Bear in mind that all St Andrews accommodation gets booked solid well in advance whenever a major golf tournament is being held and it's normally very busy anytime over summer.

BUDGET

Cairnsmill Caravan Park (☎ 473604; cairnsmill@aol.com; Largo Rd; tent site for 2 from £10; ☼ Mar-Oct) About a mile west of St Andrews on the A915, this camping ground is on a crest with brilliant views over St Andrews. There's not much space between sites – they pack 'em in.

St Andrews Tourist Hostel (☎ 479911; lee@eastgatehostel.com; Inchcape House, St Mary's Pl; dm £12; ☼ 7am-11pm) This 44-bed hostel (six- or eight-bed dorms), only five minutes' walk from the bus station, is the only backpacker accommodation in town, so it fills up quickly. The male and female dorms are clean and a little austere.

MID-RANGE

The cheapest B&Bs in St Andrews are a five- to 15-minute walk south of the centre on Largo Rd and the streets to its east. The following are more central but still reasonably priced. Note that single rooms are extremely hard to come by and should be booked in advance.

Meade B&B (☎ 477350; 5 Albany Pl; r per person £20; ✕) This family home has just one room to offer, but it should be your first port of call in town as it is an absolute bargain! The congenial owner will happily let it out to singles without charging an additional supplement – a rarity in St Andrews. The room is large, airy and in a great location, with free parking just across the road.

Fairnie House (☎ 474094; kate@fairniehouse .freeserve.co.uk; 10 Abbey St; r per person £18-35; ☒) A relaxed and friendly B&B in a Georgian townhouse near the Byre Theatre, Fairnie House has one double and two twin rooms. There's a very homely feel to this place and the communal dining room encourages conversation.

Almost every house on Murray Park and Murray Pl is a guesthouse. The area couldn't be more convenient but prices are on the high side.

Lorimer House (☎ /fax 476599; lorimersta@ talk21.com; 19 Murray Park; r per person £22-30; ☒) This very comfortable house has spacious family rooms, as well as single rooms; the top-floor bedroom has fine views.

Cameron House (☎ 472306; www.cameronhouse -sta.co.uk; 11 Murray Park; r per person £30; ☒) Cameron House is a soft and cuddly place that makes you feel right at home, especially with the teddy bears hanging off the bed posts.

TOP END

Hazelbank Hotel (☎ /fax 472466; www.hazelbank.com; 28 The Scores; s £49.50-100, d £70-118; ☒) The elegant Hazelbank is a small (10 rooms) but comfortable, family-run hotel in a fine 1898 Victorian townhouse. The rooms have king-size beds and the four sea-view rooms are delightful.

Parkland Hotel (☎ 473620; www.parklandstandrews .com; Doubledykes Rd; r per person £75-100; ☒) Housed in Kinburn Castle, a 19th-century stately home, the six-room Parkland is a great romantic hideaway only a few minutes' walk from the town centre. Ask about cheaper deals, which are sometimes available.

Old Course Hotel (☎ 474371; reservations@oldcourse hotel.co.uk; r from £225; ☒) If money's really no object, stay at this imposing, 144-room resort hotel and spa overlooking the Old Course at the western end of town. There are resident golf pros and a squad of therapists and beauticians providing massage for both body and ego. If you're planning to drop in out of the blue, it's worth noting that you need prior permission to use the helipad.

Eating

BUDGET

Cafe Jannetta (☎ 473285; 33 South St; baguettes & panini £3-4, salads £5) This informal place has outdoor seating, an impressive array of salads and terrific smoothies made with the ice-cream from next door.

B Jannetta (☎ 473285; 31 South St; 2-dip cone from £1.50) This is a St Andrews institution and on a hot weekend there is a constant stream of people outside the place feverishly licking a delicious cone before it becomes a puddle. All up you can choose from 52 varieties of ice cream. The most popular flavour? Vanilla. The weirdest? Irn Bru!

IJ Mellis (149 South St) Calling all cheese addicts! The aromas from this traditional cheesemongers will knock you flat as you stroll past. Pop in for a look – it sometimes has free tastings.

Tesco (138 Market St) is a good centrally located supermarket if you're self-catering.

MID-RANGE

Broons Bistro (☎ 478479; 119 North St; mains lunch £4.50-6.50, dinner £9-12) Housed in part of an old cinema, Broons is a friendly, humming bar-bistro with a smoky atmosphere, and kicking cocktails. There's plenty of good-value food day and night (two courses in the evening are £11), including excellent meat dishes.

Ziggy's (☎ 473686; 6 Murray Pl; mains £6.95-10.95, steaks £11.95-15.95; ☾ lunch & dinner) This small, darkened restaurant has an offbeat music recording-studio theme. There's an open kitchen and a menu that does a bit of everything, including burgers, a range of steaks, Mexican, seafood and veggie dishes.

Grill House Restaurant (☎ 470500; Inchcape House, St Mary's Pl; mains £7-10) Grill House, in the same building as St Andrews Tourist Hostel, is a funky Mexican place with décor designed by Glasgow artist Jan Nimmo. It serves great fajitas and a mean *mole poblano* (char-grilled chicken in a chilli and bitter chocolate sauce). The two-course lunch for £4.95 is a great deal.

Seafood Restaurant (☎ 479475; The Scores; mains lunch £8-12, dinner £14-17.50; ☾ noon-4pm & 6pm-late) The newly opened Seafood Restaurant occupies a stylish, glass-walled room, built out over the sea, with plush navy carpet, crisp white linen and panoramic views of St Andrews Bay. It offers top-class seafood and an excellent wine list and looks set to take over as St Andrews' finest restaurant.

Vine Leaf (☎ 477497; 131 South St; 2-course dinner £19.95; 🕑 from 7pm Tue-Sat) The Vine Leaf is one of St Andrews' best eating places, offering a gourmet menu of seafood, game, Scottish beef and vegetarian dishes in a refined atmosphere.

Doll's House (☎ 477422; 3 Church Sq; mains £8.50-12.45; 🕑 lunch & dinner) The Doll's House pips the Vine Leaf on price – the two-course lunch at £6.95 is unbeatable value, and the early-evening, two-course deal for £11.95 isn't bad either. The changing menu makes the most of fresh local fish and other Scottish produce.

TOP END

Peat Inn (☎ 840206; 3-course lunch/dinner £19.50/30; 🕑 lunch & dinner Tue-Sat) Run by master chef and wine expert David Wilson, the Peat Inn is one of the best restaurants in Scotland. Housed in a rustic country inn about 6 miles (10km) west of St Andrews, its Michelin Rosette-winning menu includes such delights as medallions of monkfish and lobster with mushrooms and artichoke hearts. To get there, head west on the A915 then turn right on the B940.

Drinking

Central Bar (Market St) The Central Bar is all polished brass and polished accents, full of students from south of the border, tourists and locals. This is the best pub in town with an impressive array of real ales.

Victoria (☎ 476964; 1 St Mary's Pl) Upstairs at the Victoria is popular with all types of students and serves good bar meals from £4.50. There's a café bar here or a lounge bar where you can sink into a sofa.

Whey Pat Tavern (cnr Argyle & Bridge Sts) This is an old-fashioned pub with bar stools and comfy bench seating. It has a range of real ales on tap and is a good place to escape the crowds.

Entertainment

Check the local *What's On* guide, published weekly and available from the TIC or its website (www.visit-standrews.co.uk).

Byre Theatre (☎ 475000; www.byretheatre.com; Abbey St) This theatre company started life in a converted cow byre in the 1930s, and is now in flash new premises making

clever use of light and space. Contact the TIC or check the website for details of performances.

The two-screen **New Picture House** (☎ 473509; North St; tickets £3.60) shows current films.

Getting There & Away

St Andrews is 55 miles (88km) north of Edinburgh and 13 miles (21km) south of Dundee.

BUS

Stagecoach Fife operates a bus service from Edinburgh to St Andrews via Kirkcaldy (£5.50, two hours, hourly). Buses to Dundee (£2.60, 30 minutes, half-hourly) and Cupar (£2.30, 20 minutes, at least hourly) also run frequently. Bus No 23 runs to Stirling (£5.20, two hours, six daily Monday to Saturday). Frequent services to East Neuk destinations include Crail (£2.30, 30 minutes) and Anstruther (£2.30, 40 minutes).

TRAIN

There is no train station in St Andrews itself, but you can take a train from Edinburgh to Leuchars, 5 miles (8km) to the northwest (£8.50, one hour, hourly), and then a bus or taxi into town.

From Leuchars, bus Nos 96 and 99 leave every 20 mins during the day (hourly in the evening) for St Andrews.

Getting Around

Ian Cowe Coachworks (ICC Rentals; ☎ 472543; carhire@ iccrentals.com; 76 Argyle St) rents small cars for £25 per day, unlimited mileage.

There are taxi ranks at the bus station and at Holy Trinity Church on South St. To order a cab, call **Golf City Taxis** (☎ 477788). **Town & Country** (☎ 840444) has taxis with wheelchair access. A taxi between Leuchars train station and the town centre costs around £8.

Spokes (☎ 77835; 37 South St) rents mountain bikes for £6.50/10.50 per half/full day.

EAST NEUK

The section of the southern Fife coast that stretches from Crail westwards to Largo Bay is known as East Neuk (*neuk* means 'corner' in Scots). There are several picturesque fishing villages and some good coastal walks in the area. Pick up a copy of the *East Neuk* bus timetable booklet from TICs.

Crail

☎ 01333 / pop 1695

One of the prettiest East Neuk villages and a favourite with artists, Crail has a much-photographed and painted harbour ringed by stone cottages with red pantiled roofs.

The **TIC** (☎ 450869; 62 Marketgate; ◌ 10am-1pm & 2-5pm Mon-Sat, noon-5pm Sun Apr-early Oct) is at the museum. The **Royal Bank** (cnr St Andrews Rd & Marketgate) nearby has an ATM.

There are far fewer fishing boats here now than there once were, but you can still buy fresh lobster (£20 a kilo) and crab (£2.50) from a kiosk at the harbour. Just to the east is a large grassed area with seating, the perfect place to munch on your shellfish while admiring the view across to the Isle of May. The village's history and involvement with the fishing industry is outlined in the **Crail Museum** (☎ 450869; 62 Marketgate; admission free; ◌ 10am-1pm & 2-5pm Mon-Sat, 2-5pm Sun Jun-Sep, 2-5pm Sat & Sun Apr & May).

Crail Gallery (☎ 450316; High St; ◌ 11am-1pm & 2-5pm Wed-Mon) is a local gallery with some terrific artists' impressions of Crail and East Neuk. There are also framed prints of St Andrews.

The 18th century **Selcraig House** (☎ 450697; www.selcraighouse.co.uk; 47 Nethergate; s £25, d £30-50) has a range of excellent rooms. On the loft-style top floor is a rather cramped but cheap double. The middle floor has a room with a four-poster bed, and you can listen to records spun on a Victorian-era gramophone in the conservatory.

Crail is 10 miles (16km) southeast of St Andrews. Stagecoach Fife bus No 95 between Leven, Anstruther, Crail and St Andrews passes through Crail hourly every day (£2.30, 30 minutes to St Andrews).

Anstruther

☎ 01333 / pop 3442

Anstruther is a vivacious, former fishing village with lots of twisting streets, interesting wynds and knick-knack shops lining Rodger and High Sts. There are many fine buildings and walking is definitely the best way to absorb the atmosphere of the place. Anstruther (often pronounced en-ster) has grown to become the main tourist centre of East Neuk.

The **TIC** (☎ 311073; Fisheries Museum; ◌ daily Apr-Oct) is the best in East Neuk. There are banks with ATMs in the town centre.

SIGHTS

The displays at the excellent **Scottish Fisheries Museum** (☎ 310628; www.scottish-fisheries-museum.org; St Ayles, Harbourhead; adult/child £3.50/2.50; ◌ 10am-4.30pm Mon-Sat, 11am-4pm Sun) include the Zulu Gallery, which houses the huge, part-restored hull of a traditional Zulu-class fishing boat, redolent with the scent of tar and timber. Afloat in the harbour outside the museum lies *The Reaper*, a fully restored Fifie-class fishing boat, built in 1902.

The mile-long **Isle of May**, 6 miles (10km) southeast of Anstruther, is a stunning nature reserve. Between April and July, the intimidating cliffs are packed with breeding kittiwakes, razorbills, guillemots, shags and around 40,000 puffins. Inland are the remains of the 12th-century **St Adrian's Chapel**, dedicated to a monk who was murdered on the island by the Danes in 875.

The five-hour excursion to the island on the **May Princess** (☎ 310103; www.isleofmayferry.com; adult/child £14/6) including two to three hours ashore, sails daily (not Friday and weather permitting) from May to October. You can make reservations and buy tickets at the harbour kiosk near the museum at least an hour before departure. Departure times vary depending on the tide – check times for the next week or so by calling, or checking the website.

SLEEPING & EATING

Gaberlunzie House (☎ 312337; 18 High St; s/d £25/40) This snug 16th-century cottage, close to the harbour, offers informal accommodation and is next door to a great pub. Gaberlunzie is an old Fife word meaning beggar, tramp or homeless person – tourists also welcome!

Spindrift (☎ /fax 310573; info@thespindrift.co.uk; Pittenweem Rd; r per person £26.50-32) The Spindrift is a top place to spoil yourself – it's a luxury, licensed small hotel in a 19th-century sea-captain's house. The hosts ensure you'll enjoy the sumptuous accommodation which is a cut above the other guesthouses on this street.

Dreel Tavern (☎ 310727; 16 High St West; mains £7; ◌ lunch & dinner) This charming old pub on the banks of the Dreel Burn serves excellent bar meals and has an outdoor beer garden in summer. There are some top-quality cask ales here including Dark Island (Orkney) and Arran Blonde.

Cellar Restaurant (☎ 310378; 24 East Green; 3-course set dinner £30) Tucked away in an alley behind the museum, the Cellar is famous for its seafood and fine wines. Inside it's elegant and upmarket. Advance bookings are essential.

There's a fresh **seafood kiosk** on the waterfront selling dressed crab (£2.50), mussels and jellied eel.

GETTING THERE & AWAY
Anstruther is 9 miles (15km) south of St Andrews. Stagecoach Fife bus No 95 runs daily from Leven (more departures from St Monans) to Anstruther and onto St Andrews (£2.30, 40 minutes, hourly) via Crail.

Around Anstruther
A magnificent example of Lowland Scottish domestic architecture, **Kellie Castle** (☎ 01333-720271; adult/child £5/3.75; ☸ castle Easter & 1-5pm Jun-Sep; garden 9.30am-sunset daily) has creaky floors, crooked little doorways and some marvellous works of art, giving it an air of authenticity. It's set in a beautiful garden and many rooms contain superb plasterwork, the Vine room being the most exquisite. The original part of the building dates from 1360; it was enlarged to its present dimensions around 1606.

The castle is 3 miles (5km) west of Anstruther on the B9171. Stagecoach bus No 95A runs from Anstruther to Grangemuir (four daily Monday to Saturday); from here it's about a 1½-mile walk to the castle.

Three miles (5km) north of Anstruther, off the B9131 to St Andrews, is **Scotland's Secret Bunker** (☎ 01333-310301; www.secretbunker .co.uk; Troy Wood; adult/child £6.95/3.95; ☸ 10am-6pm Apr-Oct). This fascinating cold war relic was to be one of Britain's underground command centres and a home for Scots leaders in the event of nuclear war. Hidden 30m underground and surrounded by nearly 5m of reinforced concrete are the austere operation rooms, communication centre and dormitories. It's very authentic and uses original artefacts of the period, which make for an absorbing exploration. A film called *The War Game*, banned by the BBC, gives a horrifying account of the realities of a nuclear war. It's graphic and definitely not for kids, but a film every world leader should be forced to watch. The Scottish CND (Campaign for Nuclear Disarmament) have

an exhibition, bringing home the realities of Britain's current nuclear Trident policy. The bunker is a gripping experience and is highly recommended.

Take Stagecoach bus No 95 to Crail, get off at the garden centre on St Andrews Rd and walk about 3 miles (5km) along the B940 to Troy Wood and the Bunker. Alternatively, the bunker runs a free **minibus** (☎ 0770 249 4935) which will pick you up from most places in East Neuk (minimum of six people required).

St Monans
☎ 01333 / pop 1435
This ancient fishing village is just over a mile west of Pittenweem and is named after a local cave-dwelling saint who was probably killed by pirates.

The **parish church**, at the western end of the village, was built in 1362 on orders from a grateful King David II, who was rescued by villagers from shipwreck in the Firth of Forth. A model of a full-rigged ship, dating from 1800, hangs above the altar. The church commands sweeping views of the firth; and the past echoes inside the church's cold, whitewashed walls.

St Monans Heritage Collection (5 West Shore; admission free; ☸ 11am-1pm & 2-4pm Tue, Thu, Sat & Sun Easter-Oct), on the harbour, is a wonderful small gallery devoted to the history of the St Monans' fishing industry through a collection of 20th-century B&W photos and several artefacts. Most of the photos were taken by a local photographer and the collection changes monthly.

You're better off staying in Anstruther as there is little accommodation here. **Green Door Cafe** (☎ 739066; 6 Station Rd; light meals £1.60-2.85; ☸ 10am-5pm Mon-Sat; ☲) is a modern café serving excellent snacks, fresh cakes, and has changing photographic exhibitions. **Itches** (☎ 730327; 16 West End; 3-course dinner £30) is a superb seafood restaurant just west of the harbour and within salt-spray distance of the sea.

Bus details for St Monans are as for Anstruther (see left).

Elie & Earlsferry
☎ 01333 / pop 1500
These two attractive villages mark the southwestern end of East Neuk. There are great sandy beaches and good walks along the coast.

Elms Guest House (☎ 330404; www.elms-elie.co.uk; 14 Park Pl, Elie; r per person £27.50) is a very relaxed and comfortable, family-run guesthouse with great rooms that get plenty of natural light. The family room has separate bedrooms for parents and kids.

Ship Inn (☎ 330246; The Toft, Elie; mains £8-10), down by Elie harbour, is a pleasant and popular place for a bar lunch. Seafood and Asian dishes feature on the menu and, on a sunny day, you can tuck in at a table outside, overlooking the wide sweep of the bay.

PERTHSHIRE & KINROSS

Perthshire & Kinross is the living, breathing heart of Scotland in more ways than one: it's the former home to the Stone of Destiny, Aberfeldy is the geographical centre of the country, and Perth is the former capital of Scotland.

The region is an absolute joy to explore – on a scale of one to 10, Perthshire rates about nine and a half. It never ceases to surprise, with its stunning castles and medieval cathedrals and its natural beauty. In a country of high winds and a thriving logging industry, Perthshire is big tree country where ancient woodlands survive among younger prosperous regeneration forests. It is this legacy that could hold the key to Scotland's environmental future and create a spark igniting a green recovery in the rest of the country.

Scenically, Perthshire and Kinross contain, in miniature, as many variations in terrain as Scotland itself. Loch Tay in Western Perthshire is a highlight of the area with picture-perfect Kenmore at its eastern head, Ben Lawers (1214m) standing guard over its northern bank and the remote, magical Glen Lyon on the other side of the strapping Ben Lawers.

GETTING AROUND

Perth and Kinross Council has a **Public Transport Traveline** (☎ 0845 301 1130) and produces a useful public transport map showing all services in the region.

Aberfeldy postbus (☎ 01887-820400) Serves remote West Perthshire.

Citylink (☎ 0870 550 5050)

Stagecoach Fife (☎ 01592-261461)

Stagecoach Perth (☎ 01738-629339)

Strathtay Scottish (☎ 01382-228345)

Trains run alongside the A9, destined for Aviemore and Inverness. The other main line connects Perth with Stirling (in the south) and Dundee and Arbroath (in the east).

KINROSS & LOCH LEVEN

☎ 01577 / pop 4681

Kinross is best known as the access point for Loch Leven Castle, which is a quintessential Scottish treasure – a castle that sits on a small island. The loch itself is the largest in the lowlands and is known for its extensive bird life.

The helpful **Heart of Scotland TIC** (☎ 863680; kinrosstic@perthshire.co.uk; ☼ daily Apr-Oct, call for winter hrs), by Junction 6 of the M90, has an exhibition on the area.

Sights

Evocative **Loch Leven Castle** (☎ 0777 804 0483; adult/child incl Kinross ferry £3.50/1.20; ☼ 9.30am-5.15pm Apr-Oct), served as a fortress and prison from the late 14th century. Its most famous captive was Mary Queen of Scots, who spent almost a year incarcerated here from 1567. Her infamous charms bewitched Willie Douglas, who managed to get hold of the cell keys to release her, then row her across to the shore. The castle is now roofless but basically intact.

The **Scottish Raptor Centre** (☎ 865650; www .scottishraptorcentre.com; Turfhills; adult/child £3/1.50; ☼ 9.30am-5.30pm) is the largest falconry in the country, and there is an impressive collection of birds of prey, especially owls. There are regular falconry displays and courses are also available. The centre is behind the TIC.

Sleeping & Eating

Turfhills House B&B (☎ 863881; s/d £30/50) Turfhills is a sumptuous, genteel, musty old place with grand Victorian furnishings, set in some lush gardens. It's next to the tourist office and makes an excellent overnight stop if you're whizzing up the A9, it's getting late in the day and you don't want to mess around in town trying to find accommodation.

Roxburghe Guest House (☎ 862498; www .roxburgheguesthouse.co.uk; 126 High St, Kinross; s/d/t per person £30/22/18) A lovely guesthouse with cool, tastefully furnished rooms in a rickety,

CENTRAL SCOTLAND

old property, Roxburghe feels like a home away from home. Prices may be up for negotiation for small groups.

Carlin Maggie's (☎ 863652; 191 High St, Kinross; lunch/dinner mains £8/£10-15; ☺ noon-2pm Tue-Sun, 6.30-9pm Tue-Sat) This is a highly recommended restaurant, specialising in seafood and vegetarian dishes. There's a three-course dinner Tuesday to Thursday for £16. Carnivores will delight in the roast trio of Angus game (beef, pigeon and duck).

Getting There & Away

Citylink and Stagecoach Fife have bus services between Perth (£3.50, 30 minutes, hourly) and Kinross. In the other direction buses go to Edinburgh (£4.90, 1½ hours, hourly).

PERTH

☎ 01738 / pop 43,450

Lodged snugly in a lush valley alongside the M90, Perth's biggest draw card is historical Scone Palace, but the city's grand Georgian buildings by the banks of the River Tay possess their own splendour. This market town was once a weaving, dyeing and glove-making centre and Scotland's capital. Today it exudes a demure pride, suggesting the town walls have not forgotten their past significance. Perth is not simply quaint though; embedded in the centuries-old architecture skirting the cobblestone streets, is a cosmopolitan vibe, reflected in imaginative cuisine, welcoming pubs, historical sites and a gallery or two. In the 1990s the town was voted the best place to live in Britain for quality of life.

History

Perth's rise in importance derives from Scone (pronounced scoon), 2 miles (3km) north of the town. In 838, Kenneth MacAlpin became the first king of a united Scotland and brought the Stone of Destiny, to Scone. An important abbey was built on the site. From this time on, all Scottish kings were invested here, even after Edward I of England stole the sacred talisman, carting it off to London's Westminster Abbey in 1296. In 1996 Prime Minister John Major persuaded the Queen to promise to return it to Scotland, but it went to Edinburgh Castle rather than Scone. There's actually some doubt about

whether Edward I stole the real stone – he might have stolen a fake!

From the 12th century, Perth was Scotland's capital, and in 1437 James I was murdered here. There were four important monasteries in the area and the town was a target for the Reformation movement in Scotland.

Orientation

Most of the town lies on the western bank of the Tay River; Scone Palace and some of the B&Bs are on the eastern bank. There are two large parks: North Inch, the scene of the infamous Battle of the Clans in 1396, and South Inch. The bus and train stations are close to each other, near the northwestern corner of South Inch.

Information

Gig@Bytes (☎ 451580; 5 St Paul's Sq; ☺ 10am-6.30pm Mon-Sat, noon-5pm Sun; £5 per hr)

Lloyds TSB (King Edward St) Has an ATM.

Perth Royal Infirmary (☎ 623311; Taymount Tce) West of the town centre.

TIC (☎ 450600; Lower City Mills, West Mill St; ☺ daily Apr-Oct, Mon-Sat Nov-Mar) An efficient place that can assist with tracking down accommodation in the area.

Sights

SCONE PALACE

Decadent **Scone Palace** (☎ 552300; adult/child £6.35/3.75; ☺ 9.30am-5.30pm Apr-Oct), 2 miles (3km) north of Perth and just off the A93 near Old Scone, was built in 1580 on a site intrinsic to Scottish history (see left). It's one of Perthshire's premier tourist attractions.

The palace's interior is a gallery of fine French furniture, including Marie Antoinette's writing table and a 16th-century needle-work hanging, worked by Mary Queen of Scots. Superb antique Chinese vases mingle with 18th- and 19th-century porcelain, and the walls drip with regal portraits of earls and countesses. Even the cornices, ceilings and walls are exquisite (the drawing room wallpaper is silk!). The earl and countess of Mansfield have owned the palace for almost 400 years and still host family functions in their sumptuous abode.

Outside, resident peacocks unfold their splendid plumage in the magnificent grounds, which incorporate a Pinetum, a wild garden, a butterfly garden and the all-important cricket pitch. Bus No 3 from

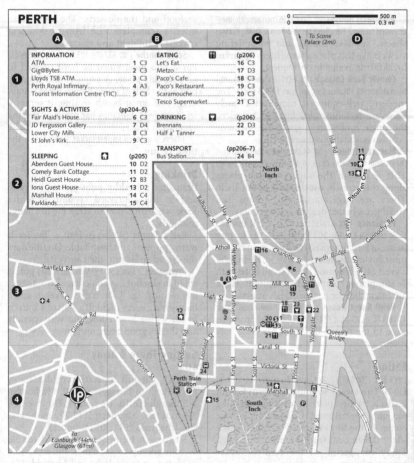

PERTH

INFORMATION		
ATM	**1**	C3
Gig@Bytes	**2**	C3
Lloyds TSB ATM	**3**	C3
Perth Royal Infirmary	**4**	A3
Tourist Information Centre (TIC)	**5**	C3

SIGHTS & ACTIVITIES		(pp204–5)
Fair Maid's House	**6**	C3
JD Fergusson Gallery	**7**	D4
Lower City Mills	**8**	C3
St John's Kirk	**9**	C3

SLEEPING		(p205)
Aberdeen Guest House	**10**	D2
Comely Bank Cottage	**11**	D2
Heidl Guest House	**12**	B3
Iona Guest House	**13**	D2
Marshall House	**14**	C4
Parklands	**15**	C4

EATING		(p206)
Let's Eat	**16**	C3
Metzo	**17**	D3
Paco's Cafe	**18**	C3
Paco's Restaurant	**19**	C3
Scaramouche	**20**	C3
Tesco Supermarket	**21**	C3

DRINKING		(p206)
Brennans	**22**	D3
Half a' Tanner	**23**	C3

TRANSPORT		(pp206–7)
Bus Station	**24**	B4

Perth comes here roughly hourly, most of the day.

ST JOHN'S KIRK
Daunting **St John's Kirk** (admission free; 10am-4pm Mon-Sat May-Sep, plus 10am-1pm Sun Jun-Sep), founded in 1126, is surrounded by cobbled streets and is still the centrepiece of the town. In 1559 John Knox preached a powerful sermon here that helped begin the Reformation, inciting a frenzied destruction of Scone abbey and other religious sites.

JD FERGUSSON GALLERY
Within the original Perth waterworks building, aptly titled the Round House, **JD Fergusson Gallery** (441944; cnr Marshall Pl & Tay St; admission free; 10am-5pm Mon-Sat) contains the most extensive collection of work by notable Scottish Colourist and Perthshire local JD Fergusson. Pieces reflect heavy French (due to Fergusson's prolonged stay across the channel) and Post Impressionist influences.

Sleeping
Aberdeen Guest House (/fax 633183; buchan@aberdeenguesthouse.fsnet.co.uk; 13 Pitcullen Cres; s/d from £20/40) A cheery place with terrific, spacious rooms and thoughtful hosts – this is a bright spark among the sea of B&Bs along this strip. Rooms are well furnished, homely and have that extra touch that comes from people who enjoy their work.

CENTRAL SCOTLAND

Iona Guest House (☎ /fax 627261; ionaguesthouse@ tinyworld.co.uk; 2 Pitcullen Cres; s/d from £20/38) Crisp sheets, spotless rooms and meandering views make this place a favourite; vegetarian breakfast is available on request.

Comely Bank Cottage (☎ 631118; comelybankcott@ hotmail.com; 19 Pitcullen Cres; s/d from £20/38 ; ✗) The modern, well-equipped rooms at Comely Bank are recommended for solo travellers; the single rooms are a good size. Genuine Scottish hospitality is guaranteed.

Marshall House (☎ 442886; gallagher@marshall -guest-house.freeserve.co.uk; 6 Marshall Pl; s/d £30/40) This is one of the superior-value places along this stretch, overlooking South Inch. There are large, tartan-clad rooms and you'll get a better deal on a longer stay.

Parklands (☎ 622451, fax 622046; 2 St Leonard's Bank; s/d from £79/99; ✗) Parklands, the former home of lord provosts (mayors), is one of the most luxurious places to stay in Perth, and a great little hideaway. It's a small hotel with 14 sumptuous rooms and a restaurant. There are often cheaper package deals available.

Heidl Guest House (☎ 635031; www.heidl.co.uk; 43 York Pl; s £20-24, d £34-50) A solid old favourite, close to the centre, the Heidl has good, tidy rooms.

Eating

Let's Eat (☎ 643377; 77 Kinnoul St; starters £4-6, mains £10-15) This award-winning and very pleasant bistro is the best place in town for splashing out on a special meal. Outstanding cuisine comes in the form of creative dishes with a slight Italian bent (Scottish pastrami aside). Enjoy an aperitif on the comfy couches before indulging your palate.

Paco's Café (☎ 629341; 16 St John's Pl; breakfast £4-6, mains £6-8; ◷ 8.30am-7pm Mon-Sat, 10am-5pm Sun) Paco's is a great spot for a cup of coffee, breakfast or meal any time of the day. It's trendy dining alfresco, or inside among the cheeses and salamis of the continental deli.

Paco's Restaurant (☎ 622290; 3 Mill St; mains £6.50-12) is the place to migrate to at dinner time – there's a huge selection of meals (steaks burgers, pizza, pasta, seafood), including good choices for vegetarians.

Metzo (☎ 626016; 33 George St; 3-course dinner £12.95, mains £8-12; ◷ lunch & dinner Mon-Sat, dinner Sun) Metzo is a new kid on the block and is proving popular with diners. The service is excellent and it's noted as being very good value for money. Highlights include the seafood and the desserts. The cool, clean interior (complete with leopard-skin seat covers) is ambient and relaxed.

Scaramouche (☎ 637479; 103 South St; lunches £6) For a pub meal you'd be hard-pressed to go past this place. A popular and friendly pub at the hub of street life on Perth's main drag, with great booth seating, it serves a wide range of delicious bar meals, including vegetarian dishes.

There's a **Tesco supermarket** (South St) in the town centre.

Drinking

Perth has a healthy pubs-per-capita ratio and in the courtyard around St John's Kirk you won't have to stray far to change draughts.

Half a' Tanner (St John's Pl) Half a' Tanner is warm, popular and hospitable. On fine days the crowd spills into the courtyard.

Brennans (St John's St; ◷ Mon-Sat) This pub is small in size but big on personality – there's live music from 9.30pm on weekends and a happy buzz every night. It's a bit of a warren inside with a low ceiling, but very friendly and there's good beers on tap.

Getting There & Away

BUS
Scottish Citylink operates regular buses from Perth to Glasgow (£6.30, 1½ hours), Edinburgh (£6.10, 1½ hours), Dundee (£4, 35 minutes), Aberdeen (£12.70, 2¼ hours) and Inverness (£11.30, 2¾ hours).

Stagecoach buses serve Dunkeld (£2.20, 40 minutes, up to six daily), Pitlochry (£3, one hour, up to six daily) and Aberfeldy (£3, 1¼ hours, up to six daily). They also service Crieff (£2.20, 45 minutes, every hour or two), St Fillans (£3, 1¼ hours, three daily Monday to Saturday) via Crieff and Comrie; and Dunning (£1.80, 40 minutes, eight daily Monday to Saturday) via Forteviot.

Strathtay Scottish buses travel from Perth to Blairgowrie (£2.40, 45 minutes, hourly Monday to Saturday) and Dundee (£2.60, 1¾ hours, hourly).

TRAIN
There's a train service from Glasgow's Queen St (£9.40, one hour, hourly Monday to Saturday, two hourly Sunday), and a rather erratic service from Edinburgh (£9.40, 1½ hours). Other rail destinations

include Stirling (£8, 30 minutes, one or two per hour) and Pitlochry (£8.30, 30 minutes, nine daily, less on Sunday).

STRATHEARN

West of Perth, the wide *strath* (valley) of the River Earn was once a great forest where medieval kings hunted. The whole area is known as Strathearn, a very attractive region of undulating farmland, hills and lochs. The Highlands begin in the western section of Strathearn.

Dunning

☎ 01764 / pop 900

If you think you've entered spooky country around here – you may just be right. On the way into Dunning, about a mile west of the town by the B8062, there's a strange **cross** on a pile of stones with the words 'Maggiewall burnt here 1657 as a witch'. We'd recommend keeping away from bonfires.

The village is dominated by the 12th-century Norman tower of **St Serfs church**, but most of the building dates from 1810. The magnificent 9th-century **Dupplin Cross**, one of the earliest Christian stone crosses in Scotland, was originally near Forteviot (3 miles/5km from Dunning). It's now the regal centrepiece of St Serfs Church and Historic Scotland provides a guided talk on the mysterious monolith.

A wonderful, eccentric little nook-and-cranny pub, **Kirkstyle Inn** (☎ 684248; Kirkstyle Sq; mains £5-14) has style and atmosphere – the food's not half bad either. Book ahead on weekends as it's very popular.

Historic Dunning is about 8 miles (13km) southwest of Perth. Stagecoach bus No 17 runs from Perth to Forteviot and Dunning (£1.80, 40 minutes, eight daily, Monday to Saturday). Docherty's Midland Coaches runs between Dunning and Auchterarder (£1.30, 15 minutes, three daily Monday to Friday).

Auchterarder

☎ 01764 / pop 3945

Four miles (6km) west of Dunning in a rich agricultural area overlooked by the Ochil Hills, the small, neat town of Auchterarder meanders along a winding High St. There's a **TIC** (☎ 663450; 90 High St; ⓧ Mon-Sat Apr-early Jul, Sep & Oct, daily Jul-Aug) with an interesting **heritage centre** (admission free) detailing wide-

ranging aspects of local history. There are some absorbing B&W pictures of the town and nearby Dunning. **Whitelaw's antique shop** (125 High St) almost doubles as a museum of 18th- and 19th-century furniture.

Gleneagles Hotel (☎ 662231; www.gleneagles.com; Auchterarder; s/d from £185/260) Highly rated Gleneagles Hotel, just over 2 miles (3km) west of Auchterarder, is a splendid place with three championship golf courses. Room charges include full use of the extensive leisure facilities. The most expensive room is the £1500 Royal Lochnagar Suite, complete with antiques, silk-lined walls and hand-woven carpets. The hotel even has its own train station, 50 minutes (£9.80) from Glasgow, and there's complimentary transport between the station and hotel. However, if you can afford to stay here, you can afford the limousine from Glasgow airport (£130). Gleneagles has also earned a reputation as a very child-friendly hotel, making it ideal for families. There's plenty here to keep kids entertained including a nursery with all the latest gizmos.

Docherty's Midland Coaches runs buses from Auchterarder to Dunning (£1.30, eight minutes, three daily Monday to Friday), Stirling (£1.80, 40 minutes, four Monday to Friday) and Perth (£1.80, 40 minutes, hourly).

Crieff & Around

☎ 01764 / pop 6579

Scraping the edge of the Highlands, elegant Crieff is an old, resort-style town, as popular with tourists today as it was in Victorian times. The helpful **TIC** (☎ 652578; Town Hall, High St; ⓧ daily Apr-Oct, call for winter hrs) is in the clock tower.

The highly rated **Famous Grouse Experience** (☎ 656565; The Hosh; tours £6; ⓧ daily), at the Glenturret Distillery, has a tour of the traditional malting process. Visitors are also treated to a high-tech, interactive display.

Innerpeffray Library (☎ 652819; Innerpeffray; adult/child incl tour £2.50/50p; ⓧ 10am-12.45pm & 2-4.45pm Mon-Wed, Fri & Sat; 2-4pm Sun Mar-Oct; by appointment only Nov-Feb), about 4 miles (6km) southeast of Crieff on the B8062, is Scotland's first lending library (founded in 1680). There's a huge collection of rare, interesting and ancient books, some of them 500 years old.

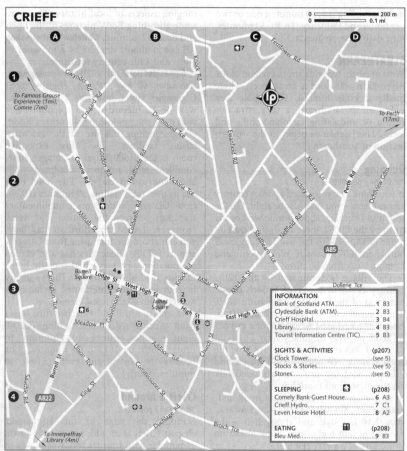

CRIEFF

To Famous Grouse
Experience (1mi);
Comrie (7mi)

To Perth
(17mi)

Dollerie Tce

To Innerpeffray
Library (4mi)

INFORMATION	
Bank of Scotland ATM	1 B3
Clydesdale Bank (ATM)	2 B3
Crieff Hospital	3 B4
Library	4 B3
Tourist Information Centre (TIC)	5 B3

SIGHTS & ACTIVITIES	(p207)
Clock Tower	(see 5)
Stocks & Stories	(see 5)
Stones	(see 5)

SLEEPING	(p208)
Comely Bank Guest House	6 A3
Crieff Hydro	7 C1
Leven House Hotel	8 A2

EATING	(p208)
Bleu Med	9 B3

SLEEPING & EATING

Comely Bank Guest House (☎ 653409; reservations@ comelybank.demon.co.uk; 32 Burrell St; r per person £18-22; ✕) The large rooms at Comely Bank achieve the tall order of being pristine without being sterile. Instead they are inviting and warm and there are good facilities for the disabled including wheelchair access.

Leven House Hotel (☎ 652529; Comrie Rd; r per person £20-24) The best way to describe Leven House is floral, floral, floral. The décor may not win any design awards, but this 1970s-era hotel offers good-value rooms and the friendly hosts make you feel right at home.

Crieff Hydro (☎ 655555; www.crieffhydro.com; Ferntower Rd; DB&B per person £45-77; ✕) An upmarket hotel, it's on the hill at the northern side of town and has one of the highest occupancy rates in Scotland. For such a classy place it's refreshingly unpretentious. The Children's Club will keep the kids happy for hours while you concentrate on grown-up activities.

Bleu Med (☎ 656161; 24 West High St; lunches £5-7, dinner mains £6-8) The years seem to drop by the wayside when you enter the Frank Sinatra-style, Bleu Med. Pizza and pasta are the specialities, but you'll also get baguettes and crepes for lunch and steaks at dinner.

GETTING THERE & AWAY

Hourly Stagecoach buses link Crieff with Perth, less frequently on Sunday (£2.30,

45 minutes). Other buses run to Comrie (£1.40, 20 minutes, roughly hourly Monday to Saturday, every two hours Sunday), St Fillans (£2.10, 35 minutes, five daily Monday to Saturday) and Stirling (£2.65, 50 minutes, four to six daily).

Upper Strathearn
☎ 01764

The Highland villages of **Comrie** (population 1839) and **St Fillans** (population 350), in upper Strathearn, are surrounded by forests and craggy, bare mountaintops where deer and mountain hares live in abundance.

Comrie has a rather tattered elegance hinting at its previous heyday. If you fancy trying to hook a big one, drop into **Drummond Trout Farm & Fishery** (☎ 670500; Comrie; 2-hour session adult/child £3.50/3; ⏱ 10am-5pm Sep-May, 10am-10pm Jun-Aug) just outside of town. It's a great place to take the kids who can fumble around in the pool while you get serious at the specimen pond. You can hire all the gear you need. Your catch will cost £1.70 a pound and cleaning is £1 per fish.

St Fillans enjoys an excellent location at the eastern end of **Loch Earn**, which reflects the silhouettes of distant, towering peaks in its steely-blue waters.

The large, cheery rooms at **St Margaret's** (☎ 670413; Braco Rd, Comrie; r without/with bathroom £18/20) are outstanding for the price. Lower floor rooms have their own sitting area in a sunny mini-conservatory. Vegetarians are catered for and the friendly owners ensure an enjoyable stay.

Comrie is 24 miles (39km) west of Perth and St Fillans is about 5 miles (8km) farther west. Stagecoach operates daily buses from Perth, via Crieff, to Comrie (£2.80, one hour, hourly) and St Fillans (£3, 1¼ hours, three daily except Sunday).

WEST PERTHSHIRE

This remote area of Perthshire is a jewel in Central Scotland's crown. It's difficult to reach via public transport buses are usually once-a-day postal services however these fabulous hills and lochs are well worth making an effort to see.

Aberfeldy & Around
☎ 01887 / pop 1895

Aberfeldy tends to get a bad rap, but we're still scratching our heads trying to figure

out why. Slightly shabby and rough around the edges it may be, but with a couple of great attractions just beyond the town and a spot deep in forest country at the geographical heart of Scotland, Aberfeldy will entice you to linger.

The helpful and knowledgeable **TIC** (☎ 820276; The Square; ⏱ daily Apr-Oct) is in an old church; there's a plan of the town on the outside wall. The **Royal Bank of Scotland** (8 The Square) has an ATM. For medical problems, there's the **cottage hospital** (☎ 820314; Old Crieff Rd).

SIGHTS

Castle Menzies (☎ 820982; Weem; adult/child £3.50/2; ⏱ 10.30am-5pm Mon-Sat & 2-5pm Sun Apr-mid Oct), 1½ miles west of town by the B846, is the impressive restored 16th-century seat of the Chief of the Clan Menzies. The Z-plan tower house is magnificently located against a backdrop of Scottish forest. And inside it doesn't disappoint. The place just smells like a castle should – musty and lived in. It reeks of authenticity, despite extensive restoration work and is a highly recommended ramble. Check out the fireplace in the dungeon-like kitchens and the gaudy great hall upstairs, with windows unfurling a ribbon of lush, green countryside extending into wooded hills beyond the estate.

Glenlyon Gallery (☎ 01887-820202; Boltachan, by Aberfeldy; ⏱ 10am-6pm) brings the wildlife and startling natural beauty of Perthshire to life with vivid paintings and sketches by a talented local artist. Some of Scotland's most priceless treasures are captured on canvas and, if you're interested, can be shipped anywhere in the world. The gallery is signposted off the B846.

SLEEPING

Tigh'n Eilean Guest House (☎ /fax 820109; www.tighneilean.com; Taybridge Dr; s/d £25/44; dinner £14; ⊠) Everything about this property screams comfort – it's a gorgeous place overlooking the Tay. Rooms have stately Victorian furnishings and there's a wonderful lounge with an open fire.

Other recommendations:

Caber-Feidh Guest House (☎ 820342; 56 Dunkeld St; r per person £18-20) The rooms with bathroom are popular so book ahead.

Innis Ghlas Guest House (☎ 820565; 25 Kenmore St; r per person £18; ⊠) This is a very friendly, cosy family home close to the centre.

GETTING THERE & AWAY

Stagecoach runs buses from Aberfeldy to Pitlochry (£2, 45 minutes, nine daily), Blairgowrie (£3.10, 1½ hours, two daily Monday to Friday) and Perth (£3, 1¼ hours, up to six daily Monday to Saturday).

Local bus operators run between Aberfeldy and Kenmore seven times daily from Monday to Saturday (no service on Sunday), three of these continue onto Fortingall, at the head of Glen Lyon.

A postbus service goes to Killin (three hours) via Kenmore, and another goes to the top of Glen Lyon, at Lubreoch, via Fortingall (both once daily Monday to Saturday).

Loch Tay

The greater part of mighty Ben Lawers (1214m), Scotland's ninth-tallest peak, looms over Loch Tay. Drop into the **visitor centre** (☎ 01567-820988; parking donation £2; ☾ 11am-5pm 19 May-14 Sep) high on the slopes of the mountain; the access road is off the A827, on the north shore of the loch and continues over a wild pass to Glen Lyon. A trail leads to the summit from the centre, but you should take a good map (OS map No 51). There is also a much easier nature trail from the visitor centre and ranger-guided walks in summer. Call by for the jaw-dropping views if nothing else.

KENMORE

The wealthy village of Kenmore, at the eastern end of Loch Tay, is about 6 miles (10km) west of Aberfeldy. It's a small but pretty place dominated by a church and clock tower. Don't forget the camera, it's the perfect place for some happy snaps. Just a quarter of a mile along the south Loch Tay road from the village, the **Scottish Crannog Centre** (☎ 01887-830583; adult/child £4.25/3; ☾ 10am-4.30pm mid-Mar–Nov) has a fascinating reconstruction of an artificial, Iron Age island-house. There are exhibits from archaeological dives of crannogs and artistic impressions of what they may have looked like.

Kenmore Hotel (☎ 01887-830205; www.kenmore hotel.com; The Square; r per person £30-55) claims to be Scotland's oldest inn and dates from 1572. Its quaint, spacious rooms are generously furnished and full of character. On the chimney piece in the bar look out for the romantic description of the

---

CRANNOGS

Usually built in a loch for defensive purposes, a crannog (from the Gaelic word *crann*, meaning 'tree') consists of an artificial rock island with timber posts and struts supporting a hut above high-water level. Crannogs were used on many lochs, including Lochs Awe, Earn and Tay, from prehistoric times up to the 18th century. Some crannogs had curious underwater causeways that could zigzag or had traps, making night-time assaults without a boat extremely difficult.

---

countryside written by Robert Burns in 1787. After a few drinks in the bar, watch out for the low doorways on your way upstairs. The **Taymouth Restaurant** (starters £5, mains £8-12; ☾ dinner) overlooks Loch Tay and the mouth-watering menu specialises in seafood creations; the service is first class.

See Aberfeldy & Around (left) for public transport options.

Fortingall & Glen Lyon

Fortingall is one of the prettiest villages in Scotland, with 19th-century thatched cottages in a very tranquil setting. It was designed by James Marjorybanks McLaren, who taught Charles Rennie Mackintosh (p111). The **church** (admission free; ☾ 10am-4pm Apr-Oct) has impressive wooden beams and a 7th-century **monk's bell**. In the churchyard, there's a 5000-year-old yew, probably the oldest tree in Europe. This tree was already ancient when the Romans camped on the meadows by the River Lyon. It's also famous as the reputed birthplace of Pontius Pilate.

Ricketty Roman bridges, Victorian lodges, a Caledonian pine forest and sheer peaks (splashed with red and orange heather) poking through swirling clouds mark the drive along the tiny road into the wonderful **Glen Lyon**. The longest enclosed glen in Scotland, it becomes wilder and more uninhabited as it snakes its way west toward Loch Lyon – few visitors penetrate its remote upper reaches, where capercaillie live in patches of pine forest. You'll need wheels, preferably the motorised kind, but if you're keen and you've the time, cycling through Glen Lyon would be a great way to experience this special place.

Invervar Lodge (☎ 01887-877206; invervar.lodge@ btinternet.com; r per person from £33) is an old Victorian hunting lodge and its isolation makes it the perfect country hideaway. Five miles (8km) from Fortingall, the Swedish hosts offer massages and reflexology after a hard day's tramping. The food here is also very good.

Part of the historic **Fortingall Hotel** (☎ /fax 01887-830367; www.fortingall.com; Fortingall; s/d £44.50/ 79) dates from 1300; there are some great rooms on the 1st floor (try room No 8). The food here is good although only dinner is available and the menu's a bit limited. Note that this hotel does not cater for families.

See Aberfeldy earlier for public transport options (p210).

Strathtummel & Loch Rannoch

The route along Lochs Tummel and Rannoch is worth doing any way you can – by foot, bicycle or car – just don't miss it! Hills of ancient birchwood and forests of spruce, pine and larch make up the Tay Forest park – the king of Scotland's forests. These wooded hills roll into the glittering waters of the lochs and while tracking along the southern side of Loch Tummel you'll be greeted by highland cattle, grand houses, startling views and a collage of greenery – a reminder of the undeniable raw beauty of Perthshire. A visit in autumn is recommended, when the birch trees are at their finest.

Queen's View Visitor Centre (☎ 01796-473123; Strathtummel; £1 parking fee; ☽ 10am-6pm Mar-Oct), at the eastern end of Loch Tummel, has a magnificent outlook towards Schiehallion

---

YEW THE OLDEST TREE?

The remarkable yew standing guard in the churchyard at Fortingall is the reason why the small *kirk* was built here. Known as the 'tree of eternity', a yew regenerates after 500 years and begins to grow again – the small kirk was established because people revered the longevity of the tree. Today this remarkable 5000-year-old yew is a shell of its former self. At its zenith it had a girth of over 17m! But souvenir hunters have reduced it to two much smaller trunks. The setting is perfect for one so ancient, with only the sound of the birds and the swishing of its veil of needles to be heard.

(1083m). There are displays and audiovisual programmes about the area, while picnic tables make an outdoor lunch an inviting option.

Kinloch Rannoch is a great base for local walks (you can walk up the popular peak Schiehallion from Braes of Foss – see the website at www.jmt.org for more information) or a take a cycle trip around **Loch Rannoch.** There's a supermarket with a few local information leaflets and a post office next door. If you're up for an easy stroll, try the **clan trail** around the loch, which has roadside notice boards about local clans. Beyond the western end of the loch you enter bleak Rannoch Moor, which extends all the way to Glen Coe (p308). The rivers and lochs on the moor are good for fishing.

SLEEPING & EATING

Kilvrecht (☎ 01350-727284; Kinloch Rannoch; site per small/large tent £3/6; ☽ Apr-Oct). This simple, basic camping ground (no electricity or showers) has terrific grassy areas for camping, picnic tables and clean toilets. If you enjoy space and your own company, head here – it's 3½ miles (5.5km) from Kinloch Rannoch on the south Loch Rannoch road.

Bunrannoch House (☎ /fax 01882-632407; bun .house@tesco.net; Kinloch Rannoch; B&B/DB&B per person £25/44) Grand Bunrannoch House is a former shooting-lodge, set back from the edge of town. It has a distinctly worn and warm design that makes you feel at home straight away. Rooms vary (some have four-poster beds).

Loch Tummel Inn (☎ 01882-634272; Strathtummel; bar suppers £5, restaurant mains £8-10; ☽ lunch & dinner) This old coaching inn is a snug spot for a good feed from a menu featuring seafood – try the chunky fish chowder. The bar is open all day for a leisurely pint in the beer garden overlooking Loch Tummel. The inn is about 3 miles (5km) from Queen's View.

Moor of Rannoch Hotel (☎ /fax 01882-633238; r per person £40; mains around £7) If you get as far as Rannoch Station (16 miles/26km west of Kinloch Rannoch) you'll be rewarded with the excellent food and lodging there.

GETTING THERE & AWAY

Elizabeth Yule Transport (☎ 01796-472290) operates a service between Kinloch Rannoch and Pitlochry (£2.40, 50 minutes, one to three daily Monday to Saturday). To Queen's View is £1.40 and to Loch Tummel Inn is £1.70.

CENTRAL SCOTLAND

The Pitlochry–Rannoch Station postbus has a once-daily service (Monday to Saturday) via Kinloch Rannoch and both sides of the loch.

ScotRail runs two to four trains daily from Rannoch Station north to Fort William (£6.30, one hour) and Mallaig, and south to Glasgow (£15, 2¾ hours).

PERTH TO AVIEMORE

There are a number of major sights strung along the A9 – which becomes a scenic treat after Pitlochry. It's the main route north to Aviemore and Inverness in the Highlands. Frequent buses and trains run along this route; most stop at the places described in this section.

Dunkeld & Birnam

☎ 01350 / pop 1005

Dunkeld and Birnam have an enviable location nestled in the heart of Perthshire's big tree country. The towns happily throb with tourists, and so they should – there are architectural delights here, including a magnificent cathedral. It's walkers in the surrounding area though who really grease the wheels of tourism, even through the winter months. Dunkeld TIC (☎ 727688; dunkeld tic@perthshire.co.uk; The Cross; ⏱ daily Apr-Oct, call for winter hrs) has to be one of the friendliest in the country. Pick up its leaflet on local walks.

SIGHTS & ACTIVITIES

Situated between open grassland dropping into the River Tay on one side and rolling hills on the other, Dunkeld Cathedral (☎ 0131-668 6800; High St; admission free; ⏱ 9.30am-6.30pm Mon-Sat & 2-6.30pm Sun Apr-Sep, 9.30am-4pm Mon-Sat & 2-4pm Sun Oct-Mar) is one of the most beautifully sited cathedrals in Scotland. Don't miss it on a sunny day, there are few more lovely places to be. Half the cathedral is still in use as a church, the rest is in ruins, and you can explore it all. The oldest part of the original church is the choir, completed in 1350. The 15th-century tower is also still standing. The cathedral was damaged during the Reformation and burnt during the Battle of Dunkeld in 1689.

Across the bridge is Birnam, made famous by Macbeth. There's not much left of Birnam Wood, but there is a small, leafy Beatrix Potter Park (the author spent childhood holidays in the area). In the park you'll find some local history on the life of the author who wrote the evergreen story of Peter Rabbit.

Loch of the Lowes Wildlife Centre (☎ 727337; Loch of the Lowes; admission by donation, £2; ⏱ 10am-5pm Apr-Sep), 2 miles (3km) east of Dunkeld off the A923, has wildlife displays mostly devoted to the majestic osprey. There's also an excellent bird-watching hide with binoculars provided, where you can see the birds nesting during breeding season.

SLEEPING & EATING

Taybank (☎ 727340; Tay Tce; www.taybank.com; s/d £20/40) The Taybank is a live music bar fielding musos from around the area who specialise in late-night jamming. There are great, simple rooms upstairs with shared bathroom. It's very friendly and once you gaze out over the Tay from the breakfast room nursing your hangover, you may not want to leave at all.

Birnam House Hotel (☎ 727462; www.birnam househotel.co.uk; Perth Rd, Birnam; r per person from £35; ⊠) This grand-looking place, with crow-stepped gables, describes itself as 'steeped in history'. Translated this means unrenovated and proud of it. It's an atmospheric place with creaky floors, lets hope it stays this way. Rooms differ in size and quality of furnishings so have a look at a few. Some have great baths and heated towel racks. The adjoining Oak Inn (mains £5-6) does hearty pub grub or you can try the restaurant inside the hotel which displays a distinctive creative flair.

GETTING THERE & AWAY

Dunkeld is 15 miles (24km) north of Perth. Citylink buses between Glasgow/Edinburgh (£4.50, two hours, at least three daily) and Inverness stop at the train station (by Birnam). Birnam to Perth (£4.60) or Pitlochry (£4.30) takes 20 minutes.

Strathtay Scottish has a bus between Blairgowrie and Aberfeldy, via Dunkeld (£1.60, twice-daily Monday to Friday); there's no bus to Aberfeldy during school holidays.

Trains run to Glasgow (£9.90, 1 hours, nine daily Monday to Saturday, four on Sunday) and Inverness (£16.60, 1 hours, eight daily Monday to Saturday, five on Sunday).

Pitlochry

☎ 01796 / pop 2564

Teeming with tourists, Pitlochry manages to absorb its annual influx of visitors and

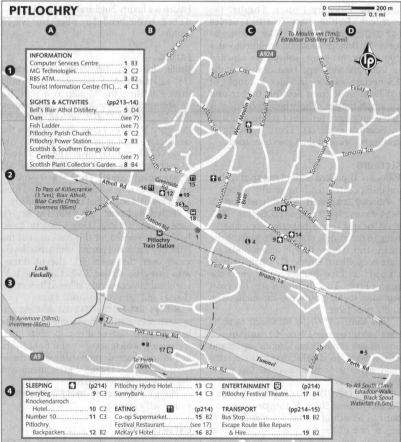

PITLOCHRY

INFORMATION	
Computer Services Centre	**1** B3
MG Technologies	**2** C2
RBS ATM	**3** B2
Tourist Information Centre (TIC)	**4** C3

SIGHTS & ACTIVITIES	(pp213–14)
Bell's Blair Athol Distillery	**5** D4
Dam	(see 7)
Fish Ladder	(see 7)
Pitlochry Parish Church	**6** C2
Pitlochry Power Station	**7** B3
Scottish & Southern Energy Visitor Centre	(see 7)
Scottish Plant Collector's Garden	**8** B4

SLEEPING	(p214)
Derrybeg	**9** C3
Knockendarroch Hotel	**10** C2
Number 10	**11** C3
Pitlochry Backpackers	**12** B2
Pitlochry Hydro Hotel	**13** C2
Sunnybank	**14** C3

EATING	(p214)
Co-op Supermarket	**15** B2
Festival Restaurant	(see 17)
McKay's Hotel	**16** B2

ENTERTAINMENT	(p214)
Pitlochry Festival Theatre	**17** B4

TRANSPORT	(pp214–15)
Bus Stop	**18** B2
Escape Route Bike Repairs & Hire	**19** B2

retain the charm of a Highland town. Clever trick. The main drag is always busy but with all the wonderful sights nearby, you won't need to spend long on it anyway. It's an excellent place to base yourself if you want to explore the region and has good transport connections if you're long on time and short on wheels.

INFORMATION

Computer Services Centre (☎ 473711; 67 Atholl Rd; ⏰ 9.30am-5.30pm Mon-Fri, 12.30-5.30pm Sat) Internet access for 6p per minute; opposite the Royal Bank.

MG Technologies (☎ 474141; 26 Bonnethill Rd; ⏰ 9am-10pm) Internet access for £1.50 per 15 minutes.

Post office (Atholl Rd)

Royal Bank of Scotland (Atholl Rd) Has an ATM.

TIC (☎ 472215; pitlochrytic@perthshire.co.uk; 22 Atholl Rd; ⏰ daily Apr-Oct, Mon-Sat Nov-Mar) Sells the useful publication *Pitlochry Walks* (50p), which lists four short and four long local walks.

SIGHTS

If you fancy a tour of a whisky distillery, Pitlochry has two. **Bell's Blair Athol Distillery** (☎ 482003; Atholl Rd; tour incl voucher redeemable against purchases £4; ⏰ 1-4pm Mon-Fri Jan-Easter, Nov & Dec; 9.30am-5pm Mon-Sat Easter-Jun; 9.30am-5pm Mon-Sat, noon-5pm Sun Jun-Sep; 10am-4pm Mon-Fri Oct) is at the southern end of town. The **Edradour Distillery** (☎ 472095; admission free; ⏰ 9.30am-5pm Mon-Sat, noon-5pm Sun Mar-Oct; call to confirm winter hrs) is proudly Scotland's smallest distillery, 2½ miles (4km) east of Pitlochry on the A924.

CENTRAL SCOTLAND

At the Pitlochry Festival Theatre, the excellent **Scottish Plant Collector's Garden** (☎ 484626; adult/child £3/1; ☻ 10am-5pm Mon-Sat Apr-late Oct, 11am-5pm Sun May-Oct) commemorates 300 years of plant collecting. Opened in 2003 the new-age landscaping in the 2.5-hectare garden includes a couple of pavilions built from Scottish timber and an amphitheatre. The whole collection is based on plants brought back to Scotland by Scottish explorers. There is plenty of seating to drink in the views over town.

SLEEPING

Pitlochry is packed with places to stay, but anything central tends to be a bit pricey.

Pitlochry Backpackers (☎ 470044; www.scotlands-top-hostels.com; 134 Atholl Rd; dm £11, t & d from £25) A great backpackers in the perfect spot, smack-bang in the middle of town overlooking the main strip. The well-kept accommodation here is excellent. Dorms are small (four or six beds) and the doubles rival some of the town's B&Bs. The communal area has great windows looking out onto the main drag, and a pool table.

Sunnybank (☎ 473014; ellson@onetel.net.uk; 19 Lower Oakfield; r per person £18-25; ✗) Austrian-run Sunnybank certainly has a sunny aspect and offers fresh, good-value rooms in a large modern house. Some rooms have that alpine thing going on.

Derrybeg (☎ 472070; www.derrybeg.co.uk; 18 Lower Oakfield; r per person £18-27; ✗) Single rooms are hard to ferret out in this town and Derry-beg is one of the few places in town that caters to solo travellers. It's quite genteel and there are also self-catering apartments available.

Number 10 (☎ 472346; www.pitlochry-guesthouse .co.uk; 10 Atholl Rd; r per person £25-32; ✗) You'll get a warm welcome at this Victorian villa which has sparkling, tastefully furnished rooms. The real pull, however, is the breakfast which must rate as the best in town, with just about every palate leaving satisfied.

Knockendarroch Hotel (☎ 473473; www.knocken darroch.co.uk; Higher Oakfield; DB&B per person £42-68; ✗) The Knockendarroch Hotel oozes elegance and class. Go on, spoil yourself – all this travelling is hard work! Traditional Scottish dinners are included in the price, as is a complimentary glass of sherry.

Pitlochry Hydro Hotel (☎ 472666; gm.pit@barbox .net; Knockard Rd; r per person £30-42.50; ✗) The Hydro is a luxury hotel and very good value – it's been recommended by wheelchair-bound visitors.

EATING

Moulin Inn (☎ 01796-472196; Moulin; starters £2.50-4.25, mains £6-8; ☻ from noon) Just a mile from Pitlochry, the Moulin is a gem. It's an atmospheric little inn that was trading here long before visitors arrived in nearby Pitlochry. It makes a great spot to escape the crowds for a meal or an afternoon drink – you could walk here from town. The hotel brews its own ales – the smooth, reddish Atholl Ale is particularly good. There's a reasonably priced menu with simple home-cooked food and a specials board that changes regularly.

Festival Restaurant (☎ 484626; Foss Rd; 2-/3-course set dinner £18.50/21.50; ☻ 6.30pm for dinner) Booking is advised for this restaurant at the Pitlochry Festival Theatre, which has lovely views over the town. It's elegant dining with first-class service. Dishes like the wild Highland game casserole, followed by Scottish cheeses and oatcakes go down a treat.

McKay's Hotel (☎ 473888; 138 Atholl Rd; bar/restaurant mains £7/11) Dine in the boisterous barn of a bar here or the crisp white linen restaurant, which serves some fine dishes including charred monkfish, and rustic roast aubergine. There's a great menu and the food is freshly prepared.

There's a **Co-op supermarket** (West Moulin Rd) if you're self-catering.

ENTERTAINMENT

The well-known **Pitlochry Festival Theatre** (☎ 484626; Foss Rd; tickets £4-25) stages a different play six nights out of seven during its season from May to mid-October.

GETTING THERE & AWAY

Scottish Citylink runs approximately hourly buses between Inverness and Glasgow/Edinburgh via Pitlochry. Prices and journey times to destinations from Pitlochry are: Inverness (£8.90, two hours), Aviemore (£7, 1¼ hours), Perth (£5.60, 40 minutes), Edinburgh (£8.80, two hours) and Glasgow (£8.80, 2¼ hours).

Stagecoach runs buses to Aberfeldy (£2, 30 minutes, up to nine daily), Dunkeld (£1.90, 25 minutes, up to 10 daily Monday to Saturday) and Perth (£3, one hour, up to six daily Monday to Saturday).

Pitlochry is on the main rail line from Perth to Inverness. There are nine trains a day from Perth (£8.30, 30 minutes), fewer on Sunday.

GETTING AROUND
Escape Route (☎ 473859; 8 West Moulin Rd; full/half-day £15/9) hires bikes and does repairs. For a taxi, call **Elizabeth Yule Transport** (☎ 472290); a taxi to Blair Castle will cost you £10.

Pass of Killiecrankie
Drop into the **Killiecrankie Visitors Centre** (☎ 01796-473233; Killiecrankie; admission free, car park fee £1.60; ☼ 10am-5.30pm Apr-Jun, Sep & Oct; 9.30am-6pm Jul & Aug) in this beautiful, rugged gorge, 3½ miles (5.5km) north of Pitlochry. It has great interactive displays on the Jacobite rebellion, and local flora and fauna. There's plenty to touch, pull and open – great for kids. There are some stunning walks into the wooded gorge; keep an eye out for red squirrels.

Local buses run between Pitlochry and Blair Atholl via Killiecrankie (£1, 10 minutes, three to six daily).

Blair Castle & Blair Atholl
☎ 01796
One of the most popular tourist attractions in Scotland, magnificent **Blair Castle** (☎ 481207; Blair Atholl; castle & grounds adult/child/family £6.50/4/16.75; ☼ 9.30am-6pm Apr-Oct, call Pitlochry TIC for winter hrs) is the seat of the duke of Atholl. Set beneath forested slopes above the River Garry, this impressive whitewashed castle plays host (in May) to the parade of the Atholl Highlanders – the only private army in Europe.

Thirty rooms are open to the public, and they're packed with paintings, arms and armour, china, lace and embroidery, presenting a near-complete picture of upper-class life in the Highlands from the 16th century to the present. One of the most impressive rooms is the ballroom. The 11th (and current) duke was a distant relative (in every sense of the word – he lives in South Africa) to the 10th duke, who died a bachelor in 1996. The duke returns to his inheritance every May to review the Atholl Highlanders.

Blair Castle is 7 miles (13km) north of Pitlochry, and a mile from Blair Atholl village. For a great cycle, walk or drive take

the stunning road to **Glenfender**, from Blair Atholl village. It's about 3 miles (5km) on a long, windy uphill track to a farmhouse, the views of snowcapped peaks along the way are spectacular.

The gothic **Atholl Arms Hotel** (☎ 01796-481205; Blair Atholl; s/d from £35/40), a pub near the train station, has comfy rooms and sometimes does special deals.

Local buses run a service between Pitlochry and Blair Atholl (£1.30, 20 minutes, three to six daily). Two buses a day (Monday to Saturday) go directly to the castle. There's a train station in the village, but not all trains stop here.

For a continuation of this route, see The Cairngorms section, p300.

BLAIRGOWRIE & GLENSHEE
☎ 01250 / pop 8500
The route along the A93 through Glenshee is one of the most spectacular drives in the country. The meandering burns and soaring peaks, splotched with glaring snow, tend to dwarf open-mouthed drivers – it's surprising there aren't more accidents along this road! Blairgowrie and Braemar (p240) are the main accommodation centres for the Glenshee ski resort, although there's a small settlement 5 miles (8km) south of the ski runs at **Spittal of Glenshee**.

There's a helpful **TIC** (☎ 872960; blairgowrietic@perthshire.co.uk; 26 Wellmeadow; ☼ daily Apr-Oct, Mon-Sat Nov-Mar) with plenty of walking information. You'll find two **banks** (High St) with ATMs, just behind the TIC.

Sights
In Blairgowrie itself there are many walks that the TIC can advise you on – if you're interested in Blairgowrie's sordid past, pick up the *Walk with the Ghosts* leaflet.

Alyth is a charming little village with a small canal and some exquisite stone bridges about 5 miles (8km) east of Blairgowrie. Ask the TIC for the *Walk Old Alyth* leaflet; there are lots of historical buildings, including church ruins dating from 1296. If you're looking to escape the rain, perusing the displays on local history at **Alyth Museum** (☎ 01738-632488; Commercial St; admission free; ☼ 1-5pm Wed-Sun May-Sep) is a fine way to pass an hour or so.

Off the A94 and 8 miles (13km) east of Blairgowrie, **Meigle** is worth the trip for those with a fascination for Pictish stones. The tiny **Meigle Museum** (☎ 01828-640612; adult/child £2/0.75; ⏱ 9.30am-12.30 pm & 1.30-6.30pm Apr-Sep) has 26 such carved stones from the 7th to 10th century, all found in the local area. The pieces range from the Nordic to the exotic – they include a Viking head stone and, bizarrely, a carving of a camel.

Skiing

Glenshee ski resort (☎ 01339-741320; www.ski-glenshee.co.uk), on the border of Perthshire and Aberdeenshire, has 38 pistes and is one of Scotland's largest skiing areas. After a good fall of snow and when the sun burns through the clouds, you'll be in a unique position to drink in the beauty of this country; the skiing isn't half bad either. The chair lift can whisk you up to 910m, near the top of **The Cairnwell** (933m). Whenever there's enough snow in winter it opens daily (it's usually closed in summer, but check with the TIC). A one-day lift pass and ski hire costs from £34, although it's cheaper for beginners and if you're hiring over two or more days.

Sleeping & Eating

Ben Blair (☎ 872393; Balmoral Rd; r per person £16; ✗) At this well-kept family home you'll receive old-fashioned hospitality in cosy surrounds and be sent on your way with a smile and a hearty breakfast.

Angus Hotel (☎ 872455; www.theangushotel.com; 46 Wellmeadow; r per person from £35) The Angus Hotel is a little poky but the rooms are just

fine, each complete with desk and telephone. Some bedrooms have a very sunny aspect but the bathrooms in the singles are not big enough for more than one. There's also a good **restaurant** here – try the local poached Tay salmon.

Drumnacree House (☎ 01828-632194; derek@drumnacreehouse.co.uk; St Ninian's Rd, Alyth; r per person from £30; ✗) This wonderful hotel, in an old Victorian mansion, specialises in providing a concoction of comforts. All the rooms are a good size, all with bath and some with shower. Book in advance. The **Oven Bistro** restaurant here has an outstanding reputation.

Spittal of Glenshee Hotel (☎ 885215; Spittal of Glenshee; dm £12-13.50, r per person from £25) This hotel is a very 'Scottish experience' – it's a great old country lodge that has burned down numerous times, but don't worry; the insurers have calculated the next likely fire won't be until 2029! There's also a good bar and a bunkhouse (without cooking facilities).

Getting There & Away

Strathtay Scottish operates a service from Perth to Blairgowrie (£2.40, 50 minutes, roughly hourly). There's also a bus from Blairgowrie to Dundee (£2.60, 50 minutes, six to eight daily Monday to Saturday).

The only service from Blairgowrie to the Glenshee area, about 30 miles (48km) away, is the postbus to Spittal of Glenshee (no Sunday service).

CENTRAL SCOTLAND

Northeast Scotland

Many visitors to Scotland pass by the country's northeastern corner in their headlong rush to the tourist honey-pots of Pitlochry, Loch Ness and Skye. The ones who do venture in this direction are usually royalty watchers heading for the Queen's summer pad at Balmoral, or the late Princess Margaret's birthplace at Glamis Castle. Shame. They're missing out on a part of the country that is as beautiful and diverse as (though very different from) the more obvious attractions of the western Highlands and islands.

The great elbow of land jutting into the North Sea between the Firth of Tay and the Moray Firth comprises a broad mantle of fertile lowlands, fringed with forests, draped around the barren shoulders of the Grampian Mountains. The coastline alternates between long, sandy beaches and rugged, bird-haunted cliffs, dotted here and there with impossibly picturesque little fishing villages.

Within its bounds you will find two of Scotland's four largest cities, a thriving indigenous culture where the old Scottish dialect known as the Doric still survives, and the greatest concentration of Scottish Baronial castles anywhere in the country. It was here, in the 19th century, that the Aberdeen Angus breed of beef cattle was perfected, and where the barley for Speyside malt whiskies was first grown. It's home to a rich array of local food such as the Arbroath smokie and Finnan haddie, the Forfar bridie and Aberdeen rowie, and to delicious Cullen skink. There are distillery tours, Highland games, heritage railways, Pictish relics, superb hill walking, and the only bronze statue of a comic-book character anywhere in Scotland.

HIGHLIGHTS

- Soaking up the views from the hills around beautiful **Glen Clova** (p228)

- Meeting **Desperate Dan** (p220) face to face in Dundee's City Square

- Discovering the delights of Scottish Baronial architecture at **Craigievar Castle** (p241)

- Puzzling over the meaning of the mysterious **Pictish stones** of Angus (p229)

- Relishing the royal heritage of fairytale **Glamis Castle** (p225)

- Sitting in the sun in the beautiful Renaissance garden at **Edzell Castle** (p229)

- Pub-crawling among the glittering granite streets of **Aberdeen** (p231)

- Being initiated into the mysteries of malt whisky making on a Speyside **distillery tour** (p246)

- Admiring art in perfect peace in Banff's exquisite baroque **Duff House** (p246)

- POPULATION: 780,000
- AREA: 10,979 SQ KM

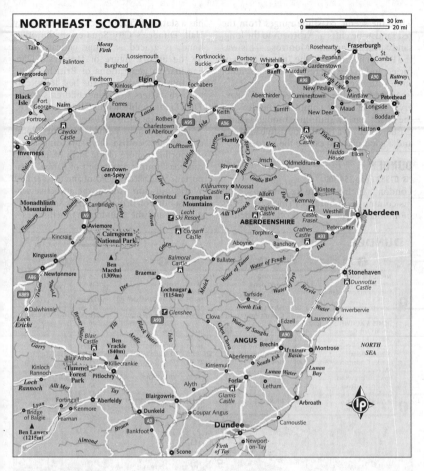

NORTHEAST SCOTLAND

GETTING AROUND

Scottish Citylink (☎ 0870 550 5050; www.citylink.co.uk) buses serve the Dundee to Aberdeen route only. **Strathtay Scottish** (☎ 01382-227201) in Dundee and **Stagecoach Bluebird** (☎ 01224-212266) in Aberdeen are the main regional bus operators, with services linking all the main towns and cities. **Royal Mail postbuses** (☎ 0845 774 0740) run to remote communities in the Angus Glens and Deeside, charging on average £2 to £5 for single journeys.

From June to September, **Moray Council** (☎ 01343-562534) operates the **Strathspey Stroller** bus service which runs from Cullen, on the Banffshire coast, to the Cairngorm Mountain Railway via Buckie, Spey Bay, Fochabers, Elgin, Dufftown, Grantown-on-Spey and Aviemore (£5, 3¼ hours, one a day, Saturday and Sunday only).

The Dundee–Inverness railway line passes through Arbroath, Montrose, Stonehaven, Aberdeen, Huntly and Elgin.

DUNDEE & ANGUS

Angus is a region of fertile farmland stretching north from Dundee – Scotland's fourth-largest city – to the Highland border. It's an attractive area of broad *straths* (valleys) and low, green hills contrasting with the rich, red-brown soil of freshly ploughed fields. Romantic glens finger their way into the foothills of the Grampian Mountains, while the scenic coastline ranges from the red sandstone cliffs of Arbroath to the long, sandy beaches around Montrose. This was the Pictish heartland of the 7th and 8th centuries, and many interesting Pictish symbol stones survive here (p229).

Apart from the crowds visiting Discovery Point in newly confident Dundee and the coach parties shuffling through Glamis Castle, Angus is a bit of a tourism backwater and a good place to escape the hordes.

DUNDEE
☎ 01382 / pop 154,700

London's Trafalgar Square has Nelson on his column, Edinburgh's Princes St has its monument to Sir Walter Scott, and Belfast

has a statue of Queen Victoria outside City Hall. Dundee's City Square, on the other hand, is graced – rather endearingly – by the bronze figure of Desperate Dan. Familiar to generations of British school children, Dan is one of the best-loved cartoon characters from the children's comic *The Dandy,* published by Dundee firm DC Thomson since the 1930s.

The city enjoys perhaps the finest location of any Scottish city, spreading along the northern shore of the Firth of Tay, and can boast tourist attractions of national importance in Discovery Point and the Verdant Works museum. Add in the attractive seaside suburb of Broughty Ferry, some lively nightlife and the Dundonians themselves –

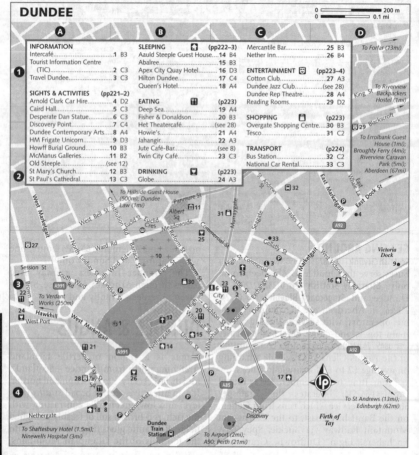

DUNDEE

0 _____ 200 m
0 _____ 0.1 mi

INFORMATION	
Intercafé.................................1	B3
Tourist Information Centre	
(TIC)....................................2	C3
Travel Dundee.........................3	C3

SIGHTS & ACTIVITIES	(pp221–2)
Arnold Clark Car Hire..............4	D2
Caird Hall...............................5	C3
Desperate Dan Statue..............6	C3
Discovery Point.......................7	C4
Dundee Contemporary Arts......8	A4
HM Frigate Unicorn.................9	D3
Howff Burial Ground..............10	B3
McManus Galleries.................11	B2
Old Steeple.......................(see 12)	
St Mary's Church...................12	B3
St Paul's Cathedral................13	C3

SLEEPING	(pp222–3)
Aauld Steeple Guest House....14	B4
Abalree.................................15	B3
Apex City Quay Hotel............16	D3
Hilton Dundee......................17	C4
Queen's Hotel......................18	A4

EATING	(p223)
Deep Sea.............................19	A4
Fisher & Donaldson...............20	B3
Het Theatercafé...............(see 28)	
Howie's................................21	A4
Jahangir...............................22	A3
Jute Café-Bar...................(see 8)	
Twin City Café......................23	C3

DRINKING	(p223)
Globe..................................24	A3

Mercantile Bar......................25	B3
Nether Inn............................26	B4

ENTERTAINMENT	(pp223–4)
Cotton Club..........................27	A3
Dundee Jazz Club.............(see 28)	
Dundee Rep Theatre..............28	A4
Reading Rooms......................29	D2

SHOPPING	(p223)
Overgate Shopping Centre.......30	B3
Tesco...................................31	C2

TRANSPORT	(p224)
Bus Station...........................32	C2
National Car Rental...............33	C3

To Forfar (13mi)
To Riverview Backpackers Hostel (1mi)
To Errolbank Guest House (1mi); Broughty Ferry (4mi); Riverview Caravan Park (5mi); Aberdeen (67mi)
To Hillside Guest House (500m); Dundee Law (1mi)
To Verdant Works (250m)
To Shaftesbury Hotel (1.5mi); Ninewells Hospital (3mi)
To St Andrews (13mi); Edinburgh (62mi)
To Airport (2mi); A90; Perth (21mi)

Victoria Dock
Firth of Tay
Tay Rd Bridge
RRS Discovery
Dundee Train Station

among the friendliest, most welcoming and most entertaining people you'll meet – and Dundee is definitely worth a stopover.

History

During the 19th century Dundee grew from its trading port origins to become a major player in the shipbuilding, whaling, textile and railway engineering industries. Dundonian firms owned and operated most of the jute mills in India, and the city's textile industry employed as many as 43,000 people – little wonder Dundee earned the nickname 'Juteopolis' (jute is a natural fibre used in making ropes and sacking).

Dundee is often called the city of the 'Three Js' – jute, jam and journalism. According to legend, it was a Dundee woman, Janet Keillor, who invented marmalade in the late 18th century; her son founded the city's famous Keillor jam factory. Jute is no longer produced, and when the Keillor factory was taken over in 1988, production was transferred to England. Journalism still thrives, however, led by the family firm of DC Thomson. Best known for children's comics such as *The Beano*, Thomson is now the city's largest employer.

In the late 19th and early 20th centuries Dundee was one of the richest cities in the country – there were more millionaires per head of population here than anywhere else in Britain – but the textile and engineering industries declined in the second half of the 20th century, leading to high unemployment and urban decay.

In the 1960s and '70s Dundee's cityscape was scarred by ugly blocks of flats, office buildings and shopping centres linked by unsightly concrete walkways – the view as you approach across the Tay Bridge does not look promising – and most visitors passed it by. Since the mid-1990s, however, Dundee has reinvented itself as a tourist destination and a centre for banking, insurance and new industries such as biotechnology. It also has more university students – one in seven of the population – than any other town in Europe except Heidelberg.

Orientation

The compact city centre is focussed on City Square, just 400m from the northern end of the Tay Road Bridge. The train station and Discovery Point are 300m south of City Square; the bus station is 400m to the northeast along Seagate. Immediately north of the city centre is the prominent hill of Dundee Law (174m), and 4 miles (6km) to the east is Broughty Ferry, Dundee's seaside resort.

Information

You'll find banks with ATMs on High St and Murraygate.

Intercafé (£1.50 for 30 min; ☺ 9am-5.30pm Mon-Sat, 9am-7pm Thu, 9am-4.30pm Sun) On the 1st floor of Debenhams department store in the Overgate Shopping Centre.

Main post office (Meadowside) A block north of the Overgate Shopping Centre.

Ninewells Hospital (☎ 660111; 24-hr casualty) At Menzieshill, west of the city centre.

TIC (☎ 527527; www.angusanddundee.co.uk; 21 Castle St; ☺ 9am-6pm Mon-Sat, noon-4pm Sun Jun-Sep; 9am-5pm Mon-Sat Oct-May) Just east of City Square; sells CalMac ferry tickets and Citylink and National Express bus tickets.

Sights

CITY CENTRE

The heart of Dundee is **City Square**, flanked to the south by the 1930s façade of **Caird Hall**, gifted to the city by a textile magnate and now home to the City Chambers. A more recent addition to the square, unveiled in 2001, is a bronze statue of **Desperate Dan**, the lantern-jawed hero of the children's comic *The Dandy* (he's clutching a copy in his right hand).

Pedestrianised High St leads west into Nethergate, flanked to the north by **St Mary's Parish Church**. Most of the church dates from the 19th century, but the **Old Steeple** (☎ 206790; adult/child £2/1.75; ☺ 10am-5pm Mon-Sat, noon-4pm Sun Apr-Sep; 11am-4pm Mon-Sat, noon-4pm Sun Oct-Mar) was built around 1460. A guided tour takes you through the bell-ringers' chamber and up to the belfry for a grand view over the city (closed for renovation at the time of research).

DISCOVERY POINT

The three masts of Captain Robert Falcon Scott's famous polar expedition vessel the **RRS Discovery** (☎ 201245; www.rrsdiscovery.com; Discovery Quay; adult/child £6.25/3.85; ☺ 10am-6pm Mon-Sat, 11am-6pm Sun Apr-Oct; 10am-5pm Mon-Sat, 11am-5pm Sun Nov-Mar; closed 25 & 26 Dec, 1 & 2 Jan) dominate the riverside to the south of the city centre. The ship was built in Dundee in 1900, with a hull at least half a metre thick to survive the pack ice, and sailed for the Antarctic in 1901 where she spent two winters trapped in the ice. Rescued by the efforts of Peter Scott (son of Robert) and the Maritime Trust, she was restored to her 1925 condition and given a berth in Dundee in 1986, where she became a symbol of the city's regeneration.

Exhibitions and audiovisual displays in the main building provide a fascinating history of both the ship and Antarctic exploration, but *Discovery* herself – afloat in a protected dock – is the star attraction. You can visit the bridge, the galley and the mahogany-panelled officers' wardroom, and poke your nose into the cabins used by Scott and his crew.

A joint ticket that gives entry to both Discovery Point and the Verdant Works costs £10.95/7.

HM FRIGATE UNICORN

Unlike the polished and much-restored *Discovery*, Dundee's other floating tourist attraction retains the authentic atmosphere of a salty old sailing ship. Built in 1824, the 46-gun **HM Frigate Unicorn** (☎ 200893; Victoria Dock; adult/child £3.50/2.50; ♥ 10am-5pm Apr-Sep; noon-4pm Wed-Fri, 10am-4pm Sat & Sun Oct-Mar) is the oldest British-built ship still afloat – perhaps because it never saw action. By the mid-19th century, sailing ships were outclassed by steam and the *Unicorn* served as a gunpowder store, then later as a training vessel. When it was proposed to break up the ship for scrap in the 1960s, a preservation society was formed.

Wandering around the four decks gives you an excellent impression of what it must have been like for the crew forced to live in such cramped conditions. The *Unicorn* is berthed in Victoria Dock, just northeast of the Tay Road Bridge. The entry price includes a guided tour (also available in French and German).

VERDANT WORKS

One of Europe's finest industrial museums, the **Verdant Works** (☎ 225282; www .verdantworks.com; West Henderson's Wynd; adult/child £5.95/3.85; ♥ 10am-6pm Mon-Sat, 11am-6pm Sun Apr-Oct; 10.30am-4.30pm Wed-Sat, 11am-4.30pm Sun Nov-Mar; closed 25 & 26 Dec, 1 & 2 Jan) explores the history of Dundee's jute industry. Housed in a restored jute mill complete with original machinery still in working condition, the museum's interactive exhibits and computer displays follow the raw material from its

origins in India through to the manufacture of a wide range of finished products from sacking to rope to wagon-covers for the pioneers of the American West.

MCMANUS GALLERIES

Housed in a solid Victorian Gothic building designed by Gilbert Scott in 1867, **McManus Galleries** (☎ 432084; Albert Sq; admission free; ♥ 10.30am-5pm Mon-Sat, till 7pm Thu, 12.30-4pm Sun) contains the city's museum and art collection. The exhibits cover the history of the city from the Iron Age to the present day, plus an impressive display of Scottish Victorian paintings, furniture and silver. Look out for the display on William McGonagall, Scotland's worst poet, whose lines commemorating the Tay Rail Bridge disaster of 1879 are truly awful.

DUNDEE CONTEMPORARY ARTS

The focus for the city's emerging Cultural Quarter – the city council's new name for the West End – is **Dundee Contemporary Arts** (☎ 606220; www.dca.org.uk; Nethergate; admission free; ♥ galleries & shop 10.30am-5.30pm Tue, Wed, Sat & Sun, 10.30am-8pm Thu & Fri; print studio 11am-9pm Tue-Thu, 11am-6pm Fri & Sat), a centre for modern art, design and cinema. The galleries here exhibit work by contemporary UK and international artists, and there are printmakers' studios where you can watch artists at work, or even take part in craft demonstrations and workshops. There's also the Jute Café-Bar (p223).

DUNDEE LAW

It's worth making the climb up **Dundee Law** (174m) for great views of the city, the two Tay bridges, and across to Fife. The **Tay Rail Bridge** – at just over 2 miles (3km) long, it was the world's longest when it was built – was completed in 1887, replacing an earlier bridge whose stumps can be seen alongside. The original bridge collapsed during a storm in 1879, less than two years after it was built, taking a train and 75 lives along with it. The 1½-mile (2km) Tay Road Bridge was opened in 1966.

Dundee Law is a short walk northwest of the city centre, along Constitution Rd.

Sleeping

Most of Dundee's city centre hotels are business-oriented, and offer lower rates at the weekend. The main concentrations of B&Bs are along Broughty Ferry Rd and Arborath Rd east of the centre, and on Perth Rd to the west. If you don't fancy a night in the city, consider staying at nearby Broughty Ferry (p225).

BUDGET

Aauld Steeple Guest House (☎ 200302; 94 Nethergate; s £21-23, d £36-38; ✗) Just as central as the Abalree, but a little more upmarket, the Aauld Steeple has spacious double and family rooms, some with views of St Mary's Church.

Abalree (☎ 223867; 20 Union St; s/d £18/30) This is a basic B&B – there are no rooms with bathrooms, though all have TV – but it couldn't be more central. It's therefore popular, so book ahead.

University of Abertay (☎ 308059; accommo@ abertay.ac.uk; Bell St; apt £15 per person; ☿ Jun-Aug; P) During the summer holidays the university offers self-catering apartments for two to eight persons in various parts of the city.

Riverview Backpackers Hostel (☎ 450565; 127 Broughty Ferry Rd; dm £10, tents £2.50) This ramshackle 10-bed hostel – a little run down and seedy-looking – is a 15-minute walk east of the bus station on the main road towards Broughty Ferry.

Riverview Caravan Park (☎ 535471; riverview caravan@btinternet.com; Marine Dr; Monifieth; tent or campervan site £10-12; ☿ Apr-Oct) This is the nearest camping ground and is attractively sited near the beach, 5 miles (8km) east of the city centre.

MID-RANGE

Shaftesbury Hotel (☎ 669216; reservations@shaftes bury-hotel.co.uk; 1 Hyndford St; s £51-66, d £68-80; ✗) The family-run, 12-room Shaftesbury is a Victorian mansion built for a jute baron and has many authentic period features including a fine marble fireplace in the dining room. It's 1½ miles (2km) west of the city centre, just off Perth Rd.

Hillside Guest House (☎ 223443; info@tildab.co.uk; 43 Constitution St; s/d £24/42; ✗ P) Hillside is an elegant Victorian villa with spacious bedrooms (two with private bathroom, two with shared bathroom) and an original conservatory. It's off Constitution Rd, 500m north of the city centre.

Errolbank Guest House (☎ 462118; 9 Dalgleish Rd; s £25-30, d £44-48; ✗ P) A mile east of the city centre, just north of the road to Broughty Ferry, Errolbank is a lovely Victorian house with small but tastefully furnished rooms with bathroom.

Queen's Hotel (☎ 322515; enquiries@queenshotel -dundee.com; 160 Nethergate; s £42-72, d £60-90; ✗ P) Despite having been Best Westernised, this grand Victorian hotel in the heart of the lively West End retains some period charm, and is only a few minutes' walk from the city centre.

TOP END

Apex City Quay Hotel (☎ 202404; dundee@apexhotels .co.uk; 1 W Victoria Dock Rd; r £40-75; ✗ P 🛋) The Apex is a new hotel overlooking the city's redeveloped waterfront, with the sort of stylish, spacious, sofa-equipped rooms that make you want to stay in in the evening and munch chocolate in front of the TV. If you can drag yourself away from your room, there are spa treatments, saunas and Japanese hot tubs to enjoy.

Hilton Dundee (☎ 229271; Earl Gray Pl; s/d from £59/78; ✗ P 🛋) The Hilton is right on the waterfront, beside the Tay Road Bridge, and has a leisure club and a restaurant with views over the Tay.

Eating

There's a growing number of good places to eat in Dundee, especially in the West End.

BUDGET

Twin City Café (☎ 223662; 4 City Sq; mains £4-6; ☿ 7.30am-6pm Mon-Sat, 10.30am-5pm Sun) A pleasant café on the main square with outdoor tables in summer, Twin City offers good salads and sandwiches, including tasty veggie stuff such as falafel and hummus wraps.

Jahangir (☎ 202022; 1 Session St; mains £5-7; ☿ noon-midnight Sun-Thu, noon-1am Fri & Sat) It's worth going to this curry house for the décor alone – pure Hollywood Moghul, with an over-the-top tent and a fountain complete with goldfish and carp (no, they're not on the menu).

Self-caterers should head for the **Tesco supermarket** (☿ 7am-midnight Mon-Fri, 7am-10pm Sat, 10am-7pm Sun) on Murraygate.

Other recommendations:

Deep Sea (81 Nethergate; ☿ 9.30am-6.30pm Mon-Sat) The oldest and best fish and chip shop in Dundee.

Fisher & Donaldson (12 Whitehall St; ☿ 6.30am-5pm Mon-Sat) An excellent bakery and patisserie with an upmarket café attached.

MID-RANGE

Jute Café-Bar (☎ 606220; DCA, Nethergate; lunch mains £7-9, dinner £8-12; ☿ 10.30am-9.30pm) The industrial-chic restaurant in the Dundee Contemporary Arts centre serves excellent pastas and salads, as well as more adventurous fusion cuisine; shame that the picture-window view over the Tay is blocked by a few ugly buildings.

Howie's (☎ 200399; 25 South Tay St; 3-course lunch/dinner £8/15; ⏱ noon-2.30pm & 6-10pm) The reliable Edinburgh chain has opened in Dundee with a mellow, candle-lit dining room serving Howie's trademark good-value bistro cuisine, and excellent house wine at only £8.90 a bottle.

Het Theatercafé (☎ 206699; Tay Sq; mains £5-10; ⏱ café 10am-late; restaurant noon-3pm & 5-7pm Mon, noon-3pm & 5-9pm Tue-Thu, noon-3pm & 5-10pm Fri & Sat) The city's arty types hang out in this continental-style coffee-bar and restaurant in the foyer at the Dundee Rep Theatre. Great sandwiches and pizzas as well as tasty steaks, fishcakes and veggie dishes.

Drinking

There are many lively pubs, especially in the West End and along West Port. The large, stylish **Nether Inn** (☎ 349970; 134 Nethergate), with its comfy couches, pool table and drinks promos, is popular with students, while the **Mercantile Bar** (☎ 225500; 100-108 Commercial St) is another lively city-centre pub. The **Globe** (☎ 224712; 53-57 West Port) serves good bar meals from noon to 7.30pm (6pm Sunday) and often has live music.

Entertainment

Dundee's nightlife may not be as hot as Glasgow's, but there are plenty of places to go – pick up a copy of the *Accent* what's-on guide from the TIC, or check out the Events and Entertainment section of www.dundee.com. Tickets for most events are on sale at the Dundee Contemporary Arts centre.

Caird Hall (☎ 434940; www.cairdhall.co.uk; 6 City Sq; ⏱ box office 9am-4.30pm Mon-Fri, 9.30am-1pm Sat) The Caird Hall hosts regular concerts of classical music, as well as organ recitals, rock bands, dances, fetes and fairs. Check its website for details of coming events.

Dundee Rep Theatre (☎ 223530; www.dundee reptheatre.co.uk; Tay Sq; ⏱ box office 10am-6pm or start of performance) Dundee's main venue for the performing arts, the Rep is home to Scotland's only full-time repertory company and to the Scottish Dance Theatre.

Cotton Club (☎ 200299; www.thecottonclub.biz; 60 Brown St; cover £2.50-10; ⏱ 8pm-2.30am Tue-Sun) The Cotton Club is a new live music, clubbing and comedy venue, successor to the late, lamented Doghouse Bar. Live local and UK bands, with the occasional big name, plus club nights Thursday to Saturday.

Reading Rooms (☎ 0790 535 3301; www.thereading rooms.co.uk; 57 Blackscroft; cover £3-8; ⏱ 10pm-2.30am Fri & Sat) This is the venue to check out for some of Scotland's best club nights, as well as occasional live bands.

Dundee Jazz Club (☎ 206699; Het Theatercafé, Dundee Rep, Tay Sq; cover £4.50; ⏱ 10.30pm-late Fri) The Jazz Club brings the top names in Scottish jazz to the foyer of the Dundee Rep Theatre on Friday nights.

If you're around in early July, look out for the **Dundee Blues Bonanza**, a two-day festival of free blues and rock (second weekend in July).

Getting There & Away

The Tay Road Bridge linking Dundee and Fife costs 80p per car southbound, but is toll-free for northbound traffic.

AIR

Dundee airport (☎ 662200; Riverside Dr) is 2½ miles (4km) west of the city centre. There are daily scheduled services to London City airport with ScotAirways. A taxi to the airport takes five minutes and costs £2.50.

BUS

National Express (☎ 0870 580 8080; www.gobycoach .com) operates two direct services a day from London to Dundee (£32, 10½ hours).

Citylink (☎ 0870 550 5050; www.citylink.co.uk) has hourly buses from Dundee to Edinburgh (£8.40, 1¾ hours), Glasgow (£8.50, 2¼ hours), Perth (£4.40, 35 minutes) and Aberdeen (£8.80, two hours). Some Aberdeen buses travel via Arbroath, others via Forfar. You can change at Perth for buses to Oban.

Strathtay Scottish (☎ 227201) operates buses to Perth (one hour, hourly), Blairgowrie (one hour, hourly), Forfar (40 minutes, once or twice an hour), Kirriemuir (one hour, half-hourly), Brechin (1¼ hours, 10 daily, change at Forfar) and Arbroath (one hour, half-hourly). They sell a Day Rover ticket (adult/child £5.50/3.50) that allows unlimited travel on their buses for one day.

Stagecoach Fife (☎ 01334-474328) bus No 99 runs to St Andrews (30 minutes, every 20 minutes) Monday to Saturday only.

TRAIN

Trains run to Dundee from Edinburgh (£15.70, 1¼ hours) and Glasgow (£20.70, 1½ hours) at least once an hour, Monday to Saturday; hourly on Sunday from Edinburgh, every two hours on Sunday from Glasgow.

Trains from Dundee to Aberdeen (£18.30, 1¼ hours) travel via Arbroath and Stonehaven. There are around two trains an hour, fewer on Sunday.

Getting Around

The city centre is compact, and is easy to get around on foot. For information on local public transport, call **Travel Dundee** (☎ 201121; Forum Centre, 92 Commercial St). City bus fares cost 40p to £1 depending on distance; buy your ticket from the driver (exact fare only – no change given).

Phone **Discovery Taxis** (☎ 732111) if you need a cab. If you'd like to drive yourself, rental companies in Dundee include **Arnold Clark** (☎ 225382; East Dock St) and **National Car Rental** (☎ 224037; 45-53 Gellatly St).

BROUGHTY FERRY

☎ 01382

This attractive seaside suburb, known locally as 'The Ferry', is 4 miles (6km) east of Dundee city centre. It has a castle, a long, sandy beach and a number of good places to eat and drink, and is handy for the golf courses at nearby Carnoustie.

Sights

Broughty Castle Museum (☎ 436916; Castle Green; admission free; ☻ 10am-4pm Mon-Sat, 12.30-4pm Sun Apr-Sep; 10am-4pm Tue-Sat, 12.30-4pm Sun Oct-Mar) occupies a 16th-century tower house that looms imposingly over the harbour, guarding the entrance to the Firth of Tay, and includes a fascinating exhibit on Dundee's whaling industry.

Sleeping

Fisherman's Tavern (☎ 775941; www.fishermans -tavern-hotel.co.uk; 10-16 Fort St; s/d £39/62; ☒) A delightful 17th-century cottage just a few paces from the seafront, the Fisherman's was converted to a pub in 1827. It has 11 luxurious rooms, most with bathroom, and an excellent pub-restaurant (see Eating & Drinking on right).

Auchenean (☎ 774782; 177 Hamilton St; s/d £20/40; ☻ Mar-Oct; ☒ ℗) This is a pleasant detached house in a quiet back street, five minutes' walk from the beach in the eastern part of Broughty Ferry.

Homebank (☎ 477481; 9 Ellieslea Rd; s/d £25/50; ☒ ℗) Close to the yacht club in the western part of Broughty Ferry, Homebank is a grand Victorian mansion set in a lovely walled garden.

Hotel Broughty Ferry (☎ 480027; 16 W Queen St; s/d £60/80; ☒ ℗ ⟐) The swankiest place to stay, this hotel is only five minutes' stroll from the waterfront, and it has a sauna and solarium as well as a small, heated pool.

Eating & Drinking

Fisherman's Tavern (☎ 775941; 10-16 Fort St; mains £5-7; ☻ lunch noon-3pm, dinner 6-9pm) The Fisherman's – a maze of cosy nooks and open fireplaces – is a lively pub where you can wash down local seafood with a choice of Scottish real ales.

Ship Inn (☎ 779176; 121 Fisher St; mains £6-12; ☻ food served noon-2pm & 5-10.30pm Mon-Fri, noon-10.30pm Sat & Sun) Overlooking the seafront around the corner from the Fisherman's is the snug, wood-panelled, 19th-century Ship Inn, which serves top-notch dishes ranging from gourmet haddock and chips to venison steaks.

Visocchi's (☎ 779297; 40 Gray St; mains £5-7; ☻ 9.30am-7.30pm Mon-Thu, 9.30am-9.30pm Fri & Sat, 9.30am-5.30pm Sun) Visocchi's – a 70-year-old institution – is a traditional, family-run Italian café that sells delicious home-made ice cream, good coffee and a range of pastas and pizzas.

Getting There & Away

Bus Nos 7 to 12 (£1, 20 minutes) run from Dundee High St to Broughty Ferry several times an hour Monday to Saturday, and hourly on Sunday.

GLAMIS CASTLE & VILLAGE

Looking every inch the Scottish Baronial castle, with its forest of pointed turrets and battlements, **Glamis Castle** (☎ 01307-840393; adult/child £6.20/3.10; ☻ 10.30am-5.30pm Apr-Oct; last entry 4.45pm) was the legendary setting for Shakespeare's *Macbeth*. The Grampian Mountains provide a spectacular backdrop for the family home of the earls of Strathmore and Kinghorne. A royal residence since 1372, the Queen Mother (born Elizabeth Bowes-Lyon) spent her childhood at Glamis (pronounced glams) and Princess Margaret (the Queen's sister) was born here.

The five-storey, L-shaped castle was given to the Lyon family in 1372, but was significantly altered in the 17th century. Inside, the most impressive room is the drawing room, with its arched plasterwork ceiling. There's a display of armour and weaponry in the haunted crypt and frescoes in the chapel (also haunted). Duncan's Hall is where King Duncan was murdered in *Macbeth*. You can also look round the royal apartments, including the Queen Mother's bedroom. The one-hour guided tours depart every 15 minutes.

The **Angus Folk Museum** (NTS; ☎ 01307-840288; Kirkwynd, Glamis; adult/child £3/2; ☺ noon-5pm Jul & Aug, Fri-Tue Apr-Jun & Sep), in a row of 18th-century cottages just off the flower-bedecked square in Glamis village, houses a fine collection of domestic and agricultural relics.

Glamis Castle is 12 miles (19km) north of Dundee. There are two to four buses a day from Dundee (£2, 35 minutes) to Glamis, operated by Strathtay Buses; some continue to Kirriemuir.

ARBROATH
☎ 01241 / pop 22,800

Arbroath is an old-fashioned seaside resort and fishing harbour – source of the famous Arbroath smokies (smoked haddock). No visit is complete without buying a pair of smokies and eating them while sitting beside the harbour.

The town has a **TIC** (☎ 872609; Market Pl; ☺ 9.30am-5.30pm Mon-Sat, 10am-3pm Sun Jun-Aug; 9am-5pm Mon-Fri, 10am-5pm Sat Apr, May & Sep; 9am-5pm Mon-Fri, 10am-3pm Sat Oct-Mar), post office and several banks with ATMs.

Sights

The magnificent, red-sandstone ruins of **Arbroath Abbey** (☎ 878756; Abbey St; adult/child £2.50/1; ☺ 9.30am-6.30pm Apr-Sep; 9.30am-4.30pm Mon-Sat, 2-4.30pm Sun Oct-Mar), founded in 1178 by King William the Lion, dominate the town centre. It is thought that Bernard of Linton, the abbot here in the early 14th century, wrote the famous Declaration of Arbroath in 1320 asserting Scotland's right to independence from England (see the boxed text on p27).

The **Arbroath Museum** (☎ 875598; Ladyloan; admission free; ☺ 10am-5pm Mon-Sat; 2-5pm Sun Jul & Aug), housed in the elegant Signal Tower, covers local history including the textile and fishing industries. The tower was originally used to communicate with the construction team working on the Bell Rock Lighthouse 12 miles (19km) offshore, built between 1807 and 1811 by the famous engineer Robert Stevenson (grandfather of writer Robert Louis Stevenson).

At St Vigeans, about a mile north of the town centre, is the excellent **St Vigeans Museum** (☎ 0131 668 8600; admission free; ☺ key available 9.30am-6.30pm Apr-Sep; 9.30am-4.30pm Mon-Sat, 2-4.30pm Sun Oct-Mar). Its collection of Pictish and medieval sculptured stones includes crosses and human and animal carvings. The museum is unstaffed – the key is kept at cottage No 7.

If you fancy catching your own fish, the **Marie Dawn** (☎ 873957) and **Girl Katherine II** (☎ 874510) offer three-hour sea-angling trips out of Arbroath harbour for £12 per person, including tackle and bait.

The coast northeast of Arbroath consists of dramatic cliffs riven by inlets, caves and natural arches. An excellent walk follows a path along the top of the cliffs for 3 miles (5km) to the quaint fishing village of **Auchmithie**.

Sleeping & Eating

Scurdy House (☎ 872417; 33 Marketgate; s/d £20/32) Colourful flower baskets single out this spick and span B&B halfway between harbour and abbey.

Seaton B&B (☎ 430424; 2 Seaton Rd; r per person £22) An attractive Victorian villa close to the start of the cliff-top walk to Auchmithie.

Sugar & Spice Tearoom (☎ 437500; 9-13 High St; mains £2-5; ☺ 10am-4pm Mon-Sat, noon-4pm Sun) With its flounces, frills and waitresses in black and white uniforms, this tearoom verges on the twee. However, it's child-friendly – there's an indoor play area and a wendy-house out the back – and the tea and scones are sublime. You can even try an Arbroath smokie, grilled with lemon butter. The best places to eat are not in town, but a few miles to the north.

But'n'Ben Restaurant (☎ 877223; 1 Auchmithie; ☺ noon-3pm, 4-5.30pm & 7-10pm Mon & Wed-Sat, noon-5.30pm Sun) Above the harbour in Auchmithie, this cosy, tartan-clad cottage restaurant serves the best of local seafood.

Gordon's Restaurant (☎ 830364; Main St, Inverkeillor; 3-course lunch/dinner £19/31; ☺ noon-1.45pm Wed-Sun, 7-9pm Tue-Sun) Six miles (10km) north of Arbroath, in the tiny and unpromising-looking village of Inverkeillor, is this hidden gem – an intimate and rustic eatery serving gourmet-quality Scottish cuisine.

Getting There & Away

There are frequent buses from Dundee to Arbroath (see Dundee Getting There & Away, p224), but the scenic train journey along the coast (£3.40, 20 minutes, half-hourly) is the better option. Trains continue from Arbroath to Aberdeen (£14.10, 50 minutes) via Montrose and Stonehaven.

GN Wishart (☎ 828747) bus No 140 runs from Arbroath to Auchmithie (£2, 15 minutes, six to eight daily Monday to Saturday, two Sunday).

MONTROSE

☎ 01674 / pop 11,800

Despite its broad main street of Victorian buildings, attractive seaside setting, and reputation as a golfing and seaside resort, Montrose exudes an austere and slightly down-at-heel atmosphere. It sits at the mouth of the River South Esk, where its industrial harbour serves the North Sea oil industry, and is backed by the broad, tidal mud flats of Montrose Basin, a rich feeding ground for thousands of resident and migrant birds.

Montrose Basin Wildlife Centre (☎ 676336; Rossie Braes; adult/child £2.50/1.50; ☼ 10.30am-5pm Apr-Oct) at the southern edge of town has indoor and outdoor hides and viewing platforms with high-powered binoculars where you can zoom in on the local wildlife. In summer you can see curlews, oystercatchers and eider ducks – and perhaps an otter if you're lucky – and in autumn the basin is invaded by huge flocks of migrant geese.

More attractive than Montrose's town beach is the lovely, 2-mile (3km) strand of **Lunan Bay** to the south, overlooked by the dramatic ruin of **Red Castle**.

Montrose lies on the Dundee to Aberdeen railway line.

FORFAR

☎ 01307 / pop 13,200

Forfar, the county town of Angus, is the home of Scotland's contribution to the world of fast food: the **Forfar bridie**. A shortcrust pastry turnover filled with minced beef and onion, it was invented in Forfar in the early 19th century. If you fancy trying one, head for **James McLaren & Son** (☎ 462762; 8 The Cross; ☼ 8am-4.30pm Mon-Wed, Fri & Sat, 8am-1pm Thu), a family bakery bang in the centre of town, which has been selling tasty, home-baked bridies since 1893.

Strathtay Scottish buses from Dundee to Kirriemuir travel via Forfar. See Getting There & Away under Dundee (p224) for details.

ABERLEMNO

Five miles (8km) northeast of Forfar, on the B9134, are the mysterious **Aberlemno Pictish stones**, some of Scotland's finest sculptured stones. By the roadside there are three 7th-to 9th-century slabs with various symbols, including the z-rod and double disc, and in the churchyard at the bottom of the hill there's a magnificent 8th-century stone displaying a Celtic cross, interlace decoration, entwined beasts and, on the reverse, scenes of the Battle of Nechtansmere. (See the Pictish Symbol Stones boxed text on p229 for more information.) The stones are covered up from November to March; otherwise there's free access at all times.

KIRRIEMUIR

☎ 01575 / pop 6000

Known as the Wee Red Town because of its close-packed, red sandstone houses, Kirriemuir is famed as the birthplace of JM Barrie (1860–1937), writer and creator of the much-loved **Peter Pan**. A willowy bronze statue of the 'boy who wouldn't grow up' graces the intersection of Bank and High Sts.

The town has a **TIC** (☎ 574097; Cumberland Close; ☼ 10am-5pm Mon-Sat Apr-Sep), banks and a post office.

Sights

JM Barrie's Birthplace (☎ 572646; 9 Brechin Rd; adult/child £5/3.75; ☼ noon-5pm Jul & Aug, noon-5pm Fri-Tue May, Jun & Sep) is the town's big attraction, a place of pilgrimage for Peter Pan fans from all over the world. The two-storey house where Barrie was born has been furnished in period style, and preserves Barrie's writing desk and the wash-house at the back that served as his first 'theatre'. The ticket also gives admission to the **Camera Obscura** (☼ noon-5pm Apr-Sep) on the hilltop northeast of the town centre.

The old Town House opposite the Peter Pan statue dates from 1604 and houses the **Gateway to the Glens Museum** (☎ 575479; admission free; ☼ 10am-5pm Mon-Wed, Fri & Sat, 1-5pm Thu; 2-5pm Sun Jul & Aug), a useful introduction to local history, geology and wildlife for those planning to explore the Angus Glens.

Sleeping & Eating

Airlie Arms Hotel (☎ 572847; info@airliearms-hotel.co.uk; St Malcolm's Wynd; s £30-35, d £55-60; ✕ P) This attractive old coaching inn has luxurious, refurbished rooms and a stylish, candle-lit café-bar called the **Wynd** (☽ 8am-9.30pm).

Visocchi's (☎ 572115; 37 High St) A proudly old-fashioned family café that serves good coffee and great home-made ice cream.

Other recommendations:

Crepto (☎ 572746; Kinnordy Pl; B&B per person £24)

Woodlands (☎ 572582; 2 Lisden Gardens; B&B per person £24)

Getting There & Away

Strathtay Scottish operates bus services from Dundee (£4.50, 1¼ hours, hourly Monday to Saturday, every two hours Sunday) via Glamis (20 minutes, two a day Monday to Saturday) and Forfar (25 minutes).

A **Royal Mail postbus** (☎ 0845 774 0740) runs from Kirriemuir to Glen Clova (two a day Monday to Friday, one Saturday).

ANGUS GLENS

The northern part of Angus is bounded by the Grampian Mountains, where five scenic valleys cut into the hills: Glens Isla, Prosen, Clova, Lethnot and Esk. All have attractive scenery, though each glen has its own distinct personality. Glen Clova and Glen Esk are the most beautiful while Glen Lethnot is the least frequented. You can get detailed information on walks in the Angus Glens from the TIC in Kirriemuir (p227) and from the Clova Hotel in Glen Clova (see right).

Glen Isla

At Bridge of Craigisla at the foot of the glen, 3 miles (5km) north of Alyth (p215) is a spectacular, 24m waterfall called **Reekie Linn**; the name Reekie (Scottish for 'smoky') comes from the billowing spray that rises from the falls.

A 5-mile (8km) hike beyond the road-end at Auchavan leads into the wild and mountainous upper reaches of the glen where the **Caenlochan National Nature Reserve** protects rare alpine flora on the high plateau.

A **Royal Mail postbus** (☎ 0845 774 0740) runs from Blairgowrie (p215) to Auchavan (once daily except Sunday).

Glen Prosen

Near the foot of Glen Prosen, 6 miles (10km) north of Kirriemuir, there's a good forest walk up to the **Airlie monument** on Tulloch Hill (380m); start from the eastern road, about a mile beyond Dykehead.

From Glenprosen Lodge, at the head of the glen, a five-hour (9 miles/15km) hike along the **Kilbo Path** leads over a pass between Mayar (928m) and Driesh (947m) and descends to Glendoll Lodge at the head of Glen Clova.

A **Royal Mail postbus** (☎ 0845 774 0740) runs from Kirriemuir to Glenprosen Lodge (once daily except Sunday).

Glen Clova

The longest and loveliest of the Angus Glens stretches north from Kirriemuir for 20 miles (32km), broad and pastoral in its lower reaches but growing narrower and craggier as the steep, heather-clad Highland hills close in around its head.

The minor road beyond the Clova Hotel ends at a Forestry Commission car park (£1.50 per car) with toilets and a picnic area, which is the trailhead for a number of strenuous hikes through the hills to the north.

Jock's Road is an ancient footpath that was much used by cattle drovers, soldiers, smugglers and shepherds in the 18th and 19th centuries; 700 Jacobite soldiers passed this way on their retreat in 1746, en route to final defeat at Culloden. From the car park the path strikes west along Glen Doll, then north across a high plateau (900m) before descending steeply into Glen Callater and on to Braemar (15 miles/24km, five to seven hours). The route is hard-going and should not be attempted in winter; you'll need OS 1:50,000 maps Nos 43 and 44.

An easier, but still strenuous, circular hike starts from the Clova Hotel, making a circuit of the scenic *corrie* (glacial hollow) that encloses **Loch Brandy** (6 miles/10km, four hours).

The **Clova Hotel** (☎ 01575-550350; hotel@clova .com; Glen Clova; bar meals £5-8; s/d £40/70; P) is a lovely old drover's inn near the head of the glen, and a great place to get away from it all. As well as 10 comfortable, rustic rooms with bathrooms, it has a more basic bunkhouse out the back (£10 per person), a climbers' bar with a roaring log fire, and a lovely conservatory with views across the glen. Food is served from noon to 9pm.

Just 50m beyond the hotel **Brandy Burn House** (☎ 550253; Glen Clova; r per person £20) is a welcoming farmhouse B&B. Its neighbour, cosy little

PICTISH SYMBOL STONES

The Romans permanently occupied only the southern half of Britain up to 410. Caledonia, north of the firths of Forth and Clyde, was mostly left alone, especially after the mysterious disappearance of the Ninth Legion.

Caledonia was the homeland of the Picts, about whom little is known. In the 9th century they were culturally absorbed by the Scots, leaving a few archaeological remains, a scattering of Pictish place names beginning with 'Pit', and hundreds of mysterious standing stones decorated with intricate symbols, mainly in the northeast. The capital of the ancient Southern Pictish kingdom is said to have been at Forteviot in Strathearn, and Pictish symbol stones are to be found throughout this area and all the way up the eastern coast of Scotland into Sutherland and Caithness.

It's believed that the stones were set up to record Pictish lineages and alliances, but no-one is sure yet exactly how the system worked. The stones fall into three groups: Class I, the earliest, are rough blocks of stone, carved with any combination from a basic set of symbols; Class II are decorated with a Celtic cross as well as symbols; and Class III, dating from the end of the Pictish era (790–840), have only figures and a cross.

Local tourist offices provide a free leaflet titled the *Angus Pictish Trail*, which will guide you to the main Pictish sites in the area. The finest assemblage of stones in their natural outdoor setting is at **Aberlemno** (p227), and there are excellent indoor collections at **St Vigeans Museum** (p226) and the **Meigle Sculptured Stone Museum** (p215). The **Pictavia** interpretive centre at Brechin (p231) provides a good introduction to the Picts and their sculpture.

The Pictish Trail by Anthony Jackson lists 11 driving tours, while *The Symbol Stones of Scotland* by the same author provides more detail on the history and meaning of the Pictish stones.

Stables Café-Bar (☎ 550203; Glen Clova; ⊙ 11am-11pm; ▣), serves tea, coffee, cakes, beer and spirits. It also has free Internet access.

The Glen Clova postbus (☎ 0845 774 0740) departs Kirriemuir post office at 8.30am and 3.10pm Monday to Friday, 8.30am only on Saturday. The morning run goes all the way to the head of the glen (£5, 2½ hours), the afternoon one only as far as Clova Hotel.

Glen Lethnot

This glen is noted for the **Brown and White Caterthuns** – two extraordinary Iron Age hill forts, defended by ramparts and ditches, perched on twin hilltops at its southern end. A minor road crosses the pass between the two summits, and it's an easy walk to either fort from the parking area in the pass; both are superb viewpoints. If you don't have a car, you can walk from Brechin (6 miles/10km) or from Edzell (5 miles/8km).

Glen Esk

The most easterly of the Angus Glens, Glen Esk, runs for 15 miles (24km) from Edzell to lovely **Loch Lee**, surrounded by beetling cliffs and waterfalls. Ten miles (16km) up the glen from Edzell is **Glenesk Folk Museum** (The Retreat; ☎ 01356-670254; adult/child £2/1;

⊙ noon-6pm Jun-Oct; noon-6pm Sat-Mon Easter-May), an old shooting lodge that houses a fascinating collection of antiques and artefacts documenting the local culture of the 17th, 18th and 19th centuries.

Five miles (8km) further on the public road ends at **Invermark Castle**, an impressive ruined tower guarding the southern approach to the Mounth, a hill track to Deeside.

EDZELL

☎ 01356 / pop 785

The picturesque village of Edzell, with its broad main street and grandiose monumental arch, dates from the early 19th century when Lord Panmure decided that the original medieval village, a mile to the west, spoiled the view from Edzell Castle. The old village was razed and the villagers moved to this pretty, planned settlement.

Lord Panmure's predecessors as owners of **Edzell Castle** (☎ 648631; adult/child £3/1; ⊙ 9.30am-6.30pm Apr-Sep; 9.30am-4.30pm Mon-Wed & Sat, 9.30am-1pm Thu, 2-4.30pm Sun Oct-Mar) were the Lindsay earls of Crawford, who built the 16th-century L-plan tower house. Sir David Lindsay, a cultured and well-travelled man, laid out the castle's beautiful **Pleasance** in 1604 as a place of contemplation and learning. Unique in Scotland, this

ABERDEEN

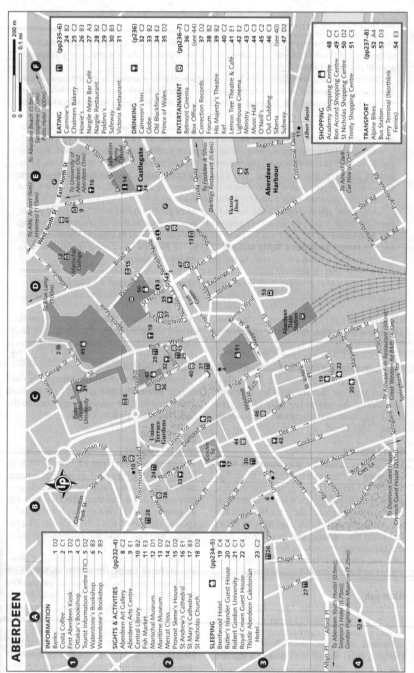

INFORMATION
Banks..	1	D2
Costa Coffee.............................	2	C1
First Aberdeen Kiosk.................	3	D2
Ottakar's Bookshop..................	4	C3
Tourist Information Centre (TIC)...	5	D2
Waterstone's Bookshop............	6	B3
Waterstone's Bookshop............	7	B3

SIGHTS & ACTIVITIES   (pp232–4)
Aberdeen Art Gallery................	8	C2
Aberdeen Arts Centre...............	9	E1
Central Library.........................	10	B2
Fish Market..............................	11	E3
Marischal Museum....................	12	D1
Maritime Museum.....................	13	D2
Mercat Cross............................	14	E2
Provost Skene's House..............	15	D2
St Andrew's Cathedral..............	16	E1
St Mary's Cathedral..................	17	B3
St Nicholas Church...................	18	D2

SLEEPING   (pp234–5)
Brentwood Hotel......................	19	C4
Butler's Islander Guest House....	20	C4
Robert Gordon University..........	21	C1
Royal Crown Guest House.........	22	C4
Thistle Aberdeen Caledonian		
Hotel.....................................	23	C2

EATING   (pp235–6)
Carmine's.................................	24	B2
Chalmers Bakery.......................	25	C2
Howie's.....................................	26	B3
Nargile Meze Bar Café..............	27	A3
Nargile Restaurant...................	28	B2
Poldino's...................................	29	C2
Safeway....................................	30	B3
Victoria Restaurant...................	31	C2

DRINKING   (p236)
Cameron's Inn..........................	32	C2
Globe..	33	B2
Old Blackfriars.........................	34	E2
Prince of Wales........................	35	D2

ENTERTAINMENT   (pp236–7)
Belmont Cinema.......................	36	C2
Box Office..........................	(see 44)	
Correction Records..................	37	D2
Forum.......................................	38	B2
His Majesty's Theatre...............	39	B2
Kef..	40	E1
Lemon Tree Theatre & Café.......	41	E2
Lighthouse Cinema...................	42	C3
Ministry....................................	43	C3
Music Hall................................	44	C3
O'Neill's...................................	45	C3
Out Clubbing...........................	46	C3
Siberia...............................	(see 40)	
Subway....................................	47	D2

SHOPPING
Academy Shopping Centre........	48	C2
Bon Accord Shopping Centre....	49	C1
St Nicholas Shopping Centre.....	50	D2
Trinity Shopping Centre............	51	C3

TRANSPORT   (pp237–8)
Alpine Bikes.............................	52	A4
Bus Station...............................	53	D3
Ferry Terminal (Northlink		
Ferries).................................	54	E3

Renaissance walled garden is lined with niches for nesting birds, and sculptured plaques illustrating the cardinal virtues, the arts and the planetary deities.

Two miles (3km) north of Edzell the B966 to Fettercairn crosses the River North Esk at Gannochy Bridge. From the layby just over the bridge, a blue-painted wooden door in the stone wall gives access to a delightful footpath that leads along the wooded river gorge for 1½ miles (2.5km) to a scenic spot known as the **Rocks of Solitude**.

Inchcape (☎ 647266; alison.mcm@btinternet.com; High St; r £18 per person; ✕ P) is an attractive Edwardian villa with comfortable rooms (all with bathroom), while the **Panmure Arms Hotel** (☎ 648950; www.panmurearmshotel .co.uk; 52 High St; s/d £43/60; bar meals £7-8; ✕ P) is a pretty, Tudoresque place that serves excellent bar meals (noon-2pm Monday to Friday, noon-9pm Saturday and Sunday).

Strathtay Scottish buses from Brechin to Laurencekirk stop at Edzell (£1.20, 15 minutes, three a day Monday to Friday).

BRECHIN
☎ 01356 / pop 7200
The name of the local football team, Brechin City, proclaims this diminutive town's main claim to fame – as the seat of **Brechin Cathedral** (now demoted to a parish church) it has the right to call itself a city, albeit the smallest one in Scotland. Adjacent to the cathedral is a 32m-high **round tower** built around 1000 as part of a Celtic monastery. It is of a type often seen in Ireland, but one of only three that survive in Scotland. Its elevated doorway, 2m above the ground, has carvings of animals, saints and a crucifix.

Housed nearby in the 18th-century former town hall, court room and prison, **Brechin Museum** (☎ 622687; St Ninian's Sq; admission free; ✕ 9am-5pm Mon-Fri, 10am-noon Sat) records the history of the round tower, cathedral and town.

The town's (OK, city's) picturesque Victorian railway station dates from 1897, and is now the terminus of the restored **Caledonian Railway** (☎ 377760; www.caledonianrail way.co.uk; 2 Park Rd; adult/child £5/3 return), which runs steam trains along a 3½ mile (5.5km) stretch of track to Bridge of Dun. Trains run on Sunday from late May to mid-September, certain Saturdays in July and August, and at Easter and Christmas. From Bridge of Dun it's a 15-minute walk to the **House of Dun** (NTS;

☎ 810264; adult/child £7/5.25; ✕ noon-5pm Jul & Aug, noon-5pm Fri-Tue May, Jun & Sep), a beautiful Georgian country house built in 1730.

Adjoining Brechin Castle Centre (a gardening and horse-riding centre on the A90 just west of Brechin), is **Pictavia** (☎ 626241; www.pictavia.org.uk; adult/child £3.25/2.25; ✕ 9am-5.30pm Mon-Sat, 10.30am-5.30pm Sun), an interpretive centre telling the story of the Picts, and explaining current theories about the mysterious carved symbol stones they left behind. It's worth making a trip here before going to see the Pictish stones at Aberlemno (p227).

Getting There & Away
Citylink buses between Dundee and Aberdeen stop at Clerk St in Brechin (see Dundee Getting There & Away, p224, for more information). Strathtay Scottish buses depart from South Esk St to Forfar (30 minutes, hourly), Aberlemno (15 minutes, six a day) and Edzell.

MW Nicoll (☎ 01561-377262) buses link Brechin and Stonehaven (55 minutes, two to five a day).

ABERDEENSHIRE & MORAY

Since medieval times Aberdeenshire and its northwestern neighbour Moray have been the richest and most fertile regions of the Highlands. Aberdeenshire is famed for its Aberdeen Angus beef cattle, its many fine castles, and the properous 'granite city' of Aberdeen. Moray's main attractions are the Speyside whisky distilleries that line the valley of the River Spey and its tributaries.

ABERDEEN
☎ 01224 / pop 197,300
Aberdeen is the powerhouse of the northeast, fuelled by its offshore riches, its economy linked inextricably to the fortunes of North Sea oil and gas. Oil money has made the city as expensive as London and Edinburgh, and there are hotels, restaurants and clubs with prices to match the depth of petroleum industry pockets. Fortunately, most of the cultural attractions, such as the excellent Maritime Museum and the Art Gallery, are free.

Known throughout Scotland as the granite city, much of the town was built using silvery grey granite hewn from the now abandoned Rubislaw Quarry, at one time the biggest artificial hole in Europe. On a sunny day the granite glitters prettily, but with low, grey clouds scudding in off the North Sea, it can be hard to tell where the city stops and the sky begins.

The city is a good base for exploring northeastern Scotland with Royal Deeside easily accessible to the west, Dunottar Castle to the south, sandy beaches to the north, and whisky country to the northwest.

History

Aberdeen was a prosperous trading and fishing port centuries before oil was considered a valuable commodity. After the townspeople supported Robert the Bruce against the English at the Battle of Bannockburn in 1314, the king rewarded the town with land for which he had previously received rent. The money was diverted into the Common Good Fund, to be spent on town amenities, as it still is today: it finances the colourful floral displays that have won the city numerous awards.

The name Aberdeen is a combination of two Pictish-Gaelic words, *aber* and *devana*, meaning 'the meeting of two waters'. The area was known to the Romans, and was raided by the Vikings when it was already an important port trading in wool, fish, hides and fur. By the 18th century, paper and rope-making, whaling and textile manufacture were the main industries, and in the 19th century it became a major herring-fishing centre.

Since the 1970s Aberdeen has been the main focus of the UK's offshore oil industry, home to oil company offices, engineering yards, a bustling harbour filled with supply ships, and the world's busiest civilian heliport. Unemployment rates, once among the highest in the country, are now among the lowest.

Orientation

Central Aberdeen is built on a ridge that runs east–west to the north of the River Dee. Union St, the main shopping street, runs along the crest of this ridge between Holborn Junction in the west and Castlegate in the east. The bus and train stations are next to each other, between Union St and the river. A half mile east of the centre lies Aberdeen Beach. Old Aberdeen is just over a mile to the north of the centre.

Information

BOOKSHOPS

Ottakar's (☎ 592440; 3-7 Union Bridge; ⏰ 9am-6pm Mon & Wed-Sat, 10am-6pm Tue, 11am-5pm Sun)
Waterstone's (☎ 571655; 236 & 269 Union St; ⏰ 9.30am-6pm Mon-Wed, Fri & Sat, 9.30am-8pm Thu, 11am-6pm Sun)

INTERNET ACCESS

Costa Coffee (☎ 645504; 31-33 Loch St; £1.80 per 15 min; ⏰ 8am-6pm Mon-Sat, 8am-7.30pm Thu, 10am-5pm Sun) On the north side of the Bon Accord Shopping Centre.
Central Library (☎ 652500; Rosemount Viaduct; free; ⏰ 9am-8pm Mon-Thu, 9am-5pm Fri & Sat) Sessions limited to 30 minutes.

MEDICAL SERVICES

Aberdeen Royal Infirmary (☎ 681818; Foresterhill) About a mile northwest of the western end of Union St.

MONEY

There are banks with ATMs all over the city centre.

POST

The main post office is in the St Nicholas shopping centre on Upperkirkgate.

TOURIST INFORMATION

TIC (☎ 288828; info@agtb; 23 Union St; ⏰ 9am-7pm Mon-Sat, 10am-4pm Sun Jul & Aug; 9am-5pm Mon-Sat, 10am-4pm Sun Jun & Sep; 9am-5pm Mon-Sat Oct-May) On the corner of Union St and Shiprow.

Sights

ABERDEEN HARBOUR

Aberdeen has a busy, working harbour crowded with survey vessels and supply ships servicing the offshore oil installations and car ferries bound for Orkney and Shetland. From dawn until about 8am the **fish market** on Albert Basin operates as it has for centuries.

Overlooking all this nautical bustle is the **Maritime Museum** (☎ 337700; Shiprow; admission free; ⏰ 10am-5pm Mon-Sat, noon-5pm Sun), centred on a three-storey replica of a North Sea oil production platform, with exhibits explaining all you ever wanted to know about the petroleum industry. Other galleries, some situated in Provost Ross's House, the oldest building in the city, cover the shipbuilding, whaling and fishing industries. Sleek and speedy Aberdeen clippers were a 19th-century shipyard speciality used by British tea merchants for the transportation of emigrants to Australia and,

NORTHEAST SCOTLAND

on the return journey, the import of tea, wool and exotic goods (opium, for instance).

UNION ST

Union St is the city's main thoroughfare, lined with solid, Victorian granite buildings. The oldest area is **Castlegate**, at the eastern end, where the castle once stood. When it was captured from the English for Robert the Bruce, the password used by the townspeople was 'Bon Accord', which is now the city's motto.

In the centre of Castle St stands the 17th-century **Mercat Cross**, bearing a sculpted frieze of portraits of Stuart monarchs. The Baronial heap towering over the eastern end of Castle St is the **Salvation Army Citadel**, which was modelled on Balmoral Castle.

On the northern side of Union St, 300m west of Castlegate, is **St Nicholas Church**, the so-called 'Mither Kirk' (Mother Church) of Aberdeen. The granite spire dates from the 19th century, but there has been a church on this site since the 12th century; the early 15th-century St Mary's Chapel survives in the eastern part of the church.

Surrounded by concrete and glass office blocks in what was once the worst slum in Aberdeen is **Provost Skene's House** (☎ 641086; Guestrow; admission free; ☒ 10am-5pm Mon-Sat, 1-4pm Sun), a late-medieval, turreted town house occupied in the 17th century by the provost (the Scottish equivalent of a mayor) Sir George Skene. It was also occupied for six weeks by the duke of Cumberland on his way to Culloden in 1746. The tempera-painted ceiling with its religious symbolism, dating from 1622, is unusual for having survived the depredations of the Reformation. It's a period gem featuring earnest-looking angels, soldiers and St Peter with crowing cockerels.

MARISCHAL COLLEGE

Across Broad St from Provost Skene's House is **Marischal College**, founded in 1593 by the 5th Earl Marischal, and merged with King's College (founded 1495) in 1860 to create the modern University of Aberdeen. The huge and impressive façade in Perpendicular Gothic style – unusual in having such elaborate masonry hewn from notoriously hard-to-work granite – dates from 1906 and is the world's second-largest granite structure (after L'Escorial near Madrid). It now houses the university's science faculty.

Founded in 1786, the **Marischal Museum** (☎ 274301; Marischal College; Broad St; admission free; ☒ 10am-5pm Mon-Fri, 2-5pm Sun) houses a fascinating collection of material donated by graduates and friends of the university over the centuries. In one room, the history of northeastern Scotland is depicted through its myths, customs, famous people, architecture and trade. The other gallery gives an anthropological overview of the world, incorporating objects from vastly different cultures, arranged thematically (Polynesian wooden masks alongside gas masks, and so on). There are the usual Victorian curios, an Indian kayak found in the local river estuary and Inuit objects collected by whalers. Go through the arch from Broad St, straight across the quadrangle and up the stairs; the museum is on the 1st floor.

ABERDEEN ART GALLERY

Behind the grand façade of **Aberdeen Art Gallery** (☎ 523700; Schoolhill; admission free; ☒ 10am-5pm Mon-Sat, 2-5pm Sun) is a cool, marble-lined space exhibiting the work of contemporary Scottish and English painters, such as Gwen Hardie, Stephen Conroy, Trevor Sutton and Tim Ollivier. There are also several landscapes by Joan Eardley, who lived in a cottage on the cliffs near Stonehaven in the 1950s and '60s, and painted tempestuous oils of the North Sea and poignant portraits of slum children. Among the Pre-Raphaelite works upstairs, look out for the paintings of Aberdeen artist William Dyce (1806–64), ranging from religious works to rural scenes.

Downstairs is a large, empty, circular, white room, with fish-scaled balustrades evoking the briny origins of Aberdeen's wealth, commemorating the 165 people who lost their lives in the Piper Alpha oil rig disaster in 1988.

ABERDEEN BEACH

Just half a mile east of Castlegate is a spectacular 2-mile (3km) sweep of clean, golden sand stretching between the mouths of the Rivers Dee and Don. At one time Aberdeen Beach was a good, old-fashioned British seaside resort, but the availability of cheap package holidays has lured Scottish holidaymakers away from its somewhat chilly delights. On a warm summer's day though, it's still an excellent beach.

The Esplanade sports several traditional seaside attractions, including **Codona's**

Amusement Park (☎ 595910; Beach Blvd; admission free, pay per ride; 🕐 1pm-late Jun-Aug; 1pm-late Fri-Sun Mar-May & Sep-Nov), complete with stomach-churning waltzers, dodgems, a roller-coaster, log flume and haunted house. The adjacent **Sunset Boulevard** (☎ 595910; admission free, pay per game; 🕐 10am-midnight) is the indoor alternative, with ten-pin bowling, arcade games, dodgems and pool tables.

Halfway between the beach and the city centre is **Satrosphere** (☎ 640340; 179 Constitution St; adult/child £5.25/3.75; 🕐 10am-5pm Mon-Sat, 11.30am-5pm Sun), a hands-on, interactive science centre.

You can get away from the fun fair atmosphere by walking north towards the more secluded part of the beach. There's a **bird-watching hide** on the south bank of the River Don, between the beach and King St, which leads back south towards Old Aberdeen.

Bus Nos 14 and 15 (eastbound) from Union St go to the beach; or you can walk from Castlegate in 10 minutes.

OLD ABERDEEN

Just over a mile north of the city centre is the district called Old Aberdeen. The name is misleading – although Old Aberdeen is certainly old, the area around Castlegate is older. It was originally called Aulton, from the Gaelic for 'village by the pool', and this was anglicised in the 17th century to Old Town.

It was here that Bishop Elphinstone established King's College, Aberdeen's first university, in 1495. The 16th-century **King's College Chapel** (☎ 272137; College Bounds; admission free; 🕐 9am-4.30pm Mon-Fri) is easily recognisable by its crown spire; the interior is largely unchanged, with impressive stained-glass windows and choir stalls. The nearby **King's College Visitor Centre** (☎ 273702; College Bounds; admission free; 🕐 10am-5pm Mon-Sat, 2-5pm Sun) houses a multimedia display on the university's history and a pleasant coffee shop.

The 15th-century **St Machar's Cathedral** (☎ 485988; The Chanonry; admission free; 🕐 9am-5pm) with its massive twin towers is a rare example of a fortified cathedral. According to legend, St Machar was ordered to establish a church where the river takes the shape of a bishop's crook, which it does just here. The cathedral is best known for its impressive heraldic ceiling, dating from 1520, which has 48 shields of kings, nobles, archbishops and bishops. Sunday services are held at 11am and 6pm.

Bus No 20 from Littlejohn St (just north of Marischal College) runs to Old Aberdeen every 10 to 20 minutes.

GORDON HIGHLANDERS MUSEUM

The excellent **Gordon Highlanders Museum** (☎ 311200; St Lukes, Viewfield Rd; adult/child £2.50/1.50; 🕐 10.30am-4.30pm Tue-Sat, 1.30-4.30pm Sun Apr-Oct) records the history of one of the British Army's most famous fighting units, described by Winston Churchill as 'the finest regiment in the world'. Originally raised in the northeast of Scotland by the 4th duke of Gordon in 1794, the regiment was amalgamated with the Seaforths and Camerons to form the Highlanders regiment in 1994. The museum is about a mile west of the western end of Union St – take bus No 14 or 15 from Union St.

Sleeping

There are clusters of B&Bs on Bon Accord St and Springbank Tce (both 400m southwest of the train station), and along Great Western Rd (the A93, a 25-minute walk southwest of the centre). They're usually more expensive than the Scottish average and, with all the oil industry workers here, single rooms are at a premium. Prices tend to be lower at the weekend.

BUDGET

Aberdeen Youth Hostel (SYHA; ☎ 0870 004 1100; 8 Queen's Rd; dm £11-13) This hostel, set in a granite Victorian villa, is a mile west of the train station. Walk west along Union St and take the right fork along Albyn Place until you reach a roundabout; Queen's Rd continues on the western side of the roundabout.

Dunrovin Guest House (☎ 586081; www.dunrovin guesthouse.co.uk; 168 Bon Accord St; s/d £23/37, r with bathroom £30/46; ✗ **P**) Dunrovin is a typical, granite Victorian house with eight rooms; the upstairs rooms are bright and airy, and the friendly owners will provide a veggie breakfast if you wish.

During the university summer holidays some colleges let rooms to visitors:

Robert Gordon University (☎ 262134; www.scotland 2000.com/rgu; Business & Vacation Accommodation Service, Schoolhill, Aberdeen AB10 1FR; 6-8 person flats from £100 for 2 nights; 🕐 mid-Jun–mid-Aug; ✗) Flats comprise six to eight single rooms with shared bathroom, lounge and kitchen, close to the city centre.

University of Aberdeen (☎ 272664; www.abdn.ac.uk
/catering; Conference Office, King's College, Old Aberdeen
AB24 3FX; s/d £30/45; ☷ mid-Jun–mid-Aug; ☒)
Single and twin rooms with bathroom in the heart of Old
Aberdeen.

MID-RANGE

Royal Crown Guest House (☎ 586461; www.royal
crown.co.uk; 111 Crown St; s £23-36, d £36-50; ☒)
The Royal Crown has eight small but nicely
furnished rooms, and is only five minutes'
walk from the train station (though up a
steep flight of stairs).

Butler's Islander Guest House (☎ 212411; www
.butlersguesthouse.com; 122 Crown St; s £26-40, d £40-46;
☐ ☒) Just across the street from the Royal
Crown, Butler's is a cosy place with a big
breakfast menu that includes fresh fruit
salad, kippers and kedgeree as alternatives
to the traditional fry-up.

Brentwood Hotel (☎ 595440; www.brentwood
-hotel.co.uk; 101 Crown St; s £37-77, d £54-87;
☐ ☒ ☐) The friendly and flower-bedecked Brentwood, set in a granite town
house, is one of the best hotels in the area,
comfortable and conveniently located, but
often full during the week.

Strathisla Guest House (☎ 321026; www.strathisla
-guesthouse.co.uk; 408 Great Western Rd; s/d £28/42;
☒ ☐) The child-friendly Strathisla is a
spacious, granite, terraced house with five
warm and welcoming rooms with bathroom.
It's 1½ miles southwest of Union St.

Other recommendations:

Crynoch Guest House (☎ 582743; crynoch@btinternet
.com; 164 Bon Accord St; r per person £22-32; ☐)
Penny Meadow Private Hotel (☎ 588037;
pennymeadow@amserve.com; 189 Great Western Rd; r per
person £25-35)
Kildonan Guest House (☎ 316115; dey@kildonan
.fsbusiness.co.uk; 410 Great Western Rd; s/d from £26/40;
☒ ☐)

TOP END

Thistle Aberdeen Caledonian Hotel (☎ 0870 333
9151; www.thistlehotels.com/aberdeencaledonian; 10-14
Union Tce; s £39-124, d £56-144; ☒ ☐) This is a
fine old Victorian hotel with bags of character, bang in the city centre. The hotel's Terrace Restaurant, and a good number of its
rooms, overlook Union Terrace Gardens.

Simpson's Hotel (☎ 327777; www.simpsonshotel
.co.uk; 59 Queen's Rd; s £75-120, d £85-130; ☒ ☐)
Simpson's, a mile west of Union St, is a
stylish boutique hotel with a Mediterranean

theme, all terracotta and aqua. It's aimed
at both business and private guests, and is
totally wheelchair-accessible.

Patio Hotel (☎ 633339; www.patiohotels.com;
Beach Blvd; s £35-162, d £45-165; ☒ ☐ ☒) Part
of a Norwegian hotel chain, the attractively
modern Patio is a 10-minute walk northeast
of Castlegate, and only a few minutes' stroll
from the beach. It has a pool, sauna, gym
and solarium.

Eating

BUDGET

Carmine's (☎ 624145; 32 Union Tce; pizza £4-8,
3-course lunch £4.50; ☷ noon-5.30pm Mon-Sat) Carmine's is famed for good, inexpensive Italian food including the best pizzas in town;
the lunch deal is available noon to 2pm
Monday to Friday.

Lemon Tree Café (☎ 621610; 5 W North St; mains
£4-7; ☷ noon-4pm Thu-Sun) The lively café-bar at
the theatre does excellent coffee, cakes and
light meals, good sandwiches and veggie
dishes, and delicious home-made puddings.
There's live music on Friday and Sunday.

Nargile Meze Bar Café (☎ 454203; 3-5 Rose St;
mains £3-5; ☷ noon-3pm & 5.30-10.30pm Mon-Thu,
noon-3pm & 5.30-11pm Fri & Sat) If you don't want
the full, sit-down, linen-tablecloth treatment at Nargile (see under Mid-Range
below), you can sample the delights of
Turkish cuisine at their café and takeaway
outlet, just off Union St.

Victoria Restaurant (☎ 621381; 140 Union St;
mains £5-6.50, 2-course lunch £5.95; ☷ 9am-5pm Fri-
Wed, 9am-6.30pm Thu) The Victoria, above the
Jamieson & Carry jewellery shop, is a traditional, posh Scottish tearoom with delicious
fresh soups, salads and sandwiches.

Chalmers Bakery (☎ 626344; 14 Back Wynd;
snacks 50p-£3.50; ☷ 7am-5.30pm Mon-Fri, 7am-5pm
Sat) This bakery, close to Union St, offers
excellent and inexpensive takeaway grub
such as home-made soups, *stovies* (stewed
potatoes, onions and sausage), sandwiches,
pastries and cakes.

Ashvale Fish Restaurant (☎ 596581; 42-48 Great
Western Rd; takeaways £2-4, sit-in mains £6-9; ☷ 11.45am-
11pm) The Ashvale, an upmarket fish and chip
shop, is well known outside the city, having
won several awards. Try some mushy peas
with your haddock and chips – they taste
much better than they sound.

Self-caterers will find large supermarkets
at Bridge of Dee and Bridge of Don. There's

NORTHEAST SCOTLAND

also a convenient **Safeway** (7.30am-10pm Mon-Sat, 10am-7pm Sun) supermarket on Union St near the Music Hall.

MID-RANGE

Nargile Restaurant (636093; 77-79 Skene St; mains £8-12; noon-3pm & 5.30-10.30pm Mon-Thu, noon-3pm & 5.30-11pm Fri & Sat) An Aberdeen institution for more than a decade, and probably the best Turkish restaurant in Scotland, Nargile serves tasty spreads of *mezes* (starters) followed by delicious, melt-in-the-mouth kebabs and marinated meats. At the time of research there were plans to open a new Nargile in Aberdeen's West End.

Howie's (639500; 50 Chapel St; 2-course lunch/dinner £7.95/15.50; noon-2.30pm & 6-10pm) The Aberdeen branch of the well-known Edinburgh chain of restaurants is a chic bistro dishing up great value 'modern Scottish' cuisine and very reasonably priced house wine.

Poldino's (647777; 7 Little Belmont St; lunch mains £5-6, dinner £8-14; noon-2.30pm & 6-10.45pm Mon-Sat) Poldino's is another long-established Aberdeen eatery, an upmarket, Italian family restaurant that never fails to impress with its quality of food and service.

TOP END

Silver Darling (576229; Pocra Quay; North Pier; mains £16-19; noon-1.45pm Mon-Fri & 7-9.30pm Mon-Sat) The Silver Darling (an old Scottish nickname for herring) is housed in the former Customs office, with picture windows overlooking the sea at the entrance to Aberdeen harbour. Here you can enjoy fresh Scottish seafood prepared by a top French chef while you watch the porpoises playing in the harbour mouth. Bookings are recommended.

Drinking

Aberdeen is a great city for a pub crawl – it's more a question of knowing when to stop than where to start. There are lots of pre-club bars in and around Belmont St, with more traditional pubs scattered throughout the city centre.

Globe (624258; 13-15 North Silver St; noon-3pm & 5-11pm Mon-Wed, noon-midnight Thu-Sat, 12.30pm-midnight Sun) This lovely Edwardian-style pub with wood panelling and white marble-topped tables, decked out with old musical instruments, is a great place for a quiet lunchtime or afternoon drink. It serves good coffee as well as real ales and

malt whiskies, and has live music Thursday to Sunday. Plus probably the poshest pub toilets in the country.

Prince of Wales (640597; 7 St Nicholas Lane) Tucked down an alley off Union St, Aberdeen's best-known pub boasts the longest bar in the city and a great range of real ales and good-value pub grub. Quiet in the afternoons, but standing-room only in the evenings.

Cameron's Inn (644487; 6 Little Belmont St) Known as Ma Cameron's, this is Aberdeen's oldest pub, established in 1789. It has a pleasantly old-fashioned atmosphere, with lots of wood, brick and stone, and a range of excellent real ales and malt whiskies.

Old Blackfriars (581922; 52 Castlegate) This is one of the most attractive traditional pubs in the city, with a lovely stone and timber interior and a relaxed atmosphere – a great place for an afternoon pint.

Blue Lamp (647472; 121 Gallowgate) A long-standing feature of the Aberdeen pub scene, the Blue Lamp is a favourite student hang-out – a dark, but not dingy, drinking den with good beer, good craic, and a jukebox selection that hasn't been changed since Elvis died.

Entertainment

CINEMA

Lighthouse Cinema (0845 602 0266; 10 Shiprow; adult/child £5.90/3.50) The Lighthouse is a seven-screen multiplex that shows mainstream, first-run films, conveniently located just off Union St.

Belmont (listings 343534; bookings 343536; 49 Belmont St; adult/child £5.70/3.70) The Belmont is a great little arthouse cinema, with a lively programme of cult classics, director's seasons, foreign films and mainstream movies. There's also a Saturday morning kids club, with a children's movie screened at 11.30am.

NIGHTCLUBS

Aberdeen's normally lively club scene was in a state of flux at the time of research – check out what's happening in a local record shop such as **Correction Records** (13 Correction Wynd). For Belmont St pubs and clubs, check out www.belmont-street.com.

Kef (648000; 9 Belmont St; cover £5 Sat; 11pm-2am Sun-Thu, 11pm-3am Fri & Sat) Formerly known as Lava, but now refurbished with a Turkish theme – there are booths with lots of rugs and cushions to lie around on – this is Aberdeen's coolest venue, with club nights seven days a week, regular big-name DJs and live bands. Crank it up beforehand in **Siberia**, a vodka bar in the same building.

Ministry (☎ 211661; 16 Dee St; cover £3-8; ☯ 10.30pm-2am Sun-Thu, 10.30pm-3am Fri & Sat) Housed in a deconsecrated church, this has been the city's best-known club for five or six years now. It has student nights with drinks promos on Monday and Wednesday, DJs on Friday and Saturday and a monthly Wicked club night with top UK DJs on Sunday, though serious clubbers slag it off as being full of poseurs.

O'Neill's Pub (☎ 621456; 9 Back Wynd; cover £2-4; ☯ till 2am Sun-Thu, 3am Fri & Sat) Upstairs at O'Neill's you're guaranteed a wild night of pounding, hardcore Irish rock, indie and alternative tunes; downstairs is a quieter bar with live music and soothing pints of Murphy's stout.

Two of the city's best club nights are the electro-funk disco **Kia-Aura** (www.kia-aura.com), held fortnightly on Friday at the **Subway** (☎ 869879; Hotel Metro, 17 Market St; cover £6; ☯ 11pm-3am), and the once-a-month **Vegas** (www.vegasscotland.co.uk) at the **Forum** (☎ 633336; 3 Skene Tce; cover £5; ☯ 10.30pm-3am).

At the time of research **Out Clubbing** (☎ 212527; 7 Crown St; cover £2-4 after 11pm, £4-6 after midnight; ☯ 10pm-2am Wed-Sun, till 3am Fri & Sat), above Sal's Bar, was the city's only gay venue.

THEATRE & CONCERTS

His Majesty's (☎ 637788; Rosemount Viaduct) The city's main theatre hosts everything from ballet and opera to musicals and pantomimes.

Arts Centre (☎ 635208; King St) The Arts Centre stages regular drama productions in its theatre, and changing exhibitions in its gallery.

Lemon Tree (☎ 642230; www.lemontree.org; 5 West North St) The Lemon Tree theatre has an interesting programme of dance, music and drama, and often has rock, jazz and folk bands playing. It also has an excellent café (see Eating, p235).

You can book tickets for most concerts and other events at the **Box Office** (☎ 641122; ☯ 9.30am-6pm Mon-Sat) next to the **Music Hall** (☎ 632080; Union St), the main venue for classical music concerts.

Getting There & Away

AIR

Aberdeen Airport (☎ 722331) is at Dyce, 6 miles (10km) northwest of the city centre. The presence of the oil industry ensures there are regular flights to numerous Scottish and UK destinations, including Orkney and Shetland, and international flights to the Netherlands, Norway and Denmark.

Bus No 27 runs regularly from Union St to the airport (£1.30, 35 minutes). A taxi from the airport costs £10 to £12.

BUS

The bus station is in Guild St, next to the train station.

National Express runs direct buses from London (£36.50, 12 hours) twice daily, one of them overnight. **Citylink** runs direct services to Dundee (£8.80, two hours), Perth (£12.30, 2½ hours), Edinburgh (£15.40, 3¼ hours) and Glasgow (£17.80, 4¼ hours).

Stagecoach Bluebird (☎ 212266) is the main local bus operator. Bus No 10 runs hourly to Inverness (£10.50, 3¾ hours) via Huntly, Keith, Fochabers, Elgin (£8, two hours) and Nairn. Service No 201 runs every half-hour (hourly on Sunday) to Crathes Castle gate (45 minutes), continuing once an hour (less frequently on Sunday) to Ballater (1¾ hours) and every two hours to Crathie (for Balmoral Castle) and Braemar (£6.80, 2¼ hours).

Other local buses serve Stonehaven, Peterhead, Fraserburgh, Banff and Buckie.

TRAIN

There are several trains a day from London's King's Cross to Aberdeen (£98, 7½ hours); most involve a change of train at Edinburgh.

Other destinations served from Aberdeen by rail include Edinburgh (£24.50, 2½ hours), Glasgow (£31.60, 2¾ hours), Dundee (£18.30, 1¼ hours) and Inverness (£19.20, 2¼ hours).

BOAT

The ferry terminal is a short walk east of the train and bus stations. **Northlink Ferries** (☎ 0845 6000 449; www.northlinkferries.co.uk) runs car ferries from Aberdeen to Orkney and Shetland (see p371 for more details).

Getting Around

BUS

First Aberdeen (☎ 650065) is the main city bus operator. Its free leaflet gives details of all the main routes and bus stops. Fares range from 60p to £1.30; pay the driver as you board the bus.

The most useful services are Nos 18, 19 and 24 from Union St to Great Western Rd (the latter two continue to Cults), No 27 from the bus station to the youth hostel and the airport, and No 20 for Marischal College and Old Aberdeen.

A FirstDay ticket (adult/child £2.50/1.70) allows unlimited travel from time of purchase until midnight on all First Aberdeen buses.

CAR
For rental cars try **Arnold Clark** (☎ 249159; Girdleness Rd) or **LCH Car Hire** (☎ 594248; Arch 3, Palmerston Rd).

TAXI
The main city-centre taxi ranks are at the train station, and on Back Wynd, off Union St. To order a taxi, phone **ComCab** (☎ 353535).

BICYCLE
Mountain bikes can be rented from **Alpine Bikes** (☎ 211455; 64 Holburn St; ☷ 9am-6pm Mon-Sat, till 8pm Thu, 11am-5pm Sun), which charges £15 a day during the week and £30 for a weekend (Friday evening to Monday morning).

STONEHAVEN
☎ 01569 / pop 9580

Originally a small fishing village, Stonehaven has been the county town of Kincardineshire since 1600 and is now a thriving, child-friendly seaside resort. The most attractive part of town is the picturesque cliff-bound harbour, where you'll find a couple of appealing pubs and the town's oldest building, the **Tolbooth**, built around 1600 by the Earl Marischal. Nearby, parts of the **Mercat Cross** date from 1645.

There's a **TIC** (☎ 762806; 66 Allardice St; ☷ 10am-7pm Mon-Sat, 1-6pm Sun Apr-Oct) near Market Square in the town centre.

A pleasant, 15-minute walk along the cliff-tops south of the harbour leads to the spectacular ruins of **Dunnottar Castle** (☎ 762173; adult/child £3.50/1; ☷ 9am-6pm Mon-Sat, 2-5pm Sun Easter-Oct; 9am-dusk Mon-Fri Nov-Mar; last admission 30 mins before closing) spread out across a grassy promontory rising 50m above the sea. As dramatic a film set as any director could wish for, it was used for Franco Zeffirelli's *Hamlet*, starring Mel Gibson. The original fortress was built in the 9th century; the keep is the most substantial remnant, but the drawing room (restored in 1926) is more interesting.

Sleeping & Eating
Grahams (☎ 763517; 71 Cameron St; r per person £18) This welcoming B&B is near the central town square.

Beachgate House (☎ 763155; www.beachgate .co.uk; Beachgate Lane; s/d £32/48; ☒ Ⓟ) This luxurious modern bungalow is right on the seafront; two of its three rooms have sea views.

Marine Hotel (☎ 762155; 9-10 The Shore; mains £7-13; ☷ food served noon-2pm & 5-9pm) This harbour-side hotel is an excellent real-ale pub with a great 1970s jukebox and good bar meals, including fresh seafood specials.

Tolbooth Restaurant (☎ 762287; Old Pier; mains £13-18; ☷ noon-2pm & 6-11pm Wed-Sun) Overlooking the harbour, this is one of the best seafood restaurants in the region – reservations are recommended.

Carron Restaurant (☎ 760460; 20 Cameron St; snacks £2-5, mains £5-7; ☷ 9am-7pm Mon-Sat, noon-7pm Sun) This perfectly preserved Art Deco tearoom is straight out of the 1930s, complete with bow-fronted terrace, iron fanlights, a player piano and original tiled toilets. Just the place for high tea on a summer afternoon.

Getting There & Away
Stonehaven is served by the frequent buses travelling between Aberdeen (£3, 45 minutes, hourly) and Dundee (£7, 1½ hours). The more expensive trains to Dundee are faster (£9.80, 55 minutes, hourly).

DEESIDE
The valley of the River Dee – often called Royal Deeside because of the royal family's holiday home at Balmoral – stretches westward from Aberdeen to Braemar, closely paralleled by the A93. From Deeside north to Strathdon (p241) is serious castle country – there are more examples of fanciful Scottish Baronial architecture here than anywhere else in Scotland.

The Dee, famed for its hugely expensive salmon fishing, has its source in the Cairngorm Mountains west of Braemar, the starting point for long hikes into the hills.

Crathes Castle
The atmospheric, 16th-century **Crathes Castle** (☎ 01330-844525; adult/child £7/5.25; ☷ 10.30am-5.30pm Apr-Sep, 10.30am-4.30pm Oct, last admission 45 min before closing) contains original painted

ceilings and furnishings. The extensive **gardens** include 300-year-old yew hedges and colourful herbaceous borders.

The castle is on the A93, 16 miles (25.5km) west of Aberdeen, on the main Aberdeen to Ballater bus route.

Ballater
☎ 01339 / pop 1450

Ballater is an attractive little village on the banks of the Dee; note the crests on the shop fronts proclaiming 'By Royal Appointment' – the village is a major supplier of provisions for nearby Balmoral Castle. You can drool over the manufacture of traditional Scottish sweeties at **Dee Valley Confectioners** (☎ 755499; Station Sq; admission free; 🕑 9am-noon & 2-4.30pm Mon-Thu Apr-Oct).

When Queen Victoria visited Balmoral Castle she would alight from the royal train at Ballater's **Old Royal Station** (☎ 755306; Station Sq; admission free; 🕑 9.30am-7pm Jul & Aug, 9.30am-6pm Jun & Sep, 10am-5pm Oct-Mar). The station has been beautifully restored and now houses a museum, a good restaurant and a TIC.

The village also has a supermarket and a bank with an ATM.

As you approach Ballater from the east the hills start to close in, and there are many pleasant **walks** in the surrounding area. The steep woodland walk up **Craigendarroch** (400m) takes just over an hour. **Morven** (871m) is a more serious prospect, taking around six hours, but offers good views from the top. Ask at the TIC for more information. Also see Hiking in the Directory chapter (p403).

Accommodation here is fairly expensive and budget travellers usually head for Braemar. Good B&Bs include **Celicall** (☎ 755699; 3 Braemar Rd; r £19-20 per person; ⊠ Ⓟ) and the elegant **Coyles Hotel** (☎ 755064; coyleshotel@sol.co.uk; 43 Golf Rd; s/d £28/44; ⊠ Ⓟ).

Stagecoach Bluebird bus No 201 runs from Aberdeen to Ballater (£5.80, 1¾ hours, hourly) and continues to Braemar.

Balmoral Castle

Eight miles (13km) west of Ballater lies **Balmoral Castle** (☎ 01339-742334; adult/child £5/1; 🕑 10am-5pm Apr-Jul), the Queen's Highland holiday home, screened from the road by a thick curtain of trees. Built for Queen Victoria in 1855 as a private residence for the royal family, it kicked off the revival of the Scottish Baronial style of architecture that characterises so many of Scotland's 19th-century country houses.

Dedicated royal-watchers will love the place; otherwise it's hard to justify braving the crowds and the admission fee just for a lot of photographs of smiling royals, a few pieces of art, some stuffed animals and the odd regimental memento. Only a small part of the castle is open to the public; don't expect to see the Queen's private quarters!

The big, pointy-topped mountain that looms above Balmoral is **Lochnagar** (1150m), immortalised in verse by Lord Byron, who spent his childhood in Aberdeenshire:

> England, thy beauties are tame and domestic
> To one who has roamed o'er the mountains afar.
> O! for the crags that are wild and majestic:
> The steep frowning glories of dark Lochnagar.

Balmoral is beside the A93 at Crathie and can be reached on the Aberdeen to Braemar bus (see Getting There & Away under Braemar, p240).

Braemar
☎ 01339 / pop 400

Braemar is a little village with a grand location, a broad plain ringed by mountains where the Dee valley and Glen Clunie meet. In winter this is one of the coldest places in the country – temperatures as low as minus 29°C have been recorded – and during spells of severe cold hungry deer wander the streets looking for a bite to eat. Braemar is an excellent base for hill walking, and there's skiing at nearby Glenshee (p215).

The helpful **TIC** (☎ 741600; The Mews, Mar Rd; 🕑 10am-1.30pm & 2-5.30pm Mon-Sat, noon-5pm Sun Apr-Oct; 10.30am-5pm Mon-Sat, noon-5pm Sun Nov-Mar) has lots of useful information on walks in the area. There's a bank with an ATM in the village centre, and a couple of outdoor equipment shops.

SIGHTS & ACTIVITIES

Just north of the village, turreted **Braemar Castle** (☎ 741219; adult/child £3.50/1.50; 🕑 10am-6pm Sat-Thu Easter-Oct, daily Jul & Aug) dates from 1628 and was a government garrison after the 1745 Jacobite rebellion.

The **Braemar Highland Heritage Centre**
(☎ 741944; Mar Rd; admission free; ☼ 9am-6.30pm Jul &
Aug, 10am-6pm Jun & Sep, 10am-5.30pm Mon-Sat, noon-5pm
Sun Mar-May; call for winter hr), beside the TIC, tells
the story of the area with displays and video.

An easy walk from Braemar is up **Creag
Choinnich** (538m), a hill to the east of the village above the A93. The route is waymarked
and takes about 1½ hours. For a longer
walk (three hours) and superb views of the
Cairngorms, head for the summit of **Morrone**
(859m), southwest of Braemar. Ask at the TIC
(p239) for details of these and other walks.

SPECIAL EVENTS

On the first Saturday in September Braemar
is invaded by 20,000 people, including the
royal family, for the annual **Braemar Gathering** (☎ 755377; www.braemargathering.org; adult/child
£6/2) Highland games. Bookings for ringside
and grandstand seats (£12-20) are essential.
See the Braemar Gathering boxed text on
this page for more information.

SLEEPING

Braemar Youth Hostel (SYHA; ☎ 0870 004 1105; 21 Glenshee Rd; dm £10-11; ☼ late Dec-Oct) This hostel is
housed in a grand former shooting lodge just
south of the village centre on the A93 to Perth.

Rucksacks (☎ 741517; 15 Mar Rd; dm £7-8.50) An
excellent alpine-style bunkhouse with comfy
beds, a drying room, a laundry and even a
sauna, Rucksacks is understandably popular
with walkers and climbers. Non-guests are
welcome to use the laundry (£2) and even
the showers (£1), and the friendly owner is a
fount of knowledge about the local area.

Braemar Lodge (☎ 741627; info@braemarlodge
.co.uk; Glenshee Rd; s/d £50/70; ✗ P) The nicest place to stay in Braemar is this classy
Victorian shooting lodge on the southern
outskirts of the village. It has a good restaurant and a cosy lounge bar well stocked
with a range of malt whiskies.

Other recommendations:
Craiglea (☎ 741641; Hillside Dr; r £20 per person;
✗ P) A homely B&B cottage.
Wilderbank (☎ 741651; Kindrochit Dr; s/d £25/38;
✗ P) Comfortable and modern B&B.
Schiehallion House (☎ 741679; 10 Glenshee Rd; s
£21, d £38-46; ✗ P) Spacious and welcoming.

EATING

Fife Arms Hotel (☎ 741644; Mar Rd; bar meals £6-10;
☼ lunch & dinner) The Fife Arms is a climbers'

BRAEMAR GATHERING

There are Highland games in many towns
and villages throughout the summer, but
the best known is the Braemar Gathering,
which takes place on a 12-acre site on the
first Saturday in September. It's a major
occasion, organised annually by the Braemar Royal Highland Society since 1817.
Events include highland dancing, pipers,
tug-of-war, a hill race up Morrone, tossing
the caber, hammer- and stone-throwing
and the long jump. International athletes
are among those who take part.

These types of events took place infor-
mally in the Highlands for many centuries
as tests of skill and strength, but they were
formalised around 1820 due to the rise
of Highland romanticism initiated by Sir
Walter Scott and King George IV. Queen
Victoria attended the Braemar Gathering in
1848, starting a tradition of royal patronage
that continues to this day.

---

favourite, a grand old pub with a roaring
log fire in winter. Bar meals are served in
the spacious lounge bar.

Gathering Place Bistro (☎ 741234; Mar Rd; mains
£9-12, steaks £15; ☼ 5pm-late Tue-Sun) This bright
and breezy bistro is an unexpected corner
of culinary excellence with a welcoming
dining room and sunny conservatory,
tucked below the main road junction at the
entrance to the village.

GETTING THERE & AWAY

There are several Stagecoach Bluebird buses
a day from Aberdeen to Braemar (£6.80, 2¼
hours, every two hours). The drive from
Perth to Braemar is beautiful, but there is
no public transport on this route.

Inverey

Five miles (8km) west of Braemar is the tiny
settlement of Inverey. Numerous mountain
walks start from here, including the adventurous hike through the **Lairig Ghru** pass to
Aviemore (see the Mountain Walks in the
Cairngorms boxed text on p305).

The **Glen Luibeg** circuit (15 miles/24km,
six hours) is a good day hike. Start from the
woodland car park 250m beyond the Linn of
Dee, a narrow gorge about 1½ miles (2.5km)
west of Inverey, and follow the footpath and

track to Derry Lodge and Glen Luibeg – there are beautiful remnants of the ancient Caledonian pine forest here. Continue westwards on a pleasant path over a pass into Glen Dee, then follow the River Dee back down to the linn. Take OS 1:50,000 map sheet No 43.

A good short walk (3 miles/5km, 1½ hours) begins at the **Linn of Quoich** – a waterfall that thunders through a narrow slot in the rocks. Head uphill on a footpath on the east bank of the stream, past the impressive rock scenery of the **Punch Bowl** (a giant pothole), to a modern bridge that spans the narrow gorge, and return via an unsurfaced road on the far bank.

The **Inverey Youth Hostel** (SYHA; ☎ 0870 004 1126; dm £9.50; ⊙ May-Sep) provides basic digs in a cosy little cottage.

A Royal Mail postbus runs from Braemar to the youth hostel (£2, 15 minutes), Linn of Dee (20 minutes) and Luibeg (30 minutes). It departs from Braemar post office at 1.20pm Monday to Saturday.

STRATHDON

The valley of the River Don, home to many of Aberdeenshire's finest castles, stretches westward from Kintore, 13 miles (21km) northwest of Aberdeen, taking in the villages of Kemnay, Monymusk, Alford (*ah*-ford) and tiny Strathdon. The A944 parallels the lower valley; west of Alford, the A944, A97 and A939 follow the river's upper reaches.

Stagecoach Bluebird bus No 220 runs from Aberdeen to Strathdon village via Alford (1¼ hours, two a day Monday to Saturday). You'll need your own transport to reach Craigievar or Corgarff castles and the Lecht.

Castle Fraser

The impressive 16th-century **Castle Fraser** (NTS; ☎ 01330-833463; adult/child £7/5.25; ⊙ 11am-5.30pm Jul & Aug, noon-5.30pm Fri-Tue Apr-Jun & Sept), 3 miles (5km) south of Kemnay, looks rather like a French chateau and is reputedly the most photographed castle in Scotland.

Alford

☎ 01975 / pop 1925

Alford has a **TIC** (☎ 562052; Old Station Yard, Main St; ⊙ 10am-5pm Mon-Sat, 12.45-5pm Sun Jul & Aug; 10am-1pm & 2-5pm Mon-Fri, 10am-noon & 1-5pm Sat, 1-5pm Sun Apr, May, Sep), banks with ATMs and a supermarket. The **Grampian Transport Museum** (☎ 562292; adult/child £4.50/2.25; ⊙ 10am-5pm Apr-Sep, 10am-4pm

Oct) houses a fascinating collection of vintage cars, buses, steam engines, trams and even a snowplough. There's also a small railway museum at the TIC; the narrow-gauge **Alford Valley steam railway** (☎ 562811; ⊙ 1-5pm Jun-Aug; 1-5pm Sat & Sun Apr, May & Sep) runs from here to Haughton County Park (adult/child £2/1).

For B&B, try **Bydland** (☎ 563613; 18 Balfour Rd; r per person £20) or the **Forbes Arms Hotel** (☎ 562108; Bridge of Alford; s/d £38/56), a mile west at Bridge of Alford.

Craigievar Castle

The most spectacular of the Strathdon castles, **Craigievar Castle** (☎ 01339-883280; adult/child £9/6.50; ⊙ noon-5.30pm Fri-Tue Apr-Sep), 9 miles (14.5km) south of Alford, has managed to survive pretty much unchanged since its completion in the 17th century, a superb example of the original Scottish Baronial style. The lower half is a plain tower house, the upper half sprouts corbelled turrets, cupolas and battlements – an extravagant statement of its builder's wealth and status.

Kildrummy Castle

Nine miles (14.5km) west of Alford lie the interesting and extensive remains of 13th-century **Kildrummy Castle** (☎ 01975-571331; adult/child £2.20/75p; ⊙ 9.30am-6.30pm Apr-Sep, 9.30am-4.30pm Mon-Sat, 2-4.30pm Sun Oct-Mar), former seat of the Earl of Mar. After the 1715 Jacobite rebellion, the earl was exiled to France and his castle fell into ruin.

If you fancy a night of luxury head for the **Kildrummy Castle Hotel** (☎ 01975-571288; boo kings@kildrummycastlehotel.co.uk; s £80-90, d £140-175; ✗ P) across the river, a splendid Baronial hunting lodge complete with original oak panelling, log fires and four-poster beds.

Corgarff Castle

In the wild upper reaches of Strathdon, near the A939 from Corgarff to Tomintoul, is the impressive tower house of **Corgarff Castle** (☎ 01975-651460; adult/child £3/1; ⊙ 9.30am-6.30pm Apr-Sep; 9.30am-4.30pm Sat, 2-4.30pm Sun Oct-Mar). The tower house dates from the 16th century, but the star-shaped defensive curtain wall was added in 1748 when the castle was converted to a military barracks in the wake of the Jacobite rebellion.

Jenny's Bothy (☎ 01975-651449; jenboth@talk21 .com; dm £8) is an excellent year-round bunkhouse; look out for the sign by the main road, then follow the old military road (drivable) for three-quarters of a mile.

Lecht Ski Resort

At the head of Strathdon the A939 crosses the Lecht pass (637m), where there's a small skiing area with lots of short easy and intermediate runs. **Lecht 2090** (☎ 01975-651440; www.lecht.co.uk) hires out skis, boots and poles for £14, or a snowboard and boots for £17; a lift pass is £20 for a day. A two-day package including ski hire, lift pass and instruction costs £75.

The ski centre opens in summer too, when you can ski or board on the dry ski slope (£10 for two hours, including equipment hire), or rent go-karts and quad bikes (£7.50 a session) or just take a trip up on the chairlift (£4 return).

NORTHERN ABERDEENSHIRE

North of Aberdeen, the Grampian Mountains fall away to rolling agricultural plains pocked with small, craggy volcanic hills. This fertile lowland corner of northeastern Scotland is known as Buchan, a region of traditional farming culture immortalised by Lewis Grassic Gibbon in his trilogy, *A Scots Quair*, based on the life of a farming community in the 1920s. The old Scots dialect called the Doric lives on in everyday use here – if you think the Glaswegian accent is difficult to understand, just try listening in to a conversation in Peterhead or Fraserburgh.

The Buchan coast alternates between rugged cliffs and long, long stretches of sand, dotted with picturesque little fishing villages such as Pennan, where parts of the film *Local Hero* were shot.

Haddo House

Haddo House (☎ 01651-851440; Tarves; adult/child £7/5.25; ☿ 11am-4.30pm Jun-Aug) was designed by William Adam in 1732, and is best described as a classic English stately home transplanted to Scotland. It's 19 miles (30km) north of Aberdeen, near the town of Ellon.

Stagecoach Bluebird buses run hourly Monday to Saturday from Aberdeen to Tarves/Methlick, stopping at the end of the Haddo House driveway; it's a mile-long walk from bus stop to house.

Fyvie Castle

Though a magnificent example of Scottish Baronial architecture, **Fyvie Castle** (☎ 01651-

891266; adult/child £7/5.25; ☿ 11am-5pm Jul & Aug, noon-5pm Fri-Tue Apr-Jun & Sep) is probably more famous for its ghosts, which include a phantom trumpeter and the mysterious Green Lady.

The castle is 8 miles (13km) south of Turriff; a bus runs hourly every day from Aberdeen to Banff and Elgin via Fyvie village, a mile from the castle.

Peterhead

☎ 01779 / pop 17,950

Peterhead's sprawling harbour stands as testimony to a once-great fishing industry. Not much more than a decade ago, the high-tech trawlers operating from here were so productive that they supported a Ferrari-driving fishing community with a large disposable income. Overfishing and EU quotas and restrictions have now led to a point where the entire industry is in danger of disappearing, and the town is turning to tourism and North Sea oil for salvation.

Peterhead Maritime Heritage (☎ 473000; The Lido; South Rd; adult/child £3/2; ☿ 11am-4pm Mon-Sat, noon-4pm Sun Apr-Oct) documents the town's involvement in the whaling and fishing industries and their replacement by North Sea oil. The central **Arbuthnot Museum** (☎ 477778; St Peter St; admission free; ☿ 11am-1pm & 2-4.30pm Mon-Sat, closes 1pm Wed) has wide-ranging displays of local and Arctic interest.

Recommended places to stay include the **Carrick Guest House** (☎ 470610; carrickhouse@uk online.co.uk; 16 Merchant St; s/d £25/44; ☒ P) with six bedrooms (all with attached bathroom), and the comfortable, recently modernised **Palace Hotel** (☎ 474821; info@palacehotel.co.uk; Prince St; s/d £50/70; ☒ P), which is the town's top accommodation.

Stagecoach Bluebird buses run from Aberdeen to Peterhead every 30 minutes Monday to Saturday and hourly on Sunday (£4.50, 1¼ hours).

Fraserburgh

☎ 01346 / pop 12,450

Fraserburgh, affectionately known to local people as the Broch, is Europe's largest shellfish port. Like Peterhead, it has suffered from the general decline of the fishing industry. The harbour can be interesting when it's crowded with boats, and there are good sandy beaches east of the town. There's a **TIC** (☎ 518315; ☿ Apr-Sep), a supermarket and banks with ATMs.

The **Scottish Lighthouse Museum** (☎ 511022; Kinnaird Head; adult/child £4.75/2; ☻ 10am-6pm Mon-Sat, 11am-6pm Sun Jul & Aug; 11am-5pm Mon-Sat, noon-5pm Sun Apr-Jun, Sep & Oct; 11am-4pm Mon-Sat, noon-4pm Sun Nov-Mar) provides a fascinating insight into the network of lights that safeguard the Scottish coast, and the men and women who built and maintained them. Guided tours take you to the top of the bizarre-looking Kinnaird Head lighthouse, a converted 16th-century castle.

Maggie's Hoosie (☎ 514761; 26 Shore St, Inverallochy; admission free; ☻ 2-4.30pm daily Apr-Sep), 4 miles (6.5km) east of Fraserburgh, is a traditional fishwife's cottage with earthen floors and original furnishings, a timeless reminder of a bygone age.

Overnight options include **Clifton House B&B** (☎ 518365; 131 Charlotte St; s/d £19/35) and **Coral Haven Guest House** (☎ 519187; 53 Saltoun Pl; r per person £22).

Stagecoach Bluebird buses run hourly to Fraserburgh from Aberdeen (£4.90, 1½ hours) and Peterhead (£1.10, 40 minutes).

Pennan

Pennan is a picturesque harbour village tucked beneath red sandstone cliffs, 12 miles (19km) west of Fraserburgh. The whitewashed houses are built gable-end-on to the sea here, and the waves break just a few metres away on the other side of the road. It's no longer a working fishing village – only one boat occasionally uses the harbour, and the owner lives in Fraserburgh; most of the cottages are now holiday homes.

The **Pennan Inn** (☎ 01346-561201; mains £6-10; d £45) featured in the film *Local Hero*, as did the red telephone box outside, though one of the houses further along the sea-front to the east doubled for the exterior of the fictional hotel. The rooms are comfy if a bit on the small side, but the restaurant is good and the bar is a lively little place on a Friday night.

Stagecoach Bluebird buses from Fraserburgh to Banff stop at the Pennan road end (25 minutes, two a day, Saturday only), 350m south of (and a steep climb uphill from) the village.

Gardenstown & Crovie

The fishing village of **Gardenstown** (or Gamrie, pronounced *game*-rey), founded

by Alexander Garden in 1720, is unusual in being built on a series of cramped terraces tumbling down the steep cliffs above the tiny harbour. Drivers should beware of severe gradients and hairpin bends in the village, parts of which can only be reached on foot. **Crovie**, half a mile to the east, is even more claustrophobically picturesque.

Huntly
☎ 01466 / pop 4400

An impressive ruined castle and an attractive main square make this small town worth a stopover between Aberdeen and Elgin. The **TIC** (☎ 792255; The Square; ☻ 9.30am-6pm Mon-Sat, 10am-3pm Sun Easter-Oct) is on the main square, next to a bank with an ATM.

Castle St (beside the Huntly Hotel) runs north from the town square to an arched gateway and tree-lined avenue that leads to 16th-century **Huntly Castle** (☎ 793191; adult/child £3/1; ☻ 9.30am-6.30pm Apr-Sep; 9.30am-4.30pm Mon-Wed & Sat, 9.30am-1pm Thu, 2-4.30pm Sun Oct-Mar), the former stronghold of the Gordons on the banks of the River Deveron. Over the main door is a superb carving that includes the royal arms and the figures of Christ and St Michael.

There are a couple of hotels on the main square, and a handful of B&Bs in the surrounding streets; travellers have recommended the hospitable **Hillview** (☎ 794870; Provost St; r per person £16; ☒ ℗) and its tasty breakfast pancakes.

If you want to spoil yourself, continue along the drive beyond the castle to the **Castle Hotel** (☎ 792696; www.castlehotel.uk.com; s £48-58, d £68-88; ☒ ℗), a splendid 18th-century mansion set amid acres of parkland. It's comfortably old-fashioned, with a grand wooden staircase, convoluted corridors, the odd creaky floorboard and rattling sash window, but must be among the most affordable country house hotels in Scotland.

Stagecoach Bluebird bus No 10 from Aberdeen to Inverness passes through Huntly (£5.80; 1¼ hours, hourly). There are also regular trains from Aberdeen to Huntly (£7.80, one hour, every two hours), continuing to Inverness.

Elgin
☎ 01343 / pop 20,800

Elgin has been the provincial capital of Moray for the past eight centuries, and

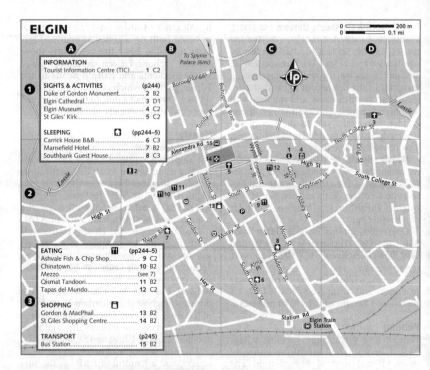

ELGIN

0 — 200 m
0 — 0.1 mi

INFORMATION
Tourist Information Centre (TIC)........ 1 C2

SIGHTS & ACTIVITIES (p244)
Duke of Gordon Monument............... 2 B2
Elgin Cathedral.................................. 3 D1
Elgin Museum................................... 4 C2
St Giles' Kirk.................................... 5 C2

SLEEPING (pp244–5)
Carrick House B&B............................ 6 C3
Mansfield Hotel................................ 7 B2
Southbank Guest House.................... 8 C3

EATING (pp244–5)
Ashvale Fish & Chip Shop................... 9 C2
Chinatown..................................... 10 B2
Mezzo.................................... (see 7)
Qismat Tandoori.............................. 11 B2
Tapas del Mundo............................. 12 C2

SHOPPING
Gordon & MacPhail.......................... 13 B2
St Giles Shopping Centre.................. 14 B2

TRANSPORT (p245)
Bus Station.................................... 15 B2

To Spynie
Palace (6mi)

To Spynie
Palace (6mi)

Elgin Train
Station

was an important town in medieval times. Dominated by a monument to the 5th duke of Gordon, erected in 1839, which crowns Lady Hill west of the centre, Elgin's main attraction is its impressive ruined cathedral.

The **TIC** (☎ 542666; 17 High St; ☺ 9am-6pm Mon-Sat, 11am-4pm Sun Apr-Oct; 9am-5pm Mon-Sat Nov-Mar) is a short distance east of the pedestrianised High St, which splits to pass either side of St Giles' Kirk. The bus station is a block north of the High St, but the train station is 900m south of the centre.

The post office is in the Tesco supermarket on Batchen Lane, just south of High St.

SIGHTS
Many people think that the ruins of **Elgin Cathedral** (☎ 547171; adult/child £3/1; joint ticket with Spynie Palace £3.50/1.20; ☺ 9.30am-6.30pm Apr-Sep, 9.30am-4.30pm Mon-Wed & Sat, 9.30am-1pm Thu, 2-4.30pm Sun Oct-Mar), known as the 'lantern of the north', are the most beautiful and evocative in Scotland. Consecrated in 1224, the cathedral was burned down in 1390 by the infamous Wolf of Badenoch, the illegitimate son of Robert II, following

his excommunication by the bishop. The octagonal chapter house is the finest in the country.

Palaeontologists and Pict lovers might like to visit **Elgin Museum** (☎ 543675; 1 High St; adult/child £2/50p; ☺ 10am-5pm Mon-Fri; 11am-4pm Sat, 2-5pm Sun Apr-Oct) where the highlights are its collections of fossil fish and Pictish carved stones.

Spynie Palace (☎ 546358; adult/child £2.20/75p; ☺ 9.30am-6.30pm Apr-Sep; 9.30am-4.30pm Sat, 2-4.30pm Sun Oct-Mar), 2 miles (3km) north of Elgin, was the residence of the medieval bishops of Moray until 1686. The massive tower house has lovely views over Spynie Loch.

Not a sight as such, but a sight for sore eyes perhaps, **Gordon & MacPhail** (☎ 545110; 58-60 South St; ☺ 9am-5pm Mon-Sat) is the world's largest specialist malt whisky dealer. Over a century old and offering around 450 different varieties, its Elgin shop is a place of pilgrimage for whisky connoisseurs.

SLEEPING & EATING
Mansfield Hotel (☎ 540883; www.themansfield.com; Mayne Rd; s £60-70, d £90-110; ☒ ℗) Centred on

a 19th-century manse (minister's house), the recently refurbished and expanded Mansfield offers elegant accommodation in both stylish modern rooms and traditional suites with four-poster beds. There's an excellent restaurant, and a cosy Whisky Lounge with leather sofas and armchairs to retire to after dinner.

Carrick House B&B (☎ 569321; kevin@scotbandb .co.uk; 13 South Guildry St; r per person £20-24; ☒ P) A fine Georgian house with warm décor and an open fire in the lounge, the Carrick's three bedrooms have crisp white linen, plump pillows and bedside reading lamps.

Southbank Guest House (☎ 547132; bizzybell@ handbag.com; 36 Academy St; r per person £23-35; ☒ P) The family-run, 11-room Southbank is in a spacious Georgian town house in a quiet street south of the centre.

Mezzo (☎ 540883; cnr Hay and South Sts; mains £6-8; ☽ noon-2.30pm & 6-9.30pm Mon-Thu, noon-9.30pm Fri & Sat, 5-9.30pm Sun) This stylish new bar-restaurant is part of the Mansfield Hotel complex, and serves tasty bistro fare including several good veggie options.

Tapas del Mundo (☎ 549737; High St; mains £4-6; ☽ 5-10pm) Part of Flanagan's Bar, tucked up a narrow wynd on the southern side of High St near the TIC, this place serves good Spanish food – they do an all-you-can-eat buffet for £10 on Wednesday and Sunday.

Other recommendations:

Ashvale (11 Moss St) A fish and chip shop.

Chinatown (☎ 552332; 210 High St)

Qismat Tandoori (☎ 541461; 204 High St; set lunch Mon-Sat £3.95)

GETTING THERE & AWAY

Stagecoach Bluebird runs buses to Banff and Macduff (£7.50, one hour), Dufftown (£3.60, 30 minutes), Inverness (£7, one hour) and Aberdeen (£8, 2¼ hours).

Elgin is on the Aberdeen to Inverness railway line.

Dufftown

☎ 01340 / pop 1450

Rome may be built on seven hills, but Dufftown's built on seven stills, say the locals. Founded in 1817 by James Duff, 4th earl of Fife, Dufftown is 14 miles (22.5km) west of Huntly and is a good place to start the Malt Whisky Trail (see the boxed text on p246).

The **TIC** (☎ 820501; ☽ 10am-1pm & 2-6pm Mon-Sat, 1-6pm Sun Easter-Oct) is in the clocktower in

the main square; the adjacent **museum** has some interesting local items.

SIGHTS & ACTIVITIES

With seven working distilleries nearby, Dufftown has been dubbed Scotland's malt whisky capital. The **Whisky Shop** (☎ 821097; 1 Fife St) stocks hundreds of single malts and a huge range of bottled Scottish beers, and runs tasting sessions at 7pm on Wednesday evenings in July and August. Ask at the TIC about the **Seven Stills Tour**, a guided tour of Dufftown's local distilleries.

At the northern edge of town is the **Glenfiddich Distillery Visitor Centre** (☎ 820373; admission free; ☽ 9.30am-4.30pm Mon-Fri, plus 9.30am-4.30pm Sat, noon-4.30pm Sun Easter–mid-Oct). Visitors are guided through the process of distilling and can see the whisky being bottled – the only Highland distillery where this is done on the premises. There's no entry charge – your free dram really is free.

The nearby 13th-century **Balvenie Castle** (☎ 820121; adult/child £1.50/50p; ☽ 9.30am-6.30pm Apr-Sep) was built by Alexander 'the Black' Comyn. It was transformed into a stately home after 1550 and was visited by Mary Queen of Scots in 1562. Note the moat and external latrine chutes.

The **Keith and Dufftown Railway** (☎ 821181; www.keith-dufftown.org.uk; Dufftown Station) is a heritage railway line running for 11 miles (18km) from Dufftown to Keith. Trains hauled by 1950s diesel motor units run on Saturdays and Sundays from June to mid-October; a return ticket costs £8 for an adult, £4 for a child. There are plans to run 1930s Pullman dining cars, starting in summer 2004.

SLEEPING & EATING

Davaar (☎ 820464; davaar@cluniecameron.co.uk; 17 Church St; r per person £20) This is a recommended B&B, just across the street from the TIC.

Commercial Hotel (☎ 820313; 4 Church St; r per person £18) Has *ceilidhs* on Thursday evening and whisky-tasting sessions on Tuesday from June to September.

Fife Arms Hotel (☎ 820220; fandbhotel@bush internet.com; 2 The Square; bar meals £5-8; s £25-27, d £40-44; ☒ P) This cosy hotel is the best of all. Its restaurant dishes up tasty steaks, including ostrich and kangaroo.

A Taste of Speyside (☎ 820860; 10 Balvenie St; mains £10-13; ☽ 12.30-9pm Mon-Sat) This upmarket

THE MALT WHISKY TRAIL

A visit to a Scotch whisky distillery should be part of any trip to Scotland – around 40 distilleries around the country open their doors to visitors.

In some distilleries, showing tourists around has become a slick marketing operation complete with promotional videos, free drams, gift shops that rival Harrods in size and glitziness, and an admission charge of around £4 (in most places this is refundable if you buy something in the shop).

In Aberdeenshire & Moray seven Speyside distilleries – Benromach, Cardhu, Dallas Dhu, Glenfiddich, Glen Grant, The Glenlivet, and Strathisla – and Speyside Cooperage (where oak casks are made) promote themselves as the **Malt Whisky Trail** (www.maltwhiskytrail.com), a pleasant, signposted 70-mile (113km) drive. Local TICs provide a leaflet and map outlining the trail.

The **Isle of Islay** (p263), with its distinctively smoky and peaty malts, is another good place for a whisky tour. There are seven working distilleries on the island – Ardbeg, Bowmore, Bunnahabhain, Bruichladdich, Caol Ila, Lagavulin and Laphroaig – and all are open to visitors.

Recommended distillery tours include Glenfiddich, The Glenlivet and Strathisla on Speyside; Highland Park on Orkney; and Bowmore on Islay. The latter two are among the few remaining places that still malt their own barley – most distilleries now buy in their malt from independent maltings and visitors rarely see this part of the process.

restaurant, just downhill from the TIC, prepares traditional Scottish dishes using fresh local produce.

GETTING THERE & AWAY

Stagecoach Bluebird buses link Dufftown to Elgin (£3.80, 50 minutes, hourly), Huntly, Aberdeen and Inverness.

On summer weekends, you can take a train from Aberdeen or Inverness to Keith, and then ride the Keith and Dufftown Railway (see Sights, p245) to Dufftown.

Tomintoul

☎ 01807 / pop 320

This high-altitude village (345m) lies on the A939, roughly midway between Strathdon and Grantown-on-Spey (p306). The A939 between Cockbridge (near Corgarff in Aberdeenshire) and Tomintoul is usually the first in Scotland to be blocked by snow when winter closes in. The village is a good base for hikes into the eastern Cairngorms, and for the nearby Lecht Ski Resort (p342). There's a **TIC** (☎ 580285; ☹ 10am-4pm Mon-Sat Easter-Oct) on the Square.

Tomintoul Museum (☎ 673701; The Square; admission free; ☹ 10am-4pm Mon-Sat Jun-Sep; 10am-4pm Mon-Fri May & Oct) has displays on a range of local topics. The surrounding Glenlivet Estate has lots of walking and cycling trails; the estate's **information centre** (☎ 580283; Main St) distributes free maps of the area.

A spur of the **Speyside Way** long-distance footpath (see boxed text, p248) between Buckie

and Aviemore runs from Tomintoul to Ballindalloch, 15 miles (24km) to the north.

Accommodation for walkers includes the **Tomintoul Youth Hostel** (☎ 0870 004 1152; Main St; dm £10.50; ☹ Apr-Sep), housed in the old village school, and the **Tomintoul Bunkhouse** (☎ 01343-548105; The Square; dm £9). The small, family-run **Glenavon Hotel** (☎ 580218; enquiries@glenavon-hotel.co.uk; The Square; s/d £25/40; ☒ ℗) is a more comfortable alternative.

GETTING THERE & AWAY

Infrequent buses connect Tomintoul with Elgin (£1¼ hours, one on Thursday only) and Dufftown (40 minutes, one on Tuesday, two on Saturday); these services are operated by **Roberts of Rothiemay** (☎ 01466-711213) and **WW Smith** (☎ 01542-882113).

Banff & Macduff

☎ 01261 / combined pop 7750

A popular seaside resort, the twin towns of Banff and Macduff lie either side of Banff Bay at the mouth of the River Deveron. Banff is an attractive little town and Macduff is a busy fishing port.

The **TIC** (☎ 812419; High St; ☹ Apr-Oct) is beside St Mary's car park in Banff.

SIGHTS

Duff House (☎ 818181; adult/child £4.50/3.50; ☹ 11am-5pm Apr-Oct, 11am-4pm Thu-Sun Nov-Mar) is an impressive baroque mansion on the southern edge of Banff (upstream from the bridge, and across from the TIC). Built between 1735 and 1740 as the seat of the earls of Fife, it was designed by William Adam and bears similarities to that Adam masterpiece, Hopetoun House (p100). Since being gifted to the town in 1906 it has served as a hotel, a hospital and a POW camp, but after extensive refurbishment it opened as an art gallery. One of Scotland's hidden gems, it houses a superb permanent collection of Scottish art.

The **Banff Museum** (☎ 622906; High St; admission free; ⏱ 2-4.30pm Mon-Sat Jun-Sep) has an award-winning display on local wildlife, geology and history, and Banff silver. Just off Carmelite St in Banff is the medieval ruin of **St Mary's Kirk** and an interesting graveyard. Nearby, the **Market Arms Bar**, built in 1585, is the oldest continuously occupied building in Banff.

The centrepiece of **Macduff Marine Aquarium** (☎ 833369; 11 High Shore; adult/child £2.75/2; ⏱ 10am-5pm) is a 400,000L open-air tank, complete with kelp-coated reef and wave machine. Marine oddities on view include the brightly coloured cuckoo wrasse, the warty-skinned lumpsucker and the vicious-looking wolf fish.

Two miles (3km) west of Banff is the quiet, picturesque fishing village of **Whitehills**, with narrow lanes and rows of neatly painted cottages gable-end-on to the sea.

SLEEPING

Banff Links Caravan Park (☎ 812228; Banff; tents & campervans £8-10; ⏱ Apr-Oct) This campground is beside the beach, half a mile west of town.

Bryvard Guest House (☎ 818090; bryvard@hotmail .com; Seafield St, Banff; r £24 per person) The Bryvard is a delightful Edwardian town house with four bedrooms (three with bathroom). It's on the A98 west of the town centre.

County Hotel (☎ 815353; enquiries@thecountyhotel .com; 32 High St, Banff; s/d £35/65; ⊠ ⓟ) Housed in an attractive Georgian mansion, the County offers fine dining to complement its fine décor.

GETTING THERE & AWAY

Stagecoach Bluebird buses run from Banff to Elgin (£7.20, one hour, hourly) and Aberdeen, and less frequently to Fraserburgh.

Portsoy

☎ 01261 / pop 1730

The pretty fishing village of Portsoy has an attractive 17th-century harbour and a maze of narrow streets lined with picturesque cottages. An ornamental stone known as **Portsoy marble** – actually a beautifully patterned green and pale pink serpentine – was quarried near Portsoy in the 17th and 18th centuries, and was reputedly used in the decoration of some rooms in the Palace of Versailles.

Each year on the last weekend in June or first weekend in July, Portsoy harbour is home to the **Scottish Traditional Boat Festival** (☎ 842951; www.thebpl.co.uk/boatfest), a lively gathering of historic wooden sailing boats accompanied by sailing races, live folk music, crafts demonstrations, street theatre and a food festival.

The 12-room **Boyne Hotel** (☎ 842242; enquiries@ boynehotel.co.uk; 2 North High St; r per person £22) is a cosy and atmospheric place to stay.

Portsoy is 8 miles (13km) west of Banff; the hourly bus between Elgin and Banff stops here.

Fordyce

This well-preserved historic village lies about 3 miles (5km) southwest of Portsoy. The main attractions are the 13th-century **St Tarquin's Church** with its extraordinary canopied Gothic tombs, and the impressive 16th-century tower house of **Fordyce Castle**. The castle is not open to the public, but its whitewashed west wing provides atmospheric **self-catering accommodation** (☎ 01261-843722; www.fordycecastle.co.uk; £325-425 a week, £225 for three nights in low season) for up to four persons.

The nearby **Joiner's Workshop & Visitor Centre** (☎ 01771-622906; admission free; ⏱ 10am-6pm Thu-Mon) has a collection of woodworking tools and machinery, and stages woodwork demonstrations by a master joiner.

Fochabers & Around

☎ 01343 / pop 1500

Fochabers sits beside the last bridge over the River Spey before it enters the sea 4 miles (6.5km) to the north. The town has a pleasant square, with a church and clock tower dated 1798, and a handful of interesting antique shops.

West of the bridge over the Spey is **Baxters Highland Village** (☎ 820666; admission free; ⏱ 9am-5.30pm Apr-Dec; 10am-4pm Jan-Mar), which charts the history of the Baxter family and their well-known brand of quality Scottish foodstuffs, which began in 1868 when they opened their first shop in Fochabers. There's a factory tour with cookery demonstrations on weekdays.

Four miles (6.5km) north of Fochabers, at the mouth of the River Spey, is the tiny village of **Spey Bay**. It's the starting point for the Speyside Way long-distance footpath (see the boxed text below), and home to the **Tugnet Ice House** (☎ 01309-673701; admission free; 🕙 11am-4pm May-Sep) salmon-fishing museum, and the **Moray Firth Wildlife Centre** (☎ 820339; admission free; 🕙 10.30am-5pm Apr-Oct, 10.30am-7pm Jul & Aug), which has an exhibit on the Moray Firth dolphins.

Bluebird Stagecoach buses run from Fochabers to Aberdeen (£7.60, two hours) and Inverness (£7.50, 1¾ hours).

Findhorn
☎ 01309 / pop 885

The attractive village of Findhorn lies at the mouth of the River Findhorn, just east of the Findhorn Bay nature reserve. It's a great place for bird-watching, seal-spotting and coastal walks.

Findhorn Heritage Centre (☎ 630349; admission free; 🕙 2-5pm Wed-Mon Jun-Aug; 2-5pm Sat & Sun May & Sep), housed in a former salmon-fisher's bothy at the northern end of the village, records the history of the settlement. The beach is just over the dunes north of the centre. At low tide, you can see seals hauled out on the sandbanks off the mouth of the River Findhorn.

Hippies old and new should check out the **Findhorn Foundation** (☎ 690311; www.findhorn.org; 🕙 9am-12.30pm & 2-5pm Mon-Fri, 2-5pm Sat & Sun May-Aug; Mon-Fri only Mar, Apr, Sep & Oct; 9am-12.30pm Mon-Fri Nov-Feb). The Foundation is an international spiritual community, founded in 1962; there's a small permanent population of around 150, but the community receives thousands of visitors each year.

With no formal creed, the community is dedicated to cooperation with nature, 'dealing with work, relationships and our environment in new and more fulfilling ways' and fostering 'a deeper sense of the sacred in everyday life'. Projects include eco-friendly houses, a biological sewage-treatment plant and a wind-powered generator. Guided tours (£1) are available at 2pm Monday, Wednesday and Friday March to October, and on Saturday and Sunday as well from June to August.

The **Crown & Anchor** (☎ 690243; 44 Findhorn; mains £6-12; r £25 per person; P) is a friendly 18th-century hotel and pub that serves excellent bar meals, including fresh seafood. Kids will love the toy train that carries meal orders from the bar to the kitchen.

Findhorn's other pub, the **Kimberley Inn** (☎ 690492; mains £5-12; food served noon-10pm), also does good bar meals.

Culbin Forest

On the western side of Findhorn Bay is **Culbin Forest**, a vast swathe of Scots and Corsican pine that was planted in the 1940s to stabilise the shifting sand dunes that buried the Culbin Estate in the 17th century. The forest is a unique wildlife habitat, and is criss-crossed by a maze of walking trails.

Forres

The tidy town of Forres, 4 miles (6.5km) south of Findhorn, is famous for **Sueno's Stone**, a remarkable, 6.5m-high Pictish stone. It is the tallest and most elaborately carved Pictish stone in Scotland, dating from the 9th or 10th century, and is thought to depict a battle between the Picts and invading Scots or Vikings. It's protected from the elements by a huge plate-glass box.

THE SPEYSIDE WAY

This long-distance footpath follows the course of the River Spey, one of Scotland's most famous salmon-fishing rivers. It starts at Buckie and first follows the coast to Spey Bay, east of Elgin, then runs inland along the river to Aviemore in the Cairngorms (with branches to Tomintoul and Dufftown). At only 66 miles (106km), it can be done in three or four days. With more time it could be combined with some hill walking in the Cairngorms.

This route has also been dubbed the 'Whisky Trail' as it passes near a number of distilleries, including The Glenlivet and Glenfiddich, which are open to the public. If you stop at them all, the walk may take considerable longer than the usual three or four days!

The Speyside Way guidebook by Jacquetta Megarry and Jim Strachan (£10.99) describes the route in detail; there's also a *Speyside Way* leaflet produced by **Moray Council Ranger Service** (☎ 01340-881266).

Check out the route at www.speysideway.org.

NORTHEAST SCOTLAND

Southern Highlands & Islands

The region covered in this chapter coincides with the old county of Argyllshire, whose name comes from the Gaelic *earra-ghaidheal* – the seaboard of the Gael. And what a seaboard! Though measuring only 155 miles (250km) north to south, Argyll's convoluted coastline is a staggering 2300 miles (3700km) in length.

Nowhere else in Scotland are land and sea so intimately interlaced as in the Highlands and islands of the southwest. Long sea lochs such as Loch Fyne and Loch Long – deep glacier-gouged valleys flooded by the sea – penetrate up to 40 miles (64km) inland. To the west, a flotilla of islands lies moored off the coast, as varied and fascinating as they are beautiful.

In summer, swallows and house martins swoop along the strand line, scooping insects from the air, while black-and-white oystercatchers police the sandy beaches, their strident 'pleep-pleep-pleep' calls a feature of Argyllshire evenings.

The very air feels balmy – warmed by the Gulf Stream, Argyll is famous for its mild climate. Palm trees grow on the promenades, and exotic subtropical species are cultivated in botanic gardens.

The sense of history is tangible too. The region is rich in prehistoric sites and is home to important religious and political centres of the past, including Dunadd, Finlaggan and the sacred island of Iona.

HIGHLIGHTS

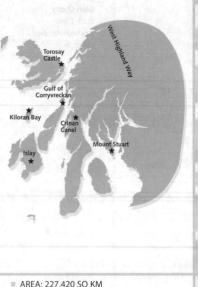

- Trying not to gawp open-mouthed as you walk through the opulent marble-clad halls of **Mount Stuart** (p257)

- Strolling along the **Crinan Canal** (p260) on a sunny day, perhaps stopping to help the yachties to open and close the lock gates

- Riding a high-speed motorboat through the white water and tidal whirlpools of the **Gulf of Corryvreckan** (p269)

- Sitting by a log fire, sampling some of **Islay's** (p263) finest single malt whiskies, having just visited the distillery where they were made

- Watching the sun sink into the Atlantic from the remote, golden-sand beach of **Kiloran Bay** (p269) on Colonsay

- Downing a pint after completing the 96 miles (154km) of the **West Highland Way** (p253) long-distance footpath

- Wandering through the beautiful gardens at **Torosay Castle** (p277) on the Isle of Mull

■ POPULATION: 4.7 MILLION	■ AREA: 227,420 SQ KM

OCH LOMOND & AROUND

The 'bonnie banks' and 'bonnie braes' of Loch Lomond have long been Glasgow's rural retreat – a scenic region of hills, lochs and healthy fresh air within easy reach of Scotland's largest city. Since the 1930s Glaswegians have made a regular weekend exodus to the hills, by car, by bike and on foot, and today the loch's popularity shows no sign of decreasing.

The region's importance was recognised when it became the heart of the **Loch Lomond & the Trossachs National Park** (☎ 01389-722600; www.lochlomond-trossachs.org) – Scotland's first national park, created in 2002.

LOCH LOMOND

Loch Lomond is the largest lake in mainland Britain and, after Loch Ness, perhaps the most famous of Scotland's lochs. Its proximity to Glasgow (only 20 miles/32km away) means that the tourist honey-pots of Balloch, Loch Lomond Shores and Luss get pretty crowded in summer. The main tourist focus is on the western shore of the loch, along the A82, and at the southern end, around Balloch, which can be a nightmare of jet skis and motorboats. The eastern shore is a little quieter.

Loch Lomond straddles the Highland border and its character changes as you

---

GAELIC & NORSE PLACE NAMES

Throughout the Highlands and islands of Scotland the indigenous Gaelic language has left a rich legacy of place names, often intermixed with Old Norse names left behind by the Viking invaders who occupied the western and northern islands between the 8th and 13th centuries. The spelling is now anglicised but the meaning is still clear once you know what to look for. Here are a few of the more common Gaelic and Norse names and their meanings.

Gaelic place names

ach, auch – from *achadh* (field)
ard – from *ard* or *aird* (height, hill)
avon – from *abhainn* (river or stream)
bal – from *baile* (village or homestead)
ban – from *ban* (white, fair)
beg – from *beag* (small)
ben – from *beinn* (mountain)
buie – from *buidhe* (yellow)
dal – from *dail* (field or dale)
dow, **dhu** – from *dubh* (black)
drum – from *druim* (ridge or back)
dun – from *dun* or *duin* (fort or castle)
glen – from *gleann* (narrow valley)
gorm – from *gorm* (blue)
gower, gour – from *gabhar* (goat), eg Ardgour (height of the goats)
inch, **insh** – from *inis* (island, water-meadow or resting place for cattle)
inver – from *inbhir* (river mouth or meeting of two rivers)
kil – from *cille* (church), as in Kilmartin (Church of St Martin)
kin, ken – from *ceann* (head), eg Kinlochleven (head of Loch Leven)
kyle, kyles – from *caol* or *caolas*, a narrow sea channel

more, vore – from *mor* or *mhor* (big), eg Ardmore (big height), Skerryvore (big reef)
strath – from *srath* (broad valley)
tarbert, tarbet – from *tairbeart* (portage), meaning a narrow neck of land between two bodies of water, across which a boat can be dragged
tay, ty – from *tigh* (house), eg Tyndrum (house on the ridge)
tober – from *tobar* (well), eg Tobermory (Mary's well)

Norse place names

a, ay, ey – from *ey* (island)
bister, buster, bster – from *bolstaor* (dwelling place, homestead)
geo – from *gja* (chasm)
holm – from *holmr* (small island)
kirk – from *kirkja* (church)
pol, poll, bol – from *bol* (farm)
quoy – from *kvi* (sheep fold, cattle enclosure)
sker, skier, skerry – from *sker* (rocky reef)
ster, sett – from *setr* (house)
vig, vaig, wick – from *vik* (bay, creek)
voe, way – from *vagr* (bay, creek)

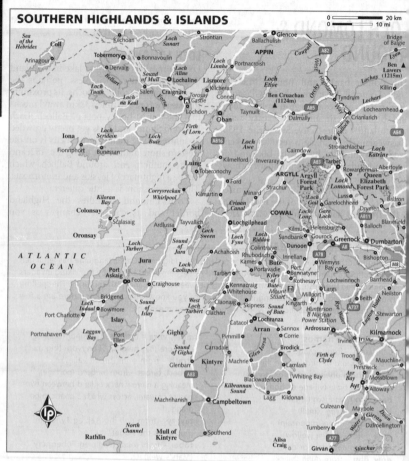

SOUTHERN HIGHLANDS & ISLANDS

move north across it. The southern part is broad and island-studded and fringed by woods and lowland meadows, but north of Luss the loch narrows, occupying a deep trench gouged out by glaciers during the Ice Age, with 900m mountains crowding in on either side.

Orientation

Loch Lomond is 22 miles (35km) long and varies in width from 1 to 5 miles (1.6km to 8km). The A82 along the western shore is the main road north from Glasgow to Fort William. The minor road along the eastern shore, reached from Balloch via Drymen, ends at Rowardennan. The West Highland Way walking trail also follows the eastern shore.

Information

Balloch TIC (☎ 08707 200607; Balloch Rd; ☼ Apr-Oct)
Drymen TIC (☎ 08707 200611; Drymen Library, The Square; ☼ May-Sep)
National Park Gateway Centre (☎ 08707 200631; www.lomondshores.com; Loch Lomond Shores, Balloch; ☼ 10am-7pm Apr-Jun & Sep, 10am-8pm Jul & Aug, 10.30am-4.30pm Oct-Mar)
Tarbet TIC (☎ 08707 200623; ☼ Apr-Oct) At the junction of the A82 and A83.

Activities
WALKS

The big walk around here is the **West Highland Way** (p253), which runs along the eastern shore of the loch. There are shorter lochside walks at Firkin Point on the

WEST HIGHLAND WAY

This classic hike – the country's most popular long-distance path – stretches for 95 miles (153km) through some of Scotland's most spectacular scenery, from Milngavie (pronounced mull-*guy*), on the northwestern fringes of Glasgow, to Fort William.

The route begins in the lowlands but the greater part of the trail is among the mountains, lochs and fast-flowing rivers of the western Highlands. After following the eastern shore of Loch Lomond and passing Crianlarich and Tyndrum, the route crosses the vast wilderness of Rannoch Moor and reaches Fort William via Glen Nevis, in the shadow of Britain's highest peak, Ben Nevis.

The path is easy to follow, making use of old drovers' roads (along which Highland cattle were once driven to lowland markets), an old military road (built by troops to help subdue the Highlands in the 18th century) and disused railway lines.

Best done from south to north, you'll need about six or seven days to complete it. Many people round it off with an ascent of Ben Nevis (p316).

You need to be properly equipped with good boots, maps, a compass, and food and drink for the northern part of the walk. Midge repellent is also essential.

The West Highland Way by Robert Aitken comes with a 1:50,000 OS route map and is the most comprehensive guidebook. The Harveys map *West Highland Way* is also handy and contains useful additional tourist information.

Accommodation shouldn't be too difficult to find, though between Bridge of Orchy and Kinlochleven it's limited. In summer, book B&Bs in advance. There are some youth hostels and bunkhouses on or near the path, and it's possible to camp in some parts. A free accommodation list is available from TICs.

For more information check out the website at www.west-highland-way.co.uk.

---

western shore and at several other places around the loch.

Rowardennan is the starting point for an ascent of **Ben Lomond** (974m), a popular five- to six-hour round trip. The route starts at the car park just past the Rowardennan Hotel.

BOAT TRIPS

The main centre for boat trips is Balloch, where **Sweeney's Cruises** (☎ 01389-752376; Balloch Rd) offers a range of trips including a one-hour cruise around the islands (adult/child £5.20/1.50, departs hourly), and a daily 2½-hour cruise (£7.50/3.50, departs 2.30pm) to Luss village, allowing 30 minutes ashore. The company also runs hourly cruises from Loch Lomond Shores.

Cruise Loch Lomond (☎ 01301-702356) is based in Tarbet and offers trips to Inversnaid and Rob Roy MacGregor's cave (see the boxed text on p186 for more on Rob Roy).

The mail boat, run by **Balhama Boatyard** (☎ 01360-870214; The Boatyard, Balmaha), cruises from Balmaha to the loch's four inhabited islands, departing at 11.30am and returning at 2pm with a one-hour stop on Inchmurrin (adult/child £7/3.50). Trips depart Monday to Saturday in July and August, and Monday, Thursday and Saturday in May, June and September).

OTHER ACTIVITIES

The mostly traffic-free **Clyde and Loch Lomond Cycle Way** links Glasgow to Balloch (20 miles/ 32km), where it links with the new **West Loch Lomond Cycle Path**, which continues along the loch shore to Tarbet (10 miles/16km).

At Loch Lomond Shores (see below) you can hire canoes (£15/10 per hour/half-hour) and bicycles (£7/10/15 for two hours/ four hours/a day), take a **guided canoe trip** on the loch or go **pony trekking** (£1 a ride).

Western Shore

The town of **Balloch**, which straddles the River Leven where it exits the southern end of Loch Lomond, is the loch's main population centre and transport hub. A Victorian resort once thronged by day-trippers transferring between the train station and the steamer quay, it was sidelined somewhat by the A82 bypass, which allowed drivers to shoot through without stopping, but may be revived by the Loch Lomond Shores development.

Opened in 2003, **Loch Lomond Shores** (☎ 01389-722406; www.lomondshores.com) is a new 'gateway centre' for Loch Lomond, offering a large national park information centre, various visitor attractions, outdoor activities and boat trips. However, in keeping with the times, the heart of the development is a large shopping mall. The vintage paddle steamer **Maid of the Loch** (☎ 01389-711865; admission free; ☺ 10am-4pm Easter-Oct), built in 1953, is moored here while awaiting full restoration – you can nip aboard for a look around.

Unless it's raining, give Loch Lomond Shores a miss and head for the little picture-postcard village of **Luss**. Take a stroll among the pretty cottages with roses around their doors, built by the local laird in the 19th century for the workers on his estate, and pop into the **Clan Colquhoun Visitor Centre** (☎ 01389-850564; adult/child £1/free; ☺ 10.30am-6pm Easter-Oct) for some background history before enjoying a cuppa at the **Coach House** (below).

SLEEPING & EATING

Loch Lomond Youth Hostel (SYHA; ☎ 0870 004 1136; Arden; dm £12.50-14; ☺ Mar-Oct) Forget about roughing it, this is one of the most impressive hostels in the country – an imposing 19th-century country house set in beautiful grounds overlooking the loch. It's 2 miles (3km) north of Balloch and very popular, so book in advance in summer. And yes, it is haunted.

Drover's Inn (☎ 01301-704234; the droversinn@ aol.com; Inverarnan; r from £23; per meals £6-8; P) This is one pub you shouldn't miss – a low-ceilinged howff with smoke-blackened stone, bare wooden floors spotted with candle wax, barmen in kilts and an ancient hallway festooned with moth-eaten stag's heads. Accommodation varies from basic rooms with shared bath in the old building to modern rooms (with bathrooms) in the annexe. There are also decent bar meals.

Ardlui Hotel (☎ 01301-704243; info@ardlui.co.uk; Ardlui; s/d £55/90; P) If the Drover's is a little rough for your taste, nip down the road to the plush Ardlui Hotel, a comfy country house hotel at the northern end of the loch.

Coach House Coffee Shop (☎ 01436-860341; Luss; snacks £2-4, mains £9; ☺ 10am-6pm) Fitted out with chunky pine furniture and a deep, deep sofa in front of a rustic fireplace, the Coach House is easily the best place to eat

on Loch Lomond. The menu includes coffee and tea, home-baked cakes, scones and ciabatta sandwiches, and more substantial offerings such as haggis.

Viewing Gallery Café (☎ 01389-722416; Drumkinnon Tower, Loch Lomond Shores; snacks £3-5, mains £5-9) With tables arranged in front of floor-to-ceiling windows, this elegant café at the top of the Drumkinnon Tower makes the most of the superb views along the loch to Ben Lomond. The eating options range from tea and a scone to salads and smoked salmon.

Eastern Shore

The road along the loch's eastern shore passes through the attractive village of **Balmaha**, where you can hire boats (p255) or take a cruise on the mail boat (p253). There are several picnic areas along the lochside; the most attractive is at **Millarochy Bay**, 1½ miles north of Balmaha, which has a nice gravel beach and superb views across the loch to the Luss hills.

The road ends at **Rowardennan**, but the West Highland Way footpath continues along the shore of the loch. It's 7 miles (11km) to the Inversnaid Hotel, which is reached by road from the Trossachs (p186), and 15 miles (24km) to Inverarnan on the main A82 road at the northern end of the loch.

SLEEPING & EATING

Forestry Commission Cashel Campsite (☎ 01360-870234; Rowardennan; site per person £3.80-4.90; ☺ Apr-Oct) This is the most attractive camping ground in the area and is 3 miles (5km) north of Balmaha, by the loch.

Oak Tree Inn (☎ 01360-870357; info@oak-tree-inn.co.uk; Balmaha; s/d £40/56, dm £20; mains £6-8; ✗ P) An attractive chalet-style hotel built in slate and timber, the child-friendly Oak Tree has eight luxurious rooms with bathroom, and two, four-bed bunkrooms. The rustic restaurant, dominated by a roaring log fire, dishes up hearty meals such as sausage and mash, haggis, and vegetable lasagne.

Highland Way Hotel (☎ 01360-870270; Balmaha; s/d £30/48; bunkhouse d £28; ✗ P) Across the road from the Oak Tree, the Highland Way has a walkers' bunkhouse around the back, with drying room and 12 basic twin and double rooms.

Rowardennan Youth Hostel (☎ 0870 004 1148; Rowardennan; dm £10.50-12; ❤ Mar-Oct) Housed in an attractive Victorian lodge, this hostel has a superb setting right on the loch shore.

Rowardennan Hotel (☎ 01360-870273; www.row ardennanhotel.com; Rowardennan; s/d £60/90; bar meals £5-7; P) Originally an 18th-century drovers inn, the sprawling Rowardennan Hotel has comfortable, refurbished rooms, two big bars (often crowded with rain-sodden hikers) and a beer garden (often crowded with midges).

Getting There & Away

First Glasgow bus Nos 204 and 205 run from Argyle St in central Glasgow to Balloch and Loch Lomond Shores (£2.50, 1½ hours, three or four an hour). Citylink buses from Glasgow to Oban and Fort William stop at Luss (£5.40, 55 minutes, six a day), Tarbet (65 minutes) and Ardlui (1¼ hours).

There are frequent trains from Glasgow to Balloch (£3.30, 45 minutes, two an hour) and a less frequent service on the West Highland line from Glasgow to Oban and Fort William, with stops at Arrochar & Tarbet and Ardlui (£9.50, 1½ hours, three or four daily).

Getting Around

H-A-D Coaches (☎ 01501-820598) bus No 309 runs from Balloch to Balmaha (20 minutes, every two hours).

A Rural Rover ticket (£3.50) gives unlimited travel for a day on most buses in the Loch Lomond and Helensburgh area. Buy the ticket from the driver on the first bus you board.

Balmaha Boatyard (☎ 01360-870214; The Boatyard, Balmaha) offers boat hire for £8/22 an hour/day with oars only, or £13/37 with outboard motor, or take a cruise around the islands on the mail boat (see Activities, p253).

The Rowardennan Hotel (see above) operates a passenger ferry across the loch between Rowardennan and Inverbeg (£3, three daily Easter to September).

HELENSBURGH

☎ 01436 / pop 16,500

Named in the 18th century after the wife of Sir James Colquhoun of Luss, with the coming of the railway in the mid-19th century Helensburgh became a popular seaside retreat for wealthy Glasgow families. Their spacious Victorian villas now populate the neat grid of streets that covers the hillside above the Firth of Clyde, but none can compare with the splendour of **Hill House** (☎ 673900; Upper Colquhoun St; adult/child £7/5.25; ❤ 1.30-5.30pm Apr-Oct). Built in 1902 for the Glasgow publisher Walter Blackie, it is perhaps Charles Rennie Mackintosh's finest creation – its timeless elegance feels as chic today as it no doubt did when the Blackies moved in a century ago.

Helensburgh has ferry connections with Gourock (p132) and a frequent train service to Glasgow (£3.90, 40 minutes, two an hour).

ARROCHAR

☎ 01301 / pop 650

The village of Arrochar has a wonderful location, looking across the head of Loch Long to the jagged peaks of **The Cobbler** (881m). The mountain takes its name from the shape of its north peak (the one on the right), which looks like a cobbler hunched over his bench. The village has several hotels and shops, a bank and a post office.

If you want to climb the Cobbler, start from the roadside car park at Succoth near the head of Loch Long. A steep uphill hike beside the woods is followed by an easier section as you traverse southwest into the valley below the triple peaks. Then it's steeply uphill again to the saddle between the north and central peaks. The central peak (to the south) is the highest point, but it's awkward to get to – scramble through the hole and along the ledge to reach the airy summit. The north peak (to the right/north) is an easy walk. Allow five to six hours for the return trip.

There's good camping at **Ardgartan Caravan & Campsite** (☎ 702293; Ardgartan; tent or campervan site £6.60-9.40; Apr-Oct) at the foot of Glen Croe.

The black-and-white, 19th-century **Village Inn** (☎ 702279; Arrochar) is a lovely spot for lunch, or just a pint of ale – the beer garden has a great view of The Cobbler.

Citylink buses from Glasgow to Inveraray and Campbeltown call at Arrochar and Ardgartan (£6.30, 1¼ hours, three a day). See Getting There & Away under Loch Lomond (see left) for trains to Arrochar & Tarbet station.

SOUTH ARGYLL

COWAL

The remote Cowal peninsula is cut off from the rest of the country by the lengthy fjords of Loch Long and Loch Fyne, more accessible by boat than by car. It's a region of rugged hills and narrow lochs, with only a few small villages; the scenery around Loch Riddon is particularly enchanting. The only town on the mainland is the old-fashioned holiday resort of Dunoon.

From Arrochar, the A83 to Inveraray loops around the head of Loch Long and climbs up Glen Croe. The pass at the head of the glen is called the **Rest and be Thankful** – when the original military road through the glen was repaired in the 18th century, a stone was erected at the top inscribed 'Rest, and be thankful. This road was made, in 1748, by the 24th Regt...Repaired by the 93rd Regt. 1786'. A copy of the stone can be seen at the far end of the parking area at the top of the pass.

There's a Forest Enterprise **visitor centre** (☎ 702432; Ardgartan; admission free; ☼ 10am-5pm Apr-Oct) at the foot of the glen, with information on various walks in the Cowal peninsula.

As you descend Glen Kinglas on the far side of the Rest and be Thankful, the A815 forks to the left; this is the main overland route into Cowal. From Glasgow, the most direct route is by ferry from Gourock to Dunoon.

Dunoon & Around

☎ 01369 / pop 9060

Like Rothesay on the Isle of Bute, Dunoon is a Victorian seaside resort that owes its existence to the steamers that once carried thousands of Glaswegians on pleasure trips 'doon the watter' (down the water) in the 19th and 20th centuries. Like Rothesay's, Dunoon's fortunes declined in recent decades when cheap foreign holidays stole its market, but whereas the Bute resort appears to be recovering Dunoon is still a bit down in the dumps.

The **TIC** (☎ 08707 200629; 7 Alexandra Pde; ☼ 9am-6pm Mon-Fri, 10am-5pm Sat & Sun) is on the waterfront 100m north of the pier.

Dunoon hosts the annual **Cowal Highland Gathering** (☎ 703206; www.cowalgathering.com) in

mid-August; the spectacular finale traditionally features 1000 bagpipers playing en masse.

The town's main attraction is still, as it was in the 1950s, strolling along the **promenade**, licking an ice-cream cone and watching the yachts at play in the Firth of Clyde. On a small hill above the seafront is a statue of **Highland Mary** (1763–86), one of the great loves of Robert Burns' life. She was born near Dunoon, but died tragically young; her statue gazes longingly across the firth to Burns' home territory in Ayrshire.

The **Benmore Botanic Garden** (☎ 706261; Benmore; adult/child £3/1; ☼ 10am-6pm Apr-Sep, till 5pm Mar & Oct), 7 miles (11km) north of Dunoon, was originally planted in the 19th and early 20th centuries. It contains the country's finest collection of flowering trees and shrubs, including Bhutanese and Chilean rainforest specimens, and is entered along a spectacular avenue of giant Californian redwoods, planted in 1863.

If you want to stay the night in Dunoon, you can experience some of its former elegance at **Belmont House** (☎ 701287; daphne perks@tiscali.co.uk; 2 Edward St, West Bay; r per person £30-50; ☒ Ⓟ), a large Victorian villa overlooking the bay south of the ferry pier. One of the rooms has a huge four-poster bed, and you can help yourself to the sherry decanter in the lounge.

Chatters (☎ 706402; 58 John St; mains £6-8; ☼ 10am-3pm & 6-10pm Wed-Sat) is a pretty little cottage restaurant serving traditional Scottish dishes, and is easily the best place to eat in Dunoon. The two-/three-course lunch (£9/11) is excellent value.

Black of Dunoon (☎ 702311; 113 George St), a bakery halfway along the main street, is famous for its traditional Scottish shortbread.

Dunoon is served by two competing ferry services from Gourock (p132) – the CalMac ferry is better if you are travelling on foot and want to arrive in the town centre.

Tighnabruaich

☎ 01700 / pop 200

Sleepy little Tighnabruaich (pronounced tinna-*broo*-ach), a small colony of seaside villas built by wealthy Glasgow families and one of the most attractive villages on the Firth of Clyde, was once a regular stop for Clyde steamers.

The old wooden pier is still occasionally visited by the paddle steamer *Waverley*, and the link with the sea continues in the **Tighnabruaich Sailing School** (☎ 811717; www.tssargyll.co.uk; ☽ May-Sep). It offers dinghy sailing and windsurfing courses – a half-day's instruction for an adult/child costs £30/26. Customers can camp at the school for £3 a night.

ISLE OF BUTE

☎ 01700 / pop 7350

The peaceful island of Bute lies pinched between the thumb and forefinger of the Cowal peninsula, separated from the mainland by a narrow, scenic strait known as the Kyles of Bute. The Highland Boundary Fault cuts through the middle of the island so that, geologically speaking, the northern half is in the Highlands and the southern half in the central lowlands – a metal arch on Rothesay's Esplanade marks the fault line.

The **Isle of Bute Discovery Centre** (☎ 505156; info@rothesay.visitscotland.com; The Esplanade, Rothesay) in Rothesay's restored Winter Garden provides tourist information. There's Internet access at the **Harbour Café** (☎ 505166; 16 East Princes St, Rothesay; mains £8-13; ☽ 11am-5pm Mon-Sat, noon-4pm Sun, 6.30-10pm Fri & Sat) for £2.50 per 30 minutes.

The five-day **Isle of Bute Jazz Festival** is held over the first weekend of May, and in late July there's the **ButeLive** (www.butelive.co.uk) music and arts festival.

Rothesay

From the mid-19th century until the 1960s Rothesay – once dubbed the Margate of the Clyde – was one of the most popular holiday resorts in Scotland, its Esplanade thronged with day-trippers disembarking from the numerous steamers crowded round the pier, its hotels filled with elderly holidaymakers and convalescents taking advantage of its famously mild climate.

The fashion for foreign holidays that took off in the 1970s saw the town's fortunes decline, and by the late 1990s it had become dilapidated and despondent. But in the last few years a nostalgia-fuelled resurgence of interest in Rothesay's holiday heyday has seen many of its Victorian buildings restored and a new feeling of optimism in the air.

Just two blocks inland from the pier are the splendid, moated ruins of 13th-century **Rothesay Castle** (☎ 502691; King St; adult/child £2.20/75p; ☽ 9.30am-6.30pm Mon-Sat, 2-6.30pm Sun Apr-Sep; 9.30am-4.30pm Mon-Wed, 9.30am-1pm Thu, 2-4.30pm Sun Oct-Mar). Once a favourite residence of the Stuart kings, it is unique in Scotland in having a circular plan, with four massive round towers. The landscaped moat, with its manicured turf, flower gardens and lazily cruising ducks, makes a picturesque setting.

There aren't too many places where a public toilet would count as a tourist attraction, but Rothesay pier's **Victorian toilets** (adult/child 10p/free), dating from 1899, are a monument to lavatorial luxury, a disinfectant-scented temple of marbled black porcelain, glistening green and cream tiles and gleaming copper pipes. The attendant will escort ladies into the hallowed confines of the gents for a look around while the facilities are unoccupied. HRH Prince Charles, the Prince of Wales, visited the loos in 1998 in his official capacity (just under a pint, allegedly) as the duke of Rothesay.

The most interesting displays in **Bute Museum** (☎ 505067; Stuart St; adult/child £1.20/40p; ☽ 10.30am-4.30pm Mon-Sat, 2.30-4.30pm Sun Apr-Sep; 2.30-4.30pm Tue-Sat Oct-Mar) are those recounting the history of the famous Clyde steamers. Other displays cover the natural history, archaeology and geology of the island,

Gardeners will enjoy the beautifully restored **Victorian Fernery** (☎ 504555; Ascog Hall; Ascog; adult/child £2.50/free; ☽ 10am-5pm Wed-Sun mid-Apr–mid-Oct) at Ascog Hall, on the southern edge of town.

Mount Stuart

The Stuart earls of Bute are direct descendants of Robert the Bruce and have lived on the island for 700 years. When a large part of the family seat was destroyed by fire in 1877 the 3rd marquess of Bute, John Patrick Crichton-Stuart (1847–1900) – one of the greatest architecture patrons of his day – commissioned Sir Robert Rowand Anderson to build **Mount Stuart** (☎ 503877; adult/child £7/3; ☽ 11am-5pm Wed & Fri-Mon Easter & May-Aug), the finest neo-Gothic stately home in Scotland.

The heart of the house is the stunning **Marble Hall**, a three-storey extravaganza of Italian marble that soars 25m to a dark blue vault spangled with constellations of golden stars representing the signs of the zodiac. The design and decoration reflect the third marquess' fascination with astrology, mythology and religion, a theme carried over into the grand **Marble Staircase** beyond, where wall panels depict the six days of the Creation, and the lavishly decorated **Horoscope Bedroom**. Here the central ceiling panel records the positions of the stars and planets at the time of the marquess's birth on 12 September 1847.

The present marquess (the 7th) is known, rather dashingly, as Johnny Dumfries (b. 1958) and was once, even more dashingly, a Formula One and Le Mans racing driver. Mount Stuart hit the headlines in 2003 when Johnny's pal Stella McCartney – daughter of ex-Beatle Sir Paul – held her wedding there.

Yet another highlight is the **Marble Chapel**, built entirely out of dazzling white Carrara marble with a dome lit to spectacular effect by a ring of ruby-red stained-glass windows.

You could easily spend half a day here, wandering from one eye-popping magnificent room to the next; just keep one hand free to stop your jaw from repeatedly hitting the floor.

Mount Stuart is 5 miles (8km) south of Rothesay. **Western Buses** (☎ 502076) runs bus No 90 hourly from Rothesay to Mount Stuart.

Southern Bute

In the southern part of Bute you'll find the 12th-century ruin of **St Blane's Chapel**, with a 10th-century tombstone in the graveyard. There are good sandy **beaches** at Kilchattan Bay in the south, and at Scalpsie and Ettrick Bays on the west coast. You can often spot seals basking at low tide off **Ardscalpsie Point**.

Island Walk

The best walk on Bute is from the ferry pier at Rhubodach to the northern tip of the island, where you can watch yachts negotiate the rocky narrows at the Burnt Islands.

Just around the point are the **Maids of Bute**, two rocks painted to look like old women. The story goes that the distinctively shaped (but then unpainted)

rocks were first noticed by the skipper of a pleasure steamer in the early 20th century, who always pointed them out to the passengers on his boat. Frustrated that the tourists could never see the resemblance, he sent a deckhand ashore with a couple of tins of paint to give them some clothes and recognisable faces. No one is quite sure who now maintains the maids, but every time the paint begins to peel, it's not long before a fresh coat brightens them up.

You can retrace your steps to Rhubodach (two hours round trip), or continue south along the west coast of the island (some rough walking) to Ettrick Bay (allow five hours).

Sleeping & Eating

Commodore (☎ 502178; 12 Battery Pl, Rothesay; s/d £30/36; ✕) This harbour-side guesthouse has fine views and – Aussies take note – Vegemite on the breakfast table.

Moorings (☎ 502277; fjhbute@aol.com; 7 Mountstuart Rd, Rothesay; s/d £28/40; P) A little further east along the bay, this is a delightful Victorian lodge with more good harbour views.

Ascog Farm (☎ 503372; Ascog; r per person £20; P) All the rooms at this peaceful farmhouse B&B have been laid out in accordance with the rules of feng shui. It's 3 miles (5km) south of Rothesay.

Harbour Café (☎ 505166; 16 East Princes St; mains £8-13; ☺ 11am-5pm Mon-Sat, noon-4pm Sun, 6.30-10pm Fri & Sat) This newly renovated, smart eatery overlooks the harbour and offers everything from a good cappuccino to excellent haddock and chips. There are also good veggie dishes.

Getting There & Around

CalMac ferries ply between Wemyss Bay (p132) and Rothesay (car/passenger £13.85/ 3.45, 35 minutes, hourly). Another ferry crosses the short stretch of water between Rhubodach in the north of the island and Colintraive (car/passenger £7/1.10, 5 minutes, frequently) in Cowal.

Stagecoach Western buses run several times a week from Rothesay to Tighna-bruaich and Dunoon via the ferry at Colintraive. On Monday and Thursday a bus goes from Rothesay to Portavadie, where there's a ferry to Tarbert in Kintyre.

Cycling on Bute is excellent – the roads are well surfaced and fairly quiet. You can hire a bike from the **Mountain Bike Centre** (☎ 502333; 24 East Princes St, Rothesay) for £7/12 per half/full day.

INVERARAY

☎ 01499 / pop 700

You can spot Inveraray long before you get there – its neat, whitewashed buildings stand out from a distance on the shores of Loch Fyne. It's a planned town, built by the duke of Argyll when he revamped his nearby castle in the 18th century. The **TIC** (☎ 08707 200616; Front St) is on the seafront, and has Internet access for £1 per 10 minutes.

Sights

Inveraray Castle (☎ 302203; adult/child £5.50/3.50; ☺ 10am-5.45pm Mon-Thu & Sat, 1-5.45pm Sun Apr–mid-Oct; plus 10am-5.45pm Fri Jul & Aug) has been the seat of the dukes of Argyll – chiefs of Clan Campbell – since the 15th century. The 18th-century building, with its fairytale turrets and fake battlements, houses an impressive armoury hall, its walls patterned with a collection of more than 1000 pole arms, dirks, muskets and Lochaber axes. The castle is 500m north of town, entered from the A819 Dalmally road.

The Georgian **Inveraray Jail** (☎ 302381; Church Sq; adult/child £5.75/2.80; ☺ 9.30am-6pm Apr-Oct; 10am-5pm Nov-Mar), in the centre of town, is an award-winning, interactive, tourist attraction. You can sit in on a trial, try out a cell and discover the harsh torture meted out to unfortunate prisoners. The attention to detail – including a life-size model of an inmate squatting on a 19th-century toilet – more than makes up for the sometimes tedious commentary.

The *Arctic Penguin*, a three-masted schooner built in 1911 and one of the world's last surviving iron sailing ships, is permanently moored in Inveraray harbour and houses the **Inveraray Maritime Museum** (☎ 302213; The Pier; adult/child £3/1.50; ☺ 10am-6pm Apr-Sep, 10am-5pm Oct-Mar), with interesting photos and models of the old Clyde steamers and a display about Para Handy (p40). Kids will love exploring below decks – there's a special play area in the bowels of the ship.

Sleeping & Eating

Inveraray Youth Hostel (☎ 0870 004 1125; Dalmally Rd; dm £11; ☺ Apr-Sep) To get to this hostel, which is housed in a comfortable, modern bungalow, go through the arched entrance on the seafront and it's set back on the left of the road about 100m further on.

Breagha Lodge (☎ 302061; breagha.lodge@virgin.net; The Avenue; r per person £20-25; ☒ ℗) A modern house on the south side of town.

Old Rectory (☎ 302280; s/d £20/38; ℗) A nine-roomed guesthouse facing the loch; breakfast is served in a conservatory overlooking the garden.

Claonairigh House (☎ 302160; Bridge of Douglas; r £18-25 per person; ☒ ℗) This grand 18th-century house is set in 3 hectares of garden on the riverbank (salmon-fishing available) 4 miles (6km) south of town on the A83.

Argyll Hotel (☎ 302466; www.the-argyll-hotel.co.uk; Front St) Dating from 1750, the large and comfortably modernised Argyll dominates Inveraray's seafront, and offers elegant rooms with excellent views over the loch.

George Hotel (☎ 302111; Main St East) The wood-panelled bar, with its rough stone walls, flagstone floor and peat fires, is a good place for a bar lunch.

Loch Fyne Oyster Bar (☎ 600236; Clachan, Cairndow; mains £6-11; ☺ 9am-9pm) The best place to eat is the Loch Fyne Oyster Bar, 6 miles (10km) north of Inveraray in Cairndow. The rustic-themed restaurant is housed in a converted byre, and the menu includes local seafood and salmon. The neighbouring shop sells packaged seafood to take away.

Getting There & Away

Citylink buses run from Glasgow to Inveraray (£7.20, 1¾ hours, six a day Monday to Saturday, two Sunday). Three of these buses continue to Lochgilphead and Campbeltown (£7.90, 2½ hours); the others continue to Oban (£6.20, 1¼ hours).

LOCHGILPHEAD

☎ 01546 / pop 2600

Lochgilphead sits at the head of a long tidal flat, facing down Loch Fyne towards the peaks of Arran. There's not much to see in the town itself, but there's plenty of interest in the surrounding area. The Crinan Canal brushes the western edge of the village on its way to the west coast (you can easily walk from here to Crinan in a day), and Kilmartin Glen is just 8 miles (13km) to the north.

There's a **TIC** (☎ 602344; Lochnell St; ☼ Apr–Oct) on the seafront, a post office, supermarket, and two banks with ATMs.

There are Citylink buses from Glasgow to Lochgilphead (£8, 2½ hours, three daily), continuing to Campbeltown (£6.20, 1¾ hours). There's also a bus to Oban (£3.70, 1½ hours, one daily Monday to Saturday).

CRINAN CANAL
☎ 01546

The scenic Crinan Canal runs from Ardrishaig (2 miles south of Lochgilphead) to Crinan. Completed in 1801, the 9-mile (14km) canal allows seagoing vessels – mostly yachts – to take a short-cut from the Firth of Clyde and Loch Fyne to the west coast of Scotland, avoiding the long and sometimes dangerous passage around the Mull of Kintyre. You can easily walk the full length of the canal towpath in a day.

Gemini Cruises (☎ 830238; www.gemini-crinan .co.uk; Kilmahuaig; adult/child £11/7.50), a half-mile west of the Crinan Hotel, runs two-hour boat trips to the spectacular Gulf of Corryvreckan (p269), where strong tidal currents create Britain's biggest **whirlpool**. They will also ferry groups across to Ardlussa on Jura (£50 for up to 12 passengers and bicycles, 30 minutes, by prior arrangement).

The plush **Cairnbaan Hotel** (☎ 603668; cairnbaan .hotel@virgin.net; Cairnbaan; s/d £70/115; bar meals £6-10; ✗ Ⓟ), halfway along the canal, serves delicious bar meals, including haddock and chips and char-grilled venison burgers, in a comfortable conservatory.

The even more luxurious **Crinan Hotel** (☎ 830261; www.crinanhotel.com; Crinan), overlooking Loch Crinan at the northwestern end of the canal, has one of Scotland's finest (and most expensive) seafood restaurants.

The coffee shop on the western side of the canal basin at Crinan has great home-baked cakes and scones.

KILMARTIN GLEN
☎ 01546

This magical glen is the focus of one of the most concentrated areas of prehistoric sites in Scotland. Burial cairns, standing stones, stone circles, hill forts and cup-and-ring marked rocks litter the countryside – within a 6-mile radius (10km) of Kilmartin village there are 25 sites with standing stones and

over 100 rock carvings. In the 6th century Irish settlers founded the kingdom of Dalriada, which eventually united with the Picts in 843 to create the first Scottish kingdom; their capital was the hill fort of Dunadd.

There's a shop and post office in Kilmartin village.

Sights
The oldest monuments at Kilmartin date from 5000 years ago and comprise a linear cemetery of **burial cairns** that run south of Kilmartin village for 1½ miles. There are also ritual monuments (two stone circles) at **Temple Wood**, three-quarters of a mile southwest of Kilmartin.

Kilmartin Churchyard contains some 10th-century Celtic crosses and lots of medieval grave slabs carved with the effigies of knights. Next door, the **Museum of Ancient Culture** (☎ 510278; www.kilmartin.org; Kilmartin House; adult/child £4.50/1.50; ☼ 10am-5.30pm) is a fascinating centre for archaeology and landscape interpretation with artefacts from local sites, reconstructions, interactive displays and guided tours. The project was partly funded by midges – the curator exposed himself in Temple Wood on a warm summer's evening and was sponsored per midge bite!

The hill fort of **Dunadd**, 3½ miles (5km) south of Kilmartin village, was the royal residence of the first kings of Dalriada, and may have been where the Stone of Destiny (p63) was originally located. The faint rock carvings of a wild boar and two footprints with an ogham inscription could have been used in some kind of inauguration ceremony. The prominent little hill rises straight out of the boggy plain of the Moine Mhor Nature Reserve. A slippery path leads to the summit where you can gaze out on much the same view that the kings of Dalriada enjoyed 1300 years ago.

At **Kilmichael Glassary** (a mile east of Dunadd) and **Achnabreck** (half a mile south) there are rock faces carved with elaborate designs – like ripples from a pebble dropped into a pond – known to archaeologists as cup and ring marks. Their purpose and meaning is unknown.

Just over a mile north of Kilmartin are the extensive remains of the 16th-century tower house **Carnassarie Castle**, former seat of the bishops of the Western Isles, with some excellent carved stonework.

Sleeping & Eating

Burndale B&B (☎ 510235; alan-hawkins@burndale -kilmartin.freeserve.co.uk; s/d £25/44) Set in an old manse (minister's house), this B&B is just three minutes' walk from the Museum of Ancient Culture.

Kilmartin Hotel (☎ 510250; info@kilmartin -hotel.com; s/d £35/56; P) Though the rooms are rather cramped, this hotel is popular and has a restaurant and a small, atmospheric bar; there's folk music here some weekends.

Cairn Bar & Restaurant (☎ 510254; mains £11-16; ☻ 6.30-10pm Wed-Mon Apr-Sep, Thu-Sun Oct-Mar) Near the Kilmartin, this restaurant serves good bar meals and restaurant dinners.

Getting There & Away

The Lochgilphead to Oban bus stops at Kilmartin (£1.80, 15 minutes, one daily Monday to Saturday), as does the return bus from Oban (£3.80, 1¼ hours).

KINTYRE

The Kintyre peninsula – 40 miles (64km) long and 8 miles (13km) wide – is almost an island, with only a narrow isthmus at Tarbert connecting it to the wooded hills of Knapdale. During the Norse occupation of the Western Isles, the Scottish king decreed that the Vikings could claim as their own any island they could circumnavigate in a longship. So in 1098 the wily Magnus Barefoot stood at the helm while his men dragged their boat across this neck of land, thus validating his claim to Kintyre.

Tarbert

☎ 01880 / pop 1500
The attractive fishing village and yachting centre of Tarbert is the gateway to Kintyre. There's a **TIC** (☎ 820429; Harbour St; ☻ Apr-Oct), a Co-op supermarket and two banks with ATMs near the head of the harbour.

SIGHTS

An Tairbeart Arts Centre (☎ 821116; Campbeltown Rd; admission free; ☻ 10am-5pm) is at the southern edge of the village and has galleries of crafts and contemporary arts, as well as displays

about local natural history and human interaction with the environment.

The crumbling, ivy-covered ruins of **Tarbert Castle**, built by Robert the Bruce in the 14th century, overlook the harbour – you can reach it via a signposted footpath beside the Ann R Thomas Gallery on Harbour St.

FESTIVALS & EVENTS

Tarbert is a lively little place, and never more so than during the annual **Scottish Series Yacht Race**, held over five days around the last weekend in May, when the harbour is crammed with hundreds of visiting yachts. The **Tarbert Seafood Festival** is held on the first weekend in July, and the **Tarbert Music Festival** on the third weekend in September.

SLEEPING & EATING

There are plenty of B&Bs and hotels, but be sure to book ahead during festivals and major events.

Anchor Hotel (☎ 820577; anchorhotel@lochfyne -scotland.co.uk; Harbour St; r per person £30-35; bar meals £7-12) This has a perfect location overlooking the harbour and serves excellent meals, both in the bar and the restaurant. Room 7 has a grand half-tester bed (like a sawn-off four-poster) and a lovely sea view.

Columba Hotel (☎ 820808; www.columbahotel.com; East Pier Rd; s/d £37/74; bar meals £6-9; 3-course dinner £22 P) A 10-minute walk from the village centre along the southern side of the harbour, this peaceful hotel has a restaurant that serves top Scottish cuisine.

Victoria Hotel (☎ 820236; Barmore Rd; bar meals £6-11; ☻ food served noon-2pm & 6-9.30pm) The bright yellow Victoria overlooks the head of the harbour and is popular with yachties.

Anchorage Restaurant (☎ 820881; Harbour St; mains £12-17; ☻ dinner daily Apr-Oct, closed Sun & Mon Nov-Mar) Serves excellent local seafood, game and meat dishes with a Mediterranean flavour.

GETTING THERE & AWAY

Tarbert is served by the Citylink buses that run from Campbeltown to Glasgow and Oban.

CalMac runs a small car ferry from Tarbert to Portavadie on the Cowal peninsula (car/passenger £13.35/2.90, 25 minutes, hourly April to September).

The Kennacraig ferry terminal on West Loch Tarbert, 5 miles (8km) south of Tarbert, has ferries to the islands of Islay (p263) and Colonsay (p268).

Skipness

☎ 01880 / pop 100

The tiny village of Skipness is on the east coast of Kintyre, about 13 miles (21km) south of Tarbert, in a pleasant and quiet setting with great views of Arran. There's a post office and general store in the village.

Beyond the village rise the substantial remains of 13th-century **Skipness Castle**, a former possession of the Lords of the Isles, strikingly built of dark green local stone trimmed with red-brown Arran sandstone. The tower house was added in the 16th century and was occupied until the 19th. From the top you can see the roofless, 13th-century **St Brendan's Chapel** down to the shore; the kirkyard contains some excellent carved grave slabs.

Skipness Seafood Cabin (☎ 760207; sandwiches £1-2, mains £5-7.50; ⊗ 11am-6pm Sun-Fri late May-Sep), in the grounds of nearby Skipness House, serves tea, coffee and home baking, as well as local fish and shellfish dishes. In fine weather you can eat at outdoor picnic tables with grand views of Arran.

There's a waymarked **forest walk** through the remote hills from Tarbert to Skipness (9 miles/14km, four to five hours); pick up a free map from the TIC at Tarbert.

Local bus No 448 runs between Tarbert and Skipness (35 minutes, two to four a day Monday to Saturday).

At Claonaig, 2 miles (3km) west of Skipness, there's a daily car ferry to Lochranza (p155) on the Isle of Arran (car/passenger £19/4.25, 30 minutes, seven to nine daily).

Isle of Gigha

☎ 01583 / pop 120

Gigha (pronounced *ghee*-a) is a low-lying island 6 miles (10km) long by about a mile wide. It's famous for its sandy beaches and the subtropical plants that thrive in the mild climate at **Achamore Gardens** (☎ 505254; Achamore House; adult/child £2/1; ⊗ 9am-dusk). Locally made Gigha cheese is sold in many parts of Argyll.

Post Office House (☎ 505251; r per person £20-25; ⊗ P), at the top of the hill above the

ferry slip, is a lovely Victorian house that contains the island post office and shop as well as a B&B.

Gigha Hotel (☎ 505254; hotel@isle-of-gigha.co.uk; s/d £38/60; 4-course dinner £25 ⊗), 100m south of the post office, is the island's only hotel, and has a good restaurant and bar.

There's also a range of self-catering cottages available (www.isle-of-gigha.co.uk). Camping is not allowed on the island.

CalMac runs a daily ferry from Tayinloan in Kintyre to Gigha (passenger £5, bicycle £2, car £18.85, 20 minutes, hourly Monday to Saturday, six on Sunday) – only return tickets are available.

You can rent bikes from Post Office House or the Gigha Hotel for £3 an hour or £10 a day.

Mid-Kintyre

At Glenbarr, 6 miles (10km) south of Tayinloan, is the **Glenbarr Abbey Visitor Centre** (☎ 01583-421247; adult/child £2.50/2; ⊗ 10am-5pm Wed-Mon Easter-Oct). This 18th-century house has a large collection of clothes, thimbles and china, and a pair of gloves worn by Mary Queen of Scots. It is a centre for the Clan Macalister. The laird of Glenbarr himself will take you on an entertaining guided tour.

On the east coast of Kintyre is the pretty village of **Carradale**, with a shop and post office. The **Network Heritage Centre** (☎ 01586-431296; admission free; ⊗ 10am-5pm Mon-Sat, 12.30-5pm Sun Jul & Aug; 10am-5pm Tue, Wed, Fri & Sat, 12.30-4pm Sun Easter-Jun & Sep-mid-Oct) in Carradale is housed in an old school house, and has fishing, farming and forestry displays. There are several interesting ruins in the area including a vitrified Iron Age fort on the eastern point of Carradale Bay, and the 12th-century **Saddell Abbey** (5 miles/8km south), founded by Somerled, Lord of the Isles.

Campbeltown

☎ 01586 / pop 6000

Campbeltown, with its ranks of gloomy grey council houses, feels like an Ayrshire mining town that's been dumped incongruously on the shores of a beautiful Argyllshire harbour. Once a thriving fishing port and whisky-making centre, industrial decline and the closure of the former air force base at nearby Machrihanish has seen the town slip into decline. It's now a low-key holiday resort and feels a very long way from anywhere else, but it's worth stopping to see the Davaar cave painting.

The **TIC** (☎ 552056) is beside the harbour. There are plenty of shops and banks in the nearby town centre.

SIGHTS
There were once no fewer than 32 distilleries in the Campbeltown area, but most closed down in the 1920s. Today **Springbank Distillery** (☎ 552085; tours by arrangement 2pm Mon-Thu) is the only survivor. It is also the only distillery in Scotland that distills, matures and bottles all its whisky on the one site.

One of the most unusual sights in Argyll is in a cave on the southern side of the island of **Davaar**, at the mouth of Campbeltown Loch. Painted on the wall of the cave is an eerie painting of the Crucifixion by local artist Archibald MacKinnon, dating from 1887. You can walk to the island at low tide across a shingle bar called the Dhorlinn (allow at least 1½ hours for the round trip), but make sure you're not caught by a rising tide – check tide times with the TIC before you set off.

The **Mull of Kintyre Music Festival** (☎ 551053; www.mokmf.com), held in Campbeltown in late August, is a popular event featuring traditional Scottish and Irish music.

GETTING THERE & AWAY
Citylink buses run from Campbeltown to Glasgow (£12.40, 4½ hours) via Tarbert, Inveraray, Arrochar and Loch Lomond; and to Oban (£13.40, four hours, three a day), changing buses at Inveraray.

Mull of Kintyre
A narrow winding road, about 18 miles (29km) long, leads south from Campbeltown to the Mull of Kintyre, passing some good sandy beaches near Southend. The name of this remote headland has been immortalised in Paul McCartney's famous song – the former Beatle owns a farmhouse in the area. A lighthouse marks the spot closest to Northern Ireland, whose coastline is often visible only 12 miles (19km) away across the North Channel.

ISLE OF ISLAY
☎ 01496 / pop 3400
The most southerly of the Inner Hebrides, Islay (pronounced *isle*-a) is best known for its single malt whiskies, which have a distinctive smoky flavour. There are seven distilleries, all of which welcome visitors and offer guided tours.

With a list of over 250 recorded bird species, Islay also attracts bird-watchers. It's an important wintering ground for thousands of white-fronted and barnacle geese. As well as the whisky and the wildfowl, there are miles of sandy beaches, great scenery and pleasant walking.

Islay's whisky industry contributes around £100 million a year to the government in excise duty and VAT; that's about £30,000 for every man, woman and child on the island. Little wonder that the islanders complain about lack of government investment.

Orientation & Information
There are two ferry terminals on the island, both served by ferries from Kennacraig in West Loch Tarbert – Port Askaig on the east coast, opposite Jura, and Port Ellen in the south. Islay airport lies midway between Port Ellen and Bowmore.

The island's **TIC** (☎ 810254; The Square; ☒ Mar-Oct) is in Bowmore.

There are post offices in all the main towns and Internet access at the **MacTaggart Community CyberCafé** (☎ 302693; 30 Mansfield Pl; £1 per 30 min; 11am-10pm Mon-Fri, 10am-10pm Sat, noon-9pm Sun) in Port Ellen.

The **Mactaggart Leisure Centre** (☎ 810767; School St) has a coin-operated laundrette (wash £3, dry £1.50).

There's a camping ground and bunkhouse at Kintra, near Port Ellen, and a youth hostel in Port Charlotte. If you want to camp elsewhere, ask permission first. Camping is prohibited on the Ardtalla and Dunlossit estates on the eastern side of Islay.

Port Ellen & Around
Port Ellen is the main point of entry for Islay. It has a **grocery store** (☒ 8am-8pm Mon-Sat, noon-7.30pm Sun), a pub and a bank (no ATM, closed most afternoons and all day Wednesday). While there's nothing to see in the town itself, the coast stretching

northeast from Port Ellen is one of the loveliest parts of the island.

There are three **whisky distilleries** in close succession: **Laphroaig** (☎ 302418; tours 10.15am & 2.15pm Mon-Fri); **Lagavulin** (☎ 302400; tours 10am, 11.30am & 2.30pm Mon-Fri); and **Ardbeg** (☎ 302244; tours 11.30am & 2.30pm daily Jul & Aug, Mon-Fri Sep-Jun). All guided tours are £2.

A pleasant bike ride leads past the distilleries to the roofless **Kildalton Chapel**, 8 miles (13km) northeast of Port Ellen. In the kirkyard is the exceptional late-8th-century **Kildalton Cross**, the only remaining Celtic High Cross in Scotland. There are carvings of biblical scenes on one side and animals on the other. There are also several extraordinary grave slabs around the chapel, some carved with swords and Celtic interlace patterns.

The **Ardmore Islands**, off the southeastern corner of Islay near Kildalton, are a wildlife haven and home to the second largest colony of common seals in Europe.

SLEEPING & EATING

Kintra Farm (☎ 302051; margaret@kintrafarm.co.uk; Kintra; tent sites £4-7, dm £7-9, B&B per person £18; Apr-Sep) At the southern end of Laggan Bay, Kintra offers B&B in the farmhouse, a bunkhouse, and a small but beautiful campsite on buttercup-sprinkled turf amid the dunes.

Glenmachrie Farmhouse (☎ 305260; glenmachrie@lineone.net; s/d £50/70, DB&B per person £60;) This delightful country guesthouse is 4 miles (6km) north of Port Ellen, near the airport and Machrie Golf Links. Dinner is a superb four-course affair using fresh local produce (veggie dishes available) with sunset views from the dining room. (Note that credit cards not accepted – cash or cheque only.)

MacTaggart Community CyberCafe (☎ 302693; 30 Mansfield Pl; mains £2-5; 11am-10pm Mon-Fri, 10am-10pm Sat, noon-9pm Sun, food served till 6.30pm) Offers snacks, salads, baked potatoes, tea, coffee and cakes – to eat in or take away.

Old Kiln Cafe (☎ 302244; mains £5-7; 10am-4pm daily Jul & Aug, 10am-4pm Mon-Fri Sep-Jun) Housed in the former malting kiln at Ardbeg Distillery, this is the nicest place to eat in the area. It serves hearty home-made soups, sandwiches and home baking, including delicious clootie dumpling with ice cream.

Other recommendations:

Trout Fly Guest House (☎ 302204; Charlotte St, Port Ellen; r per person £22-25;) Pleasant, three-room B&B just two minutes' walk from the ferry terminal.

Mrs McGillivray (☎ 302420; Frederick Cres, Port Ellen; s/d £18/34; Apr-Oct) Good-value B&B half a mile north of the ferry terminal; has two clean, spacious rooms.

Bowmore

The attractive Georgian village of Bowmore was laid out in 1768 to replace the village of Kilarrow, which was ruining the view from the laird's house. Its centrepiece is the distinctive **Round Church** at the top of Main St, built in circular form to ensure that the devil had no corners to hide in.

Bowmore is in the centre of the island, 10 miles (16km) from both Port Askaig and Port Ellen, and is the island's capital. It has a **TIC** (☎ 810254; The Square; Mar-Oct), two banks with ATMs, and a **Co-op supermarket** (8am-8pm Mon-Sat, noon-7.30pm Sun).

Bowmore Distillery (☎ 810441; School St; adult/child £2/1; tours 10.30am & 2pm Mon-Sat May-Sep, Mon-Fri Oct-Apr) is the only distillery on the island that still malts its own barley – the tour, which begins with an overblown 10-minute marketing video, is redeemed by a look at (and taste of) the germinating grain laid out in golden billows on the floor of the malting shed.

If the weather's bad, there's always the **Mactaggart Leisure Centre** (☎ 810767; School St; pool adult/child £2.20/1.40; 12.30-9.30pm Tue, 2-9pm Wed, 12.30-9pm Thu & Fri, 10am-6pm Sat, 10.30am-5.30pm Sun), with a 25m pool, a sauna and a fitness centre.

You can hire **bikes** at the post office, near the church at the top of Main St, for £10 a day.

SLEEPING & EATING

Lambeth House (☎ 810597; Jamieson St; r per person £20;) Simple, good-value B&B accommodation; it also offers a two-course evening meal for £6.

Meadowside (☎ 810497; Birch Dr; r per person £16-18) A neat modern house with a warm welcome; the two guest rooms share a bathroom.

Harbour Inn (☎ 810330; harbour@harbour-inn.com; The Square; s/d £55/95; lunch mains £6-9, dinner mains £12-17;) The plush seven-room Harbour Inn is the poshest place in town, with a good restaurant serving fresh local lobster and scallops, steak, lamb and Jura venison.

Lochside Hotel (☎ 810244; ask@lochsidehotel.co.uk; 19 Shore St; r per person £40; ✗) The bar at the Lochside has around 400 malts on offer, including a 29-year-old Black Bowmore (50% ABV) for £150 a nip! The hotel runs speciality malt whisky weekends from £125 per person (including three nights' dinner and B&B and whisky tours).

Cottage Restaurant (☎ 810422; 45 Main St; snacks £2-4, mains £4-7; ☯ 10am-4pm Mon-Sat, 6-8pm Fri & Sat) An old-fashioned tearoom with tartan wallpaper and a line in healthy home-cooked food as well as the traditional artery-clogging café favourites such as sausage and chips.

Port Charlotte

Eleven miles (18km) from Bowmore, on the opposite shore of Loch Indaal, is the attractive village of Port Charlotte. It has a **shop** (☯ 9am-12.30pm & 1.30-5.30pm Mon-Sat, 11.30am-1.30pm Sun) and post office, and you can hire **bikes** from the house opposite the Port Charlotte Hotel.

Islay's long history is charted in detail in the **Museum of Islay Life** (☎ 850358; adult/child £2/1; ☯ 10am-5pm Mon-Sat, 2-5pm Sun Easter-Sept; 10am-4pm Mon-Sat Oct-Easter), housed in the former Free Church. Prize exhibits include an illicit still, 19th-century crofters furniture, and a set of leather boots once worn by the horse that pulled the lawnmower at Islay House (so it wouldn't leave hoof-prints on the lawn!).

The **Islay Wildlife Information Centre** (☎ 850288; adult/child £2/1; ☯ 10am-3pm Mon, Tue, Thu & Fri Apr-Oct), next to the youth hostel, has a useful reference library and displays on the island's natural history.

Closed since 1993, the **Bruichladdich Distillery** (☎ 850221; tour £3; ☯ tours 10.30am & 2.30pm Mon-Sat) at the northern edge of the village was recently re-opened with all its original Victorian equipment restored to working condition.

SLEEPING & EATING

Islay Youth Hostel (SYHA; ☎ 0870 004 1128; dm £10; ☯ Apr-Sep) This modern and comfortable hostel is housed in a former distillery building with views over the loch.

Port Charlotte Hotel (☎ 850360; info@ portcharlottehotel.co.uk; s/d £59/100; mains £12-17; ✗ P) This lovely old Victorian hotel overlooking the sea has a stylish, candle-lit restaurant serving local seafood, Islay beef, venison and duck. The bar is well stocked with Islay malts and real ales, and has a nook at the back with a view over the loch.

Croft Kitchen (☎ 850230; mains lunch £5-9, dinner £11-15; ☯ snacks 10am-6pm, lunch noon-3pm, dinner 6.30-8.30pm) This laid-back little bistro serves snacks during the day and quality meals in the evening. It's opposite the Museum of Islay Life.

Loch Indaal Hotel (☎ 850202; mains £3-5; ☯ food served noon-2pm & 6-8.30pm) Just south of the Port Charlotte Hotel; does good-value bar meals.

Loch Gruinart

Seven miles (11km) north of Port Charlotte is **Loch Gruinart Nature Reserve**, where you can hear corncrakes in summer and see huge flocks of migrating ducks, geese and waders in spring and autumn; there's a hide with wheelchair access. The nearby **RSPB Information Centre** (☎ 850505; admission free; ☯ 10am-5pm Apr-Oct; 10am-4pm Nov-Mar) offers two- to three-hour guided walks around the reserve (£2 per person, 10am Thursday and 6pm Tuesday in August).

Three miles (5km) north of the reserve, at **Kilnave Chapel**, is a Celtic stone cross made from an improbably thin slab; though less elaborate than the cross at Kildalton, it is more delicate.

The beach at **Killinallan**, northeast of the reserve, is one of Islay's best. You can walk for miles along the **raised beaches** on the coast to its north.

Portnahaven

Six miles (10km) southwest of Port Charlotte the road ends at **Portnahaven**, another pretty village that was purpose-built as a fishing harbour in the 19th century. A mile north of the village is the world's first commercially viable, wave-powered electricity generating station, which was built on the cliffs that are open to the Atlantic swell. The 500kW plant – known as 'Limpet' (land-installed, marine-powered energy transformer) – provides enough electricity to power 200 island homes.

Finlaggan

Lush meadows swathed in buttercups and daisies slope down to reed-fringed Loch

Finlaggan, the medieval capital of the Lords of the Isles. This bucolic setting was once the most important settlement in the Hebrides, the central seat of power of the Lords of the Isles from the 12th to the 16th century. From the little island at the northern end of the loch the descendants of Somerled administered their island territories and entertained visiting chieftains in their great hall. Little remains now except the tumbled ruins of houses and chapel, but the setting is beautiful and the history fascinating. A wooden walkway leads over the reeds and water lilies to the island, where information boards describe the remains.

Finlaggan Visitor Centre (☎ 810629; admission free; ☷ 1-4.30pm daily May-Sep; 1-4.30pm Tue, Thu & Sun Apr; 1-4pm Tue & Thu Oct), in a nearby cottage, explains the site's history and archaeology. The island itself is open at all times.

Finlaggan is 3 miles (5km) southwest of Port Askaig; buses stop at the road-end, from where it's a 15-minute walk to the loch.

Port Askaig & Around

Port Askaig is little more than a hotel, a shop and a ferry pier, set in a picturesque nook halfway along the Sound of Islay, the strait that separates Islay and Jura.

There are two distilleries within easy reach: **Caol Ila Distillery** (☎ 840207; admission £3; tours by appointment Mon-Fri), pronounced cull ee-la, just a half-mile walk north of the ferry pier; and **Bunnahabhain Distillery** (☎ 840646; ☷ 10am-4pm Mon-Fri Mar-Oct; by appointment Nov-Feb), pronounced boo-na-ha-ven, 3 miles (5km) north of Port Askaig. Both enjoy a wonderful location with great views across to Jura.

Port Askaig Hotel (☎ 840245; hotel@portaskaig .co.uk; s £30-40, d £72; ☐) is beside the ferry pier. The beer garden is a popular spot to sit and watch the comings and goings at the quay.

Tours

Seafari Islay (☎ 840273; www.seafari-islay.co.uk) can arrange customised tours by sea to visit some or all of Islay and Jura's distilleries in a single day, as well as bird-watching trips, coastal exploration, and trips to Jura's remote west coast and the Corryvreckan whirlpool.

Festivals & Events

The **Islay Festival** (Feis Ile; www.ileach.co.uk/festival), held at the end of May, is a week-long

celebration of traditional Scottish music and includes the **Islay Whisky Festival** (www .islaywhiskyfestival.com). Events include *ceilidhs*, pipe band performances, distillery tours and whisky tastings.

The annual three-day **Islay Jazz Festival** (☎ 810044; www.ileach.co.uk/jazz) takes place over the second weekend in September and sees a varied line-up of international talent playing at various venues across the island.

Getting There & Away

British Airways flies from Glasgow to Islay twice on weekdays and once on Saturday (from £100 return, 40 minutes).

CalMac (☎ 302209) runs ferries from Kennacraig in West Loch Tarbert to Port Ellen (passenger/car £7.55/55, 2¼ hours, one to three a day) and Port Askaig (same fare, two hours, one to three a day). On Wednesday only in summer the ferry continues from Port Askaig to Colonsay (£4/20.65, 1¼ hours) and Oban (£10.85/ 53, 4¾ hours).

Getting Around

A bus service runs between Ardbeg, Port Ellen, Bowmore, Port Charlotte, Portnahaven and Port Askaig (only one bus on Sunday). The timetable is so complex that there's a danger you'll miss your bus while trying to work it out – get a copy from the TIC.

Taxis are available in both **Bowmore** (☎ 810449) and **Port Ellen** (☎ 302155).

You can hire **bikes** in Bowmore (p264) and Port Charlotte (p265).

ISLE OF JURA
☎ 01496 / pop 200

Jura lies off the coast of Argyll – long, dark and low like a vast Viking longship, its billowing sail the distinctive triple peaks of the Paps of Jura. It's a magnificently wild and lonely island, the perfect place to get away from it all – as George Orwell did in 1948. Orwell wrote his masterpiece *1984* while living at the remote farmhouse of Barnhill in the north of the island, describing it in a letter as 'a very un-get-at-able place'.

Jura takes its name from the Old Norse *dyr-a* (deer island) – an apt appellation as the island supports a population of around

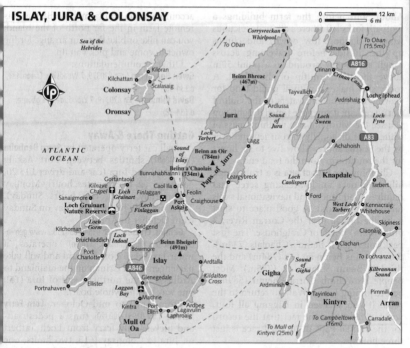

ISLAY, JURA & COLONSAY

6000 red deer, which outnumber their human cohabitants by 30 to one. Most of the island is occupied by deer-stalking estates and access to the hills may be restricted during the stalking season (July to February); the Jura Hotel can provide details of areas to be avoided.

The community-run **Jura Service Point** (☎ 820161; Craighouse; ⏰ 10am-1pm Mon-Fri), 400m north of the Jura Hotel, provides tourist information and Internet access. **Jura Stores** (☎ 820231; Craighouse; ⏰ 9am-1pm & 2-5pm Mon-Fri, 9am-1pm & 2-4.30pm Sat) is the island's only shop.

Apart from the superb wilderness walking, there's not much to do on the island apart from visit the **Isle of Jura Distillery** (☎ 820240; admission free; ⏰ by appointment) or wander around the attractive walled gardens of **Jura House** (adult/child £2/free; ⏰ dawn-dusk) at the southern end of the island; a **tea tent** (⏰ 11am-5pm Mon-Fri Jun-Aug) here sells hot drinks, home baking, crafts and plants.

The bar at the Jura Hotel is a very sociable place to spend the evening, and

there are regular *ceilidhs* held throughout the year where visitors are made very welcome; check the notice board outside Jura Stores for announcements.

Walking

There are very few proper footpaths on Jura, and any off-the-beaten-path exploration will involve rough going through giant bracken, knee-deep bogs and thigh-high tussocks. The only real trail is **Evans' Walk**, a stalkers' path that leads for 5 miles (8km) from the main road through a pass in the hills to a hunting lodge above the beautiful sandy beach at Glenbatrick Bay. The path leaves the road 4 miles (6km) north of Craighouse (just under a mile north of the bridge over the Corran River); allow five hours for the round trip.

Another walk is to a viewpoint for the **Corryvreckan whirlpool** (p269), the great tidal race at the northern end of the island between Jura and Scarba. From the northern end of the public road at Lealt you hike along a 4WD track past Barnhill to Kinuachdrachd Farm (6 miles/10km).

About 30m before the farm buildings a footpath forks left (there's an inconspicuous wooden signpost low down) and climbs up the hillside before traversing across rough and boggy ground to a point 50m above the northern tip of the island. A rocky slab makes a natural grandstand for viewing the turbulent waters of the Gulf of Corryvreckan; if you have timed it right, you will see the whirlpool as a writhing mass of white water diagonally to your left and over by the Scarba shore. Allow five to six hours for the round trip from the road end.

Climbing the **Paps of Jura** is a truly tough hill walk over ankle-breaking scree that requires good fitness and navigational skills (allow eight hours). A good place to start is by the bridge over the Corran River, 3 miles (5km) north of Craighouse. The first peak you reach is Beinn a'Chaolais (734m), the second is Beinn an Oir (784m) and the third is Beinn Shiantaidh (755m). Most people also climb Corra Bheinn (569m), before joining Evans' Walk to return to the road. If you succeed in bagging all four, you can reflect on the fact that the record for the annual Paps of Jura fell race is just three hours!

There are easier **short walks** (one or two hours) east along the coast from Jura House, and north along a 4WD track from Feolin. *Jura – A Guide for Walkers* by Gordon Wright (£2) is available from the TIC in Bowmore, Islay.

Sleeping & Eating

Places to stay on the island are very limited, so book ahead – don't rely on just turning up and hoping to find a bed. Most of Jura's accommodation is in self-catering cottages let by the week.

You can camp for free in the field below the Jura Hotel (ask at the bar first, and pop a donation in the bottle); there are toilets, hot showers (£1 coin needed) and a laundry in the block behind the hotel.

Jura Hotel (☎ 820243; jurahotel@aol.com; Craighouse; s £47-62, d £70-100; bar meals £6-10; 3-course dinner £18; ☒ food served noon-2pm & 6.30-9pm; ℗) The 18-room Jura is the most comfortable place to stay on the island; ask for a room at the front with a view of the bay. It serves decent bar and restaurant meals.

Kinuachdrachd Farm (☎ 07899-912116; joanmikekd@ hotmail.com; dm £7, d £35) There is bunkhouse accommodation and farmhouse B&B at this remote farm in the far north of the island; you can hike or bike there, or arrange for the owner to come and pick you up.

Other recommendations:

Gwen Boardman (☎ 820379; 7 Woodside, Craighouse; d £34-38)

David Gilmour (☎ 820319; 7 Woodside, Craighouse; d £34-38)

Getting There & Away

A small car ferry operated by **Serco Denholm** (☎ 840681) shuttles between Port Askaig (on Islay) and Jura (car and driver £13.20, passenger £2, five minutes, hourly Monday to Saturday, every two hours Sunday). There are only two ferries a day on Sunday from October to April.

Gemini Cruises (☎ 01546-830238; www.gemini-crinan.co.uk; Kilmahumaig, Crinan) operates a water-taxi service on demand and will take passengers from Crinan on the mainland to Ardlussa at the northern end of Jura (£50 one way for the whole boat).

From April to mid-October, **Lorn Ferry Service** (☎ 01951-200320) runs a pedestrian-and bicycle-only ferry from Loch Tarbert on Jura to Colonsay (£15, two hours, one a day Tuesday and Friday). Prior booking is essential.

Getting Around

Charles MacLean (☎ 820314) runs a minibus service between Feolin and Craighouse, timed to coincide with ferry arrivals and departures at Feolin. One or two of the runs continue north as far as Inverlussa.

You can hire bikes from the Jura Hotel (see left).

ISLE OF COLONSAY
☎ 01951 / pop 106

Legend has it that when St Columba set out from Ireland in 563, his first landfall was Colonsay. But on climbing a hill he found he could still see the distant coast of his homeland, and pushed on further north to found his monastery in Iona, leaving behind only his name (Colonsay means 'Columba's Isle').

Colonsay is a connoisseur's island, a little jewel box of varied delights, none exceptional but each exquisite – an ancient priory, a woodland garden, a golden beach – set amid a Highland landscape in miniature:

JONATHAN SMITH

Arched stone gateway, **Edzell** (p229)

A piper at the door, **Glamis Castle** (p225)

JONATHAN SMITH

JONATHAN SMITH

Flowers in a wall at Edzell Castle, **Edzell** (p229)

Spectacular scenery on the road to **Glen Shiel** (p345)

Pretty fishing village of **Ullapool** (p340)

B&B accommodation, **Inverness** (p291)

The Orkney Island Ferry at **John o'Groats** (p371)

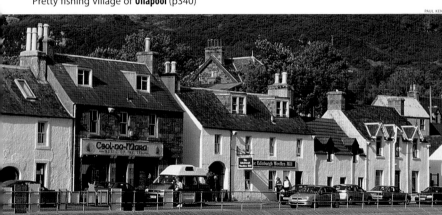

THE SCOTTISH MAELSTROM

It may look innocuous on the map, but the Gulf of Corryvreckan – the 1000m-wide channel between the northern end of Jura and the island of Scarba – is home to one of the three most notorious tidal whirlpools in the world (the others are the Maelstrom in Norway's Lofoten Islands, and the Old Sow in Canada's New Brunswick).

The tide doesn't just rise and fall twice a day, it flows – dragged around the earth by the gravitational attraction of the moon. On the west coast of Scotland, the rising tide – known as the flood tide – flows northwards. As the flood moves up the Sound of Jura, to the east of the island, it is forced into a narrowing bottleneck jammed with islands and builds up to a greater height than the open sea to the west of Jura. As a result, millions of gallons of sea water pour westwards through the Gulf of Corryvreckan at speeds of up to 8 knots – an average sailing yacht is going fast at 6 knots.

The Corryvreckan whirlpool forms where this mass of moving water hits an underwater pinnacle, which rises from the 200m-deep sea bed to within just 28m of the surface, and swirls over and around it. The turbulent waters create a magnificent spectacle, with white-capped breakers, bulging boils and overfalls, and countless miniature maelstroms whirling around the main vortex.

Corryvreckan is at its most violent when a flooding spring tide, flowing west through the gulf, meets a westerly gale blowing in from the Atlantic. In these conditions, standing waves up to 5m high can form and dangerously rough seas extend more than 3 miles west of Corryvreckan, a phenomenon known as the Great Race.

You can see the whirlpool by making the long hike to the northern end of Jura (check tide times at the Jura Hotel), or by taking a boat trip from Islay (p263), Easdale (p276) or Crinan (p260).

rugged, rocky hills, cliffs and sandy strands, machair and birch woods, even a trout loch. Here, hill walkers bag 'McPhies' – defined as 'eminences in excess of 300ft' (90m) – instead of Munros (p403). There are 22 in all; the super competitive will bag them all in one day.

Orientation & Information

The ferry pier is at **Scalasaig**, the main village, where you'll find a **shop** (☉ 9am-5.30pm Mon-Fri, 9am-4pm Sat), post office and public telephone. There's no TIC and no bank or ATM on the island. General information is available at the CalMac waiting room beside the ferry pier, and there's Internet access at the Colonsay Hotel.

The tiny **Colonsay Bookshop** (☎ 200232) at Kilchattan, on the west side of the island, has an excellent range of books on Hebridean history and culture.

Sights & Activities

If the tides are right don't miss the chance to walk across the half-mile of cockleshell-strewn sand that links Colonsay to the smaller island of Oronsay. Here you can explore the 14th-century ruins of **Oronsay Priory**, one of the best-preserved medieval priories in Scotland. There are

two beautiful late-15th-century stone crosses in the kirkyard, but the highlight is the collection of superb 15th- and 16th-century carved grave slabs in the Prior's House; look for the ugly little devil trapped beneath the sword-tip of the knight on the right-hand one of the two horizontal slabs. The island is accessible on foot for about 1½ hours either side of low water, and it's a 45-minute walk from the road-end on Colonsay to the priory. There are tide tables posted at the ferry terminal in Scalasaig.

The **Woodland Garden** (☎ 200211; admission free; ☉ dawn-dusk) at Colonsay House, 1½ miles north of Scalasaig, is tucked in an unexpected fold of the landscape and famous for its outstanding collection of hybrid rhododendrons and unusual trees. The formal walled garden around the mansion, which has a terrace café, opens 9am to 5pm Wednesday and Friday only, Easter to September.

There are good sandy beaches at several points around the coast but **Kiloran Bay** in the northwest, a scimitar-shaped strand of dark golden sand, is outstanding. If there are too many people here for you, walk the 3 miles (5km) north to beautiful **Balnahard Bay**, accessible only on foot or by boat.

Kevin and Christa Byrne (☎ 200320; byrne@ colonsay.org.uk) offer guided tours on foot (£10 an hour for up to eight people) or by minibus (£30 an hour), and boat trips for fishing (£15 per person) or whale-watching (£20 per person).

Sleeping & Eating

Short-stay accommodation on Colonsay is limited and should be booked before coming to the island. Camping on the island is not allowed.

Keepers Backpackers Lodge (☎ 200312; dm £8.50, tw £20) Set in a former gamekeeper's house near Colonsay House, this lodge is about 30 minutes' walk from the ferry terminal (you can arrange to be picked up at the pier). Bikes can be hired for £5 per day.

Seaview Guesthouse (☎ 200315; s/d £36/60; (P)) This peaceful farmhouse is in Kilchattan, at the southwestern end of Loch Fad, 3 miles (5km) from the pier. Packed lunches are available for an extra £4.

Isle of Colonsay Lodges (☎ 200320; chalets@ colonsay.org.uk; s/d £25/40) These comfortable and modern holiday chalets are just 10 minutes' walk from the ferry pier at Scalasaig. You can check last-minute availability at www .colonsay.org.uk/newother/chalets.html.

Isle of Colonsay Hotel (☎ 200316; colonsay .hotel@pipemedia.co.uk; s £80-95, d £13-150; mains £8-12; ☻ lunch noon-2pm, dinner 6-9pm 🖵 ☒ (P)) The island's most luxurious option is this characterful old inn that dates from the 18th century. You can eat in the lounge bar or the excellent restaurant.

Pantry (☎ 200325; ☻ 9am-8pm Mon-Fri, 9am-6pm Sat, 2.30-8pm Sun) Serves light meals, snacks and ice creams and is beside the ferry pier. It's open daily April to September, and on the days the ferry calls the rest of the year.

Getting There & Around

CalMac operates car ferries to Colonsay from Oban (passenger/car £10.65/52, 2¼ hours) once daily except on Tuesday and Saturday.

On Wednesday only (April to September) there's a service from Colonsay to Islay's Port Askaig (passenger/car £4/20.65, 1¼ hours, one a day) and on to Kennacraig on the Kintyre peninsula. A day trip to Colonsay from Port Askaig or Kennacraig allows you about five hours on the island.

The island's only bus (☎ 200341) meets the ferry and makes a circular tour around the island.

OBAN & MULL

OBAN

☎ 01631 / pop 8120

Oban is a peaceful waterfront town on a delightful bay, with sweeping views to Kerrera and Mull. OK, that first bit about peaceful is true only in winter; in summer the town centre is a heaving mass of humanity, its streets jammed with holidaymakers, day-trippers and travellers headed for the islands of Mull, Coll, Tiree and the Outer Hebrides.

There's not a lot to see in the town itself, but it's an appealingly busy place with some excellent restaurants and lively pubs.

Orientation

The bus, train and ferry terminals are all grouped conveniently together next to the harbour on the southern edge of the bay. Argyll Square is one block east of the train station, and George St, the main drag, runs north along the promenade to North Pier. From the pier, Corran Esplanade runs round the northern edge of the bay.

Information
EMERGENCY
Lorn & Islands District General Hospital (☎ 567500; Glengallan Rd) Southern end of town.

INTERNET ACCESS
Café na Lusan (☎ 567268; 9 Craigard Rd; £1 per 15 min, £3.50 per hr)
Oban Backpackers Lodge (☎ 562107; Breadalbane St; £2 per 15 min, £5 per hr)
TIC (☎ 563122; Argyll Sq; £1 per 10 min)

POST
Post office (☻ 8am-6pm Mon-Sat, 10am-4pm Sun) In the Tesco supermarket on Lochside St.

TOURIST INFORMATION
TIC (☎ 563122; info@oban.org.uk; Argyll Sq; 9am-9pm Mon-Sat, 9am-7pm Sun Jul & Aug; 9am-5.30pm Mon-Sat, 9am-5pm Sun May, Jun & Sep; 9am-5.30pm Mon-Sat Oct-Apr) Just east of the train station.

Sights

Crowning the hill above the town centre is **McCaig's Tower** (admission free; ☻ 24 hr), built at the end of the 19th century (see boxed text on p275). To reach it on foot, make the steep climb up Jacob's Ladder (a flight of stairs)

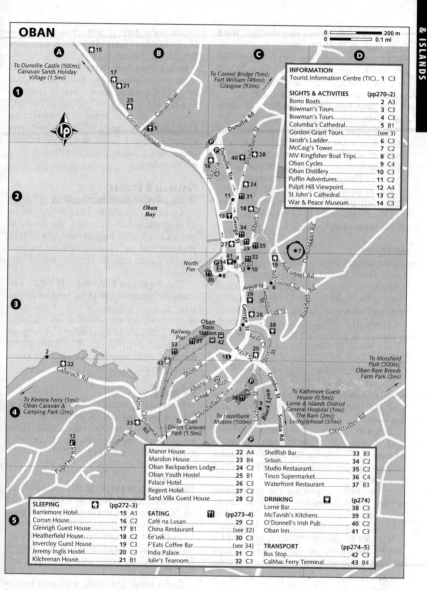

OBAN

0 — 200 m
0 — 0.1 mi

To Dunollie Castle (500m);
Ganavan Sands Holiday
Village (1.5mi)

To Connel Bridge (5mi);
Fort William (49mi);
Glasgow (93mi)

Oban Bay

North Pier

Railway Pier

Oban Train Station

Gallanach Rd

To Kerrera Ferry (1mi);
Oban Caravan &
Camping Park (2mi)

To Oban
Divers Caravan
Park (1.5mi)

To Hazelbank
Motors (100m)

To Kathmore Guest
House (0.5mi);
Lorne & Islands District
General Hospital (1mi);
The Barn (2mi);
Lochgilphead (37mi)

To Mossfield
Park (200m);
Oban Rare Breeds
Farm Park (2mi)

INFORMATION	
Tourist Information Centre (TIC)..	**1** C3

SIGHTS & ACTIVITIES	(pp270–2)
Borro Boats..............................	**2** A3
Bowman's Tours.........................	**3** C3
Bowman's Tours.........................	**4** C3
Columba's Cathedral...................	**5** B1
Gordon Grant Tours.....................	(see 3)
Jacob's Ladder...........................	**6** C3
McCaig's Tower..........................	**7** C2
MV Kingfisher Boat Trips............	**8** C3
Oban Cycles..............................	**9** C4
Oban Distillery...........................	**10** C3
Puffin Adventures.......................	**11** C2
Pulpit Hill Viewpoint...................	**12** A4
St John's Cathedral.....................	**13** C3
War & Peace Museum..................	**14** C3

SLEEPING	(pp272–3)
Barriemore Hotel........................	**15** A1
Corran House............................	**16** C2
Glenrigh Guest House.................	**17** B1
Heatherfield House.....................	**18** C2
Invercloy Guest House................	**19** C3
Jeremy Inglis Hostel...................	**20** C3
Kilchrenan House.......................	**21** B1
Manor House..............................	**22** A4
Maridon House...........................	**23** B4
Oban Backpackers Lodge............	**24** C2
Oban Youth Hostel.....................	**25** B1
Palace Hotel..............................	**26** C3
Regent Hotel.............................	**27** C2
Sand Villa Guest House...............	**28** C3

EATING	(pp273–4)
Café na Lusan............................	**29** C2
China Restaurant........................	(see 32)
Ee'usk......................................	**30** C3
F'Eats Coffee Bar.......................	(see 34)
India Palace...............................	**31** C2
Julie's Tearoom..........................	**32** C3
Manor House..............................	**22** A4
Maridon House...........................	**23** B4
Oban Backpackers Lodge............	**24** C2
Oban Youth Hostel.....................	**25** B1
Palace Hotel..............................	**26** C3
Regent Hotel.............................	**27** C2
Sand Villa Guest House...............	**28** C3
Shellfish Bar..............................	**33** B3
Sirloin......................................	**34** C2
Studio Restaurant.......................	**35** C2
Tesco Supermarket.....................	**36** C4
Waterfront Restaurant.................	**37** B3

DRINKING	(p274)
Lorne Bar.................................	**38** C3
McTavish's Kitchens...................	**39** C3
O'Donnell's Irish Pub..................	**40** C2
Oban Inn..................................	**41** C3

TRANSPORT	(pp274–5)
Bus Stop...................................	**42** C3
CalMac Ferry Terminal................	**43** B4

from Argyll St and then follow the signs. The views over the bay are worth the effort. **Pulpit Hill**, to the south of the bay, is another excellent viewpoint; the footpath starts to the right of Maridon House B&B on Dunuaran Rd.

Oban Distillery (☎ 572004; Stafford St; admission £3.50; ☒ 9.30am-8.30pm Mon-Fri, 9.30am-5pm Sat,

noon-5pm Sun Jul-Sep; 9.30am-5pm Mon-Sat Easter-Jun & Oct; 9.30am-5pm Mon-Fri Nov-Easter) has been producing Oban single malt whisky since 1794. There are guided tours available year-round (last tour begins one hour before closing time), but even without a tour it's still worth visiting the small exhibition in the foyer.

Military buffs should visit the little **War & Peace Museum** (North Pier; admission free; ☼ 10am-4pm & 7-9pm Mon-Sat Jul & Aug, 10am-4pm Mon-Sat Sep-Jun), which chronicles Oban's role in WWII as a base for Catalina seaplanes and as a marshalling area for Atlantic convoys.

The **Oban Rare Breeds Farm Park** (☎ 770608; New Barran Farm, Glencruitten; adult/child £6/4; ☼ 10am-5.30pm late Mar-Oct, 10am-7.30pm mid-June–Aug) is a favourite with children, who get to meet all kinds of animals at close quarters, such as rabbits, goats, cows, deer and even llamas. The farm maintains rare breeds of domesticated animals, including Tamworth pigs, Shetland and Soay sheep and longhorn cattle; it's 2 miles (3km) east of the town centre.

Activities

It's a pleasant 20-minute **walk** north from Oban Youth Hostel along the coast road to Dunollie Castle, built by the MacDougalls of Lorn in the 13th century and unsuccessfully besieged for a year during the 1715 Jacobite rebellion. It's always open and very much a ruin. You can continue along this road to the beach at Ganavan Sands, 2½ miles from Oban.

A TIC leaflet lists local **bike rides**. They include a 7-mile (11km) Gallanach circular tour, a 16-mile (25km) route to the Isle of Seil and routes to Connel, Glenlonan and Kilmore.

You can hire sailing dinghies, rowboats and motorboats at **Borro Boats** (☎ 563292; Gallanach Rd; ☼ 10am-6pm May-Sep). A Wayfarer sailing dinghy costs £24.50/49 for two hours/a day.

If you fancy exploring the underwater world, **Puffin Adventures** (☎ 571190, 566088; George St) offers a 1½ hour Try-a-Dive package (£42.50) for complete beginners.

The **MV Kingfisher** (☎ 563138; adult/child £5/2.50; ☼ departs hourly 10am-2pm) offers boat trips to spot seals and other marine wildlife, departing from the North Pier slipway.

Tours

From April to October, **Bowman's Tours** (☎ 563221; 3 Stafford St) offers a Three Isles day trip from Oban that visits Mull, Iona and Staffa (adult/child £35/17.50, 10 hours, 10am Saturday to Thursday); the crossing to Staffa is weather dependent. A shorter day trip visits Mull and Iona only (£27/

13.50, eight hours) and departs daily at 10am. **Bowman's Tours** (☎ 566809) has another Branch on Queens Park Pl.

Gordon Grant Tours (tickets from Bowman's Tours) runs a whale-watching tour (adult/child £38/19), departing from Oban at 10am on Sunday (early May to late July). The trip takes in a ferry crossing to Craignure on Mull, travel by coach to Fionnphort, and a cruise around Staffa and the Treshnish Isles, plus a landing on Lunga to visit a puffin colony.

Festivals & Events

During **West Highland Yachting Week** (☎ 563309; www.whyw.co.uk) at the end of July/beginning of August, Oban becomes the focus of one of Scotland's biggest yachting events. Hundreds of yachts cram into the harbour and the town's bars are jammed with thirsty sailors.

The **Argyllshire Gathering** (☎ 562671; www.obangames.com; adult/child £8/4), held over two days in late August, is one of the most important events on the Scottish Highland games calendar and includes a prestigious pipe band competition. The main games are held at Mossfield Park on the eastern edge of town.

Sleeping

Despite having lots of B&B accommodation, Oban's beds can still fill up quickly in July and August so try to book ahead. If the town is full, consider staying at Connel, 4 miles (8km) to the north (p285).

BUDGET

Oban Backpackers Lodge (☎ 562107; oban@scotlands-top-hostels.com; Breadalbane St; dm £11-12; ☼ Mar-Oct; ☐ ✗) This is a friendly place with a good vibe and an attractive communal area with lots of sofas and armchairs. From the train station, walk 800m north along George St, past the cinema, and veer right into Breadalbane St.

Corran House (☎ 566040; enquiries@corranhouse.co.uk; 1 Victoria Cres; dm £10-11; tw £26; ☐ P) The family-friendly Corran House has a nice waterfront location and offers big comfy beds in four- and six-bed dorms as well as twin and double rooms. Facilities include a kitchen, a laundry and bike hire.

Jeremy Inglis Hostel (☎ 565065; jeremyinglis@mctavishs.freeserve.co.uk; 21 Airds Cres; dm £6, s £11-12;

d £13-15; ✗) This bargain place is more of a basic B&B than a hostel – most 'dorms' have only two or three beds, and are decorated with books, flowers and cuddly toys, and the price includes a continental breakfast. The kitchen is a little cramped, but the owner is friendly and knowledgeable (and makes delicious home-made jam).

Oban Youth Hostel (SYHA; ☎ 562025; Corran Esplanade; dm £10.50-13; ✗ P) Oban's SYHA hostel is set in a grand Victorian villa on the Esplanade, three-quarters of a mile north of the train station, with great views across Oban Bay.

Palace Hotel (☎ 562294; George St; s £17.50-25, d £32-50; ✗) The Palace is a small, old-fashioned but friendly hotel right in the centre of town. The rooms are a bit small but are good value, especially the ones with harbour views.

There are several camping grounds in the Oban area.

Oban Divers Caravan Park (☎ 562755; info@ obandiver.co.uk; Glenshellach Rd; site per tent/campervan/ car/person £8/8/1/50p; ☿ Mar-Oct), The closest to the train station, this caravan park is 1½ miles south of town in Glenshellach.

Oban Caravan & Camping Park (☎ 562425; info@ obancaravanpark.co.uk; Gallanachmore Farm; sites £9-10; ☿ Apr-Oct) This campground has a superb location overlooking the Sound of Kerrera, 2½ miles (4km) south of Oban.

Ganavan Sands Holiday Village (☎ 566479; www .ganavansands.com; Ganavan Rd; sites per campervan/ person £12/1; ☿ Mar-Oct) Ganavan is mainly a self-catering chalet park, but also has 30 sites for tourers. The lovely sandy beach makes it a good place for kids.

MID-RANGE

Kilchrenan House (☎ 562663; info@kilchrenan house.co.uk; Corran Esplanade; s £30-35, d £56-70; ✗ P) You'll get a warm welcome at the Kilchrenan, an elegant Victorian villa built for a textile magnate in 1883. Most of the 10 rooms have views across Oban Bay, but Nos 5 and 9 are the best – No 5 has a huge freestanding bath tub, perfect for soaking weary bones.

Invercloy Guest House (☎ 562058; Ardconnel Tce; s £18-23, d £36-50; ✗) Set on a quiet street high above town and close to McCaig's Tower, the good-value Invercloy has crisp white linen and grand views of the CalMac ferry chugging across the harbour – shame about

the dirty great industrial chimney stack in the way!

Maridon House (☎ 562670; maridonhse@aol.com; Dunuaran Rd; r per person £18-22; ✗) The bright blue, flower-bedecked Maridon House has eight rooms (all with bath), and is only a few minutes' walk from the ferry terminal. The owners are very helpful and will provide a vegetarian breakfast if you ask.

Heatherfield House (☎ 562681; heatherfield@ dial.pipex.com; Albert Rd; s/d £40/50; ✗ P) The homely Heatherfield House is set in a converted 1870s rectory and has five rooms (all with bath), including one family room with a bathroom designed for guests with limited mobility.

Other recommendations:

Barriemore Hotel (☎ 566356; reception@barriemore -hotel.co.uk; Corran Esplanade; s £25-45, d £45-80; ✗ P)

Glenrigh Guest House (☎ 562991; glenrigh.guesthouse@ virgin.net; Corran Esplanade; s £25-30, d £46-60; ✗ P)

Kathmore Guest House (☎ 562104; wkathmore@ aol.com; Soroba Rd; s £25-35, d £40-48; ✗ P)

Sand Villa Guest House (☎ 562803; sandvilla@holidayo ban.co.uk; Breadalbane St; r per person £17.50-22.50; ✗)

TOP END

Regent Hotel (☎ 562341; regent@british-trust-hotels .com; Corran Esplanade; s £55-75, d £95) One part traditional Victorian and three parts 1930s Art Deco on the outside, and fully refurbished with all mod-cons on the inside, the Regent has a great waterfront location right in the centre of town.

Manor House (☎ 562087; manorhouseoban@ aol.com; Gallanach Rd; s £60-85, d £70-116; ✗ P) Built in 1780 for the duke of Argyll as part of his Oban estates, the Manor House is now one of Oban's finest hotels. It has small but elegant rooms in Georgian style, a posh bar frequented by local and visiting yachties, and a fine restaurant serving Scottish and French cuisine.

Eating

There's no shortage of places to eat in Oban. Most are strung out along the bay between the train station and the North Pier, and along George St.

BUDGET

Shellfish Bar (Railway Pier; sandwiches £2.20-2.50; ☿ 9am-6pm) If you want to savour superb Scottish seafood without the expense of an upmarket restaurant, head for Oban's famous seafood stall – it's the green shack on the quayside. Here you can buy fresh and cooked seafood to take away – prawn sandwiches, dressed crab and fresh oysters for only 50p each.

Julie's Tearooms (☎ 565952; 37 Stafford St; sandwiches £2-3.50; ☯ 10am-5pm Mon-Sat) Nip into Julie's (opposite the distillery) for coffee and cake, tea and a scone, or some delicious Luca's ice cream.

Café na Lusan (☎ 567268; 9 Craigard Rd; snacks £2.5-5, mains £6-8.50; ☯ 10am-5pm Mon, 10am-10pm Tue-Sat, noon-4pm Sun) This is a neat little café with great background music, good coffee, sandwiches, organic food and veggie meals – and Internet access to boot.

F'Eats Coffee Bar (☎ 571000; The Warehouse, John St; light meals £2-3.50; ☯ 9am-5pm Mon-Sat, 10am-4pm Sun) This stylish café and bar with comfy purple sofas serves tasty panini, baguettes and focaccia, as well as home-made soup and great cappuccino.

MID-RANGE

Ee'usk (☎ 565666; North Pier; lunch mains £7-9, dinner £11-17; ☯ lunch 11am-4pm, dinner 6-10pm) A brand-new development on the North Pier houses bright and modern Ee'usk (it's how to pronounce *iasg*, the Gaelic word for fish). Tall picture windows allow diners on two levels to enjoy views over the harbour to Kerrera and Mull while sampling a seafood menu ranging from crisp-battered haddock to Thai fishcakes. A tad overpriced, perhaps, but both food and location are first class.

Sirloin (☎ 565666; 104 George St; mains £10-16; ☯ noon-2pm & 6-10pm) Move along please vegetarians, nothing for you here... As the name suggests, steaks are the star attraction in this appealing bistro, along with good old-fashioned comfort food such as sausage and mash, and clootie dumpling, all served with a dash of modern style.

Waterfront Restaurant (☎ 563110; Waterfront Centre, Railway Pier; mains lunch £5-8, dinner £7-16; ☯ 10.30am-2.15pm & 5.30-9.30pm) The stylish, minimalist Waterfront, housed in the converted seamen's mission, serves seafood freshly landed at the quay just a few metres away.

Studio Restaurant (☎ 562030; Craigard Rd; mains £10-14, 3-course dinner £13.95; ☯ 6-10pm) This snug little place, up the hill off George St, deserves the good reputation it holds. Scottish cuisine includes paté and oatcakes,

crab claws with garlic butter, roast Angus beef, and Scottish cheeses. The set three-course dinner costs £11.95 before 6.30pm.

Other recommendations:
India Palace (☎ 566400; 146 George St; mains £6-12; ☯ noon-2pm & 5pm-midnight)
China Restaurant (☎ 563575; 39 Stafford St; mains £7.50-8.50; ☯ noon-2pm & 5-10.30pm)

Drinking & Entertainment

Oban Inn (☎ 562484; Stafford St; bar meals £6) The lively Oban Inn, overlooking the harbour by the North Pier, is the best pub in town. It's a traditional bar with wood panelling, brass rails and stained glass, and has real ales, a wide range of single malt whiskies and good bar food – the *moules frites* (mussels and chips) are a local favourite.

O'Donnells Irish Pub (☎ 656421; Breadalbane St; ☯ 2pm-1am Sun-Thu, 2pm-2am Fri & Sat) This Irish bar, opposite Oban Backpackers, has live entertainment – usually Celtic music – most nights.

The Barn (☎ 564618; Lerags; ☯ 11am-11pm Mon-Sat, noon-11pm Sun Apr-Oct; 11am-11pm Mon-Sat Nov-Mar) This family-friendly pub, with an outdoor beer garden and children's play area, is in a lovely country setting 2 miles (3km) south of Oban. It does bar meals with a special children's menu and some good veggie options.

McTavish's Kitchens (☎ 563064; George St; adult/child £4/2 for show only, £2/1 if dining; ☯ shows 8pm & 10pm May-Sep) The nightly 'Scottish show' here caters to the kilts-and-tartan tourist market, with Scottish country dancing, live bands, piping, fiddle music and Gaelic songs.

Lorne Bar on Stevenson St is popular with Oban's late-teens and twenty-somethings, and stays open till 2am Thursday to Saturday.

Getting There & Away

BOAT

CalMac ferries link Oban with the islands of Kerrera (p275), Mull (p276), Coll (p283), Tiree (p283), Lismore (p286) and Colonsay (p268).

BUS

Citylink buses run to Oban from Glasgow (£12.20, three hours, four daily) via Inveraray; from Fort William (£7.60, 1½ hours, four daily Monday to Saturday), with connections to Inverness; and from

MCCAIG'S FOLLY

McCaig's Tower – a bizarre landmark on top of a hill overlooking Oban harbour – is vaguely reminiscent of Rome's Colosseum. Its construction was commissioned in 1890 by local worthy John Stuart McCaig, an art critic, philosophical essayist and banker, who had the philanthropic intention of providing work for unemployed stonemasons.

However, work was abandoned in 1900 when over £5000 had been spent. A planned 29m-high central tower was never built and the bronze statues of family members stipulated by McCaig's will were never installed. As a result, the unfinished monument came to be known as McCaig's Folly. Its best feature is the stunning view of Mull from the seaward arches.

Perth (£8.60, three hours, twice daily Friday to Monday) via Tyndrum and Killin.

West Coast Motors (☎ 570500) bus No 423 runs from Oban to Lochgilphead (£3.70, 1¾ hours, four daily Monday to Friday, two on Saturday) via Kilmartin Glen.

TRAIN

Oban is at the end of a scenic route that branches off the West Highland line at Crianlarich. There are up to three trains a day from Glasgow to Oban (£15.50, three hours).

The train's not much use for travelling north from Oban. To reach Fort William requires a detour via Crianlarich – take the bus instead.

Getting Around

BICYCLE

Oban Cycles (☎ 566996; 29 Lochside St; ☼ 9am-5.30pm Mon-Sat), opposite Tesco supermarket, rents bikes for £10 a day.

Hazelbank Motors (☎ 566476; Lynn Rd; ☼ 8.30am-5.30pm Mon-Sat) rent bicycles for £2/10 per hour/day.

BUS

The main bus stop is outside the train station. **Oban & District Buses** (☎ 570500) is the local company; bus Nos 1 and 401 run from the train station to Ganavan Sands via Oban Youth Hostel (60p, five minutes, every 20 minutes). Bus No 431 connects the train station with the Kerrera ferry and Oban

Caravan & Camping Park (15 minutes, two daily Monday to Saturday late May to September).

CAR

Hazelbank Motors (see above) rents small cars from £35/195 a day/week including VAT, insurance and CDW.

TAXI

There's a taxi rank outside the train station. Otherwise call **Oban Taxis** (☎ 564666) or **Kennedy's Taxis** (☎ 564172).

AROUND OBAN
Isle of Kerrera
☎ 01631 / pop 40

Some of the best **walking** in the area is on Kerrera, which faces Oban across the bay. There's a 6-mile (10km) circuit of the island (two to three hours), which follows tracks or paths (use OS map No 49) and offers the chance to spot wildlife such as Soay sheep, wild goats, otters, golden eagles, peregrine falcons, seals and porpoises. At **Lower Gylen**, at the southern end of the island, there's a ruined castle.

Kerrera Bunkhouse & Tea Garden (☎ 570223; www.kerrerabunkhouse.com; Lower Gylen; dm £8) is a charming six-bed bothy in a converted 18th-century stable, a 40-minute walk south from the ferry (keep left at the fork just past the telephone box). Booking is recommended. You can get snacks and light meals at the nearby Tea Garden (open April to September only).

The 10-bed **Ardentrive Farm Hostel** (☎ 567180; joyce-glen@whsmithnet.co.uk; Ardentrive Farm; dm £8) is on a working farm at the northern end of the island, just south of the yacht marina.

There's a daily passenger **ferry** (☎ 563665) to Kerrera from Gallanach, about 2 miles (3km) southwest of Oban town centre, along Gallanach Rd (adult/child £3/1.50 return, bicycle 50p, 10 minutes). From April to September it runs half-hourly from 10.30am to 12.30pm and 2pm to 6pm every day, plus 8.45am Monday to Saturday. Call to check winter ferry times.

Isle of Seil
☎ 01852 / pop 506

The small island of Seil, 10 miles (16km) south of Oban, is best known for its connection to the mainland – the so-called

Bridge over the Atlantic, designed by Thomas Telford and opened in 1793. The bridge has a single stone arch and spans the narrowest part of the tidal Clachan Sound.

On the west coast of the island is the pretty conservation village of **Ellanbeich**, with its whitewashed cottages, 4 miles (6.5km) from the bridge. The village was built to house workers at the local slate quarries, but the industry collapsed in 1881 when the sea flooded the main quarry pit, which can still be seen. The **Scottish Slate Islands Heritage Trust** (☎ 300449; Ellanbeich; adult/child £1.50/25p; ☾ 10.30am-5.30pm Apr-Oct, 10.30am-7pm May-Aug) displays fascinating old photographs illustrating life in the village in the 19th and early 20th centuries.

Just offshore from Ellanbeich is the small island of Easdale, which has more old slate-workers' cottages and the interesting **Easdale Island Folk Museum** (☎ 300370; adult/child £2.25/50p; ☾ 10.30am-5.30pm Apr-Oct). The museum has displays about the slate industry and life on the islands in the 18th and 19th centuries. Climb to the top of the island (a 38m peak!) for a great view of the surrounding area.

Coach tours flock to the **Highland Arts Studio** (☎ 300273; Easdale; ☾ 9am-9pm Apr-Sep; 10am-6pm Oct-Mar), a crafts and gift shop and a shrine to the eccentric output of the late 'poet, artist and composer' C John Taylor. Please, try to keep a straight face.

Sea.fari Adventures (☎ 300003; Easdale Harbour) runs a series of exciting two-hour boat trips in high-speed RIBs (rigid inflatable boats) to the Corryvreckan whirlpool (p269), the slate island of Belnahua (see right) and the remote Garvellach Islands (adult/child £22/16.50). A 15-minute spin around Easdale costs £4.50/3.

GETTING THERE & AROUND
Oban & District Buses (☎ 01631-570500) runs buses at least twice daily, except Sunday, from Oban to Ellanbeich and on to North Cuan for the ferry to Luing (see right).

Argyll & Bute Council (☎ 01631-562125) operates the daily passenger-only ferry service from Ellanbeich to Easdale (£1 return, bicycles free, five minutes). Most runs are on request, at the times displayed on the pier. To call the boat to Ellanbeich pier, sound the hooter during daylight, or switch on the light at night.

Isle of Luing
☎ 01852 / pop 180

Luing (pronounced ling), about 6 miles (10km) long and 1½ miles wide (2.5km), is separated from the southern end of Seil by the narrow Cuan Sound. There are two attractive villages – **Cullipool** at the northern end and **Toberonochy** in the east – but Luing's main pleasures are scenic.

The **slate quarries** of Cullipool were abandoned in 1965. About 1½ miles out to sea you can see the remains of the extensively quarried slate island of **Belnahua** – workers used to live on this remote and desolate rock. You can get a closer look on a boat trip from Easdale (see left).

There are two Iron Age forts, the better being **Dun Leccamore**, about a mile north of Toberonochy. In Toberonochy itself are the ruins of the late medieval **Kilchatton Church** and a graveyard with unusual slate gravestones.

You can visit both villages, the fort, the ruined chapel and the scenic west coast on a pleasant 8-mile (13km) circular walk.

GETTING THERE & AROUND
A small **car ferry** (☎ 01631-562125) runs from Cuan (on Seil) to Luing (return car/passenger £5.80/1.10, bicycles free, five minutes, two an hour Monday to Saturday); a passenger-only ferry runs on Sunday too.

There's a Monday to Saturday **postbus** (☎ 01463-256200) service around Luing that connects to Ellanbeich on Seil.

Isle of Luing Bike Hire (☎ 314256) in Cullipool rents bikes for £10/6 a day/half-day.

ISLE OF MULL
pop 2600

It's easy to see why Mull is so popular with tourists. As well as having superb mountain scenery, two castles, a narrow-gauge railway and being on the route to the holy Isle of Iona, it's also a charming and endearing place.

Despite the number of visitors who flock to the island, it seems to be large enough to absorb them all; many stick to the well-worn route from Craignure to Iona, returning to Oban in the evening. If you're looking for budget accommodation, there's not much of it on Mull, so you'd be advised to take a tent.

Orientation

About two-thirds of Mull's population lives in and around Tobermory, the island's capital, in the north. Craignure, at the southeastern corner, has the main ferry terminal and is where most people arrive. Fionnphort is at the far western end of the long Ross of Mull peninsula, and is where the ferry to Iona departs.

Information

The **hospital** (☎ 01680-300392) is centrally located at Salen.

You can check email (£1 per 15 minutes) at the Spar shop next to the Mishnish Hotel (p278) or at the SYHA hostel, both in Tobermory. The island's only bank (with an ATM) is also in Tobermory .

There are post offices and grocery stores in most villages – the Co-op supermarket in Tobermory is the best place for provisions.

There are TICs at **Craignure** (☎ 812377; ⏱ 8.30am-7pm Mon-Thu, 8.30am-5.15pm Fri, 9am-5pm Sat, 10am-5pm Sun) and **Tobermory** (☎ 302182; The Pier; ⏱ 9am-5.30pm Apr-Oct).

Craignure & Around
☎ 01680

There's not much at Craignure other than the ferry terminal, the hotel and the pub, so hop onto the **Mull Railway** (☎ 812494; Old Pier Station; adult/child £3.50/2.50; ⏱ Apr-Oct), a miniature steam train that will take you 1½ miles south to Torosay Castle.

Torosay Castle & Gardens (☎ 812421; adult/child £4.50/1.50; ⏱ house 10.30am-5.30pm Easter–mid-Oct; gardens 10.30am-dusk) is a rambling Victorian mansion in the Scottish Baronial style. 'Take your time but not our spoons' advises the sign, and you're left to wander at will.

Two miles (3km) beyond Torosay is **Duart Castle** (☎ 812309; adult/child £4/2; ⏱ 10.30am-6pm May–mid-Oct, 11am-4pm Fri-Sun Apr), a formidable fortress dominating the Sound of Mull. The seat of the Clan Maclean, this is one of the oldest inhabited castles in Scotland – the central keep was built in 1360. It was bought and restored in 1911 by war hero Sir Fitzroy Maclean and has damp dungeons, vast halls and bathrooms equipped with ancient fittings.

B&Bs within 10 minutes' walk of the ferry include **Linnhe View** (☎ 812369; linnheview@ yahoo.co.uk; s £25, d £40-50; ✗ P) and **Aon a'Dha** (☎ 812318; r from £16; ✗ P).

Shieling Holidays (☎ 812496; www.shielingholidays .co.uk; sites for 2 people/car £11/1.50, dm £9; ⏱ late Mar-Oct) is a well-equipped camping ground less than 10 minutes' walk from the ferry.

Tobermory
☎ 01688 / pop 750

Tobermory, the island's main town and a major yachting centre, is a picturesque little fishing port with brightly painted houses around a sheltered harbour.

Places to go on a rainy day include **Mull Museum** (☎ 302493; Main St; adult/child £1/20p; ⏱ 10am-4pm Mon-Fri, 10am-1pm Sat Easter-Oct), which records the history of the island, and the **Tobermory Distillery** (☎ 302645; adult/ child £2.50/1; ⏱ 10.30am-4pm Mon-Fri Easter-Oct), which offers guided tours.

The Hebridean Whale & Dolphin Trust's **Marine Discovery Centre** (☎ 302620; 28 Main St; admission free; ⏱ 10am-5pm Mon-Fri, 11am-4pm Sun Apr-Oct; 11am-5pm Mon-Fri Nov-Mar) has displays, videos and interactive exhibits on whale and dolphin biology and ecology.

Somewhere out in Tobermory Bay is the wreck of a Spanish galleon that sank here in 1588. Rumours of a cargo of gold have kept treasure-hunters looking ever since.

SLEEPING

Tobermory has dozens of B&Bs, but the place can still be booked solid in July and August, especially at weekends.

Tobermory Campsite (☎ 302624; angus.williams@ supanet.com; Newdale, Dervaig Rd; tent sites per person £3.50; ⏱ Mar-Oct) The nearest place to camp is this quiet, country campground a mile west of town on the road to Dervaig.

Tobermory Youth Hostel (SYHA; ☎ 0870 004 1151; Main St; dm £10-11; ⏱ Mar-Oct) This smallish hostel (39 beds) has a great location right on the waterfront. Bookings are recommended.

34 Main St (☎ 302530; 34 Main St; s/d £10/20) This B&B has two neat and cosy attic rooms for a bargain, room-only rate.

Ulva House Hotel (☎ 302044; info@ulvahousehotel .co.uk; Strongarbh; r per person £35-45) The snug, six-room Ulva House is a lovely Victorian villa overlooking the harbour from above the ferry terminal. The food is top notch (evening meals available), and the log fires in the lounge and bar will warm your toes after a day's hike.

Western Isles Hotel (☎ 302012; wihotel@aol.com; s £49, d £99-174; ✗ P) One of the top hotels on Mull, this grand Victorian pile commands the heights above the harbour. It has luxurious rooms and a great conservatory bar-restaurant and terrace with panoramic views.

EATING & DRINKING

Back Brae Restaurant (☎ 302422; Back Brae; mains £8-14; ☺ 6pm-late) This snug and atmospheric restaurant is also the village's oldest and specialises in Scottish seafood, beef, lamb and venison. There are vegetarian dishes and a children's menu.

MacGochan's (☎ 302350; Ledaig; mains £4-7; ☺ food served noon-10pm) A lively pub beside the car park at the southern end of the waterfront, MacGochan's does good bar meals. It also holds outdoor barbecues on summer evenings, offers a weekend brunch (11am to 2.30pm) and there's live music in the bar every weekend.

Mishnish Hotel (☎ 302009; Main St; bar meals £6-12; ☺ food served noon-2pm & 6-9pm) You can't miss the virulently yellow façade of this hotel; it's a favourite hang-out for visiting yachties and a good place for a bar meal. The 'Mish', as it's known, is a fine traditional pub that has escaped the deluge of gambling machines afflicting so many of Scotland's watering holes. Toast your toes by the open fire, burrow into a booth with a book, or challenge the locals to a game of pool.

Other recommendations:

Pisces (☎ 302012; wihotel@aol.com; meals £20-25) This is a superb seafood restaurant at the Western Isles Hotel.

Water's Edge (meals per person excl wine £20-25) For truly posh nosh, try this harbour-side restaurant in the Tobermory Hotel.

North Mull

☎ 01688

With only 43 seats, **Mull Little Theatre** (☎ 400245; www.mulltheatre.com; Dervaig; adult/child £12/9; shows at 8.30pm Apr-Sep) is Scotland's smallest theatre, but it enjoys a reputation for staging excellent productions. The theatre is 8 miles (13km) west of Tobermory at Dervaig.

The **Old Byre Heritage Centre** (☎ 400229; Dervaig; adult/child £3/1.50; ☺ 10.30am-6.30pm Easter-Oct) brings Mull's heritage and natural history to life through a series of tableaux and a half-hour film show; prize for most bizarre exhibit goes to the 40cm-long model of a midge. The centre's **tearoom** serves good, inexpensive snacks, including soup, and clootie dumplings.

Mull's best silver-sand beach, flanked by cliffs and with views out to Coll and Tiree, is at **Calgary**, about 4 miles (6km) west of Dervaig.

SLEEPING & EATING

Calgary Bay camping (sites per person £3) There's a very basic campground at the southern end of the beach at Calgary Bay.

Calgary Hotel (☎ 400256; www.calgary.co.uk; Calgary; s £38-50, d £60-80; ☒ ℗) The Calgary provides delightfully rustic accommodation a few minutes' walk from the sandy beach at Calgary Bay. There are also two lovely self-catering loft apartments available for £360 per week (sleeping two to four people).

Bellachroy Hotel & Pub (☎ 400314; booking@ bellachroy.co.uk; Dervaig; r per person £20-28) The seven-room Bellachroy is an atmospheric 17th-century droving inn. The bar, known as the Bear Pit, is a focus for local social life and serves good-value bar meals. Dinner, bed and breakfast is available for an extra £12.50.

Druimard Country House & Restaurant (☎ 400345; www.druimard.co.uk; Dervaig; d DB&B £130-170; ☒ ℗) Near the theatre, this Victorian country house offers luxurious but homey accommodation and excellent food. Its four-course dinners are available to non-guests for £29.50 per person.

Central Mull

☎ 01680

The central part of the island, between the Craignure–Fionnphort road and the narrow isthmus between Salen and Gruline, contains the island's highest peak, Ben More and some of its wildest scenery (see the Walking on Mull boxed text, p281).

At Gruline, near the head of Loch na Keal, is the **MacQuarrie Mausoleum**. Sir Lachlan MacQuarrie (1762–1824) was born on Mull and served as governor of New South Wales in Australia from 1809 to 1821.

The narrow B8035 road along the southern shore of Loch na Keal squeezes past some impressive cliffs before cutting south towards Loch Scridain. About a mile along the shore from Balmeanach, where the road climbs away from the coast, is **Mackinnon's Cave**, a deep and spooky fissure in the basalt cliffs that was once used as a refuge by Celtic monks; a big, flat rock inside, known as Fingal's Table, may have been their altar.

MULL, COLL & TIREE

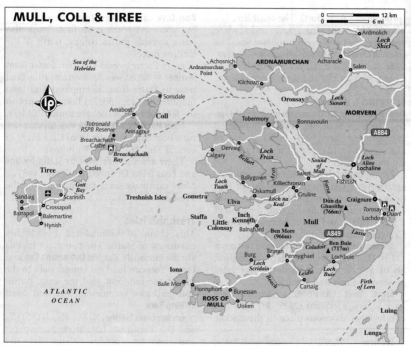

Balmeanach Park Caravan & Camping Site
(☎ 01680-300342; sites per person £4.50; ☼ Mar-Oct)
is a peaceful camping ground 10 minutes'
walk from the Fishnish–Lochaline ferry,
on the main road between Craignure and
Tobermory.

There's also a very basic **campground** (sites
per person £3) at Killiechronan, half a mile
north of Gruline. Toilets and water are a
five-minute walk away.

Isle of Ulva
☎ 01688 / pop 30
Ulva, just off the west coast of Mull, has
good walking and mountain-biking, a
9th-century Viking fort, and an old chapel
with a graveyard. A short walk north of
the ferry landing is **Sheila's Cottage Heritage
Centre** (☎ 500241; admission included in ferry ticket;
☼ 9am-5pm Mon-Fri Easter-Oct, 9am-5pm Sun Jun-Aug),
a reconstruction of a traditional thatched
crofter's cottage with displays about the
history of the island.

At the **Boathouse** tearoom, beside the ferry
landing, you can savour locally harvested
oysters washed down with Guinness.

An interpretative centre upstairs has
information on walks and natural history.

The two-minute ferry crossing (adult/
child £4/2 return) runs on demand during
Heritage Centre opening hours.

South Mull
☎ 01681
The road from Craignure to Fionnphort
climbs through some wild and desolate
scenery before reaching the southwestern
part of the island, which consists of a long
peninsula called the Ross of Mull. The Ross
has a spectacular south coast with black
basalt cliffs, which give way farther west to
pink granite crags and white-sand beaches.
The cliffs reach their highest at Malcolm's
Point, near the superb **Carsaig Arches** (p281).

The little village of **Bunessan** has a hotel,
tearoom, pub and some shops, and is home
to the **Ross of Mull Historical Centre** (☎ 700659;
admission £1; ☼ 10am-4.30pm Mon-Fri Apr-Oct; by
arrangement Nov-Mar), which covers local history,
geology, archaeology, genealogy and wildlife.

At the western end of the Ross, 38
miles (61km) from Craignure, is **Fionnphort**

(pronounced *finn*-afort). The coast here is a beautiful blend of pink granite rocks, white sandy beaches and vivid turquoise sea. The **Columba Centre** (☎ 700660; admission free; ☉ 11am-5.30pm May-Sep) has displays about the life of St Columba, the Celts and the history of Iona.

SLEEPING & EATING

Fidden Farm (☎ 700427; sites per person £2; ☉ Apr-Sep) There's a basic but beautifully situated campground here, 1¼ miles south of Fionnphort (continue on the road past the Columba Centre).

Pennyghael Hotel (☎ 704288; www.pennyghaelhotel.com; Pennyghael; r per person £37-41; ☉ Mar-Oct) This delightful, six-room country hotel is set in a 17th-century farmhouse, near the head of Loch Scridain and about halfway between Craignure and Fionnphort.

Ardness House (☎ 700260; Bunessan; r per person £18-24) This spacious modern bungalow, about a mile west of Bunessa, has great views over Loch na Lathaich.

Argyll Arms (☎ 700240; argyllarms@isleofmull.co.uk; Bunessan; r per person £28-35; Ⓟ) This is a comfortable six-room place in the middle of the village.

Seaview (☎ 700235; john@seaviewmull.f9.co.uk; Fionnphort; s £20-27, d £36-48; ☒ Ⓟ) Barely a minute's walk from the Iona ferry, the Seaview has grand views across to the island.

Staffa House (☎ 700677; Fionnphort; s £20-44, d £36-50; ☉ Mar-Oct; ☒ Ⓟ) Readers have recommended this for its charm and hospitality. The house is packed with antiques, and there's a lovely view of Iona from the conservatory dining room.

Keel Row (☎ 700458; Fionnphort; bar meals £6-10) It may look like an ordinary cottage, but Keel Row, next door to Seaview, is a cosy pub with wooden floors, stone walls, good bar meals and home-made snacks.

Isle of Staffa
☎ 01681

Felix Mendelssohn, who visited Staffa in 1829, was inspired to compose his Hebrides Overture after hearing the sound of the waves echoing in the impressive and cathedral-like **Fingal's Cave**; the cave walls and surrounding cliffs are composed of vertical, hexagonal basalt columns that look like pillars (Staffa is Norse for 'Pillar Island'). You can land on the island and walk into the cave via a causeway. Nearby

Boat Cave can be seen from the causeway, but you can't reach it on foot. Staffa also has a sizeable puffin colony, north of the landing place.

From Easter to mid-October, **Gordon Grant Marine** (☎ 700388; www.staffatours.com) runs boat trips to Staffa from Fionnphort and Iona (adult/child £15/7.50, 2½ hours). Tours on the **MV Iolaire** (☎ 700358) are similar (£14/7).

Turus Mara (☎ 08000 858786; www.turusmara.com) runs boat trips to Staffa from Ulva Ferry in central Mull (£15/7.50, 3½ hours).

There are also day trips to Staffa by bus and boat from Oban via Craignure (p272). More expensive tours take in Iona and the Treshnish Isles as well as Staffa.

Treshnish Isles

This chain of uninhabited islands lies northwest of Staffa. The two main islands are the curiously shaped **Dutchman's Cap** and **Lunga**. You can land on Lunga, walk to the top of the hill, and visit the shag, puffin and guillemot colonies on the west coast at **Harp Rock**.

Gordon Grant Marine (☎ 700388) sails to Staffa and the Treshnish Isles from Fionnphort and Iona on Tuesday, Wednesday and Thursday from late April to July (£27/13.50, six hours). **Turus Mara** (☎ 08000 858786) sails from Ulva Ferry to the Treshnish Isles/Staffa daily from late May to late August (£38.50/19.50, six hours).

Tours

See p272 for details of day tours to Mull and Iona by ferry and bus. There are also several companies running wildlife and whale-watching tours – booking for these is strongly advised.

Travellers have recommended the 7½-hour Land Rover tours offered by **Mull Wildlife Expeditions** (☎ 01688-500121; Ulva Ferry). The cost (adult/child £29.50/23.50) includes a picnic lunch. You'll have a chance to spot golden eagles, peregrine falcons, hen harriers, red deer, seals, otters, and perhaps dolphins and porpoises. Tours leave from Tobermory at 10am and from Craignure an hour later, returning to Craignure for the 5pm ferry so that you can make a day trip from Oban.

Sea Life Surveys (☎ 01688-400223; Tobermory) runs whale-watching trips to the waters north and west of Mull. An all-day whale

WALKING ON MULL

More information on the following walks can be obtained from the TICs in Oban (p270), Craignure and Tobermory.

Ben More

The highest peak on the island, Ben More (966m) has spectacular views across to the surrounding islands when the weather is clear. If it's overcast or misty, wait until the next day because Mull's weather is notoriously changeable. A trail leads up the mountain from Loch na Keal, by the bridge on the B8035 over the Abhainn na h-Uamha – the river 8 miles (13km) southwest of Salen. Return the same way or continue down the narrow ridge to the eastern top, A'Chioch, then descend to the road via Gleann na Beinn Fhada. The glen can be rather wet and there's not much of a path. Allow five to six hours for the round trip.

Carsaig Arches

One of the best walks on Mull is along the coast west of Carsaig Bay to the Carsaig Arches at Malcolm's Point. There's a good path below the cliffs all the way from Carsaig, but it becomes a bit rough and exposed near the arches – the route climbs and then traverses a very steep slope above a vertical drop into the sea. You'll see spectacular rock formations on the way, including one that looks like a giant slice of Christmas cake. The arches are two sea-cut rock formations. One, nicknamed the 'keyhole', is a freestanding rock stack; the other, the 'tunnel', is a huge natural arch. The western entrance is hung with curtains of columnar basalt – an impressive place. Allow three to four hours' walking time plus at least an hour at the arches.

Burg

At the tip of the remote Ardmeanach peninsula there is a remarkable, 50-million-year-old **fossil tree** preserved in the basalt lava flows of the cliffs, reached via a strenuous 7-mile (11km) hike. A 4WD track leads from the car park at Tiroran to a house at Burg; the last 2.5 miles to the tree is on a very rough coastal path. About 500m before the tree, a metal ladder allows you to climb down to the foreshore, which is only accessible at low tide– check tide times at Tobermory TIC before setting off. Allow six to seven hours for the round trip.

Other Walks

In the east there's good walking on **Beinn Talaidh** (762m) and **Dùn da Ghaoithe** (766m). Beinn Talaidh is easiest to reach by its southern ridge; look out for the aircraft wreckage near the top. Allow about four hours for the return trip. Dùn da Ghaoithe can be ascended from various places including Scallastle, about one mile north of Craignure. Allow around five hours.

watch (£45, or £48 in July and August) gives up to six hours at sea (not recommended for kids under 12). The 4½-hour family whale-watch is geared more to young children and costs £32/28 (£35/30 in July and August).

Duncan's Island Tours (☎ 302194; 50 Main St; Tobermory) offers day trips by minibus to Iona, and to Ulva and Calgary beach (£20 per person).

Festivals & Events

The annual **Mull Music Festival** (☎ 01688-302383) takes place on the last weekend of April and includes Celtic music and Irish folk music. The **Mull Highland Games & Dance** (☎ 01688-302001) is a one-day event in late July.

The **Tour of Mull Rally** (☎ 01688-302133), part of the Scottish Championship, is in early October. More than 100 cars are involved and public roads are closed for parts of the weekend.

Getting There & Away

There are daily CalMac ferries from Oban to Craignure (passenger/car £3.75/33.50, 40 minutes, every two hours). There's another car ferry link between Fishnish, on the east coast of Mull, and Lochaline (£2.35/10.15, 15 minutes, at least hourly).

A third **CalMac car ferry** (☎ 01688-302017) links Tobermory to Kilchoan on the Ardnamurchan peninsula (£3.60/19, 35 minutes, seven a day Monday to Saturday); from June to August there are also five sailings on Sunday.

Getting Around

Public transport on Mull is limited. **Bowman's Coaches** (☎ 01680-812313) is the main operator, connecting the ferry ports and main villages. The routes useful for visitors are Craignure–Tobermory (£6 return, one hour, six daily Monday to Saturday, two Sunday) and Craignure–Fionnphort (£9 return, 1¼ hours, five daily Monday to Saturday, one Sunday).

There's also a Royal Mail postbus from Salen to Burg (Kilninian) via Ulva Ferry. **RN Carmichael** (☎ 01688-302220) runs buses from Tobermory to Dervaig (five a day) and Calgary (four a day); there are only two buses Saturday and none Sunday.

There's a **taxi** (☎ 01688-302204) service based in Tobermory.

You can hire bikes from a number of places for around £10 to £13 per day. In Salen, try **On Yer Bike** (☎ 01680-300501); it also has an outlet in the craft shop near the ferry terminal in Craignure. In Tobermory, try **Brown's Hardware Shop** (☎ 01688-302020; Main St) or Mrs MacLean at **Tom-A-Mhuillin** (☎ 01688-302164; Salen Rd).

ISLE OF IONA
☎ 01681 / pop 130

From the moment you step off the ferry from Fionnphort you will notice the hushed, reverent atmosphere that pervades this sacred island. If the hordes of day-trippers piling off the tour buses in summer make it hard to appreciate, the solution is to spend a night here. Once the crowds have gone you can wander round the ancient graveyard where 48 of Scotland's early kings, including Macbeth, are buried, attend an evening service, or walk to the top of the hill north of the abbey and gaze south towards Ireland, as St Columba must have done.

The spiritual heart of the island is **Iona Abbey** (☎ 700512; adult/child £2.80/1.20; ⊗ 9.30am-6.30pm Apr-Sep, 9.30am-4.30pm Nov-Mar), which

houses some of Britain's most outstanding stone carvings. A replica of the beautiful **St John's Cross** stands just outside St Columba's shrine – the massive 8th-century original is in the abbey's **Infirmary Museum** along with many other fine examples of early Christian and medieval carved stones. The spectacular nave, dominated by high stone arches and wooden beams, is a highlight of the abbey – sitting outside is a bench with 'Be Still' carved into the woodwork, which sums up the mood nicely.

St Columba sailed from Ireland and landed on Iona in 563 before setting out to bring Christianity to Scotland. He established a monastery on the island and it was here that the Book of Kells – the prize attraction of Dublin's Trinity College – is believed to have been transcribed. It was taken to Kells in Ireland when Viking raids drove the monks from Iona.

The monks returned and the monastery prospered until its destruction during the Reformation. The ruins were given to the Church of Scotland in 1899, and by 1910 a group of enthusiasts called the Iona Community had reconstructed the abbey. It's still a flourishing spiritual group holding regular courses and retreats.

The short walk from the ferry pier to the abbey leads through a ruined 13th-century **nunnery** with fine cloistered gardens.

The nearby **Iona Heritage Centre** (☎ 700576; admission £1.50; ⊗ 10.30am-4.30pm Mon-Sat Apr-Oct) covers the history of Iona, crofting and lighthouses; the centre's coffee shop serves delicious home baking.

SLEEPING & EATING

Iona Hostel (☎ 700781; info@ionahostel.co.uk; dm £12.50) This hotel has stunning views out to Staffa and the Treshnish Isles and, on a clear day, as far as the Isle of Skye. Rooms are clean and functional, and the well-equipped lounge/kitchen area has an open fire. It's at the far northern end of the island – to get there, turn right off the ferry and follow the road for 1½ miles to the end.

Argyll Hotel (☎ 700334; reception@argyllhoteliona .co.uk; s £48, d £60-104; ⊗ Apr-Oct; ✗) The quaint Argyll offers the island's most luxurious accommodation, complete with roaring log fire.

Shore Cottage (☎ 700744; enquiries@shorecottage .co.uk; r per person £23-37; ✗) Travellers have recommended this attractive modern house with three rooms (all with bathroom). Breakfast is served in a conservatory with great views across the sea to Mull.

Other recommendations:

Bishop's House (☎ 700800; r per person £23-31; ☺ Mar-Nov) For good B&B try this place near the abbey.

Iona Cottage (☎ 700579; r per person £22) Directly in front of the ferry landing.

GETTING THERE & AROUND

The ferry from Fionnphort to Iona (£3.50 return, five minutes, hourly) runs daily. There are also various interesting day trips available from Oban (p272) and Mull (p280) to Iona .

You can hire bikes from the craft shop above the pier.

ISLE OF COLL

☎ 01879 / pop 172

This lovely island, about 12 miles (19km) long and 3 miles (5km) wide, has a good sunshine record but can be very windy. On the west coast the wind has formed sand dunes up to 30m high. Crossapol beach is one of the best spots on Coll.

At **Totronald RSPB reserve** (☎ 230301), on the west coast of the island, there's a free information centre (open year-round); listen for the corncrakes on the machair. Two nearby castles, both known as **Breachachadh Castle**, were built by the Macleans. There was a clan battle here in 1593.

Coll Stores and the Corner Shop sell groceries; both are in the island's only village, **Arinagour**, where the ferry docks. There's also a post office, and Coll Ceramics – a pottery with art exhibitions.

Garden House Camping & Caravan Site (☎ 230374; Uig; sites per person £5; ☺ May-Sep) is a basic campground with toilets and cold water only, 4½ miles (7km) south of Arinagour. Dogs are not allowed.

There are several places offering B&B, including **Taigh Solas** (☎ 230333; taigh .solas@virgin.net; r £20-24; ✗) in Arinagour, and **Achamore** (☎ 230430; jimachamore@hotmail.com; r per person £20-24; ✗), 1½ miles north of Arinagour.

Coll Hotel (☎ 230334; collhotel@aol.com; Arinagour; s £30-50, d £50-90; mains lunch £5-9, dinner £8-15; ✗ P), the island's only hotel, has a really good restaurant serving lobster and scallops, the local specialities.

Getting There & Around

A CalMac car ferry runs from Oban to Coll (passenger/car £12/70, 2¾ hours, one daily) and Tiree (£12/70, 3¾ hours). You can sail between Coll and Tiree (£3.10/17.85, one hour) on the same ferry.

Mountain bikes can be hired in Arinagour from **Tammie Hedderwick** (☎ 230382; £8 per day) and from the B&Bs listed earlier.

ISLE OF TIREE

☎ 01879 / pop 765

Low-lying Tiree (pronounced tye-*ree*; from the Gaelic *tiriodh,* meaning 'land of corn') is a fertile sward of lush, green machair liberally sprinkled with yellow buttercups, much of it so flat that, from a distance, the houses seem to rise straight out of the sea. It is one of the sunniest places in Scotland, but also one of the windiest – cyclists soon find that although the island is flat, heading west usually feels like going uphill. One major benefit – the constant breeze keeps Tiree almost midge-free.

The surf-lashed coastline is scalloped with broad, sweeping beaches of white sand, hugely popular with windsurfers and kite-surfers. Most visitors, however, come for the bird-watching, beachcombing and lonely coastal walks.

The ferry arrives at **Gott Bay**, towards the eastern end of the island. The airport is right in the centre. There's a bank (without ATM), post office and Co-op supermarket in **Scarinish**, the main village, a half-mile south of the ferry pier. An Iodhlann (see below) has free Internet access.

Sights

In the 19th century Tiree's population was 4500, most of whom emigrated to Canada, the USA, Australia and New Zealand. **An Iodhlann** (☎ 220793; www.tireearchive.com; Scarinish; admission free; ☺ 10.30am-3.30pm Mon-Fri) is a historical and genealogical library and archive, where many of the estimated 38,000 descendants of Tiree emigrants come to trace their ancestry. The centre stages a **summer exhibition** (adult/child £3/free; ☺ 2-5pm Jul-Sep) on island life and history.

At **Sandaig**, in the far west of the island, is the **Island Life Museum** (admission free; ☺ 2-4pm Mon-Fri Jun-Sep), a row of picturesque thatched cottages each restored as a 19th-century crofter's home.

The picturesque harbour and hamlet of **Hynish**, near the southern tip of the island, was built in the 19th century to house workers and supplies for the construction of the Skerryvore Lighthouse, which stands 10 miles (16km) offshore. **Skerryvore Lighthouse Museum** (admission free; daylight hrs) occupies the signal tower above the harbour, which was once used to communicate by semaphore with the lighthouse building site.

For the best view on the island, walk up nearby **Ben Hynish** (141m) which is capped by a conspicuous radar station known locally as the Golf Ball.

Activities

Reliable wind and big waves have made Tiree one of Scotland's top windsurfing venues – the annual Tiree Wave Classic competition is held here in October. **Wild Diamond Windsurfing** (220399; www.tireewindsurfing.com), based at Loch Bhasapoll in the northwest of the island, runs courses and rents equipment. A two-hour 'taster' session costs £12, and a beginners course (five hours over two days) costs £40 including equipment hire.

You can also try **sand-yachting** (220317; one hour £15) on Gott Bay beach at low tide.

Sleeping & Eating

Millhouse Hostel (220435; tireemillhouse@yahoo.co.uk; Cornaigmore; dm £12, tw £30) Housed in a converted barn next to an old water mill, this comfortable hostel is 5 miles (8km) from the ferry pier.

Kirkapol (220729; www.kirkapoltiree.co.uk; Gott Bay; s/d with bathroom £28/52;) Six homey rooms in a converted 19th-century church overlooking the island's biggest beach.

Glassary (220684; Sandaig; s/d £35/64;) Tiree's poshest restaurant, the Glassary is at the other end of the island; the tables in the conservatory have views of the Atlantic. There are also six comfortable bedrooms.

Scarinish Hotel (220308; Scarinish; s/d £30/50;) A classic Scottish hostelry of the old school, with creaky floorboards, gurgling plumbing and a bar full of half-cut locals. But it *is* convenient for the ferry.

Café Tyrii (snacks £2.50-3.50; 11am-4.30pm Mon-Sat) Two miles (3km) west of Scarinish in Baugh, this friendly tearoom serves delicious home-made soups, sandwiches, cakes and scones; for those suffering from latte deprivation, it even has a real espresso machine.

There are no official camping grounds on Tiree but it's possible to camp for free almost anywhere on the island, provided that you ask permission from the farmer or crofter who owns the land.

Getting There & Around

British Airways flies from Glasgow to **Tiree airport** (220309) daily from Monday to Saturday (around £110 return). Ferry connections and fares are the same as for Coll (p283).

You can rent bicycles from **Neil MacLean** (220428; Kenovay) and cars from **Tiree Motor Company** (220469; Crossapol). For a taxi, call **Island Cabs** (220344).

NORTH ARGYLL

LOCH AWE

Loch Awe is one of Scotland's most beautiful lochs, with rolling forested hills around its southern end and spectacular mountains in the north. The loch lies between Oban and Inveraray and is the longest in Scotland – about 24 miles (39km) long – but less than a mile wide for most of its length.

At its northern end, the loch widens out and there are several islands you can visit: **Inishail** has a ruined church and **Fraoch Eilean** has a broken-down castle. For details of boat hire, contact **Oban TIC** (01631-563122; info@oban.org.uk).

Also at the northern end of Loch Awe are the scenic ruins of **Kilchurn Castle** (admission free; closed winter), built in 1440 and one of Scotland's finest. It's accessible by foot along a rough track from the A85. Otherwise **Loch Awe Steam Packet Company** (01866-833333; adult/child £4/3; 10am-5pm Apr-Nov) sails hourly steamboats from Lochawe village pier to the castle, allowing 40 minutes at the castle.

Nearby **Dalmally**, popular with anglers, has a train station, post office, shop and hotel.

At its southern end, Loch Awe escapes to the sea through the narrow **Pass of Brander**, where Robert the Bruce defeated the MacDougalls in battle in 1309. In the pass, by the A85, you can visit **Cruachan power**

station (☎ 01866-822618; Lochawe; adult/child £3.50/
1.50; ⏰ 9.30am-5pm Easter-July & Sep-early Nov, 9.30am-
6pm Aug). Electric buses take you more than
half a mile inside Ben Cruachan allowing
you to see the pump-storage hydro-electric
scheme in action.

Climbing Bren Cruachan

You can climb **Ben Cruachan** (1126m) from
the Cruachan power station (above). A
complete traverse of the ridge, mostly a
walk with some easy scrambling, can take
as long as nine hours. The quickest route –
about six hours – follows the path from the
power station steeply uphill to the dam,
then left around the reservoir to its head.
From there, go westwards up to the pass
below Meall Cuanail, then northwards up a
steep boulder field to the summit (return by
the same route). This is no mere ramble –
you must be well equipped with hiking
boots, waterproofs, food and water.

Getting There & Away

Citylink buses from Glasgow to Oban go
via Dalmally, Lochawe village and Cruachan
power station. Trains from Glasgow to Oban
stop at Dalmally and Lochawe village.

GLEN ORCHY

The A85 goes east from Dalmally, up bleak
Glen Lochy to Tyndrum, but a more scenic
route follows beautiful **Glen Orchy** to Bridge
of Orchy and **Loch Tulla**. The A82 Glasgow
to Fort William road passes Loch Tulla,
but the western side is quiet and you'll
see remnants of the ancient **Caledonian pine
forest** here.

Bridge of Orchy Hotel (☎ 01838-400208; Bridge
of Orchy; s/d £50/85; dm £10; ☒ Ⓟ) is a convivial
country hotel in the heart of the mountains.
It also has a large bunkhouse (without a
kitchen); breakfast is available for £5.50.

Getting There & Away

Bridge of Orchy is served by the Glasgow
to Fort William Citylink bus. Trains from
Glasgow to Fort William stop at Bridge of
Orchy.

LOCH ETIVE

Loch Etive is one of Scotland's most
beautiful sea lochs, extending for 17 miles
(27km) from Connel to Kinlochetive and
flanked by some impressive mountains,

including Ben Cruachan (above) and Ben
Starav (1078m).

Connel

☎ 01631 / pop 500

At Connel Bridge, 5 miles (8km) north
of Oban, Loch Etive is joined to the sea
by a narrow channel partly blocked by
an underwater rock ledge. When the tide
falls – as it does twice a day – millions of
tons of water pour out of the loch and over
the ledge, creating spectacular white-water
rapids known as the **Falls of Lora**.

Dunstaffnage Castle (☎ 01631-562465; Dunstaffnage;
adult/child £2.20/75p; ⏰ 9.30am-6.30pm Apr-Sep; 9.30am-
4pm Mon-Wed & Sat, 9.30am-noon Thu, 2-4pm Sun Oct-Mar)
is 2 miles (3km) west of Connel and easily
reached by bus from Oban. It was built
around 1260 on a rock plinth, and captured
by Robert the Bruce during the Wars of
Independence in 1309. The nearby ruins of
the 13th-century **chapel** are slightly creepy –
perhaps the skulls carved in the stonework
are watching you.

The friendly **Dunstaffnage Arms Hotel**
(☎ 01631-710666; Connel; mains £6-16) does home-
made bar meals and specialises in local
seafood.

Buses between Oban and Fort William
or Glasgow, and trains between Oban and
Glasgow, all stop in Connel.

Taynuilt

☎ 01866 / pop 700

One of the region's most unusual historical
sights is **Bonawe Iron Furnace** (☎ 822432;
adult/child £2.80/1; ⏰ 9.30am-6.30pm daily Apr-Sep;
9.30am-4pm Mon-Wed & Sat, 9.30am-noon Thu & 2-4pm
Sun Oct-Mar), near Taynuilt. Dating from 1753,
it was built by a Cumbrian iron-smelting
company from the English Lake District
because of the abundance of birchwood in
the area. The wood was made into charcoal,
which was needed for smelting the iron. To
produce Bonawe's annual output of 700 tons
of pig iron took 10,000 acres of woodland.
A fascinating self-guided tour leads you
around the various parts of the site.

Loch Etive Cruises (☎ 822430), at the end
of the road that passes the entrance to
Bonawe, runs cruises to the head of Loch
Etive and back between one and three times
a day from April to October. There are 1½-
hour and three-hour cruises (£5 and £8
respectively); you may spot eagles, otters,

seals and deer, and at the head of the loch you can see the famous Etive slabs – usually dotted with rock climbers.

Taynuilt is 6 miles (10km) east of Connel. Citylink buses and trains to and from Oban stop here.

APPIN & AROUND

The **Scottish Sea Life & Marine Sanctuary** (☎ 720386; Barcaldine; adult/child £6.95/4.95; ⏰ 10am-6pm Apr-Sep), 8 miles (13km) north of Oban on the shores of Loch Creran, provides a haven for orphaned seal pups. As well as the seal pools there are tanks with herring, rays and flatfish, touch pools and displays on Scotland's marine environment.

Glen Creran, at the head of Loch Creran, is a pleasant glen with several walks. North of Loch Creran, you come to **Appin**, with the villages of Portnacroish and Port Appin. At Portnacroish, there's a wonderful view of **Castle Stalker** perched on a tiny offshore island – Monty Python buffs will recognise it as the castle that appears in the final scenes of the film *Monty Python and the Holy Grail.* Port Appin, a couple of miles off the main road, is a pleasant spot with a passenger ferry to the island of Lismore (see below).

The delightfully quaint **Pierhouse Hotel** (☎ 01631-730302; pierhouse@btinternet.com; Port Appin; s £45-60, d £65-85; mains £12-18; ✗ P) sits on the waterfront above the ferry pier for Lismore. Two of the 10 rooms have four-poster beds, and there is an atmospheric restaurant serving excellent seafood and game.

Citylink buses between Oban and Fort William stop at the marine sanctuary and Appin.

LISMORE

☎ 01631 / pop 146

The first thing you notice about the island of Lismore is how green it is – there's no heather here. Much of it consists of limestone, which makes for very fertile soil; the Gaelic name Lios Mor means 'Great Garden'.

Lismore is long and narrow – 10 miles (16km) long and just over a mile wide – with

a road running almost its full length. There are a few scattered communities and two ferry terminals, one halfway up the east coast at **Achnacroish**, the other at **Point**, the island's northernmost tip. **Clachan**, a scattering of houses midway between Achnacroish and Point, is the nearest the island comes to a village. There's a shop and post office between Achnacroish and Clachan; its advertised 'special offer' – one free piece of gossip with every £20 spent.

Lismore is a place to relax and enjoy the scenery. However, if you're feeling energetic, the best walk on the island runs from Kilcheran, at the southern end of the road, up to the top of **Barr Mor** (127m), then southwest along the ridge to the southern tip of the island, returning to Kilcheran by a 4WD track. It's about 6 miles (10km) for the round trip. Allow three to four hours to fully appreciate the fantastic views of the surrounding mountains.

The ruins of 13th-century **Castle Coeffin** have a lovely setting on the west coast, half a mile from Clachan. **Tirefour Broch**, where the double walls reach 3m in height, is directly opposite on the east coast.

There is no short-stay accommodation on Lismore. However, there are several self-catering options advertised on the Web (www.isleoflismore.com).

Getting There & Around

A CalMac car ferry runs from Oban to Achnacroish, with two to five sailings Monday to Saturday (passenger/car £2.65/£22.10, 50 minutes).

Argyll & Bute Council (☎ 01546-604695) operates the passenger-only ferry from Port Appin to Point (£1, 10 minutes, hourly, daily). Bicycles are carried for free.

A Royal Mail postbus runs the length of the island once a day Monday to Saturday, calling at Point at 12.40pm.

Lismore is great for cycling; contact **Peter McDougall** (☎ 760213) to hire bikes from the Point ferry terminal (£10/6 per day/half-day).

Central & Western Highlands

CONTENTS

CENTRAL & WESTERN HIGHLANDS

Seen from the summit of Cairngorm at sunset, the serried ridges of the central and western Highlands recede towards the horizon. Except for a small area of coastal plain around Inverness, this region is entirely mountainous, stretching from the high, subarctic plateau of the Cairngorms and the great, hump-backed hills of the Monadhliath to the more rugged, rocky peaks of Glen Coe, the Mamores and Ardgour. And, hunching its great, cliff-bound shoulders above the mass of lesser hills, is Ben Nevis (1344m), the highest summit in the British Isles.

Not surprisingly, this part of the country is an adventure playground for outdoor sports enthusiasts. Aviemore, Glen Coe and Fort William draw hordes of hill walkers and rock climbers in summer, and skiers, snowboarders and ice climbers in winter.

Inverness, the Highland capital, provides a spot of urban sophistication before you strike south through the forests and lochs of the Great Glen, stopping perhaps to check Loch Ness for any monsterish disturbances.

From Fort William, the aptly named Road to the Isles skirts one of Europe's last great wilderness areas before reaching the gorgeous beaches of Arisaig and Morar. Here the beguiling silhouettes of the Small Isles draw your eye to the west, where the Hebrides lie beckoning on the horizon.

HIGHLIGHTS

- Breathing in the scent of Scots pines as you wander through the Caledonian forest at **Rothiemurchus** (p302) in Cairngorms National Park

- Admiring the magnificent mountain scenery of spectacular **Glen Coe** (p308)

- Snowboarding off the back of **Aonach Mor** (p315) at Nevis Range on a perfect winter's day

- Getting away from it all in the remote **Knoydart Peninsula** (p320)

- Thundering across Glenfinnan Viaduct on the **Jacobite steam train** (p312), with Loch Shiel bathed in autumn sunshine

- Reaching the summit of **Ben Nevis** (p316), Britain's highest peak

- Watching the sun set behind the Small Isles from one of **Arisaig's** (p319) silver-sand beaches

- Marvelling at the Edwardian extravagance of **Kinloch Castle** (p321) on the Isle of Rum

- Seeing the whole west coast and islands laid out before you from the summit of the **Sgurr of Eigg** (p322)

- Hiking among the hills, lochs and forests of beautiful **Glen Affric** (p296)

■ POPULATION: 140,000	■ AREA: 9660 SQ KM

CENTRAL & WESTERN HIGHLANDS

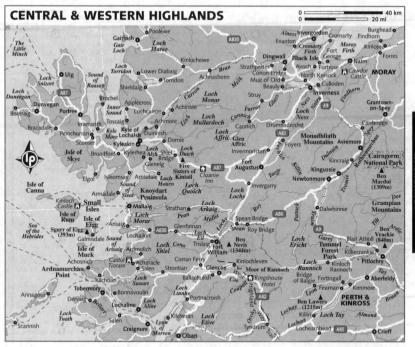

GETTING AROUND

Scottish Citylink (☎ 0870 550 5050) buses run from Perth to Inverness and from Glasgow to Fort William, and also link Inverness to Fort William along the Great Glen. **Rapsons/Highland Country** (☎ 01463-71055; www .rapsons.com) is the main regional bus company, with offices in Aviemore, Inverness and Fort William. Their Cairngorm Day Rover ticket (adult/child £5/3) gives one day's unlimited travel on Rapsons buses in the region covering Newtonmore, Aviemore and Grantown-on-Spey.

Two railway lines serve the region: the Perth–Aviemore–Inverness line in the east, and the Glasgow–Fort William–Mallaig line in the west.

INVERNESS & THE GREAT GLEN

Inverness is the capital of the Highlands and one of the fastest growing towns in Britain. It's a major transport hub and jumping-off point for exploring the central, western and northern Highlands, the Moray Firth coast and the Great Glen.

The Great Glen is a geological fault running in an arrow-straight line across Scotland from Fort William to Inverness. The glaciers of the last Ice Age eroded a deep trough along the fault line that is now largely filled by a series of lochs – Linnhe, Lochy, Oich and Ness. The glen has always been an important communication route – General George Wade built a military road along the southern side of Loch Ness in the early 18th century, and in 1822 the various lochs were joined together by the Caledonian Canal to create a cross-country waterway. The modern A82 road along the glen was completed in 1933 – a date that coincides neatly with the first modern sightings of the Loch Ness Monster (see the Strange Spectacle on Loch Ness boxed text, p299).

INVERNESS

☎ 01463 / pop 44,100

Inverness, the main city and shopping centre of the Highlands, has a great location

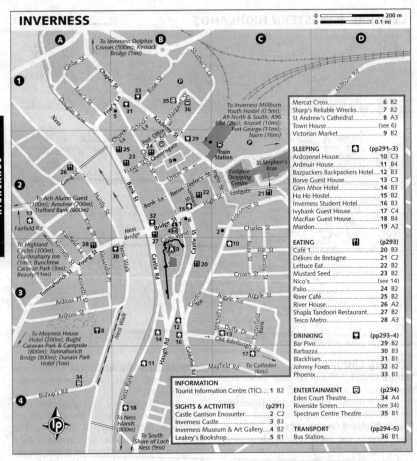

INVERNESS

Mercat Cross.................................6	B2
Sharp's Reliable Wrecks...............7	B2
St Andrew's Cathedral..................8	A3
Town House................................(see 6)	
Victorian Market..........................9	B2
SLEEPING (pp291–3)	
Ardconnel House..........................10	C3
Ardmuir House.............................11	B4
Bazpackers Backpackers Hotel....12	B3
Borve Guest House.......................13	C3
Glen Mhor Hotel..........................14	B2
Ho Ho Hostel...............................15	B2
Inverness Student Hotel...............16	B3
Ivybank Guest House...................17	C4
MacRae Guest House...................18	B4
Mardon......................................19	A2
EATING (p293)	
Café 1...20	B3
Délices de Bretagne....................21	C2
Lettuce Eat.................................22	B2
Mustard Seed.............................23	B2
Nico's...(see 14)	
Palio...24	B2
River Café...................................25	B2
River House................................26	A2
Shapla Tandoori Restaurant.........27	B2
Tesco Metro................................28	B3
DRINKING (pp293–4)	
Bar Pivo.....................................29	B2
Barbazza....................................30	B3
Blackfriars..................................31	B1
Johnny Foxes.............................32	B1
Phoenix......................................33	B1
ENTERTAINMENT (p294)	
Eden Court Theatre.....................34	A4
Riverside Screen.........................(see 34)	
Spectrum Centre Theatre.............35	B1
TRANSPORT (pp294–5)	
Bus Station.................................36	B1

INFORMATION
Tourist Information Centre (TIC)....1 B2

SIGHTS & ACTIVITIES (p291)
Castle Garrison Encounter.............2 C2
Inverness Castle...........................3 B3
Inverness Museum & Art Gallery....4 B2
Leakey's Bookshop.......................5 B1

---

astride the River Ness at the northern end of the Great Glen. In summer it overflows with visitors intent on monster-hunting at nearby Loch Ness, but it's worth a visit in its own right for a stroll along the picturesque River Ness and a cruise on the Moray Firth in search of its famous bottlenose dolphins.

The town was probably founded by King David in the 12th century but thanks to its often violent history, few buildings of real age or historical significance have survived – much of the older part of town dates from the period following the completion of the Caledonian Canal in 1822.

Orientation

The broad and shallow River Ness, which flows a short 6 miles (10km) from Loch Ness into the Moray Firth, runs through the heart of town. The town centre lies on the eastern bank, at the foot of the castle hill, with the bus and train stations next to each other a little to the north.

Information

Leakey's (☎ 239947; Greyfriars Hall, Church St; ☑ 10am-5.30pm Mon-Sat) An excellent second-hand bookshop with a good café.

Main post office (☑ 9am-5.30pm Mon-Fri, 9am-6pm Sat) On Queensgate.

New City Laundrette (☎ 242507; 17 Young St; ☑ 8am-8pm Mon-Fri, 8am-6pm Sat, 10am-4pm Sun) Charges £3 a load, £1.40 to dry, and has Internet access for £1 per 20 minutes.

TIC (☎ 234353; inverness@host.co.uk; Castle Wynd; ☺ 9am-8pm Mon-Sat, 9.30am-5pm Sun) Beside Inverness Museum, just off Bridge St. Contains a bureau de change, CalMac ferry office and accommodation booking service; it also sells tickets for tours and cruises. It has Internet access for £2 per 20 minutes.

Sights

The hill above the town centre is topped by the picturesque Baronial turrets of **Inverness Castle**, a pink sandstone confection dating from 1847 that replaced a medieval castle blown up by the Jacobites in 1746. It serves today as the Sheriff's Court. Between the castle and the TIC is **Inverness Museum & Art Gallery** (☎ 237114; Castle Wynd; admission free; ☺ 9am-5pm Mon-Sat) with wildlife dioramas, geological displays, period rooms with historic weapons, Pictish stones and a missable art gallery.

But save the museum for a rainy day – the main attraction in Inverness is a leisurely stroll along the river to the **Ness Islands**. Planted with mature Scots pine, fir, beech and sycamore, and linked to the river banks and each other by elegant Victorian footbridges, the islands make an appealing picnic spot. They're a 20-minute walk south of the castle – head upstream on either side of the river, and return on the opposite bank. On the way you'll pass the red sandstone towers of **St Andrew's Cathedral**, dating from 1869, and the modern **Eden Court Theatre**, which hosts regular art exhibits, both on the west bank.

Castle Garrison Encounter (☎ 243363; 3 Connel Court; Ardconnel St; adult/child £4/3; ☺ 10am-5pm Mon-Sat, 2.30-4.30pm Sun Mar-Oct) is another rainy-day alternative, where actors playing characters from the Hanoverian garrison depict life during the Jacobite uprising of 1745-46. Or you could opt for a spot of retail therapy in the **Victorian Market**, a shopping mall that dates from the 1890s and has rather more charm than its modern equivalents.

Tours

WALKING TOURS

Guided walking tours of the town (adult/child £4/2) leave from outside the TIC and last 1¼ hours; check with the TIC for details.

Davy the Ghost Tours (mobile ☎ 07730-831069; adult/child £6/4; ☺ departs 7pm) offers 1¼-hour tours led by an '18th-century ghost' in

period costume. Expect tales of the town's horrific past, including ghosts, witches, murders and hangings. Tours depart from the blackboard outside the TIC.

BUS & TAXI TOURS

From late May to September, **City Sightseeing** (☎ 224000; adult/child £5/2.50; ☺ every 30 min, 10am-4.30pm) runs 45-minute, hop-on-hop-off bus tours around Inverness, departing from Bridge St. There's also a longer tour (1½ hours, five a day) out to Culloden (p295), Cawdor Castle (p296) and Fort George (p295) for £8.50/3.50. Tickets remain valid all day.

From June to early September, **John O'Groats Ferries** (☎ 01955-611353; adult/child £45/22.50; ☺ departs 7.30am) runs daily tours (lasting 13½ hours) by bus and passenger ferry from Inverness to Orkney.

Tartan Taxis (☎ 233033) has a wide range of day tours to places as far afield as Skye and the Cairngorms. Fares per car (with up to four people) include £42 for a three-hour trip to Fort George and Culloden, and £60 for a four-hour circular tour around Loch Ness.

CRUISES

The **Jacobite Queen** (☎ 233999; Glenurquhart Rd; adult/child £12/10; ☺ 10am & 2pm) departs from Tomnahurich Bridge for a 3½-hour cruise on Loch Ness; you can buy tickets at the TIC and catch a free minibus to the boat. A two-hour cruise to Urquhart Castle (p298) including admission fee and time ashore costs £10/7.50.

Inverness Dolphin Cruises (☎ 717900; Shore St Quay, Shore St; adult/child £10/7.50; ☺ every 90 min, 10.30am-6pm Mar-Oct) offers 1½-hour wildlife cruises to look for dolphins, seals and bird life. Sightings aren't guaranteed but the commentaries are excellent, and on a fine day it's good just being out on the water. Follow the signs to Shore St Quay from the far end of Chapel St or catch the free shuttle bus that leaves from the TIC 15 minutes before sailings.

Sleeping

Inverness has a good range of backpacker accommodation, and there are lots of guesthouses and B&Bs along Old Edinburgh Rd and Ardconnel St on the east side of the river, and on Kenneth St and Fairfield Rd on the west bank; all are within 10 minutes' walk of the centre.

The town fills up quickly in July and August, so either pre-book your accommodation or get an early start looking for somewhere to stay.

BUDGET

Inverness Millburn Youth Hostel (SYHA; ☎ 0870 004 1127; Victoria Dr; dm £11.50-13.50; ✗ P) Inverness' modern 166-bed hostel is 10 minutes' walk northeast of the town centre. With its comfy beds and flashy stainless steel kitchen, some reckon it's the best hostel in the country. Booking is essential, especially at Easter and in July and August.

Bazpackers Backpackers Hotel (☎ 717663; bazmail@btopenworld.com; 4 Culduthel Rd; dm £9-11; tw £24-28; 🖳 ✗) This may be Inverness's smallest hostel (30 beds), but it's the most popular with LP readers – a friendly, quiet place with a wood-burning stove, a small garden and great views, though the dorms can be a bit cramped.

Inverness Student Hotel (☎ 236556; inverness@ scotlands-top-hostels.com; 8 Culduthel Rd; dm £11-12; 🖳) More of a grungy, party place than nearby Bazpackers, but with comfy beds and views across the River Ness. It's a 10-minute walk from the train station, just past the castle.

Ho Ho Hostel (☎ 221225; hohohostel@hotmail.com; 23a High St; dm £9, tw £24; 🖳) Set in a former gentlemen's club in a fine old Victorian building, this is another lively, party-crowd hostel. The entrance is in an alley between High St and Baron Taylor's St, only a few minutes' walk from the train station.

Bught Caravan Park & Campsite (☎ 236920; Bught Lane; tent £4.50-8, car £2, campervan £11.70; 🌣 Apr-Sep) A mile southwest of the town centre near Tomnahurich Bridge, this is the nearest camping ground.

Bunchrew Caravan Park (☎ 237802; tent £4.50-7.50, campervan £10; 🌣 Mar-Nov) This enjoys a much more attractive setting among trees on the shore of the Beauly Firth, 3 miles (5km) west of the city centre on the A862 to Beauly.

MID-RANGE

Ardconnel House (☎ 240455; racowe@lineone.net; 21 Ardconnel St; s £25-40; d £48-56; ✗) The six-room Ardconnel is a readers' favourite, with comfortable rooms with bathroom, and owners who have the knack of being welcoming and helpful without being in your face all the time.

Ivybank Guest House (☎ 232796; ivybank@talk21 .com; 28 Old Edinburgh Rd; s £25-60; d £50-64; ✗ P) Ivybank is a splendid detached villa – a small mansion, really – with bags of character. Set in a large, wooded garden, it's been lovingly restored by its owner. A magnificent mahogany staircase leads to luxurious bedrooms, one with a four-poster bed, another with a bathroom in a turret.

Ach Aluinn (☎ 230127; info@achaluinn.com; 27 Fairfield Rd; s £25-35; d £45-60; ✗ P) This large, detached house is bright and homely, and offers all you might want from a guesthouse – private bathroom, TV, reading lights, comfy beds with two pillows each, and an excellent breakfast.

MacRae Guest House (☎ 243658; joycemacrae@ hotmail.com; 24 Ness Bank; s £35; d £44-52; ✗ P) Travellers have recommended this pretty, flower-bedecked, Victorian house on the eastern bank of the river. One room is wheelchair-accessible, and vegetarian breakfasts are available.

Trafford Bank (☎ 241414; www.traffordbankguest house.co.uk; 96 Fairfield Rd; s £45-55; d £55-80; ✗ P) Lots of word-of-mouth rave reviews for Trafford Bank, an elegant Victorian villa that was once home to a bishop, just a mitre-toss from the Caledonian Canal and only 10 minutes' walk from the town centre. The luxurious rooms include fresh flowers and fruit, bathrobes and fluffy towels – ask for the Tartan Room, with its wrought-iron king-size bed and Victorian roll-top bath.

Other recommendations:

Amulree (☎ 224822; 40 Fairfield Rd; s £19-25, d £40-50; ✗) Comfortable, four-bedroom Victorian B&B less than 10 minute's walk west of the centre.

Ardmuir House Hotel (☎ 231151; hotel@ardmuir .com; 16 Ness Bank; s/d £36/60; ✗) Small, family-run Georgian hotel with a pleasant, riverside setting.

Borve Guest House (☎ 234728; wilma@theborve .com; 9 Old Edinburgh Rd; s £25-37, d £46-64; ✗) Attractive Victorian house with sunny, south-facing rooms. A five-minute walk south of the city centre.

Mardon (☎ 231005; mardon37kst@aol.com; 37 Kenneth St; s £15-21, d £32-44) Friendly B&B with six cosy rooms (all with bathroom) just five minutes west of the centre.

Moyness House Hotel (☎ 233836; stay@moyness .co.uk; 6 Bruce Gardens; r per person £33-37; ✗ P)

Elegant Victorian villa with a beautiful garden and peaceful setting 10 minutes' walk southwest of the town centre.

TOP END

Glen Mhor Hotel (☎ 234308; www.glen-mhor.com; 9-12 Ness Bank; s £59-75, d £88-118; ☒ P) The large and elegant Glen Mhor is spread across four separate riverside properties, all with luxurious bedrooms and views across the Ness to the cathedral. There are two excellent restaurants – Nico's (see Eating, below) and the Riverview, serving Scottish and international cuisine in a dining room with crisp white linen.

Dunain Park Hotel (☎ 230512; www.dunainpark hotel.co.uk; Dunain Park; r per person £79-99; ☒ P ☒) Staying at this sumptuous country house hotel is like being in an antiques show-room, what with its Victorian four-poster beds, Georgian-style furniture and Italian marble bathrooms, all set in beautiful wooded grounds just five minutes' stroll from the Caledonian Canal and River Ness. The hotel is on the A82 to Fort William a mile southwest of Inverness.

Eating

BUDGET

Délices de Bretagne (☎ 712422; 6 Stephen's Brae; light meals £2-5; ☽ 9am-5pm Mon-Sat; 10am-5pm Sun) *Très français* – this café brings a little corner of Brittany to the Highlands, serving tasty Breton galettes (savoury pancakes) and excellent coffee.

River Café (☎ 714884; 10 Bank St; lunch mains £5-7, dinner £8-13; ☽ 10am-9.30pm Tue-Sat, 10am-8.30pm Sun & Mon) This is good place to drop in for a pot of tea and a scone after a stroll along the river; there's a restaurant upstairs with more filling fare such as casseroles and lasagne.

Shapla Tandoori Restaurant (☎ 241919; 2 Castle Rd; 3-course lunch £5.95, mains £8-12; ☽ noon-2.30pm & 6-11pm) Head upstairs and choose a table by the window, where you can enjoy a tasty curry with a splendid view over the river.

Lettuce Eat (☎ 715064; 7 Lombard St; sandwiches £1.50-2.50; ☽ 7am-3.30pm Mon-Sat) This is a good place for inexpensive sandwiches, baguettes, salads and the like.

Tesco Metro (☽ 7.30am-10pm Mon-Sat, 9am-6pm Sun) is a supermarket on King St for self-caterers.

MID-RANGE & TOP END

Mustard Seed (☎ 220220; 16 Fraser St; mains £10-15; ☽ noon-3pm & 6-10pm) This bright and bustling bistro brings a dash of big-city style to Inverness and is one of the most popular restaurants in town. Grab a table on the upstairs balcony if you can – it's the best outdoor lunch spot in Inverness, with a great view across the river. It's best to book at weekends and on any day in July and August. From 6pm to 7pm you can get a two-course dinner with one drink for £10.95.

Café 1 (☎ 226200; 75 Castle St; mains £8-14; ☽ noon-2pm & 6-9pm Mon-Sat) Café 1 is the Mustard Seed's main rival in the style stakes, with candle-lit tables amid elegant blonde-wood and wrought-iron décor, serving an international menu based on quality Scottish produce, from succulent Aberdeen Angus steaks to vegetables in Thai red curry sauce.

Nico's (☎ 234308; Glen Mhor Hotel; 9-12 Ness Bank; mains £10-18; ☽ noon-2pm & 5-9.30pm, till 10.30pm Fri & Sat) A wood-panelled bistro where the menu concentrates on Scottish shellfish and steaks, Nico's is a local favourite. On Sunday from 12.30pm to 3.30pm a brunch or roast is £5.95.

River House (☎ 222033; 1 Greig St; lunch & early evening mains £7-9.50; 2-/3-course dinner £24/28; ☽ noon-2pm & 5.30-9.30pm Tue-Sun) The River House is an elegant restaurant of the pol-ished-wood and crisp white-linen variety, serving the best of British venison, beef, lamb, duck and seafood. The early evening menu is available from 5.30pm to 7pm.

Palio (☎ 711950; 26 Queensgate; mains £5-8; ☽ noon-late Mon-Sat, noon-5.30pm Sun) If you're looking for the best pizza in town, look no further than this stylish Italian restaurant.

Drinking

Phoenix (☎ 233685; 108 Academy St) This is the best of the traditional pubs in the city centre, with a mahogany horseshoe bar, a comfortable, family-friendly lounge and good food at both lunchtime and in the evening. Real ales on tap include the rich and fruity Orkney Dark Island.

Blackfriars (☎ 233881; 93-95 Academy St) Black-friars is a friendly, traditional pub with good bar meals and live music most nights. It's popular with backpackers, and is a good place to meet other travellers.

Barbazza (☎ 243342; 5-9 Young St) Barbazza pulls in a young crowd – it probably has the highest pierced belly-button count in Inverness. It serves booze-absorbing grub such as baked potatoes, burgers and nachos. There are regular DJs, and drinks promos from 8pm to 11pm Wednesday and Sunday.

Bar Pivo (☎ 713307; 38-40 Academy St) The latest addition to the Inverness drinking scene is this Czech-style bar – no less than three Czech beers on draught, another six in bottles, and half of the industrial-chic bar area made up to look like a Prague metro station. DJs play Thursday to Sunday.

Johnny Foxes (☎ 236577; 26 Bank St) Stuck beneath the ugliest building on the riverfront, Johnny Foxes is a big and boisterous Irish bar, with a wide range of food served all day and live music every night.

Clachnaharry Inn (☎ 239806; 17-19 High St; Clachnaharry) Just over a mile northwest of the centre, on the bank of the Caledonian Canal just off the A862, this is a delightful old coaching inn serving good food and excellent real ales.

Entertainment

Eden Court Theatre (☎ 234234; www.eden-court .co.uk; Bishop's Rd; ⏱ box office 10am-8.30pm Mon-Sat) Inverness' main cultural venue has a busy programme of drama, dance and music, an excellent cinema (see Riverside Screen below), and a good bar and restaurant. Pick up a programme from the foyer or check the website.

Spectrum Centre Theatre (☎ 0800 015 8001; Margaret St; ⏱ 8.30pm Mon-Thu Jun & Jul, 8.30pm Mon-Fri Aug) From June to August this theatre stages 'Scottish Showtime', an evening of traditional Scottish music, song and dance aimed squarely at the tourist market.

Riverside Screen (☎ 221718; Ness Walk; adult/child £4.80/3) Part of the Eden Court Theatre complex, Inverness' art-house cinema screens both recent films and old classics.

Warner Village (☎ 711175; Inverness Retail & Business Park; Eastfield Way; adult/child £5.80/4) This is a seven-screen multiplex cinema way out on the eastern edge of town, just south of the A96 to Nairn.

Getting There & Away

AIR

Inverness airport (☎ 01667-464000) is at Dalcross, 10 miles (16km) east of town on the A96 to Aberdeen. There are flights to Glasgow, Edinburgh, Stornoway, Benbecula, Orkney, Shetland and London.

For more information, see the Transport chapter, p416.

BUS

National Express (☎ 0870 580 8080; www.gobycoach .com) operates a direct overnight bus from London to Inverness (£36.50, 13 hours, one daily), with more frequent services requiring a change at Glasgow.

Scottish Citylink (☎ 0870 550 5050; www.citylink .co.uk) has direct connections to Glasgow (£15.50, four hours, four daily), Edinburgh (£15, four hours, five daily), Fort William (£8.20, two hours, five daily), Ullapool (£7, 1½ hours, two daily except Sunday), Portree on the Isle of Skye (£11, 3½ hours, two daily) and Thurso (£11, 3½ hours, four daily).

Buses to Aberdeen (£10.50, 3¾ hours, hourly) are operated by Stagecoach Bluebird, while Rapsons/Highland Country bus No 15 serves Aviemore (£4.50, 1¾ hours, three daily Monday to Friday) via Grantown-on-Spey.

TRAIN

There is one direct train daily from London to Inverness (£99, eight hours); others require a change at Edinburgh. There are several direct trains a day from Glasgow (£31.60, 3½ hours), Edinburgh (£31.60, 3¼ hours) and Aberdeen (£19.20, 2¼ hours), and three daily Monday to Saturday (one or two on Sunday) to Thurso and Wick (£12.50, four hours).

The line from Inverness to Kyle of Lochalsh (£14, 2½ hours, four daily Monday to Saturday, two Sunday) offers one of Britain's great scenic train journeys.

Getting Around

TO/FROM THE AIRPORT

The twice-daily airport bus connects with the Stornoway and London flights (£2.50, 20 minutes). A taxi costs around £11.

BICYCLE

There are some great cycling opportunities out of Inverness. Rental outlets include **Highland Cycles** (☎ 234789; 16a Telford St; ⏱ 9am-5.30pm Mon-Sat), which charges £12 for 24 hours.

BUS

Rapsons/Highland Country (☎ 710555) operates local services and buses to places around

Inverness, including Nairn, Forres, the Culloden battlefield, Beauly, Dingwall and Lairg. A Tourist Trail Rover ticket costs £6 and gives unlimited travel for a day on buses serving Culloden, Cawdor Castle, Fort George and Nairn.

CAR

The TIC has a handy Car Hire leaflet. The big boys charge from £35 per day, or you could try **Sharp's Reliable Wrecks** (☎ 236694; Inverness train station) for cheaper cars from £20 per day.

TAXI

Call **Central Taxis** (☎ 222222).

AROUND INVERNESS
Culloden

The Battle of Culloden in 1746, the last pitched battle ever fought on British soil, saw the defeat of Bonnie Prince Charlie and the end of the Jacobite dream; 1200 Highlanders were slaughtered by government forces in a 68-minute rout. The duke of Cumberland, son of the reigning king George II and leader of the Hanoverian army, won the label Butcher Cumberland for his brutal treatment of the defeated Scottish forces. The battle sounded the death knell of the old clan system, and the horrors of the Clearances soon followed. The sombre moor where the conflict took place has scarcely changed in the ensuing 258 years.

The **Culloden visitor centre** (☎ 01463-790607; adult/child £5/3.75; ☼ 9am-7pm Jul & Aug; 9am-6pm Apr-Jun, Sep & Oct; 11am-4pm Nov, Dec, Feb & Mar) screens a 15-minute audiovisual presentation on the battle, but it's not worth the money – the guided tours of the battlefield (£3/2) are much better value.

Culloden is 6 miles (10km) east of Inverness. See p294 for details of bus services.

Fort George

The headland guarding the Moray Firth narrows opposite Fortrose is occupied by the magnificent and virtually unaltered 18th-century artillery fortification of **Fort George** (☎ 01667-462777; adult/child £5/3.50; ☼ 9.30am-6.30pm Apr-Sep; 9.30am-4.30pm Mon-Sat, 2-4.30pm Sun Oct-Mar). One of the finest examples of its kind in Europe, it was completed in 1769 as a base for George II's army of occupa-

tion in the Highlands. The mile-plus walk around the ramparts offers fine views out to sea and back to the Great Glen. Given its size, you'll need at least two hours to do the place justice. The fort is off the A96 about 11 miles (18km) northeast of Inverness.

Nairn
☎ 01667 / pop 8420

Nairn is a popular seaside resort with a good sandy beach, but there's not a great deal to see. The town has a **TIC** (☎ 452763; 62 King St; ☼ Apr-Oct), banks with ATMs and a post office.

The most attractive part of Nairn is the old fishing village of **Fishertown**, down by the harbour. **Nairn Museum** (☎ 458531; Viewfield House; adult/child £2/50p; ☼ 10am-4.30pm Mon-Sat Mar-Oct), a few minutes' walk from the TIC, has displays on the history of Fishertown, as well as on local archaeology, geology and natural history.

You can spend many pleasant hours wandering along the **East Beach**, which is one of the finest in Scotland.

The big event in the town's calendar is the **Nairn Highland Games** (www.nairnhighlandgames .co.uk), held in mid-August. Also in August is the week-long **Nairn International Jazz Festival**. Contact the TIC for details of both events.

SLEEPING & EATING

Havelock House Hotel (☎ 455500; Crescent Rd; r per person £25; ☒ ℗) Originally built as a summer residence for the emir of Jaipur after he was exiled from India in 1857, this hotel has five recently refurbished rooms, all with bathroom. There's a neat little restaurant specialising in Scottish seafood and venison.

Windsor Hotel (☎ 453108; www.windsor-hotel .co.uk; 16 Albert St; s/d £43/80; ☒ ℗) This elegant hotel is a comfortable modern place that aims mainly at the golfing market; the bar serves good pub grub.

Other recommendations:

Braighe (☎ 453285; braighe@aol.com; Albert St; r per person £18; ☒)

Brightmony Farm House (☎ 455550; Auldearn; r per person £18; ℗) In a rural setting, 2 miles (3km) east of town.

GETTING THERE & AWAY

Stagecoach Bluebird buses run hourly (less frequently on Sunday) from Inverness to

Aberdeen via Nairn. The town also lies on the Inverness to Aberdeen railway line; there are five to seven trains a day from Inverness (£3.50, 20 minutes).

Cawdor

Cawdor Castle (☎ 01667-404615; adult/child £6.10/3.30; 🕑 10am-5pm May–mid-Oct), the 14th-century home of the Thanes of Cawdor, is reputedly the castle of Shakespeare's *Macbeth* and was the scene of Duncan's murder in the play – a bit of poetic licence from the bard, since the central tower dates from the 14th century (the wings were 17th-century additions) and Macbeth died in 1057. The castle is 5 miles (8km) southwest of Nairn.

Cawdor Tavern (☎ 01667-404777; bar meals £5-8) in the nearby village is worth a visit, though it can be difficult deciding what to drink as it stocks over 100 varieties of whisky. There's also reasonable pub food, with tempting daily specials.

Brodie Castle

Brodie Castle (☎ 01309-641371; adult/child £5/3.75; 🕑 11am-5.30pm Mon-Sat, 1.30-5.30pm Sun Apr-Sep), set in 70 hectares of parkland, has several highlights including an early 19th-century library with more than 6000 peeling, dusty volumes. There are some wonderful clocks, a huge Victorian kitchen and a 17th-century dining room with wildly extravagant moulded plaster ceilings depicting mythological scenes. Best of all is the chance to chat with the ageing laird, who sometimes dons a National Trust badge and mingles with the visitors.

The Brodies have been living here since 1160 but the present structure dates mostly from 1567, with many additions over the years.

The castle is 8 miles (13km) east of Nairn. Stagecoach Bluebird buses run from Inverness to Brodie (£4.60, 45 minutes, hourly) via Culloden.

WEST OF INVERNESS
Beauly

☎ 01463 / pop 1160

In 1584 Mary Queen of Scots is said to have given this village its name when she exclaimed, in French: *'Quel beau lieu!'* (What a beautiful place!). Founded in 1230 the red sandstone **Beauly Priory** (☎ 01667-460232; admission free; 9.30am-6.30pm mid-Jun–Sep) is now an

impressive, mostly roofless ruin. A small information kiosk next door has information on the history of the priory.

The attractive and centrally located **Priory Hotel** (☎ 782309; reservations@priory-hotel.com; The Square; s/d £48/90; 🗶 P) has bright, modern rooms and an excellent restaurant. For B&B, try **Ellangowan** (☎ 782273; Croyard Rd; r per person £15; P), a few minutes' walk from the priory.

Stagecoach Inverness runs buses from Inverness to Beauly (£3.20, hourly Monday to Saturday, four on Sunday), and the town lies on the Inverness–Thurso railway line.

Strathglass & Glen Affric

☎ 01456

The broad valley of **Strathglass** extends about 18 miles (29km) inland from Beauly, followed by the A831 to **Cannich**, the only village in the area, where there's a grocery store and a post office.

About 5 miles (8km) west of Beauly, at the Aigas Dam on the River Beauly, there's a **fish lift** (🕑 10am-3pm Mon-Fri mid-Jun–early Oct) where you can watch migrating salmon take advantage of a dam bypass.

Several long and narrow valleys lead west from Strathglass into an almost roadless wilderness. **Glen Affric**, one of the most beautiful glens in Scotland, extends deep into the hills beyond Cannich. The upper reaches of the glen, recently designated as Glen Affric National Nature Reserve, is a scenic wonderland of shimmering lochs, rugged mountains and native Scots pine, home to pine marten, wildcat, otter, red squirrel and golden eagle.

From the parking area and picnic site at the eastern end of **Loch Affric** there are several short walks along the river and the loch shore. The circuit of Loch Affric (10 miles/16km, allow five hours) follows good paths right around the loch and takes you deep into the heart of some very wild scenery. Contact Inverness TIC (p291) for more information.

It's possible to walk all the way from Cannich to Loch Duich on the west coast (35 miles/56km) in two days, spending the night at the remote Glen Affric Youth Hostel (see p297).

SLEEPING & EATING

Cougie Lodge (☎ 415459; peteland@knockfin.com; Cougie; dm £8, tent site per person £5) The tiny, six-bed lodge is hidden away in the forest to the south of Loch Beinn a'Mheadhoin, 9 miles (14km) southwest of Cannich (go through Tomich and continue on a forest road beyond Plodda Falls car park). It makes a good overnight stop if you're walking from Cannich to Glen Affric Youth Hostel. You can also camp here.

Glen Affric Youth Hostel (☎ 0870 155 3255; Allt Beithe, Glen Affric; dm £10.50; ☽ Apr-Oct) This remote and rustic hostel is set amid magnificent scenery at the halfway point of the cross-country walk from Cannich to Ratagan Youth Hostel on the west coast. Facilities are basic and you'll need to take all supplies with you. Book in advance.

Kerrow House (☎ 415243; hilary@kerrow-house .demon.co.uk; Cannich; s £24-38, d £44-52; ☒ Ⓟ) This wonderful Georgian hunting lodge has bags of old-fashioned character. The house was once the home of Highland author Neil Gunn, and has spacious grounds with 3½ miles (5km) of private trout fishing. It's a mile south of Cannich on the minor road along the east side of the River Glass.

Tomich Hotel (☎ 415399; tomich@tomich.co.uk; Tomich; s £54-64, d £77-87; ☒ Ⓟ ☎) About 3 miles (5km) southwest of Cannich on the southern side of the river, this Victorian hunting lodge is a good place to eat. It has eight comfortable rooms with bathroom and – a bit of a surprise out here in the wilds – a small, heated indoor swimming pool.

Other recommendations:

Cannich Youth Hostel (SYHA; ☎ 0870 004 1108; Cannich; dm £10; ☽ Apr-Oct)

Glen Affric Backpackers (☎ 01456-415263; Charrein Lodge; dm £6)

Cannich Caravan Park (☎ 415364; Cannich; tents £6).

GETTING THERE & AWAY

Rapsons/Highland Country buses run from Inverness to Cannich (45 minutes, five a day Monday to Friday, two Saturday) via Drumnadrochit.

From July to mid-September, **Ross's Minibuses** (☎ 01463-761250) runs from Beauly train station to Cannich (30 minutes, one a day Thursday to Tuesday), and from Cannich to Loch Affric car park (30 minutes, two a day Tuesday to Thursday). The rest of the year there are only two buses a week from Beauly to Cannich, on Tuesday and Thursday.

Black Isle

The Black Isle – a peninsula rather than an island – is linked to Inverness by the Kessock Bridge.

Rapsons/Highland Country runs buses from Inverness to Fortrose and Rosemarkie (£3.30, 30 minutes, hourly Monday to Saturday); most continue to Cromarty (£4.90, 55 minutes).

FORTROSE & ROSEMARKIE

At **Fortrose Cathedral** you'll find the vaulted crypt of a 13th-century chapter house and sacristy, and a ruinous 14th-century southern aisle and chapel. **Chanonry Point**, 1½ miles (2km) to the east, is a favourite dolphin-spotting vantage point.

In Rosemarkie, the **Groam House Museum** (☎ 01381-620961; admission free; ☽ 10am-5pm Mon-Sat, 2-4.30pm Sun Easter & May-Sep; 2-4pm Sat & Sun Oct-Apr) has a superb collection of Pictish stones engraved with designs similar to those on Celtic Irish stones.

From the northern end of Rosemarkie's High St a short but pleasant signposted walk leads you through the gorges and waterfalls of the **Fairy Glen**.

CROMARTY

The Cromarty Firth, north of the Black Isle, is often dotted with huge offshore oil rigs lying at anchor; some are mothballed, others waiting for maintenance work at the Nigg Bay shipyards before being towed out to the North Sea.

The pretty village of Cromarty at the northeastern tip of the Black Isle has lots of 18th-century stone houses, two stores, a post office and a bank (without ATM).

The 18th-century **Cromarty Courthouse** (☎ 01381-600418; Church St; adult/child £3/2; ☽ 10am-5pm Apr-Oct; noon-4pm Nov, Dec & March) details the town's history using contemporary references. It's very engaging – kids will love the talking mannequins.

Next to the Courthouse is **Hugh Miller's Cottage** (☎ 01381-600245; Church St; adult/child £2.50/ 1.90; ☽ noon-5pm Easter-Sep; noon-5pm Sun-Wed Oct). Miller (1802-56) was a local stonemason and amateur geologist who later moved to Edinburgh and became a famous journalist and newspaper editor.

From Cromarty harbour, **Dolphin Ecosse** (☎ 01381-600323; www.dolphinecosse.co.uk; per person £20) runs 2½-hour boat trips into the Moray

Firth to see bottlenose dolphins and other wildlife.

Several places offer a bed for the night, including **Mrs Robertson** (☎ 01381-600488; 7 Church St; r per person £16).

LOCH NESS

Deep, dark and narrow, Loch Ness stretches for 23 miles (37km) between Inverness and Fort Augustus. Its bitterly cold waters have been explored extensively for Nessie, the elusive Loch Ness monster, and although some visitors get lucky, most see only her cardboard cut-out form at the monster exhibitions. The congested A82 road runs along the northwestern shore, while the more tranquil and extremely picturesque B862 follows the southeastern shore. A complete circuit of the loch is about 70 miles (113km) – travel anti-clockwise for the best views.

Walking & Cycling

The 73-mile (118km) **Great Glen Way** (www .greatglenway.com) is Scotland's newest long-distance footpath, stretching from Inverness to Fort William where walkers can connect with the West Highland Way (see the boxed text on p253). It is described in detail in *The Great Glen Way* by Jacquetta Megarry.

The footpath shares some sections with the 80-mile (129km) **Great Glen Cycle Route**, a waymarked mountain-bike route that follows canal tow-paths and gravel tracks through forests, avoiding roads where possible.

The climb to the summit of **Meallfuarvonie** (699m), on the northwestern shore of Loch Ness, makes an excellent short hill walk: the views along the Great Glen from the top are superb. It's a 6-mile/10km round trip so allow about three hours. Start from the car park at the end of the minor road leading south from Drumnadrochit to Bunloit.

Drumnadrochit

☎ 01456 / pop 810

Seized by monster madness, its gift shops bulging with Nessie cuddly toys, Drumnadrochit is a hot-bed of beastie fever, with two monster exhibitions battling it out for the tourist dollar.

The prominent **Loch Ness 2000 Exhibition Centre** (☎ 450573; www.loch-ness-scotland.com; adult/

child £5.95/4.50; 9am-8pm Jul & Aug, 9am-6pm Jun & Sep, 9am-5.30pm Oct, 9.30am-5pm Easter-May, 10am-3.30pm Nov-Easter) is the better of the two Nessie-themed attractions, featuring a 40-minute audiovisual presentation, plus exhibits of equipment used in the various underwater monster hunts.

The nearby **Original Loch Ness Monster Centre** (☎ 450342; adult/child £3.50/3; 9am-8pm Jul & Aug; 10am-5.30pm Apr-Jun, Sep & Oct; 10am-4pm Nov-Mar) shows a superficial 30-minute Loch Ness video (with multilingual headsets), but its main function is to sell you tacky Loch Ness Monster souvenirs.

One-hour monster-hunting cruises, complete with sonar and underwater cameras, aboard the **Nessie Hunter** (☎ 450395), operate from Drumnadrochit. They depart from 9.30am to 6pm daily, from Easter to October, and cost £8/5 for an adult/child.

Urquhart Castle

Urquhart Castle (☎ 450551; adult/child £5.50/1.20; 9.30am-6.30pm Apr-Sep, 9.30am-4.30pm Mon-Sat & 2-4.30pm Sun Oct-Mar) commands a brilliant location with outstanding views (on a clear day), but the meagre ruins make it hard to justify the steep admission fee – there's a widespread feeling that Historic Scotland is just cashing in on the castle's reputation as a Nessie-sighting hot spot.

The castle was repeatedly sacked and rebuilt over the centuries. It was finally blown up in 1692 to prevent the Jacobites from using it, and its remains perch dramatically on the edge of the loch. The five-storey tower house at the northern point is the most impressive remaining fragment and offers wonderful views across the water.

Sleeping & Eating

There are numerous B&Bs in and around Drumnadrochit, but single rooms are in short supply.

Loch Ness Backpackers Lodge (☎ 450807; info@lochness-backpackers.com; Coiltie Farmhouse, East Lewiston; dm £9.50, d £27) This neat, friendly hostel has six-bed dorms, one double room and a large barbecue area. It's about three-quarters of a mile from Drumnadrochit, along the A82 towards Fort William; turn left where you see the sign for Loch Ness Inn, just before the bridge.

Loch Ness Youth Hostel (SYHA; ☎ 0870 004 1138; dm £10.50-11.50; Apr-Oct) This hostel is housed

STRANGE SPECTACLE ON LOCH NESS

Highland folklore is filled with tales of strange creatures living in lochs and rivers, notably the kelpie (water horse) that lures unwary travellers to their doom. The use of the term 'monster', however, is a relatively recent phenomenon whose origins lie in an article published in the *Inverness Courier* of 2 May 1933, entitled 'Strange Spectacle on Loch Ness'.

The article recounted the sighting of a disturbance in the loch by Mrs Aldie Mackay and her husband: 'There the creature disported itself, rolling and plunging for fully a minute, its body resembling that of a whale, and the water casading and churning like a simmering cauldron.'

The story was taken up by the London press and sparked off a rash of sightings that year, including a notorious on-land encounter with London tourists Mr and Mrs Spicer on 22 July 1933, again reported in the *Inverness Courier:*

It was horrible, an abomination. About fifty yards ahead, we saw an undulating sort of neck, and quickly followed by a large, ponderous body. I estimated the length to be 25 to 30 feet, its colour was dark elephant grey. It crossed the road in a series of jerks, but because of the slope we could not see its limbs. Although I accelerated quickly towards it, it had disappeared into the loch by the time I reached the spot. There was no sign of it in the water. I am a temperate man, but I am willing to take any oath that we saw this Loch Ness beast. I am certain that this creature was of a prehistoric species.

The London newspapers couldn't resist. In December 1933 the *Daily Mail* sent Marmaduke Wetherall, a film director and big-game hunter, to Loch Ness to track down the beast. Within days he found 'reptilian' footprints in the shoreline mud (soon revealed to have been made with a stuffed hippopotamus foot, possibly an umbrella stand). Then in April 1934 came the famous 'long-necked monster' photograph taken by the seemingly reputable Harley St surgeon Colonel Kenneth Wilson. The press went mad and the rest, as they say, is history.

In 1994, however, Christian Spurling – Wetherall's 90-year-old stepson – revealed that the most famous photo of Nessie ever taken was in fact a hoax, perpetrated by his stepfather with Wilson's help. Today, of course, there are those who claim that Spurling's confession is itself a hoax. And, ironically, the researcher who exposed the surgeon's photo as a fake still believes whole-heartedly in the monster's existence.

Hoax or not, there's no denying that the bizarre mini-industry that has grown up around Loch Ness and its mysterious monster since that eventful summer 70 years ago is the strangest spectacle of all.

in a big lodge overlooking Loch Ness, and many of the dorms have loch views. It's at Glenmoriston, 13 miles (21km) down the loch towards Fort Augustus. Buses from Inverness to Fort William stop nearby.

Drumbuie Farm (☎ 450634; s/d £26/42) On the right as you enter Drumnadrochit from Inverness, this B&B has spacious, tidy rooms, some overlooking the loch; the double has a four-poster bed.

Gillyflowers (☎ 450641; gillyflowers@cali.co.uk; s/d per person £35/44) This B&B is a renovated 18th-century farmhouse on the southern edge of Drumnadrochit village. The three luxury rooms have en suite bathrooms.

Borlum Farm Caravan & Camping Park (☎ 450220; r per person £4) Rates are the same per person for a tent or campervan in this caravan park, half a mile southeast of Drumnadrochit.

Near the Drumnadrochit village green are the pleasant **Glen Café Bar** (☎ 450282), and the more expensive, nonsmoking **Fiddler's Café Bar** (☎ 450678), which serves traditional Highland fare such as venison casserole and plenty of interesting Scottish beers.

Getting There & Away

Scottish Citylink buses from Inverness to Fort William run along the Great Glen; those headed for Skye turn off at Invermoriston. There are bus stops at Drumnadrochit (£4.90, 30 minutes), Urquhart Castle car park (£4.90, 35 minutes) and Loch Ness Youth Hostel (£6.30, 45 minutes, seven or eight daily).

FORT AUGUSTUS

☎ 01320 / pop 510

Fort Augustus, at the junction of four old military roads, was originally a government garrison and the headquarters of General George Wade's road-building operations in the early 18th century. Today it's a neat and picturesque little place, often overrun by tourists in summer.

There's a **TIC** (☎ 366367; ✆ Easter-Oct) in the central car park, an ATM and a bureau de change (in the post office) beside the canal. **Neuk Internet Café** (☎ 366208), a few doors along, has Internet access for £1.50 per 15 minutes.

Sights & Activities

At Fort Augustus, boats using the **Caledonian Canal** are raised and lowered 13m by a 'ladder' of five consecutive locks. It's fun to watch, and the neatly landscaped canal banks are a great place to soak up the sun or compare accents with fellow tourists. The promontory between the canal and the River Oich affords a fine view over Loch Ness. The **Caledonian Canal Heritage Centre** (☎ 366493; admission free; ✆ 10am-5pm Apr-Oct), beside the lowest lock, showcases the history of the canal.

Between 1729 and 1742, as part of a plan to pacify the Highlands, General Wade built a fort at the point where the River Tarff joined Loch Ness. Although it was captured, and later damaged, by the retreating Jacobites, it remained occupied until 1854. In 1876 Benedictine monks took over the building and founded **Fort Augustus Abbey**. The abbey closed down and the monks departed in 1998, but the monks' burial ground, cloisters and gardens remained open to the public until 2003 when the abbey was sold to a London property developer for conversion to luxury apartments. A local preservation trust (www .theabbeytrust.co.uk) hopes to negotiate continued public access to the grounds.

The **Royal Scot** (☎ 366277; adult/child £6/3; hourly departures 10am-5pm Mar-Nov) offers 50-minute cruises on Loch Ness accompanied by the latest high-tech sonar equipment so you can keep an underwater eye open for Nessie.

Sleeping & Eating

Morag's Lodge (☎ 366289; lizpp@radicaltravel.com; Bunnoich Brae; dm £11, d £36) This clean, colourful and well-run hostel has spacious communal areas and great views of Fort Augustus' hilly surrounds.

Caledonian House (☎ 366236; Station Rd; r per person £23) This B&B is in a lovely spot overlooking the canal.

Lorien House (☎ 366736; lorienhouse@aol.com; Station Rd; s/d £25/40) A cut above your usual B&B, the bathrooms here come with bidets and the breakfasts with smoked salmon.

Lovat Arms Hotel (☎ 366206; lovatarms@ipw.com; Fort Augustus; s/d £40/80; ✗ Ⓟ) The bedrooms are spacious and elegantly furnished, while the lounge is equipped with a log fire, comfy armchairs and grand piano. It's up the hill to the south of the canal bridge.

Fort Augustus Caravan & Camping Park (☎ 366618; tent/campervan per person £4.50) Just south of the village on the western side of the road to Fort William.

Lock Inn (☎ 366302; mains £7-10; food served noon-9pm) A superb little pub on the canal bank, with a vast range of malt whiskies and a tempting menu that includes Orkney salmon and Highland venison.

Getting There & Away

Scottish Citylink buses from Inverness to Fort William stop at Fort Augustus (£7.40, 1¼ hours, five or six daily).

THE CAIRNGORMS

The recently established Cairngorms National Park encompasses the highest landmass in Britain – a broad mountain plateau, riven only by the deep valleys of the Lairig Ghru and Loch Avon, with an average altitude of over 1000m and including five of the six highest peaks in the UK. This wild mountain landscape of granite and heather has a sub-Arctic climate and supports rare alpine tundra vegetation and high-altitude bird species such as snow bunting, ptarmigan and dotterel.

The harsh mountain environment gives way lower down to scenic glens softened by beautiful open forests of native Caledonian pine, home to rare animals and birds such as pine marten, wildcat, red squirrel, osprey, capercaillie and crossbill.

This is prime hill-walking territory, but even couch potatoes can enjoy a taste of the high life by taking the Cairngorm Mountain Railway (p305) up to the edge of the Cairngorm plateau.

BETHUNE CARMICHAEL

Perched on the edge of Loch Ness, **Castle Urquhart** (p298)

The largest house in the Highlands, **Dunrobin Castle** (p329)

MANFRED GOTTSCHALK

NICOLA WELLS

Headstones in the ruins of an old church, **Elgol** (p349)

BRYN T▸

The Shetland's most impressive archeological site, **Jarlshof** (p395)

DAVID TIPLING

One of a population of 250,000 puffins at **Hermaness** (p398)

The famous sandstone stack, **Old Man of Hoy** (p382)

GRANT

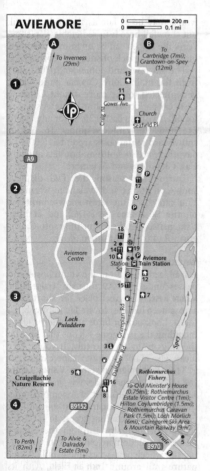

AVIEMORE

☎ 01479 / pop 2400

Aviemore is the gateway to the Cairngorms. It is the region's main centre for transport, accommodation, restaurants and shopping. It's not the prettiest town in Scotland by a long stretch – the main attractions are in the surrounding area – but when bad weather puts the hills off limits Aviemore fills up with hikers, cyclists and climbers (plus skiers and snowboarders in winter) cruising the outdoor equipment shops or recounting their latest adventures in the cafés and bars around town. Add in tourists and locals and the eclectic mix makes for a lively little town.

Map Legend

INFORMATION

Aviemore Photographic....................	**1** B3
Ottakar's Bookshop........................	**2** B3
Tourist Information Centre (TIC)......	**3** B3

SIGHTS & ACTIVITIES (pp301–2)

Aviemore Kart Raceway..................	**4** A2
Rothiemurchus Fishery...................	**5** B4
Strathspey Steam Railway...............	**6** B3

SLEEPING 🏠 (pp302–3)

Ardlogie Guest House.....................	**7** B3
Aviemore Bunkhouse......................	**8** B4
Aviemore Youth Hostel...................	**9** A4
Cairngorm Hotel............................	**10** B3
Dunroamin...................................	**11** B1
Kinapol Guest House......................	**12** B3
Ravenscraig Guest House................	**13** B1

EATING 🍴 (p303)

Coffee Corner...............................	**14** B3
Hamblett's...................................	**15** B3
Old Bridge Inn..............................	**16** B4
Ski-ing Doo..................................	**17** B2
Tesco Supermarket........................	**18** B2

DRINKING 🍷 (p303)

Café Mambo.................................	**19** B3

SHOPPING

Speyside Sports............................	(see 6)

Orientation

Aviemore is on a loop off the A9 Perth–Inverness road; almost everything of note is to be found along the main drag, Grampian Rd. The train station and bus stop are towards the southern end.

The Cairngorm skiing area and mountain railway lie 9 miles (14km) east of Aviemore along the B970 and its continuation through Coylumbridge and Glenmore.

Information

There's a cluster of ATMs outside the Tesco supermarket on Grampian Rd, and currency exchange at the post office and the TIC.

Aviemore Photographic (☎ 810371; The Mall, Grampian Rd; £1 per 10 min; ☀ 8.30am-8pm) You can check email here.

Old Bridge Inn (☎ 811137; 23 Dalfaber Rd; £1 per 30 min; ☀ 11am-11pm Sun-Thu, 11am-midnight Fri & Sat) You can also check email here.

Ottakar's (☎ 810797; 87 Grampian Rd; ☀ 9am-5.30pm Mon-Sat, 11am-5pm Sun) For books and maps.

TIC (☎ 810363; aviemore@host.co.uk; Grampian Rd; ☀ 9am-7pm Mon-Fri, 9am-6pm Sat, 9am-5pm Sun Jul & Aug; 9am-5pm Apr-Jun, Sep & Oct; 9am-5pm Mon-Sat Nov-Mar) Office is 500m south of the village centre.

Sights

Aviemore's train station is home to the **Strathspey Steam Railway** (☎ 810725; www.strath speyrailway.co.uk), which operates steam trains on a section of restored line between Aviemore and Broomhill, 10 miles (16km) to the northeast, via Boat of Garten (p306). There are four or five trains daily from June to September, and a more limited service in April, May, October and December; a return ticket from Aviemore to Broomhill costs £8.40/4.20 for an adult/child. At the time of writing, work was continuing on an extension to Grantown.

Activities
FISHING
Fishing permits for salmon, sea trout and brown trout on the Aviemore stretch of the River Spey are available from **Speyside Sports** (☎ 810656; 2 Station Sq); they're only available to people who are staying in local accommodation. A day permit costs around £20; numbers are limited, so it's best to book in advance.

Rothiemurchus Fishery (☎ 810703; Rothiemurchus Estate, Inverdruie) at the southern end of the village has a loch where you can cast for rainbow trout; buy permits (from £12.50 a day) at the Fish Farm Shop in Inverdruie. If you're a fly-fishing virgin, they offer a one-hour beginner's package, including tackle hire and basic instruction, for £7.50.

You can also fish for brown trout and pike on **Loch Morlich** (p304) – permits are available from the warden's office at Glenmore Camping & Caravan Site (p305).

GO-KARTING & QUAD BIKING
If bad weather keeps you off the hills, there are motorised alternatives for getting wet and dirty. You can burn some rubber at the **Aviemore Kart Raceway** (☎ 810722; Aviemore Centre; £4-5 per session; ◷ 9am-10pm Jun-Sep, 10am-5pm Oct-May), or join a cross-country quad bike trek at **Alvie & Dalraddy Estate** (☎ 810330; Dalraddy Holiday Park; per person £28), 3 miles (5km) south of Aviemore on the B9152 (call first).

SKIING
Aspen or Val d'Isere it ain't, but with 19 runs and 23 miles (37km) of piste **Cairngorm Mountain** (☎ 861261; www.cairngormmountain.com) is Scotland's biggest ski area. When the snow is at its best and the sun is shining you can close your eyes and imagine you're in the Alps; sadly, low cloud and horizontal sleet are more common. The season usually runs from December until the snow melts,

which may be as late as the end of April, but snowfall here is upredictable – in some years the slopes can be open in November, but closed for lack of snow in February.

The ski tows and funicular (p305) start from the main Coire Cas car park, which is connected to the more distant Coire na Ciste car park by free shuttle bus. A ski pass for one/five days costs £25/99 for adults and £15.50/62 for children under 16. Ski or snowboard rental costs around £15.50/12 a day; there are lots of rental outlets at Coire Cas, Glenmore and Aviemore.

During the season the TIC displays snow conditions and avalanche warnings. You can check the latest snow conditions on the **Ski Hotline** (☎ 861261) and at http://ski.visitscotland.com, or tune into Cairngorm Radio Ski FM on 96.6MHz.

WALKING
A trail leads west from the youth hostel and passes under the A9 into the **Craigellachie Nature Reserve**, a great place for short hikes across steep hillsides covered in natural birch forest. Look out for birds and other wildlife, including the peregrine falcons that nest on the crags from April to July. If you're very lucky, you may even spot a capercaillie.

The **Rothiemurchus Estate Visitor Centre** (☎ 810858; Inverdruie; admission free; ◷ 9am-5.30pm), a mile southeast of Aviemore along the B970, provides a free *Visitor Guide & Footpath Map* detailing access to 50 miles (80km) of footpaths through the estate's beautiful Caledonian pine forests, including the wheelchair-accessible 4-mile (6km) nature trail around **Loch an Eilein**, with its ruined castle and peaceful pine woods. See also the Mountain Walks in the Cairngorms boxed text on p305.

Sleeping
BUDGET
Aviemore Bunkhouse (☎ 811181; www.aviemore-bunkhouse.com; Dalfaber Rd; dm £12; ☐ ✗ **P**) This brand-new independent hostel, next door to the excellent Old Bridge Inn, provides accommodation in bright, modern six- or eight-bed dorms, each with private bathroom, and one twin/family room (£29/38). There's a drying room, secure bike storage and wheelchair-accessible dorms. From the train station, cross the pedestrian bridge and walk south on Dalfaber Rd.

Aviemore Youth Hostel (SYHA; ☎ 0870 004 1104; 25 Grampian Rd; dm £11-13; ☐ ☒ ℗) Aviemore Youth Hostel offers upmarket hostelling in a well-equipped building near the TIC, five minutes' walk from the village centre. There are four- and six-bed rooms, and the doors stay open till 2am.

Kinapol Guest House (☎ 810513; Dalfaber Rd; s £28-32, d £32-36; ℗) The Kinapol is a modern bungalow, across the tracks from the train station. All three rooms have shared bathrooms.

Ardlogie Guest House (☎ 810747; Dalfaber Rd; s £25, d £36-50; ☒ ℗) Also handy for the train station, the five-room Ardlogie has great views over the Spey towards the Cairngorms, and guests get free use of the local Country Club's pool, spa and sauna.

The nearest camping ground to Aviemore is **Rothiemurchus Caravan Park** (☎ 812800; Coylumbridge; tent £6) at Coylumbridge, 1½ miles (2.5km) along the B970.

MID-RANGE

Old Minister's House (☎ 812181; Rothiemurchus; r per person £28-35; ☒ ℗) This former manse dates from 1906 and has four rooms with a homely, country farmhouse feel. It's in a lovely setting amid Scots pines on the banks of the River Druie just three-quarters of a mile southeast of Aviemore.

Dunroamin (☎ 810698; lorraine.sheffield@virgin .net; Craig na Gower Ave; s £20-40, d £32-50; ☒ ℗) Dunroamin is a pleasant modern bungalow with three rooms with TV and private bathroom. It's on a quiet street a short walk north of the village centre.

Ravenscraig Guest House (☎ 810278; ravenscrg@ aol.com; Grampian Rd; r per person £20-26; ☒ ℗) A large, flower-bedecked Victorian villa with 12 recently refurbished ensuite rooms, Ravenscraig offers veggie breakfasts in an attractive conservatory breakfast room.

Cairngorm Hotel (☎ 810233; www.cairngorm.com; Grampian Rd; s/d £32/63; ☐ ℗) Better known as the Cairn, this hotel is easily located as it's the fine old granite building with the pointy turret opposite the train station. It's a welcoming place with comfortable rooms and a determinedly Scottish atmosphere, all tartan carpets and stags' antlers, though thankfully they've thrown away the background music tape they once had that included *Viva España* played on the bagpipes.

TOP END

Hilton Coylumbridge (☎ 810661; www.coylumbridge .hilton.com; Coylumbridge; s £70-140, d £80-120; ☒ ℗ ☜) This modern, low-rise Hilton, set amid the pine woods just outside Aviemore, is a wonderfully child-friendly family hotel with indoor and outdoor play areas and a creche.

Eating & Drinking

Hamblett's (☎ 810300; 72 Grampian Rd; lunch mains £4-7; dinner £8-11; ☒ 11.30am-10pm) The only modern, bistro-style restaurant in Aviemore, Hamblett's varied menu includes delicious home-made soups, pasta dishes and imaginative vegetarian options.

Old Bridge Inn (☎ 811137; 23 Dalfaber Rd; bar meals £6; mains £9-14; ☒ food served noon-2pm & 6-9pm, till 9.30pm Fri & Sat) The Old Bridge has a snug bar, complete with roaring log fire in winter, and a cheerful, chalet-style restaurant at the back serving quality Scottish cuisine.

Coffee Corner (☎ 810564; 85 Grampian Rd; snacks £2-4; ☒ 9am-5pm) This cosy café is a good place to relax with the newspapers and a steaming mug of coffee on a rainy day. They do good breakfasts, scones and ice cream sundaes.

Ski-ing Doo (☎ 810392; 9 Grampian Rd; mains £5-10, steaks £12-14; ☒ 1pm-late Mon, Tue & Thu-Sat; 5.30pm-late Sun) A long-standing Aviemore institution, the child-friendly Ski-ing Doo (it's a pun ... oh, ask the waiter!) is a favourite with family skiers, an informal place offering a range of hearty, home-made burgers, chillis and juicy steaks.

Cairngorm Hotel (☎ 810233; Grampian Rd; mains £6-12; ☒ food served 9am-9.30pm) The Cairn has a coffee shop that serves full fry-up breakfasts (9am till noon), and a lounge and restaurant that does decent bar meals and dinners. The bar is a popular meeting place for locals, and often has folk music sessions in the evenings.

Café Mambo (☎ 811670; The Mall, Grampian Rd; mains £5-7; ☒ food served noon-8.30pm Mon-Thu, noon-7.30pm Fri & Sat, 12.30-8.30pm Sun) The Mambo is the snowboarders' alternative to the crustily traditional Cairn – a chill-out café in the afternoon, it turns into a clubbing and live band venue in the evenings.

For self-caterers, Aviemore has an enormous **Tesco** (☒ 8am-10pm Mon-Sat, 9am-6pm Sun) supermarket. For smoked trout, venison, pâté and other picnic delicacies head for

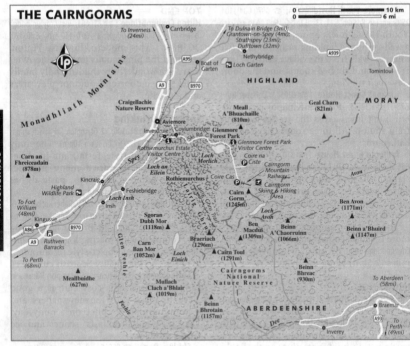

THE CAIRNGORMS

Rothiemurchus Larder (☎ 810858; Rothiemurchus Estate Visitor Centre, Inverdruie), a mile along Ski Rd.

Getting There & Away
BUS
Buses stop on Grampian Rd; buy tickets at the TIC. Scottish Citylink connects Aviemore with Inverness (£5, 45 minutes), Newtonmore (£4.50, 25 minutes), Pitlochry (£6.80, 1¼ hours), Perth (£9.80, two hours), Glasgow (£13, 3¼ hours) and Edinburgh (£13, 3¼ hours).

Rapsons/Highland Country buses link Aviemore with Carrbridge (15 minutes) and Grantown-on-Spey (£3.90, 35 minutes, hourly).

TRAIN
There are direct train services to Glasgow/Edinburgh (£30.60, 2¾ hours, three daily) and Inverness (£7.40, 40 minutes, nine daily).

Getting Around
Rapsons/Highland Country (☎ 811211) buses run from Aviemore to Cairngorm (£2.80, seven

daily June to September and mid-December to April; three a day Monday to Friday in May and October to mid-December) and to Coylumbridge (every 40 minutes Monday to Saturday).

Several places in Aviemore, Rothiemurchus Estate and Glenmore have mountain bikes for rent; most charge £10 to £15 per day.

AROUND AVIEMORE
Loch Morlich
Loch Morlich, 6 miles (10km) east of Aviemore, is surrounded by some 2000 hectares of pine and spruce forest that make up the Glenmore Forest Park. Its attractions include a sandy beach (at the east end) where you'll find the popular **Loch Morlich Watersports Centre** (☎ 861221; Glenmore; ⏰ 9am-5pm May-Oct) which rents out Canadian canoes (£14 an hour), kayaks (£7), windsurfers (£15), sailing dinghies (£18) and rowing boats (£14).

The park's **visitor centre** (☎ 861220) has a small exhibition on the Caledonian forest and sells the *Glen More Forest Guide Map*, detailing local walks. The circuit of Loch Morlich (one hour) makes a pleasant short outing; the trail is pram- and wheelchair-friendly.

The warden at the neighbouring **Cairngorm Reindeer Centre** (☎ 861228; Glenmore; adult/child £6/3; walks at 11am, plus 2.30pm Jun-Aug) will take you on a tour to see and feed Britain's only herd of reindeer, who are very tame and will eat out of your hand.

Glenmore Lodge (☎ 861256; www.glenmorelodge.org.uk; Glenmore; s/d £27/36; **P**) is one of Britain's leading adventure sports training centres, offering courses in hill walking, rock climbing, ice climbing, canoeing, mountain biking and mountaineering. The centre's comfortable B&B accommodation is available to all, even if you're not taking a course, as is the indoor-climbing wall, gym and sauna.

Cairngorm Lodge Youth Hostel (SYHA; ☎ 0870 004 1137; Glenmore; dm £11-12; ☷ closed Nov–mid-Dec) is set in a former shooting lodge and enjoys a great location at the east end of Loch Morlich; pre-booking is essential.

Campers can set up a base at **Glenmore Caravan & Camping Site** (☎ 861271; Glenmore; tents & campervans £7.70-12.90; ☷ closed Nov–mid-Dec), an attractive lochside site with pitches amid the Scots pines.

Cairngorm Mountain Railway

Aviemore's newest attraction is the **Cairngorm Mountain Railway** (☎ 861261; adult/child £8/5 return; ☷ 10am-4.30pm May-Oct), a funicular train that will whisk you to the edge of Cairngorm plateau (1085m) in just eight minutes. The bottom station is at the Coire Cas car park at the end of Ski Rd; at the top is an exhibition, a shop (of course) and a restaurant. Unfortunately, for environmental and safety reasons, you're not allowed out of the top station in summer, not even to walk down – you must return to the car park on the funicular.

The **Ptarmigan Restaurant** (☎ 861261; 3-course dinner £28; ☷ 6.30-10.30pm Fri-Sun late Jun-Sep) in the top station is Britain's highest restaurant, and offers – weather permitting – a spectacular sunset dining experience. The menu combines traditional Scottish ingredients with contemporary styles. Book as far in advance as possible.

Kincraig & Glen Feshie

The **Highland Wildlife Park** (☎ 01540-651270; Kincraig; adult/child £7.50/5; ☷ 10am-7pm Jun-Aug, till

MOUNTAIN WALKS IN THE CAIRNGORMS

The climb from the car park at the Coire Cas ski area to the summit of **Cairn Gorm** (1245m) takes about two hours (one way). From there, you can continue south across the high-level plateau to Ben Macdui (1309m), Britain's second-highest peak. This can take eight to 10 hours return from the car park and is a serious undertaking, for experienced and well-equipped walkers only.

The **Lairig Ghru trail**, which can take eight to 10 hours, is a demanding 24-mile (39km) walk from Aviemore across the Lairig Ghru pass (840m) to Braemar. An alternative to doing the full route is to make the six-hour return hike up to the summit of the pass and back to Aviemore. The path starts from Ski Rd, a mile east of Coylumbridge.

Warning – the Cairngorm plateau is a sub-Arctic environment where navigation is difficult and weather conditions can be severe, even in mid-summer. Hikers must have proper equipment and know how to use a map and compass. In winter it is a place for experienced mountaineers only.

6pm Apr-May & Sep-Nov, till 4pm Dec-Mar, last entry 2 hr before closing) near Kincraig, 6 miles (10km) southwest of Aviemore, features a drive-through safari park and animal enclosures that offer the chance to get close to native wildlife that is rarely seen in the wild, such as wildcat, capercaillie, pine marten, white-tailed sea eagle and red squirrel, as well as species that once roamed the Scottish hills but have long since disappeared, including wolf, lynx, wild boar, beaver and European bison. Visitors without cars get driven around by staff (at no extra cost).

At Kincraig the Spey widens into **Loch Insh**, home of the **Loch Insh Watersports Centre** (☎ 01540-651272; Kincraig), which offers canoeing, windsurfing, sailing, bike hire and fishing, as well as B&B accommodation from £18.50 per person in comfortable rooms with attached bathrooms. The food here is good, especially after 6.30pm when the lochside café metamorphoses into a restaurant.

Beautiful, tranquil **Glen Feshie** extends south from Kincraig, deep into the Cairngorms, with Scots pine woods in its upper reaches surrounded by big, heathery hills. The 4WD track to the head of the glen makes a great mountain-bike excursion (25 miles/ 40km round trip).

Glen Feshie Hostel (☎ 01540-651323; glenfeshie hostel@totalise.co.uk; Glen Feshie; dm £9), about 5 miles (8km) south of Kincraig, is a cosy, independent 14-bed hostel popular with hikers. Rates include bed linen and a steaming bowl of porridge to start the day.

Carrbridge
☎ 01479 / pop 540

Carrbridge, 7 miles (11km) northeast of Aviemore, is a good alternative base for exploring the region. It takes its name from the graceful old bridge (spotlit at night), built in 1717, over the thundering rapids of the Dulnain.

The **Landmark Forest Heritage Park** (☎ 01479-841613; adult/child £7.95/5.95; ⏱ 10am-5pm, till 6pm Apr–mid-Jul, till 7pm mid-Jul–Aug), set in a forest of Scots pines, is a theme park with a difference; the theme is timber. The main attractions are the Treetop Trail, a raised walkway through the forest canopy that allows you to view red squirrels, crossbills and crested tits, the wooden viewing tower and the steam-powered sawmill.

Good places to stay include the **Struan House Hotel** (☎ 841242; www.struanhousehotel.co.uk; s/d £28/49; P), with its snug bar and roaring log fire, and the similarly styled **Cairn Hotel** (☎ 841212; cairn.carrbridge@lineone.net; Main Rd; s/d £28/48; P), where a single room with shared bathroom costs only £20.

Carrbridge Bunkhouse Hostel (☎ 841250; jonesbunk@aol.com; dm £7) is a cosy, wood-panelled forest cabin, complete with hot showers, drying room and sauna. It's just off the A938 at Bogroy, on the western edge of the village.

Rapsons/Highland Country run four or five buses daily (Monday to Saturday) from Inverness to Carrbridge (£3.40, 45 minutes) and onwards to Grantown-on-Spey (£2.30, 20 minutes).

Boat of Garten
☎ 01479 / pop 570

Boat of Garten is known as the Osprey Village because these rare and beautiful birds of prey nest nearby at the **RSPB Loch Garten Osprey Centre** (☎ 831694; Tulloch, Nethy-

bridge; adult/child £2.50/1.50; ⏱ 10am-6pm Apr-Aug). The ospreys migrate here each spring from Africa and nest in a tall pine tree – you can watch from a hide as the birds feed their young. The centre is signposted about 2 miles (3km) east of the village.

Fraoch Lodge (☎ 831331; Deshar Rd; dm £7.50, d £24; ✗ P) provides luxury hostel-style accommodation in a Victorian town house. There's a lounge with an open fire and a self-catering kitchen, and a lift to and from the hostel can be arranged.

The **Old Ferryman's House** (☎ 831370; s/d £22/44; ✗ P) is a charming cottage B&B on the riverbank on the far side of the bridge to the east of the village (follow the signs to Nethybridge), while the **Boat Hotel** (☎ 831258; www.boathotel.co.uk; s/d £53/105; ✗ P) is a luxurious country hotel with a superb restaurant.

Boat of Garten is 8 miles (13km) northeast of Aviemore. The best way to get here is on the Strathspey Steam Railway (p301).

GRANTOWN-ON-SPEY
☎ 01479 / pop 2170

Grantown (pronounced granton) is an elegant Georgian town on the banks of the Spey geared towards the needs of anglers and retirees. Thronged with tourists in summer, it reverts to a quiet backwater in winter. Most hotels can kit you out for a day of fly-fishing or put you in touch with someone who can. There's a **TIC** (☎ 872773; 54 High St; ⏱ Mar-Oct), a bank, ATMs and a post office.

Sleeping & Eating
Brooklynn (☎ 873097; brooklynn@woodier.com; Grant Rd; s £18-24, d £40-52; ✗ P) This beautiful Victorian villa features original stained glass and wood-panelling, and seven spacious, luxurious rooms (all doubles have private bathrooms). The food – dinner is available as well as breakfast – is superb too.

Culdearn House Hotel (☎ 872106; www.culdearn .com; Woodlands Terrace; d £110; ✗ P) Yet another plush Victorian villa (Grantown is full of them) with corniced ceilings, marble fireplaces and original wood panelling, this hotel has an excellent restaurant, with log fire and candle-lit tables. Note that children under 10 are not welcome.

Good B&Bs include **Stonefield House** (☎ 872197; High St; r per person from £16), with basic rooms above a tearoom, and **Bank**

House (☎ 873256; 1 The Square; r per person £20) in a former Bank of Scotland building.

The **Coffee House & Ice Cream Parlour** (High St) is a traditional family café that sells delicious home-made ice cream.

Getting There & Away

Rapsons/Highland Country buses run between Grantown-on-Spey and Aviemore (£3.90, 35 minutes, hourly) and Inverness (£4.30, 1¼ hours, two or three daily except Sunday).

KINGUSSIE

☎ 01540 / pop 1410

The gracious old Speyside town of Kingussie (pronounced kin-yewsie) sits at the foot of the great heather-clad humps of the Monadhliath Mountains. The town is best known as the home of the excellent Highland Folk Museum.

Sights

The open-air **Highland Folk Museum** (☎ 661307; Duke St; adult/child £1/50p; ♥ 9.30am-5.30pm Mon-Sat Apr-Sep, till 4.30pm Oct) comprises a collection of historical buildings and relics revealing many aspects of Highland culture and lifestyle. The museum is laid out like a village and includes a traditional thatch-roofed Isle of Lewis blackhouse, a water mill and a 19th-century corrugated-iron shed for smoking salmon. Live actors in period costume give demonstrations of traditional crafts. There's another section of the museum at nearby Newtonmore.

Perched dramatically on a river terrace and clearly visible from the main A9 road, the roofless **Ruthven Barracks** (admission free; ♥ 24 hr) was one of four garrisons built by the British government after the first Jacobite rebellion of 1715 as part of a Hanoverian scheme to take control of the Highlands. Ironically, the barracks were last occupied by Jacobite troops awaiting the return of Bonnie Prince Charlie after the Battle of Culloden. Learning of his defeat and subsequent flight, they destroyed the barracks before taking to the glens. The ruins are spectacularly floodlit at night.

Walking

The Monadhliath Mountains, northwest of Kingussie, attract fewer hikers than the nearby Cairngorms and make an ideal destination for walkers seeking peace and solitude. However, during the deer-stalking season (August to October), you'll need to check with the TIC before setting out.

The recommended six-hour circular walk to the 878m summit of **Carn an Fhreiceadain**, above Kingussie, begins north of the village. It continues to Pitmain Lodge and along the Allt Mor river before climbing to the cairn on the summit. You can then follow the ridge east to the twin summits of Beinn Bhreac before returning to Kingussie via a more easterly track.

Sleeping & Eating

Lairds Bothy Hostel (☎ 661334; 68 High St; dm £9) Behind the Tipsy Laird pub in the town centre, this hostel has four family rooms and several plain eight-bed dorms.

Homewood Lodge (☎ 661507; jennifer@homewood-lodge-kingussie.co.uk; Newtonmore Rd; s/d £25/40; ✗ P) On the western outskirts of town, this elegant Victorian lodge offers exceptional value. The double rooms have exquisite views of the Cairngorms – a nice way to wake up in the mornings!

Hermitage (☎ 662137; Spey St; r per person £23; ✗ P) All style and sophistication, but in a laid-back way, the Hermitage is a lovely old house with plenty of character, and five comfortable rooms with bathroom.

Osprey Hotel (☎ 661510; www.ospreyhotel.co.uk; Ruthven Rd; s/d £39/50; ✗ P) Overlooking the town's flower-filled memorial gardens, this cosily old-fashioned Victorian town house has eight brightly refurbished rooms and serves tasty home cooking at breakfast and dinner.

Cross (☎ 661166; www.thecross.co.uk; Tweed Mill Brae, Ardbroilach Rd; 5-course dinner £40; ♥ closed Tue; ✗ P) Housed in a converted water mill beside the Allt Mor burn, the Cross is one of the finest restaurants in the Highlands. The intimate, low-raftered dining room has an open fire and a patio overlooking the stream, and serves the likes of Scottish seafood and local lamb accompanied by a superb wine list. If you want to stay the night, there are nine stylish bedrooms to choose from (dinner B&B £115 per person).

Tipsy Laird (☎ 661334; High St; mains £7-12) This snug bar and restaurant serves large portions of better than average pub grub.

La Cafetière (☎ 661020; 54 High St) The most attractive of the High St cafés, this is the place to go for a cappuccino.

Getting There & Away

Kingussie is on the main Edinburgh/Glasgow to Inverness rail and bus routes, and all trains and many Scottish Citylink buses stop here.

There are Citylink buses to Aviemore (£3.70, 25 minutes, five to seven daily) and Inverness (£6.50, one hour, six to eight Monday to Saturday, three Sunday). Rapsons/Highland Country runs a once-daily service (Monday to Friday only) between Newtonmore and Inverness, calling at Kingussie, Kincraig, Aviemore and Carrbridge, with more frequent buses (school days only) between Kingussie and Aviemore.

From the train station at the southern end of town there are trains to Edinburgh (£30.60, 2½ hours, seven a day Monday to Saturday, two Sunday) and Inverness (£7.40, one hour, eight a day Monday to Saturday, four Sunday).

NEWTONMORE

☎ 01540 / pop 980

Three miles (5km) southwest of Kingussie is the peaceful backwater of Newtonmore. The excellent **Highland Folk Museum** (☎ 661307; adult/child £5/3; ☽ 10.30am-5.30pm Apr-Aug), at the northern end of the village, is a sister establishment to the museum of the same name in Kingussie. The Newtonmore site includes a reconstructed village with wattle and daub cottages, a school and a farm, and on-site demonstrations of woodcarving, spinning and peat-fire baking. You'll need two to three hours to make the most of a visit here.

As a popular hill-walking base camp, Newtonmore is well endowed with budget accommodation. **Newtonmore Hostel** (☎ 673360; www.highlandhostel.co.uk; Main St; dm £10, d £24; ☐ (P)), in the heart of town, is a bright, modern, bungalow-style place with two eight-bed dorms and a double room, and a TV lounge with wood-burning stove.

Strathspey Mountain Hostel (☎ 673694; strathspey@newtonmore.com; Main St; dm £10; ☐ ✗ (P)) is a snug 19th-century cottage with two six-bunk dorms and two triple rooms, all with bedside reading lights – a nice touch. You can rent bikes here (from £5 a day), and the friendly owners can provide lots of information on local hiking and biking routes.

There's a **TIC** (☎ 673253; ☽ Easter-Oct) at Ralia, beside the A9 1½ miles (2.5km) south of Newtonmore.

Rapsons/Highland Country runs a twice-daily service Monday to Friday (once on Saturday) between Newtonmore and Aviemore (£2.50, 25 minutes).

DALWHINNIE

The remote village of Dalwhinnie, bypassed by the main A9 road, straggles along its single street in glorious isolation amid wild and windswept scenery. From a distance you can spot the distinctive twin pagoda-shaped roofs of the malt kiln at **Dalwhinnie Distillery** (☎ 672219; tours £3; ☽ 9.30am-5pm Mon-Sat Jun-Sep plus 12.30-4pm Sun Jul & Aug; 11am-4pm Mon-Sat Oct; 9.30am-5pm Mon-Fri Easter-May; 1-4pm Mon-Fri Nov-Easter). It is the highest in Scotland (326m above sea level) and one of the most remote.

Three or four trains a day on the Glasgow/Edinburgh to Inverness line stop at Dalwhinnie's tiny station, 600m from the distillery.

WEST HIGHLANDS

This area extends from the bleak blanket-bog of Rannoch Moor to the west coast beyond Glen Coe and Fort William, and includes the southern reaches of the Great Glen. The scenery is grand throughout, with high and wild mountains dominating the glens. Great expanses of moor alternate with lochs and patches of commercial forest. Fort William, at the inner end of Loch Linnhe, is the only town in the area.

GLEN COE

Scotland's most famous glen is also one of the grandest and, in bad weather, the grimmest. The approach to the glen from the east, watched over by the rocky pyramid of Buachaille Etive Mor – the Great Shepherd of Etive – leads over the Pass of Glencoe and into the narrow upper valley. The southern side is dominated by three massive, brooding spurs, known as the Three Sisters, while the northern side is enclosed by the continuous steep wall of the knife-edged Aonach Eagach ridge. The main road threads its lonely way through the middle of all this mountain grandeur, past deep gorges and crashing waterfalls, to the more pastoral lower reaches of the glen around Loch Achtriochtan and Glencoe village.

Glencoe was written into the history books in 1692 when the resident MacDonalds were murdered by the Campbells in what became known as the Glencoe Massacre (see the boxed text on p310).

Walking

There are several short, pleasant walks around **Glencoe Lochan**, near the village. To get there, turn left off the minor road to the youth hostel, just beyond the bridge over the River Coe. There are three walks (40 minutes to an hour), all detailed on a signboard at the car park. The artificial lochan was created by Lord Strathcona in 1895 for his homesick Canadian wife Isabella and is surrounded by a North American-style forest.

A more strenous hike, but well worth the effort on a fine day, is the climb to the **Lost Valley**, a magical mountain sanctuary still haunted by the ghosts of murdered MacDonalds (only 2.5 miles/4km round trip, but allow three hours). A rough path from the car park at Allt na Reigh (on the A82, 6 miles/10km east of Glencoe village) bears left down to a footbridge over the river, then climbs up the wooded valley between Beinn Fhada and Gearr Aonach (the first and second of the Three Sisters). The route leads steeply up through a maze of giant, jumbled, moss-coated boulders before emerging – quite unexpectedly – into a broad, open valley with a half-mile-long meadow as flat as a football pitch. Back in the days of clan warfare, the valley – invisible from below – was used for hiding stolen cattle; its Gaelic name, Coire Gabhail, means 'corrie of capture'.

The summits of Glen Coe's mountains are for experienced mountaineers only. Details of hill-walking routes can be found in the Scottish Mountaineering Club's guidebook *Central Highlands* by Peter Hodgkiss.

East of the Glen

A few miles east of Glencoe proper, on the south side of the A82, is the car park and base station for the **Glencoe Ski Centre** (☎ 01855-851226; www.ski-glencoe.co.uk) where commercial skiing in Scotland first began back in 1956.

The **chair lift** (adult/child £4.50/3; ⏲ 9.30am-4.30pm Thu-Mon May-Sep) continues to operate in summer – there's a grand view over Rannoch Moor from the top station. In winter a lift pass costs £20 a day and equipment hire is £16 a day.

Two miles (3km) past the ski centre, a minor road leads along peaceful and beautiful **Glen Etive**, which runs southwest for 12 miles (19km) to the head of Loch Etive (p285). On a hot summer's day, the River Etive contains many tempting pools for swimming in, and there are lots of good picnic sites. Wild camping is allowed here too.

The remote **King's House Hotel** (☎ 01855-851259; www.kingy.com; Glencoe; bar meals £6-10; s/d from £22/44; Ⓟ) claims to be one of Scotland's oldest licensed inns, dating from the 17th century. It lies on the old military road from Stirling to Fort William (now followed by the West Highland Way; see boxed text on p253), and after the Battle of Culloden it was used as a Hanoverian garrison – hence the name, King's House. The hotel serves good pub food – it's famous for its haggis, neeps and tatties (haggis, mashed turnip and mashed potato). The lounge bar has a picture window with a stupendous view of Buachaille Etive Mor, a great place to sit and admire the scenery with a glass of malt whisky.

Glencoe Village

☎ 01855 / pop 360

The slightly glum little village of Glencoe stands on the south shore of Loch Leven at the western end of the glen, 16 miles (26km) south of Fort William. The small, thatched **Glencoe Folk Museum** (☎ 811664; Glencoe; adult/child £2/free; ⏲ 10am-5.30pm Mon-Sat mid-May–Sep) houses a varied collection of military memorabilia, farm equipment and tools of the woodworking, blacksmithing and slate-quarrying trades.

About 1½ miles east of the village, towards the glen, is the **Glencoe Visitor Centre** (☎ 811307; Inverigan; adult/child £3.50/2.60; ⏲ 10am-6pm Easter-Oct). A modern facility with an eco-tourism angle, the centre provides comprehensive information on the geological, environmental and cultural history of Glencoe via high-tech interactive and audiovisual displays, and tells the story of the Glencoe Massacre in all its gory detail.

THE GLENCOE MASSACRE

The brutal murders that took place here in 1692 were particularly shameful, perpetrated as they were by one Highland clan on another, with whom they were lodging as guests.

In an attempt to quash remaining Jacobite loyalties among the Highland clans, King William III had ordered that all chiefs take an oath of loyalty to him by the end of the year (1691). Maclain, the elderly chief of the MacDonalds of Glencoe, was late in setting out to fulfil the king's demand and going first to Fort William rather than Inveraray made him later still.

The secretary of state for Scotland, Sir John Dalrymple, declared that the MacDonalds should be punished as an example to other Highland clans, some of whom had not bothered to take the oath. A company of 120 soldiers, mainly of the Campbell clan, were sent to the glen. It was a long-standing tradition for clans to provide hospitality to passing travellers and, since their leader was related to Maclain by marriage, the troops were billeted in MacDonald homes.

After they'd been guests for 12 days, the order came for the soldiers to put to death all MacDonalds aged under 70. Some Campbells alerted the MacDonalds to their intended fate, while others turned on their hosts at 5am on 13 February, shooting Maclain and 37 other men, women and children. Some died before they knew what was happening, while others fled into the snow, only to die of exposure.

The ruthless brutality of the incident caused a public uproar and after an enquiry several years later, Dalrymple lost his job. There's a monument to Maclain in Glencoe village and members of the MacDonald clan still gather here on 13 February each year.

You can learn basic summer and winter mountaineering skills with Paul Moore from **Glencoe Guides** (☎ 811402). Costs start from £125 per day (one to four people). Paul also offers rock climbing courses and guiding on hard winter climbs (maximum two clients per trip) for more advanced parties.

SLEEPING & EATING

Glencoe Youth Hostel (SYHA; ☎ 811219; Glencoe; dm £11-12) A 1½-mile walk from the village along the minor road on the northern side of the river, it is popular with hikers but feels a little institutional.

Leacantuim Farm Bunkhouse (☎ 811256; Glencoe; dm £11-12) Near the youth hostel, this bunkhouse is basic, clean and laid-back.

Red Squirrel Campsite (tent site per person £5) This popular camping ground is also run by the Leacantuim Farm people. It's farther along the Glencoe road.

Clachaig Inn (☎ 811252; info@clachaig.com; Clachaig, Glencoe; bar meals £6-10; s £32, d £26-40; ⊠ P) This comfortable, 20-room inn is 2½ miles (4km) southeast of the village and has long been a favourite haunt of hill walkers and climbers.

Glencoe Guest House (☎ 811244; info@theglencoe guesthouse.com; Strathlachlan; r per person £17-24; ⊠ P) A modern bungalow on the outskirts of the village, this guesthouse is in a peaceful setting on the banks of the River Coe.

The lively **Boots Bar** (☎ 811252; info@clachaig .com; Clachaig, Glencoe), round to the right of the Clachaig Inn, is for the great unwashed – it serves good pub grub and has live Scottish, Irish and blues music several times a week. Head for the lounge bar (to the left; no boots allowed) to escape the fug of beer and sweaty socks. You can rent bikes here for £12 a day.

GETTING THERE & AWAY

Rapsons/Highland Country and Scottish Citylink buses run between Fort William and Glencoe (£3.70, 30 minutes, up to seven a day Monday to Saturday). Citylink buses also run to Glasgow (£10.90, 2½ hours, four a day).

KINLOCHLEVEN

☎ 01855 / pop 900

Kinlochleven is hemmed in by high mountains at the head of the beautiful fjord-like Loch Leven, about 7 miles (11km) east of Glencoe village. The aluminium smelter that led to the town's development in the early 20th century has now closed, and the opening of the Ballachulish Bridge in the 1970s allowed the main road to by-pass the place completely. A ray of hope was provided by the opening of the West Highland Way (see the boxed text on p253) which now brings a steady stream of hikers through the village.

The **Aluminium Story Visitor Centre** (☎ 831663; Linnhe Rd; admission free; ✆ 10am-1pm & 2-5pm Mon-Fri Apr-Sep; 10am-1pm Mon, Wed & Fri, 10am-2pm & 6-8pm Tue & Thu Oct-Mar) tells the interesting story of the British Aluminium Company smelter (which opened in 1908) and the Blackwater Reservoir hydroelectric scheme that powered it.

The final section of the **West Highland Way** stretches for 14 miles (22km) from Kinlochleven to Fort William. There are easier walks up the glen of the River Leven, through pleasant woods to the Grey Mare's Tail waterfall, and harder mountain hikes into the Mamores.

The 40-bed **Blackwater Hostel** (☎ 831253; enquiries@blackwaterhostel.co.uk; Lab Rd; dm £11) has spotless, pine-panelled dorms with attached bathrooms and TV. The adjacent camping ground offers pitches for £4 per person.

Mamore Lodge Hotel (☎ 831213; info@mamore lodgehotel.co.uk; Kinlochleven; s £25-35, d £48-70; P) occupies a spectacular situation, high on a hillside 200m above Kinlochleven. Built in 1905 as a shooting lodge for shipping magnate Frank Bibby, its guest list included Viscount Churchill and King Edward VII. The rooms retain their original and ageing pine panelling, giving the place a slightly worn-out air – its not to everyone's taste – but the views more than compensate for the rather spartan décor.

Rapsons/Highland Country buses run to Kinlochleven from Fort William (£2.90, 15 minutes, seven a day Monday to Saturday) and Glencoe village.

FORT WILLIAM
☎ 01397 / pop 9910

Basking on the shores of Loch Linnhe amid magnificent mountain scenery, Fort William has one of the most enviable settings in the country. If it wasn't for the busy dual carriageway crammed between the town centre and the loch, and one of the highest rainfall records in the country, it would be almost idyllic. Even so, it's not a bad little town, and its easy access by rail and bus makes it a good place to base yourself for exploring the surrounding mountains and glens.

Magical Glen Nevis begins near the northern end of the town and wraps itself around the southern flanks of Ben Nevis (1344m) – Britain's highest mountain and

a magnet for hikers and climbers. The glen is also popular with movie-makers – parts of the films *Braveheart*, *Rob Roy* and *Harry Potter & the Sorcerer's Stone* were filmed here.

History

There's little left of the original fort from which the town takes its name – it was pulled down in the 19th century to make way for the railway. The first castle here was built by General Monk in 1654 and called Inverlochy, but the meagre ruins by the loch are of the fort built in the 1690s by General Mackay and named after King William III. In the 18th century it became part of a chain of garrisons (along with Fort Augustus and Fort George) that controlled the Great Glen in response to the Jacobite rebellions.

Originally a tiny fishing village called Gordonsburgh, the town took its present name with the opening of the railway in 1901 which, along with the building of the Caledonian Canal, soon saw it grow into a tourist centre. This has been consolidated in the last three decades by the huge increase in popularity of climbing, skiing and other outdoor sports.

Orientation

The town straggles along the shore of Loch Linnhe for around 3 miles (5km). The compact town centre is centred on High St and Cameron Sq, 200m southwest of the train and bus stations, and is easy to get around on foot. Glen Nevis and Ben Nevis (p315) are 3 miles (5km) north of the town centre.

Information

There are banks with ATMs in the High St. There are left-luggage lockers at the train station, costing £2.50/3 per 24 hours for a medium/large locker.

Belford Hospital (☎ 702481; Belford Rd) Opposite the train station.

Nevisport (☎ 704921; High St; ✆ 9am-7pm) Has a huge range of outdoor equipment, and books and maps for mountaineers. There is Internet access in the downstairs bar in Nevisport (£1 per 10 min).

TIC (☎ 703781; fortwilliam@host.co.uk; Cameron Sq; ✆ 9am-8pm Mon-Sat & 10am-6pm Sun) Has a good range of books and maps. There is Internet access here also (£1 per 20 min).

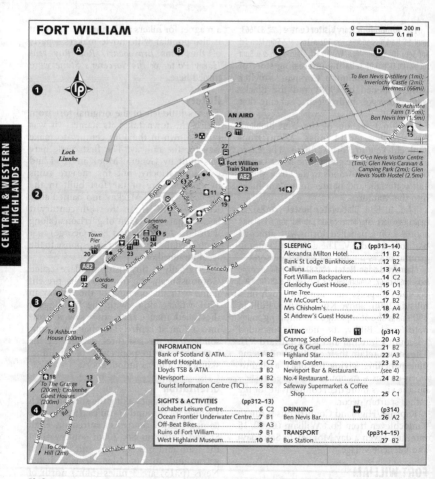

FORT WILLIAM

0 _____ 200 m
0 _____ 0.1 mi

To Ben Nevis Distillery (1mi);
Inverlochy Castle (2mi);
Inverness (66mi)

To Achintee
Farm (1.5mi);
Ben Nevis Inn (1.5mi)

To Glen Nevis Visitor Centre
(1mi); Glen Nevis Caravan &
Camping Park (2mi); Glen
Nevis Youth Hostel (2.5mi)

AN AIRD

Loch
Linnhe

Fort William
Train Station

Town
Pier

Cameron
Sq

To Ashburn
House (300m)

Gordon
Sq

To The Grange
(200m); Crolinnhe
Guest Houses
(200m)

To Cow
Hill (2mi)

INFORMATION	
Bank of Scotland & ATM	1 B2
Belford Hospital	2 C2
Lloyds TSB & ATM	3 B2
Nevisport	4 B2
Tourist Information Centre (TIC)	5 B2

SIGHTS & ACTIVITIES	(pp312–13)
Lochaber Leisure Centre	6 C2
Ocean Frontier Underwater Centre	7 B1
Off-Beat Bikes	8 A3
Ruins of Fort William	9 B1
West Highland Museum	10 B2

SLEEPING	(pp313–14)
Alexandra Milton Hotel	11 B2
Bank St Lodge Bunkhouse	12 B2
Calluna	13 A4
Fort William Backpackers	14 C2
Glenlochy Guest House	15 D1
Lime Tree	16 A3
Mr McCourt's	17 B2
Mrs Chisholm's	18 A4
St Andrew's Guest House	19 B2

EATING	(p314)
Crannog Seafood Restaurant	20 A3
Grog & Gruel	21 B2
Highland Star	22 A3
Indian Garden	23 B2
Nevisport Bar & Restaurant	(see 4)
No.4 Restaurant	24 B2
Safeway Supermarket & Coffee Shop	25 C1

DRINKING	(p314)
Ben Nevis Bar	26 A2

TRANSPORT	(pp314–15)
Bus Station	27 B2

Sights

Fort William is home to the world's leading centre for training commercial divers, which in 2003 opened a new visitor attraction, the **Ocean Frontier Underwater Centre** (☎ 702930; An Aird; ☼ 10am-6pm; last admission 4.30pm). The centre is filled with interactive exhibits charting the history of underwater exploration, including piloting ROVs (remotely operated vehicles) and the chance to take a trip in Morzh, a miniature two-man submarine.

The small but fascinating **West Highland Museum** (☎ 702169; Cameron Sq; adult/child £2/50p; 10am-4pm Mon-Sat Oct-May; 10am-5pm Mon-Sat Jun-Sep, plus 2-5pm Sun Jul & Aug) is packed with all manner of Highland memorabilia. Look out for

the secret portrait of Bonnie Prince Charlie. After the Jacobite rebellions all things Highland were banned, including pictures of the exiled leader. This tiny painting looks like nothing more than a smear of paint until placed next to a cylindrical mirror, which then reflects a credible likeness of the prince.

A tour of the **Ben Nevis Distillery** (☎ 702476; Lochy Bridge; adult/child £2/1; ☼ 9am-Mon-Fri Sep-Jun; 9am-7.30pm Mon-Fri & 10am-4pm Sat Jul & Aug) makes for a warming rainy-day alternative to exploring the hills.

From mid-June to late September or early October, the **Jacobite Steam Train** (☎ 01463-239026; www.westcoastrailway.co.uk; adult/child £24/14 day return) makes the scenic run from Fort William to Mallaig, departing Fort William at 10.20am Monday to Friday (and Sunday in August), returning from Mallaig at 2.10pm. There's a brief stop at Glenfinnan station (p318), and you get 1½ hours in Mallaig (p319). Classed as one of the great railway journeys of the world, the route crosses the historic Glenfinnan Viaduct, made famous in the film *Harry Potter & the Chamber of Secrets* – the Jacobite's owners supplied the steam locomotive and rolling stock used in the film.

Activities

The **Lochaber Leisure Centre** (☎ 704359; Belford Rd; pool £2.30, wall £2.70; ☺ 10am-9pm Mon-Fri, 10am-6pm Sat & Sun) has a swimming pool, indoor climbing wall, gym and other leisure facilities.

You can hike from the town centre to the summit of **Cow Hill** (287m) in about 1½ hours, for a superb view of Ben Nevis, the Great Glen and Loch Linnhe. From the roundabout at the end of High St, head south along Lundavra Rd for three-quarters of a mile and turn left after Lochview Dr onto an unsurfaced road that leads to the TV mast at the top of the hill. Halfway to the summit another path descends the far side of the hill into Glen Nevis, from where you can return to town along the road (total 2½ hours).

For details of walking and cycling routes through the Great Glen, see p298.

Tours

Glengarry Mini Tours (☎ 01809-501297) offers half- or full-day tours around Lochaber and Glencoe, starting at £8 for a four-hour afternoon tour.

Seal Island Cruises (☎ 703919; adult/child £7.50/ 4) operate 1½-hour boat trips on the loch from the Town Pier. There are three trips a day, plus an evening cruise with buffet at 7pm on summer weekdays.

Sleeping

It's best to book well ahead in summer, especially for hostels. See also Sleeping & Eating in the Glen Nevis section (p315).

BUDGET

Fort William Backpackers (☎ 700711; fortwilliam@ scotlands-top-hostels.com; Alma Rd; dm £10-11; ☐ ☒) A 10-minute walk from the bus and train stations, this hostel is lively and welcoming if perhaps a tad dishevelled, and enjoys a hillside location with great views.

Calluna (☎ 700451; info@fortwilliamholiday.co.uk; Heathercroft; dm £9.50-10, tw £20-22; ☒ ℗) Run by well-known mountain guide Alan Kimber and wife Sue, the Calluna is geared to hikers and climbers, with three four-bed bunkrooms, five twin rooms and an excellent drying room for your soggy hiking gear. Phone for a free pick-up from the train station.

Bank Street Lodge Bunkhouse (☎ 700070; booking@accommodation-fortwilliam.com; Bank St; dm £10-12) Part of a modern hotel and restaurant complex, the Bank Street Lodge offers the most central budget beds in town, only 250m from the train station. It has kitchen facilities and a drying room.

MID-RANGE

Lime Tree (☎ 701806; info@limetreestudio.co.uk; Achintore Rd; r per person £20-35; ☒ ℗) More interesting than your average B&B is this 19th-century former manse, now an 'art gallery with rooms' decorated throughout with the artist-owner's atmospheric Highland landscapes.

Mrs Chisholm's (☎ 705548; 5 Grange Rd; s £20-25, d £28-33) Mrs Chisholm has just two plain but cosy rooms with shared bathroom, but readers have recommended her for hospitality, comfort and good value.

St Andrew's Guest House (☎ 703038; Fassifern Rd; r per person £18-24; ℗) Set in a lovely 19th-century building that was once a rectory and choir school, St Andrew's retains period features such as carved masonry, wood panelling and stained-glass windows, and has spacious and stylish rooms with stunning views.

Glenlochy Guest House (☎ 702909; enquiries@ glenlochy.co.uk; Nevisbridge; s £25-35, d £40-60; ☒ ℗) Set in a huge garden beside the River Nevis, and convenient to Glen Nevis and the end of the West Highland Way, the Glenlochy has 12 good-value rooms.

Alexandra Milton Hotel (☎ 702241; www .miltonhotels.com; The Parade; s £30-45, d £60-135; ☒ ℗) A large, traditional, family-oriented hotel bang in the middle of town, the refurbished Alexandra is stylish and comfortable and has a good leisure club.

Other recommendations:
Mr McCourt's (☎ 703756; 6 Caberfeidh, Fassifern Rd; s £25-40, d £36-50) Vegetarian breakfast is provided on request.

Ashburn House (☎ 706000; ashburn.house@tiny world.co.uk; Achintore Rd; s £30-40, d £60-90; ✗ P) Victorian villa opposite the sailing club.

TOP END

Grange (☎ 705516; joan@grangefortwilliam.com; Grange Rd; r per person £43-48; ✗ P) An exceptional 19th-century villa set in its own landscaped grounds, the Grange is crammed with antiques and fitted with log fires, chaises longues and Victorian roll-top baths. The Turret Room, with its window seat in the turret overlooking Loch Linnhe, is our favourite.

Crolinnhe (☎ 702709; info@crolinnhe.co.uk; Grange Rd; s £76-80, d £80-110; ✗ P) If you can't get into the Grange try the neighbouring Crolinnhe, another grand 19th-century villa with lochside location and sumptuous accommodation. A vegetarian breakfast is provided on request.

Inverlochy Castle Hotel (☎ 702177; www.inver lochycastlehotel.co.uk; Torlundy; s £205-290, d £290-475; ✗ P) If your pockets are deep enough you can hob-nob with celebrities in the wonderfully grand Inverlochy Castle, an opulent Victorian creation completed in 1865. One of Scotland's finest country house hotels, it has everything you'd expect to find in a Victorian gentleman's country retreat – hunting trophies, log fires, a billiard room and a walled garden. It's set in 200 hectares of private grounds, 3 miles (5km) north of Fort William.

Eating

No 4 (☎ 704222; 4 Cameron Sq; lunch mains £6-9, dinner £9-16; 11am-5pm & 6.30-9.30pm) Easily the best-value restaurant in town, No 4 has a quiet, farmhouse feel, with an attractive, sunny conservatory and a couple of outdoor tables. The food is wholesome and fresh, ranging from hearty home-made soups to steaks, seafood and vegetarian dishes. It's tucked away in a corner to the right (west) of the TIC.

Crannog Seafood Restaurant (☎ 705589; Town Pier; mains £13-16; noon-2.30pm & 6-9.30pm) The Crannog vies with No 4 for the accolade of Fort William's best restaurant, but easily wins the prize for best location. It's perched on the Town Pier, giving diners an uninterrupted view down Loch Linnhe as they feast on fresh seafood.

Grog & Gruel (☎ 705078; 66 High St; mains £7-14; bar meals noon-9pm, restaurant 5pm-late) The Grog & Gruel is a lively Tex-Mex bar and restaurant, with a crowd-pleasing (and belly-bursting) menu of tasty enchiladas, burritos, fajitas, burgers, steaks and pizza.

Nevisport Bar & Restaurant (☎ 704921; High St; mains £5.50-8; bar 11am-late, restaurant 5pm Mon-Sat, 9am-4.30pm Sun) The downstairs bar-restaurant at the outdoor equipment shop is a mountaineering extravaganza, festooned with climbing memorabilia and portraits of celebrity climbers. Chicken, fish and steak dominate the menu, but there are several veggie options too.

Other recommendations:

Indian Garden Restaurant (☎ 705011; 88 High St; mains £5-8) Good for curries.

Highland Star (☎ 703905; 155 High St; mains £5-8) Chinese food.

Self-caterers can stock up at the **Safeway Supermarket** (An Aird; 8am-9pm Mon-Sat, 9am-7pm Sun) next to the train station. Inside, the **Safeway Coffee Shop** (mains £2-3; 8am-9pm Mon-Fri, 9am-6pm Sat & Sun) is handy for travellers on a tight budget.

Drinking

Ben Nevis Bar (☎ 702295; 105 High St) The Ben Nevis, whose lounge bar enjoys a good view over the loch, exudes a relaxed, jovial atmosphere where climbers and tourists can work off left-over energy jigging to live music (several nights a week) or belting out their karaoke favourites (Tuesday).

Nevisport Bar (☎ 704921; Airds Crossing) Downstairs at the Nevisport complex, this bar tempts walkers and climbers in with real ales and, on the second Saturday of each month, free blues, folk and jazz performances.

Getting There & Away

Fort William lies 146 miles (235km) from Edinburgh, 104 miles (167km) from Glasgow and 66 miles (106km) from Inverness.

BUS

Scottish Citylink (☎ 0870 550 5050) has direct buses to Glasgow (£13, three hours, four daily), Edinburgh (£18, 3¾ hours, one daily direct) – both via Glencoe and Crianlarich – Oban (£7.60, 1½ hours, four daily), Inverness (£8.20, two hours, five daily) and Portree on the Isle of Skye (£15.50, three hours, three daily).

Shiel Buses (☎ 01967-431272) runs one bus daily, except Sunday, to/from Mallaig (£4, 1¼ hours) via Glenfinnan (£2, 35 minutes).

Rapsons/Highland Country (☎ 702373) runs buses to Kinlochleven (£2.90, 50 minutes, six daily) via Inchree, Onich, Ballachulish and Glencoe (£2.30, 40 minutes).

CAR
The TIC has a leaflet listing car hire companies. **Easydrive Car Hire** (☎ 701616; www.easy drivescotland.co.uk; Unit 36A, Ben Nevis Industrial Estate, Ben Nevis Dr) has small cars from £32/185 a day/week including tax and unlimited mileage.

TRAIN
The spectacular West Highland line runs from Glasgow to Mallaig via Fort William. There are two or three trains daily from Glasgow to Fort William (£18, 3¾ hours), and four or five daily between Fort William and Mallaig (£7.50, 1½ hours). Travelling from Edinburgh (£30.50, five hours), you have to change at Glasgow's Queen St station.

There's no direct rail connection between Oban and Fort William – you have to change at Crianlarich, so it's faster to use the bus.

An overnight sleeper service connects Fort William and London Euston (£65 seated, £109 sharing a twin berth cabin, 13 hours).

Getting Around
From late May to late September, **Rapsons/Highland Country** (☎ 702373) bus No 42 runs from the bus station up Glen Nevis to the youth hostel (£1.20, 10 minutes, hourly Monday to Saturday, four daily Sunday) and continuing to the Lower Falls (20 minutes).

There's a **taxi rank** (☎ 702545 or 773030) at the corner of High St and The Parade.

Off-Beat Bikes (☎ 704008; 117 High St; ☺ 9am-5.30pm) rents out mountain bikes for £10/15 for a half/full day.

AROUND FORT WILLIAM
Glen Nevis
You can walk from Fort William to scenic Glen Nevis in an hour or so. The **Glen Nevis Visitor Centre** (☎ 01397-705922; ☺ 9am-6pm Easter–mid-Oct) is a mile up the glen and pro-

vides information on walking and advice on climbing Ben Nevis.

From the car park at the far end of the road along Glen Nevis, there's an excellent walk through the spectacular Nevis Gorge to **Steall Meadows**, a verdant valley dominated by a 100m-high bridal-veil waterfall. You can reach the foot of the falls by crossing the river on a wobbly, three-cable wire bridge – one cable for your feet and one for each hand – a real test of balance!

SLEEPING & EATING
Glen Nevis Caravan & Camping Park (☎ 702191; www.glen-nevis.co.uk; tent site per 1/2/3 persons £7/9.50/11.50, car £2, campervan £8, extra persons £2; ☺ Mar-Oct) This big, well-equipped site is a popular base camp for exploring the surrounding mountains.

Glen Nevis Youth Hostel (SYHA; ☎ 0870 004 1120; dm £11-13) Large, impersonal and reminiscent of a school camp, this hostel is 3 miles (5km) from Fort William, beside one of the starting points for the tourist track up Ben Nevis.

Ben Nevis Inn (☎ 702240; www.ben-nevis-inn .co.uk; Achintee; dm £9; 🖳 🅿) A good alternative is this great barn of a pub with a comfy 20-bed hostel downstairs. It's at the Achintee start of the path up Ben Nevis, and only a mile from the end of the West Highland Way.

Achintee Farm (☎ 702240; achintee.accom@ glennevis.com; Achintee; dm £10, r per person £25-35) An attractive farmhouse B&B which also has a small bunkhouse.

GETTING THERE & AWAY
From June to September, Rapsons/Highland Country bus No 42 runs from Fort William bus station to Glen Nevis Youth Hostel (£1.80, 10 minutes, 11 a day Monday to Saturday, four Sunday) and continues to the Lower Falls (3 miles/5km beyond the hostel).

Nevis Range
The **Nevis Range ski area** (☎ 01397-705825; www.nevisrange.com), 6 miles (10km) north of Fort William, spreads across the northern slopes of Aonach Mor (1221m). The gondola that gives access to the bottom of the ski area at 655m operates year-round from 10am to 5pm; a return trip costs £7.50/4.60 for an adult/child (15 minutes each way).

CLIMBING BEN NEVIS

As the highest peak in the British Isles, Ben Nevis (1344m) attracts many would-be ascensionists who would not normally think of climbing a Scottish mountain – a staggering (often literally) 70,000 people reach the summit each year.

Although anyone who is reasonably fit should have no problem climbing Ben Nevis on a fine summer's day, an ascent should not be undertaken lightly. Every year people have to be rescued from the mountain. You will need proper walking boots (the path is rough and stony, and there may be soft, wet snowfields on the summit), warm clothing, waterproofs, a map and compass, and plenty of food and water.

Here are a few facts to mull over before you go racing up the tourist track: the summit plateau is bounded by 700m-high cliffs and has a sub-Arctic climate; at the summit it can snow on any day of the year; the summit is wrapped in cloud nine days out of 10; in thick cloud, visibility at the summit can be 10m or less; in such conditions the only safe way off the mountain requires careful use of a map and compass to avoid walking over those 700m cliffs.

The tourist track (the easiest route to the top) was originally called the Pony Track. It was built in the 19th century for the pack ponies that carried supplies to a meteorological observatory on the summit that was manned continuously from 1883 to 1904.

There are three possible starting points for the tourist track – Achintee Farm; the footbridge at Glen Nevis Youth Hostel; and, if you have a car, the car park at Glen Nevis Visitor Centre. The path climbs gradually to the shoulder at Lochan Meall an t-Suidhe (known as the Halfway Lochan), then zigzags steeply up beside the Red Burn to the summit plateau. The highest point is marked by a trig point on top of a huge cairn beside the ruins of the old observatory; the plateau is scattered with countless smaller cairns, stones arranged in the shape of people's names and, sadly, a fair bit of litter.

The total distance to the summit and back is 8 miles (13km); allow four or five hours to reach the top, and another 2½ to three hours for the descent. Afterwards, as you celebrate in the pub with a pint, consider the fact that the record time for the annual Ben Nevis Hill Race is just under 1½ hours – up *and* down. Then have another pint.

At the top there's a restaurant and a couple of walking routes through nearby **Leanachan Forest**. During the ski season a one-day lift pass costs £22/12.25; a one-day package including equipment hire, lift pass and four hours' instruction costs £36.

A competition-class **downhill mountain bike trail** (11am-3pm mid-May–Sep) – for experienced riders only – runs from the Snowgoose restaurant to the base station; bikes are carried on a rack on the gondola cabin. A single trip with your own bike costs £9.75; including bike hire it's £25. There are also 25 miles (40km) of waymarked mountain-bike trails in the nearby forest.

Rapsons/Highland Country buses run from Fort William's bus station to Nevis Range (£2, 15 minutes, three or four a day).

Corpach to Loch Lochy

Corpach lies at the southern entrance to the Caledonian Canal, 3 miles (5km) north of Fort William. There's a classic picture-postcard view of Ben Nevis from the mouth of the canal. Nearby is the award-winning **Treasures of the Earth** (01397-772283; Corpach; adult/child £3/2.75; 9.30am-7pm Jul-Sep;10am-5pm Oct-Dec & Feb-Jun) exhibition, a rainy-day diversion with a great collection of gemstones, minerals, fossils and other geological curiosities.

A mile east of Corpach, at Banavie, is **Neptune's Staircase**, an impressive flight of eight locks that allows boats to climb 20m to the main reach of the Caledonian Canal. The B8004 road runs along the west side of the canal to Gairlochy at the south end of Loch Lochy, offering superb views of Ben Nevis; the canal towpath on the east side makes a great walk or bike ride (6½ miles/10km).

From Gairlochy the B8005 continues along the west side of Loch Lochy to Achnacarry and the **Clan Cameron Museum** (01397-712480; adult/child £3/free; 1.30-5pm Easter–mid-Oct, 11am-5pm Jul & Aug), which records the history of the clan and its involvement with the Jacobite rebellions.

From Achnacarry the Great Glen Way and Great Glen Cycle Route (p298) continue along the roadless western shore of Loch Lochy, and a dead-end minor road leads west along lovely **Loch Arkaig**.

Glen Spean & Glen Roy

Near Spean Bridge, at the junction of the B8004 and A82 2½ miles (4km) east of Gairlochy stands the **Commando Memorial**, which commemorates the WWII special forces soldiers who trained in this area.

Four miles (6.5km) further east, at Roy Bridge, a minor road leads north up Glen Roy, which is noted for its intriguing, so-called **parallel roads**. These prominent horizontal terraces contouring around the hillside are actually ancient shorelines formed during the last Ice Age by the waters of an ice-dammed glacial lake. The best viewpoint is 3 miles (5km) up Glen Roy.

ARDGOUR & ARDNAMURCHAN

The drive from **Corran Ferry**, 8 miles (13km) south of Fort William, to Ardnamurchan Point, the most westerly place on the British mainland, is one of the most beautiful in the western Highlands, especially in late spring and early summer when much of the narrow, twisting road is lined with the bright pink and purple blooms of rhododendrons. A car ferry (car £5.20, passenger free; 10 minutes, two an hour) crosses to Ardgour at Corran Ferry.

The road clings to the northern shore of Loch Sunart, passing through the pretty villages of **Strontian** – which gave its name to the element strontium, first discovered in ore from the nearby lead mines in 1790 – and **Salen**.

The road from Salen to Ardnamurchan Point is only 25 miles (40km) long, but it'll take you 1½ hours each way. It's a dipping, twisting, low-speed roller-coaster of a ride through sun-dappled native woodlands draped with lichen and fern. Just when you're getting used to the views of Morvern and Mull to the south, it makes a quick detour to the north for a panorama over the islands of Rum and Eigg.

Sights

Midway between Salen and Kilchoan is the fascinating **Ardnamurchan Natural History Centre** (☎ 01972-500209; Glenmore; adult/child £2.50/1.50;

10.30am-5.30pm Mon-Sat, noon-5.30pm Sun Easter-Oct). Devised by local photographer Michael MacGregor, it brings you face to face with the flora and fauna of the Ardnamurchan peninsula – the Living Building is designed to attract local wildlife and you'll have the opportunity to see pine marten, red deer and local bird life.

The scattered crofting village of **Kilchoan**, the only village of any size west of Salen, is best known for the scenic ruins of 13th-century **Mingary Castle**. The village has a **TIC** (☎ 01972-510222; Pier Rd; Easter-Oct), a shop and a hotel.

The final 6 miles (10km) of road ends at the 36m-high, grey granite tower of **Ardnamurchan Lighthouse**, built in 1849 by the Stevensons to guard the westernmost point of the British mainland. The **Kingdom of Light Visitor Centre** (☎ 01972-510210; by Kilchoan; adult/child £2.50/1.50; 10am-5pm Apr-Oct) will tell you more than you'll ever need to know about lighthouses, but the main attraction here is the expansive view over the ocean. This is a superb sunset viewpoint, provided you don't mind driving back in the dark.

Sleeping

Strontian Hotel (☎ 01967-402029; strontianhotel@supanet.com; Strontian; s £30-35, d £45-55;) This attractively modernised six-bedroom country inn dates from 1808.

Salen Inn (☎ 431661; info@thesalen-ardnamurchan.co.uk; Salen; s/d £28/46; P) A traditional Highland pub with views over Loch Sunart, the Salen has three rooms upstairs in the pub and another three rooms (each with attached bathroom) in a modern chalet out the back. The cosy lounge has a roaring fire and comfy sofa, and the bar meals, including seafood, venison and other game dishes, are very good.

You can camp at **Resipole Caravan Park** (☎ 01967-431235; Resipole; tents £7.50, with car £8-10). Alternatively, **Kilchoan House Hotel** (☎ 01972-510200; k.mews@btinternet.com; Kilchoan; r per person £28, tent site per person £2.50; Mar-Oct; P) will let you pitch a tent in their garden; ask at the bar first.

Getting There & Away

Shiel Buses (☎ 01967-431272) run between Fort William and Kilchoan (one daily Monday to Saturday). For details of ferries between Kilchoan and Tobermory, see p282.

SALEN TO LOCHAILORT

The A861 road from Salen to Lochailort passes through the low, wooded hills of Moidart. A minor road (signposted Dorlin) leads west from the A861 at Shiel Bridge to a picnic area looking across to the picturesque roofless ruin of 13th-century **Castle Tioram** (admission free; ⊗ 24 hr). The castle sits on a tiny island in Loch Moidart, connected to the mainland by a narrow strand that is submerged at high tide (the castle's name, pronounced *chee*-ram, means 'dry'). It was the ancient seat of the Clanranald Macdonalds, but the Clanranald chief ordered it to be burned (to prevent it falling into the hands of Hanoverian troops) when he set off to fight for the Jacobite side in the 1715 rebellion. At the time of research it was closed to the public while the owner and Historic Scotland wrangled over plans for its future.

As the A861 curls around the north shore of Loch Moidart you will see a line of five huge beech trees between the road and the shore. Known as the **Seven Men of Moidart** (two have been blown down by gales and replaced with saplings), they were planted in the late 18th century to commemorate the seven local men who accompanied Bonnie Prince Charlie from France and acted as his bodyguards at the start of the 1745 rebellion.

Shiel Buses (☎ 01967-431272) has a service from Fort William to Acharacle via Lochailort.

ROAD TO THE ISLES

The 46-mile (74km) A830 from Fort William to Mallaig is traditionally known as the Road to the Isles, as it leads to the jumping-off point for ferries to the Small Isles and Skye. This is a region steeped in Jacobite history, having witnessed both the beginning and the end of Bonnie Prince Charlie's doomed attempt to regain the British throne.

The final section of this scenic route, between Arisaig and Mallaig, has recently been upgraded to a fast straight road. Unless you're in a hurry, opt for the old coastal road (signposted Alternative Coastal Route).

Between the A830 and the A87 far to the north lies Scotland's 'Empty Quarter', a rugged landscape of wild mountains and lonely sea lochs roughly 20 miles (32km) by 30 miles (48km) in size, mostly unin-habited and penetrated only by two minor roads (along Lochs Arkaig and Quoich). If you want to get away from it all, this is the place to go.

Glenfinnan

☎ 01397

Glenfinnan is hallowed ground for fans of Bonnie Prince Charlie, and its central shrine is the **Glenfinnan Monument**. This tall column, topped by a statue of a kilted Highlander, was erected in 1815 on the spot where the Young Pretender first raised his standard and rallied the clans on 19 August 1745, marking the start of the ill-fated campaign that would end in disaster 14 months later. The setting, at the north end of Loch Shiel, is hauntingly beautiful.

The nearby **Glenfinnan Visitor Centre** (☎ 722250; adult/child £2/1; ⊗ 9.30am-5.30pm Jul & Aug; 10am-5pm Apr-Jun, Sep & Oct) recounts the story of the '45, as the Jacobite rebellion of 1745 is known, when the prince's loyal clansmen marched and fought from Glenfinnan south to Derby, then back north to final defeat at Culloden.

A half-mile beyond the visitor centre is **Glenfinnan Station Museum** (☎ 722295; adult/child 50/25p; ⊗ 9.30am-4.30pm Jun-Sep), a shrine of a different kind whose object of veneration is the great days of steam on the West Highland line. The famous 21-arch **Glenfinnan Viaduct**, just south of the station, was built in 1901, and featured in the movie *Harry Potter & the Chamber of Secrets*.

The **Glenfinnan Highland Games** (☎ 722324) are held on the Saturday nearest 19 August.

Two converted railway carriages at Glenfinnan Station house the **Sleeping Car Bunkhouse** (☎ 722295; dm £8-10) and the atmospheric **Railway Carriage Restaurant** (☎ 722295; snacks £1-3, mains £5-10; ⊗ 9.30am-5pm, dinner by reservation Fri & Sat), which serves home-baked cakes and real leaf tea.

Prince's House Hotel (☎ 722246; www.glenfinnan .co.uk; s £40-45, d £70-120; ⊗ P) is a delightful old coaching inn dating from 1658 and recently refurbished; it is a good place to pamper yourself – ask for the spacious, tartan-clad Stuart Room if you want to stay in the oldest part of the hotel. There is no documentary evidence that Bonnie Prince Charlie actually stayed here in 1745, but it was the only sizeable house in Glenfinnan at that time, so...

Arisaig & Morar
☎ 01687

The 5 miles (8km) of coast between Arisaig and Morar is a fretwork of rocky islets, inlets and gorgeous silver-sand beaches backed by dunes and machair, with stunning sunset views across the sea to the silhouetted peaks of Eigg and Rum. The **Silver Sands of Morar**, as they are known, draw crowds of bucket-and-spade holidaymakers in July and August, when the many camping grounds scattered along the coast are filled to overflowing. Fans of the movie *Local Hero* still make pilgrimages to the beach at **Camusdarach**, just south of Morar, which starred in the film as Ben's beach.

Loch nan Uamh (pronounced loch nan *oo*-ah, meaning the loch of the caves) washes the southern shores of Arisaig; this was where Bonnie Prince Charlie first set foot on the Scottish mainland on 11 August 1745, on the shingle beach at the mouth of the Borrodale burn. Just 2 miles (3km) to the east of this bay, on a rocky point near a parking area, the **Prince's Cairn** marks the spot where he finally departed Scottish soil, never to return, on 19 September 1746.

Garramore House (☎ 450268; South Morar; mains £9-12; s/d £30/56; **P**) was built as a hunting lodge in 1840 and served as a Special Operations Executive HQ during WWII. Today it's a wonderfully atmospheric guesthouse and restaurant set in lovely woodland gardens with great views to the Small Isles and Skye.

The **Old Library** (☎ 450651; Arisaig; snacks £4-5, mains £10-13; ☉ 11.30am-2.30pm Wed-Mon, 6.30-9.30pm) is a charming restaurant set in converted 200-year-old stables overlooking the waterfront in Arisaig village. The eclectic menu ranges from fajitas to vegetable tajine to beef in ale pie.

There are at least half a dozen camping grounds between Arisaig and Morar; all are open in summer only, and are often full in July and August, so book ahead. **Camusdarach Campsite** (☎ 450221; camdarach@aol.com; South Morar; site for 2 people £10; ☉ mid-Mar–mid-Oct) is a small and beautiful site with good facilities, only three minutes' walk from the *Local Hero* beach.

Mallaig
☎ 01687 / pop 800

If you're travelling between Fort William and Skye you may find yourself overnighting in the bustling fishing and ferry port of Mallaig. Indeed, it makes a good base for a series of day trips by ferry to the Small Isles and Knoydart. There's a **TIC** (☎ 462170), a bank with ATM, a **Co-op supermarket** (☉ 8am-10pm), and Internet access at **Got-IT** (☎ 460011; Harbour Bldg; ☉ 9.30am-5pm Mon-Sat, 10.30am-2pm Sun).

The village's rainy-day attractions consist of **Mallaig Marine World** (☎ 462292; The Harbour; adult/child £2.75/1.50; ☉ 9.30am-6pm Mon-Sat, 11am-5pm Sun Jun-Sep; 9.30am-5.30pm Mon-Sat, 11am-5pm Sun Oct-May, closed Sun Nov-Mar), a child-friendly aquarium with touch-pools and hands-on exhibits, and **Mallaig Heritage Centre** (☎ 462085; Station Rd; adult/child £1.80/90p; ☉ 9.30am-4.30pm Mon-Sat, 12.30-4.30pm Sun), which covers the archaeology and history of the region, including the heart-rending tale of the Highland Clearances in Knoydart.

The **MV Grimsay Isle** (☎ 462652) offers customised sea-fishing trips and seal-watching tours.

SLEEPING & EATING
Sheena's Backpacker's Lodge (☎ 462764; Harbour View; mains £2-6; dm £11) A friendly, 12-bed hostel in an old house overlooking the harbour. On a sunny day the hostel's garden terrace café, with its flowers, greenery and cosmopolitan backpacker staff, feels more like the Med than Mallaig.

Moorings Guest House (☎ 462225; mooringsguesthouse@talk21.com; East Bay; s/d £25/36; ✗) Just beyond the tourist office, this B&B overlooks the harbour.

Springbank Guest House (☎ 462459; East Bay; r per person £16-18; **P**) Another decent B&B that also overlooks the harbour.

Cabin Seafood Restaurant (☎ 462207; Main St; mains £5-10) A first-class seafood restaurant with a wood-panelled dining room and a cosy, traditional feel.

Fish Market (☎ 462299; Station Rd; mains £7-15; ☉ 11.45am-2.45pm & 6-9pm) A bright, modern bistro-style restaurant with excellent food and some tables with a view of the harbour.

GETTING THERE & AWAY
Shiel Buses (☎ 01967-431272) run from Fort William to Mallaig (£4, 1¼ hours, one a day Monday to Friday) via Glenfinnan (£2, 35 minutes), Arisaig and Morar.

The beautiful West Highland railway links Mallaig to Fort William (£7.50, 1½ hours) and Glasgow (£21, 5¼ hours, four a day Monday to Saturday, two Sunday). In summer vintage steam trains (p312) operate between Fort William and Mallaig.

Ferries run from Mallaig to the Small Isles (see right), the Isle of Skye (p347) and Knoydart (see below).

KNOYDART PENINSULA

☎ 01687 / pop 70

The Knoydart Peninsula is the only sizeable area in Britain that remains inaccessible to the motor car, cut off by miles of rough country and the embracing arms of Lochs Nevis and Hourn – Gaelic for the lochs of Heaven and Hell. No road penetrates this wilderness of rugged hills – **Inverie**, its sole village, can only be reached by ferry from Mallaig, or on foot from the remote road-end at Kinloch Hourn (a tough 16-mile/26km hike).

The main reasons for visiting are to climb the remote 1020m peak of **Ladhar Bheinn** (pronounced *laar*-ven), which affords some of the west coast's finest views, or just to enjoy the feeling of being cut off from the rest of the world. There are no shops, no TV and no mobile phone reception.

There are a couple of walkers' bunkhouses near Inverie, including the recently renovated **Knoydart Foundation Bunkhouse** (☎ 462242; bunkhouse@knoydart.fsnet.co.uk; Inverie; dm £7.50), 15 minutes' walk east of the ferry pier, and the atmospheric **Torrie Shieling** (☎ 462669; Inverie; dm £15), a 20-minute walk to the west.

The very basic **Barrisdale Bothy** (☎ 01599-522302; Barrisdale; dm £2.50), 6 miles (10km) west of Kinloch Hourn on the footpath to Inverie, has sleeping platforms without mattresses – you'll need your own sleeping bag and foam mat.

The **Pier House** (☎ 01687-462347; info@thepier houseknoydart.co.uk; Inverie; r per person £30; ✕) is the first place you'll see when you walk off the ferry. A guesthouse and restaurant, it offers B&B in its four homely bedrooms, and is famous for its superb seafood, venison and vegetarian dishes.

The neighbouring **Old Forge** (☎ 462267; Inverie) is listed in the Guinness Book of Records as Britain's most remote pub. It's very sophisticated – as well as having real ale on tap, there's an Italian coffee machine

for those wilderness lattes and cappuccinos, and the house special is a platter of langoustines with aioli dipping sauce. In the evening you can sit by the fire, pint of beer in hand, and join the impromptu ceilidh that seems to take place just about every night.

Getting There & Away

A Royal Mail postbus runs from Invergarry post office (on the A82, halfway along the Great Glen) to Kinloch Hourn (£5, two hours, one a day Monday, Wednesday and Friday), departing at 11.55am.

A passenger ferry operated by **Bruce Watt Cruises** (☎ 462320; www.knoydart-ferry.co.uk) links Mallaig to Inverie (£6/8 single/return, 45 minutes, two a day) on Monday, Wednesday and Friday.

SMALL ISLES

The scattered jewels of the Small Isles – Rum, Eigg, Muck, and Canna – lie strewn across the silvery blue cloth of the Cuillin Sound to the south of the Isle of Skye. Their distinctive outlines enliven the glorious views from the beaches of Arisaig and Morar.

Rum is the biggest and boldest of the four, a miniature Skye of pointed peaks and dramatic sunset silhouettes. Eigg is the most pastoral and populous, dominated by the miniature sugarloaf mountain of the Sgurr. Muck is a botanist's delight with its wildflowers and unusual alpine plants, and Canna is a craggy bird sanctuary made of magnetic rocks.

If your time is limited and you can only visit one island, choose Eigg; it has the most to offer in a day trip.

GETTING THERE & AWAY

The main ferry operator is **CalMac** (☎ 01687-462403; www.calmac.co.uk), which operates a passenger-only ferry from Mallaig to Eigg (£8.80 return, 1¼ hours, five a week), Muck (£13.55 return, 1½ hours, four a week), Rum (£13.05 return, 1¼ hours, five a week) and Canna (£14.50 return, two hours, four a week). You can also hop between the islands without returning to Mallaig, but the timetable is complicated and it requires a bit of planning. You would need at least five days to visit all four. A bicycle costs £2 extra on all routes.

From May to September **Arisaig Marine** (☎ 01687-450224; www.arisaig.co.uk) operates day cruises from Arisaig harbour to Eigg (£15 return, one hour, six a week), Rum (£19 return, 2½ hours, two or three a week), and Muck (£15 return, two hours, three a week). The trips include whale-watching, with up to an hour for close viewing. Sailing times allow four or five hours ashore on Eigg, two hours on Muck or Rum.

ISLE OF RUM
☎ 01687 / pop 30

The Isle of Rum – the biggest and most spectacular of the Small Isles – was once known as the Forbidden Island. Cleared of its crofters in the early 19th century to make way for sheep, from 1888 to 1957 it was the private sporting estate of the Bulloughs, a nouveau-riche Lancashire family whose fortune was made in the textile industry. Curious outsiders who ventured too close to the island were liable to find a gamekeeper's shotgun pointing in their direction.

The island was sold to the Nature Conservancy in 1957. Since then it has been a reserve noted for its deer, wild goats, ponies, golden and white-tailed sea eagles, and a 120,000-strong nesting colony of Manx shearwaters. Its dramatic, rocky mountains – known as the Rum Cuillin for their similarity to the peaks on neighbouring Skye – draw hill walkers and climbers.

Kinloch, where the ferry lands, is the island's only settlement; it has a small grocery shop, post office and public telephone. There's a tearoom in the village hall, which is open for day-trippers. The hall itself is open at all times for people to shelter from the rain (or the midges!).

Sights & Activities

When George Bullough – a dashing, Harrow-educated cavalry officer – inherited Rum along with half his father's fortune in 1891, he became one of the wealthiest bachelors in Britain. He blew half his inheritance on building his dream bachelor pad – the ostentatious **Kinloch Castle** (☎ 462037; adult/child £3/1.50; guided tours only, to coincide with ferry times). He shipped in pink sandstone from Dumfriesshire and 250,000 tonnes of Ayrshire topsoil for the gardens, and paid his workers a shilling extra a day to wear tweed kilts – just so they'd look more picturesque. He kept hummingbirds in the greenhouses and alligators in the garden, and entertained guests with an orchestrion, the Edwardian equivalent of a Bose hifi system. Since the Bulloughs left, the castle has survived as a perfect time capsule of upper-class Edwardian eccentricity. The guided tour should not be missed.

The only part of the island that still belongs to the Bullough family is the **Bullough Mausoleum** in Glen Harris, a miniature Greek temple that wouldn't look out of place on the Acropolis; Lady Bullough was laid to rest here alongside her husband and father-in-law in 1967, having died at the age of 98. Glen Harris is a 10-mile (16km) round trip from Kinloch, on a rough 4WD track – allow four to five hours' walking.

There's some great coastal and mountain walking on the island, including a couple of easy, waymarked **nature trails** in the woods around Kinloch. The climb to the island's highest point, **Askival** (812m), is a strenuous hike and involves a bit of rock scrambling (allow six hours for the round trip from Kinloch).

Sleeping & Eating

Accommodation on Rum is strictly limited, and if you want to stay overnight on the island, you have to contact the **reserve office** (☎ 462026) in advance.

Kinloch Campsite (£3 per person) Near the castle, this is the only place on the island where camping is allowed. The only facilities are toilets and a water supply, and there's not much in the way of level ground! Book in advance with the reserve office.

Kinloch Castle (☎ 462037; dm £12) Has 45 hostel beds in its rear wing. There's also a small restaurant offering breakfast (£3.50 to £5.50) and dinner (£10) to guests and non-guests alike.

ISLE OF EIGG
☎ 01687 / pop 70

The Isle of Eigg made history in 1997 when it became the first Highland estate to be bought out by its inhabitants. The island is now owned and managed by the Isle of Eigg Heritage Trust, a partnership among the islanders, Highland Council and the Scottish Wildlife Trust.

The ferry landing is at Galmisdale in the south. **An Laimhrig** (☎ 482416; www.isleofeigg.org), the building above the pier, houses a post office, grocery store, craft shop and tearoom. You can hire bikes here too.

Walking

The island takes its name from the Old Norse egg (edge), a reference to the **Sgurr of Eigg** (393m), an impressive mini-mountain that towers over Galmisdale. Ringed by vertical cliffs on three sides, it's composed of pitchstone lava with columnar jointing similar to that seen on the Isle of Staffa and at the Giant's Causeway in Northern Ireland.

The climb to the summit (allow three to four hours for the round trip) begins on the stony road leading up from the pier, which continues uphill through the woods to a red-roofed cottage. Go through the gate to the right of the cottage and turn left; just 20m along the road a cairn on the right marks the start of a boggy footpath that leads over the eastern shoulder of the Sgurr, then traverses beneath the northern cliffs until it makes its way up onto the summit ridge.

On a fine day the views from the top are magnificent – Rum and Skye to the north, Muck and Coll to the south, Ardnamurchan Lighthouse to the southeast and Ben Nevis shouldering above the surrounding mountains on the eastern horizon. Take binoculars – on a calm summer's day there's a good chance of seeing minke whales feeding down below in the Sound of Muck.

A shorter walk (2 miles/3km; allow 1½ hours round trip, and bring a torch) leads west from the pier to the spooky and claustrophobic **Uamh Fraing** (the Massacre Cave). Start as for the Sgurr of Eigg, but half a mile from the pier turn left through a gate and into a field. Follow the 4WD track and fork left before a white cottage to pass below it. A footpath continues across the fields to reach a small gate in a fence; go through it and descend a ridge towards the shore.

The cave entrance is tucked inconspicuously down to the left of the ridge. The entrance is tiny – almost a hands-and-knees job – but the cave opens out inside and runs a long way back. Go right to the back, turn off your torch, and imagine the cave packed shoulder to shoulder with terrified men, women and children. Then imagine the

panic as your enemies start piling timber into the entrance. Almost the entire population of Eigg – around 400 people – sought refuge in this cave when the MacLeods of Skye raided the island in 1577. In an act of inhuman cruelty, the raiders lit a fire in the narrow entrance and everyone inside died of asphyxiation. There are more than a few ghosts floating around in here.

Other good walks are to the deserted crofts of **Grulin** on the southwest coast (two hours round trip), and north to Laig Beach with its famous **singing sands** – the sand makes a squeaking noise when you walk on it (three hours return). You can get more information on island walks from the craft shop in An Laimhrig (p321).

Sleeping

All accommodation should be booked in advance.

Glebe Barn (☎ 482417; www.glebebarn.co.uk; Galmisdale; dm £12, d £26) There's excellent bunkhouse accommodation with kitchen, laundry and drying rooms.

Lageorna (☎ 482405; lageorna@isleofeigg.org; Cleadale; r per person £16) Good B&B accommodation.

Kildonnan House (☎ 482446; Kildonnan; r per person £18) Another homely B&B.

An Laimhrig (☎ 482416; www.isleofeigg.org) The craft shop takes fees for camping near the head of the bay at Galmisdale (£3 per tent); you use the showers and toilets at the pier.

You can also camp at **Sue Holland's Croft** (☎ 482480; £4 per tent) at Cleadale in the north of the island.

ISLE OF MUCK

☎ 01687 / pop 34

The tiny island of Muck, measuring just 2 miles by 1 mile, has exceptionally fertile soil, and the island is carpeted with wildflowers in spring and early summer. It takes its name from the Gaelic muc (pig), and pigs are still raised there.

Ferries call at the southern settlement of **Port Mor**. There's a tearoom and craft shop above the pier, which also acts as an information centre.

It's an easy 15-minute walk along the island's only road from the pier to the sandy beach at **Gallanach** on the northern side of the island. A longer and rougher hike (1½ hours round trip) goes to the top of **Beinn**

Airein (137m) for the best views. Puffins nest on the cliffs at the western end of Camas Mor, the bay to the south of the hill. On Wednesday in summer you can take a **guided tour** (£1; ☿ departs 1.30pm) around the island by tractor and trailer.

The cosy six-bed **Isle of Muck Bunkhouse** (☎ 462042; dm £10.50), with its oil-fired Rayburn stove, is just above the pier, as is the welcoming eight-room **Port Mhor Guesthouse** (☎ 462365; r per person £35); the evening meals here are available to non-guests (£15, book in advance).

You can **camp** on the island for free – ask at the craft shop first.

ISLE OF CANNA
☎ 01687 / pop 16

The roadless island of Canna is a moorland plateau of black basalt rock, just 5 miles long and 1¼ miles wide (8km by 2km). **Compass Hill** (143m), at the northeastern corner, contains enough magnetite (an iron oxide mineral) to deflect the magnetic compasses in passing yachts.

The ferry arrives at the hamlet of **A'Chill** at the eastern end of the island, where tourists have left extensive graffiti on the rock face south of the harbour. There's a tearoom and craft shop by the harbour and a tiny post office in a hut.

You can walk to **An Coroghon**, just east of the ferry pier, a medieval stone tower perched atop a sea cliff, and continue to Compass Hill, or take a longer hike along the southern shore past a **Celtic cross** and the remains of the 7th-century **St Columba's Chapel**.

The island is owned by the NTS and there are no hotels or B&Bs. Contact the **warden** (☎ 462466) for permission to camp, or write to the Holidays Secretary, NTS, Wemyss House, 28 Charlotte Sq, Edinburgh EH2 4ET for details of self-catering accommodation.

CENTRAL & WESTERN
HIGHLANDS

Northern Highlands & Islands

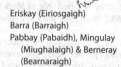

The northern Highlands conjure up most visitors' romantic notion of Scotland. Vast, wild expanses punctuated by endless, steely-blue lochs and towering mountain ranges with snow trickling down their peaks, which are often lost in swirling cloud and mist. This is truly an astonishing part of Scotland, with jaw-dropping scenery that will sear itself in your mind. It's powerful country and you can almost feel the desolation and tragedy of the Clearances – the silence is deafening. But the romanticism of the region is inescapable too and if you've ever heard the call of the wild, you're likely to be mesmerised here. There's something unique and Scottish in all of this – an elusive quality that furrows brows before the penny drops. It's the ethereal light that squeezes through the clouds and tangos over Europe's northern fringe, illuminating its rugged splendour and changing its appearance by the hour, or sometimes by the minute.

The stunning scenery extends offshore to the Isle of Skye, where the jagged peaks of the Cuillin Hills tear at the mist and the ghosts of Bonnie Prince Charlie and Flora Macdonald haunt the hallways of Dunvegan Castle. And that magical light intensifies as you head west to the Outer Hebrides – the 'isles at the edge of the sea' – with their landscapes of peat bog, lochan and bare, glaciated gneiss, softened by glittering beaches, wildflower-strewn machair, and the outlines of ruined blackhouses settling into the turf like fossil shapes in a slab of rock.

NORTHERN HIGHLANDS & ISLANDS

HIGHLIGHTS

■ Ogling at the splendour of **Dornoch Cathedral** (p329) and the castles of **Dunrobin** (p329) and **Eilean Donan** (p345)

■ Grappling with the Highlands' mighty peaks in the stunning mountainous playgrounds of **Inverpolly** (p339), **Assynt** (p339) and **Glen Torridon** (p343)

■ Hiking among the jagged peaks of Skye's spectacular **Cuillin Hills** (p349)

■ Taking a boat trip to experience the brooding grandeur of **Loch Coriusk** (p349)

■ Meditating on the meaning of the mysterious **Standing Stones of Callanish** (p361)

■ POPULATION: 175,000   ■ AREA: 20,000 SQ KM

EAST COAST

In both landscape and character, the east coast is where the real barrenness of the Highlands begins to unfold. A gentle splendour and a sense of escapism mark the route along the twisting A9, as it heads north for the last of Scotland's far-flung mainland, population outposts. With only a few exceptions, the tourism frenzy is left behind once the road traverses Cromarty Firth and snakes its way along wild and pristine coastline.

While the interior is dominated by the vast and mournful Sutherland mountain range, along the coast great heather-covered hills heave themselves out of the wild North Sea. Rolling farmland, dominated by miles of stone fencing, crawling its way over hills and pastureland, drops suddenly into the icy waters and the only interruptions en route are the small, historic towns moored precariously on the coast's edge.

GETTING AROUND

The region is well served by buses, and trains follow the coast up to Wick then across to Thurso. **Citylink** (☎ 0870 550 5050) runs regular services from Inverness through to Wick, stopping at most towns on the A9 and A99 along the way, before taking the short cut inland to Thurso. **Rapsons/Highland Country** (☎ 01463-222244) operates buses from Wick to Thurso, via the coast and John O'Groats.

STRATHPEFFER

☎ 01997 / pop 918

Charming Strathpeffer has a certain faded grandeur in its creaking old pavilions and grandiose hotels – there's a whisper of days gone by in the streets, which are interspersed among some lush greenery.

The village was a fashionable spa in Victorian and Edwardian times when chic society folk congregated here to splash about in the sulphurous waters.

The self-service **TIC** (☎ 421000; The Square; ☺ 10am-5pm Mon-Sat Easter-Nov) is in Square Wheels Bike Shop, which also hires mountain bikes for £12 per day. You'll find a supermarket and a post office nearby.

Sights

The renovated **Pump Room** (☎ 420124; Strathpeffer; adult/child £2.50/1) has some splendid

displays showing the bizarre lengths Victorians went to in the quest for a healthy glow. It's open by previous arrangement for groups.

At the old Victorian train station is the **Highland Museum of Childhood** (☎ 421031; adult/child £2/free; ☺ 10am-5pm Mon-Sat, 2-5pm Sun Apr-Jun, Sep & Oct; 10am-7pm Mon-Fri, 10am-5pm Sat, 2-5pm Sun Jul & Aug). It has a wide range of social history displays about childhood in the Highlands. Most importantly it has activities for the kids including a dressing-up box and a toy train.

Sleeping

Craigvar (☎ 421622; www.craigvar.com; The Square; r per person £25-35; ☒) Luxury living is what you'll find in this delightful Georgian town house. All the little extras that mark out a classy place are here, such as a welcome drink, bathrobes and fresh fruit. Couples should go for the Blue Room with its sensational four-poster bed – you'll need to collapse back into it after the gourmet breakfast.

Highland Hotel (☎ 421457; fax 421033; 2-nights per person from £50) Many of the old spa hotels have fallen into neglect, but this one has been renovated. It's a magnificent, European chateau-style building overlooking the TIC, with a wood-panelled lobby and lounge, plus lovely wooded grounds. Book in advance for the best deals.

Getting There & Away

Stagecoach Inverness operates buses from Inverness to Strathpeffer (£3, 45 minutes, hourly Monday to Saturday, four on Sunday). The Inverness to Gairloch and Durness buses, plus some Inverness to Ullapool buses, also run via Strathpeffer.

TAIN

☎ 01862 / pop 3511

Tain is Scotland's oldest royal burgh and was an important pilgrimage centre. It has a couple of excellent attractions, making it a desirable spot to break a journey along the east coast. The High St has a post office and banks.

Tain Through Time (☎ 894089; adult/child £3.50/2.50; ☺ 10am-5pm Apr-Jun, Sep & Oct; 10am-6pm Jul & Aug) is a fascinating heritage centre, which describes the history of Tain as a place of pilgrimage. The actors dressed in period costume make it fun for the kids as well.

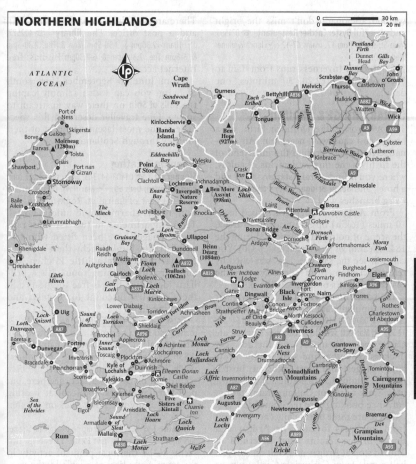

NORTHERN HIGHLANDS

On the northern edge of town is the excellent **Glenmorangie Distillery & Visitor Centre** (☎ 892477; tours £2; ☺ 9am-5pm Mon-Fri year-round, plus 10am-4pm Sat, noon-4pm Sun Jun-Aug), which produces some of the finest single malts in the Highlands. For proof, knock back a dram of the sherry- or Madeira-wood finish.

Rooms are of a high standard at the bustling **St Duthus Hotel** (☎ 894007; Tower St; s/d £24/50, d with bathroom £60; mains £6-7). The bathrooms are spotless and the snazzy dining area has a cheery vibe; there's also a beer garden which doubles as a playground for the kids.

Citylink buses from Inverness to Thurso pass through Tain (four daily). There are up to three trains daily to Inverness (£8.50, one hour) and Thurso (£10.60, 2½ hours).

PORTMAHOMACK
☎ 01862 / pop 608

A former fishing village, Portmahomack is now quiet and relaxing, making it a great spot to kick back and chill out.

Tarbat Discovery Centre (☎ 871351; Tarbatness Rd; adult/child £3.50/1; ☺ 10am-5pm May-Sep, 2-5pm Mar, Apr & Oct-Dec) has some excellent carved Pictish stones and medieval grave slabs. There are good coastal walks at **Tarbat Ness**, 3 miles (5km) northeast of the village; the headland is marked by a tall, red-and-white striped lighthouse.

If you're staying, try the friendly and comfortable **Caledonian Hotel** (☎ 871345; www .caleyhotel.co.uk; Main St; s £30-35, d £45-59) overlooking the village's sandy beach. If you're a seafood aficionado don't miss the bright and cheerful **Oyster Catcher Restaurant** (☎ 871560; Main St; snacks from £2, mains £7-12; ☺ lunch & dinner Wed-Sun).

Stagecoach Inverness runs from Tain to Portmahomack (£2.20, 30 minutes, one daily).

BONAR BRIDGE & AROUND

The A9 crosses the Dornoch Firth, on a bridge and causeway, near Tain. An alternative route goes around the inner end of the firth via the tiny settlements of **Ardgay**, where you'll find a train station, shop and a hotel, and **Bonar Bridge**, where the A836 to Lairg branches west.

From Ardgay, a single-track road leads 10 miles (16km) up Strathcarron to **Croick**, the scene of notorious evictions during the 1845 Clearances (see boxed text, p330). You can still see the sad messages scratched by refugee crofters from Glencalvie on the eastern windows of Croick Church.

If a youth hostel could attract a five-star rating, opulent **Carbisdale Castle Youth Hostel** (SYHA; ☎ 0870 004 1109; Culrain; dm adult/child £14.75/ 12.50; ☺ Mar-Oct) would score six. Carbisdale Castle was built in 1914 for the dowager duchess of Sutherland – it is now Scotland's biggest and most luxurious hostel, its halls studded with statues. It's 10 minutes' walk north of Culrain train station. Advance bookings are recommended.

There are three buses daily (not Sunday) from Inverness to Lairg via Ardgay and Bonar Bridge. Trains from Inverness to Thurso stop at Ardgay and Culrain (£10.40, half a mile from Carbisdale Castle) two or three times daily.

LAIRG

☎ 01549 / pop 904

Lairg is an attractive village strung out quite a way – it makes for an idyllic afternoon wander, although the tranquillity can be rudely interrupted by the sound of military jets heard whining and cracking overhead. At the southern end of Loch Shin, it's the gateway to the remote mountains and loch-speckled bogs of central Sutherland. The A836 from Lairg to Tongue passes Ben Klibreck (961m) and Ben Loyal (764m).

Lairg has a seasonal **TIC** (☎ 402160; Ferry-croft Countryside Centre; ☺ 9.30am-5pm Jun-Aug) on the far side of the river from the village.

There are also shops, a bank (with ATM), and a post office. The **library** (☎ 402577; ☺ 10am-12.30pm & 2.30-5pm Mon & Thu, 2.30-5pm & 6-8pm Tue, 2.30-5pm & 6-7.30pm Fri) has free Internet access.

From June to September, just south of Lairg, you can watch salmon leaping the **Falls of Shin** on their way upstream to spawn. One traveller described this spectacle as the most fascinating part of their journey through Scotland.

Sleeping & Eating

Sleeperzzz (☎ 01408-641343; www.sleeperzzz.com; Rogart Station; beds £9; ☺ Mar-Nov) Nine miles (14km) east of Lairg, at Rogart train station, is this charming and unique hostel. Ten compartments in two 1st-class railway carriages have been fitted with two comfortable bunks each; there's also a compartment with a little kitchen and another with a dining room. It's a brilliant idea! Bike hire is free to guests and there's a 10% discount for cyclists and train travellers.

Crask Inn (☎ 411241; Crask; r per person £20; 3-course dinner £12) The small and remote Crask Inn, 13 miles (21km) north of Lairg on the A836, is notorious for being the coldest place in Scotland. In December 1995 a record low of -30°C was recorded here, but peat-burning stoves and central heating keep the inn cosy. Roast venison is often on the menu.

Nip Inn (☎ 402243; www.nipinn.co.uk; Main St; r per person £22-27; bar meals from £5.50) The Nip Inn seems to be the focal point of activity in the town. Sip a beer at a table by the window while watching the hustle and bustle of Highland life.

Getting There & Away

From Lairg single-track roads run north to Tongue, Laxford Bridge (between Durness and Kylesku) and Ledmore (between Kylesku and Ullapool).

Stagecoach Inverness buses run from Inverness to Tain (£5.70, one hour, half-hourly); MacLeods then pick up the link from Tain to Lairg (£2.80, 30 minutes, four daily Monday to Saturday).

Trains from Inverness to Thurso stop at Lairg (£10.40, 1½ hours) and Rogart (£10.40, 1¾ hours) two or three times daily in each direction.

NORTHERN HIGHLANDS & ISLANDS

DORNOCH

☎ 01862 / pop 1206

It's difficult to believe that Scotland's last executed witch perished in a vat of boiling tar in Dornoch in 1722, because today this graceful village is all happy families. On the coast, 2 miles (3km) off the A9, this symphony in sandstone bewitches visitors with flowers, greenery and affable locals at every turn.

The **TIC** (☎ 810916; 9.30am-5.30pm Mon-Sat, 10am-4pm Sun Apr-Oct, call for winter hr;) in the main square doubles as a coffee shop.

Sights

The town is clustered around the 13th-century **Dornoch Cathedral**, which is shaped like a crucifix. The criss-cross of light streaming through adjacent stained-glass windows creates a powerful effect. The original building was destroyed in 1570 during a clan feud. Despite some patching up, it wasn't completely rebuilt until 1837.

Sleeping

Dornoch Castle Hotel (☎ 810216; www.dornochcastlehotel.com; Castle St; garden s/d £45/60, castle r £110; dinner mains £12-16, bar meals £6.50) Fancy a night in a castle? Then try this grand, 16th-century former bishop's palace. The stately rooms vary considerably, but you're unlikely to be disappointed no matter what you choose – ask for a room number at random! In the evening toast your toes in the cosy bar before dining in style at the first-rate restaurant.

Rosslyn Villa (☎ 810237; Castle St; r per person £15-18;) This excellent place proves that the best B&Bs come with simplicity and a smile.

Trevose Guest House (☎ 810269; trevose@amserve.net; Cathedral Sq; s/d £25/40;) This great B&B claims primo location on the village green, across from the cathedral.

Getting There & Away

Citylink has services to/from Inverness (£6, 1¼ hours, four to five daily) and Thurso (£8, 2¼ hours, four to five daily), stopping in the Square at Dornoch.

GOLSPIE

☎ 01408 / pop 1404

Crying gulls and the faint whiff of pungent seaweed greets visitors to Golspie. The beach is nothing to rave about, but the nearby castle is a different story.

Golspie is basically one street and a beach, with a couple of supermarkets, banks and a post office. It's the starting point for some good walks. One trail leads north along the coast for 5 miles (8km) to Brora, passing the remains of the Iron Age broch of **Carn Liath** about halfway along. The other trail climbs steeply above the village to the summit of **Ben Bhraggie** (394m), which is crowned by a massive monument to the duke of Sutherland, erected in 1834 and visible for miles around.

Sights

One mile north of Golspie is mighty **Dunrobin Castle** (☎ 01408-633177; adult/child £6.25/5; 10.30am-5.30pm daily Jul & Aug; 10.30am-4.30pm Mon-Sat, noon-5.30pm Sun Jun & Sep; 10.30am-4.30pm Mon-Sat, noon-4.30pm Sun Apr, May & Oct), the largest house in the Highlands (187 rooms). Although it dates back to around 1275 and additions were made in the mid-1600s and late 1700s, most of what you see today was built in French style between 1845 and 1850. One of the homes of the earls and dukes of Sutherland, it's richly furnished and offers an intriguing insight into their opulent lifestyle.

Judging by the numerous hunting trophies and animal skins, much of the family's energy seems to have gone into shooting things. The house also displays innumerable gifts from farm tenants (probably grateful they weren't victims of the 'shift over for sheep programme'). Behind the house, magnificent formal gardens slope down to the sea, and a summer house offers an eclectic museum of archaeological finds, natural-history exhibits and more big-game trophies.

Getting There & Away

Buses between Inverness and Thurso stop in Golspie. There are also trains from Inverness (£11.40, two hours, two or three daily).

HELMSDALE

☎ 01431 / pop 861

The town of Helmsdale is pretty and petite surrounded by stunning, undulating coastline and the River Helmsdale – one of the best salmon rivers in the Highlands.

CROFTING & THE CLEARANCES

In many parts of the Highlands and islands you will see clusters of ruined cottages crumbling amid the bracken – all that remains of deserted farming communities. Up to the 19th century the most common form of farming settlement here was the *baile*, a group of a dozen or so families who farmed the land granted to them by the local chieftain in return for military service and a portion of the harvest. The arable land was divided into strips called *rigs*, which were allocated to different families by annual ballot so that each took turns at getting the poorer soils; this system was known as *runrig*. The families worked the land communally, and their cattle shared the common grazing.

But this lifestyle was swept away in the wake of the Highland Clearances (p30), which took place between around 1750 and the 1880s. Following the ban on private armies, clan chiefs no longer needed military service from their tenants, and saw sheep farming as far more profitable than collecting rent from poverty-stricken farmers. Tens of thousands of tenant farmers were evicted from their homes and their land.

Those who chose not to emigrate or move to the cities to find work were forced to eke a living from narrow plots of marginal agricultural land, often close to the coast, a form of smallholding that became known as crofting. The small patch of land barely provided a living, and had to be supplemented by other work such as fishing and kelp-gathering. The close-knit community of the *baile* was replaced by the widely scattered cottages of the crofting settlements that you can still see today.

When economic depression hit in the late 19th century, many crofters couldn't pay their rent. This time, however, they resisted expulsion, instead forming the Highland Land Reform Association and their own political party. Their resistance led to several of their demands being acceded to by the government; the Crofters' Holdings Act of 1886 provided for security of tenure, fair rents and eventually the supply of land for new crofts.

Today the Scottish Highlands are, in many parts, a graveyard of broken communities, which ceased living and breathing more than 200 years ago. Evidence of the cruel evictions is everywhere and the human tragedy has scarred this majestic landscape. While economic recovery is in full swing, the human cost is irrecoverable and the desolation of the countryside is in harmony with the poor souls lost to starvation, poverty and estrangement from their ancestral lands.

Crofting tenancies still exist and complex regulations now protect the crofters. The Land Reform Act, passed in 2003, gave crofters the absolute right to buy their tenancy and a law abolishing feudal tenure is planned for late 2004, which will end 900 years of feudalism.

For tourist information, go to the **Strath Ullie Crafts & Information Centre** (☎ 821402; The Harbour, Shore St; ☑ 9am-5.30pm Apr-Oct, 10am-4.30pm Mon-Sat Nov-Mar).

Sights & Activities

The excellent **Timespan Heritage Centre** (☎ 821327; Dunrobin St; adult/child £4/2; ☑ 9.30am-5pm Mon-Sat, noon-5pm Sun Easter-Jun & Sep–mid-Oct; 9.30am-6pm Jul & Aug) has a model of Barbara Cartland, the late queen of pulp romance novels (she holidayed here for over 60 years). There's also a free gallery upstairs overlooking the river, featuring fine exhibitions from local artists.

Fishing for a good time starts with throwing in your line, and **Bridge Hotel Tackle Shop** (☎ 821102; Dunrobin St) will help you do just that. It rents out fly rods for £20 per day,

and river fishing for trout or salmon costs £17 per day (loch fishing is cheaper).

Sleeping & Eating

Helmsdale Youth Hostel (SYHA; ☎ 0870 004 1124; cnr A9 & Old Caithness Rd; dm adult/child £9/7.75; ☑ mid-May–Sep) This hostel is particularly good for groups and has large, 12-bed dorms and a cavernous dining hall. It gets busy; book well ahead for July and August.

Belgrave Arms Hotel (☎ 821242; www.belgrave armshotel.com; cnr Dunrobin St & A9; s/d £20/48) The Belgrave has a genuine feel to it – a slightly musty odour and creaky floorboards. Importantly, though, the rooms are fresh and well-maintained.

La Mirage (7 Dunrobin St; snacks £1.50-3, mains £6-13) Proprietor Nancy Sinclair has gone to great lengths to become Cartland's double.

Accordingly, her restaurant's décor oozes pink kitsch, and is a draw card in itself. The menu boasts standard grills and vegetarian options, as well as fish done both cheap and classy.

Getting There & Away
Buses from Inverness and Thurso stop in Helmsdale, as do trains (£11.40, 2½ hours, two daily Monday to Saturday, one Sunday).

HELMSDALE TO LATHERON
About 7 miles (11km) north of Helmsdale a 15-minute walk east from the A9 (signposted) takes you to **Badbea**, where the ruins of crofts are perched on the cliff top. The **Berriedale Braes**, 2½ miles (4km) beyond the Badbea parking area, is a difficult section of the A9, with steep gradients and hairpin bends.

Dunbeath has a spectacular setting in a deep glen – it makes a good stop on the way to the northern towns. There are a couple of shops and a **heritage centre** (☎ 01593-731233; The Old School; adult/child £2/free; ☼ 10am-5pm Easter-Oct), with displays about the history of Caithness, including crofting and fisheries. There are also exhibitions, including the crash of the Sunderland flying boat near Dunbeath in 1942.

The friendly, laid-back **Kingspark Llama Farm** (☎ 01593-751202; Berriedale; s/d from £16/32), on a working llama farm, is a good choice for accommodation in the area.

At the **Clan Gunn Heritage Centre & Museum** (☎ 015932-731370; Latheron; adult/child £2/1; ☼ 11am-1pm & 2-4pm Mon-Sat Jun & Sep, 11am-1pm & 2-4pm Mon-Sat, 2-4pm Sun Jul & Aug), in Latheron, 3 miles (5km) north of Dunbeath on the A9, you'll learn that a Scot, not Christopher Columbus, discovered America – but you might take this claim with a pinch of salt! Even if you don't want to go in, it's worth pulling into the car park on a fine day to admire the stunning views.

LYBSTER & AROUND
☎ 01593
Lybster is a purpose-built fishing village dating from 1810, with a pretty harbour area surrounded by grassy cliffs. The major crowd-pleaser here is the **Waterlines Visitor Centre** (☎ 721520; Lybster; adult/child £2/50p; ☼ 11am-5pm Mon-Sat, noon-5pm Sun May-Sep). It

has a heritage exhibition, a smokehouse, giving visitors a whiff of the kippering process, and CCTV beaming live pictures of nesting sea birds from nearby cliffs. It's child-friendly and after a visit you can sit on outdoor benches and munch on some home-baking while admiring the views across the harbour

At Ulbster, 5 miles (8km) north of Lybster on the A9, is **Whaligoe Steps**, a spectacular staircase cut into the cliff face giving access to a tiny natural harbour ringed by vertical cliffs and echoing with the cackle of nesting fulmars. The path begins at the end of the minor road beside the telephone box, opposite the road signposted 'Cairn of Get'. The **Cairn o'Get**, a prehistoric burial cairn, is a mile northwest of Ulbster.

There are several interesting prehistoric sites near Lybster. Five miles to the northwest of Lybster, on the minor road to Achavanich, just south of Loch Stemster, are the 40 or so **Achavanich Standing Stones**.

A mile east of Lybster on the A9, a turnoff leads north to the **Grey Cairns of Camster**. Dating from between 4000 and 2500 BC, these burial chambers are hidden in long, low mounds rising from an evocatively desolate stretch of moor. The Long Cairn measures 60m by 21m. You can enter the main chamber, but must first crawl into the well-preserved **Round Cairn**. The Round Cairn has a corbelled ceiling. Afterwards, you can continue 7 miles (11km) north on this remote road to approach Wick on the A882.

Back on the A9, the **Hill o'Many Stanes**, another 2 miles (3km) beyond the Camster turn-off, is a curious, fan-shaped arrangement of 22 rows of small stones probably dating from around 2000 BC.

Getting There & Away
Citylink buses between Thurso and Inverness run via Lybster (£3.50, one hour, up to four daily), Latheron and Dunbeath. Rapsons/Highland Country runs frequently from Wick to Ulbster, Lybster, Dunbeath and Berriedale.

WICK
☎ 01955 / pop 7333
Wick is a place you should spend at least a night. It takes a wee while to dig under the façade of this seemingly dismal place, with its boarded-up buildings, to enjoy its

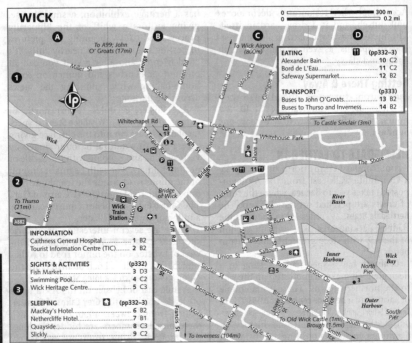

WICK

admirable attractions. It's probably the most economically depressed town in the north – it certainly has that atmosphere – but it also has a fascinating history and a grittiness that takes a while to appreciate.

Information

The friendly **TIC** (☎ 602596; Whitechapel Rd; 🕑 10am-5pm Mon-Sat, 10am-4pm Sun Jun-Sep; 10am-5pm Mon-Sat Apr, May & Oct) is on the road leading to the Safeway supermarket car park off High St.

Sights

WICK HERITAGE CENTRE

The town's award-winning local **museum** (☎ 605393; 18-27 Bank Row; adult/child £2/50p; 🕑 10am-5pm Mon-Sat May-Sep) deserves all the praise heaped upon it. It tracks the rise and fall of the herring industry, and displays everything from fishing equipment to complete herring fishing boats.

The Johnston photographic collection is the museum's star exhibit. From 1863 to 1977, three generations of Johnstons photographed everything that happened

around Wick, and the 70,000 photographs are an amazing portrait of the town's life. The museum even displays the Johnstons' photo studio. Prints of their superb early photos are for sale.

CASTLES

A path leads a mile south of town to the ruins of 12th-century **Old Wick Castle** (free admission), with the spectacular cliffs of the **Brough** and the **Brig**, as well as **Gote o'Trams**, a little farther south. In good weather, it's a fine coastal walk to the castle, but take care on the final approach. Three miles (5km) northeast of Wick is the magnificently located cliff-top ruin of **Castle Sinclair**.

Sleeping & Eating

Slickly (☎ 602356; 2 Shore Lane; r per person £15) Just off the High St, Slickly is a traditional, welcoming house with good value rooms that share a bathroom. There's a communal breakfast in the morning in a sun-filled glass conservatory.

Nethercliffe Hotel (☎ 60204; fax 605691; Louisburgh St; s/d £35/50) The Nethercliffe, signposted off the main drag, is a very friendly, small hotel with good-value rooms exhibiting warmth and old-fashioned décor. The cosy little watering hole here does decent bar lunches.

MacKay's Hotel (☎ 602323; fax 605930; Union St; s/d £55/80) The renovated MacKay's is Wick's best hotel. Rooms vary in layout and size so ask to see a few. The 2.75m-long Ebenezer Pl, the shortest street in Britain, runs past one end of the hotel.

Quayside (☎ 603229; www.quayside.co.uk; 25 Harbour Quay; r per person £16.50-22) This homely place is also recommended; it's down by the harbour

Bord de L'Eau (☎ 604400; 2 Market St; starters £4, mains £7-12; ☺ lunch Tue-Sat, dinner Tue-Sun) This serene, upmarket French restaurant is the best place to eat in Wick by a mile. It overlooks the river and serves dishes such as escargot, and red snapper with a chive and shallot butter sauce. The menu is very meat-driven.

Alexander Bain (☎ 609920; Market Pl; dishes £5-7; ☺ lunch & dinner) This is the only pub serving food on weeknights in town. It's a fairly humourless, cavernous place in the middle of the pedestrianised High St, attracting a cross-section of tourists, families and rag-tag locals. The food dabbles in pastas, salads, burgers, steaks and wraps.

Getting There & Away
Wick is a transport gateway to the surrounding area. **Logan Air** (☎ 602294) flies between Edinburgh and Wick airport (£168, one hour, one daily Monday to Saturday) and onto Kirkwall (£32, 25 minutes, one daily Monday to Saturday) on Orkney. **Eastern Airways** (☎ 01652 680 600) flies to Aberdeen (£51, plus taxes, 35 minutes, twice daily).

Citylink operate buses to/from Inverness (£11, three hours, four daily) and Thurso (£2.50, 40 minutes, four daily). **Rapsons/Highland Country** (☎ 01847-893123) runs the connecting service to John o'Groats (£2.30, 40 minutes, up to four daily Monday to Saturday) for the passenger ferry to Burwick, Orkney.

Trains service Wick from Inverness (£12.50, four hours, one or two daily).

JOHN O'GROATS
☎ 01955 / pop 512
Everything about John o'Groats screams tourist trap. The main attraction is a car park surrounded by shoddy craft and souvenir shops. There's even a booth where you can get your mug shot taken beside an arrowed sign with the name and distance of your home town. Give them a challenge and say you're from Hobart.

Two miles (3km) east of John o'Groats is the much better **Duncansby Head**, which is home to many sea birds at the start of summer. A path leads to **Duncansby Stacks**, spectacular natural rock formations soaring 60m above the sea. There is a series of narrow inlets and deep coves on this wonderful stretch of coast.

Even if you're hell-bent on staying… don't!

Getting There & Away
Rapsons/Highland Country run buses between John o'Groats and Wick (£2.30, 40 minutes, up to four buses daily, Monday to Saturday). There are also up to five services Monday to Saturday to/from Thurso.

From May to September, the passenger ferry MV *Pentland Venture*, operated by **John o'Groats Ferries** (☎ 01955-611353; www.jogferry.co.uk), shuttles across to Burwick in Orkney (adult/child return £26/13); a coach tour of Orkney mainland, including the ferry fare, is £34/17. Ninety-minute wildlife cruises to the island of Stroma or Duncansby Head cost £14.

MEY
The latest attraction on Scotland's northern tourist beat, and a big crowd puller, is the **Castle of Mey** (☎ 01847-851227; www.castleofmey.org.uk; adult/child £5/3; ☺ 11am-4.30pm Tue-Sat, 2-5pm Sun, late May-Jul & mid-Aug–mid-Oct). It's about 6 miles (10km) from John o'Groats, off the A836 to Thurso and holds a special place in the hearts of many Scots, being the former home of the late Queen Mother. Hardened royal buffs will get a kick out of items of memorabilia and pictures of the late Queen Mum, but for everyone else there's not that much to see inside. Outside in the castle grounds, though, there's an unusual walled garden worth a stroll, and lovely views over the Pentland Firth.

The nearby **Castle Arms Hotel** (☎ 01847-851244; www.castlearms.co.uk; Mey; s/d £42/64), a former 19th-century coaching inn, has a friendly bar downstairs and decent rooms upstairs. If you haven't had enough of the royals there's a room decked out with pictures of the late Queen Mother.

DUNNET HEAD

Let's put a common misconception to rest. Contrary to popular belief, naff John o'Groats is not the British mainland's most northerly point; that honour goes to Dunnet Head, 10 miles (16km) to the west. The head is marked by a lighthouse that dates from 1832.

Just southwest of Dunnet Head is a magnificent stretch of sandy beach, at the southern end of which lies the tiny harbour of **Castlehill**, where a heritage trail explains the evolution of the local flagstone industry.

Situated on the minor road that leads to Dunnet Head, **Dunnet Head B&B & Tearoom** (☎ 01847-851774; brsparks@dunnethead.co.uk; r per person £18.50-21.50; meals under £8; ☼ Easter-Sep; ☒ ☐) offers good, inexpensive food, including meals for vegetarians, and has a comfortable rooms and an onsite caravan.

NORTH & WEST COAST

Quintessential Highland country such as this, marked by single-track roads, breathtaking emptiness and a wild, fragile beauty, is rarely seen on the modern, crowded, highly urbanised island of Britain. You could get lost up here for weeks – and that probably still wouldn't be enough time.

Carving its way from Thurso to Glencoul, the north and northwest coastline is a feast of deep inlets, forgotten beaches and surging peninsulas. Within the rugged confines, the deep interior is home to vast, empty spaces, enormous lochs and some of Scotland's highest peaks. After curving inland and delving in between the mountains of the Assynt, where remote landscapes merge with secluded and welcoming towns, the road emerges at the charming coastal village of Ullapool. This northernmost slab of the Highlands is the stuff of coastal-drive dreams.

GETTING AROUND

Public transport in the northwest is, well, pretty awful. Getting to Thurso or Kyle of Lochalsh by bus or train is easy, but following the coast between these places, especially from October to May, is when the fun really starts. **Royal Mail postbuses** (☎ 08457-740740; www.postbus.royalmail.com) run year-round; fares vary, but long journeys are usually good value at around £4 or £5. See their website for details of routes, which cover most towns in this section.

From late May to September, **Rapsons/Highland Country** (☎ 01847-893123) runs a service once-daily (except Sunday) from Thurso to Durness (£7.50, 2½ hours). The rest of the year there are Monday to Saturday services from Thurso to Bettyhill; from where you can change to a postbus to Tongue, and then back to a Rapsons/Highland Country service to Durness.

From late May to mid-September **Tim Dearman Coaches** (☎ 01349-883585; www.timdearman coaches.co.uk) runs buses from Inverness to Durness (£15.40, five hours, one daily Monday to Saturday) via Ullapool and Lochinver.

An alternative is to come up from Inverness via Lairg. Apart from trains (Monday to Saturday in winter, see Inverness Getting There & Away, p294), **Stagecoach Inverness** (☎ 01463-239292) operates to/from Tain (£5.70, 1¼ hours, half-hourly) and **McLeods Coaches** (☎ 01408-641354) operates a connecting service to Lairg (£2.80, 45 minutes, four daily Monday to Saturday).

There are regular Citylink buses between Inverness and Ullapool. **Westerbus** (☎ 01445-712255) runs every Thursday year-round between Ullapool and Gairloch.

The once-daily (except Sunday) Westerbus service from Inverness to Gairloch, runs via Kinlochewe and Achnasheen, or via Dundonnell on Monday, Wednesday and Saturday. The route via Dundonnell provides a link between Ullapool and Gairloch (via Braemore Junction). The Achnasheen–Kinlochewe–Torridon postbus can be used in conjunction with the Westerbus, taking you from Gairloch to Kinlochewe and Torridon (at least one day after the Ullapool to Gairloch leg).

From Torridon, the **MacLennan bus service** (☎ 01520-755239) goes to Strathcarron once daily (except Sunday) from June to September, or Monday, Wednesday and Friday the rest of the year.

THURSO & SCRABSTER

☎ 01847 / pop 7737

The mainland's most northerly town, Thurso is a bleak, rather depressing place where

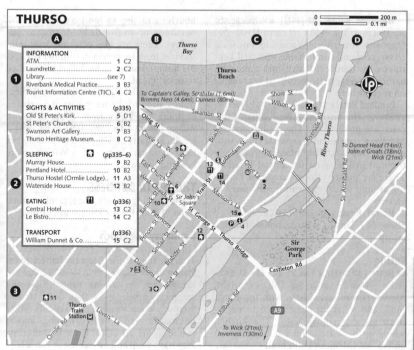

THURSO

INFORMATION	
ATM	1 C2
Laundrette	2 C2
Library	(see 7)
Riverbank Medical Practice	3 B3
Tourist Information Centre (TIC)	4 C2

SIGHTS & ACTIVITIES	(p335)
Old St Peter's Kirk	5 D1
St Peter's Church	6 B2
Swanson Art Gallery	7 B3
Thurso Heritage Museum	8 C2

SLEEPING	(pp335–6)
Murray House	9 B2
Pentland Hotel	10 B2
Thurso Hostel (Ormlie Lodge)	11 A3
Waterside House	12 B2

EATING	(p336)
Central Hotel	13 C2
Le Bistro	14 C2

TRANSPORT	(p336)
William Dunnet & Co	15 C2

prams seem to rule the streets – you get the impression young people either leave or simply have more *bairns* here. It's useful as a service centre, though, and as an overnight stop en route to Orkney – the view across Pentland Firth to Hoy beckons visitors to a more appealing location.

Ferries cross from Scrabster, 2½ miles (4km) west of Thurso, to Orkney. Tiny Scrabster, little more than a collection of BP oil storage containers, revolves around its port.

Information

ATM (cnr Olrig & Rotterdam Sts)

Library (☎ 893237; Davidson's Lane; ◷ 10am-6pm Mon & Wed, 10am-8pm Tue & Fri, 10am-1pm Thu & Sat) Has free Internet access.

Riverbank medical centre (☎ 892027; Janet St)

Post office (Co-op supermarket, Grove Lane)

TIC (☎ 892371; Riverside Rd; ◷ Mon-Sat Apr-Oct, Sun late May-Sep)

Sights & Activities

Thurso Heritage Museum (☎ 892459; High St; adult/child £1/25p; ◷ 10am-1pm & 2-5pm Mon-Sat Jun-

Sep) displays Pictish and Christian carved stones, fossils and a reconstruction of a croft interior. There's also an excellent photographic display and exhibitions on accomplished Thurso locals, including the botanist and geologist Robert Dick.

Thurso is an unlikely **surfing** centre, but the nearby coast has arguably the best and most regular surf on mainland Britain. There's an excellent right-hand reef break on the eastern side of town, directly in front of Lord Thurso's castle (closed to the public), and another shallow reef break 5 miles (8km) west at Brimms Ness.

North of Scrabster harbour, there's a fine **cliff walk** along Holborn Head. Take care in windy weather.

Sleeping

Thurso Hostel (Ormlie Lodge; ☎ /fax 896888; Ormlie Rd; s/d £9/15) Scruffy Ormlie Lodge is a student hall of residence a few minutes' walk from the train station. It has an excellent, if slightly ragged, range of budget accommodation, set to improve with the renovations that were underway at the time of writing.

Waterside House (☎ 894751; waterside.house@tinyonline.co.uk; 3 Janet St; r per person £15-20; ✗) Opposite the river, Waterside house is classy, cool and comfortable with well-kept rooms; the more expensive ones come with bathroom. Vegetarian breakfast is available on request here.

Pentland Hotel (☎ 893202, fax 892761; Princes St; s/d £39/70) The business-style rooms in this place are great value. They're big enough to have a couch and a separate nook with a desk. It's a stylish place, surprisingly tranquil inside given its central location. There are plenty of open areas for lounging around while you wait for the ferry to Orkney.

Murray House (☎ 895759; 1 Campbell St; s/d £20/46; ✗) This is a professional, friendly set up.

Eating

Le Bistro (☎ 893737; 2 Traill St; lunch £3-5.50, dinner £8-11; ✤ lunch & dinner Tue-Sat) This is a bright, Mediterranean-style bistro with top-notch food, and wins the 'best place to eat in town' award hands down. The kitchen whips up both traditional (Cullen skink) and exotic (Mexican chilli bean crepe) fare and service comes with a smile. For those cursed with a sweet tooth, the desserts are wonderful.

Central Hotel (☎ 893129; Traill St; mains £2-6) The old Central dabbles in a little bit of everything and makes a fair go at a fisherman's pie – also on offer are panini, sandwiches, grills, pizzas and curries. The elderly lounge upstairs overlooks the main drag and makes a good spot for a coffee and a read of the newspaper.

Captain's Galley (☎ 894999; The Harbour, Scrabster; mains £13-16; ✤ lunch & dinner Tue-Sat) This classy diner, metres from the pier, dishes out posh seafood and has a changing menu, depending on the day's catch. If you're a serious seafood connoisseur, try the medley of Scrabster market fish.

Getting There & Around

Thurso is 290 miles (464km) from Edinburgh, 130 miles (208km) from Inverness and 21 miles (34km) from Wick.

From Inverness, Citylink buses operate via Wick to Thurso (£11, 3½ hours, four daily). Rapsons/Highland Country operates a service to Wick (£2.50, 45 minutes, hourly) and also to John o'Groats (£2.20, one hour, up to five daily Monday to Saturday). There are two or three daily train services from Inverness in summer (£12.50, 3½ hours), but space for bicycles is limited so book ahead.

It's a 2-mile (3km) walk from Thurso train station to the ferry port at Scrabster, or there are buses from Olrig St (80p). **William Dunnet & Co** (☎ 893101) rents cars; a small car starts at £25 per day, plus 8p per mile – you can drop it off in Wick if you're heading that way.

THURSO TO DURNESS

It's 80 winding and often spectacular coastal miles (128km) from Thurso to Durness.

Dounreay & Melvich

On the coast 10 miles (16km) west of Thurso, there's the **Dounreay Nuclear Power Station Visitor Centre** (☎ 01847-802572; Dounreay; admission free; ✤ 10am-4pm May-Oct), spewing company propaganda that only Homer Simpson would swallow. It's actually rather humorous, and worth dropping into if you're in the area. Just beyond Dounreay, **Reay** has a shop and an interesting little harbour dating from 1830. **Melvich** overlooks a fine beach and there are great views from **Strathy Point** (a 2-mile/3km drive from the coast road, then a 15-minute walk).

Bettyhill (Am Blaran Odhar)

☎ 01641 / pop 553

The pleasing panorama of a sweeping, sandy beach and surrounding velvety green hills with bulbous, rocky outcrops makes a sharp contrast to the sad history of this area. Bettyhill is a crofting community of resettled tenant-farmers kicked off their land during the Clearances.

Bettyhill **TIC** (☎ 521342; ✤ Apr-Oct) has limited information on the area but Elizabeth's Cafe here serves good home-cooked food. There's also a shop and post office.

Strathnaver Museum (☎ 521418; Clachan; adult/child £1.90/50p; ✤ 10am-1pm & 2-5pm Mon-Sat Apr-Oct, by arrangement at other times), in an old church, tells the sad story of the Strathnaver Clearances. The museum contains memorabilia of Clan Mackay, various items of crofting equipment and a 4000-year-old beaker.

Dunveaden (☎ 521273; Bettyhill; r per person £16-18, campsite £7) is a friendly B&B and camping ground on the main road and opposite the grocery store. **Bettyhill Hotel** (☎ /fax 521352; www.bettyhillhotel.co.uk; Bettyhill; r per person £20-30) has a range of rooms culminating in the spacious 12A, which has been refurbished and has great views over the sandy beach fringing Torrisdale Bay.

From Bettyhill, the B871 turns south for Helmsdale, through **Strathnaver**, where the Clearances took place.

Coldbackie & Tongue
☎ 01847 / pop 445

The wonderful beach at Coldbackie is overlooked by the Watch Hill viewpoint. Only 2 miles (3.25km) farther on is Tongue, with the evocative 14th-century ruins of **Castle Varrich**, once a Mackay stronghold. Tongue has a shop, post office, bank and petrol station.

Down by the causeway, **Tongue Youth Hostel** (☎ 611301; Tongue; dm adult/child £10/8.50; ☺ Apr-Sep) offers bunkers plenty of room to move in spacious dorms and has a spectacular location with great views of the Kyle of Tongue.

Looking for peace and quiet? Look no further! **Mrs MacIntosh** (☎ 611251; 77 Dalcharn; s/d £15/26), just east of Coldbackie and off the A836, is a little cottage surrounded by heather-clad, rolling, green peaks. Snug rooms and home-spun hospitality is what you can expect.

Ben Loyal Hotel (☎ 611216, fax 611212; Tongue; s/d from £30/50; mains £6-9.50) has good rooms and the restaurant seems to drag patrons from miles around with its delicious, filling meals prepared with local produce and lots of TLC. Try the rich venison and cranberry pie or Kyle of Tongue oysters. It makes a great pit stop, even if you're just after a cup of coffee or a well-poured pint of Guinness.

Tongue to Durness

From Tongue it's 37 miles (59km) to Durness – you can take the causeway across the **Kyle of Tongue** or the beautiful old road which goes around the head of the kyle. A detour to **Melness** and **Port Vasgo** may be rewarded with the sight of seals on the beach.

Continuing west, the road crosses a desolate moor past **Moine House** (a ruin built as a shelter for travellers in 1830) to the northern end of **Loch Hope**. A 10-mile

(16km) detour south along the loch leads to **Dun Dornaigil**, a well-preserved broch in the shadow of **Ben Hope** (927m). If you'd like to bag this Munro (p405), it's a three- to four-hour round trip along the route from the car park, which is 2 miles (3km) before the broch, near a large barn.

Beyond Loch Hope, on the main road, **Heilam** has stunning views out over **Loch Eriboll**, Britain's deepest sea inlet and a shelter for ships during WWII.

DURNESS (DIURANAIS)
☎ 01971 / pop 353

The scattered village of Durness (www .durness.org) is strung out along cliffs, which rise from a series of pristine beaches. It has one of the finest locations in Scotland. When the sun shines, the effects of blinding white sand, the cry of sea birds and the lime-coloured seas combine in a magical way. The only blight is the sometimes constant thumping from the Ministry of Defence (MOD) range on Cape Wrath, which can shatter the tranquillity of this northern outpost.

Orientation & Information

What's known as Durness is really two villages strung along the main road: Durness, in the west, and Smoo, a mile to the east. The friendly **TIC & Visitor Centre** (☎ 511259; ☺ Mon-Sat Apr-Oct, Sun Apr-Sep; half day Mon-Fri Nov-Mar) organises guided walks in summer. There are also displays here on folk and natural history.

Durness has two stores (Mace has an ATM), a petrol station, a **health centre** (☎ 511273) and a travelling bank (11.10am to 12.45pm every Tuesday). **Balnakeil Bistro** (Balnakeil Craft Village; £1 per 30 min) has Internet access.

Sights & Activities

A mile east of the village centre there's a path from near the SYHA hostel down to **Smoo Cave**. The vast cave entrance stands at the end of an inlet, or geo, and a river cascades through its roof into a flooded cavern, then flows out to sea. There's evidence the cave was inhabited around 6000 years ago. You can take a **boat trip** (£3/1.50) into the floodlit cave, although after heavy rain the waterfall can make it impossible to get past.

If you're a Beatles fan, drop by the **John Lennon memorial** in the newly created garden by the village hall. His song, 'In my Life' from the Rubber Soul album is about Durness.

Durness has several beautiful **beaches**. One of the best is Sangobeg, but there's also a 'secret beach' just to the east, which can't be seen from the road. The sea offers great **windsurfing**. Around the coast, there are wrecks, caves, seals and whales. Enquire at the TIC for **trout-fishing** permits.

The disused radar station at **Balnakeil**, less than a mile up a minor road from Durness, has been turned into a hippy craft village, with a bookshop, restaurants, art and craft workshops and the innovative **Lotte Globe Pottery Studio** (☎ 511354).

Sleeping & Eating

Sango Sands Oasis (☎ 511222; fax 511205; Durness; site per person £4.25) Pitch your tent on the northern edge of the country and dangle your feet over the precipice, admiring the sweeping views over the Atlantic's twinkling waters.

Lazy Crofter Bunkhouse (☎ 511202; fiona@visitmackays.com; Durness; dm £10) This hostel has neat sung-as-a-bug bunks and great facilities. There's hot showers, no curfews and small dorms. Check in at MacKays Hotel next door.

Braemar (☎ 511284; Durness; r per person £15) No-frills accommodation here comes in the way of three clean upstairs rooms and a guests' TV lounge. You'll get a peaceful night's kip, a decent breakfast and be whisked out nice and early in the morning.

Smoo Falls (☎ 511228; www.smoofalls.com; Smoo; s £25, d £18-21; ✗) Friendly Smoo Falls is a working croft that has tastefully furnished rooms with a touch of class; the breakfast uses local produce and is a fine way to start the day.

MacKays Hotel (☎ 511202; www.visitmackays.com; Durness; d £60-70; ✗) This recently refurbished hotel has tastefully decorated rooms and an air of sophistication. The deluxe rooms have super king-size beds and big showers – they're worth the extra 10 quid.

Loch Croispol Bookshop & Restaurant (☎ 511777; 17c Balnakeil Craft Village; lunch & snacks £2-5, 2/3-course dinner £10/13.50; ☼ 10am-8.30pm Thu-Tue, 10am-5pm Wed) At this place you can feed your body and your mind. Set among books on all things Scottish are a few tables where you can enjoy an excellent dinner over a bottle of wine, with mellow vibes in the

background. There's access for people with disabilities, and stuff to amuse the kids.

DURNESS TO ULLAPOOL

It's 69 miles (110km) from Durness to Ullapool, with plenty of diversions along the way. The road to Ullapool has jaw-dropping scenery – dangerous on single-track roads as drivers struggle to tear their eyes away from vast, desolate plains spliced with rivulets of burns, towering peaks and giant rocky outcrops.

Rugged **Cape Wrath** is crowned by a lighthouse (dating from 1827) and stands close to the sea-bird colonies on Clo Mor Cliffs, the highest coastal cliffs on the mainland. Getting to Cape Wrath involves a **ferry** (☎ 01971-511376) ride across the Kyle of Durness (£4 return, two hours) and a connecting **minibus** (☎ 01971-511287) for the 11 miles to the cape (£6.50 return, 40 minutes one way). Contact the TIC before setting out to make sure the ferry is running.

Kinlochbervie was one of Scotland's premier fish-landing ports and there's a lovely beach at **Oldshoremore**, a crofting settlement about 2 miles (3km) northwest of Kinlochbervie. The outlook from the **Kinlochbervie Hotel** (☎ 521275; www.thekinlochberviehotel.com; Kinlochbervie; r per person £37-55; 3-course dinner £19.95) must be the envy of almost every hotel in Scotland!

Scourie is a pretty crofting community. If you're looking to spoil yourself, **Scourie Lodge** (☎ 502248; Scourie; s/d £40/60; dinner £17.50; ✗), in a gorgeous building overlooking the bay, has three luxurious rooms and a garden with possibly the most northerly palm trees in the world.

Ferries (☎ 502347; adult/child £7/3.50; ☼ half-hourly, 9.30am-2pm Mon-Sat, Apr–mid-Sep) go out to the important **Handa Island** sea-bird sanctuary from Tarbet, 6 miles (10km) north of Scourie

Kylesku & Loch Glencoul
☎ 01971

Cruises on steely-blue Loch Glencoul pass treacherous-looking mountains, seal colonies and the 213m-drop of **Eas a'Chual Aulin**, Britain's highest waterfall. In summer, the **MV Statesman** (☎ 01571-844446) runs two-hour trips twice daily (except Saturday) from Kylesku Old Ferry Pier for £10/5. There are also trips to the lovely **Kerrachar Gardens** (ferry £10, admission £2.50), which are only accessible by boat.

While you wait for the ferry you can enjoy a pint and tuck into a superb bar meal in the **Kylesku Hotel** (☎ 502231; kyleskuhotel@ lycos.co.uk; Kylesku; s/d £40/70; mains £8.50), overlooking the pier.

The Old Man of Stoer

It's roughly a 30-mile (48km) detour off the A894 to the Point of Stoer and the Rhu Stoer Lighthouse (1870) and back to the main road again. Along the coast road you need to be prepared for single-track roads, blind bends, summits and sheep. The rewards are spectacular views, pretty villages and excellent beaches. From the lighthouse, it's a good one-hour cliff walk to the Old Man of Stoer, a spectacular sea stack.

There are more good beaches between Stoer and Lochinver, including one at Achmelvich. **Achmelvich Youth Hostel** (SYHA; ☎ 0870 004 1102; Achmelvich; dm adult/child £9.50/8; ❤ Apr-Sep) is about 1½ miles from the Lochinver–Drumbeg postbus route, and 4 miles (7km) from Lochinver. It is a small place sheltered by rocky hills, has basic dorms and is close to the beach.

Lochinver & Assynt
☎ 01571 / pop 639

The busy little fishing port of Lochinver is a popular port of call for tourists, with its laid-back attitude, good facilities, striking scenery and award-winning visitor centre.

The **TIC & visitor centre** (☎ 844330; Main St) has an interpretive display on the story of Assynt, from flora and fauna to clans, conflict and controversy. There's a supermarket in town, a post office, bank (with an ATM), a petrol station and a **doctor** (☎ 844755).

The Lochinver–Lairg road (A837) meets the Durness road (A894) at **Skiag Bridge**, by Loch Assynt, about 10 miles (16km) east of Lochinver. Half a mile south of here, by the loch, there's the ruin of the late 15th-century MacLeod stronghold, **Ardvreck Castle**. There are wonderful summer sunsets over the castle and the loch.

The stunningly shaped hills of Assynt are popular with walkers and include peaks such as Suilven (731m), Quinag (808m), Ben More Assynt (998m) and Canisp (846m). Ask at the TIC for details of walking routes.

SLEEPING

Ardglas (☎ 844257; ardglas@btinternet.com; Inver, Lochinver; r per person £17) The comfortable Ardglas is a bastion in the hospitality trade with modern rooms, a decent size single and top views from the guests' lounge. It's efficient yet laid-back.

Albannach (☎ 844407; the.albannach@virgin.net; Baddidarroch, Lochinver; DB&B per person £95-102) The Albannach is sheer indulgence and decadence on a grand scale. You'll find roaring fireplaces, furniture found only in antique shops and a demure, sophisticated atmosphere. It makes a great hideaway to whisk off that someone special to.

Inchnadamph Lodge (☎ 822218; www.inch-lodge .co.uk; Inchnadamph; dm £10.95, d £16.95-18.50, all include breakfast; 🖳) By the Lochinver–Lairg road, this place is a friendly 50-bed lodge with plenty of rustic accommodation. Most rooms are spacious and clean and there's a separate music/TV lounge for late partying. The facilities here are excellent and it's very popular with groups.

Mrs Ross (☎ 844401; 1 Bayview Tce, Lochinver; r per person £16; 🗙) This B&B has home-spun vibes and tidy rooms

Inverpolly Nature Reserve

The Inverpolly Nature Reserve has numerous glacial lochs and the three peaks of Cul Mor (849m), Stac Pollaidh (613m) and Cul Beag (769m). **Stac Pollaidh** is one of the most exciting walks in the area, with some good scrambling on its narrow sandstone crest. It takes just three hours on a round trip from the car park on Loch Lurgainn.

Achiltibuie
☎ 01854 / pop 290

Serene Achiltibuie has a magnificent setting, sheltered from the west by the wonderfully named Summer Isles. In the village, there's a post office and general store.

About 5 miles (8km) northwest, The Achiltibuie **Smokehouse** (☎ 622353; Altandhu; admission free; ❤ 9.30am-5pm Mon-Sat Easter-Oct) smokes all sorts of things, from cheese to eel and salmon. You can watch the processing and buy the results in the shop.

Summer Isles Cruises (☎ 622200) operates boat trips to the Summer Isles from Achiltibuie. The 3½-hour trips cost £15/7.50 for adult/children, and you get one hour ashore on **Tanera Mor**, where the post office issues its own stamps.

The rudimentary 20-bed **Achininver Youth Hostel** (SYHA; ☎ 0870 004 110; Achininver, Achiltibuie; dm adult/child £9.50/8; ☺ mid-May–Sep) has an out-of-the-way location at the southern end of Achiltibuie.

Summer Isles Hotel (☎ 622282; summerisleshotel@ aol.com; Achiltibuie; s £69-106 d £108-140; bar meals £7-12, 5-course dinner £40; ☺ Apr-Oct) makes a great spot to take a break from urban dwelling and treat that someone special. The rooms are excellent as is the food and there's an extensive wine list.

Spa Coaches (☎ 01997-421311) operates buses Monday to Saturday from Reiff, Badenscallie (half a mile, from the hostel) and Achiltibuie to Ullapool (three daily Monday to Friday, one Saturday).

ULLAPOOL
☎ 01854 / pop 1308

Ullapool's harbour-side façade is postcard-perfect and, on a sunny day, its surrounding rocky slopes are mirrored in the glassy veneer of its bay. A ferry service links Ullapool to Stornoway on the Isle of Lewis, churning a consistent trade of overnighters in its wake. There are few attractions, but piles of accommodation, delectable seafood and a couple of good watering holes.

Information

Bank of Scotland (West Argyle St) Has an ATM.
Library (☎ 612543; ☺ 9am-5pm Mon-Fri, plus 6-8pm Tue & Thu, closed Mon & Wed during holidays) Free Internet access.
Mountain Man Supplies (☎ 613323; West Argyle St) Opposite the Ullapool Museum; good for outdoor equipment.
Royal Bank of Scotland (cnr Ladysmith & Argyle Sts) Has an ATM.
TIC (☎ 612135; ullapool@host.co.uk; 6 Argyle St; ☺ daily Apr-Sep, Mon-Sat Oct, Mon-Fri Nov-Mar) Efficient and helpful.

Sights

Ullapool Museum & Visitor Centre (☎ 612987; 7-8 West Argyle St; adult/child £3/50p; ☺ 9.30am-5.30pm Mon-Sat Apr-Oct, 11am-3pm Mar, 10am-4pm Sat Nov-Feb) is in a converted Telford Parliamentary church. An audiovisual presentation, interactive exhibits and various other displays chart the history of Loch Broom and its people.

Rhue Studio (☎ 612460; Rhue; admission free; ☺ 10am-6pm Mon-Sat Apr-Sep, call for details Oct-Mar), 2½ miles (4km) northwest of Ullapool, displays and sells the excellent art of contemporary landscape painter James Hawkins. The vivid and reflective works take a moment to adjust to, but they are wonderful interpretations. His work on the Outer Hebrides is breathtaking.

Walking

Ullapool is a great centre for hill walking. There are only a few paths in the area – the good one up **Gleann na Sguaib** heads for the top of Beinn Dearg from Inverlael, at the inner end of Loch Broom. Ridge-walking on the **Fannichs** is relatively straightforward and many different routes are possible. The TIC can supply you with all the information and maps you need.

Sleeping

Broomfield Holiday Park (☎ 612664; sross@ broomfield.com; West Lane; sites £5-9; ☺ May-Oct) On an inviting verge of Loch Broom, this camping ground has lawns manicured with nail scissors, pesky midges and good facilities.

West House Hostel (Scotpackers; ☎ /fax 613126; West Argyle St; dm/d £10/30; ☐) This rambling backpackers has got the right idea. Small, spacious dorms (some with private bathroom) have comfy bunks, and doubles have TV and hot-drink facilities. It's clean, well run and very friendly. You can even sit outside in summer as there is a midge buster!

Sea Breezes (☎ 612148; 2 West Tce; s/d £25/40; ☒) The recommended Sea Breezes is a brilliant choice – you couldn't buy better views from the double room, and the single is an excellent size. It's personable, laid-back and virtually impossible to leave disappointed. Booking ahead is advisable.

Eilean Donan Guest House (☎ 612524; edonan@ ullapoolholidays.com; 14 Market St; s/d £22/40; 2-/3-course dinners £15.50/18.50; ☒) This top-class guesthouse has an open fire in the sitting room for those blustery evenings, a full-blown restaurant and excellent rooms with bathroom. It's in a lovely, tree-lined street a few minute's walk from the seafront.

Ferry Boat Inn (☎ 612366; www.ferryboat-inn .com; Shore St; r per person £32-35) The vivacious

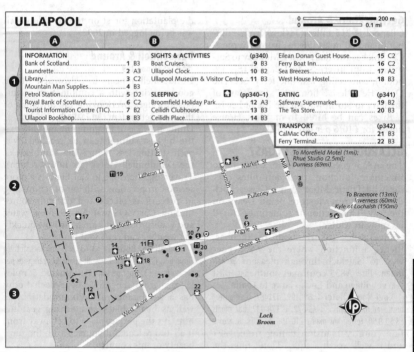

ULLAPOOL

| 0 | 200 m |
| 0 | 0.1 mi |

INFORMATION	
Bank of Scotland......................	1 B3
Laundrette...............................	2 A3
Library.....................................	3 C2
Mountain Man Supplies...........	4 B3
Petrol Station..........................	5 D2
Royal Bank of Scotland............	6 C2
Tourist Information Centre (TIC)...	7 B2
Ullapool Bookshop...................	8 B3

SIGHTS & ACTIVITIES	(p340)
Boat Cruises............................	9 B3
Ullapool Clock........................	10 B2
Ullapool Museum & Visitor Centre...	11 B3

SLEEPING	(pp340-1)
Broomfield Holiday Park............	12 A3
Ceilidh Clubhouse...................	13 B3
Ceilidh Place..........................	14 B3

Eilean Donan Guest House.........	15 C2
Ferry Boat Inn..........................	16 C2
Sea Breezes.............................	17 A2
West House Hostel...................	18 B3

EATING	(p341)
Safeway Supermarket...............	19 B2
The Tea Store..........................	20 B3

TRANSPORT	(p342)
CalMac Office..........................	21 B3
Ferry Terminal.........................	22 B3

To Morefield Motel (1mi);
Rhue Studio (2.5mi);
Durness (69mi)

To Braemore (13mi);
Inverness (60mi);
Kyle of Lochalsh (150mi)

Loch
Broom

Ferry Boat is the liveliest place in town. The stylish, tastefully furnished rooms here get snapped up quickly in summer. Book in advance if you want a room with a view of Loch Broom – the alternative is looking at a brick wall.

Ceilidh Place (☎ 612103; reservations@ceilidh.demon .co.uk; 14 West Argyle St; r per person £45-65; Clubhouse beds £15-20; ☒ ☐) The Ceilidh Place exudes warmth and class. Take your pick from the individually designed rooms in this nook-and-cranny hotel. Price depends upon size, position (view), facilities and how long you stay. Nearby, the **Ceilidh Clubhouse** (☎ 612103; West Lane) has upmarket dorms with reputedly the best showers in Scotland.

Eating

Morefield Motel (☎ 612161; North Rd; mains £7.50-12) This sedate motel serves outstanding local seafood, including langoustine, salmon, swordfish and lobster, in its lounge bar. It has a deservedly fine reputation and is popular with locals and tourists alike. The Seafood Rendezvous for two should only be attempted if you've been fasting. The motel is off the A835, a mile north of the harbour (follow Mill St).

Ceilidh Place (☎ 612103; 14 West Argyle St; mains £11.50-16.50) This restaurant serves good and inventive dishes catering for most palates – the venison with chilli and chocolate offers both a sweet and spicy fix. Unfortunately the soulless setting of the restaurant lets the place down. In contrast it comes to life in summer, serving as Ullapool's main entertainment centre.

Ferry Boat Inn (☎ 612366; Shore St; bar meals £4.50-8, 2-/3-course dinner £16.50/19.95) The Ferry Boat, recommended by readers, slaps together a delectable menu by putting a creative spin on traditional fare. The mushrooms are shitake and the sauce is vermouth. This cosy pub is also the best watering hole in town.

Tea Store (☎ 612995; Argyle St; snacks & light meals £1.50-3.65; ☼ 8am-5pm Mon-Sat, 10am-4pm Sun) This is a decent coffee nook for a light meal and a read of the newspaper; a bumper breakfast is £6.

For self-catering, the large Safeway supermarket is next to the car park north of Seaforth Rd.

Getting There & Around

Ullapool is 215 miles (344km) from Edinburgh and 60 miles (96km) from Inverness. Citylink has two daily buses, Monday to Saturday, from Inverness to Ullapool (£7, 1½ hours), connecting with the ferry. See The Outer Hebrides section, p357, for details of the ferry to Stornoway on the Isle of Lewis.

Bikes can be hired from West House hostel for £10/6 per day/half-day.

ULLAPOOL TO THE EAST COAST

The A835 goes south from Ullapool to Braemore Junction, then continues over the wild Dirrie More to the Glascarnoch dam, with great views of Beinn Dearg on the way. This section is sometimes closed by snow in winter.

Five miles (8km) south of Inchbae, there's a junction where the A832 goes west to Gairloch through pleasant **Strath Braan**. The A835 continues southeast, past Garve village and Loch Garve to **Contin**.

Coul House Hotel (☎ 01997-421487; coulhouse@ bestloved.com; Contin; s £54-72, d £78-142; bar meals £3.50-8.50, restaurant mains £10-15; ✗) is a very fine country mansion dating from 1821 and is well worth a squiz. Don't miss the MacKenzie sitting room where huge rooms reveal a ribbon of green countryside.

Ullapool to Inverness buses follow this route and stop off at Contin, Garve and Aultguish. Trains from Inverness to Kyle of Lochalsh stop at Garve.

ULLAPOOL TO KYLE OF LOCHALSH

Although it's less than 50 miles (80km) as the crow flies from Ullapool to Kyle of Lochalsh, it's more like 150 miles along the circuitous coastal road – but don't let that put you off – it's a deliciously remote region and there are fine views of beaches and bays backed by mountains all the way along.

Falls of Measach

The A832 doubles back to the coast from the A835, 12 miles (19km) from Ullapool. Just before the junction, the Falls of Measach ('ugly' in Gaelic) spill 45m into the spectacularly deep and narrow Corrieshalloch Gorge. You can cross from side to side on a wobbly suspension bridge, built by Sir John Fowler of Braemore. The thundering falls and misty vapours rising from the gorge are very impressive – a shame about

the plantation forest on the far side which was being logged in 2003.

Dundonnell & Around
☎ 01854 / pop 169

Dundonnell appears half-drowned after a good soaking with a combination of imposing ridges overlooking the lowlands of this tiny settlement. **An Teallach** (1062m), at Dundonnell, is a magnificent mountain – the highest summit can be reached by a path starting less than 500m southeast of the Dundonnell Hotel (six hours return). Traversing the ridge to Sail Liath is a more serious proposition, with lots of scrambling in precarious places and difficult routefinding. Carry OS map No 19, food, water and waterproofs – it's amazing how quickly the weather can turn foul here.

Badrallach Bothy (☎ 633281; michael.stott2@ virgin.net; Croft 9, Badrallach; flr space £4, campsite per person from £3, r per person £25) Situated 7 miles (11km) from the A832, Badrallach Bothy has a good range of accommodation, as well as boats, bikes and fishing gear for hire. It's the perfect place to get away from it all and reacquaint yourself with the rural beauty of this country.

Gairloch & Around
☎ 01445 / pop 1061

Gairloch is a group of villages (comprising Auchtercairn, Strath and Charlestown) around the inner end of a loch of the same name. The surrounding area has beautiful sandy beaches, good trout-fishing and birdwatching. Hill walkers also use Gairloch as a base for the Torridon hills and An Teallach.

There are shops and takeaways in Strath and Auchtercairn, a petrol station in Auchtercairn and a bank (with an ATM) between Auchtercairn and Charlestown. For a doctor, call the **Auchtercairn health centre** (☎ 712229).

SIGHTS & ACTIVITIES

The excellent **Heritage Museum** (☎ 712287; Auchtercairn; adult/child £3/50p; ✆ 10am-5pm Mon-Sat Apr-Sep, 10am-1.30pm Mon-Fri Oct), near the TIC, creates a vivid impression of life in the West Highlands from the time of the Picts to the present. You can see a typical crofting cottage, schoolroom and shop.

The **Gairloch Marine Life Centre** (☎ 712636; Pier Rd, Charlestown; admission free; ✆ 9.30am-4pm

Mon-Fri, noon-3.30pm Sat-Sun Easter-Sep) has audiovisual and interactive displays, lots of charts and photos, and knowledgeable staff. From here, **Gairloch Marine Cruises** (☎ 712636; cruises per adult/child £14/12) sail up to four times daily (weather permitting) from Easter to September; during the two-hour trip you may see basking sharks, porpoises and Minke whales.

SLEEPING & EATING

Rua Reidh Lighthouse Hostel (☎ 771263; ruareidh@ netcomuk.co.uk; by Melvaig; dm/d £8.50/24) At the end of the road, 13 miles (21km) from Gairloch, this excellent hostel will give you a taste of a lighthouse-keeper's life. It also does good meals for £12.50 (by reservation). Buses from Gairloch run as far as Melvaig, then it's a 3-mile (5km) hike along the road to the lighthouse.

Oakwood B&B (☎ 712069; 1 Braeside Rd; r per person £15.50-18.50; ✗) Opposite the golf course and within walking distance of Gairloch Pier and, more importantly, the Old Inn (great pub!), Oakwood is a friendly, helpful place. The double and twin are both immaculately kept and the owners can provide good information on outdoor activities in the area, especially hill walking.

Myrtle Bank Hotel (☎ 712004; www.myrtlebank hotel.co.uk; Low Rd; r per person £36-44; bar meals £8.50-13) The add-on conservatory gives this hotel good natural light. The rooms are exceptionally large (some with partitioned sitting areas) and most have gorgeous sea views – you can just about smell the spray of the salt water, as the white caps come rippling into the bay. The kitchen does lots of dishes for carnivores and a couple for vegetarians and there's an extensive wine list.

Strath Stores (☎ 712499; Strath; lunch £1.60-2.40) Drop into this first-rate grocery store for a freshly prepared sandwich or baguette.

Loch Maree & Victoria Falls

Loch Maree is sprinkled with islands and a series of peaks line its northern shore culminating in 980m-high Slioch. The A832 runs alongside the loch.

The Victoria Falls (commemorating Queen Victoria's 1877 visit) tumble down to the loch between Slattadale and Talladale. Look for the 'Hydro Power' signs to find it.

Kinlochewe to Torridon

KINLOCHEWE & AROUND

Tiny Kinlochewe is a good base for outdoor activities. You'll find an outdoor-equipment shop, a petrol station with a tearoom and a shop/post office which runs a café in summer. Check out the **Beinn Eighe Visitor Centre** (☎ 01445-760254; admission free; ☯ 10am-5pm Easter-Oct), a mile north of Kinlochewe, with interactive displays (good for kids too) on local geography, ecology, flora and fauna and walking routes.

There's a basic, free **camping ground** (☎ 01445-760254) 1½ miles north of the village. **Hillhaven** (☎ 01445-760204; hillhaven@ kinlochewe.info; Kinlochewe; s/d £30/50; ✗) is an excellent, friendly B&B that organises hawk-flying displays.

Kinlochewe Hotel (☎ 01445-760253; kinlochewe hotel@tinyworld.co.uk; Kinlochewe; dm £10, r per person without/with bathroom £27.50/30; bar meals £5 to £11) has a bunkhouse with one no-frills dorm with 12 beds, a decent kitchen and clean bathrooms. Make sure you check in at the hotel before venturing into the bunkhouse. The hotel's traditional bar meals include baked salmon (£7.95).

East of Kinlochewe, the single-track A832 continues to Achnasheen, where there's a train station.

TORRIDON & AROUND

Westwards, the A896 follows Glen Torridon, overlooked by multiple peaks, including Beinn Eighe (1010m) and Liathach (1055m). The drive along Glen Torridon is one of the most breathtaking in Scotland. Mighty, brooding mountains, often partly obscured by clumps of passing clouds, seemingly drawn to their peaks like magnets, loom over the tiny, winding, single-track road.

The road reaches the sea at Torridon, where a **Countryside Centre** (☎ 01445-791221; Torridon Mains; donation adult/child £2/1; ☯ 10am-6pm May-Sep) offers information on walks in the rugged area.

The **camping ground** (☎ 01445-791313; Torridon; site £4) here has good showers and you get a grassy patch to pitch your tent with stunning views and wide-open, exhilarating space.

The modern, grey, squat **Torridon Youth Hostel** (SYHA; ☎ 0870 004 1154; Torridon; dm adult/ child £11/9.50; ☯ Mar-Oct, 28 Dec-1 Jan) is near the countryside centre and is used mainly by outdoor enthusiasts.

Magnificent **Loch Torridon Country House Hotel** (☎ 01445-791242; www.lochtorridonhotel.com; Torridon; s £60-104, d £97-315; 4-course dinner £39), complete with clock tower, is a class act and one of the best places to stay in Scotland. Sweeping views, roaring log fires, stag heads and ornate furnishings – you get the idea! Activities on offer include hill walking, clay-pigeon shooting, sea kayaking, fly-fishing and archery.

The A896 continues westwards to lovely **Shieldaig**, which boasts an attractive main street of whitewashed houses. **Tigh an Eilean Hotel** (☎ 01520-755251; Shieldaig; bar meals £6-10, 3-course dinner £32) dishes out locally caught seafood so fresh it may still be squirming on your plate.

Applecross

A long side trip abandons the A896 to follow the coast road to the delightfully remote seaside village of Applecross, surrounded by bare crags and with stunning views across to the Isle of Raasay. The scenery around here is exceptional.

You can pitch your tent at the **Applecross Camp Site & Flower Tunnel** (☎ 01520-744268; sites from £9; pizza from £4; ☻ Easter-Oct), which also has a licensed pizza restaurant in a flower-filled conservatory.

The family-run **Applecross Inn** (☎ 01520-744262, fax 744400; Shore St; r per person from £25; bar meals £7-11) is warm and welcoming and does some of the best pub grub in the West Highlands. Specials change daily.

Turning inland from Applecross, the road climbs to the Bealach na Ba pass (626m), then drops steeply to rejoin the A896. This winding, precipitous road can be closed in winter. The A896 runs south from Shieldaig to **Kishorn**, where there's a general store and post office, and spectacular views westwards to the steep sandstone Applecross hills.

Kishorn Seafood & Snack Bar (☎ 01520-733240; Kishorn; seafood £4-15) has outstanding seafood in a simple eatery. The squat lobster (£4.70) is particularly good and the shellfish platter (£16) allows a taste of some of their best dishes.

Lochcarron

The appealing, whitewashed village of Lochcarron is a veritable metropolis with two supermarkets, a bank (with an ATM), a post office and a petrol station.

If you're interested in the local wildlife drop into **WildAid** (☎ 722380; www.wildaid.co.uk; The White House, Main St). WildAid is a wildlife conservation organisation working at a grassroots level across the country. At Lochcarron it has a small gallery with wildlife and landscape prints on display. It also acts as an informal information centre, now that the town TIC has closed.

There's a range of very good, warm, bright rooms at **Castle Cottage** (☎ 01520-722564; Main St; r per person £20-23; ☒) – the best is the downstairs double with a huge, sparkling bathroom. The rooms upstairs, however, have better views (except for the single).

If you stay at the small, quiet **Rockvilla Hotel** (☎ 01520-722379; rockvillahotel@btinternet.com; Main St; r £60-65; mains £7-14) choose room Nos 1 or 2 – they are slightly cheaper, have private facilities and views to die for! The hotel kitchen does wonderful fresh seafood (try the seared sea bass or roasted monkfish) and is renowned for its scallops.

Plockton

☎ 01599 / pop 428

Plockton is so idyllic it could be designed by Hollywood, but there's nothing fake about the grandeur and beauty of this set. Maybe that's why the popular TV series *Hamish Macbeth* was filmed here. There's something Hawaii-esque about the view over the harbour – the small, protected bay dotted with mini islands and surrounded by rocky mountains carpeted in greenery. The main street of this delightful town is lined with palms and whitewashed houses, each house with a seagull perched on its chimney-stack.

ACTIVITIES

Calum's Seal Trips (☎ 544306; adult/child £5/3) runs seal-watching cruises; there are swarms of seals just outside the harbour and the trip comes with an excellent commentary. Trips leave daily at 10am, noon, 2pm and 4pm.

Cycling is a great way to explore the area and **Plockton Cycle Hire** (☎ 544255; Plockton Cottages, Frithard Rd) rents bikes for £8/12, for a half/full day.

SLEEPING & EATING

Plockton Station Bunkhouse (☎ 544235; mickcoe@ btinternet.com; Nessun Dorma; dm £8.50-10) This bunkhouse is in the former station building and gets lots of light in the comfortable, well-equipped common areas upstairs. It's modern and very convenient for the train.

Manse (☎ 544442; www.paintings-in-plockton.com; Innes St; r per person £26-31; ☒) The Manse is delightfully decadent. It's a place to spoil yourself, and proudly claims to be the most expensive B&B in town… for good reason. One double has a four-poster bed and a huge black and white tiled bathroom with freestanding bathtub. The manse doubles as an art gallery, with the owner's work lining much of the wall space. If that's not enough, it's also handy for falling out of the Plockton Inn across the road!

Craig Highland Farm (☎ /fax 544205; Plockton; r per person from £15, cottages for 2-6 persons per week £138-420) This is a delightful, if raggedy, conservation centre about 2 miles (3km) east of Plockton. It's ramshackle and improvised, but has loads of personality. There are excellent self-catering cottages – also rented out as B&B rooms. If you don't want to stay, you can still visit the farm for £1.50; the kids will love the llamas.

Plockton Hotel (☎ 544274; Harbour St; r per person £30-40; starters £4.75, mains £7.50-12) The black-painted Plockton serves popular pub food. The menu features seafood but also has a bit of variety with game dishes like Highland venison casserole or Talisker whisky pâté. It's sophisticated dining in elegant surrounds.

Haven Hotel (☎ 544223; Innes St; starters £4.85, mains £13.20) Some of the best food in Plockton is to be had at the Haven Hotel. It has a delectable menu – you'll need a drink just to read through it. Suffice to say that local produce is used to create culinary heaven.

KYLE OF LOCHALSH
☎ 01599 / pop 739

Before the Skye Bridge opened, Kyle of Lochalsh (normally just called Kyle) was the main jumping-off point for trips to the Isle of Skye. Now, however, its many B&B owners have to watch most of their trade whizzing past without stopping. If you get stuck here on the way to Skye, take advantage of the good facilities the town has to offer.

The **TIC** (☎ 534198/534390; ☷ 9am-5.30pm Mon-Sat Easter-Oct), beside the main sea-front car park, stocks information on Skye. In the village, you'll find two supermarkets, two banks with ATMs and a post office.

There's a string of B&Bs just outside of town on the road to Plockton. **A Chromraich** (☎ 534210; Stoney Rd; r per person £15-20) is a good choice. This old-fashioned place provides homely accommodation in rooms that share a bathroom. The best place to eat in town is the **Waverley** (☎ 534337; Main St; starters £4.50, mains £8-14; ☷ dinner). This superb restaurant is an intimate place with excellent service. There's a nightly bargain three-course dinner for £9.75.

Kyle can be reached by bus and train from Inverness (see Getting There & Away, p294), and by three daily direct Citylink buses from Glasgow (£19.50, 5½ hours).

The 82-mile (131km) train ride between Inverness and Kyle of Lochalsh (£14, 2½ hours, up to four daily) is one of Scotland's most scenic rail routes.

KYLE TO THE GREAT GLEN

It's 55 miles via the A87 from Kyle to Invergarry, which lies between Fort William and Fort Augustus, on Loch Oich (see The Great Glen section in the Central Highlands chapter, p289).

Eilean Donan Castle

Photogenically sited at the entrance to Loch Duich, near Dornie village, **Eilean Donan Castle** (☎ 555202; Dornie; adult/child £4.50/3.40; ☷ 10am-6pm mid-Mar–Nov) is one of Scotland's most evocative castles, and must be represented in millions of photo albums. It's on an offshore islet, magically linked to the mainland by an elegant, stone-arched bridge. It's very much a re-creation inside with an excellent introductory exhibition. Keep an eye out for the photos of scenes from the movie *Highlander* filmed in the castle. There's also a sword used at the battle of Culloden in 1745. The castle was ruined in 1719 after Spanish Jacobite forces were defeated at the Battle of Glenshiel and was rebuilt between 1912 and 1932.

Citylink buses from Fort William and Inverness to Portree stop opposite the castle and by the bridge at Dornie.

Glen Shiel & Glenelg

From Eilean Donan Castle, the A87 follows Loch Duich into spectacular Glen Shiel, with 1000m-high peaks soaring up on both sides of the road. At Shiel Bridge, a narrow side road goes over the **Bealach Ratagain** (pass) to Glenelg, where there's still a ferry to Skye.

There are several good walks in the area, including the low-level route from Morvich to Glen Affric Youth Hostel (p297), via spectacular **Gleann Lichd** (four hours each way). A traverse of the **Five Sisters of Kintail** is a classic and none-too-easy expedition; start a mile east of the Glen Shiel battle site and finish at Shiel Bridge (eight to 10 hours). For more information on these walks, contact the TIC at Kyle of Lochalsh (p345).

From the Bealach Ratagain, there are great views of the Five Sisters. Continue past Glenelg to the two fine ruined Iron Age **brochs**, Dun Telve and Dun Troddan. Dun Telve still stands to a height of 10m, making it the second best-preserved broch in Scotland, after Mousa in Shetland.

From Glenelg round to the road-end at **Arnisdale**, the scenery becomes even more spectacular, with great views across Loch Hourn to Knoydart.

Ratagan Youth Hostel (SYHA; ☎ 0870 004 1147; Shiel Bridge; dm adult/child £11/9; ✆ Mar-Oct; ▫) is a particularly good hostel. It has excellent facilities and a to-die-for spot by Loch Duich. If you want a break from munro-bagging, this is the place.

Don't miss the wacky **Glenelg Inn** (☎ 01599-522273, fax 522283; Glenelg; DB&B per person from £60; bar meals £8-12) with its kilt-clad proprietor, excellent accommodation and delicious meals.

Citylink buses between Fort William, Inverness and Skye operate along the A87. There's a postbus operating once daily, except Sunday, from Kyle to Arnisdale via Shiel Bridge and Glenelg.

Cluanie Inn

Beyond the top of Glen Shiel, the A87 passes the remote, but welcoming, **Cluanie Inn** (☎ 01320-340238; www.cluanie.co.uk; Glenmoriston; r per person £25.50-49.50; bar meals £6-10), which has tourist information at reception. It's a classy lodge and very popular with outdoor enthusiasts. There's even a four-poster bed, spa and sauna in here. Bar meals for hungry walkers include freshly shot haggis for £6.95.

From the inn, you can walk along several mountain ridges, bagging munros to your heart's content. There's a low-level

route through to Glen Affric Youth Hostel (see the Central Highlands chapter, p297), which takes three hours, but it gets very wet at certain times of year.

ISLE OF SKYE

pop 8850

The Isle of Skye (an t-Eilean Sgiathanach in Gaelic) takes its name from the old Norse *sky-a*, meaning 'cloud island' – no doubt a reference to the often mist-enshrouded Cuillin Hills. It's the biggest of Scotland's islands, a 50-mile (80km) long smorgasbord of velvet moors, jagged mountains, sparkling lochs and towering cliffs. The stunning scenery is the main attraction, but when the mist closes in there are plenty of castles, crofting museums and cosy pubs and restaurants to retire to.

Along with Edinburgh and Loch Ness, Skye is one of Scotland's top three tourist destinations, but the hordes tend to stick to Portree, Dunvegan and Trotternish and it's almost always possible to find peace and quiet in the island's farther flung corners. Come prepared for changeable weather: when it's fine it's very fine indeed, but all too often it isn't.

Information

Portree and Broadford are the main population centres.

INTERNET ACCESS

Portree TIC (☎ 01478-612137; portree@host.co.uk; Bayfield Rd, Portree; £1 per 20 min)

Sligachan Hotel (☎ 650204; Sligachan; www.sligachan.co.uk; £1 per 15 min)

Columba 1400 Community Centre (☎ 01478-611400; Staffin, Trotternish; £1.50 per 20 min; ✆ 10.30am-4.30pm Mon-Sat)

MEDICAL SERVICES

Portree Hospital (☎ 01478-613200) There's a casualty department and dental surgery here.

MONEY

Only Portree and Broadford have banks with ATMs. Portree's TIC also has a currency exchange desk.

TOURIST INFORMATION

Broadford TIC (☎ 01471-822361; The Car Park, Broadford; 9am-5.30pm Mon-Sat, 11am-4pm Sun Apr-Oct; 9am-4.30pm Mon-Sat Nov-Mar)

Dunvegan TIC (☎ 01470-521581; 2 Lochside, Dunvegan; 9am-5.30pm Mon-Sat, 11am-4pm Sun Apr-Oct; 9am-4.30pm Mon-Sat Nov-Mar)

Portree TIC (☎ 01478-612137; portree@host.co.uk; Bayfield Rd, Portree; 9am-5.30pm Mon-Sat, 11am-4pm Sun Apr-Oct; 9am-4.30pm Mon-Sat Nov-Mar)

Activities
WALKING
Skye offers some of the finest – and in places the roughest and most difficult – walking in Scotland. There are many detailed guidebooks available, including a series of four walking guides by Charles Rhodes, available from the Aros Centre and the TIC at Portree. You'll need Ordnance Survey (OS) 1:50,000 maps No 23 and 32. Don't attempt the longer walks in bad weather or in winter.

Easy low-level routes include: Torrin to Luib (two hours); Sligachan to Kilmarie via Camasunary (four hours); and Portnalong to Talisker via Fiskavaig (four hours return). Harder walks, but still on good paths, are: Kilmarie to Coruisk via the 'Bad Step', a rocky slab above the sea that you have to scramble across (at least four hours return).

Skye Walking Holidays (☎ 01470-552396; www.skyewalks.co.uk; Duntulm Castle Hotel, Trotternish) organises week-long walking holidays, but individual walkers are welcome to join their guided walks for £24 a day.

CLIMBING
The Cuillin Hills are a playground for rock climbers, and the traverse of the Cuillin Ridge – a two-day expedition – is the finest mountaineering expedition in the British Isles. There are several mountain guides who can provide instruction and introduce inexperienced climbers safely to the harder routes. Agencies include **Cuillin Guides** (☎ 01478-640289; www.cuillin-guides.co.uk) and **Skye Highs Mountain Guiding** (☎ 01471-822116; www.skyeguides.co.uk).

WATERSPORTS
There is superb sea kayaking in the sheltered coves and sea lochs around the coast of Skye. **Whitewave Outdoor Centre** (☎ 542414; www.white-wave.co.uk; Linicro, Kilmuir; Mar-Oct) and **Skyak Adventures** (☎ 01471-833428; www.skyakadventures.com; 13 Camuscross, Isleornsay) provide kayaking instruction, guiding and equipment hire for both beginners and experts.

Organised Tours
There are several operators who offer guided tours of Skye, covering history, culture and wildlife, including **Red Deer Travel** (☎ 01478-612142) and **Isle of Skye Tour Guide Co** (01471-844440; www.isle-of-skye-tour-guide.co.uk). Rates are around £10 an hour for up to six people.

Getting There & Away
BOAT
Despite the bridge, there are still two ferry links between Skye and the mainland.

CalMac (☎ 01471-844248; www.calmac.co.uk) operates the Mallaig to Armadale ferry (driver/passenger £3, car £16.50, 30 minutes, eight or nine a day). It's very popular in July and August, so book ahead if you're travelling by car.

Skye Ferry (☎ 01599-511302; www.skyeferry.co.uk) runs a tiny vessel (six cars only) on the short Glenelg to Kylerhea crossing, from Easter to October only (car and passengers £6, motorcycle £3, pedestrian 70p, bicycle £1, five minutes, on demand). The ferry operates from 9am to 7.45pm Monday to Saturday and 10am to 5.45pm Sunday from mid-May to August (till 5.45pm Monday to Saturday in September and October). From Easter to mid-May it operates from 9am to 5.45pm Monday to Saturday only.

BUS & CAR
The Isle of Skye became permanently tethered to the Scottish mainland when the Skye Bridge was opened in 1995. The one-way bridge tolls are £5.70/2.90/11.40 for a car/motorcycle/car and caravan from May to September, and £4.70/2.40/9.40 October to April

Citylink runs direct buses from Glasgow to Portree and Uig (£21, seven hours, three a day) via Crianlarich, Fort William and Kyle of Lochalsh and Thurso. Buses also run from Inverness to Portree (£11, 3½ hours) twice-daily.

Getting Around
Getting around the island by public transport can be a pain, especially if you want to explore away from the main Kyleakin–

NORTHERN HIGHLANDS & ISLANDS

Portree road. And here, as in much of the Highlands, public transport dwindles to nothing at weekends, particularly in winter and even more dramatically (or so it seems) when it rains.

Rapsons/Highland Country (☎ 01478-612622; www.rapsons.co.uk) operates the main bus routes on the island, linking all the main villages and towns. It offers a good-value Skye Rover ticket, giving unlimited travel for one/three days for £6/15.

You can order a taxi from **Kyle Taxi Company** (☎ 01599-534323), or rent a car from **Portree Coachworks** (☎ 01478-612688; www.portree coachworks.co.uk) from £36 a day.

KYLEAKIN (CAOL ACAIN)
☎ 01599 / pop 100
Poor wee Kyleakin had the carpet pulled from under it when the Skye Bridge opened – it went from being the gateway to the island, to a backwater bypassed by the main road. It's now a pleasant, peaceful little place, with a harbour used by wildlife cruise boats.

Seacruise (☎ 534760) charges £5.50/3.50 for one-hour cruises to see seals, a shipwreck and an otter sanctuary. There's also a two-hour evening cruise to Eilean Donan Castle (£10/5; p345).

The village is something of a backpacker ghetto, with three hostels in close proximity. The homely **Dun Caan Independent Hostel** (☎ 534087; www.skyerover.co.uk; Castle View; dm £10), in a fine old pine-panelled house overlooking the harbour, has the best location.

Friendly **Skye Backpackers** (☎ 534510; skye@ scotlands-top-hostels.com; Benmhor; dm £10-12) pulls in the party crowd, but the boxy **Kyleakin International Hostel** (SYHA; ☎ 0870 004 1134; dm £10-12.50) lacks atmosphere, despite its sea views.

The **Pier Coffee House** (☎ 534641; snacks £2-3), down by the harbour, is the place to go for tea and scones.

A shuttle bus runs half-hourly between Kyle of Lochalsh and Kyleakin (£1.70, five minutes), and there are one to three buses daily (except Sunday) to Broadford and Portree.

BROADFORD (AN T-ATH LEATHANN)
☎ 01471 / pop 1050
Broadford is a service centre for the scattered communities of southern Skye. The long, straggling village has a 24-hour petrol

station, a large supermarket, a laundrette, a bank with ATM, and a **hospital** (☎ 822137). **Broadford Books** (☎ 822748; Old Post Office; ⏰ 9.15am-5pm Mon-Sat) sells a wide range of fiction as well as books of local interest.

There are lots of B&Bs in and around Broadford, and the village is well placed for exploring southern Skye by car. Recommended B&Bs include **Berabhaigh** (☎ 822372; berabhaigh@freeuk.com; 3 Limepark; s £22-30, d £36-50; ✗ Ⓟ), a lovely old croft house with views over the bay, and neighbouring **Limestone Cottage** (☎ 822142; 4 Lime Park; s £30-35, d £36-50; ✗), a delightful, ivy-clad cottage.

Broadford has several places to eat, but one really stands out. **Creelers** (☎ 822281; Lower Harrapool; mains £10-14; ⏰ noon-10pm Thu-Tue) is a small, bustling, no-frills restaurant that serves some of the best seafood on Skye. Book ahead, and if you can't get a table nip around to the back door, where you'll find **Ma Doyle's Takeaway**, for seafood to go.

Daily Citylink buses to Portree stop at Broadford. You can hire bikes from **Fairwinds Bicycle Hire** (☎ 822270) near the Broadford Hotel for £7 a day.

SLEAT
If you cross over the sea to Skye on the ferry from Mallaig you arrive in Armadale, at the southern end of the long, low-lying peninsula known as Sleat (pronounced slate). There's not much to see in Sleat itself, but it provides a magnificent grandstand for ogling the surrounding scenery – take the steep and twisting minor road that loops through **Tarskavaig** and **Tokavaig** for stunning views of the Isle of Rum, the Cuillin Hills and Bla Bheinn.

ARMADALE
☎ 01471 / pop 150
Armadale, where the Mallaig ferry docks, has a grocery store and post office. Just along the road is the part-ruined Armadale Castle, former seat of Lord Macdonald of Sleat and home to the **Museum of the Isles** (☎ 844305; Armadale; adult/child £4.50/3.50; ⏰ 9am-5.30pm Apr-Oct), which will tell you all you ever wanted to know about Clan Donald. The ticket also gives admission to the lovely castle gardens.

Sea.fari (☎ 822361) runs two-hour rigid inflatable boat (RIB) trips around the area for £15 per person. Longer trips can be arranged to places such as Canna or Rum, but you'll need cast-iron buttocks.

The no-frills **Armadale Youth Hostel** (☎ 0870 004 1103; dm £10.50; ◯ Apr-Sep) has a great location on the north side of the ferry harbour, while the rustic **Flora MacDonald Hostel** (☎ 844440; The Glebe, Kilmore; dm £9) is 3 miles (5km) north of the ferry, on a farm full of Highland cattle and Ersikay ponies.

The **Pasta Shed** (☎ 844264; The Pier, Armadale; mains £5-9), beside the ferry pier, is a cute little conservatory with some outdoor tables. It serves good seafood dishes, pizza and sandwiches.

There are four to six buses a day (Monday to Saturday) from Armadale to Broadford and Portree.

ISLEORNSAY

This pretty harbour, 8 miles (13km) north of Armadale, is opposite Sandaig Bay on the mainland, where Gavin Maxwell lived and wrote his much-loved memoir *Ring of Bright Water*. **Gallery An Talla Dearg** (☎ 01767-650444; ◯ 9am-5pm Mon-Fri, 9am-1pm Sat Aug & Sep) exhibits and sells winsome sculptures of otters and other animals and birds.

Hotel Eilean Iarmain (☎ 833332; Isleornsay; s/d £68/90; bar meals £7-9; **P**) is a charming old Victorian hotel with log fires, an excellent restaurant and 12 luxurious rooms, many with sea views. The hotel's cosy, wood-panelled bar serves delicious, gourmet-style bar meals – try the crunchy, salmon-filled fishcakes.

ELGOL (EALAGHOL)

On a clear day, the journey along the road from Broadford to Elgol is one of the most scenic on Skye. It takes in two classic postcard panoramas – the view of Bla Bheinn across Loch Slapin (near Torrin), and the superb view of the entire Cuillin range from Elgol pier.

Aquaxplore (☎ 0800 731 3089; adult/child £20/15, 2½ hours) runs high-speed boat trips from Elgol harbour to the remote **Loch na Cuilce**, an impressive inlet surrounded by acres of bare rock slabs. You might see seals, otters and porpoises here and, on a calm day, you can clamber ashore to make the short hike to **Loch Coruisk** in the heart of the Cuillin Hills. There are longer trips to Rum, Canna and Sanday with the chance of seeing Minke whales.

There's a postbus from Broadford to Elgol (£4, 40 minutes, two a day Monday to Friday, one Saturday), departing Broadford at 10.45am and 3.40pm, and departing Elgol at 2.40pm and 8.07am.

CUILLIN HILLS

☎ 01478

The Cuillin Hills are Britain's most spectacular mountain range. Though small in stature (**Sgurr Alasdair**, the highest summit, is only 993m), the peaks are near-alpine in character, with knife-edge ridges, jagged pinnacles, scree-filled gullies and acres of naked rock. While they are a paradise for experienced

---

FLORA MACDONALD

The Isle of Skye was home to Flora MacDonald, who became famous for helping Bonnie Prince Charlie escape his defeat at the Battle of Culloden.

Flora was born in 1722 at Milton in South Uist, where a memorial cairn marks the site of one of her early childhood homes. After her mother's abduction by Hugh MacDonald of Skye, Flora was reared by her brother and educated in the home of the Clanranald chiefs.

In 1746, she helped Bonnie Prince Charlie escape from Benbecula to Skye disguised as her Irish maidservant. With a price on the prince's head, their little boat was fired on, but they managed to land safely and Flora escorted the prince to Portree where he gave her a gold locket containing his portrait before setting sail for Raasay.

Waylaid on the way home, the boatmen admitted everything. Flora was arrested and imprisoned in the Tower of London. She never saw or heard from the prince again.

In 1747, she returned home, marrying Allan MacDonald of Skye and going on to have nine children. Dr Johnson stayed with her in 1773 during his journey around the Western Isles, but later poverty forced her family to emigrate to North Carolina. There her husband was captured by rebels. Flora returned to Kingsburgh on Skye where she died in 1790 and was buried in Kilmuir churchyard, wrapped in the sheet in which both Bonnie Prince Charlie and Dr Johnson had slept.

mountaineers, the higher reaches of the Cuillin are off-limits to the majority of walkers.

There are plenty of good low-level walks that are within the ability of most walkers. One of the best (on a fine day) is the steep climb from Glenbrittle campground to **Coire Lagan** (at least three hours round trip). The impressive upper corrie contains a little lochan for bathing, and the surrounding cliffs are a playground for rock climbers – bring along your binoculars.

There are two main bases for exploring the Cuillin – Sligachan to the north, and Glenbrittle to the south.

Sleeping & Eating

Sligachan Hotel (☎ 650204; www.sligachan.co.uk; Sligachan; s/d £50/70; bunkhouse per person £9; ☐ ☒ Ⓟ) The Slig, as it has been known to generations of climbers, is a near village in itself, encompassing a posh hotel, a bunkhouse, self-catering cottages, a big barn of a bar (complete with kids' playroom) and an adventure playground. **Seamus's Bar** (mains £5-10; ☼ food served 8am-11pm) dishes up decent bar meals, but if you fancy something a little more upmarket, the hotel's **Cairidh Seafood Restaurant** (mains £10-16; ☼ noon-2pm & 7-9pm) can oblige.

Across the road from the hotel there's a basic **campground** (☎ 650333; site per person £4).

At the southern end of the Cuillin you have the choice of the Scandinavian-style, timber **Glenbrittle Youth Hostel** (SYHA; ☎ 0870-004 1121; Glenbrittle; dm £11; ☼ Apr-Sep), or the **campground** (☎ 640404; site per person £3.50, plus per car £1.75) down by the sea. Beware – the midges can be diabolical.

Getting There & Away

Sligachan, on the main Kyle–Portree road, is easily accessible by bus. Glenbrittle is a bit harder to reach. From Monday to Saturday, local buses run twice a day from Portree to Glenbrittle via Sligachan and Carbost. Hitching to Glenbrittle can be slow, especially late in the day.

MINGINISH
☎ 01478

Loch Harport, to the north of the Cuillin, divides the Minginish peninsula from the rest of Skye. The village of Carbost is home to the smooth, sweet and smoky Talisker malt whisky, produced at **Talisker Distillery**

(☎ 614308; Carbost; admission £3.50; ☼ 9.30am-5pm Mon-Sat Easter-Oct, 2-5pm Mon-Fri Nov-Easter). This is the only distillery on Skye; the guided tour includes a free dram. Magnificent **Talisker Bay**, 5 miles (8km) west of Carbost, has a sandy beach, sea stack and waterfall.

The **Old Inn** (☎ 640205; Carbost; s/d £27/53; dm £10; ☼ food served 6.30-10pm; Ⓟ) has a lovely location overlooking Loch Harport. Its bright, refurbished rooms are complemented by a comfortable chalet-style bunkhouse. The bar is a favourite with walkers and climbers from Glenbrittle.

Three miles (5km) north of Carbost is the **Skyewalker Independent Hostel** (☎ 640250; Fiskavaig Rd, Portnalong; dm £8), housed in the old village school. There's a tiny **camping ground** (sites per person £2.50) out the back.

There are two or three buses a day from Portree to Carbost via Sligachan.

PORTREE (PORT RIGH)
☎ 01478 / pop 1920

Portree is Skye's largest and liveliest town. The harbour is very pretty, the houses are gaily painted and there are great views of the surrounding hills. Its name (from the Gaelic for King's Harbour) commemorates James V, who came here in 1540 to pacify the local clans.

Information

Bank of Scotland (☼ 9am-12.30pm & 1.30-5pm Mon-Fri) Has an ATM

Post office (☼ 9am-5.30pm Mon-Sat) Has currency-exchange facilities.

TIC (☎ 612137; Bayfield Rd) Opens year-round, including Sunday from late May to mid-October.

Sights & Activities

On the southern edge of Portree, the **Aros Experience** (☎ 613649; Viewfield Rd; adult/ child £3/2; ☼ 9am-6pm) is a combined book and gift shop, restaurant, theatre and cinema. The price of a ticket gets you a look at some fascinating, live CCTV images from local sea eagle and heron nests, and a viewing of a strangely commentary-free wide-screen video of Skye's impressive scenery (it's worth waiting for the aerial shots of the Cuillin). The centre is a useful rainy-day retreat, with an indoor soft play area for children.

An Tuireann Art Centre (☎ 613306; Struan Rd; admission free; ☼ 10am-5pm Mon-Sat), half a mile west of town on the B885, is an appealing gallery that

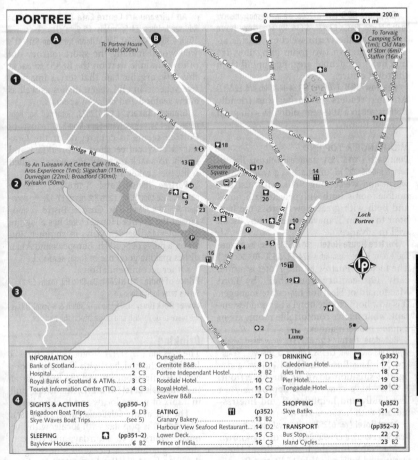

PORTREE

NORTHERN HIGHLANDS & ISLANDS

hosts changing exhibitions of contemporary art. It also has an excellent café (p352).

Brigadoon Boat Trips (☎ 613718; adult/child £10/6.50) runs wildlife cruises (two hours, three daily) to the Sound of Raasay. Porpoises, seals and eagles are commonly seen, and you can explore sea caves in the boat. Fishing trips can also be arranged.

Skye Waves (☎ 612461; adult/child £20/15) has exciting, two-hour boat trips in high-speed RIBs. Even if you don't see any wildlife, it's a blast just zipping around. Both companies operate from Portree harbour.

Festivals & Events

The annual **Isle of Skye Highland Games** (☎ 612608) are held in Portree in early August.

Sleeping

BUDGET

Torvaig Camping (☎ 612209; Torvaig; tent site £7; ⊗ Apr-Oct) This is the closest camping ground. It's a mile north of town on the A87 to Uig.

Portree Independent Hostel (☎ 613737; The Green; dm £10-11; ⊗) Housed in the former post office near Somerled Sq, this is a rambling two-storey hostel with cosy dorms and double rooms and a huge open kitchen and dining area.

Bayview House (☎ 613340; Bayfield; r per person £15; ⊗ P) This is a modern house with spartan but sparkling clean rooms, some with sea and mountain views. The bathrooms have power showers. At this price and location, it's a bargain.

Grenitote B&B (☎ 612808; e.a.matheson@amserve
.net; 9 Martin Cres; s £20-25, d £36-40) Readers have
appreciated the warm welcome at this attractive, modern two-room bungalow, It's
in a quiet residential area, just uphill from
the town centre.

Seaview B&B (☎ 611123; 4 Mill Rd; s/d £20/32)
Another readers' favourite, this friendly
B&B is set in a 100-year-old villa with great
views of Raasay.

MID-RANGE & TOP END

Dunsgiath (☎ 612851; stay@dunsgiath.com; The Harbour; d £40-56; ✗) Dunsgiath is a wonderfully
warm and welcoming B&B, with just two
double rooms, both with private bathrooms
and both with great views across the harbour to Beinn Tianavaig and Raasay. Book
well in advance.

Portree House Hotel (☎ 613713; enquiry@portree
house.com; Home Farm Rd; s £24-28, d £50-70; ✗ Ⓟ)
The focus of Portree House Hotel is a fine,
early 19th-century house built by Lord
Macdonald of Sleat for his estate manager.
It is now home to the hotel's bar and restaurant, while its five comfortable rooms are in
a quiet, modern annex.

Rosedale Hotel (☎ 613131; www.rosedalehotel
skye.co.uk; Beaumont Cres; s £40-46, d £68-98; ✓ Apr-
Nov; ✗) The Rosedale Hotel enjoys a delightful situation down by the waterfront.
Readers have commented approvingly on
its friendly and helpful staff and fine restaurant with harbour views.

Royal Hotel (☎ 612525; info@royal-hotel-skye.com;
Bank St; s £45-55, d £75-90; ✗) Formerly known
as MacNab's Inn, the historic Royal Hotel
was visited by James V in 1540, and Bonnie
Prince Charlie and Flora MacDonald parted
company in a room here shortly before the
prince left for Raasay. Recently refurbished,
it is now modern and luxurious and many
rooms have a view across the harbour.

Eating

Harbour View Seafood Restaurant (☎ 612069; 7
Bosville Tce; mains £12.50-17; ✓ noon-2.30pm & 5-10pm)
The Harbour View is Portree's most congenial place to eat. It has a homely dining
room with a log fire in winter, books on the
mantelpiece and bric-a-brac on the shelves.
And on the table, superb Scottish seafood,
such as fresh Skye oysters, poached scallops
with orange and coriander sauce, and seared
salmon with tarragon and lemon butter.

An Tuireann Art Centre Café (☎ 613306; Struan
Rd; sandwiches £4-5, mains £6-9; ✓ snacks served
10am-4.30pm Mon-Sat, lunch noon-3pm Mon-Sat) It's
well worth making the short journey out
of town (a mile west on the B885) to eat at
this arty, organic café that serves imaginative vegetarian and vegan dishes as well as
a few seafood and chicken specials.

Granary Bakery (☎ 612873; Somerled Sq; light
meals £3-4.50; ✓ 8.30am-5pm Mon-Sat) Most of
Portree seems to congregate at the Granary's cosy coffee shop at breakfast and
lunch, to snack on tasty sandwiches, filled
rolls, pies, cakes and pastries.

Portree House Hotel (☎ 613713; enquiry@
portreehouse.com; Home Farm Rd; mains £7-12; ✓ noon-
3pm & 5.30-9.30pm) The Garden Bistro restaurant at the Portree House Hotel has a log fire
in winter and garden views in summer, and
serves a range of Scottish, European and Asian
dishes making good use of local seafood.

Other recommendations:

Prince of India (☎ 612681; Bayfield Rd; mains £5-8)
Serves tasty Indian food

Lower Deck (Quay St; ✓ noon-2.30pm & 6-9pm) This is
the place to go for fish and chips; it's on the harbour.

Drinking

The **Isles Inn** (☎ 612129; Somerled Sq) features a
Jacobean-themed bar with flagstone floor
and open fires; both it and the lively bar at
the **Tongadale Hotel** (☎ 612115; Wentworth St) pull
in a mix of young locals and backpackers.

The bar at the **Caledonian Hotel** (☎ 612641;
Wentworth St) is popular with locals, with live
music Thursday to Saturday, and you can
almost guarantee a weekend sing-song in
the waterfront **Pier Hotel** (☎ 612094; Quay St).

Shopping

Skye Batiks (☎ 613331; The Green; ✓ 9am-9pm Mon-
Fri, 9am-6pm Sat & Sun) is a cut above the average gift shop, selling a range of interesting
crafts that includes carved wood, jewellery
and batik fabrics with Celtic designs.

Getting There & Around

The main bus stop is in Somerled Square.
There are three to five buses a day from
Portree to Sligachan (15 minutes), Broadford (35 minutes) and Dunvegan Castle (40
minutes), and six a day on a circular route
around Trotternish (in both directions)
taking in Flodigarry (20 minutes), Kilmuir
(1¼ hours) and Uig (30 minutes).

You can hire bikes at **Island Cycles** (☎ 613121; The Green; £10 a day; ☺ 9.30am-5pm).

DUNVEGAN (DUN BHEAGAIN) & DUIRINISH
☎ 01470

Dunvegan Castle (☎ 521206; Dunvegan; adult/child £6.50/4; ☺ 10am-5pm Easter-Oct, 11am-4pm Oct-Easter), seat of the chief of Clan MacLeod, is Skye's most famous historic building. It has played host to Samuel Johnson, Sir Walter Scott and, most famously, Flora Macdonald (p349). The oldest parts are the 14th-century keep and dungeon, but most of it dates from the 17th to 19th centuries.

In addition to the usual castle stuff – swords, silver and family portraits – there are some interesting artefacts, most famous being the **Fairy Flag**, a diaphanous, silk banner that dates from sometime between the 4th and 7th centuries. Bonnie Prince Charlie's waistcoat and a lock of his hair, donated by Flora Macdonald's granddaughter, share a room with **Rory Mor's Drinking Horn**, a beautiful 16th-century vessel of Celtic design that could hold half a gallon of claret. Upholding the family tradition back in 1956, the present chief downed the contents in one minute and 57 seconds 'without setting down or falling down' – note that in his portrait in the dining room he is most definitely sitting down.

It's worth making the long drive beyond Dunvegan on single-track roads to Waterstein to see the spectacular sea cliffs of **Waterstein Head**, and to walk down to **Neist lighthouse** with its views to the Outer Hebrides.

The **Stein Inn** (☎ 592362; angus.teresa@steininn.co.uk; Stein, Waternish; s/d £31/49; P) is an old country inn dating from 1790, with a handful of rooms (all with sea views), a lively little bar, and a delightful beer garden beside the loch, a real suntrap on summer afternoons. It's on the B886 road along the Waternish peninsula, about 8 miles (13km) north of Dunvegan.

Next door is one of Skye's most romantic restaurants, the **Lochbay Seafood Restaurant** (☎ 592235; Stein, Waternish; mains £8-18; ☺ noon-2.30pm & 6.30-9pm Mon-Fri Easter-Oct, plus 6.30-9pm Sat Aug-Oct), a cosy farmhouse kitchen of a place with terracotta tiles and a wood-burning stove. The menu includes most things that live in a shell or swim.

In Colbost, halfway between Dunvegan and Waterstein, is the **Three Chimneys** (☎ 511258; Colbost, Dunvegan; s/d £155/190; 3-course lunch/dinner £24/42; ✗ P), another superb romantic retreat combining a gourmet restaurant in a candlelit crofter's cottage with sumptuous five-star rooms in the house next door. Book well in advance.

TROTTERNISH
☎ 01470

The Trotternish peninsula to the north of Portree has some of Skye's most beautiful – and bizarre – scenery.

East Coast

First up is the 50m-high, pot-bellied pinnacle of crumbling basalt known as the **Old Man of Storr**, prominent above the road 6 miles (10km) north of Portree. You can hike up to its foot from the car park in the woods at the northern end of Loch Leathan (one hour round trip). This seemingly unclimbable pinnacle was scaled in 1955 by English mountaineer Don Whillans. North again, near Staffin (Stamhain), is the spectacular **Kilt Rock**, a stupendous cliff of columnar basalt whose vertical ribbing has been fancifully compared to the pleats of a kilt.

Staffin Bay is dominated by the dramatic basalt escarpment of the **Quiraing**, whose impressive land-slipped cliffs and pinnacles constitute one of Skye's most remarkable landscapes. From a parking area at the highest point of the minor road between Staffin and Uig you can hike north to the Quiraing in half an hour. The adventurous (and energetic) can scramble up to the left of the slender pinnacle called the **Needle** to find a hidden, grass-topped plateau known as the **Table**.

Flora Macdonald (p000) lived in a farmhouse at **Flodigarry** in northeast Trotternish from 1751 to 1759. The farmhouse and its pretty garden is now part of the delightful **Flodigarry Country House Hotel** (☎ 552203; www.flodigarry.co.uk; Flodigarry; s £76-85, d £118-170; ✗ P). The hotel's bar – whose décor is strangely reminiscent of a Turkish bathhouse – has great views over the Inner Sound, and serves excellent haddock and chips.

If the hotel is too expensive for you, the nearby **Dun Flodigarry Hostel** (☎ 552212; hostel@flodigarry.f9.co.uk; Flodigarry; dm £9, d £20) has the same superb views, and you can still visit the hotel bar for a pint.

West Coast

The peat-reek of crofting life in the 18th and 19th centuries is preserved in a gathering of thatched cottages at the **Skye Museum of Island Life** (☎ 552206; Kilmuir; adult/child £1.75/50p; ☼ 9.30am-5.30pm Mon-Sat Apr-Oct). Behind the museum is Kilmuir Cemetery, where a tall Celtic cross marks the **grave of Flora Macdonald**; the cross was erected in 1955 to replace her original memorial, of which 'every fragment was removed by tourists'.

Whichever way you arrive at **Uig** (pronounced oo-ig), the picture-perfect bay, ringed by steep hills, rarely fails to impress. If you have time to kill while waiting for a ferry to the Outer Hebrides, you can visit the **Isle of Skye Brewery** (☎ 542477; The Pier), which sells four locally brewed and bottled beers.

Just south of Uig, a minor road (signposted 'Sheader and Balnaknock') leads in a mile or so to the **Fairy Glen**, a strange and enchanting natural landscape of miniature conical hills, rocky towers, ruined cottages and a tiny roadside lochan.

There's a cluster of B&Bs in Uig, as well as the **Uig Youth Hostel** (SYHA; ☎ 0870 004 1155; Uig; dm £10.50; ☼ late Apr-Sep) and a lovely old coaching inn, the **Uig Hotel** (☎ 542205; Uig; s £30-34, d £49-57; P).

Whitewave Outdoor Centre (☎ 542414; www .white-wave.co.uk; Linicro, Kilmuir; snacks £1-4.50; B&B £17.50-20 per person) has a warm and welcoming little café serving home-made soups, cakes and sandwiches, and a wicked chocolate fudge brownie. It also offers B&B, and kayaking and windsurfing instruction.

ISLE OF RAASAY

☎ 01478 / pop 163

There are several good walks on Raasay, the rugged, 10-mile-long island that lies off Skye's east coast, including one to the flat-topped conical hill of **Dun Caan** (443m). Forest Enterprise publishes a free leaflet (available from the TICs in Portree or Kyle of Lochalsh) with suggested walks and forest trails.

The extraordinary ruin of **Brochel Castle**, perched on a pinnacle at the northern end of Raasay, was home to Calum Garbh MacLeod, an early-16th-century pirate. At the battle of Culloden in 1746, Raasay supplied Bonnie Prince Charlie with around 100 fighting men and 26 pipers, but the people paid dearly for their Jacobite sympathies when victorious government forces arrived and proceeded to murder, rape and pillage their way across the island.

Set in the former laird's residence, **Raasay Outdoor Centre** (☎ 660266, 660200; Raasay House; B&B £21 per person, campsite per person £5) welcomes backpackers and overnight guests as well as people attending outdoor activity courses.

Raasay Youth Hostel (SYHA; ☎ 660240; Creachan Cottage; dm £9.50; ☼ Apr-early Sep) is set in a rustic cottage high on the hillside overlooking Skye. It's a long hike from the ferry pier but makes a good base for exploring the island.

Other island accommodation includes the lovely old **Isle of Raasay Hotel** (☎ 660222; info@isleofraasayhotel.co.uk; Borodale House, Inverarish; d £58-70; P), just above the ferry pier, and **Mrs MacKay's B&B** (☎ 660207; 6 Oskaig Park; s/d £23/35), 3 miles (5km) to the north.

A CalMac **ferry** (passenger/bicycle/car £2.50/1/9.85) runs from Sconser, on the Portree–Broadford road, to the southern end of Raasay (15 minutes, hourly Monday to Saturday). There are no petrol stations on the island.

OUTER HEBRIDES

pop 26,500

A professor of Spanish and a professor of Gaelic met at a conference and began discussing the relative merits of their respective languages. 'But tell me,' said the Spanish professor, 'do you have a Gaelic equivalent for the Spanish phrase *mañana, mañana*?' The Hebridean professor thought for a while, then replied, 'No, I do not think that we have in the Gaelic a word that conveys such a pressing sense of urgency'.

An old joke perhaps, but one which hints at the slower pace of life you can expect to find in the Gaelic-speaking communities of the Outer Hebrides, a place where the morning papers arrive in the afternoon and almost everything – in Lewis and Harris at least – closes down on Sundays.

Isolated, windswept and irresistibly romantic, the Outer Hebrides – also known as the Western Isles, or Na h-Eileanan an

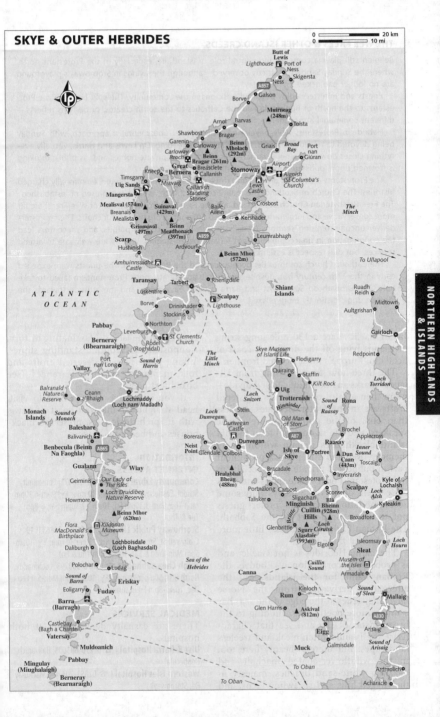

SKYE & OUTER HEBRIDES

0 — 20 km
0 — 10 mi

Butt of Lewis
Lighthouse Port of Ness
Ness
Skigersta
Borve
Galson
Muirneag (248m)
Tolsta
Arnol   Barvas
Shawbost   Bragar
Garenin   Bragar
Carloway   **Beinn Mholach (292m)**
Carloway Broch   Griais
Kneep   **Beinn Bragar (261m)**   Broad Bay   Port nan Giúran
Timsgarry   **Great Bernera**   Breasclete   Callanish   Stornoway
Uig Sands   Miavaig   *Callanish Standing Stones*   Airport   Aignish (St Columba's Church)
Mangersta   *Lews Castle*
Mealisval (574m)   Baile Ailein   Crosbost
Breanais   **Suinaval (429m)**
Mealista   Kershader
Griomaval (497m)   **Beinn Meadhanach (397m)**   Leumrabhagh
Scarp   Ardvourlie
Hushinish   **Beinn Mhor (572m)**
Amhuinnsuidhe Castle   Rhenigidale   To Ullapool
Taransay   Tarbert   *The Minch*
Shiant Islands
Luskentyre   Ruadh Reidh
Borve   **Scalpay**   Midtown
Drinishader   *Lighthouse*   Aultgrishan
Stockinish
Pabbay   Northton   Gairloch
Leverburgh   *St Clements Church*   *The Little Minch*   Redpoint
Berneray (Bhearnaraigh)   Rodel (Roghadal)
Vallay   Port nan Long   *Sound of Harris*   Skye Museum of Island Life
Flodigarry
Balranald Nature Reserve   Ceann a' Bhaigh   Quiraing   Staffin
Monach Islands   *Sound of Monach*   Lochmaddy (Loch nam Madadh)   *Loch Snizort*   **Trotternish**   Kilt Rock   *Loch Torridon*
Baleshare   Uig   Uig   *Hinnisdal*   Old Man of Storr   **Rona**
Balivanich   Stein   *Sound of Raasay*
Benbecula (Beinn Na Faoghla)   *Loch Dunvegan*   Brochel
Gualann   **Wiay**   *Dunvegan Castle*   **Raasay**   Applecross
Geirinis   *Our Lady of The Isles*   Boreraig   Dunvegan   *Isle of Skye*   Portree   **Dun Caan (443m)**   *Inner Sound*
Howmore   *Loch Druidibeg Nature Reserve*   Neist Point   Colbost   Glendale   *Oisr*   Peinchorran   Toscaig   Kyle of Lochalsh
Flora MacDonald's Birthplace   **Beinn Mhor (620m)**   **Healabhal Bheag (488m)**   Bracadale   Sconser   Inverarish   **Scalpay**   *Loch Alsh*
Kildonan Museum   Portnalong   Carbost   **Bla Bheinn (928m)**   Kyleakin
Lochboisdale (Loch Baghasdail)   Talisker   Sligachan   **Minginish**   **Cuillin Hills**   Broadford
Daliburgh   Glenbrittle   *Loch Coruisk*   Isleornsay   *Loch Hourn*
Polochar   Ludag   *Sea of the Hebrides*   **Sgurr Alasdair (993m)**   Elgol   **Sleat**   *Museum of the Isles*
Sound of Barra   **Eriskay**   **Canna**   *Cuillin Sound*   Armadale
Eoligarry   **Fuday**   Kinloch   *Sound of Sleat*   Mallaig
Barra (Barragh)   **Rum**   Arisaig
Castlebay (Bagh a Chaistell)   Glen Harris   **Askival (812m)**   Cleadale   *Sound of Arisaig*
Vatersay   Muldoanich   Cladale   **Eigg**
Mingulay (Miughalaigh)   **Pabbay**   **Muck**   Galmisdale   Ardmolich
Berneray (Bearnaraigh)   To Oban   Acharacle

ATLANTIC OCEAN

To Oban

NORTHERN HIGHLANDS & ISLANDS

THE WEE FREES & OTHER ISLAND CREEDS

Religion still plays a complex and central role in island life, especially in the Protestant north, where the Sunday Sabbath is strictly observed – although the swings in Stornoway's playground are no longer padlocked on a Sunday.

Priests and ministers enjoy powerful positions in the community. The split between the Protestants to the north of Benbecula and the Catholics to the south creates, or perhaps reflects, a different communal atmosphere.

Hebridean Protestants have developed a distinctive fundamentalist approach, with Sunday being devoted to religious services, prayer and Bible reading. On Lewis and Harris, virtually everything closes down. In general, social life is restricted to private homes and, as public drinking is frowned upon, pubs are mostly uninspiring.

The Protestants are further divided into three main sects with convoluted, emotionally charged histories. The Church of Scotland, the main Scottish church, is state-recognised or 'established'. The Free Presbyterian Church of Scotland and the Free Church of Scotland (or Wee Frees) are far more conservative and intolerant, permitting no ornaments, organ music or choirs. Their ministers deliver uncompromising sermons (usually in Gaelic) from central pulpits, and precentors lead the congregation in unaccompanied but fervent psalm-singing. Visitors are welcome to attend services, but due respect is essential.

The Catholic Church south of Benbecula survived the Reformation. The priests were expelled early in the 17th century but, despite several missionary attempts, Protestantism failed to take hold. The Sabbath on South Uist and Barra is more easy-going, and the attitude towards the 'demon drink' distinctly more relaxed.

Iar in Gaelic – are a 130-mile long string of islands lying off the northwest coast of Scotland, Europe's most isolated frontier.

The three-hour ferry crossing from Ullapool marks an important cultural divide – more than a third of Scotland's registered crofts are in the Outer Hebrides, no less than 60% of the population are Gaelic speakers, and the rigours of life in the old island blackhouses remain within living memory. Religion still plays a prominent part in public and private life, especially in the Protestant north where shops and pubs close their doors on Sundays and some accommodation providers prefer guests not to arrive or depart on the Sabbath. The Roman Catholic south is a little more relaxed about these things.

The name Hebrides is not Gaelic, and is probably a corruption of Ebudae, the Roman name for the islands. But the alternative derivation from the Norse *havbredey* (isles at the edge of the sea) has a much more poetic ring, alluding to the broad vistas of sky and sea that characterise the islands' often bleak and treeless landscapes. But there is beauty here too, in the wildflower-coated machair and dazzling white-sand beaches, majesty in the rugged hills and sprawling lochs, and

mystery in the islands' fascinating history, signposted by Neolithic standing stones, Viking place names, deserted crofts and folk memories of the Clearances (see boxed text p330).

If you only have a short time to visit, head straight for the west coast of Lewis with its prehistoric sites, preserved blackhouses and beautiful beaches.

Information
INTERNET ACCESS
Community Library (☎ 01871-810471; Community School, Castlebay, Barra; £2 per 30 min; ☷ 9am-4.30pm Mon-Thu, 9am-3.30pm Fri, 10am-12.30pm Sat, 6-8pm Tue & Thu)

Stornoway Public Library (☎ 01851-708631; 19 Cromwell St, Stornoway, Lewis; £2 per 30 min; ☷ 10am-5pm Mon-Wed & Sat, 10am-6pm Thu & Fri)

Taigh Chearsabhagh (☎ 01876-500293; Lochmaddy, North Uist; 50p per 20 min; ☷ 10am-5pm Mon-Sat Feb-Dec, 10am-8pm Fri in summer)

MEDICAL SERVICES
There are casualty departments at both hospitals.

Uist & Barra Hospital (☎ 01870-603603; Balivanich, Benbecula)

Western Isles Hospital (☎ 01851-704704; MacAulay Rd, Stornoway)

MONEY

There are banks with ATMs in Stornoway (Lewis), Tarbert (Harris), Lochmaddy (North Uist), Balivanich (Benbecula), Lochboisdale (South Uist) and Castlebay (Barra).

TOURIST INFORMATION

Barra (☎ 01871-810336; Main St, Castlebay)
Harris (☎ 01859-502011; Pier Rd, Tarbert)
Lewis (☎ 01851-703088; www.witb.co.uk; Western Isles Tourist Board, 26 Cromwell St, Stornoway)
North Uist (☎ 01876-500321; Pier Rd, Lochmaddy)
South Uist (☎ 01878-700286; Pier Rd, Lochboisdale)

Getting There & Away

AIR

There are airports at Stornoway (Lewis), Benbecula and Barra.

There are flights to Stornoway from Edinburgh (£140 return, daily) and Inverness (£130 return, daily) and from Glasgow (£140 return, Monday to Saturday only). There are also two flights a day (weekdays only) between Stornoway and Benbecula (£121 return).

There are daily flights from Glasgow to Barra and Benbecula (£140 return). At Barra, the planes land on the hard sand beach at low tide, so the timetable depends on the tides.

Airlines serving the Western Isles:
British Airways (☎ 08457 799977; www.british airways.com)
bmi (☎ 0870 60 70 555; www.flybmi.com)
Highland Airways (☎ 01851-701282; www.highland airways.co.uk)

FERRY

CalMac (☎ 0870 565 0000) runs car ferries from Ullapool to Stornoway (Lewis); from Uig (Isle of Skye) to Lochmaddy (North Uist) and Tarbert (Harris); and from Oban to Castlebay (Barra), continuing to Lochboisdale (South Uist).

Route	Car	Driver/ Passenger	Duration (hrs)
Ullapool–Stornoway	£67	£13.70	2¾
Uig–Tarbert	£43	£8.95	1½
Uig–Lochmaddy	£43	£8.95	1¾
Oban–Lochboisdale	£72	£19.70	6¾
Oban–Castlebay	£72	£19.70	4¾

From Monday to Saturday there are two or three ferries a day to Stornoway, two a day to Tarbert and Lochmaddy, and one a day to Castlebay and Lochboisdale; on Sundays there are ferries (same frequency) to Castlebay, Lochboisdale and Lochmaddy, but none to Tarbert and Stornoway. Advance booking for cars is essential in July and August; foot and bicycle passengers should have no problems. The fare for a bicycle is only £1 or £2 on top of the passenger fare.

There are 12 different Island Hopscotch tickets for set routes in the Outer Hebrides, offering a saving of around 10% (they're valid for one month).

Getting Around

Despite their separate names, Lewis and Harris are actually one island. Berneray, North Uist, Benbecula, South Uist and Eriskay are all linked together by road bridges and causeways. There are car ferries between Harris and Berneray, and between Eriskay and Barra.

BICYCLE

Many visiting cyclists plan to cycle the length of the archipelago, but if you're one of them, remember that the wind is often strong (you hear stories of people pedalling downhill and freewheeling uphill), and the prevailing direction is from the southwest – so south to north is usually the easier direction. There are few serious hills, except for a stiff climb on the main road just north of Tarbert.

Bikes can be hired for around £8.50 a day or £30 a week.
Alex Dan's Cycle Centre (☎ 01851-704025; www.heb rideancycles.co.uk; 67 Kenneth St, Stornoway, Lewis)
Barra Cycle Hire (☎ 01871-810284; 29 St Brendan's Rd, Castlebay, Barra)
Rothan Cycles (☎ 01870-620283; www.rothan.com; 9 Howmore, South Uist)

BUS

Bus transport is extremely limited, although a bare-bones service allows crofters to get to the shops in the morning and return in the afternoon; there are no buses at all on Sundays. You can pick up timetables from the TICs, or call **Stornoway bus station** (☎ 01851-704327) for information about Lewis and Harris services. Visitors without their own transport should anticipate a fair amount of hitching and walking.

CAR

Most roads are single-track, but the main hazard is posed by sheep wandering about or sleeping on the road. Petrol stations are far apart, usually closed on Sunday, and about 10% more expensive than on the mainland.

Cars can be hired from around £20 per day.

Arnol Car Rentals (☎ 01851-710548; Arnol, Lewis)

Ask Car Hire (☎ 01870-602818; Liniclate, Benbecula)

Gaeltech Car Hire (☎ 01859-520460; Leverburgh, Harris)

Laing Motors (☎ 01878-700267; Lochboisdale, South Uist)

Mackinnon Self Drive (☎ 01851-702984; 18 Inaclete Rd, Stornoway, Lewis)

Maclennan Brothers Ltd (☎ 01870-602191; Balivanich, Benbecula)

LEWIS (LEODHAIS)

☎ 01851 / pop 19,634

The northern part of Lewis is dominated by the desolate expanse of the Black Moor, a vast, undulating peat bog dimpled with glittering lochans, well seen from the Stornoway–Barvas road. The coastal fringes have some arable land and are surprisingly densely populated, though not particularly attractive.

The old blackhouses may have gone, but most smallholdings still follow a traditional pattern dating back to medieval times. Most are narrow strips of land, designed to give everyone an equal share of good and bad soil, running from the foreshore (with its valuable seaweed, used as fertiliser), across the machair (the

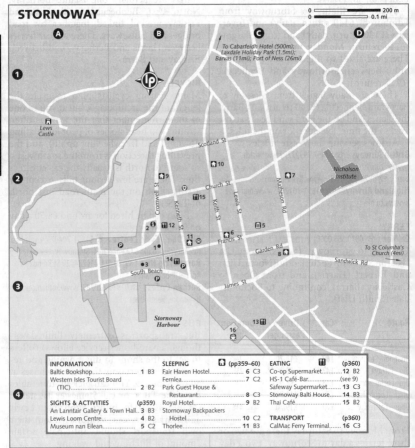

STORNOWAY

To Cabarfeidh Hotel (500m);
Laxdale Holiday Park (1.5mi);
Barvas (11mi); Port of Ness (26mi)

Lews Castle

Scotland St

Nicholson Institute

Church St

Cromwell St

Kenneth St

Keith St

Lewis St

Matheson Rd

To St Columba's Church (4mi)

Francis St

Garden Rd

Sandwick Rd

South Beach

James St

Stornoway Harbour

INFORMATION		SLEEPING 🛏 (pp359–60)		EATING 🍴 (p360)	
Baltic Bookshop	1 B3	Fair Haven Hostel	6 C3	Co-op Supermarket	12 B2
Western Isles Tourist Board		Fernlea	7 C2	HS-1 Café-Bar	(see 9)
(TIC)	2 B2	Park Guest House &		Safeway Supermarket	13 C3
		Restaurant	8 C3	Stornoway Balti House	14 B3
SIGHTS & ACTIVITIES	(p359)	Royal Hotel	9 B2	Thai Café	15 B2
An Lanntair Gallery & Town Hall	3 B3	Stornoway Backpackers			
Lewis Loom Centre	4 B2	Hostel	10 C2	TRANSPORT	(p360)
Museum nan Eilean	5 C2	Thorlee	11 B3	CalMac Ferry Terminal	16 C3

grassy sand dunes that provide the best arable land) to the poorer sheep-grazing land on hill or moor. Nowadays, few crofts are economically viable, so most islanders supplement their income from the land with fishing, tweed-weaving, and work on oil rigs and fish farms.

Lewis's finest scenery is on the west coast, from Barvas southwest to Mealista, where the rugged landscape of hill, loch and sandy strand is reminiscent of the northwestern Highlands. The Outer Hebrides' most evocative historic sites – Callanish Standing Stones, Dun Carloway, and Arnol Black-house Museum – are also to be found here.

Stornoway (Steornabhagh)
pop 5600

Stornoway is the bustling 'capital' of the Outer Hebrides and the only real town in the whole archipelago. It's a surprisingly busy little place, with cars and people swamping the centre on weekdays. Though set on a beautiful natural harbour, the town isn't going to win any prizes for beauty or atmosphere, but it's a pleasant enough introduction to this remote corner of the country.

Stornoway is the Outer Hebrides' administrative and commercial centre, home to the Western Isles Council (Comhairle nan Eilean Siar) and the islands' Gaelic TV and radio stations.

There's an airport and a car ferry link with Ullapool (p342).

INFORMATION

There are banks with ATMs and a post office, all near the tourist office.

Baltic Bookshop (☎ 702802; 8-10 Cromwell St; ☺ 9am-5.30pm Mon-Sat) Good for books and maps.

Western Isles Tourist Board (☎ 703088; www.witb.co.uk; 26 Cromwell St; ☺ 9am-6pm & 8.30-9.30pm Mon, Tue & Thu, 9am-8pm Wed & Fri, 9am-5pm & 8.30-9.30pm Sat) A short walk from the ferry pier.

SIGHTS

The **Museum nan Eilean** (☎ 703773; Francis St; admission free; ☺ 10am-5.30pm Mon-Sat; shorter winter hr) should be your first stop on a visit to Lewis. The main exhibition strings together a loose history of the Outer Hebrides from the earliest human settlements some 9000 years ago to the 20th century, exploring traditional island life and the changes inflicted by progress and technology.

An Lanntair Arts Centre (☎ 703307; South Beach; admission free; open 10am-5.30pm Mon-Sat), in the old Town Hall, hosts changing exhibitions of contemporary art and is worth a look to see what's showing.

The **Lewis Loom Centre** (☎ 704500; 3 Bayhead St; adult/child £1/50p; ☺ Mon-Sat) houses an exhibition on the history of Harris tweed; the 40-minute guided tour (£2.50 extra) includes spinning and weaving demonstrations.

Lews Castle, the imposing Baronial mansion across the harbour, was built in the 1840s. It served as home to the local college for 40 years but has lain empty since 1997.

The roofless ruin of the 14th-century **St Columba's Church** (Aignish; admission free; ☺ 24 hr), 4 miles (7km) east of town on the Eye peninsula, contains the interesting grave slabs of Roderick McLeod, 7th clan chief, (around 1498) and his daughter (1503). Hourly buses (not Sunday) to Point pass nearby.

FESTIVALS & EVENTS

The annual **Hebridean Celtic Festival** (www.hebceltfest.com), a four-day extravaganza of folk/rock/Celtic music is held in the second half of July in the grounds of Lews Castle.

SLEEPING

Laxdale Holiday Park (☎ 703234; gordon@laxdaleholidaypark.force9.co.uk; 6 Laxdale Lane; tent £4.50-6, campervan £6-7, plus £1.50-2 per person; dm £9-10, d £32-36 ☺ Apr-Oct; P) This campground, 1½ miles north of town off the A857, has a pleasant and peaceful woodland setting. There's also a bunkhouse that stays open year-round.

Fair Haven Hostel (☎ 705862; hebsurf@madasafish.com; 17 Keith St; dm £10, s/d £15/30) The Fair Haven is a friendly and easy-going hostel operated by Hebridean Surf Holidays, and is often used by groups who don't mind squeezing in together – for the rest of us it can be a bit cramped. You can hire bikes and surfing equipment, and arrange transport and historical bus tours.

Stornoway Backpackers Hostel (☎ 703628; 47 Keith St; dm £9) This is a small, laid-back place with spacious six-bed dorms (single-sex and mixed), though the whole place is a little grubby. It's a five-minute walk from the ferry and bus station. The price includes a fairly basic breakfast but there's also a self-catering kitchen.

Fernlea (☎ 702125; maureenmacmillan@amserve.com; 9 Matheson Rd; s/d £22/44; ☒ P) Set in a tastefully restored Victorian terraced house, and only five minutes' walk from the ferry, Fernlea has four rooms with private bathrooms.

Thorlee (☎ 703250; cnr Cromwell St & South Beach; s/d £15/30) Thorlee's warm, spacious rooms with views over the harbour are an absolute bargain. Check in at the County Hotel around the corner on Francis St.

Park Guest House (☎ 702485; 30 James St; d £42-58; ☒) A charming Victorian villa with a conservatory and nine luxurious rooms (most with bathroom), the Park is comfortable and central and has the added advantage of an excellent restaurant (see Eating, below).

Royal Hotel (☎ 702109; royal@calahotels.com; Cromwell St; s/d £54/72; ☒ P) The Royal is the most appealing of Stornoway's hotels, with many of the rooms enjoying a view of the harbour. Ask to see your room first, though, as some are a bit cramped.

Cabarfeidh Hotel (☎ 702604; cabarfeidh@ calahotels.com; Manor Park; s/d £72/92; ☒ P) Owned by the same company as the Royal, the Cabarfeidh is bigger and more luxurious and is handy for the golf course, but lacks the Royal's old-fashioned character. It has one room that is wheelchair-accessible.

EATING

Thai Café (☎ 701811; 27 Church St; mains £5-6; ☺ noon-2.30pm & 5-11pm Mon-Sat) Here's a surprise – authentic and inexpensive Thai food in the heart of Stornoway. This spick-and-span little restaurant has a genuine Thai chef, and serves some of the most delicious and best-value food in the Hebrides. There's no liquor licence, so BYOB.

Park Guest House (☎ 702485; 30 James St; mains £13-16; ☺ 5.30-9pm Tue-Sat) The Park's restaurant specialises in local shellfish, game and lamb, simply prepared, allowing the flavour of the food to speak for itself. It offers a good-value two-course dinner for £11.95 between 5.30pm and 7pm.

An Lanntair Café (☎ 703307; South Beach; light meals £3-5; ☺ 10am-5pm Mon-Sat) The cosy and appealing upstairs café at An Lanntair gallery serves good coffee and tasty deli-style sandwiches and light meals.

HS-1 Café-Bar (☎ 702109; Cromwell St; mains £5-8, snacks £3-6; ☺ food served noon-4pm & 5-9pm Mon-Sat, 5-9pm Sun) Bright, brash and young at heart, this café-bar dishes up foundation food for drinking sessions – fajitas, steaks and na-

chos – as well as healthier stuff like baked potatoes and tortilla wraps.

If you fancy a curry, **Stornoway Balti House** (☎ 706116; 24 South Beach St; mains £6-7; ☺ noon-2.30pm & 6-11pm) is the place to go.

For self-catering, there's a big **Safeway** supermarket (Shell St) and a **Co-op** (Cromwell St). Both are closed on Sunday.

GETTING THERE & AWAY

There are buses from Stornoway to Tarbert (£3, one hour, five a day Monday to Saturday) and Leverburgh (£3.90, two hours, five a day Monday to Saturday).

Maclennan Coaches (☎ 702114) Westside Circular bus No W2 runs a circular route from Stornoway through Callanish, Carloway, Garenin and Arnol; the timetable means you can visit one or two of the sites in a day. A one-day Rover ticket costs £5.

For details on CalMac ferries, see p357.

Butt of Lewis (Rubha Robhanais)

The Butt of Lewis (no snickering please) – the extreme northern tip of the Hebrides – is windswept and rugged, with a lighthouse, pounding surf and large colonies of nesting fulmars on the high cliffs. There's a bleak sense of isolation here, with nothing but the grey Atlantic between you and Canada.

Just before the turn-off to the Butt at Eoropie (Eoropaidh), **St Moluag's Church** (Teampull Mholuidh) is an austere, barn-like structure believed to date from the 12th century, but still used by the Episcopal Church. The main settlement here is **Port of Ness** (Port Nis) with its attractive harbour and a sandy beach popular with surfers.

Arnol Blackhouse Museum

One of Scotland's most evocative historic buildings, the **Arnol Blackhouse Museum** (☎ 710395; Arnol; adult/child £3/1; ☺ 9.30am-6.30pm Mon-Sat Apr-Sep; 9.30am-4.30pm Mon-Sat Oct-Mar; last admission 30 min before closing) is not so much a museum as a perfectly preserved fragment of a lost world. Built in 1885, this traditional blackhouse – a combined byre, barn and home – was inhabited until 1964 and has not been changed since the last inhabitant moved out. The staff faithfully rekindle the central peat fire every morning so you can experience the distinctive peat-reek; there's no chimney, and the smoke finds its own way out through the turf roof, windows and door – spend too long inside and you might feel like you've been kippered! The museum is just off the A858, about 3 miles (5km) west of Barvas.

At nearby **Bragar**, a pair of whalebones form an arch by the road, with the rusting harpoon that killed the whale dangling from the centre.

Garenin (Na Gearrannan)

The picturesque and fascinating **Gearrannan Blackhouse Village** is a cluster of nine restored thatch-roofed blackhouses perched above the exposed Atlantic coast. One of the cottages is home to the **Blackhouse Museum** (☎ 643416; Garenin; adult/child £2/1; ♥ 10am-5.30pm Mon-Sat Apr-Oct), a traditional 1955 blackhouse with displays on the village's history, while another houses the **Taigh an Chocair Restaurant** (☎ 643416, 710506; ♥ 11am-5pm Mon-Sat, dinner Thu-Sat); dinner is by booking only.

Garenin Crofters' Hostel (dm £7.50/5.50 adult/child) occupies one of the village blackhouses, and is one of the most atmospheric hostels in Scotland (or anywhere else for that matter).

The other houses in the village are let out as self-catering **holiday cottages** (☎ 643416; www.gearrannan.co.uk; Garenin; d per night £64, per week £224-330), offering the chance to stay in a unique and luxurious modernised blackhouse with attached kitchen and lounge. There's a minimum five-night let from June to August.

Carloway (Carlabagh)

Dun Carloway (Dun Charlabhaigh) is a 2000-year-old dry-stone *broch* (defensive tower), perched defiantly above a beautiful loch with views to the mountains of North Harris. One of the best-preserved brochs in Scotland, its double walls (with internal staircase) still stand to a height of 9m and testify to the engineering skills of its Iron Age architects.

The tiny, turf-roofed **Doune Broch Centre** (☎ 643338; Carloway; admission free; ♥ 10am-5pm Mon-Sat late May–mid-Sep) nearby has interpretative displays and exhibitions about the history of the broch and the life of the people who lived there.

Callanish (Calanais)

The **Callanish Standing Stones** (☎ 621422; Callanish; admission free) form one of the most complete stone circles in Britain, and one of the most atmospheric prehistoric sites anywhere. Its ageless mystery, impressive scale and undeniable beauty leave a lasting impression. Sited on a wild and secluded promontory overlooking Loch Roag, 13 large stones of beautifully banded gneiss are ranged, as if in worship, around a central monolith 4.5m high. Some 40 smaller stones radiate from the circle in the shape of a cross, with the remains of a chambered tomb at the centre. Dating from between 3800 and 5000 years ago, the stones are roughly contemporary with the pyramids of Egypt.

The nearby **Calanais Visitor Centre** (☎ 621422; Callanish; admission free; ♥ 10am-6pm Mon-Sat Apr-Sep, 10am-4pm Mon-Sat Oct-Mar) is a tour de force of discreet design. Inside is a small **exhibition** (adult/child £1.75/75p) that speculates on the origins and purpose of the stones, and an excellent **café** (snacks £1-3).

If you plan to stay the night, you have a choice of **Eshcol Guest House** (☎ 621357; neil@eshcol.com; 21 Breascleit; B&B per person £29-31; ✉ ⓟ) and neighbouring **Loch Roag Guest House** (☎ 621357; donald@lochroag.com; 22a Breascleit; B&B per person £27-30), half a mile north of Callanish. Both are modern bungalows with the same friendly owner who is very knowledgeable about the local area.

Tigh Mealros (☎ 621333; Garrynahine; mains £8-13; ♥ 7-9pm Mon-Sat), set in a sculpture garden, offers a tasty à la carte seafood menu including not-to-be-missed local scallops.

Great Bernera

This rocky island is connected to Lewis by a bridge built in 1953 – the islanders originally planned to destroy a small hill with explosives and use the material to build their own causeway. On a sunny day, it's worth making the long detour to the island's northern tip for a picnic at the perfect little sandy beach of **Bosta** (Bostadh).

To the west of the beach, an entire Iron Age village has been excavated. A guide will show you around a restored **Iron Age house** (☎ 612331; Bosta; adult/child £1.50/50p; ♥ noon-4pm Tue-Sat May-Sep).

There are four or five buses a day (Monday to Saturday) between Stornoway and the hamlet of Breacleit on Great Bernera; the bus will continue to Bosta if you ask the driver.

NORTHERN HIGHLANDS & ISLANDS

Miavaig (Miabhaig) & Mealista (Mealasta)

The B8011 road (signposted Uig, on the A858 Stornoway–Callanish road) from Garrynahine to Timsgarry (Timsgear-raidh) meanders through a scenic wilderness to some of Scotland's most stunning beaches. At **Miavaig** a loop road detours north through the Bhaltos Estate to the beautiful, mile-long white strand of **Traigh na Cnip**; there's a basic **campground** in the machair behind the beach.

Sea Trek (☎ 672464; www.seatrek.co.uk) runs adventurous day trips in a high-speed rigid-inflatable boat (RIB) from Miavaig pier to the **Flannan Isles**, a remote group of tiny, uninhabited islands 25 miles (40km) northwest of Lewis. Puffins, seals and a ruined 7th-century chapel are the main attractions, but the isles are most famous for the mystery of the three lighthouse keepers who disappeared without trace in December 1900.

From Miavaig the road continues west through a rocky defile to Timsgarry and the vast, sandy expanse of **Traigh Uige** (Uig Beach) – the famous 12th-century Lewis chess pieces made of walrus-ivory were discovered in the sand dunes here in 1831; of the 78 pieces, 67 are in the British Museum in London, and 11 in Edinburgh's National Museum of Scotland. You can buy replicas at various outlets on the island. There's a very basic **campground** (☎ 672248; tent/campervan site per person £1) on the south side of the bay (signposted 'Ardroil Beach').

The minor road that continues south from Timsgarry to **Mealista** passes a few smaller, but still spectacular, white-sand beaches; beware, though – the surf can make swimming treacherous.

Bonaventure (☎ 672474; www.bonaventurelewis .co.uk; Aird Uig; 2-/3-course lunch £7/9, dinner mains £13-14; ☺ noon-2pm Wed-Sat, 7-9pm Tue-Sat; closed Nov & Feb) has to be the most remote French restaurant in Europe, housed in a converted, pine-clad military prefab perched above a wild, cliff-bound Atlantic cove 3 miles (5km) north of Timsgarry. The food is superb – local seafood and venison prepared by the resident French chef/owner – and the setting unique. Booking is essential for both lunch and dinner. If you want to stay the night after dinner, there are three comfortable **double rooms** (B&B per person £17).

HARRIS (NA HEARADH)

☎ 01859 / pop 1866

Harris is the scenic jewel in the necklace of islands that comprise the Outer Hebrides, and combines mountains, pristine beaches, expanses of machair and weird rocky hills and coastline. The mountains of North Harris rise forbiddingly above the peat moors south of Stornoway – Clisham (799m) is the highest point. South Harris, across the narrow isthmus at Tarbert, has a fascinating variety of landscapes and lovely snow-white beaches.

Harris is famous for Harris Tweed, high-quality woollen cloth still hand-woven in islanders' homes. The industry employs around 400 weavers; Tarbert TIC can tell you about weavers and workshops you can visit.

Tarbert (An Tairbeart)

pop 480

Tarbert is a harbour village with ferry connections to Uig on Skye. It's a serene and pretty place with a spectacular location, overshadowed by mountains on the narrow neck of land that links North and South Harris

The **TIC** (☎ 502011; Pier Rd) is signposted up the hill and stays open for late ferry arrivals. Village facilities include a petrol station, bank, ATM and two general stores. The **Harris Tweed Shop** (☎ 502493; Main St) stocks a wide range of books on the Hebrides.

Rockview Bunkhouse (☎ 502626; Main St; dm £9) on the street above the harbour is a bit cell-like with its cramped dorms but has good facilities.

Waterstein House (☎ 502358; Main St; B&B per person £15) has plain, simple rooms in a very old-fashioned house (it feels like you're visiting your granny), just a few minutes' walk from the ferry.

Harris Hotel (☎ 502154; www.harrishotel.com; Tarbert; s £45-60, d £67-77; P) is a 19th-century sporting hotel, originally built for deer-stalkers visiting the North Harris Estates. Run since 1903 by four generations of the Cameron family, it offers spacious and comfortable rooms and good food; look out for JM Barrie's initials scratched on the dining room window (the author of Peter Pan visited here in the 1920s).

Firstfruits (☎ 502439; Pier Rd; ☺ 10.30am-4.30pm Mon-Sat Apr-Sep) is a cosy little cottage tea-room near the TIC – handy while you wait for a ferry.

FOR PEAT'S SAKE

Visitors to the Outer Hebrides will not fail to notice peat stacks next to many houses. These interestingly constructed stacks are designed to allow wind to blow straight through, thus assisting the drying process before the peat can be used as fuel.

Peat is extremely wet in its raw state and it can take a few months to dry out. Initially it's cut from roadside sphagnum moss bogs, and cuttings are at least a metre deep. Rectangular blocks of peat are cut using a long-handled tool called a peat-iron (*tairsgeir* in Gaelic); this is extremely hard work and causes blisters, even on hands used to manual labour. Different types of *tairsgeir* are used on the islands. In Lewis, they cut relatively short brick-shaped blocks, while in Uist the blocks are somewhat longer. The peat blocks are transported to the cutter's house, then carefully built into a stack called a *cruach-mhonach*. The blocks are balanced on top of each other in a grid pattern so that there's a maximum air space. Once the peat is dry it can be stored in a shed.

Peat fires in Hebridean homes are becoming increasingly rare due to the popularity of oil-fuelled central heating. Peat burns much more slowly than wood or coal and it produces a pleasant smell and quite a lot of heat.

North Harris

Magnificent North Harris is the most mountainous region of the Outer Hebrides. There are few roads, but many opportunities for climbing, walking and bird-watching.

The B887 leads west to **Hushinish**, where there's a lovely silver-sand beach. Just northwest of Hushinish is the uninhabited island of **Scarp**, the scene of bizarre attempts to send mail by rocket in 1934, a story recounted in the movie *The Rocket Post* (2001), which was shot in Harris.

Rhenigidale Crofters' Hostel (dm £7.50/5.50 adult/child) can be reached on foot from Tarbert (6 miles/10km, allow three hours). It's an excellent walk, but take all the necessary supplies for mountain walks (maps, protective clothing etc). Take the road to Kyles Scalpay for 2 miles (3km) and, at a bend in the road just beyond Laxdale Lochs, veer off to the left on a signposted track across the hills (marked on OS maps). The hostel is a white building standing above the road on the eastern side of the glen; the warden lives in the house closest to the shore.

The remote hamlet of Rhenigidale can also be reached by road; the **Rhenigidale Taxi Bus** (☎ 502221) will take you there, but you must book in advance.

South Harris

If you think that Scotland has no decent beaches, wait till you see the west coast of South Harris. The blinding white sands and turquoise waters of **Luskentyre** and **Scarasta** beaches would be major holiday resorts if

they were transported to somewhere with a warm climate; as it is, they're usually deserted.

The culture and landscape of the Hebrides are celebrated in the exhibition at **Seallam! Visitor Centre** (☎ 520258; Northton; adult/child £2.50/2; ☺ 9am-5pm Mon-Sat). Seallam is Gaelic for 'Let me show you'. The centre, which is in Northton, just south of Scarasta, also has a genealogical research centre for people who want to trace their Hebridean ancestry. The centre is in Northton (Taobh Tuath), just south of Scarasta.

The east coast is a complete contrast to the west – a strange, rocky moonscape of hillocky gneiss pocked with innumerable tiny lochans, the bleakness lightened here and there by the occasional splash of green around the few crofting communities. At its southernmost end stands the impressive 16th-century **St Clement's Church** (Rodel; admission free), which was abandoned in 1560 after the Reformation. Inside the echoing nave is the fascinating tomb of Alexander MacLeod, the man responsible for the church's construction. Crude carvings show hunting scenes, a castle, a galleon, and various saints, including St Clement clutching a skull.

The town of **Leverburgh** (An t-Ob) is named after Lord Leverhulme (the founder of Unilever), who bought Lewis and Harris in 1918. He had grand plans for the islands, and for Obbe, as Leverburgh was then known. It was to be a major fishing port with a population of 10,000, but the plans died with Lord Leverhulme in 1925 and the village reverted to a sleepy backwater.

Am Bothan (☎ 520251; Leverburgh; dm £13) is a quirky, chalet-style hostel with small, neat dorms and a great porch where you can enjoy morning coffee with views over the creek.

Recommended guesthouses near the ferry include **Caberfeidh House** (☎ 520276; Leverburgh; r per person £18-20) and **Sorrel Cottage** (☎ 520319; 2 Glen; r per person £20); both serve evening meals.

There's a **car ferry** (person/car £5/23.05) from Leverburgh to Berneray (1¼ hours, three or four daily Monday to Saturday), which is connected by a causeway to North Uist.

BERNERAY (BEARNARAIGH)
☎ 01876 / pop 140

The superb beaches of western Berneray are unparalleled in Scotland. The causeway to North Uist opened in October 1998, but hasn't altered the peace and beauty of this place.

The excellent thatch-roofed **Gatliff Hostel** (Baile; dm £6.50) is just under 2 miles (3km) from the causeway.

You'll get the finest island hospitality at **Burnside Croft** (☎ /fax 540235; Borve; B&B per person from £20-26; ⓨ Feb-Nov). It offers a four-course dinner for £20.

In summer, snacks are available at the **Lobster Pot**, the tearoom attached to Ardmarree Stores (near the causeway). There are two shops for groceries on Berneray.

There are Monday to Saturday **Royal Mail postbus** (☎ 01246-546329) services, and **Grenitote Travel** (☎ 560244) buses, from Berneray (Gatliff Hostel) to Lochmaddy. For details of ferries to Leverburgh (Harris), see above.

NORTH UIST (UIBHIST A TUATH)
☎ 01876 / pop 1400

North Uist, an island half-drowned by lochs, is famed for its fishing but also has some magnificent beaches on its north and west coasts. For bird-watchers this is an earthly paradise, with huge populations of wading birds – oystercatchers, lapwings, curlews and redshanks at every turn. The landscape is less wild and mountainous than Harris, but it has a sleepy, subtle appeal.

Lochmaddy (Loch nam Madadh)

There's not much to keep you in tiny Lochmaddy, but it's the first village you hit after arriving on the ferry from Harris or Skye. There's a **TIC** (☎ 500321), a couple of stores,

a Bank of Scotland with ATM, a petrol station, a post office and a pub.

The **Taigh Chearsabhagh museum & arts centre** (☎ 500293; Lochmaddy; museum adult/child £1/50p; ⓨ 10am-5pm Mon-Sat Feb-Dec, till 8pm Fri Jul & Aug) not only preserves and displays the history and culture of the Uists, but is also a thriving community centre and meeting place. The centre's lively **café** (mains £2-4) dishes up lovely home-made soups, sandwiches and cakes.

Uist Outdoor Centre (☎ 500480; Lochmaddy; dm £10) has clean, four-bed dorms and offers a range of activities including canoeing, walking, snorkelling and diving.

The **Old Courthouse** (☎ 500358; Lochmaddy; B&B £23-25 per person; ⊠ Ⓟ) is the sole guesthouse in the village and a charming one at that.

Lochmaddy Hotel (☎ 500331; info@lochmaddy hotel.co.uk; Lochmaddy; bar meals £7-10; s/d £49/90; Ⓟ) is a traditional anglers' hotel (you can buy fishing permits here) with comfortable, old-fashioned rooms, many with views of the harbour. The lively hotel bar pulls in a blend of anglers, locals and tourists, and serves excellent pub grub including seafood, venison and king-sized steaks.

Buses from Lochmaddy to Langass, Clachan na Luib, Berneray Hostel, Benbecula and Lochboisdale run twice a day Monday to Saturday.

Bharpa Langass & Pobull Fhinn

A waymarked circular path beside the Langass Lodge Hotel (just off the A867, 6 miles/10km southwest of Lochmaddy) leads to the chambered Neolithic burial tomb of **Bharpa Langass** and the stone circle of **Pobull Fhinn** (Finn's People); both are reckoned to be around 5000 years old. There are lovely views over the loch, where seals can sometimes be seen.

The delightful six-bedroom **Langass Lodge Hotel** (☎ 580285; Locheport; 2-/3-course dinner £20/25; s/d £50/80; Ⓟ) is a former shooting lodge set in splendid isolation overlooking a remote sea loch. The restaurant is noted for its fine seafood and game, including grouse, snipe and woodcock.

Balranald Nature Reserve

Bird-watchers flock to this RSPB nature reserve, 18 miles (29km) west of Lochmaddy, in the hope of spotting the rare red-necked phalarope or hearing the distinctive call of the corncrake. There's a **visitor centre** (☎ 510372; admission free; ✆ Apr-Sep) with a resident warden who offers 2½-hour guided walks (£3, 10am Tuesday and Thursday, May to August).

BENBECULA (BEINN NA FAOGHLA)
☎ 01870 / pop 1880

Squeezed between North Uist and South Uist and connected to both by causeways, Benbecula is a low-lying island that's almost as much water as land. The flat, lochan-studded landscape is best appreciated from the summit of **Rueval** (124m), the island's highest point; there's a path around the south side of the hill (signposted from the main road) that is said to be the route taken to the coast by Bonnie Prince Charlie and Flora Macdonald during the prince's escape in 1746.

A British army missile range occupies most of the island's west coast and **Balivanich** (Baile a'Mhanaich) – looking like a corner of a Glasgow housing estate planted incongruously on the machair – is the commercial centre serving the troops and their families. The village has a bank with an ATM, a post office and a large **Co-op supermarket** (✆ 8am-8pm Mon-Sat, 12.30-6pm Sun).

SOUTH UIST (UIBHIST A DEAS)
pop 2060

South Uist is the second-largest island in the Outer Hebrides, and saves its choicest corners for those who explore away from the main north-south A865 road. The low-lying west coast is an almost unbroken stretch of white-sand beach and flower-flecked machair, while the multitude of inland lochs provide excellent trout fishing. The east coast, riven by four large sea lochs, is quite hilly, with spectacular **Beinn Mhor** (620m) the highest point.

As you drive south from Benbecula you cross from the predominantly Protestant northern half of the Outer Hebrides into the mostly Roman Catholic south, a religious transition marked by the granite statue of **Our Lady of the Isles** on the slopes of Rueval, and the presence of many roadside shrines.

The North
The northern part of the island is mostly occupied by the watery expanses of Loch Bee and Loch Druidibeg. **Loch Druidibeg**

National Nature Reserve is an important breeding ground for birds like dunlin, redshank, ringed plover, greylag goose and corncrake; you can take a 5-mile (8km) self-guided hike through the reserve (pick up a leaflet from Lochmaddy or Lochboisdale TICs).

Two miles (3km) south of Loch Druidibeg is the attractive hamlet of **Howmore** (Tobha Mor), with several restored, thatched blackhouses, one of which houses the **Tobha Mor Crofters' Hostel** (dm adult/child £7.50/5.50). You can rent bikes from the **shed** (☎ 01870-620283) at the junction with the main road.

The South
☎ 01878

Kildonan Museum (☎ 710343; Kildonan; adult/child £1.50/free; open 10am-5pm Mon-Fri, plus 10am-2pm Sun Easter-Oct), 6 miles (10km) south of Howmore, explores the lives of local crofters through its collection of artefacts, an absorbing exhibition of B&W photography and first-hand accounts of harsh Hebridean conditions.

Amid the ruined blackhouses of Milton, half a mile south of the museum, a cairn marks the site of **Flora Macdonald's birthplace**.

The **Polochar Inn** (☎ 700215; polocharinn@btconnect.com; Polochar; B&B per person £35; ☒ Ⓟ), at the southern tip of South Uist, is a fine and remote old hotel with superb views across the Sound of Barra to Eriskay and Barra.

A few miles to the east is the abandoned ferry harbour at Ludag. The ferry to Barra now leaves from Eriskay, which was joined to South Uist by a £10 million causeway in 2001.

Lochboisdale (Loch Baghasdail)
☎ 01878

The ferry port of Lochboisdale in the southeast is the island's largest settlement. There's a **TIC** (☎ 700286), a bank (no ATM) and a petrol station.

Friendly **Lochside Cottage** (☎ 700472; Lochboisdale; B&B per person £20; ☒ Ⓟ), 1½ miles west of the ferry, has appealing rooms and a sun lounge barely a fishing-rod's length from its own trout loch. Nearer the pier, **Bayview** (☎ 700329; Lochboisdale; B&B per person £20; ✆ Mar-Oct; Ⓟ) is a simple place in a quiet spot overlooking the bay; it offers a room-only rate of £14 per person.

Lochboisdale Hotel (☎ 700332; hotel@lochboisdale.com; Lochboisdale; bar meals £8-11; s/d £51/76; Ⓟ),

ST KILDA

St Kilda (www.kilda.org.uk) is a collection of spectacular sea stacks and cliff-bound islands about 45 miles (72km) west of North Uist. The largest island, Hirta, measures only 2 miles by 1 mile, with huge cliffs along most of its coastline. Owned by NTS, the islands are a UNESCO World Heritage site and are the biggest sea-bird nesting site in the North Atlantic, home to more than a million birds.

History

Hirta was inhabited by a Gaelic-speaking population of around 200 until the 19th century, when the arrival of church missionaries and tourists began the gradual breakdown of St Kilda's traditional way of life. By the 1920s disease and emigration had seen the islands' economy collapse, and the 35 remaining islanders were evacuated, at their own request, in 1930. The people had survived here by keeping sheep, fishing, growing a few basic crops such as barley, and climbing the cliffs barefoot to catch sea birds and collect their eggs. Over the centuries, this resulted in a genetic peculiarity – St Kilda men had unusually long big toes.

Visiting St Kilda

Boat tours to St Kilda are a major undertaking. For a full listing of tour operators, check out the website at www.kilda.org.uk. Weather permitting, **Sea Trek** (☎ 07879-607932; www.seatrek.co.uk) offers day trips in a high-speed RIB, departing from Berneray harbour (North Uist). It's a buttock-numbing 2½ to three-hour trip in each direction, with three to four hours ashore on Hirta; the cost is £125 per person.

Western Edge Charters (☎ 01506-204053; www.westernedge.co.uk) operates more leisurely six-day expeditions on a 12m sailing yacht departing from Berneray (North Uist) and charging £545 per person.

The only way to spend any time in the islands is to join one of the two-week NTS work parties that visit St Kilda from mid-May to August. The NTS charges volunteers for doing archaeological and conservation work in and around the village ruins – you have to be physically fit and prepared to work for up to 36 hours per week. And you have to pay for the privilege – from £475 to £550 (including transport from Oban in a converted lifeboat and full board in dorm accommodation). To get an application form, send a stamped, self-addressed envelope to St Kilda Work Parties, NTS, Balnain House, 40 Huntly St, Inverness IV3 5HR. The closing date for application is 31 January.

above the ferry terminal, is old-fashioned and perhaps a tad past its glory days, with bright, seaward-facing rooms. The hotel pub serves decent bar meals.

For details of ferries from Lochboisdale to Castlebay (Barra) and Oban see p357.

ERISKAY (EIRIOSGAIGH)

☎ 01878 / pop 170

In 1745, Bonnie Prince Charlie first set foot in Scotland on the west coast of Eriskay, on the sandy beach (immediately north of the ferry terminal) still known as **Prince's Strand** (Coilleag a'Phrionnsa).

More recently, the SS *Politician* sank just off the island in 1941. The islanders salvaged much of its cargo of around 250,000 bottles of whisky and, after a binge of dramatic proportions, the police intervened and a number of the islanders landed in jail. The story was immortalised by Sir Compton Mackenzie in his book *Whisky Galore*, later made into a film.

A CalMac car ferry links Eriskay with Ardveenish (Ard Mhidhinis) at the northern end of Barra (person/car £5.35/15.80, 40 minutes, four or five daily).

BARRA (BARRAIGH)

☎ 01871 / pop 1212

With its beautiful beaches, machair-clad dunes, rugged little hills, Neolithic remains and strong sense of community, little Barra – just 14 miles (22km) in circumference – is the Outer Hebrides in miniature. For a great view of the island, walk up to the top of **Heaval** (383m), a mile northeast of Castlebay; allow two hours round trip.

Castlebay (Bagh a'Chaisteil), in the south, is the largest village. There's a **TIC** (☎ 810336), bank with ATM, post office and two grocery stores.

The village takes its name from **Kisimul Castle** (☎ 810313; Castlebay; adult/child incl ferry £3.30/1; ☽ 9.30am-6.30pm Apr-Oct), first built by the MacNeil clan in the 11th century. It was sold in the 19th century and restored in the 20th by American architect Robert MacNeil, who became the 45th clan chief; he gifted the castle to Historic Scotland in 2000 for an annual rent of £1 and a bottle of whisky (Talisker single malt, since you ask).

The **Barra Heritage Centre** (☎ 810413; Castlebay; adult/child £2/75p; ☽ 11am-4pm Mon-Fri May-Sep) has Gaelic-themed displays about the island, local art exhibitions and a tearoom. The centre manages a restored 19th-century **Thatched House** (adult/child £2/75p; ☽ 1-4pm Mon-Fri May-Sep), 3 miles (5km) north of Castlebay.

Accommodation on Barra is limited, so make a reservation before committing to a night on the island.

Dunard Hostel (☎ 810443; www.isleofbarrahostel.com; Castlebay; dm £10, d £28) is a friendly, family-run hostel with 12 beds, just five minutes' walk from the ferry terminal. The hostel can organise sea-kayaking tours for £15/25 a half/full day.

Faire Mhaoldonaich (☎ 810441; fmotacfm@aol.com; Nask; B&B per person £20-22; ✗ Ⓟ) has very comfortable rooms with great views over Castlebay; it's a mile west of Castlebay on the road to Vatersay.

Refurbished **Craigard Hotel** (☎ 810200; craigard@isleofbarra.com; Castlebay; s/d £65/80; Ⓟ) has snug rooms and a brand new conservatory with grand views across the harbour to the island south of Barra.

See p357 for details of CalMac ferries from Castlebay to Oban and Lochboisdale (South Uist) and flights to the Scottish mainland, and p365 for the ferry from Ardveenish (Ard Mhidhinis) at the northern end of Barra to Eriskay.

A **Royal Mail postbus** (☎ 01246-546329) makes a regular circuit of the island, and connects with flights at the airport.

PABBAY (PABAIDH), MINGULAY (MIUGHALAIGH) & BERNERAY (BEARNARAIGH)

These three uninhabited islands were gifted to the NTS in 2000. **Pabbay**, roughly a mile across, was abandoned in 1912. Near the ruinous settlement at the eastern end of Pabbay, there are symbol stones (probably Pictish), one with a cross, a crescent and a lily. The southwestern cliffs and an immense natural arch attract rock climbers.

The western side of **Mingulay** is characterised by sea stacks, cliffs over 200m high, huge caves and natural arches. The ruined village near the boat landing is a reminder of human occupation.

The islands are important breeding sites for sea-bird species such as fulmar, black guillemot, common and Arctic tern, great skua, puffin and storm petrel. **George McLeod** (☎ 01871-810223) in Castlebay, Barra, operates bird-watching cruises to Mingulay (usually at weekends) for around £10/20 per person without/with landing, depending on weather and numbers. Puffin season lasts from June to early August.

Orkney & Shetland Islands

ORKNEY & SHETLAND ISLANDS

Moored off the country's remote northeast coast, the Orkney and Shetland Islands are a plaything for the raging, northern Atlantic Ocean, which cuts them off from the Scottish mainland, mercilessly buffets their coastline and, in times of relative calm, reflects their raw beauty. Together, these diverse and captivating archipelagos form an antithesis to modern urban grit, and referring to them as a part of Scotland is almost deceptive.

But it's not just their geographical isolation that gives them their own devolved identity – each has a unique cultural flavour, Norse roots and a distinctive island geography. This character is accentuated by echoes of the past; the island groups are a living breathing museum, with our distant ancestors leaving behind an extraordinary diary of human development. It's this sort of fusion that makes a trip to Scotland's far-flung northern outposts not only intriguing, but a highlight of any visit to the country.

In many ways the landscape is untamed as mother nature lashes it with snarling gales. Breathtaking scenery means walking and cycling are both popular and, with at times ferocious headwinds, challenging island pursuits. The wildlife spectacle here is unparalleled in the British Isles and visitors may spot porpoises, elusive otters and seal colonies – but it is the thriving bird population that is a real draw card, with literally millions of sea birds breathing life into foreboding coastal areas. And who can resist sitting among colonies of comical puffins as they totter about their daily business.

HIGHLIGHTS

- Discovering ancient lifestyles at astonishingly well-preserved historical sites such as **Skara Brae** (p380)

- Teetering on wild cliff precipices between gales at **Eshaness** (p396)

- Uncovering ancient Norse roots in cosmopolitan **Kirkwall** (p372) and **Stromness** (p377)

- Bird-watching at deliciously peaceful **North Ronaldsay** (p387), and sitting among puffins at **Hermaness** (p398)

- Scuba-diving in Europe's premier underwater museum of sunken warships in **Scapa Flow** (p379)

ORKNEY & SHETLAND ISLANDS

- POPULATION: Orkney 19,250; Shetland 22,000
- SHETLAND SEABIRD POPULATION: millions
- AREA: Orkney 990 sq km; Shetland 1466 sq km

ORKNEY ISLANDS

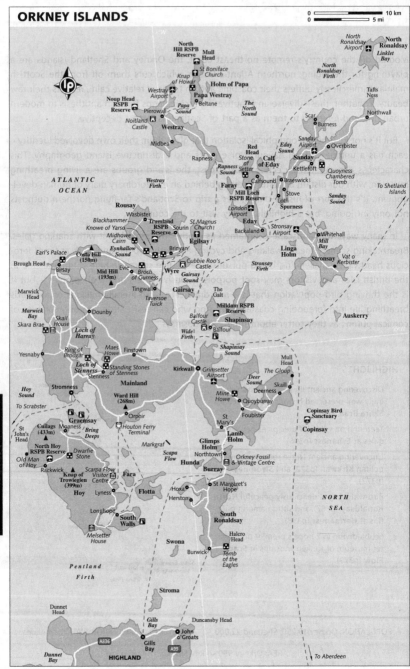

0 ——— 10 km
0 ——— 5 mi

North Hill RSPB Reserve
Mull Head
St Boniface Church
Knap of Howar
Holm of Papa
Westray Airport
Papa Westray
Papa Sound
Beltane
The North Sound
Noup Head RSPB Reserve
Pierowall
Noltland Castle
Westray
Midbea
Rapness
ATLANTIC OCEAN
Westray Firth
Rapness Sound
Red Head
Stone of Setter
Calf of Eday
Faray
Mill Loch RSPB Reserve
London Airport
Eday
Backaland
Stronsay Airport
Rousay
Wasbister
Blackhammer
Knowe of Yarso
Trumland RSPB Reserve
Sourin
St Magnus Church
Egilsay
Midhowe Cairn
Eynhallow Sound
Brinyan
Cubbie Roo's Castle
Wyre
Gairsay Sound
Earl's Palace
Costa Hill (150m)
Brough Head
Birsay
Evie
Broch of Gurness
Mid Hill (193m)
Tingwall
Gairsay
The Galt
Mildam RSPB Reserve
Shapinsay
Auskerry
Marwick Head
Marwick Bay
Skara Brae
Skail House
Dounby
Taversoe Tuick
Balfour Castle
Balfour
Loch of Harray
Yesnaby
Ring of Brodgar
Maes Howe
Finstown
Wide Firth
Shapinsay Sound
Loch of Stenness
Standing Stones of Stenness
Stenness
Mainland
Kirkwall
Grinsetter Airport
Mull Head
The Gloup
Deer Sound
Skaill
Deerness
Stromness
Ward Hill (268m)
Orphir
Mine Howe
Quoybrray
Foubister
Copinsay Bird Sanctuary
Hoy Sound
To Scrabster
Graemsay
Cuilags (433m)
Moaness
Bring Deeps
Houton Ferry Terminal
Markgraf
St Mary's
Lamb Holm
Glimps Holm
Copinsay
St John's Head
North Hoy RSPB Reserve
Dwarfie Stone
Old Man of Hoy
Rackwick
Scarpa Flow Visitor Centre
Knap of Trowieglen (399m)
Hoy
Fara
Flotta
Scapa Flow
Hunda
Burray
Northtown
Orkney Fossil & Vintage Centre
NORTH SEA
Lyness
Longhope
South Walls
Melsetter House
Hoxa
Herston
St Margaret's Hope
South Ronaldsay
Swona
Halcro Head
Burwick
Tomb of the Eagles
North Ronaldsay Airport
North Ronaldsay
Linklet Bay
North Ronaldsay Firth
Tafts Ness
Scar
Burness
Northwall
Sanday Airport
Overbister
Sanday
Kettletoft
Quoyness Chambered Tomb
Braeswick
Calfsound
Stove
Loth
Spurness
Sanday Sound
To Shetland Islands
Linga Holm
Stronsay
Whitehall
Mill Bay
Vat o Kerbister
Stronsay Firth
Pentland Firth
Stroma
Dunnet Head
Gills Bay
Duncansby Head
A836
Gills Bay
John o'Groats
A99
Dunnet Bay
HIGHLAND
To Aberdeen

ORKNEY ISLANDS

The magical Orkney archipelago, a mere 6 miles (10km) off the north coast, is a jewel in Scotland's tourism crown. When you step off that boat, you know you've entered a different realm – a significant factor in the allure of these enchanting islands. Seventeen of Orkney's 70 islands are inhabited and dramatic coastal scenery sees 300m cliffs plunge into white, sandy beaches.

Orkney contains a sliver of mankind's prehistoric existence that is found nowhere else. Prehistoric sites pepper the islands – Europe's greatest concentration – their walls of stone immune to 5000 years of climatic onslaught. The Flinstonesque furniture of Skara Brae, tomb of Maes Howe and standing stones weave a mystical milieu, while providing a snapshot of the way people worshipped, lived and perished since time immemorial. The real allure of Orkney, though, is today's civilisation which can be found in its animated contemporary culture, expressed through fine cuisine, inviting drinking holes, chatty locals and spirited festivals.

GETTING THERE & AWAY
Air
British Airways/Loganair (☎ 0845 773 3377) flies at least twice-daily (except Sunday) from Kirkwall airport to Aberdeen (£155, one hour), Edinburgh (£186, 1¾ hours), Glasgow (£150) and Inverness (£104, 45 minutes) with connections to London Heathrow (£297), Birmingham, Manchester and Belfast. There is one daily flight from Kirkwall to Sumburgh airport on Shetland (£85.50, 35 minutes). Cheaper fares are often available.

Boat
Car ferries to and from Orkney can be very busy in July and August – it's best to book ahead at these times.

FROM SCRABSTER, SHETLANDS & ABERDEEN
Northlink Ferries (☎ 0845 6000 449; www.northlink ferries.co.uk) operates ferries from Scrabster to Stromness (passenger/car and driver return £27-33/98-112, 1½ hours, three daily Monday to Friday, two on weekends). North-

link also sails from Aberdeen to Kirkwall (passenger/car and driver £32-48/£142-200, up to 7½ hours, four weekly) and onto Lerwick (passenger/car and driver £26-39/112-178, up to 7¼ hours, four weekly) on the Shetland Islands. Note: there are only three services weekly from Lerwick to Kirkwall and onto Aberdeen.

Fares vary according to low/mid/peak season and travel times vary due to winds. Ask Northlink about its saver fares, which provide discounts (a car and up to four passengers) for early departures and weekly return tickets.

FROM GILLS BAY
A shorter and less expensive car ferry crossing is offered by **Pentland Ferries** (☎ 01856-831226; www.pentlandferries.com), from Gills Bay about 3 miles (5km) west of John o'Groats, to St Margaret's Hope in Orkney (passenger/car single £10/25, one hour). There are at least three crossings daily in summer and usually two in winter.

FROM JOHN O'GROATS
During the summer period **John o' Groats Ferries** (☎ 01955-611353; www.jogferry.co.uk) operates a passenger-only ferry (p333) from John o'Groats to Burwick, on the southern tip of South Ronaldsay.

Bus
Scottish Citylink (☎ 0870 550 5050; www.citylink.co.uk) has daily coaches from Inverness to Scrabster (£11.50, 3½ hours), connecting with the ferries to Stromness. Early-morning departures from Glasgow or Edinburgh, and overnighters from London, connect with the Scrabster bus at Inverness.

John O'Groats Ferries (☎ 01955-611353; www .jogferry.co.uk) operates the summer-only Orkney bus service from Inverness to Kirkwall. Tickets (single/return £28/40, five hours) include bus travel from Inverness to John o'Groats, passenger ferry to Burwick, and another bus from Burwick to Kirkwall. There's one bus daily in May and two daily from June to early September.

GETTING AROUND
Orkney Islands Council (☎ 01856-888750) publishes the *Orkney Public Transport Timetable*, a detailed schedule of all bus, ferry and air services around and to/from Orkney, available free from TICs.

ORKNEY & SHETLAND ISLANDS

The largest island, Mainland, is joined by road-bearing causeways to Burray and South Ronaldsay. The other islands can be reached by air and ferry services.

To/From the Airport

British Airways/Loganair (☎ 0845 773 3377/ 01856-872494) operates inter-island flights between Kirkwall airport and North Ronaldsay, Westray, Papa Westray, Stronsay, Sanday and Eday. For details, see each island entry in this chapter.

Bicycle

You can hire bikes from various locations on Mainland, including **Bobby's Cycle Centre** (☎ 01856-875777; Tankerness Lane, Kirkwall; day/week £8/50) and **Orkney Cycle Hire** (☎ 01856-850255; 54 Dundas St, Stromness; per day £5-8.50).

Boat

Orkney Ferries (☎ 01856-872044; www.orkneyferries .co.uk; Shore St, Kirkwall) operates car ferries from Mainland to Hoy, Flotta and the northern Orkney islands; for details see each island section later in the chapter.

Car

There are several hire-car companies on Mainland, including **Orkney Car Hire** (☎ 01856-872866; Junction Rd, Kirkwall) and **Norman Brass Car Hire** (☎ 01856-850850; Blue Star Filling Station, North End Rd, Stromness). Small-car rates begin at around £34/70 per day/week.

To hire a camper van, contact **Orkney Motorhome Hire** (☎ 01856-874391; www.orkney-motorhome-hire.co.uk). The vans sleep two adults comfortably, but two adults and three kids at a pinch. Weekly rates are £390 from November to March, £590 in July and August, and £490 all other months.

Public Transport

Orkney Coaches (☎ 01856-870555) runs bus services on Mainland and South Ronaldsay. Most buses don't run on Sunday. Day Rover (£6) and 3-Day Rover (£15) tickets will save you money, allowing unlimited travel on Orkney Coaches bus routes.

Tours

Orkney Island Holidays (☎ 01856-711373; www .orkneyislandholidays.com; Furrowend, Shapinsay, Orkney) offers holidays based on Shapinsay, with guided tours of archaeological sites, bird-

watching, wildlife trips, and excursions to other islands. One-week, all-inclusive packages cost £699.

Wildabout Orkney (☎ /fax 01856-851011, 0777 637 8966; wildabout@orkney.com) operates tours covering Orkney's history, ecology, folklore and wildlife. Day trips run from March to October and cost £16 to £23. The minibus tours pick up at Stromness ferry terminal, and at Palace Rd and Kirkwall Youth Hostel in Kirkwall.

Discover Orkney (☎ /fax 01856-872865; 44 Clay Loan, Kirkwall) caters to individuals and small groups, offering guided tours and walks throughout the islands in the company of a qualified guide.

KIRKWALL

☎ 01856 / pop 6206

Set back from a wide bay, Orkney's capital has a distinctive character. This bustling market town with its paved main street, twisting wynds and outstanding attractions is one of Scotland's most engaging districts. Magnificent St Magnus Cathedral takes pride of place in the town centre, while the nearby Earl's and Bishop's Palaces are definitely worth a ramble. Founded in the early 11th century, the original part of town is one of the best examples of an ancient Norse town.

Orientation

Kirkwall is fairly compact and it's easy enough to get around on foot. The cathedral and most of the shops are set back from the harbour on Broad St, which changes name several times along its length.

Information

There are banks with ATMs on Broad St and Albert St.

Balfour Hospital (☎ 885400; New Scapa Rd)

Launderama (☎ 872982; 47 Albert St; ⊗ 8.30am-5.30pm Mon-Fri, 9am-5pm Sat) Does a service wash and dry for £6.

Orkney College (☎ 569000; East Rd; £4 per hr) Internet access. It's a 10-minute walk from the TIC.

Post office (Junction Rd)

Support Training (☎ 873582; cnr Junction Rd & West Tankerness Lane; £5 per hr; ⊗ 9am-7.30pm Mon-Fri, 10am-4pm Sat) Internet access.

TIC (☎ 872856; www.visitorkney.com; 6 Broad St; ⊗ Mon-Sat Oct-Apr, daily May-Sep) Has a good range of publications on Orkney. If you're travelling with kids, pick up a copy of the invaluable Child Friendly Orkney (free).

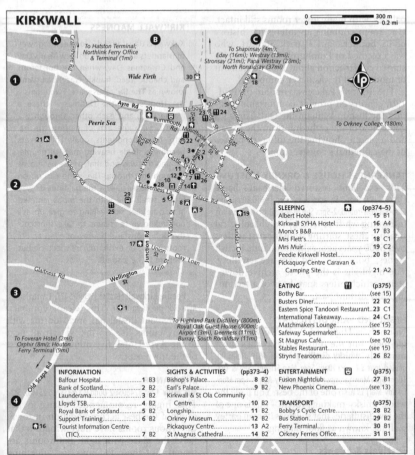

KIRKWALL

To Hatston Terminal;
Northlink Ferry Office
& Terminal (1mi)

To Shapinsay (4mi);
Eday (16mi); Westray (19mi);
Stronsay (21mi); Papa Westray (28mi);
North Ronaldsay (37mi)

Wide Firth

Ayre Rd

Peerie Sea

To Orkney College (180m)

To Foveran Hotel (2mi);
Orphir (8mi); Houton
Ferry Terminal (9mi)

To Highland Park Distillery (800m);
Royal Oak Guest House (800m);
Airport (3mi), Deerness (11mi);
Burray; South Ronaldsay (11mi)

SLEEPING	(pp374–5)
Albert Hotel............................. 15	B1
Kirkwall SYHA Hostel.............. 16	A4
Mona's B&B............................. 17	B3
Mrs Flett's.............................. 18	C1
Mrs Muir.................................. 19	C2
Peedie Kirkwell Hostel............ 20	B1
Pickaquoy Centre Caravan &	
Camping Site...................... 21	A2

EATING	(p375)
Bothy Bar............................. (see 15)	
Busters Diner........................ 22	B2
Eastern Spice Tandoori Restaurant.. 23	C1
International Takeaway........... 24	C1
Matchmakers Lounge............ (see 15)	
Safeway Supermarket............ 25	B2
St Magnus Café...................... (see 10)	
Stables Restaurant................. (see 15)	
Strynd Tearoom.................... 26	B2

ENTERTAINMENT	(p375)
Fusion Nightclub................... 27	B1
New Phoenix Cinema............ (see 13)	

INFORMATION			SIGHTS & ACTIVITIES	(pp373–4)		TRANSPORT	(p375)
Balfour Hospital................ 1	B3		Bishop's Palace.................. 8	B2		Bobby's Cycle Centre........ 28	B2
Bank of Scotland............... 2	B2		Earl's Palace..................... 9	B2		Bus Station....................... 29	B2
Launderama....................... 3	B2		Kirkwall & St Ola Community			Ferry Terminal.................. 30	B1
Lloyds TSB........................ 4	B2		Centre............................ 10	B2		Orkney Ferries Office......... 31	B1
Royal Bank of Scotland...... 5	B2		Longship.......................... 11	B2			
Support Training................ 6	B2		Orkney Museum................ 12	B2			
Tourist Information Centre			Pickaquoy Centre.............. 13	A2			
(TIC)............................ 7	B2		St Magnus Cathedral......... 14	B2			

Sights

ST MAGNUS CATHEDRAL

Founded in 1137 and constructed from local red sandstone and yellow Eday stone, fabulous **St Magnus Cathedral** (☎ 874894; admission free; ⏰ 9am-6pm Mon-Sat, 2-6pm Sun Apr-Sep; 9am-1pm & 2-5pm Mon-Sat Oct-Mar) should not be missed. The powerful atmosphere of a very ancient faith pervades the impressive interior. Epitaphs of the dead, written in a lyrical and melodramatic way, line the walls inside and emphasise the serious business of 17th- and 18th-century bereavement.

Earl Rognvald Brusason commissioned the cathedral in the name of his martyred uncle, Magnus Erlendsson, who was killed by Earl Hakon Paulsson on Egilsay in 1117.

Work began in 1137, but the building is actually the result of 300 years of construction and alteration, and includes Romanesque, transitional and Gothic styles.

During summer, 40-minute tours of the cathedral's upper levels start at 11am and 3pm on Tuesday and Thursday and cost £5 per person.

EARL'S PALACE & BISHOP'S PALACE

Near the cathedral, and on opposite sides of the street, these two ruined **buildings** (☎ 875461; adult/child £2/0.75; ⏰ 9.30am-6.30pm Apr-Sep) are worth poking around. The Earl's Palace was once known as the finest example of French Renaissance architecture in Scotland. It's the better of the two

ORKNEY & SHETLAND ISLANDS

palaces, with many lower rooms still intact. One room contains an interesting history of its builder, Earl Patrick Stewart, who was executed in Edinburgh for treason. He started construction about 1600 but ran out of money and it was never completed.

The Bishop's Palace was built in the mid-12th century to provide comfortable lodgings for Bishop William the Old. There's a good view of the cathedral from the tower, and a plaque showing the different phases of the cathedral's construction.

TANKERNESS HOUSE & ORKNEY MUSEUM

This excellent restored **merchant's house** (☎ 873191; Broad St; admission free; 🕒 10.30am-5pm Mon-Sat year-round, 2-5pm Sun May-Sep) contains an intriguing whiff of Orkney's archaeological treasure chest, starting from the first settlers over 5000 years ago; exhibits include Pictish stones, 'bone' pins and iron-age jewellery. The highlight is the photo archive downstairs, which offers snapshots of a technologically distant past.

HIGHLAND PARK DISTILLERY

Not only is Highland Park a very fine single malt, but the tour of the world's most northerly **whisky distillery** (☎ 874619; Holm Rd; guided tour £4; 🕒 10am-5pm Mon-Fri Apr, Sep & Oct; 10am-5pm Mon-Sat, noon-5pm Sun May-Aug; 1-5pm Mon-Fri Nov-Mar) is also one of the best. You'll see the whole whisky-making process – this is one of the few distilleries that still does its own barley malting, known as floor malting.

Festivals & Events

The **St Magnus Festival** (☎ 871445; www.stmagnusfestival.com) takes place in June and is a colourful celebration of music and the arts.

Sleeping

BUDGET

Pickaquoy Centre Caravan & Camping Site (☎ 879900; Pickaquoy Rd; tent sites £3.70-5.75) On the western outskirts of Kirkwall, this is an odd little windswept site with plenty of grass and decent facilities.

Kirkwall Youth Hostel (SYHA; ☎ 0871 330 8533; Old Scapa Rd; dm adult/child £10.50/8.75; 🕒 Apr-Sep) Kirkwall's well-equipped hostel is a 10-minute walk south of the bus station. Though no architectural gem, it's large (with plenty of two-bed dorms) and very friendly. You'll probably get a room to yourself.

> **KIRKWALL MADNESS**
>
> Kirkwall is transformed into a seething swell of islanders and tourists on New Year's Day and Christmas Day, when the boisterous and chaotic (read, frankly crazy) ball game known as **The Ba'** takes place. Two teams – the Uppies and the Doonies – chase a leather ball, and each other, through the streets, with the aim of getting the ba' into their opponents goal. The streets become a single heaving mass of people, striking this way and that, as the ba' moves through the throng. The game can go on for hours, especially if the ba' finds its way into a small lane with the mobs jammed in and neither side willing to give up. It's not unknown for teams to take shortcuts through shops and houses, or even across rooftops. It's an extraordinary spectacle but prepare to be jostled!

Peedie Kirkwall Hostel (☎ 875477; 1 Ayre Houses, Ayre Rd; dm from £10) This clean, compact, independent hostel has small dorms with roomy bunks. It's on the waterfront next to the Ayre Hotel, five minutes' walk west of the town centre.

MID-RANGE

Mrs Muir (☎ 874805; 2 Dundas Cres; s/d £25/40; ⊠) This highly recommended mansion has some of the best accommodation in town. Cavernous rooms have huge windows that flood the place with light. Bathrooms are shared, but these lodgings are something special.

Mrs Flett's (☎ 873160; Cumliebank, Cromwell Rd; r per person £15-17) Overlooking Kirkwall Bay, Mrs Flett's small, traditional B&B has to be the friendliest place in town. It also has the steepest staircase in town, so be careful after a few drinks. Good-sized rooms are lovingly kept and there's a tiny single upstairs for £10 – a bargain.

Mona's B&B (☎ 872440; 7 Matches Sq, Junction Rd; s £16, d £30-34; ⊠) Mona's is a welcoming place and great value. The owners, who are particularly partial to antipodean guests, offer plenty of tidy rooms and are very chatty, so it's a good spot to get some advice about what to see and do around town.

Royal Oak Guest House (☎/fax 877177; www.royaloakhouse.co.uk; Holm Rd; s/d £30/50; ⊠) The

ORKNEY & SHETLAND ISLANDS

well-run Royal Oak, near the Highland Park distillery, is a professional set-up offering modern rooms with private bathrooms and small desks that would suit business travellers or families. There's also a kitchen and laundry facilities.

TOP END

Albert Hotel (☎ 876000; www.alberthotel.co.uk; Mounthoolie Lane; s/d £49/79, with dinner £64/109; ✗) The central, child-friendly Albert Hotel has a pleasant, traditional feel to it. Functional, tidy rooms have king-size beds and you'll get a discount if you stay more than three nights. Excellent meals are served downstairs and one of the best pubs in town is also here.

Foveran Hotel (☎ 872389; www.foveranhotel.co.uk; St Ola; s/d from £48.50/77; mains £11-17; ✗) Two miles (3km) southwest of Kirkwall, the modern Foveran Hotel enjoys a peaceful location overlooking Scapa Flow. Rooms are spotless and slightly sterile but very comfortable. Only a couple of rooms have views over the water – so book ahead. Foveran would suit families or older visitors. The restaurant here is excellent.

Eating

St Magnus Café (☎ 873354; Broad St; light meals under £2; ⏱ 9.30am-6pm & 7-10pm Mon-Fri, 9.30am-4pm Sat) This foodhall-style place, in the Kirkwall and St Ola Community Centre, is a good, clean, honest eatery serving cheap food, such as toasties and bacon rolls, late. It also does breakfast (to 1.30pm) for £3.50.

Albert Hotel (☎ 876000; Mounthoolie Lane; bar suppers £4.50-8) The Albert offers a fine range of places to eat. The lively, friendly Bothy Bar and the more sedate Matchmakers Lounge dish out high-quality, scrumptious bar suppers including Louisiana wraps, fajitas and Orkney crab cakes. Or, if you're in the mood for something a bit more stylish, **Stables Restaurant** (starters £5, mains £12-16) offers an intimate dining ambience and gourmet cuisine using local produce to create some heavenly dishes.

Busters Diner (☎ 876717; 1 Mounthoolie Lane; mains £5-11; ⏱ 4.30-10pm Mon-Fri, noon-2am Sat, 12.30-10pm Sun) A perpetually busy, American-style diner churning out generous portions of hot dogs, pizza, burgers and Tex Mex such as enchiladas and tacos, Busters is popular with the younger crowd.

Bridge St, near the harbour, has several fast-food and takeaway places, including the **Eastern Spice Tandoori Restaurant** (☎ 877899; 5 Bridge St; mains £5.50-8.50), which dishes out decent curries; and the **International Takeaway** (☎ 874773; fish supper £3.50), directly across the street, which fires out some kicking kebabs.

The constant hum of the **Strynd Tearoom** (meals £2-4), in an alley beside the TIC, is a good place for a pit stop and a steaming mug of coffee.

Safeway supermarket (Pickaquoy Rd) is the best place to stock up on provisions.

Drinking & Entertainment

The **Bothy Bar** (☎ 876000; Mounthoolie Lane) in the Albert Hotel is a spirited place for a drink, with occasional live music in the evenings. On Thursday, Friday and Saturday there's Matchmakers disco, also at the Albert.

Fusion Nightclub (☎ 879489; Ayre Rd; admission club nights £2-6; ⏱ from 10pm Thur-Sat, last entry 11.45pm) is a rocking club (dress code is smart casual) catering to most musical tastes from retro and cheesy chart tunes to soul, funk and hip hop. Local DJs also spin the latest dance tunes and the club sometimes hosts live gigs.

Getting There & Away

The **airport** (☎ 886210) is 2½ miles east of the town centre. For information on flying into Orkney, see Getting There & Away, p371. For flights and ferries from Kirkwall to the northern islands, see the following island sections.

Bus No 1 runs direct from Kirkwall to Stromness (£2.35, 30 minutes, four to 12 daily); No 2 runs to Orphir and Houton (£1.50, 20 minutes, four or five daily); and No 7 from Kirkwall to Stromness via Birsay (one hour).

Bus No 6 runs from Kirkwall to Tingwall (£1.90, 30 minutes, two to four daily Monday to Saturday) and the ferry to Rousay, and on to Evie (£2.10, 35 minutes, four daily Monday to Saturday).

From May to September, bus No 10 runs between Kirkwall and the John o'Groats ferry at Burwick (£2.50, 50 minutes, four daily). From June to September, a special tourist service (bus No 8A) runs twice-daily Monday to Friday between Kirkwall and Stromness via Stenness Standing Stones, the Ring of Brodgar and Skara Brae.

EAST MAINLAND TO SOUTH RONALDSAY

☎ 01856

The sinking of the battleship HMS *Royal Oak* in 1939 – torpedoed by a German U-boat which snuck through Kirk Sound into Scapa Flow – prompted Winston Churchill to commission better defences for this important naval harbour. Causeways made of concrete blocks were laid across the channels on the eastern side of Scapa Flow, linking Mainland to the islands of Lamb Holm, Glimps Holm, Burray and South Ronaldsay. The **Churchill Barriers**, flanked by the rusting wrecks of the old blockships that once guarded the channels, now carry the main road from Kirkwall to Burwick. There are good sandy beaches by Barrier Nos 3 and 4.

East Mainland

On a farm at Tankerness is the mysterious Iron Age site of **Mine Howe** (☎ 861234; adult/child £2.50/1.50; ☽ 11am-3pm Wed & Sun May, 11am-5pm daily Jun-Aug, 11am-4pm daily early Sep, 11am-2pm Wed & Sun late Sep), discovered in 1946 but reopened by farmer Douglas Paterson in September 1999. The Howe is an eerie underground chamber whose function is unknown – the Channel 4 TV series *Time Team* carried out an archaeological dig here in 2000 and concluded that it may have had some ritual significance, perhaps an oracle or shrine. Be careful as you climb down – the stairs are narrow and wet. There are other archaeological works in the area and, presumably, many historical mysteries yet to be uncovered.

On the far eastern shore of Mainland, a mile north of Skaill, is the **Gloup**, a spectacular natural arch and sea cave. There are large colonies of nesting sea birds at **Mull Head**, and the shores of **Deer Sound** attract wildfowl.

Lamb Holm

On the tiny island of Lamb Holm, the **Italian Chapel** (☎ 781268; admission free; ☽ 9am-10pm Apr-Sep, 9am-4.30pm Oct-Mar) is all that remains of a POW camp that housed the Italian soldiers who worked on the Churchill Barriers. They built the chapel in their spare time, using two Nissen huts, scrap metal and their considerable artistic and decorative skills. One of the artists returned in 1960 to restore the paintwork. It's quite extraordinary inside and definitely worth seeing.

Burray

Sleepy Burray village, on the southern side of the island, has a general store, a post office and a couple of places to stay.

Nearby, **Orkney Fossil & Vintage Centre** (☎ 731255; Viewforth; adult/child £2/1; ☽ 10am-6pm Apr-Sep) is a quirky collection of household and farming relics and 360-million-year-old fish fossils. The fossils are from the Devonian period, which pre-dates the dinosaurs (Jurassic period) by about 200 million years.

Sands Hotel (☎ /fax 731298; Burray; r £50-70; mains £8-12) is a spiffy, refurbished 19th-century herring station, right on the pier. Rooms are bright and modern, and overlook the water. The restaurant dishes out decent nosh, and tables in the sunlit conservatory migrate outside in sunny weather.

Ankersted (☎ 731217; ankersted@tinyworld.co.uk; r per person £19) is a great place to stay with fine rooms, all with private bathroom. The upstairs lounge and balcony area overlook Watersound Bay and barrier No 4, and are exclusively for guests' use.

South Ronaldsay

The main village on South Ronaldsay is **St Margaret's Hope**, named after Margaret, the Maid of Norway, who died here in 1290 on the way from her homeland to marry Edward II of England. There are two grocery stores, a post office and several pubs.

TOMB OF THE EAGLES

This 5000-year-old chambered **tomb** (☎ 831339; Liddle Farm, Isbister; adult/child £3.50/1.50; ☽ 9.30am-6pm Apr-Oct, 10am-noon or by arrangement Nov-Mar), at the southern tip of South Ronaldsay, is run as a visitor attraction by local farmers. Their entertaining and informative tour is a real draw card and an excellent way to experience this relic of our ancestors. It's possible that sky burials occurred here; there's evidence that the bodies people had been stripped of their flesh before being put in the tomb, possibly by being placed on top of wooden platforms just outside the tomb entrance and providing the eagles with a feast. You'll also see a **burned mound**, an impressive Bronze Age kitchen. The tomb is a 20-minute walk east from Burwick.

ORKNEY & SHETLAND ISLANDS

SLEEPING & EATING

Backpacker's Hostel (☎ 831205; St Margaret's Hope; dm £10) Run by the neighbouring Murray Arms Hotel, this lovely stone cottage has one single, two twins and a six-bed dorm with comfy bunks. There's a great lounge, kitchen and good hot showers. It's an excellent set-up, particularly as the pub is right outside the front door!

Mrs Fraser (☎ 831310; St Margaret's Hope; r per person £22) On the A961, just outside of town, this place has two smashing upstairs rooms. A lot of thought has been put into guests' comfort here. There's also a huge stretch of lawn out the front overlooking the town and bay – perfect for sunbathing on those shimmering, summery Orkney days.

Creel Inn & Restaurant (☎ 831311; Front Rd, St Margaret's Hope; s/d £50/70; mains £16.80) Arguably the best restaurant in Orkney, the Creel serves fresh local produce – simply but deliciously prepared. Try the seared scallops with avocado and pink grapefruit salsa. There are also first-class rooms, some with panoramic views of the small harbour.

Wheems Hostel (☎ 831537; Eastside; dm £6.50, tent site £3; ☺ Apr-Oct) Wheems has an ageing, hippy feel to it and is a mile southeast of St Margaret's Hope. There's one basic, rustic dorm sleeping eight that has a kitchen, and hot showers are available. The friendly owner can supply you with organic produce.

Getting There & Away

Orkney Coaches bus No 4 from Kirkwall runs to Deerness in East Mainland (25 minutes, three daily Monday to Saturday), with one bus calling at Tankerness. From May to September, bus No 10 runs from Kirkwall to Burwick (£2.50, 50 minutes, four daily).

Causeway Coaches travels to St Margaret's Hope (£2, 30 minutes, four daily Monday to Friday, three on Saturday, one on Sunday) on South Ronaldsay.

SOUTH MAINLAND

☎ 01856

South Mainland, with its gently rolling landscape, is devoid of much of the archaelogical treasures of the north, but not the history. There are a few things to see at **Orphir**, a scattered community with no shop, about 9 miles (14.5km) west of Kirkwall. The **Orkneyinga Saga Centre** (admission free; ☺ 9am-5pm) has displays relating to

the Orkneyinga Saga (a story dating from 1136 about the Vikings in Orkney) and a wide-screen video show.

Just behind the centre is the **Earl's Bu** (admission free), the foundations of a 12th-century manor house belonging to the Norse earls of Orkney. There's also the remains of **St Nicholas' Church**, a unique circular building that was originally 9m in diameter. Built before 1136 and modelled on the rotunda of the Church of the Holy Sepulchre in Jerusalem, it was popular with pilgrims after the capture of the Holy Land by the First Crusade. The church remained in use until 1705, and was partly demolished in 1756. From the main road, it's a 10-minute walk to the centre. For bus details, see p375.

King Haakon of Norway beached his ship at **Houton** in 1263, after his defeat at the Battle of Largs, and he died in Orkney soon afterwards. There's not much in Houton apart from a ferry terminal and a hotel.

Roving Eye Enterprises (☎ 811360; adult/child £25/12.50; 1.20pm daily May-Aug) offers terrific boat trips, with the opportunity to view some of the rusting hulks of the German High Seas Fleet at the bottom of Scapa Flow (p379) – and you don't even get your feet wet! The boat uses a video camera attached to a remotely operated vehicle (ROV) – a technology developed for use in the offshore oil industry. The trips, which must be booked in advance, depart from Houton Pier, last around three hours and include a visit to the Scapa Flow Visitor Centre at Lyness (p382).

Bus No 2 runs from Kirkwall to Houton (25 minutes, four or five daily Monday to Saturday) via Orphir. For details of ferries from Houton to Hoy and Flotta, see p382.

STROMNESS

☎ 01856 / pop 1609

The rambling, winding streets flanking the port of Stromness have changed little since the 18th century and the flagstone-paved main street curves along the waterfront, amid attractive stone cottages. Guesthouses, pubs and eateries interrupt traditional trade along the main street, where cars and pedestrians move at the same pace. As a place to stay, many visitors prefer Stromness to Kirkwall.

Although Stromness was officially founded in 1620, it had been used as a port by the Vikings in the 12th century, as well

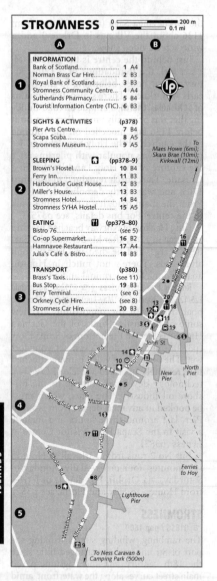

STROMNESS

0 ——————— 200 m
0 ——————— 0.1 mi

INFORMATION
Bank of Scotland.................. 1 A4
Norman Brass Car Hire.......... 2 B3
Royal Bank of Scotland.......... 3 B3
Stromness Community Centre.. 4 A4
Sutherlands Pharmacy........... 5 B4
Tourist Information Centre (TIC)..6 B3

SIGHTS & ACTIVITIES (p378)
Pier Arts Centre.................. 7 B4
Scapa Scuba...................... 8 A5
Stromness Museum.............. 9 A5

SLEEPING (pp378–9)
Brown's Hostel.................. 10 B4
Ferry Inn........................ 11 B3
Harbourside Guest House...... 12 B3
Miller's House................... 13 B3
Stromness Hotel................ 14 B4
Stromness SYHA Hostel........ 15 A5

EATING (pp379–80)
Bistro 76....................... (see 5)
Co-op Supermarket............ 16 B2
Hamnavoe Restaurant......... 17 A4
Julia's Café & Bistro........... 18 B3

TRANSPORT (p380)
Brass's Taxis.................. (see 11)
Bus Stop........................ 19 B3
Ferry Terminal................. (see 6)
Orkney Cycle Hire............. (see 8)
Stromness Car Hire............ 20 B3

To
Maes Howe (6mi);
Skara Brae (10mi);
Kirkwall (12mi)

John St

North St

New Pier

North Pier

Ferries to Hoy

Lighthouse Pier

To Ness Caravan & Camping Park (500m)

as by earlier visitors. Its importance as a trading port grew in the 18th century, and in the 19th century it was a busy centre for the herring industry.

Orientation & Information
Stromness is the point of arrival for ferries from Scrabster.

Royal Bank of Scotland (Victoria St) Near the pier; has an ATM.

Stromness Community Centre (Church Rd; £2.94–£5.88 per hr) Cheaper rates for Internet access in the evenings.

TIC (☎ 850716; stromness@visitorkney.com; ☺ 8am-5pm Mon-Fri, 10am-3pm Sat & Sun Jun-Sep; 8am-5pm Mon-Fri Oct-May) Small and friendly office at the northern end of the village in the ferry terminal.

Sights
The main occupation in Stromness is simply strolling back and forth along the narrow, atmospheric main street. It's worth poking your head inside the **Pier Arts Centre** (☎ 850209; 30 Victoria St; admission free; ☺ 10.30am-12.30pm & 1.30-5pm Tue-Sat), an exquisite gallery exhibiting 20th-century British and international art, including works by Barbara Hepworth and Ben Nicholson.

The superb **Stromness Museum** (☎ 850025; 52 Alfred St; adult/child £2.50/50p; ☺ 10am-5pm May-Sep) is full of knick-knacks belonging to maritime and natural history exhibitions covering whaling, the Hudsons Bay Company and the sunken German fleet. You can happily nose around the place for a couple of hours. Across the street from the museum is the house where local poet and novelist **George Mackay Brown** (p39) lived from 1968 until his death in 1996.

Festivals & Events
The annual **Orkney Folk Festival** (☎ 851331; www .orkneyfolkfestival.com) is a four-day event based in Stromness in the third week of May, with a programme of folk concerts, ceilidhs and informal pub sessions.

Sleeping
Ness Caravan & Camping Park (☎ 873535; tent sites £3.70-5.80) Stromness' breezy, fenced-in campground overlooks the bay at the southern end of town.

Brown's Hostel (☎ 850661; 45 Victoria St; dm £9-10) Brown's is a very popular 14-bed independent hostel, just five minutes' walk from the ferry. It opens year-round and there's no curfew. It has renovations planned, which is a good thing – the dorms are *tiny*.

Stromness Youth Hostel (SYHA; ☎ 0870 004 1150; Hellihole Rd; beds £9.50/8; ☺ May-Sep) This sedate hostel is a 10-minute walk from the ferry terminal and is a comfortable spot, but not for party animals. Facilities are clean and

DIVING SCAPA FLOW'S WRECKS

The many wrecks that litter the floor of Scapa Flow make it one of the most popular diving locations in Europe. Enclosed by Mainland, Hoy and South Ronaldsay, this is one of the world's largest natural harbours and has been used by vessels as diverse as King Hakon's Viking ships in the 13th century and the NATO fleet of today.

It was from Scapa Flow that the British Home Fleet sailed to meet the German High Seas Fleet at the Battle of Jutland on 31 May 1916. After the war, 74 German ships were interned in Scapa. Conditions for the German sailors were poor and there were several mutinies as the negotiations for the fate of the ships dragged on. When the terms of the armistice were agreed on 6 May 1919, with the announcement of a severely reduced German navy, Admiral von Reuter, who was in charge of the German fleet in Scapa Flow, decided to take matters into his own hands. On 21 June, a secret signal to scuttle the ships was passed from vessel to vessel, and the British watched incredulously as every German ship began to sink.

Most of the ships were salvaged but seven remain on the sea floor, attracting divers from all over the world. There are three battleships – the *König*, the *Kronprinz Wilhelm* and the *Markgraf* – which are all over 25,000 tonnes. The first two were subjected to blasting for scrap metal, but the *Markgraf* is undamaged and considered one of the best dives in the area. Four light cruisers (4400 to 5600 tonnes) – the *Karlsruhe*, *Dresden*, *Brummer* and *Köln* – are particularly interesting as they lie on their sides and are very accessible to divers. The *Karlsruhe*, though severely damaged, is only 10m below the surface. Its twisted superstructure has now become a huge metal reef encrusted with diverse sea life.

As well as the German wrecks, numerous other ships rest on the sea bed in Scapa Flow. HMS *Royal Oak*, which was sunk by a German U-boat in October 1939, with the loss of 833 crew, is an official war grave.

If you're interested in diving in Scapa Flow contact:

■ **European Technical Dive Centre** (ETDI; ☎ 01856-731269; www.technicaldivers.com; Garisle, Burray)

■ **Diving Cellar** (☎ 01856-850055; www.divescapflow.co.uk; 4 Victoria St, Stromness)

■ **Scapa Scuba** (☎ /fax 01856-851218; www.scapascuba.co.uk; Lifeboat House, Dundas St, Stromness)

well-looked after but it has a certain school-camp feel to it.

Miller's House (☎ 851969; millershouse@orkney.com; 7 & 13 John St; s/d £28.50/45; ✗) Miller's House also runs Harbourside Guest House a couple of doors down. They're both lovely historical houses that have been extensively renovated inside to fully exploit their light and space. The rooms in Harbourside are better but all are quite luxurious. Over summer you'll need to book in advance.

Stromness Hotel (☎ 850298; www.stromnesshotel.com; Victoria St; r per person £42; ✗) The grandest place in town, the 19th-century Stromness Hotel lords it over the harbour. Everything seems on a very imposing scale and the rooms are a bit old-fashioned, but stupendous views from the almost floor-to-ceiling windows more than compensate for its faded splendour. Room No 2 is a beauty, with brilliant harbour vistas.

Ferry Inn (☎ 850280; www.ferryinn.com; John St; s/d £32/54) The Ferry Inn has cutesy rooms with the exception of No 9, which is spacious and has good views. The lively bar downstairs will alleviate all symptoms of boredom. The Ferry Inn also runs the **annexe** (15 John St; r per person £18) across the road, which desperately requires an interior decorator, but at such a low price the rooms (with shared bathrooms) can't be faulted.

Eating

Julia's Café & Bistro (☎ 850904; 20 Ferry Rd; mains lunch £4-8, dinner £10-13; café daily, bistro dinner Wed-Sun) This light and airy eatery can get pretty frantic when the tour buses converge, but the food is worth the wait. For lunch, chow down on melts, open crab or salmon sandwiches, crisp salads and a home-made nut roast for vegetarians. Formal dinners are on the evening menu.

Bistro 76 (Orca Hotel; starters £4.60, mains £10-15) This is an intimate cellar restaurant with a stand-out menu that will entice most palates, particularly vegetarians. The all-day buffet is terrific value at £8.25.

Stromness Hotel (starters £2.75-5.25, mains £8-12) The Stromness does excellent seafood dishes (try the grilled halibut with a mango and chilli coulis) as well as hearty and healthy beef and vegetarian options. There's a large open fireplace to toast the toes in the Flattie Bar downstairs.

Hamnavoe Restaurant (☎ 850606; 35 Graham Pl; starters £5.75, mains £11-14; ☺ dinner Wed-Sun Apr-Sep) Stromness' gourmet restaurant is especially good for seafood. Self-caterers can stock up at the **Co-op Supermarket** (North End Rd).

Getting There & Away

For information on ferries to Scrabster, Lerwick and Aberdeen, see p371. For bus services, see p375.

WEST & NORTH MAINLAND

☎ 01856

This part of Orkney is sprinkled with outstanding prehistoric monuments, many of them in the care of Historic Scotland (HS). A joint admission ticket to all staffed monuments in Orkney costs £12/3.50 in summer (April to September) and £11/2.50 in winter (October to March).

Stenness

The scattered village of Stenness, about 4 miles (6.5km) northeast of Stromness, consists of little more than some houses, a petrol station and a hotel. Around it, however, are some of the most absorbing prehistoric monuments on Orkney, easily accessible using the regular bus service between Stromness and Kirkwall (p375).

Just 500m north of the Stenness crossroads, on the B9055, are the **Standing Stones of Stenness**. Only four of the original 12 mighty slabs of this prehistoric stone circle remain erect. Fenced off from the world outside, just like the sheep in the next field, the stones are impressive for their sheer size (one is over 5m high) and of course, age – they were erected around 2500 BC.

A short walk to the east are the excavated remains of **Barnhouse Neolithic Village**, thought to have been inhabited by the builders of Maes Howe.

Maes Howe

Egypt has the pyramids, Scotland has **Maes Howe** (☎ 761606; adult/child £3/1; ☺ 9.30am-6.30pm Apr-Sep; 9.30am-4.30pm Mon-Sat, 2-4.30pm Sun Oct-Mar). Constructed about 5000 years ago, Maes Howe is the finest chambered tomb in western Europe. A long, low stone passage leads into a chamber in the centre of an earth-covered mound, which is over 6.7m high, and 35m across. The size of the local sandstone slabs used, and the skill with which they were laid, is mind-boggling. During the winter solstice, Maes Howe takes on Indiana Jones-esque qualities as blood-red sunsets align themselves with the passage, striking a cairn entrance at the rear of the chamber with alarming precision. From Stone Age mystique to the age of the information superhighway, these sunsets are recorded live at www.maeshowe.co.uk in December and January.

In the 12th century, Vikings returning from the Crusades broke into the tomb, searching for treasure. They found none, but left a wonderfully earthy collection of graffiti, carved in runes on the walls of the tomb, including 'Thorni bedded Helgi' – some things never change. There's also some Viking artwork, including a crusader cross, a lion, a walrus and a knotted serpent.

Entry includes an excellent guided tour (lasting 20 minutes) filling your mind with both awe and questions about this astonishing place. Buy your ticket across the road at **Tormiston Mill**. Maeshowe is about 10 minutes' walk east of the Stenness crossroads.

Ring of Brodgar

About a mile north of Stenness, along the road towards Skara Brae, is this wide circle of **standing stones** (admission free), some over 5m tall. Thirty-six of the original 60 stones still stand among the heather. It's an impressive sight and a powerful place. These old stones, raised skyward 4500 years ago, still attract the forces of nature – on 5 June 1980 one was struck by lightning.

Skara Brae & Skaill House

A visit to extraordinary Skara Brae offers the best opportunity in Scotland for a glimpse of Stone Age life. Idyllically situated by a sandy bay 8 miles (13km) north of Stromness, and predating the pyramids of Giza and Stonehenge, **Skara Brae** (☎ 841815; Bay of Skaill; adult/child £4/1.20, joint ticket with Skaill House £5/1.30; ☺ 9.30am-6.30pm Apr-Sep; 9.30am-4.30pm Mon-Sat, 2-4.30pm Sun Oct-Mar)

POO BREW

So you like a nip of the *odd* Scottish brew and you're looking for something that packs a bit of wallop – good news. After discovering what is believed to be a 5000-year-old brewery within Skara Brae, scientists at the 2002 Orkney Science Fair meticulously recreated a stone-age beer, spicing it up with...cow dung – samplers claimed it was a potent brew, not to be served in pint mugs. The traditional method was to ferment the ale in clay pots made out of fertiliser.

Although the poo brew is not yet in mass production, perhaps you should check for whiffy qualities next time you order a pint in Orkney.

is northern Europe's best preserved prehistoric village.

Even the stone furniture – beds, boxes and dressers – has survived the 5000 years since a community lived and breathed here. It was hidden until 1850, when waves whipped up by a severe storm eroded the sand and grass above the beach, exposing the houses underneath. There's an excellent interactive exhibition and short video, arming visitors with facts and theory, which will enhance the impact of the site. The official guidebook, available from the visitor centre, includes a good self-guided tour.

The joint ticket will also get you into **Skaill House**, an early 17th-century mansion and the former home of the laird of Breckness, who discovered Skara Brae. Displays of period furniture and memorabilia include Captain Cook's dinner service.

Bus No 8A runs twice daily to Skara Brae from Kirkwall and Stromness (May to September only). It's possible to walk along the coast from Stromness to Skara Brae via Yesnaby and the Broch of Borwick (9 miles/14.5km).

Yesnaby Sea Stacks

Six miles (10km) north of Stromness are some spectacular but easy coastal walks (Stromness TIC has details). Less than half a mile south of the car park at Yesnaby is the Yesnaby Castle sea stack. Watch out during the nesting season in early summer when dive-bombing sea birds determinedly protect their nests.

Birsay

The small village of Birsay, with a shop and a post office, is 6 miles (10km) north of Skara Brae. The ruins of the **Earl's Palace** (admission free), built in the 16th century by the despotic Robert Stewart, earl of Orkney, dominate the village centre. Today it's a mass of half walls and crumbling columns, the latter climbing like dilapidated chimney stacks. Nevertheless, the size of the palace is impressive, matching the reputed ego and tyranny of its former inhabitant.

At low tide (check tide times at the shop in Earl's Palace) you can walk out to the **Brough of Birsay** (☎ 08156-841815; admission free; 🕑 9.30am-6.30pm mid-Jun–Sep), three-quarters of a mile northwest of the Earl's Palace. On the island, you'll find the extensive ruins of a Norse settlement and the 12th-century St Peter's Church.

There's **self-catering accommodation** (☎ 721321; per wk £80-100) in a couple of excellent properties scraping the water's edge. One is a small, sunlit studio-flat that sleeps two.

Evie

On an exposed headland at Aikerness, a 1½-mile walk northeast from the straggling village of Evie, you'll find the **Broch of Gurness** (☎ 751414; adult/child £3/1; 🕑 9.30am-6.30pm Apr-Sep). Built around 100 BC, it's the best-preserved example of a fortified stone tower in Orkney. Surrounding it are the shells of houses, discernable by the hearths in the centre of each. The small visitor centre helps unravel the mysteries of this ancient culture.

Eviedale Cottages & Campsite (☎ /fax 751270; colin.richardson@orkney.com; Dyke Farm, Evie; tent sites £4-7, bothy bunks £5, self-catering spaces per wk from £230; 🕑 campground open Apr-Sep) at the northern end of the village, has a small, basic, bothy with four beds (with toilet and stove, but no showers or bed linen) and a good grassed area for camping with picnic tables. Next door is self-catering accommodation in excellent, renovated farm cottages.

Woodwick House (☎ 751330, fax 751383; Evie; s £32, d £56-84) has large, stark rooms in a relaxed country house. The building is set in gorgeous gardens, where guests can catch glimpses of the sea. And when you are feeling peckish, three-course home-made dinners cost £24.

HOY

☎ 01856

Orkney's second-largest island Hoy (the name means 'High Island') got the lion's share of this archipelago's scenic beauty. Shallow turquoise bays lace the perimeter, while peat and moorland cover Orkney's highest hills. The highest point is Ward Hill (479m), in the north of Hoy. This dramatic landscape can be accessed on foot or by wheels, and will tempt hands to cameras.

Sights

The northern part of the island boasts spectacular coastal scenery, including some of Britain's highest vertical cliffs – St John's Head on the northwest coast rises 346m. Hoy is probably best known for the **Old Man of Hoy**, a 137m-high rock stack that can be seen from the Scrabster–Stromness ferry. The northern part of Hoy has been maintained as a nature reserve by the RSPB since 1983.

Lyness, on the eastern side of Hoy, was an important naval base during both world wars, when the British Grand Fleet was based in Scapa Flow. With the dilapidated remains of buildings and an uninspiring outlook towards the Oil Terminal on Flotta Island, this isn't a pretty place, but the **Scapa Flow Visitor Centre** (Lyness Interpretation Centre; ☎ 791300; adult/child £2/1; 🕙 9am-4.30pm Mon-Fri, 10.30am-4pm Sat & Sun mid-May–Sep) is a fascinating naval museum and photographic display, located in an old pumphouse that once fed fuel to the ships.

Activities

First scaled in 1966, the **Old Man of Hoy** is a rock climber's delight.

The easiest approach to the Old Man is from Rackwick Bay, a two- to three-hour walk by road from Moaness Pier through the beautiful **Rackwick Glen**. You'll pass the 5000-year-old **Dwarfie Stone**, the only example of a rock-cut tomb in Scotland and, according to Sir Walter Scott, the favourite residence of Trolld, a dwarf from Norse legend. On your return you can take the path via the **Glens of Kinnaird** and **Berriedale Wood**, Scotland's most northerly tuft of native forest.

The most popular walk climbs steeply westwards from Rackwick Bay, then curves northwards, descending gradually to the edge of the cliffs opposite the Old Man of Hoy. Allow about seven hours for the return

trip from Moaness Pier in Hoy village on the east coast where the ferries dock, or three hours from Rackwick.

Sleeping & Eating

Hoy Youth Hostel (☎ 873535 ext 2415 office hours only; Moaness; dm adult/child £7.50/6.25; 🕙 May–mid-Sep) This place has an enviable location, around 15 minutes' walk from Moaness Pier, at the base of the rugged Cuilags. You'll need your own sleeping bags and supplies for the basic, six-bed dorms.

Rackwick Youth Hostel (☎ 873535 ext 2404 office hours only; Rackwick; dm adult/child £7.70/6.70; 🕙 Apr–Sep) The Rackwick, 6 miles (10km) from the ferry at Moaness, is a snug (two four-bed dorms), clean place, popular with walkers. Once again you'll need your own sleeping bag and supplies, and the warden will collect your dosh in the evening.

There are several B&Bs on the island including **Stoneyquoy Farm** (☎ 791234; www .visithoy.com; Lyness; r per person £19; ✗), a charming farmhouse with Dutch-Orcadian hosts, comfy rooms and 'special' breakfasts. **St John's Manse** (☎ 791240; r per person £20; ✗), between Lyness and Longhope, is a recommended guesthouse with a superb double and a delightful twin.

The small, atmospheric **Stromabank Hotel** (☎ 701494; Longhope; bar meals £6) offers tasty home-cooked meals from its small menu; try the chicken breast stuffed with haggis in a whisky ginger sauce.

Groceries can be bought at the shops in Lyness and in Longhope.

Getting There & Away

Orkney Ferries (☎ 850624) runs passenger ferries between Stromness and Moaness pier (£2.85, 30 minutes, two to five daily May to September). There's a reduced schedule from October to April. In the other direction, the service departs 30 minutes after its arrival on Hoy.

There is also a **car ferry** (☎ 811397; passenger/car £2.85/8.50) to Lyness (Hoy) from Houton on Mainland (45 minutes, up to six daily Monday to Friday, two or three Saturday and Sunday). The more limited Sunday service runs from May to September.

Getting Around

Transport on Hoy is very limited. **North Hoy Transport** (☎ 791315) runs a minibus service between Rackwick and Moaness, meeting the 10am weekday ferry from Stromness. Otherwise, call the same number for a taxi service.

You can hire mountain bikes at **Moaness pier** (☎ 791225; £7 per day). Hitching is possible, but there are more sheep than cars.

NORTHERN ISLANDS

The group of windswept islands north of Mainland provides a refuge for migrating birds and a nesting ground for sea birds; there are several Royal Society for the Protection of Birds (RSPB) reserves. Some of the islands are also rich in archaeological sites, but it's the beautiful scenery, with wonderful white-sand beaches and lime-green to azure seas, that is the main attraction.

The TICs in Kirkwall and Stromness have the useful *The Islands of Orkney* brochure with maps and details of these islands. Note that the 'ay' at the end of each island name (from the Old Norse for 'island') is pronounced 'ee' (Shapinsay is pronounced *shap*-insee).

Orkney Ferries (☎ 872044) enables you to make day trips to many of the islands (except North Ronaldsay) from Kirkwall on most days of the week, but it's really worth staying for at least a few nights.

Shapinsay
☎ 01856
Just 20 minutes by ferry from Kirkwall, Shapinsay is a low-lying, intensively cultivated island with a superb castle. There are two general stores and a post office here.

Balfour Castle (☎ 711282; adult/child £16/8; tours 2.15pm Sun May-Sep), completed in 1848 in the turreted Scottish Baronial style, is Shapinsay's most impressive draw card. Guided tours must be booked in advance; the price includes the ferry, admission to the castle and afternoon tea.

About 4 miles (7km) from the pier, at the far northeastern corner of the island, is the Iron-Age **Burroughston Broch** (admission free; open at all times), one of the best-preserved in Orkney.

Girnigoe (☎ 711256; jean@girnigoe.f9.co.uk; Girnigoe; r per person £20) is a friendly farmhouse at the northern end of the island. The breakfasts, with Mrs Wallace's home-made bread and jam, are excellent and dinner is also available for £12.

Balfour Castle (☎ 711282; www.balfourcastle.com; Balfour Village; DB&B per person £100; ✕) has grand, old-fashioned, Victorian rooms with the added attraction that you are, of course, spending the night in a castle. There's also a private chapel, popular for weddings. A boat is available for residents for island trips, bird-watching and sea fishing.

Orkney Ferries (person/car £2.85/8.50) operates a ferry from Kirkwall (25 minutes, six daily Monday to Friday, four to five Saturday and Sunday, May to September). Services are limited in winter.

Rousay
☎ 01856 / pop 200
History buffs will adore this hilly island. Lying close to Mainland's northeast, it's known as 'the Egypt of the North' for its numerous archaeological sites. Most of the island is classed as a site of special scientific interest (SSSI), but it also has the important RSPB **Trumland Reserve** and three trout-fishing lochs.

Marion's shop, and a post office that looks like a hen coop, are at Sourin, 2½ miles (4km) north of the pier.

SIGHTS
West of the pier are the prehistoric burial cairns, **Taversoe Tuick**, **Blackhammer**, **Knowe of Yarso** and Midhowe Cairn.

Midhowe Cairn is an extraordinary burial cairn, containing the remains of 25 people. Dating from the 3rd millennium BC, the 'Great Ship of Death', as it's called, is the longest chambered cairn in Orkney. Bird and animal bones accompany the human remains, perhaps meant as food for the deceased. It's housed inside a modern barn-like building, about 5½ miles (9km) west of the pier, and a half-mile walk down from the road.

Nearby **Midhowe Broch** (admission free) is the best example of a broch in Orkney. The TICs on Mainland have a useful leaflet, *Westness Walk*, describing the mile-long walk from Midhowe Cairn to Westness Farm via a Norse cemetery.

SLEEPING & EATING
Rousay Farm Hostel (☎ 821252; Trumland Farm; tent sites £2.50, dm £6) On an organic farm half a mile west of the ferry, Rousay Farm offers accommodation in two tidy, but cramped

six-bed dormitories (and one single room). There are excellent self-catering facilities. Bring your own sleeping bag.

Taversoe Hotel (☎ 821325; r per person from £20) This hotel is a squat, grey cottage about 2 miles (3km) southwest of the pier, opposite the entrance to Yarso. Fortunately, the exterior belies its finer attributes – creative home cooking (free chips!), superb views of Eynhallow Sound from the restaurant and comfortable accommodation.

Pier Restaurant (☎ 821359; meals £2-5; ☑ 11am-9pm Mon-Sat) by the pier, is an ideal spot for a home-made snack or all-day breakfast.

GETTING THERE & AROUND

A small **car ferry** (☎ 751360; passenger/car £2.85/8.50) connects Tingwall on Mainland with Rousay (30 minutes, up to six daily) and the nearby islands of Egilsay and Wyre.

Bikes can be rented for £5 per day – ask at the Pier Restaurant. The island's one road makes a pleasant circuit of about 13 miles (21km).

Egilsay & Wyre

These two small islands lie east of Rousay. On **Egilsay**, a cenotaph marks the spot where Earl Magnus was murdered in 1117. After his martyrdom, pilgrims flocked to the island, and **St Magnus Church**, now roofless, was built. Today it provides a rare example of a round-towered Viking church. Much of Egilsay is an RSPB reserve; listen for the corncrakes at the southern end of the island.

Wyre is even smaller than Egilsay. It was the domain of the Viking baron Kolbein Hruga ('Cubbie Roo'); the ruins of his castle, built around 1145, and the nearby 12th-century **St Mary's Chapel**, can be visited free. Seal sightings at the beach on Wyre's western sliver are virtually certified. These two islands are reached on the Rousay–Tingwall ferry (see above).

Stronsay

☎ 01857

A peaceful and attractive island, Stronsay attracts seals, migratory birds and tourists. In the 19th century Whitehall harbour became one of Scotland's major herring ports until the collapse of the fisheries in the 1930s. Currently, Whitehall has shops, a post office and a hotel.

SIGHTS & ACTIVITIES

The old **Stronsay Fish Mart** (☎ 616267; Whitehall; admission free; ☑ 11am-5pm May-Sep) now houses a herring industry interpretation centre, designed to take visitors back (figuratively speaking) to the herring boom days, a hostel and a café.

Just across the harbour from Whitehall is the small island of **Papa Stronsay**, where Earl Rognvald Brusason was murdered in 1046. The island is owned by a monastic order, the Transalpine Redemptorists; the monks will provide **boat trips** (☎ 616389) to the island by prior arrangement.

There are good coastal walks and some sandy beaches. In the east, the **Vat o'Kirbuster** is the best example of a *gloup* (natural arch) in Orkney.

At the southern end of the island, you can visit the **seal-watch hide** on the beach near the camping barn (see below). There's also a chance to see otters at nearby **Loch Lea-shun**.

SLEEPING & EATING

Torness Camping Barn (☎ 616314; per person £5) Down at the southern end of the island, the environmentally friendly Holland Farm offers bunkhouse accommodation only a few metres from the beach. It's an excellent place – more like a bungalow – with a kitchen and toilet, that sleeps about eight, but you'll need a sleeping bag. Phone from the pier for a lift.

Stronsay Fish Mart Hostel & Cafe (☎ 616267; Whitehall; dm/r per person £10/16) Part of the island's former herring station has been converted into a 10-bed hostel with shower and kitchen. Bedding is an extra £3 if you don't have a sleeping bag. The neighbouring café serves takeaways, snacks and meals all day.

Stronsay Hotel (☎ 616473; www.stronsayhotel.com; Whitehall; r per person £25-35; pub meals from £5) The island's watering hole has been extensively refurbished and has immaculate rooms. There's also recommended pub grub in the bar (including paella and lobster).

Stronsay Bird Reserve (☎ 616363; Castle, Mill Bay; full board/B&B per person £26/17, tent sites £5) Birders in particular will enjoy staying at the friendly, comfortable Stronsay Bird Reserve, a 40-minute walk south from the ferry pier. Rates include all the tea and coffee you can drink and ensure hours of protracted conversation with the chatty owners.

GETTING THERE & AWAY

British Airways/Loganair (☎ 01856-872494) flies from Kirkwall to Stronsay (single/return £31/62, 30 minutes, two daily Monday to Saturday).

A car ferry links Kirkwall with Stronsay (passenger/car £5.65/12.70, 1½ hours, two to three daily) and Eday. There's a reduced service to Stronsay on Sunday.

Eday

☎ 01857

Eday has a hilly centre and cultivated fields around the coast. There is the impressive standing **Stone of Setter** and close by, the chambered cairns of **Braeside**, **Huntersquoy** and **Vinquoy**. Huntersquoy is a two-storey cairn, like Taversoe Tuick on Rousay. The early 17th-century **Carrick House** (☎ 622260; adult/child £2.50/1; 🕙 from 2pm Sun Jun–mid-Sep, other times by arrangement), with its floor blood-stained from a pirate skirmish, is worth a visit; there are tours every 45 minutes.

It's worth getting hold of the *Eday Heritage Walk* leaflet, which details an interesting four-hour ramble from the Community Enterprises shop up to the Cliffs of Red Head in the north of the island.

Eday Minibus Tour (☎ 622206; adult/child £18.40/ 12.50; Mon, Wed & Fri May-Aug) offers 2¼-hour guided tours from the ferry pier. Tickets don't include lunch, and Friday is the best day, as you get more time on the island.

SLEEPING & EATING

Eday Hostel (SYHA; ☎ 622283; Bay of London; dm adult/child £8/7) Four miles (6.5km) north of the ferry pier, this renovated, 24-bed hostel is reminiscent of an army barracks. You'll need your own sleeping bag, although cotton bags are provided.

Mrs Popplewell's (☎ 622248; Blett, Carrick Bay; DB&B per person £28; croft-house per person £23) Mrs Popplewell's is a charming cottage opposite the Calf of Eday. There's also a fully equipped, self-catering croft-house nearby for three people. Mrs Popplewell bakes fresh bread daily, and she serves snacks and meals at her craft shop.

GETTING THERE & AROUND

There are two flights from Kirkwall (single/ return £31/62, 30 minutes) to London airport – that's London, Eday – on Wednesday only. The ferry service from Kirkwall usually sails via Stronsay (passenger/car £5.65/12.70, 1¼ to two hours, two to three daily), but occasionally it's direct. There's also a link between Sanday and Eday (20 minutes).

Alan Stewart (☎ 622206) runs the local minibus and taxi service. He charges around £3 for a trip along the length of Eday.

Sanday

☎ 01857

Aptly named, blissfully quiet Sanday is ringed by Orkney's best beaches – with dazzling white sand of the sort you'd expect in the Caribbean. The island is almost entirely flat apart from a colossal sand dune and the cliffs at Spurness; it's 12 miles (19km) long and growing due to sand build-up.

There are several archaeological sites, the most impressive being the **Quoyness chambered tomb** (admission free), similar to Maeshowe and dating from the 3rd millennium BC. It has triple walls, a main chamber and six smaller cells. At the northeastern tip of Sanday, there's **Tafts Ness**, with around 500 prehistoric burial mounds.

There are shops and post offices at Kettletoft, Lady and Cross. A bank service is available at Kettletoft on Tuesday only.

SLEEPING & EATING

With permission, you can camp anywhere on the island.

Kettletoft Hotel (☎ /fax 600217; Kettletoft; r per person £20-25; ✗) The welcoming and family-friendly, four-room Kettletoft is an elderly statesman near the centre of the island. The pub here serves tasty bar meals for around £7.

Belsair (☎ 600206; emma@white1935.freeserve .co.uk; Kettletoft; r with bathroom per person £25) The Belsair, also at Kettletoft, has recently been taken over by an enthusiastic new owner, and nothing seems too much trouble. The tidy rooms here are good value. Bar meals and evening dinner are also available.

Quivals Rest B&B (☎ 600370, 600418; www .quivals.co.uk; Quivals; r per person £17, self-catering £30; 🖵) This comfortable guesthouse has self-catering facilities and offers car hire, bike hire and canoe trips. Kids are welcome and package deals are available.

GETTING THERE & AROUND

There are flights from Kirkwall to Sanday (single/return £31/62, 20 minutes, twice

ORKNEY & SHETLAND ISLANDS

daily Monday to Saturday) and Westray. Ferries between Kirkwall and Sanday (passenger/car £5.65/12.70, 1½ hours, two daily May to September) usually permit a day trip with about eight hours on the island.

Bernie Flett (☎ 600467) hires bicycles for £6.

Westray

☎ 01857 / pop 700

The largest of the northern islands, Westray is a jewel in the archipelago's crown. With prehistoric sites, sandy beaches and great cliff scenery, this island is a favourite. The friendly locals, great places to stay and fresh seafood will entice visitors to linger. The ferry docks at Rapness in the south of the island but Pierowall, 7 miles (11km) to the north, is the main village. It has grocery shops, a post office and a hotel. For information about island facilities, call the **Westray & Papa Westray Tourist Association** (☎ 677404; www.westraypapawestray.com).

SIGHTS

Pierowall has one of the best natural harbours in Orkney – it was once an important Viking base. The **Westray Heritage Centre** (☎ 677414; Pierowall; adult/child £2/50p; ⌚ 2-5.30pm Tue-Sat & 11.30am-5pm Sun & Mon May-Sep) has interesting displays on local history and nature.

A half-mile west of Pierowall lie the ruins of creepy **Noltland Castle** (adult/child £1.50/50p; ⌚ 9.30am-6.30pm Jun-Sep), a 16th-century fortified Z-plan tower house. The RSPB reserve at **Noup Head** coastal cliffs, in the northwest of the island, attracts vast numbers of breeding sea birds from April to July. There are big puffin colonies here and at **Castle o'Burrian**, a mile north of Rapness.

SLEEPING & EATING

With permission, you can camp almost anywhere.

Barn (☎ 677214; jharcus@thebarn.sagehost.co.uk; Chalmersquoy, Pierowall; dm £11.75/8.80, tent sites from £3; ✗) This small but excellent, modern, 13-bed hostel is heated throughout and has an inviting lounge. The price includes bed linen, shower and pristine kitchen facilities, and one room has wheelchair access.

Bis Geos Hostel (☎ 677420; www.bisgeos.co.uk; Bis Geos; beds £10; ⌚ Apr-Oct; 🖳 ✗) Bis Geos is a snug and intimate 16-bed hostel in spectacular surrounds, which guests can enjoy

from the conservatory. It's about 2 miles (3km) west of Pierowall and 30 minutes' hike from Noup Head. Facilities include showers, a phone and a kitchen and dining area. Ask here about self-catering cottages.

Pierowall Hotel (☎ 677472; www.orknet.co.uk/pierowall; Pierowall; s/d with shared bathroom £23/40, with bathroom £28/52) The comfortable, eight-room Pierowall Hotel is famous throughout Orkney for its popular fish and chips – the fish is caught fresh by the hotel's boats and is available to eat in or takeaway. Toast your toes by the coal fire in the lounge.

Friendly **Mrs Groat** (☎ 677374; Sand o'Gill; r per person £18), at the northern end of Pierowall, has two properties that she lets out as B&B or self-catering accommodation. Each property has a double plus a two-bunk bedroom – good for families.

GETTING THERE & AWAY

For information on flights, see the Sanday section (p385). A ferry service links Kirkwall with Rapness (passenger/car £5.65/12.70, 1½ hours, two to three daily, May to September). There are one to two ferries daily in winter.

There's also a passenger-only ferry from Pierowall to Papa Westray (£2.85, 25 minutes, three to six daily in summer); the crossing is free if you travel direct from the Rapness ferry. From October to April the boat sails by arrangement (☎ 677216).

Papa Westray

Known locally as Papay (pronounced *pa*-pee), this exquisitely peaceful, tiny island (4 miles long by a mile wide) attracts superlatives. It is home to Europe's oldest domestic building, the **Knap of Howar** (built about 5500 years ago), and to Europe's largest colony of arctic terns (about 6000 birds) at North Hill. Even the two-minute hop from Westray airfield is featured in the *Guinness Book of World Records* as the world's shortest scheduled air service. The island was also the cradle of Christianity in Orkney – **St Boniface's Church** was founded in the 8th century, though most of the recently restored structure dates from the 12th century.

From May to September, **Jim Davidson** (☎ 644259) runs boat trips to the **Holm of Papay**, a small island about a half-mile east of Papa Westray, for £5 per person. The main reason for a visit is to see the huge **chambered cairn**, with 16 beehive cells, and wall carvings. You enter through the roof – there's a torch so you can light your way as you crawl around in the gloomy interior.

Beltane House Hotel (☎ 644267; dm adult/child £10/8, DB&B per person £40; ✗) Owned by the local community co-op, the excellent Beltane House comprises a 16-bed SYHA-approved hostel and a guesthouse with four comfortable rooms with private bathroom. There is also a small shop and a **restaurant** (3-course lunch/dinner £7/16.50) serving Orkney beef, seafood, lamb and veggies. The hotel is just over a mile north of the ferry.

GETTING THERE & AWAY

There are two daily (three on Wednesday and one on Sunday) flights to Papa Westray (£10, 15 minutes) and North Ronaldsay (£10, 20 minutes) from Kirkwall; it's an amazing deal compared to other flights in Orkney – about twice the distance for a fraction of the price (taxes not included). For ferry details, see Westray, p386.

North Ronaldsay
☎ 01857 / pop 50

All of 3 miles (5km) long and almost completely flat, North Ronaldsay is a real outpost surrounded by rolling seas and big skies. The delicious peace and quiet and excellent bird-watching lures visitors here; the island is home to cormorant and seal colonies and is an important stopover for migratory birds. There's also a piteous colony of sheep, kept off the rich farmland by a 13 mile-long wall all round the island and forced to feed only on seaweed, which is said to give their meat a unique flavour.

Powered by wind and solar energy, the **Bird Observatory** (☎ 633200; kevin@nrbo.prestel.co .uk; dm £19.50, r per person £29.50; ✗) next to the ferry pier offers decent accommodation and ornithological activities. Rates include dinner and bed linen; under-15s are half-price, under-fours are free. There's also a shop, café and licensed lounge bar.

Garso Guest House (☎ /fax 633244; DB&B per person £25, cottage per night £25) is a comfortable B&B and self-catering cottage sleeping five at the northern end of the island, about 3 miles (5km) from the pier. Mrs Muir also offers a taxi and minibus service.

For details of flights to North Ronaldsay, see the Papa Westray section p386. There's a weekly ferry from Kirkwall on Friday (passenger/car £5.65/12.70, 2½ hours).

SHETLAND ISLANDS

The rugged and remote Shetland Islands feel like the other side of the globe from Edinburgh or Glasgow. In fact they are almost as much a part of Scandinavia as of Scotland; they were under Norse rule until 1469, when they were given to Scotland as part of a Danish princess' dowry.

Far more desolate and cut-off than Orkney, the Shetlands' far-flung location is belied by the activity and charisma of the capital Lerwick, causing you to forget the 60-plus oceanic miles between you and the mainland. There is a romanticism here intrinsic to such a self-reliant community. Once outside the humming capital, however, the isolation sweeps you off your feet – frequent thundering gales thrash across the raw landscape and mother nature whips up the wild Atlantic into white-cap frenzies that smash into coastal cliffs.

Over 100 windswept and virtually tree-less islands make up this archipelago. Mainland is the biggest island and there is first-rate walking, especially along the rugged, indented coastline.

GETTING THERE & AWAY
Unlike Orkney, Shetland is relatively expensive to get to from mainland Scotland.

Air
The oil industry ensures that air connections are good. The main airport is at Sumburgh, 25 miles (40km) south of Lerwick. There are two to four flights daily between Sumburgh and Aberdeen (£177, one hour) with **British Airways** (BA; ☎ 0845 773 3377; www.britishairways.com).

BA flies daily (except Sunday) between Orkney and Shetland (£85.50, 35 minutes). You can also fly direct from Inverness, Glasgow and Edinburgh.

Boat
Northlink Ferries (☎ 01856-851144; www.northlink ferries.co.uk) runs car ferries between Lerwick and Kirkwall in Orkney (p371).

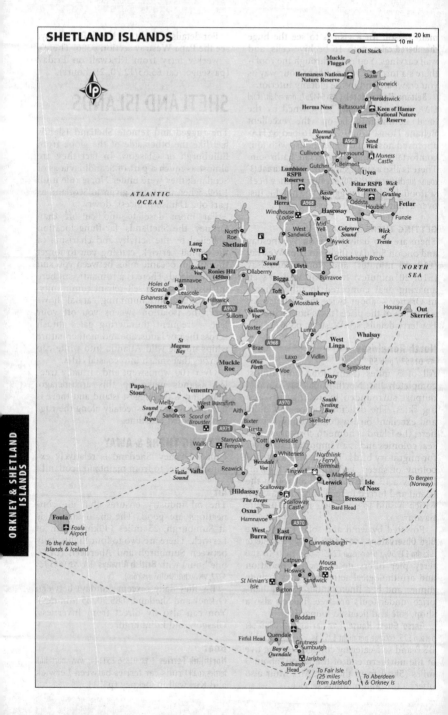

SHETLAND ISLANDS

0   20 km
0   10 mi

Out Stack

Muckle Flugga
Hermaness National Nature Reserve
Skaw
Norwick
Herma Ness
Baltasound
Haroldswick
Keen of Hamar National Nature Reserve
Unst
Bluemull Sound
A968
Sand Wick
Cullivoe
Uyeasound
Muness Castle
Lumbister RSPB Reserve
Gutcher
Belmont
Uyea
Feltar RSPB Reserve
Wick of Gruting
The Herra
Basta Voe
A968
Oddsta
Houbie
Fetlar
Windhouse Lodge
Hascosay
Tresta
Funzie
North Roe
Shetland
West Sandwick
Mid Yell
Colgrave Sound
Wick of Tresta
Lang Ayre
ATLANTIC OCEAN
Yell
Aywick
Ronas Voe
Ronies Hill (450m)
Yell Sound
Grossabrough Broch
Ollaberry
Ulsta
Holes of Scrada
Hamnavoe
Bigga
NORTH SEA
Eshaness
Leascole
Hillswick
Toft
Burravoe
Stenness
Tanwick
A970
Sullom Voe
Samphrey
Housay
Out Skerries
Sullom
Mossbank
Voxter
Lunna
St Magnus Bay
Brae
West Linga
Whalsay
Muckle Roe
Obia Firth
Laxo
Vidlin
Symbister
Voe
Dury Voe
Papa Stour
Vementry
South Nesting Bay
Melby
West Burrafirth
Aith
Sound of Papa
Sandness
Scord of Brouster
Bixter
Skellister
Tresta
A971
Cott
Walls
Stanydale Temple
Weisdale
Whiteness
Northlink Ferry Terminal
Vaila
Vaila Sound
Reawick
Weisdale Voe
Tingwall
Maryfield
Isle of Noss
Lerwick
To Bergen (Norway)
Foula
Foula Airport
Scalloway
Bressay
Hildassay
The Deeps
Scalloway Castle
Bard Head
Oxna
Hamnavoe
A970
West Burra
East Burra
Cunningsburgh
To the Faroe Islands & Iceland
Catpund
Mousa Broch
Hoswick
St Ninian's Isle
Sandwick
Bigton
Boddam
Fitful Head
Quendale
Bay of Quendale
Grutness
Sumburgh
Sumburgh Head
Jarlshof
To Fair Isle (25 miles from Jarlshof)
To Aberdeen & Orkney Is

ORKNEY & SHETLAND ISLANDS

Northlink also operates overnight car ferries from Aberdeen to Lerwick (passenger £43 to £63, car and driver £190 to £263, 12 to 14 hours, daily) departing Aberdeen at 5pm or 7pm.

For details of the ferry link between Lerwick, Torshavn (Faroe Islands) and Bergen (Norway), see the Transport chapter, p419.

GETTING AROUND

The *Shetland Transport Timetable*, an invaluable publication listing all local air, sea and bus services, costs £1 from the TIC.

Bicycle

If it's fine, cycling on the islands' excellent roads can be an exhilarating way to experience the stark beauty of Shetland. It can, however, be very windy (wind speeds of up to 194mph have been recorded!) and there are few places to shelter. You hire bikes from Eric Brown at **Grantfield Garage** (☎ 01595-692709; North Rd, Lerwick; day/week £7.50/45).

Car

The wide roads seem more like motorways after Orkney's tiny, winding lanes. Car rental is cheaper in Lerwick than at the airport.

Bolts Car Hire (☎ 693636; 26 North Rd) Small cars start from £23.60 per day.

John Leask & Son (☎ 01595-693162; leasks@zetnet .co.uk; The Esplanade)

Star Rent A Car (☎ 01595-692075; 22 Commercial Rd) Opposite the bus station.

Public Transport

There are several **bus operators** (☎ 01595-694100). Call for detailed information on services.

LERWICK

☎ 01595 / pop 6830

The consistent ebb and flow of travellers ensures that Lerwick, the only place of any size in Shetland, is a vibrant harbour town, defying its relative isolation from the rest of Scotland. It makes a handy location for some of Mainland's finest attractions and grand Victorian housing abounds.

Although the Shetland Islands have been occupied for several thousand years, Lerwick was only established in the 17th century. Dutch herring fleets began to shelter in the harbour, in preference to Scalloway, which was then the capital. A small community grew up to trade with them and by the late 19th century this was the largest herring town in northern Europe. Today, it's the main port of entry into the Shetlands and transit a point to the North Sea oil rigs.

Orientation & Information

The old harbour, which forms the focus of the town, is a 20-minute walk south of the main ferry terminal; it's now used by visiting yachts and pleasure cruisers. Commercial St, one block back from the waterfront, is the main shopping street, with the post office, and a bank with an ATM across the road.

Havly Centre (☎ 692100; 9 Charlotte St; £1 per 30 mins; ☺ 10am-3pm Mon-Fri, 10am-4.45pm Sat) Internet access available in this Christian centre and café.

Library (☎ 693868; Lower Hillhead; ☺ 10am-7pm Mon, Wed & Thurs, 10am-5pm Tues, Fri & Sat) Has free Internet access.

Manson's Dry Cleaners (☎ 695335; Kantersted Rd) Charges £7 for a wash and dry.

Shetland Times Bookshop (☎ 695531; 71 Commercial St) has every book you could possibly want to read about Shetlands, from the famous WWII Shetland Bus to spotting adorable puffins around the islands.

TIC (☎ 693434; www.shetland-tourism.co.uk; Market Cross; ☺ 8am-6pm Mon-Fri, 8am-4pm Sat & 10am-1pm Sun Apr-Sep, 9am-5pm Mon-Fri Oct-Mar) This friendly office has a good range of books and maps, and a comprehensive selection of brochures detailing Shetlands' activities. *Walks on Shetland* (£6.50), by Mary Welsh, is a good walking guide. There's also a bureau de change here.

Sights

Above the town, there are excellent views from the battlements of **Fort Charlotte** (Charlotte St; admission free; ☺ 9.30am-sunset), built in 1665 to protect the harbour from the Dutch navy.

It's worth dropping into the **Shetland Museum** (☎ 695057; Lower Hillhead; admission free; ☺ 10am-7pm Mon, Wed & Fri, 10am-5pm Tues, Thur & Sat) for an introduction to the island's 5000-year history. Inside are terrific exhibits on Shetland's fishing heritage, along with medieval pottery, grisly human remains and fine examples of Pictish stone carvings. The Monk's Stone arguably depicts the coming of Christianity to the archipelago.

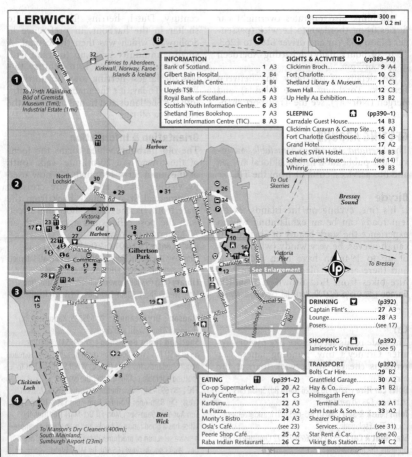

LERWICK

0 ————— 300 m
0 ————— 0.2 mi

INFORMATION
Bank of Scotland............................. **1** A3
Gilbert Bain Hospital....................... **2** B4
Lerwick Health Centre..................... **3** B4
Lloyds TSB...................................... **4** A3
Royal Bank of Scotland................... **5** A3
Scottish Youth Information Centre.... **6** A3
Shetland Times Bookshop................ **7** A3
Tourist Information Centre (TIC)....... **8** A3

SIGHTS & ACTIVITIES (pp389–90)
Clickimin Broch.............................. **9** A4
Fort Charlotte................................ **10** C3
Shetland Library & Museum............ **11** C3
Town Hall....................................... **12** C3
Up Helly Aa Exhibition.................... **13** B2

SLEEPING (pp390–1)
Carradale Guest House.................... **14** B3
Clickimin Caravan & Camp Site....... **15** A3
Fort Charlotte Guesthouse.............. **16** C3
Grand Hotel.................................... **17** A2
Lerwick SYHA Hostel...................... **18** B3
Solheim Guest House................(see 14)
Whinrig... **19** B3

DRINKING (p392)
Captain Flint's................................ **27** A3
Lounge... **28** A3
Posers......................................(see 17)

SHOPPING (p392)
Jamieson's Knitwear..................(see 5)

TRANSPORT (p392)
Bolts Car Hire................................. **29** B2
Grantfield Garage........................... **30** A2
Hay & Co....................................... **31** B2
Holmsgarth Ferry
Terminal..................................... **32** A1
John Leask & Son............................ **33** A2
Shearer Shipping
Services...................................(see 31)
Star Rent A Car.........................(see 26)
Viking Bus Station.......................... **34** C2

EATING (pp391–2)
Co-op Supermarket......................... **20** A2
Havly Centre................................... **21** C3
Karibunu.. **22** A3
La Piazza.. **23** A3
Monty's Bistro................................ **24** A3
Osla's Café................................(see 23)
Peerie Shop Café............................ **25** A3
Raba Indian Restaurant................... **26** C2

There's a lot of memorabilia and an authentic feel to the **Böd of Gremista** (☎ 695057; Gremista; admission free; ☒ 10am-1pm & 2-5pm Wed-Sun Jun–mid-Sep), a restored 18th-century fishing booth; the highlight is the chatty old salt who shows visitors around.

The fortified site of **Clickimin Broch** (admission free), just under a mile west of the town centre, was occupied from the 7th century BC to the 6th century AD. It's impressively large and its setting on a small loch gives it a feeling of being removed from the present-day – unusual given the surrounding urban encroachment.

The **Up-Helly-Aa Exhibition** (St Sunniva St; adult/child £3/1; ☒ 2-4pm Tue & Sat, plus 7-9pm Tue & Fri mid-May–mid-Sep) explains the bizarre, annual Viking fire festival (see the boxed text, 'Viking Mayhem' later).

Festivals & Events
It's well worth being here for the **Folk Festival** in April/May, or the **Fiddle & Accordion Festival** in October. See the boxed text on p391 for a description of the wacky **Up-Helly-Aa** festival, which takes place on the last Tuesday in January.

Sleeping
BUDGET
Clickimin Caravan & Camp Site (☎ 741000; Lochside; sites per small/large tent £6.20/8.40) By the loch on the western edge of town, Clickimin is a small and tidy park. Rates include the

VIKING MAYHEM

Given the connections with their Scandanavian neighbours, it's not surprising that islanders wish to honour their Norse heritage. And what better way to do it than burning a replica Viking Longship? **Up-Helly-Aa** is all about fancy dress and pageantry: about 1 costumed revellers with flaming torches lug a wooden galley through Lerwick to the designated torching site. Leading the charge is a horde of Vikings wearing sheepskins, winged helmets (think *Asterix*) and armed with axes and shields. This festival for pyros dates back to Norse times, when Vikings celebrated the rebirth of the sun at yule by torching a longship in the bay.

use of the ablutions facility in the adjacent Clickimin Leisure Centre.

Lerwick Youth Hostel (SYHA; ☎ 692114; King Harald St; dm adult/child £11/9.50; ☷ Apr-Sep) This hostel, in a grand building with modern facilities, has spacious dorms and is clean and well maintained, although the kitchen is small. It's very popular with groups so book ahead.

MID-RANGE

Most of Lerwick's B&Bs and guesthouses are small, cosy affairs with only two or three rooms.

Whinrig (Mrs Giffords; ☎ 693554; cgifford@btinternet.com; 12 Burgh Rd; r per person £22-24; ☒) This house, actually in a small lane off Burgh Rd, is a small, old-fashioned operation with two immaculate rooms. Guests are extremely well looked after and it's especially recommended for people with mobility difficulties.

Fort Charlotte Guesthouse (☎ 692140; fortcharlotte.guesth@talk21.com; 1 Charlotte St; s £20-30, d £55; ☒) This place is like *Dr Who's* Tardis – a lot bigger than it looks. In a quiet, central part of Lerwick, it has bright and cheery rooms and the best single accommodation in town. Book ahead as it's very popular. The family room is particularly good value for three (£55).

Solheim Guest House (☎ /fax 695275; 34 King Harald St; s £22-30, d £40-45; ☒) An excellent place, Solheim offers a filling breakfast, and the rooms, with shared bathrooms, are clean

and bright. Although they aren't huge, the rooms make an intelligent use of space and the whole place is very laid-back.

Carradale Guest House (☎ 692251; 36 King Harald St; s £22-35, d £44-60; ☒) Next door to Solheim, huge, beautifully furnished rooms and a concoction of comforts greet visitors at this well-kept guesthouse.

TOP END

Grand Hotel (☎ 692826; www.kgqhotels.co.uk; 24 Commercial St; s/d £65/90) The modernised Grand Hotel includes Shetland's only nightclub. This old bastion of hospitality used to take pride of place in Lerwick; nowadays it has an air of faded grandeur but the rooms are still very comfy.

Eating

Karibunu (☎ 690606; Harrison Sq; wraps from £1.50) This clean, modern place is the best spot in town for a fresh roasted coffee – just follow your nose to find it! It also does tasty pitta breads and wraps with a variety of fillings (the falafel is recommended).

Havly Centre (☎ 692100; 9 Charlotte St; light meals £2-4; ☷ 10am-3pm Mon-Fri, 10am-4.45pm Sat; ☐) The Havly Centre is a Norwegian Christian centre with an excellent café, and the staff don't quiz you on your religious beliefs. It serves mainly snacks and heavenly, gooey cakes. There are some comfy couches and toys for the kids – it's a good spot for a read of the newspaper.

Monty's Bistro (☎ 696555; 5 Mounthooly St; mains lunch £3-7, dinner £10-15; ☷ lunch & dinner Tue-Sat) Highly recommended, Monty's Bistro is possibly the best place to eat in Lerwick. The bright Mediterranean décor, cheery staff and delicious local produce all combine to make it an excellent dining experience.

Peerie Shop Café (☎ 692817; Esplanade; light meals from £3) This trendy spot has a stark, industrial décor that interior designers would kill for, and is as close as Lerwick comes to stylish. It does a mean carrot cake and the fresh sandwiches are enormous.

Osla's Café (☎ 696005; 88 Commercial St; pancakes £2.50-3.50; ☷ 9.30am-5pm Mon-Sat, 11am-4pm Sun) Osla's is a sparky little joint serving scrumptious sweet and savoury pancakes and whopping toasties.

La Piazza (mains £5.50-9; ☷ noon-2pm & 5pm-late Mon-Sat, noon-8pm Sun) Upstairs from Osla's is

ORKNEY & SHETLAND ISLANDS

the recently opened La Piazza. It's a very 'now' Italian joint (well 'now' for Shetlands – but it's actually quite stylish!) dishing out healthy portions of pasta, and pizza like Papa used to make…well almost.

Raba Indian Restaurant (☎ 695585; 26 Commercial Rd; mains £4.50-7) Located near the bus station, Raba whips up first-class curries amid token Indian wall hangings and dodgy wallpaper. It's a highly commended restaurant, rated among the top 1000 Indian restaurants in the country (which begs the question – how many *are* there?!).

Self-caterers head for the **Co-op supermarket** (Holmsgarth Rd).

Drinking

The Shetland Fiddlers play at a number of locations, and it's worth attending their sessions – enquire at the TIC.

Lounge (☎ 692231; 4 Mounthooly St) The Lounge is a friendly bar patrolled by Andy Capp characters during the day, and features a variety of live music several nights a week, including informal jam sessions.

Captain Flint's (☎ 692249; 2 Commercial Rd) Captain Flint's is a lively bar and *the* spot in town for some action. There's a cross-section of young uns, tourists and crusty locals. There's often live music here too.

Posers (☎ 692826; 24 Commercial St; cover charge £5) Posers, at the Grand Hotel, is Lerwick's only nightclub, and on Wednesday the ladies get free entry – how 1980s! Show the locals your latest moves to the booming, dated, dance music.

Shopping

Best buys are the woollen jerseys, cardigans and sweaters for which Shetland is world-famous. For bargains you must go to the factories. **Judane** (☎ 693724), on the industrial estate north past the power station, sells plain sweaters from £10 and patterned ones for £18.

At **Jamieson's Knitwear** (☎ 693114; 93 Commercial St) you'll find real Fair Isle sweaters with the distinctive OXOXO pattern, from £40.

Getting There & Around

See Getting There & Away, p387, for services to Lerwick. Ferries dock at Holmsgarth terminal, a 20-minute walk from the town centre. From Sumburgh airport, Leask's runs regular buses to meet flights (£2.10 one way).

If you need a taxi, call **Sinclair's Taxis** (☎ 694617).

BRESSAY & NOSS
☎ 01595 / pop 353

Two islands lie across Bressay Sound east of Lerwick. The 34-sq-km island of Bressay (pronounced bressah) has some interesting walks, especially along the cliffs and up Ward Hill (226m), which offers good views of the island.

Colonies of birds can be seen at the Ord and Bard Head cliffs in the south. For serious **bird-watching** though, it's worth visiting Noss, a National Nature Reserve (NNR) east of Bressay, to see the huge number of sea birds nesting on the island's 183m cliffs. Noss can only be visited from mid-May to August when Scottish Natural Heritage (SNH) operates a small visitor centre at Gungstie.

From Lerwick, **Bressaboats** (☎ 693434) runs three-hour cruises (twice-daily, not Wednesday, May to August) around Bressay and Noss for £30/20; book with the TIC.

Maryfield Hotel (☎ 820207; mains from £6), by the ferry quay, offers bar meals with seafood specialities.

GETTING THERE & AWAY

From Lerwick there are daily **ferries** (☎ 01426-980317; person/car £1.40/3.30) to Bressay (seven minutes, frequent). It's then 2½ miles across the island (some people bring rented bikes from Lerwick) to take the inflatable dinghy to Noss (£3/1.50; 10am to 5pm Tuesday, Wednesday and Friday to Sunday, mid-May to August), but check with **SNH** (☎ 693345) before leaving Lerwick as the dinghy doesn't operate in bad weather.

CENTRAL & WEST MAINLAND
Scalloway
☎ 01595 / pop 812

The former capital of Shetland, Scalloway (pronounced scallowah), on the west coast 6 miles (10km) from Lerwick, is now a busy fishing village set around bare, rolling hills. It's a little shabby, but has an air of authenticity away from the tourist hoardes. During WWII, the Norwegian resistance movement operated the **Shetland Bus** (see boxed text p393) from here, carrying arms and transporting refugees in fishing boats.

ALL ABOARD THE SHETLAND BUS

In early April, 1940, Nazi Germany mounted an unprovoked attack on Norway. Ill-prepared, Norway was quickly overrun and many small craft fleeing the German advance ended up in Shetland. The penny soon dropped that if small boats could sail to Shetlands, they could also return – so began the Shetland Bus. At first fishing boats were used, but the Germans and the weather took their toll and eventually they were replaced by three more formidable American sub-chasers. The trips were very successful, carrying agents, wireless operators and military supplies for the resistance movement and returning with refugees, recruits for the Free Norwegian Forces and, in December, Christmas trees for the treeless Shetlands!

The **Shetland Bus Memorial** in Scalloway is built of stones from both countries. The Norwegian stones are sourced from the home areas of 44 Norwegian men who died running the gauntlet between Norway and the Shetland Islands.

For more information on the Shetland Bus see www.shetland-heritage.co.uk/shetlandbus.

The small, volunteer-run **Scalloway Museum** (☎ 880675; Main St; donation requested; ☾ 9.30-11.30am, 2-4.30pm Mon, 10am-noon, 2-4.30pm Tue-Sat May-Sep) is best visited for its Shetland Bus displays, and a peek at Scalloway's glory days.

Down in the village close to the water-front, the **Scalloway Hotel** (☎ 880444; Main St; s/d £49/77) has modern, spotless rooms with small, private bathrooms. Some rooms have good views over the harbour and it may be a decent option if everything in Lerwick is full.

Buses run from Lerwick (£1.10, 25 minutes, 10 daily Monday to Saturday) to Scalloway.

Weisdale

There is an excellent gallery and café in the restored **Weisdale Mill** (☎ 01595-830400; Weisdale; admission free; ☾ 10.30am-4.30pm Tue-Sat, noon-4.30pm Sun). On the western shore of Weisdale Voe, south of the mill, are the ruins of the house where John Clunies Ross (1786–1853) was born. In 1827 he settled in the Cocos Islands in the Indian Ocean where he proclaimed himself 'king'.

The Western Side

☎ 01595

The western side of Mainland is notable for its varied scenery: bleak moors, sheer cliffs, rolling green hills and numerous cobalt-blue lochs and inlets. It's ideal for walking, cycling and fishing.

Out in the Atlantic Ocean, about 15 miles (24km) southwest of Walls, is the 8-sq-km island of **Foula** (Bird Island), which competes with Fair Isle for the title of Scotland's most isolated, inhabited island. Foula supports 42 people, 1500 sheep and 500,000

sea birds, including the rare Leach's petrel and Scotland's largest colony of great skuas, all amid dramatic cliff scenery, particularly the awesome, sheer Kame (372m). There's no shop on the island, but centrally located **Mrs Taylor's** (☎ /fax 753226; Leraback; DB&B per person £28) offers accommodation and good food.

Foula is reached by twice-weekly **ferries** (☎ 753226; return/car & driver £4.80/23.20) from Walls or Scalloway (four hours) and **flights** (☎ 840246; £38) from Tingwall and Sumburgh.

Northwest from Walls, the road crosses desolate moorland then descends through green fields before arriving at the small crofting community of **Sandness**. Visible about a mile offshore is the island of **Papa Stour**, home to huge colonies of auks, terns and skuas. It's mostly made up of volcanic rock that has eroded to form sea caves, underground passages, arches and columns. Access to the island is by ferry from West Burrafirth (£4.80 return, £23.20 for a car and driver, one hour, three or four weekly), east of Sandness; book with **W Clark** (☎ 810460).

SOUTH MAINLAND

From Lerwick, the main road south winds 25 miles (40km) down the eastern side of this long, narrow, hilly tail of land that ends at Sumburgh Head. The waters lapping against the cliffs are an inviting turquoise in many places. If it weren't for the raging, Arctic gales, you might almost be tempted to have a dip.

Sandwick & Around

☎ 01950 / pop 1352

Opposite the small scattered village of Sandwick, is the **Isle of Mousa**, an RSPB reserve, on which stands the impressive double-walled,

ORKNEY &
ISLANDS
SHETLAND

BIRD-WATCHING IN SHETLAND

For bird-watchers, Shetland is paradise. This island group is internationally famous for its bird life. As well as being a stopover for migrating Arctic species, there are huge sea-bird breeding colonies.

Out of the 24 seabird species that nest in the British Isles, 21 are found here; June is the height of the breeding season. The **Royal Society for the Protection of Birds** (RSPB; www.rspb.org.uk) maintains several reserves on south Mainland and on the island of Fetlar. There are national nature reserves at **Hermaness**, where you can't fail to be entertained by the clownish antics of the almost tame puffins and on the **Isle of Noss. Fair Isle** also supports large seabird populations.

A useful website for bird-watchers is at www.wildlife.shetland.co.uk/birds/where .html. Take care when out bird-watching as the cliff-edge sites can be dangerous. Also watch out for skuas (bonxies) that will dive-bomb you if you go near their nests. Since they aim for the highest part of your body, it's wise to walk with a stick, pointing it above your head if they approach. And don't get too close to nesting fulmars or you'll be the target for their smelly, oily spittle!

---

fortified tower, **Mousa Broch** (13m). The well-preserved broch was built from local sandstone between 100 BC and AD 100 and features in two Viking sagas as a hideout for eloping couples! The island is also home to many sea birds and waders; around 6000 storm petrels nest on Mousa, but they're only on the island at night. Common and grey seals can be seen on the beach and among the rocks at West Voe.

From mid-April to mid-September, **Tom Jamieson** (☎ 431367; www.mousaboattrips.co.uk; adult/child return £8/4) runs daily boat trips (15 minutes) from Leebitton harbour in Sandwick, allowing two hours on the island.

Back on Mainland, **Hoswick Visitor Centre** (☎ 431406; Hoswick; admission free; ☉ 10am-5pm Mon-Sat, 11am-5pm Sun May-Sep) has a great collection of old wirelesses (including the daddy of them all – the Murphy-type wireless). There are displays on fishing, whaling, weaving and...peat castin'! (See p363).

The old-style rooms with shared bathroom are pretty average at the **Barclay Arms Hotel** (☎ 431226, fax 431262; Hoswick; r per person £20), but they'd do at a pinch. However, you come here for the craic, not the comforts – there's traditional live music some nights in a great bar overlooking the water. If you'd prefer a comfy B&B, try **Solbrekke** (☎ 43141; Park Rd, Sandwick; r per person £20), which has two double rooms.

There are buses between Lerwick and Sandwick (£1.45, 25 minutes, three to seven daily).

Bigton & Around

Buses from Lerwick stop twice daily (Monday to Saturday) in Bigton on the west coast, but it's another couple of miles to the **tombolo** (a narrow isthmus) that connects Mainland with St Ninian's Isle. This geologically important site is the largest shell-and-sand tombolo in Britain and an SSSI.

Across the tombolo is **St Ninian's Isle** where you'll find the ruins of a 12th-century church, beneath which are traces of an earlier Pictish church. In 1958 during excavations, Pictish treasure, probably dating from AD 800 and consisting of 27 silver objects, was found beneath a broken sandstone slab. They're now kept in the Museum of Scotland in Edinburgh, but you can see replicas in the Shetland Museum, Lerwick.

Boddam

From this small village there's a side road that leads to the **Shetland Crofthouse Museum** (☎ 01595-695057; South Voe; admission free; ☉ 10am-1pm & 2-5pm May-Sep). When you enter, the years clunk by the wayside as you step back into a primitive existence. Built in 1870, it has been restored, thatched and furnished with 19th-century furniture and utensils. The Lerwick–Sumburgh bus stops right outside.

Quendale

South of Boddam, a minor road runs southwest to Quendale where you'll find the small but excellent, restored and fully operational 19th-century **Quendale Watermill** (☎ 01950-460969; adult/child £2/50p; ☉ 10am-5pm May-Sep), the last of Shetland's water mills.

The village overlooks a long, sandy beach to the south in the Bay of Quendale. West of the bay there's dramatic cliff scenery and **diving** in the waters between

Garth's Ness and Fitful Head and to the wreck of the oil tanker Braer off Garth's Ness.

From Lerwick there are two buses daily (Monday to Saturday).

Sumburgh

At the southern tip of Mainland, this village is home to the international airport and **Jarlshof** (☎ 01950-460112; adult/child £3/1; ☼ 9.30am-6.30pm Apr-Sep), Shetland's most impressive archaeological attraction. This large settlement, with buildings from prehistory through Norse times to the 16th century, was hidden under the sand until it was exposed by a gale at the end of the 19th century. It's a thought-provoking place, mainly in ruins, but with a fascinating, intact wheelhouse defying time. You should buy the short guide, which interprets the ruins from a number of vantage points (otherwise a fair bit of imagination is required).

Near Jarlshof you can visit **Sumburgh Head**, an RSPB reserve. The lighthouse here isn't open to the public, but you can view the many birds that inhabit the cliffs below. At various times there are puffins (over 2000 pairs), kittiwakes (1000 pairs), fulmars, guillemots (over 13,000 breed here), razorbills and cormorants. The other important bird-watching area is the **Pool of Virkie**, the bay just east of the airport.

Also east of the airport, **Grutness** is the port for the ferry to Fair Isle.

Betty Mouat's Cottage (Old Scatness, Dunrossness; beds £5; ☼ Apr-Sep) is a camping böd by the airport sleeping up to eight people. Book in advance at Lerwick TIC.

The large, upmarket **Sumburgh Hotel** (☎ 01950-460201; sumburgh.hotel@zetnet.co.uk; Sumburgh; s/d from £45/60), next to Jarlshof, has a bar and restaurant, and organises loads of activities, including fishing, cycling and pony trekking.

To get to Sumburgh from Lerwick, take the airport bus (£1.90, 45 minutes, five daily Monday to Saturday, two on Sunday) and get off at the second-last stop.

FAIR ISLE

☎ 01595 / pop 68

About halfway to Orkney, Fair Isle is one of Scotland's most remote inhabited islands. It's only three by 1½ miles in size

and probably best known for its patterned knitwear, still produced in the island's co-operative, Fair Isle Crafts.

It's also a paradise for bird-watchers, who form the bulk of the island's visitors. Fair Isle is in the flight path of migrating birds, and thousands breed here. They're monitored by the **Bird Observatory** which collects and analyses information year-round; visitors are more than welcome to participate.

The small **George Waterston Memorial Centre** (☎ 760244; Taft; donations welcome; ☼ 2-4pm Mon, 10.30am-noon Wed, 2-3.30pm Fri) has photos and exhibits on the island's natural history, crofting, fishing, archaeology and knitwear.

Fair Isle Lodge & Bird Observatory (☎ /fax 760258; full-board dm/s/d £30/42/74) offers home cooking and free guided walks; it's located about 400m from the ferry terminal.

Mrs Coull (☎ 760248l; kathleen.coull@lineone.net; Upper Leogh; DB&B per person £35), near the southern harbour, has three good rooms and the tariff includes a packed lunch.

Getting There & Away

There are **flights** (☎ 840246) to Fair Isle from Tingwall (£76 return, 25 minutes, twice daily Monday, Wednesday and Friday). There's also a return flight from Sumburgh on Saturday.

From May to September, the *Good Shepherd IV* ferry sails from Grutness (near Sumburgh) to Fair Isle (£2.40, three hours) on Tuesday, Saturday and alternate Thursdays, and from Lerwick (£2.40, 4½ hours) on alternate Thursdays. In winter, there's one return trip on Tuesday. Book with **JW Stout** (☎ 760222).

NORTH MAINLAND
Voe

Lower Voe is a pretty collection of buildings beside a tranquil bay on the southern shore of Olna Firth.

In previous incarnations, red-painted **Sail Loft** (Lower Voe; beds £5; ☼ Apr-Sep), by the pier, was a fishing shed and knitwear factory, but it's now a camping böd. The key is kept by a friendly local who works on the pier next to Sail Loft.

Try the lobster platter or local salmon in the appealing, wood-panelled **Pierhead Restaurant & Bar** (☎ 01806-588332; Lower Voe; starters

£4.50, mains £8.50-14), opposite Sail Loft, which serves top-notch seafood.

There are buses from Lerwick to Voe (£1.70, 35 mins, up to six daily Monday to Saturday, and two on Sunday during school terms).

Whalsay & Out Skerries

☎ 01806 / pop 1043

South of Voe, the B9071 branches east to Laxo, the ferry terminal for the island of **Whalsay**. This is one of the most prosperous of Shetland's islands owing to its large fishing industry whose fleet is based at the modern harbour of **Symbister**.

The Hanseatic League, a commercial association of German towns that existed between the 14th and early 18th centuries, set up trading booths at the harbour. One of these, **Pier House** (☎ 566362; Symbister; adult/child £1/free; ⊙ 9am-1pm & 2-5pm Mon-Sat Apr-Sep, other times key available at shop next door), has been restored and inside is an interesting exhibition about the island. Whalsay is popular for sea angling and for trout fishing in its lochs. There are also scenic walks in the south and east where colonies of sea birds breed and where you may catch sight of seals.

The famous poet Hugh MacDiarmid's former home, **Grieve House** (Sodom; beds £5; ⊙ Apr-Sep), is now a camping böd. Book through Lerwick TIC.

There are regular **ferries** (☎ 566259; £2.80 return) between Laxo and Symbister (30 minutes; daily).

Northeast of Whalsay, another thriving fishing community occupies the 2-sq-miles of **Out Skerries** (or just Skerries). It's made up of the three main islands of Housay, Bruray (these two connected by a road bridge) and Grunay, plus a number of islets. Their rugged cliffs teem with birdlife.

There are **ferries** (☎ 07626-983633; return passenger/car & driver £4.80/6.60) between Out Skerries and Lerwick on Tuesday and Thursday (2½ hours), and the rest of the week (except Wednesday) to Vidlin (1½ hours), about 3 miles (5km) northeast of Laxo.

Brae & Around

With its accommodation options, Brae makes a good base. Pack a bottle of your favourite poison (single malts recommended) to keep you company on those stormy nights. There's fine **walking** on the peninsula west of Brae, and to the south on the red-granite island of **Muckle Roe**, which is connected to the peninsula by a bridge. Muckle Roe also offers good **diving** off its west and north coasts.

Valleyfield Guest House (☎ 01806-522450, fax 522563; r per person £25) has good size rooms with private bathrooms (especially the singles). For families there's a double and a single with a separate entrance, giving good privacy. Valleyfield is 1½ miles south of Brae on the A970. **Drumquin Guest House** (☎ 01806-522621; Brae; r per person £25-30) is a large, laid-back place with good rooms. Breakfast is served in a sun-flooded conservatory.

Busta House Hotel (☎ 01806-522506; s/d from £75/95; 4-course dinner £28.50), just outside Brae, would make a great place to splash out – it's a luxurious, genteel, country-house hotel with a fine restaurant.

Brae Stores, near the junction in the village centre, is a supermarket and post office.

Buses from Lerwick to Eshaness and North Roe stop in Brae (£1.70, 35 minutes) up to eight times a day Monday to Saturday.

Eshaness & Hillswick

About 11 miles (18km) northwest of Brae the road ends at the red, basalt lava cliffs of Eshaness, which form some of the most impressive, wild, coastal scenery in Shetland. Howling Atlantic gales whip the ocean into a whitecap frenzy, before crashing into the base of the cliffs. When the wind subsides there is superb **walking** and panoramic views from the lighthouse (closed to the public) on the headland.

A mile east, a side road leads south to the **Tangwick Haa Museum** (☎ 503389; Tangwick Haa; admission free; ⊙ 1-5pm Mon-Fri,11am-7pm Sat & Sun May-Sep), located in a restored 17th-century house. The wonderful collection of ancient B&W photos capture the sense of community here.

At **Hamnavoe**, which you reach from another side road heading north, about 3½ miles (6km) east of Eshaness, is the small, stone **Johnny Notions Camping Böd** (dm £5; ⊙ Apr-Sep); book through Lerwick TIC. This was the birthplace of Johnny 'Notions' Williamson, an 18th-century blacksmith who inoculated several thousand people against smallpox using a serum and method he devised himself.

Built of timber brought from Norway in 1900, **St Magnus Hotel** (☎ 01806-503372, fax 503373; Hillswick; s £30-40, d £25-35) is kinda creepy and reminiscent of an episode of *Scooby-Doo*. The wooden rooms have a certain Scandanavian-chalet feel to them and are fair value. Bar lunches and local seafood dishes are available.

Down on the quay, **Booth Restaurant & Café** (☎ 01806-503348; Hillswick; ☼ May-Sep) serves vegetarian food in a hippy crofters house – actually a 300-year-old former Hanseatic trading-post house and one of Shetland's oldest buildings. All proceeds go to the local wildlife sanctuary.

Buses from Lerwick run (evenings only) to Hillswick (£2.10, 1¼ hours) and Eshaness.

THE NORTH ISLES

The North Isles are made up of the three islands of Yell, Unst and Fetlar, all connected to each other by ferry.

Yell

☎ 01957 / pop 1083

Yell is all about colours: the browns and vivid, lush greens of the peaty moor, grey clouds thudding through the skies and the steely blue waters of the North Atlantic, which are never far away. It's a desolate island with some good coastal and hill walks, especially around the **Herra peninsula**, about halfway up the west coast.

Across Whale Firth from the peninsula is **Lumbister**, where red-throated divers (called 'rain geese' in Shetland), merlins, bonxies, arctic skuas and other bird species breed. The area is home to a large otter population too. The otters are best viewed near the shores of Whale Firth, where you may also spot common and grey seals.

South of Lumbister, on the hillside above the main road, stand the reputedly haunted ruins of **Windhouse**, dating from 1707. About a mile east of here is **Mid Yell**, the island's largest village and a natural harbour. The road north to Gutcher passes **Basta Voe** where many otters inhabit the shores. In the north, around the village of **Cullovoe**, there's more good walking along the attractive coastline.

From Ulsta ferry terminal, the road leads 5 miles (8km) east to Burravoe. The **Old Haa Museum** (☎ 722339; Burravoe; admission free; ☼ 10am-4pm Tue-Thu & Sat, 2-5pm Sun late Apr-Sep) has a fascinating exhibition on local flora, fauna and history and there's a small gallery. It's given authenticity by the musty old stone building (Yell's oldest building, built in 1672) in which it's housed, and there's a genealogy centre for those whose ancestors came from these parts.

SLEEPING & EATING

Windhouse Lodge (Mid Yell; beds £5; ☼ Apr-Sep) Below the haunted ruins of Windhouse, and on the A968, you'll find this small, clean, well-kept camping böd with a pot belly stove to warm your toes. You can book beds at Lerwick TIC.

Pinewood Guest House (☎ 702427; South Aywick, East Yell; r without/with bathroom per person £19/22) Pinewood has the comforts of home in a traditional, laid-back house overlooking the islands of Fetlar, Unst and Skerries. Dinner can be arranged with advance notice.

Gutcher Post Office (☎ 744201, fax 744366; Gutcher; r per person £18; dinner £9; ✗) Friendly Gutcher Post Office has cosy rooms and is a stone's throw from the ferry pier. The owner has a definite piggy fetish! It's very cheerful and has been recommended by travellers.

While you're waiting for the ferry to Unst, you can snack at the warm, eclectic little **Wind Dog Cafe** (☎ 744321; Gutcher; snacks & light meals £1.60-2.50; ☼ 8.30am-6.30pm Mon-Fri, 9.45am-6.30pm Sat, 10am-6.30pm Sun; ☐). It serves up hot baguettes, burgers and baked potatoes and on Friday evening, pizza is on the menu.

There are **grocery stores** in Mid Yell, Aywick and Ulsta.

GETTING THERE & AWAY

Yell is connected with Mainland by **ferry** (☎ 722259; single £1.40, car & driver £3.30) between Toft and Ulsta (20 minutes, frequent). Although you don't need to book in advance, from May to September traffic is constant so it's wise to do so.

Buses leave Lerwick for Toft ferry pier (£2.10, one hour, two to four daily, Sunday during school terms only). There are connecting buses at Ulsta for other parts of the island.

Unst

☎ 01957 / pop 1067

Unst is a lot smaller than Yell, but it feels less isolated and has more of a community. It has an area of 45-sq-miles and is Scotland's northernmost inhabited island. There's a wide variety of vegetation – over 400 different plant species. Some of the most unusual examples can be seen at the 30-hectare **Keen of Hamar NNR** northeast of Baltasound.

In the northwest is the wonderfully wild and windy NNR reserve of **Hermaness**. Here you can sit on the high cliffs, commune with the thousands of sea birds and Shetland's largest colony of puffins (best seen in May and June), and gaze across the sea towards the Arctic Circle. The more energetic should take on the superb **cliff-top walk** along the west coast.

The **Hermaness Visitor Centre** (☎ 711278; Shore Station, Burrafirth; admission free; ☼ 8am-6pm late Apr–mid-Sep), near the reserve's entrance, has a seabird exhibit and provides information on the island's wildlife.

Robert Louis Stevenson wrote Treasure Island while living on Unst and the map in the novel is reputedly based on Unst. Stevenson's uncle built the lighthouse on **Muckle Flugga**, one of the group of rocks off Hermaness; another of the rocks is **Out Stack**, Scotland's most northerly point.

Unst Heritage Centre (☎ 711528; Haroldswick; adult/child £2/free, joint Unst Boat Haven ticket £3; ☼ 2-5pm May-Sep) houses a modern museum with a history of the Shetland pony, and a nostalgic look at the past. There's a re-creation of a croft house complete with box bed and, for weather-obsessed Brits, a summary of the last 170 years of weather in the Shetlands.

Unst Boat Haven (☎ 711528; Haroldswick; admission – same as Heritage Centre; ☼ 2-5pm May-Sep) is housed in a large shed and is every boaty's delight, with rowing and sailing boats, photographs of more boats, and maritime artefacts.

Scotland's oddest **bus shelter**, complete with sofa and other accoutrements, is at Baltasound – looks as though someone just got kicked out of home!

SLEEPING & EATING
Gardiesfauld Hostel (☎ 755240; www.gardiesfauld .shetland.co.uk; Uyeasound; dm adult/child £9.25/8, tent & 2 persons £6; ☼ Apr–Sep) Gardiesfauld Hostel has modern facilities, a variety of clean dorm accommodation and a family room. There's a well-equipped kitchen and a snug, communal lounge; you can also rent bikes here.

Prestegaard (☎ 755234; Uyeasound; r per person £18, with dinner £29) The rooms at the front of this large Victorian house are excellent with lovely views over the water. It's a well-kept place with a friendly host.

Baltasound Hotel (☎ 711334; www.baltasound -hotel.shetland.co.uk; Baltasound; s/d £44/68) The cottage-style rooms inside this solid place are better than the rooms in the nearby chalets, which are a bit cramped. It's also a decent watering hole popular with tourist buses. During the day it's soup and sandwiches, while dinner at night is decent nosh from £5. Try the local real ale White Wife, named after a ghostly figure seen by the A968, just south of Baltasound.

Clingera Guest House (☎ /fax 711579; Baltasound; r per person £20) This is one of the best places to stay on the island and has affable hosts and huge, immaculate, rooms with en suite bathrooms. The twin has a separate sitting room and is terrific value. The owners also rent out a couple of self-catering croft houses.

Self-caterers can stock up at **Skibhoul Store & Bakery** (Baltasound).

GETTING THERE & AWAY
Unst is connected with Yell by a small car **ferry** (☎ 722259; single/car & driver £1.40/3.30) between Gutcher and Belmont (10 minutes, frequent).

Haroldswick is 55 miles (88km) from Lerwick and, if you don't have a car, you must spend the night on Unst as buses only run once daily.

Fetlar
☎ 01957 / pop 87

Fetlar is the smallest (five miles by two miles) but most fertile of the North Isles. Much of the island is designated an SSSI. There's great bird-watching, and the 705 hectares of grassy moorland around Vord Hill (159m) in the north form the **Fetlar RSPB Reserve**. Large numbers of auks, gulls and shags breed in the cliffs. Common and grey seals can also be seen on the shores. The reserve is closed during the breeding season, from May to August; contact the **warden** (☎ 733246) at Baelans.

Scenic **walking** is possible on much of the island, especially around the bay near Tresta, at Urie and Gruting in the north, and Funzie in the east.

There's no petrol on Fetlar, but there's a shop and a post office in **Houbie**, the main village. The excellent **Fetlar Interpretive Centre** (☎ 733206; Houbie; admission free; ☯ 12.30-5pm Tue-Sun May-Sep), near the post office, has photos, audio recordings and videos on the island and its history.

Garth's Campsite (☎ 733227; Gord, Houbie; tent sites £5-7), 2½ miles (4km) from the ferry, overlooks the beach at Tresta and has great facilities. Nearby is the friendly **Gord** (☎ 733227; Gord, Houbie; r per person £25; 3-course dinner £12) the two twin rooms and one double room available here, have private bathrooms .

The shop/café in Houbie serves home-made food, including lemon chicken pie and pasta dishes.

Regular ferries (single £1.40, car and driver £3.30, 25 minutes) from Oddsta in the island's northwest connect with Gutcher on Yell and Belmont on Unst.

ORKNEY & SHETLAND ISLANDS

Directory

CONTENTS

ACCOMMODATION

For a peaceful night's slumber, Scotland provides a comprehensive choice of accommodation to suit all visitors. For budget travel (£5 to £20 per person per night), the three options are camping grounds, hostels and cheap bed & breakfasts (B&Bs). Mid-range travellers will find a plethora of comfortable B&Bs and guesthouses (£20 to £50). For top-end lodgings (£50-plus) there are some superb hotels, the most interesting being converted castles and mansions. Almost all B&Bs, guesthouses and hotels provide breakfast in the morning.

Prices tend to increase over the peak tourist season (June to mid-September). Outside of these months, and particularly over winter, special deals are often available at guesthouses and hotels. Note that smaller establishments will often close from around November to March, particularly in more remote areas.

Tourist Information Centres (TICs) have an accommodation booking service (£2 to £3, local and national), which can be handy over summer. We have listed hundreds of accommodation options throughout the book, but if you're stuck, try the **Scottish Tourist Board** (STB; www.visitscotland.com/accommodation) for assistance in booking accommodation across the country.

B&Bs & Guesthouses

B&Bs are a Scottish institution. At the bottom end you get a bedroom in a private house, a shared bathroom and a fry-up (consisting of juice, coffee or tea, cereal and cooked breakfast – bacon, eggs, sausage, baked beans and toast). Mid-range B&Bs have en suite bathrooms, TVs in each room and more variety (and healthier options) for breakfast. Almost all B&Bs provide hospitality trays (tea- and coffee-making facilities) in bedrooms. An excellent option are farm B&Bs which offer traditional Scottish hospitality, enormous breakfasts and a quiet rural setting – good for discharging urban grit. Pubs may also offer cheap (and sometimes noisy) B&B and can be good fun.

Guesthouses, often large converted private houses, are an extension of the B&B concept. They are normally more upmarket than B&Bs, offering quality food and more luxurious accommodation.

Camping & Caravan Parks

Free 'wild' camping should become a legal right under the newly passed Land Reform Bill. However, campers are obligated to camp on unenclosed land, in small numbers away from buildings and roads (see the boxed text on p404).

Commercial camping grounds are geared to caravans and vary widely in quality. A tent site costs from £4 to £12. If you plan to use a tent regularly, invest in *Scotland: Caravan & Camping* (£4.99), available from most TICs.

Homestays

A convenient and increasingly popular holiday option is to join an international house-exchange organisation. You sign up for a year and place your home on a website giving details of what you're looking for, where and for how long. You organise the house-swap yourself with people in other countries and arrange to swap homes, rent free, for an agreed holiday period. Shop around, as registration can cost from £30 to £100 depending on the organisation. Check out **Home Base Holidays** (www.homebase-hols.com) and **Home Link International** (www.homelink.org.uk).

Hostels

If you're travelling on a budget, the numerous hostels offer cheap accommodation and are great centres for meeting fellow travellers. Hostels have facilities for self-catering and many provide Internet access and arrange activities and tours.

From May to September and on public holidays, hostels can be booked out, sometimes by large groups, so phone in advance.

SCOTTISH YOUTH HOSTEL ASSOCIATION

The **SYHA** (☎ 08701 553255; reservations@syha.org.uk; www.syha.org.uk; 7 Glebe Cres, Stirling FK8 2JA) has a network of decent, reasonably priced hostels and produces a free booklet listing details of more than 70. The booklet is available from SYHA hostels and TICs. Average prices are about £11/8 for adults/children, but increase in summer.

INDEPENDENT & STUDENT HOSTELS

There are a large number of independent hostels, most with prices around £10 to £15. As they are independent, facilities vary considerably, but because they are aimed at young backpackers they can be great places to party. The free *Independent Backpackers Hostels Scotland* guide (www.hostel-scotland.co.uk), available from TICs, lists over 100 hostels in Scotland.

Hotels

Hotels normally service the top end of the scale and there are some wonderfully luxurious places, including country-house hotels in fabulous settings, and castles complete with crenellated battlements, grand staircases and the obligatory rows of stags' heads. You can expect all the perks at these places, often including, a gym, sauna, swimming pool and first-class service.

Rental Accommodation

Self-catering accommodation is very popular in Scotland. The minimum stay is usually one week in the summer peak season, three days or less at other times. Details are in the accommodation guides available from regional TICs. Alternatively, buy a copy of the STB's *Scotland: Self-Catering* (£5.99). Expect a week's rent for a two-bedroom cottage to cost from £150 in winter, £175 April to June, and £250 July to September. Places in the city range from £175 to over £700 per week.

The following are good places to start your search:

CKD Galbraith (☎ 0131-556 4422; www.ckdgalbraith.co.uk; 17 Dublin St, Edinburgh EH1 3PG) Offers a wide range of self-catering accommodation, from cottages to castles.

Highland Hideaways (☎ 01631-562056; www.highlandhideaways.co.uk; Alliance House, 1 George St, Oban, Argyll, PA34 5RU) Specialising in self-catering properties in Argyll, the west Highlands and the southern islands of the Hebrides.

Landmark Trust (☎ 01628-825925; www.landmarktrust.co.uk; Shottesbrooke, Maidenhead, Berkshire SL6 3SW, England) A building-preservation charity that restores historic buildings and lets them out as accommodation.

Something Different

Scotland offers a surprising diversity of accommodation and it's possible to bunk down on a cruise around the Hebrides (a good way to see remote St Kilda) or the Caledonian Canal; in converted churches (spooky!); in a blackhouse (primitive 19th-century living); and in an art gallery, wigwam or lighthouse. Information on specific establishments is littered throughout this guide and can also be found on the STB website listed earlier.

Simple alternative accommodation can be found at *bothies* – simple shelters, often in remote places. They are not locked, there's no charge, and you can't book. A camping barn (*böd* in Shetland) – usually a converted farm building – is where walkers can stay for around £5 per night. Take your own cooking equipment, sleeping bag and mat if you plan to stay at *bothies* or *böds*.

University Accommodation

Many Scottish universities offer their student accommodation to visitors during the holidays. Most rooms are comfortable, functional, single bedrooms, some with shared bathroom, but there are also twin and family units, self-contained flats and shared houses. Full-board, half-board, B&B and self-catering options are often available. Rooms are usually let-out late June to late September. B&B costs around £20 to £25 per person. Details are provided throughout the regional chapters.

ACTIVITIES

Scotland is a brilliant place for outdoor recreation and has something to offer everyone, from adrenalin junkies to those who prefer a short stroll after breakfast. Although walking and cycling are the most popular, there are an astonishing variety of activities available.

Most activities are well organised and have clubs and associations that can give visitors invaluable information and, sometimes, substantial discounts. The **Scottish Tourist Board** (STB; www.visitscotland.com) and **British Tourist Authority** (BTA; www.visitbritain.com) have brochures on most activities.

Detailed information can be found in the regional chapters throughout this guide.

Bird-Watching

Scotland is a bird-watcher's paradise. There are over 80 ornithologically important nature reserves managed by **Scottish Natural Heritage** (SNH; www.snh.org.uk), the **Royal Society for the Protection of Birds** (RSPB; www.rspb.org.uk) and the **Scottish Wildlife Trust** (SWT; www.swt.org.uk). Further information can be obtained from the **Scottish Ornithologists Club** (☎ 0131-653 0653; www.the-soc.org.uk; Harbour Point, Newhailes Rd, Musselburgh, Edinburgh EH21 6SJ).

Canal Boating

Canal boating can be a relaxing, scenic way to travel (on a wide, lazy section of waterway) or very hard work (on a steep section of canal).

The Forth and Clyde Canal runs 35 miles (56km) between Grangemouth in the east

PRACTICALITIES

■ Leaf through Edinburgh's *Scotsman* newspaper or Glasgow's *Herald*, the oldest daily in the English-speaking world.

■ Have a giggle at the popular Labour tabloid, the *Daily Record*, or try the *Sunday Post* for rose-tinted nostalgia.

■ Watch and listen to the national advertising-free BBC TV and radio networks.

■ BBC Radio Scotland (AM 810kHz, FM 92.4-94.7MHz) provides a Scottish point of view.

■ Zone out in front of the box to BBC1 and BBC2 and three commercial channels (ITV1, Channel Four and Channel Five). Scottish Television and Grampian TV give a Scottish perspective.

■ Buy or watch videos on the PAL system.

■ Plug into a square three-pin adapter (different from the Australian three-pin) before plugging into the electricity supply (240V, 50Hz AC).

■ Use the metric system for weights and measures, with the exception of road distances (in miles) and beer (in pints).

and Bowling near Dumbarton in the west. The 31-mile (50km) Union Canal joins central Edinburgh with Falkirk. These canals are linked by means of the mighty Falkirk Wheel (see boxed text p192).

The 60-mile (97km) Caledonian Canal, which slices through the Great Glen from Fort William to Inverness, has a mixture of canal reaches, open lochs and stunning scenery, making it fully geared to boating holidays. The main operator here is **Caley Cruisers** (☎ 01463-236328; www.caleycruisers.com; Canal Rd, Inverness IV3 8NF), which has a fleet of 40 motor cruisers ranging from two to eight berths available for hire from March to October.

Scotland's canals are owned and operated by the **British Waterways Board** (☎ 0141-332 6936; www.scottishcanals.co.uk; Canal House, 1 Applecross St, Glasgow G4 9SP), which publishes the free *Skippers' Guides* to all the canals (available online). It also publishes a list of boat-hire and canal-holiday companies.

Cycling

Travelling by bicycle is an excellent way to explore Scotland; May to October is the best time of year to do so. There are forest trails and dedicated cycle routes along canal towpaths and disused railway tracks. Depending on your energy and enthusiasm you can take a leisurely trip through idyllic farm country along peaceful country lanes, stopping at the numerous pubs along the way, or thrash about all day up steep slopes, freewheeling down the other side. Cyclists in search of the wild and remote will enjoy northwestern Scotland. Its majestic Highlands and mystical islands offer quiet pedalling through breathtaking mountainscapes. The beautiful forests, lochs, glens and hills in the central and southern areas of Scotland are more easily accessible and have an intimate charm. The gentle undulating countryside in the beautiful Borders Region (p135) is excellent cycling country.

The STB publishes a useful free booklet, *Cycle Scotland*. Many regional TICs have information on local cycling routes and places to hire bikes. They also stock cycling guides and books.

For up-to-date, detailed information on Scotland's cycle-route network contact **Sustrans** (☎ 0117-929 0888, 0131-624 7660; www.sustrans.org.uk; 162 Fountainbridge, Edinburgh EH3 9RX).

Cyclists' Touring Club (CTC; ☎ 0870 873 0060; www.ctc.org.uk; Cotterell House, 69 Meadrow, Godalming, Surrey GU7 3HS) is a membership organisation offering comprehensive information about cycling in Britain.

Fishing

Fishing – coarse, sea and game – is enormously popular in Scotland, whose waters are filled with salmon, trout (sea, brown and rainbow), pike, arctic char and many other species. Fly-fishing, in particular is a joy in Scotland's many lochs and rivers – it's a tricky but very rewarding form of fishing, closer to an art form than a sport.

For wild brown trout the close season is early October to mid-March. The close season for salmon and sea trout varies between districts; it's generally from early November to early February.

Fishing rights to most waters are privately owned and you must obtain a permit – these are often readily available at the local fishing tackle shop or hotel. Permits cost from around £15 per day but some salmon rivers – notably the Tweed, the Tay and the Spey – can be much more expensive.

There are numerous fish farms with stocked ponds where you can hire equipment and get a couple of lessons; they're particularly good for kids. One example is the Drummond Trout Farm & Fishery, p209.

The STB booklet *Fish Scotland* is a good introduction and is stocked by TICs. Other organisations that can help include the following:

Scottish Anglers National Association (☎ 01577-861116; www.sana.org.uk; The National Game Angling Academy, The Pier, Loch Leven, Kinross, KY13 8UF)

Scottish Federation of Sea Anglers (☎ 01592-657520; Unit 28, Evans Business Centre, Michelson Dve, Kirkcaldy KY1 3NB)

Golf

Scotland is the home of golf. The game has been played in Scotland for centuries and there are more courses per capita in Scotland than in any other country. Most clubs are open to visitors.

St Andrews is the headquarters of the game's governing body, the Royal and Ancient Golf Club, and the location of the world's most famous golf course, the Old Course (see boxed text p197). There are major courses around the country including at Troon (p162) and Turnberry (p162).

Official Guide to Golf in Scotland is a free magazine listing course details, costs and clubs with details of where to stay. The STB has a website dedicated to golf (www.visitscotland.com/golf/); there's a course directory and you can book online. Some regions offer a Golf Pass, costing between £50 and £90 for five days (Monday to Friday), which allows play on a range of courses.

Hang Gliding & Paragliding

There's a relatively small but growing hang gliding and paragliding scene in Scotland. The Highlands offer many impressive flying spots, complete with stunning scenery. For information and details on clubs and training schools contact the **British Hang Gliding & Paragliding Association** (www.bhpa.co.uk).

Hiking

Scotland's wild, dramatic scenery and variation in landscape has made hiking

ACCESS & THE LAW

Access to the countryside has been a thorny issue in Scotland for many years. In Victorian times, belligerent landowners attempted to prevent walkers from using well-established trails and moves to counter this led to successful litigation for the walkers and the formation of what later became the Scottish Rights of Way Society.

In January 2003, the Scottish Parliament formalised access to the countryside and passed the Land Reform (Scotland) Bill, creating statutory rights of access to land in Scotland for the first time. More information on this new legislation and on the **Scottish Rights of Way & Access Society** can be found at www.scotways.co.uk.

a thriving pastime for locals and tourists alike. There really is something for everyone, from after-breakfast strolls to the popular sport of Munro bagging (p405).

For mountain hikes, the best time is usually May to September. Winter walking in the higher areas of Scotland is 'technical' – requiring, at the very least, an ice axe, crampons and mountaineering experience.

Highland hikers should be properly equipped, and cautious, as the weather can become vicious at any time of year. After rain, peaty soil can become boggy; always wear stout shoes and carry a change of clothing.

There is a tradition of relatively free access to open country, especially on mountains and moorlands. You should, however, avoid areas where you might disrupt or disturb wildlife, lambing (generally mid-April to the end of May), or deer stalking and grouse shooting (mainly from 12 August to the third week in October).

Rights of way exist but local authorities aren't required to list and map them so they're not shown on Ordnance Survey (OS) maps. However, in its guide, *Scottish Hill Tracks*, the Scottish Rights of Way & Access Society (SRWS) publicises those routes. Access is free at all times to areas owned by the National Trust for Scotland (NTS) and to most owned by the Forestry Commission.

Some long distance routes:
Southern Upland Way (p135) 212 miles (341km); remote hills and moorlands; nine to 14 days; medium to hard

West Highland Way (p253) 95 miles (153km); spectacular scenery, mountains and lochs; six to eight days; medium
Speyside Way (p248) 84 miles (135km); follows river, whisky distilleries; five days; easy to medium
Great Glen Way (p298) 73 miles (117km); Loch Ness, canal paths, forest tracks; four days; easy
Fife Coastal Path (p178) 78 miles (126km); Firth of Forth, undulating country; five to six days; easy
St Cuthbert's Way (p135) 62 miles (100km); follows life of famous saint, six to seven days; medium
The Pilgrims Way (p135) 25 miles (40km); Machars peninsula, standing stones, burial mounds; two to three days; easy

INFORMATION

Every TIC has details (free or for a nominal charge) of suggested walks that take in local points of interest. Lonely Planet's *Walking in Scotland* is a comprehensive resource, covering short walks and long-distance paths. Its *Walking in Britain* covers Scottish walks too. For general advice, the STB produces a *Walking Scotland* brochure, describing numerous routes in various parts of the country, plus safety tips and other information.

Other useful sources:
Mountaineering Council of Scotland (☎ 01738-638227; www.mountaineering-scotland.org.uk; The Old Granary, West Mill St, Perth PH1 5QP)
Ramblers' Association Scotland (☎ 01577-861222; www.ramblers.org.uk/scotland; Kingfisher House, Auld Mart Business Park, Milnathort, Kinross KY13 9DA)
Scottish Rights of Way & Access Society (☎ 0131-558 1222; www.scotways.co.uk; 24 Annandale St, Edinburgh EH7 4AN)

Horse Riding & Pony Trekking

Seeing the country from the saddle is highly recommended, even if you're not an experienced rider. There are riding schools catering to all levels of proficiency throughout the country.

For more information:
British Horse Society (☎ 08701-202244; www.bhs.org.uk; British Equestrian Centre, Stoneleigh Park, Kenilworth, Warwickshire CV8 2XZ)
Trekking & Riding Society of Scotland (☎ 01821-650210; www.ridinginscotland.com; Steadingfield, Wolfhill, Perthshire PH2 6DA)

Rock Climbing

Scotland has a long history of rock climbing and mountaineering. The country's main rock-climbing areas include Ben Nevis

MUNROS & THE ANCIENT ART OF MUNRO BAGGING

At the end of the 19th century, an eager hill walker, Sir Hugh Munro, published a list of 545 Scottish mountains measuring over 3000ft (914m) – a height at which he believed they gained a special significance. Of these summits he classified 277 as mountains in their own right (new surveys have since revised this to a total of 284), the rest being satellites of lesser consequence (known as 'tops'). Sir Hugh couldn't have realised that his name would one day be used to describe any main mountain over the magical 3000ft mark; it is now the object (for some obsession) of many eager walkers to reach the summit (or bag) as many Munros as possible.

This peculiar practice of Munro bagging must have started soon after the list was published because by 1901 Reverend AE Robertson had bagged the lot. Between 1901 and 1981, only 250 people bagged all the Munros, but by 2003 the number of officially declared Munroists was over 2600. To the uninitiated it may seem strange that Munro baggers see a day (or longer) plodding around in mist, cloud and driving rain to the point of exhaustion as time well spent. However, for those who can add one or more ticks to their list, the vagaries of the weather are part of the enjoyment – at least in retrospect. Munro bagging is, of course, more than merely ticking names on a list. It takes you to some of the wildest, most beautiful parts of Scotland.

Once you've bagged the Munros you can move onto the Corbetts – hills over 2500ft (700m), with a drop of at least 500ft (150m) on all sides – and the Donalds, lowland hills over 2000ft (610m).

(p316), with routes up to 400m in length, Glen Coe (p309), the Cairngorms (p305), the Cuillins of Skye (p349), Arrochar (p255) and the Isle of Arran (see p154), but there are hundreds of smaller crags all over the country. One unusual feature of Scotland's rock-climbing scene is the sea stacks around the coast, most famously the 140m-high Old Man of Hoy (p382).

Rock Climbing in Scotland, by Kevin Howett, and the Scottish Mountaineering Club's regional *Rock & Ice Climbs* guides are excellent references.

More information:

Mountaineering Council of Scotland (☎ 01738-638227; www.mountaineering-scotland.org.uk; The Old Granary, West Mill St, Perth PH1 5QP)

Scottish Mountaineering Club (www.smc.org.uk)

Skiing & Snowboarding

There are five ski centres in Scotland, offering downhill and cross-country skiing and snowboarding.

Glenshee (p215; ☎ 013397-41320; www.ski-glenshee.co.uk) 920m; on the A93 road between Perth and Braemar; offers the largest network of lifts and widest range of runs in Scotland

Cairngorm Mountain (p302; ☎ 01479-861261; www.cairngormmountain.com) 1097m; has almost 30 runs spread over an extensive area

Glencoe (p309; ☎ 01855-851226; www.ski-glencoe.co.uk) 1108m; has only five tows and two chairlifts

Nevis Range (p315; ☎ 01397-705825; www.nevis-range.co.uk) 1221m; near Fort William; offers the highest

ski runs, the grandest setting, and some of the best off-piste potential in Scotland

Lecht (p242; ☎ 01975-651440; www.lecht.co.uk) 793m; the smallest and most remote centre, on the A939 between Ballater and Grantown-on-Spey

Each ski centre has its own website and contact number for snow reports and general information. There's an answerphone service for calls outside business hours.

The high season is from January to April but it's sometimes possible to ski from as early as November to as late as May. It's easy to turn up at the slopes, hire some kit, buy a day pass and off you go.

The STB's *Ski Scotland* is useful and has an accommodation list. General information can be obtained from **Snowsport Scotland** (☎ 0131-445 4151; www.snsc.demon.co.uk; Hillend, Biggar Rd, Edinburgh EH10 7EF).

For the weather-report service phone the **Ski Hotline** (☎ 09001-654, followed by 654 for all centres). Alternatively you can check the **STB website** (www.ski.visitscotland.com).

Water Sports

CANOEING

Scotland, with its islands, sea lochs and indented coastline, is ideal for sea-kayaking, while its inland lochs and Highland rivers are great for both Canadian and white-water canoeing.

For information contact the **Scottish Canoe Association** (☎ 0131-317 7314; www.scot-canoe.org;

Caledonia House, South Gyle, Edinburgh EH12 9DQ). It publishes coastal navigation sheets as well as organising tours, including introductory ones for beginners.

DIVING
It may lack coral reefs and warm, limpid waters but Scotland offers some of the most spectacular and challenging scuba diving in Europe, if not the world. The sea bed around St Abbs (p140) is Scotland's first voluntary marine nature reserve.

There are also hundreds of fascinating shipwrecks, the most famous of which lie on the bed of Scapa Flow in the Orkney Islands (p379).

For more information contact the **Scottish Sub Aqua Club** (☎ 0141-425 1021; www.scotsac.com; The Cockburn Centre, 40 Bogmoor Place, Glasgow G51 4TQ).

SURFING
You definitely have to be hardy, or equipped with a wetsuit, to do anything more than take a quick dip around Scotland's coast. However, there is some truly magnificent coastline, beautiful sandy beaches and some of the best surfing breaks in Europe.

The tidal range is large, which means there is often a completely different set of breaks at low and high tides. It's the north and west coasts, particularly around Thurso (p335) and in the Outer Hebrides (p359) that have outstanding world-class possibilities. Lewis has the best and most consistent surf in Britain, with around 120 recorded breaks and waves up to 5m. For more information contact **Hebridean Surf** (☎ /fax 01851-705862; www.hebrideansurf.co.uk; 28 Francis St, Stornoway, Lewis HS1 2ND).

BUSINESS HOURS
Shops open at least 9am to 5pm Monday to Friday, and most open Saturday too. An increasing number of shops also open Sunday, typically from 10am to 4pm. Even in small towns, supermarkets stay open until 8pm daily and a few city supermarkets are open 24 hours. In country towns, some shops have an early-closing day – usually Tuesday, Wednesday or Thursday afternoon.

Approximate standard opening hours are as follows:

Banks 9.30am-4pm Mon-Fri, some 9.30am-12.30pm Sat.
Cafes 11am-5pm; if licensed they may stay open for dinner.
Post offices 9am-5.30pm Mon-Fri, 9am-12.30pm Sat.
Pubs: 11am-11pm (some places up to midnight or 1am) Mon-Sat; 12.30-11pm Sun; noon-2pm (lunch), 6-9pm (dinner) daily.
Restaurants: 11am-3pm lunch, 6-9pm or 10pm dinner; in small towns and villages the *chippy* (fish and chip shop) is often the only place to buy food after 8pm.

CHILDREN
It's well worth asking in TICs for local family-based publications. For those going to Orkney, pick up a copy of the excellent *Child Friendly Orkney* book (free) from Kirkwall TIC, which is jam-packed full of activities, sightseeing and accommodation suggestions.

Children are generally well-received around Scotland, particularly in more traditional areas of the country such as the Highlands and islands. A lot of pubs are family-friendly these days and some have great beer gardens where the kids can run around and exhaust themselves while you have a quiet pint. Children under a certain age can often stay free with their parents in hotels, but be prepared for hotels and B&Bs that won't accept children; call ahead to get the lowdown. More hotels and guesthouses these days provide child-friendly facilities including cots. Many restaurants (especially the larger ones) have highchairs available. Nappy-changing facilities can be found in shopping centres.

The larger car hire companies can provide safety seats for children – ask when booking your car. Note that attitudes towards breast-feeding in public are generally a little conservative.

See Edinburgh for Children, p76, and Glasgow for Children, p117, for more information.

See also Lonely Planet's *Travel with Children*, by Cathy Lanigan, and check out the website at www.kids-scotland.co.uk.

CLIMATE CHARTS
'Variable' is a vague but appropriate way to describe the many moods of Scotland's cool, temperate climate. Considering how far north the country lies you might expect a colder climate, but the winds from the Atlantic are warmed by the Gulf Stream. The following climate charts give an indication of temperature and rainfall around the country.

See also the When to Go section, p13, in the Getting Started chapter.

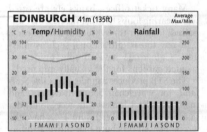

EDINBURGH 41m (135ft)

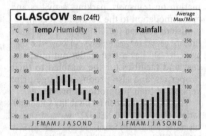

GLASGOW 8m (24ft)

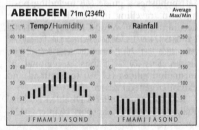

ABERDEEN 71m (234ft)

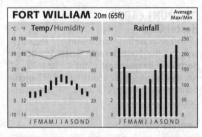

FORT WILLIAM 20m (65ft)

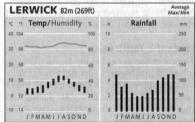

LERWICK 82m (269ft)

COURSES

With the remarkable revival of Scottish Gaelic since the 1980s, a number of courses on the language and culture are available:

Cothrom na Fèinne (☎ 01599-566240; Balmacara Mains, Kyle IV40 8DN) Residential language courses take place during the first week of the month, May to October. Individually tailored weekends are available November to April; courses start at £200.

Royal Scottish Country Dance Society (RSCDS; ☎ 0131-225 3854; www.rscds.org) In July and August, this society holds a summer school in St Andrews. Course fees begin at £107 for a week.

Sabhal Mór Ostaig (☎ 01471-888000; www.smo.uhi.ac.uk; Sleat, Isle of Skye IV44 8RQ) Offers courses in Gaelic language, song, piping and the fiddle. Courses from £125 per week plus accommodation.

CUSTOMS

Travellers arriving in the UK from other EU countries don't have to pay tax or duty on goods for personal use. The maximum amounts of tobacco and alcohol that each person can bring into the country duty-free are 3200 cigarettes, 400 cigarillos, 200 cigars, 3kg of smoking tobacco, 10L of spirits, 20L of fortified wine (eg, port or sherry), 90L of wine and 110L of beer. People under the age of 17 are not allowed to import any alcohol or tobacco.

Travellers from outside the EU can bring in, duty-free, a maximum of 200 cigarettes *or* 100 cigarillos *or* 50 cigars *or* 250g of tobacco; 2L of still table wine; 1L of spirits *or* 2L of fortified wine, sparkling wine or liqueurs; 60mL of perfume; and £145 worth of all other goods, including gifts and souvenirs. Anything over this limit must be declared to customs officers on arrival.

For details of restrictions and quarantine regulations, see the website **HM Customs and Excise** (www.hmce.gov.uk).

DANGERS & ANNOYANCES
Crime

Scotland has the usual big-city crimes (often alcohol and/or drug related), mainly in Edinburgh and Glasgow, so normal caution is advised. Don't wander around unlit city streets at night, and always be aware of who is around you late at night anywhere on the streets. Pickpockets and bag snatchers operate in crowded public places, although this isn't a common problem.

Never leave valuables in a car, and remove all luggage overnight. Report thefts to the police and ask for a statement, or your travel insurance won't pay out; bear in mind that thefts from cars may be excluded.

Midges & Clegs

The most painful problems facing visitors to the Highlands and islands are midges and clegs. The midge is a tiny, 2mm-long blood-sucking fly that is related to the mosquito. Midges are at their worst during the twilight hours, and on still, overcast days. They proliferate from late May to mid-September, but especially mid-June to mid-August – which unfortunately coincides with the main tourist season. Cover yourself up, particularly in the evening, wear light-coloured clothing (midges are attracted to dark colours) and, most importantly, use a reliable insect repellent containing DEET or DMP.

The cleg, or horse fly, is about 13mm (half an inch) in length and slate grey in colour. A master of stealth, it loves to land unnoticed on neck or ankle, and can give a painful bite. It can even bite through hair or light clothing. Unlike midges, they are most active on warm, sunny days, and are most common in July and August.

Military Jets

One of the most annoying and frightening aspects of touring the Highlands is the sudden appearance and sound of military jets. It's something you never get used to.

DISABLED TRAVELLERS

For many disabled travellers, Scotland is a strange mix of user-friendliness and unfriendliness. Most new buildings are accessible to wheelchair users, so large, new hotels and modern tourist attractions are usually fine. However, most B&Bs and guesthouses are in hard-to-adapt older buildings. This means that travellers with mobility problems may pay more for accommodation than their more able-bodied fellows.

It's a similar story with public transport. Newer buses sometimes have steps that lower for easier access, as do trains, but it's always wise to check before setting out. Tourist attractions sometimes reserve parking spaces near the entrance for disabled drivers.

Many ticket offices, banks etc are fitted with hearing loops to assist the hearing-impaired; look for the symbol of a large ear.

A few tourist attractions, such as Glasgow Cathedral, have Braille guides or scented gardens for the visually impaired.

The STB produces a guide, *Accessible Scotland*, for wheelchair-bound travellers, and many TICs have leaflets with accessibility details for their area. Perthshire TICs have the *Access For All* brochure that provides information on transport, parking, activities and accommodation in the Perthshire region.

Historic Scotland (☎ 0131 668 8600; www.historic -scotland.gov.uk; Longmore House, Salisbury Place Edinburgh EH9 1SH) has a free leaflet outlining access and facilities for the disabled to their properties, and also produces a large-print version of their promotional brochure.

The **Royal Association for Disability & Rehabilitation** (RADAR: ☎ 020-7250 3222; www.radar.org.uk; Information Dept, 12 City Forum, 250 City Rd, London EC1V 8AF) publishes a guide (£8 including postage) on travelling in the UK and has an accommodation website. **Holiday Care Service** (☎ 0845 124 9971; www.holidaycare.org.uk; Holiday Care Information Unit, 7th fl Sunley House, 4 Bedford Park, Croydon, Surrey CR0 2AP) publishes regional information guides (£7.50) to Scotland and can offer general advice.

Rail companies offer a Disabled Persons' Railcard (see the Transport chapter, p422, for more details).

DISCOUNT CARDS
Hostel Card

If you're travelling on a budget, membership of the **Scottish Youth Hostel Association/ Hostelling International** (SYHA/HI; ☎ 01786 891 400; www.syha.org.uk) is a must (annual membership over/under 18 £6/2.50, life membership £60).

Seniors Cards

Discount cards for over 60s are available for rail and bus travel (see the Transport chapter, p422, for details).

Student & Youth Cards

The most useful card is the plastic ID-style International Student Identity Card (ISIC), which displays your photograph. This can perform wonders, including producing discounts on entry to attractions and on many forms of transport.

There's a worldwide industry in fake student cards, and many places now stipulate a maximum age for student discounts or, more simply, substitute a 'youth discount' for a 'student discount'. If you're aged under 26 but not a student, you can apply for the Euro/26 card, which goes by various names in different countries, or an International Youth Travel Card (IYTC) issued by the ISTC. These cards are available through student unions, hostelling organisations or youth-oriented travel agencies.

EMBASSIES & CONSULATES
Scottish/UK Embassies & High Commissions
Australia (High Commission; ☎ 02-6270 6666; www.britaus
.net) Commonwealth Ave, Yarralumla, Canberra, ACT 2600
Canada (High Commission; ☎ 613-237 1530; www
.britainincanada.org) 80 Elgin St, Ottawa, Ontario K1P 5K7
France (Embassy; ☎ 01 44 51 31 00; www.amb-grande
bretagne.fr) 35 rue du Faubourg St Honoré, 75383 Paris
Germany (Embassy; ☎ 030-20457 0; www.britischebots
chaft.de) Wilhelmstrasse 70, 10117 Berlin
Ireland (Embassy; ☎ 01 205 3700; www.british
embassy.ie) 29 Merrion Rd, Ballsbridge, Dublin 4
Japan (Embassy; ☎ 03-5211 1100; www.uknow.or.jp)
1 Ichiban-cho, Chiyoda-ku, Tokyo 102-8381
Netherlands (Embassy; ☎ 0 70 4270 427;
www.britain.nl) Lange Voorhout 10, 2514 ED, The Hague
New Zealand (High Commission; ☎ 04 924 2888;
www.britain.org.nz) 44 Hill St, Wellington 1
South Africa (High Commission; ☎ 012 483 1200;
www.britain.org.za) 255 Hill St, Arcadia, 0002 Pretoria
USA (Embassy; ☎ 202-588 6500) 3100 Massachusetts
Ave NW, Washington DC 20008

Consulates in Scotland
Most foreign diplomatic missions are in London, but some countries also have consulates in or near Edinburgh:
Australia (☎ 0131-624 3333) 69 George St, EH2 2JG;
passport applications and document witnessing only; for
emergencies contact the Australian High Commission in
London (☎ 020-7887 5335)
Canada (☎ 0131-220 4333) Standard Life House, 30
Lothian Rd, EH1 2DH
Denmark (☎ 0131-337 6352) 215 Balgreen Rd, EH11 2RZ
France (☎ 0131-225 7954) 11 Randolph Cres, EH3 7TT
Germany (☎ 0131-337 2323) 16 Eglinton Cres, EH12 5DG
Ireland (☎ 0131-226 7711) 16 Randolph Cres, EH3 7TT
Japan (☎ 0131-225 4777) 2 Melville Cres, EH3 7HW
Netherlands (☎ 0131-220 3226) Thistle Court, 1-2
Thistle St, EH2 2HT
USA (☎ 0131-556 8315) 3 Regent Terrace, EH7 5BW

Eight countries have consulates in Lerwick, Shetland Islands: **Denmark**, **Iceland**, **Netherlands** and **Sweden** (☎ 01595-692533; Hay & Co; 66 Commercial Rd) and **Finland**, **France**, **Germany** and **Norway** (☎ 01595-692556; Shearer Shipping Services, off Commercial Rd).

FESTIVALS & EVENTS
Countless diverse events are held around the country all year. Even small villages have weekly markets, and many still enact traditional customs and ceremonies, some dating back hundreds of years.

The STB publishes a comprehensive list, *Events in Scotland*, twice a year.

The **Traditional Music & Song Association** (☎ 0131-667 5587, fax 662 915; www.tmsa.info) publishes an excellent annual listing of music, dance and cultural festivals around Scotland.

See also Festivals & Events in the Edinburgh chapter (p78).

JANUARY
Celtic Connections (☎ 353 8000; www.grch.com)
Based in Glasgow, a celebration of Celtic music and culture.
Hogmanay Celebrations to greet the New Year, including
a huge street party in Edinburgh.
The Ba' A seething swell of islanders and tourists take
part in this boisterous and chaotic ball game, New Year's
Day, Kirkwall, Orkney.
Up Helly Aa Re-enactment of a Viking fire festival (think
Asterix), last Tuesday in January, Shetland.
Burns Night Suppers all over the country celebrating
Robbie Burns, 25 January.

MARCH
Whuppity Scourie Chasing away the winter blues in Lanark.

APRIL
Rugby Sevens Seven-a-side rugby tournament, the Borders.

MAY
Beltane Fire Festival An incredibly popular, wild and
wacky pagan fire festival in Edinburgh, celebrating the end
of winter.
Spirit of Speyside Whisky Festival (www.spiritof
speyside.com) Four days of distillery tours, whisky-tasting,
food, art and outdoor activities.
Orkney Folk Festival (www.orkneyfolkfestival.com)
Concerts, ceilidhs, impromptu music sessions, workshops.

JUNE TO AUGUST
Highland Festival (www.highland-festival.co.uk)
Celebrating the magic of the Highlands.

Riding of the Marches Horse riding, with parades, brass bands etc, commemorating conflict with England, various towns in the Borders.

St Magnus Festival (www.stmagnusfestival.com) A midsummer celebration of the arts; music, literature, visual arts, Orkney.

T in the Park (www.tinthepark.com) Music festival in the footsteps of Glastonbury, held over a weekend, Kinross.

Edinburgh International and Fringe Festivals (www.eif.co.uk, www.edfringe.com) Premier international arts festivals, running for three weeks mid-August to early September.

SEPTEMBER
Braemar Gathering Kilts, cabers and bagpipes, attended by the Queen, Braemar; other games held all over Scotland, June to September

OCTOBER
Royal National Mod (www.the-mod.co.uk) Gaelic music festival competition, in various locations

FOOD
In the larger towns and cities we have ordered places to eat in this guide by neighbourhood, then price (budget up to £6, mid-range £6-20, top-end above £20), and then by the author's favourite choices in each category. In all other places, listings are by price and then by author choice. See p406 for restaurant opening hours, and the Food & Drink chapter (p50) for information about tucking into Scottish cuisine.

GAY & LESBIAN TRAVELLERS
Although many Scots are fairly tolerant of homosexuality, overt displays of affection aren't wise if conducted away from acknowledged 'gay' venues or districts – hostility may be encountered. The age of homosexual consent is 16.

Edinburgh and Glasgow have small but flourishing gay scenes. The website at www.gayscotland.com and the monthly magazine *Scotsgay* (www.scotsgay.com) keep gays, lesbians and bisexuals informed about gay-scene issues. Also check out *Gay Scotland* magazine (www.outright-scotland.org.uk/gs). Another good information source is the **GLGBT Centre** (☎ 0141-221 7203; www.glgbt.org.uk; 11 Dixon St, Glasgow); otherwise, contact the **Gay & Lesbian Switchboard** (☎ 0131-556-8997; info@lgls.org). See also the respective Gay & Lesbian boxed texts in the Glasgow and Edinburgh chapters.

HOLIDAYS
Public Holidays
Although bank holidays are general public holidays in the rest of the UK, in Scotland they only apply to banks and some other commercial offices. Bank holidays occur at the start of January, the first weekend in March, the first and last weekend in May, the first weekend in August and Christmas Day and Boxing Day.

Christmas Day, New Year's Day and 2 January, Good Friday and Easter Monday are also general public holidays. Scottish towns normally have their own spring and autumn holiday; dates vary from year to year and from town to town.

School Holidays
School holidays (two weeks over Easter, early July to late August, one week in October and two or three weeks over Christmas) are always a busy time, particularly in summer when families often go on their annual break to the countryside. As this time coincides with peak tourist season, accommodation is harder to come by and it's often worth booking ahead.

INSURANCE
This not only covers you for medical expenses, theft or loss, but also for cancellation of, or delays in, any of your travel arrangements. There's a variety of policies and your travel agent can provide recommendations. The international student travel policies handled by STA Travel and other reputable student travel organisations are usually good value.

Make sure the policy includes health care and medication in the countries you may visit on your way to/from Scotland. See also Insurance in the Health chapter (p424).

Always read the small print carefully. Some policies specifically exclude 'dangerous activities' such as scuba diving, motorcycling, skiing, mountaineering and even trekking.

You may prefer a policy that pays doctors or hospitals directly rather than forcing you to pay on the spot and claim the money back later. If you have to claim later, make sure you keep all documentation. Some policies ask you to call back (reverse charges) to a centre in your home country where an immediate assessment of your problem is made.

Not all policies cover ambulances, helicopter rescue or emergency flights home. Most policies exclude cover for pre-existing illnesses.

INTERNET ACCESS

Connecting to the Internet using your laptop is not easy in Scotland and may be expensive - see the website www.teleadapt.com for more information. You'll need a universal AC transformer, plug adapter, a global or a British PC-card modem and a US RJ-11 telephone connector.

Hotels set up for business travellers will usually have sockets for RJ-11 plugs, but at other hotels and B&Bs you'll have to ask where you can plug in your modem (be prepared for a bewildered stare).

If you don't have a laptop, the best place to check email and surf the Internet in Scotland are libraries – almost every town and village in the country has at least a couple of computer terminals devoted to the Internet, and they are free to use. Internet cafés also exist in the cities and larger towns. The Lonely Planet ekno email account service (www.ekno.com) is a good way to stay in touch with friends and family. For more information on using the Internet in Scotland see the Internet Resources section, p16, in the Getting Started chapter.

LEGAL MATTERS

The 1707 Act of Union preserved the Scottish legal system as separate from the law in England and Wales.

Police have the power to detain anyone suspected of having committed an offence punishable by imprisonment (including drugs offences) for up to six hours. They can search you, take photographs and fingerprints, and question you. You are legally required to provide your correct name and address – not doing so, or giving false details, is an offence – but you are not obliged to answer any other questions. After six hours, the police must either formally charge you or let you go. If you are detained and/or arrested, you have the right to inform a solicitor and one other person, though you have no right to actually see the solicitor or to make a telephone call. If you don't know a solicitor, the police will inform the duty solicitor for you.

The UK parliament passed the antiterrorism crime and security act, in the wake

---

WHEN YOU'RE LEGAL

In Scotland the following legal ages apply:

- Drinking alcohol – 18 years
- Driving – 17 years
- Heterosexual/homosexual sex – 16 years
- Smoking – 16 years
- Marriage – 16 years
- Voting – 18 years

---

of September 11. The legislation makes it possible for the government to detain foreigners suspected of terrorist activities, without trial.

If you need legal assistance contact the **Scottish Legal Aid Board** (☎ 0131-226 7061; www.slab.org.uk; 44 Drumsheugh Gardens, Edinburgh).

Possession of a small amount of cannabis is an offence punishable by a fine, but possession of a larger amount of cannabis, or any amount of harder drugs is much more serious, with a sentence of up to 14 years in prison. Police have the right to search anyone they suspect of possessing drugs.

You're allowed to have a maximum blood-alcohol level of 35mg/100mL when driving.

MAPS

Most bookshops stock a range of decent road atlases. If you plan to go off the beaten track, you'll need one that shows at least 3 miles to the inch (1.9km to 1cm).

Alternatively, TICs have free maps at a scale of at least one inch to 10 miles (1cm to 6.4km) which are adequate for most purposes. For general touring the clear *Collins Touring Map of Scotland* (£4.50) shows most tourist attractions.

If you're about to tackle Munros you'll require maps with far greater detail than the maps in this guide, or the ones supplied by TICs. Look out for the Collins map of the *Munros* (£4.50). The Ordnance Survey (OS) caters to walkers with a wide variety of maps at different scales. Alternatively, look out for the excellent walkers' maps published by Harveys; they're at scales of 1:40,000 and 1:25,000.

MONEY

The British currency is the pound sterling (£), with 100 pence (p) to a pound. 'Quid' is the slang term for pound.

Several Scottish banks issue their own banknotes. You shouldn't have trouble changing them in shops etc immediately south of the Scotland–England border, but elsewhere it may be difficult. All UK banks will accept them, but foreign banks will not.

Sterling is a stable currency but was fairly weak against the US dollar and the euro in the first half of 2003. Later in 2003 the pound was still weak against the euro but strengthened against the dollar. Euros are accepted in Scotland only at some major tourist attractions and a few upmarket hotels – it's always better to have sterling cash. For exchange rates see the inside front cover of this book. For information on costs see the Getting Started chapter, p14.

ATMs
Automatic teller machines (ATMs – called cashpoints in Scotland) are widespread in Scotland and you'll usually find at least one in small towns and villages. You can use Visa, MasterCard, Amex, Cirrus, Plus and Maestro to withdraw cash from ATMs belonging to most banks and building societies in Scotland.

Cash withdrawals from some ATMs may be subject to a small charge (about £1), but most are free.

Cash
Nothing beats cash for convenience – or risk. It's still a good idea, though, to travel with some local currency in cash, if only to tide you over until you get to an exchange facility. There's no problem if you arrive at Edinburgh, Glasgow, Glasgow Prestwick or Aberdeen airports; all have good-value exchange counters open for incoming flights.

Credit Cards
Visa, MasterCard, Amex and Diners Club cards are widely recognised, although some places will charge for accepting them (generally for small transactions). Charge cards such as Amex and Diners Club may not be accepted in small establishments or off the beaten track. Credit and credit/debit cards like Visa and MasterCard are more widely accepted.

Combine plastic and travellers cheques so you have something to fall back on if an ATM swallows your card or the local banks don't accept it.

Moneychangers
Be careful using bureaux de change; they may offer good exchange rates but frequently levy outrageous commissions and fees. The bureaux de change at international airports are exceptions to the rule. They charge less than most high-street banks, and cash sterling travellers cheques for free.

US dollars is probably the best currency to carry (especially if you intend further travel outside Europe), although the strengthening euro has made it an attractive alternative.

International Transfers
Money sent by telegraphic transfer (usually at a cost of about £12) should reach you within a week; by mail, allow at least two weeks. When it arrives, it will most likely be converted into local currency.

You can also transfer money by either Moneygram or Thomas Cook. American travellers can also use **Western Union** (☎ 0800 833833; www.westernunion.com).

Travellers Cheques
American Express (Amex) or Thomas Cook cheques are widely accepted and have efficient replacement policies. Bring pounds sterling to avoid changing currencies twice. In Scotland, travellers cheques are usually only accepted by banks.

Take most cheques in large denominations, say £100; commission is usually charged per cheque.

PHOTOGRAPHY & VIDEO
Both print and slide film are widely available; if there's no specialist photographic shop around, Boots, the chemist chain, is the most likely stockist. The cost for a roll of 36-exposure print film starts from £3.99, excluding processing; processing print films ranges from £4.99 to £7.99, depending on how quickly you want it back. A 36-exposure slide film costs from £6.99 (excluding processing) to £10.49 (including processing). A three-pack of 90-minute Digital 8/Hi8 video cassettes costs around £10; a three-pack of 30-minute DV-Mini cassettes costs £15.

Mathers (☎ 01204-522186) offers bulk-buy mail-order film at very good prices. A 10-pack of 24-exposure print film is £13.99, plus £2.50 postage.

Most towns have several shops where you can get print films processed in as little as one hour.

With dull, overcast conditions common throughout the whole of Scotland, high-speed film (ISO 200 or ISO 400) is useful. In summer, the best times of day for photography are usually early in the morning and late in the afternoon when the glare of the sun has passed. For expert guidance pick up a copy of Lonely Planet's *Travel Photography*.

Many tourist attractions either charge for taking photos or prohibit photography altogether. Use of a flash is frequently forbidden to protect delicate pictures and fabrics. Video cameras are often disallowed because of the inconvenience they can cause to other visitors.

POST

Mail sent within the UK can go either 1st or 2nd class. First-class mail is faster (normally next-day delivery) and more expensive (28/42p for up to 60/100g) than 2nd-class mail (20/34p). Air mail postcards/letters (40g to 60g) to European countries cost 38/69p, to South Africa, the USA and Canada 42p/£1.42 and Australia and New Zealand 42p/£1.56. An air-mail letter generally takes five days to get to the USA or Canada and around a week to Australia or New Zealand.

If you don't have a permanent address, mail can be sent to poste restante in the town or city where you're staying. Amex offices also hold card-holders' mail for free.

SOLO TRAVELLERS

Travelling by yourself in Scotland is quite easy and relatively common. Note that solo hitching anywhere in Scotland isn't wise though. The biggest nuisance for solo travellers is finding single rooms in B&Bs and guesthouses. Many accommodation owners are reluctant to let a double room (even when it's quiet) to one person without charging a supplement, particularly over the peak season when a solo traveller may be asked to pay double rates. To avoid difficulties, book ahead when you can.

The easiest place to meet other people, be it locals or tourists, is in the many pubs around the country. In small towns and villages they're usually the centre of social interaction. Although many Scots are not extroverts, they are generally very friendly and a bit of persistence will normally be rewarded. For budget travellers, hostels are an excellent way to meet other travellers.

Women travelling by themselves should encounter no extra difficulties, as long as sensible precautions observed in most western countries are adhered to – see Women Travellers, p415, for more information.

TELEPHONE

To call Scotland from abroad dial your country's international access code then ☎ 44 (the UK country code), then the area code (dropping the first 0) followed by the telephone number.

You'll mainly see two types of phone booth in Scotland: one takes money (and doesn't give change), while the other uses prepaid phone cards and credit cards. Some phones accept both coins and cards. The minimum charge is 20p.

All phones come with reasonably clear instructions in several languages. British Telecom (BT) offers phonecards for £3, £5, £10 and £20; they're widely available from retailers, including post offices and newsagents.

Some codes worth knowing are:
☎ 0345 – local call rate
☎ 0800 – toll-free call
☎ 0845 – local call rate
☎ 0870 – national call rate
☎ 0891 – premium rate
☎ 9064 – premium call rate

International Calls

Dial ☎ 155 for the international operator. To get an international line (for international direct dialling) dial 00, then the country code, area code (drop the first zero if there is one) and number. Direct dialling is cheaper, but some budget travellers prefer the operator-connected reverse-charge (collect) calls.

You can also use the Home Country Direct service to make a reverse-charge or credit-card call via an operator in your home country.

Local & National Calls

Local calls are charged by time; national calls are charged by time and distance. Daytime rates are from 8am to 6pm, Monday to Friday; cheaper rates are from 6pm to 8am Monday to Friday, and the cheap weekend rate is from midnight Friday to midnight Sunday. The latter two rates offer substantial savings.

For directory enquiries call ☎ 118500 (free from public telephones but 40p per call from a private phone). To get the operator call ☎ 100.

The *Yellow Pages* business directory (with maps) is online at www.yell.co.uk.

Mobile Phones

Codes for mobile phones usually begin with ☎ 07. The UK uses the GSM 900/1800 network, which covers the rest of Europe, Australia and New Zealand, but isn't compatible with the North American GSM 1900 (though some North Americans have GSM 1900/900 phones that work in Scotland). If you have a GSM phone, check with your service provider about using it in the UK, and beware of calls being routed internationally (very expensive for a 'local' call). You can also rent a mobile phone – ask a TIC for details – or buy a 'pay-as-you-go' phone for as little as £40.

TIME

See World Time Zones map, p426.

TOURIST INFORMATION

The national tourist board, **Scottish Tourist Board/Visit Scotland** (STB; ☎ 0131-332 2433; www.visitscotland.com; 23 Ravelston Tce, Edinburgh EH4 3TP), deals with enquiries made by post and telephone only.

Most larger towns have tourist information centres (TICs) that open 9am or 10am to 5pm Monday to Friday, and at weekends in summer. In small places, particularly in the Highlands, TICs only open from Easter to September.

Regional tourist boards are a handy source of information when you are planning your trip and will usually post information, including their regional accommodation guides.

Aberdeen & Grampian Tourist Board (☎ 01224-288825/8; www.castlesandwhisky.com; Exchange House, 26-28 Exchange St, Aberdeen, AB11 6PH)

Angus & Dundee Tourist Board (☎ 01382-527527; www.angusanddundee.co.uk; 21 Castle St, Dundee DD1 3AA)

Argyll, the Isles, Loch Lomond, Stirling & Trossachs Tourist Board (☎ 0870 720 0629; www.visit scottishheartlands.org; 7 Alexandra Pde, Dunoon, PA23 8AB)

Ayrshire & Arran Tourist Board (☎ 01292-678100; www.ayrshire-arran.com; 15 Skye Rd, Prestwick KA9 2TA)

Scottish Borders Tourist Board (☎ 0870 608 0404; www.scot-borders.co.uk; Shepherds Mill, Whinfield Rd, Selkirk TD7 5DT)

Dumfries & Galloway Tourist Board (☎ 01387-253862; www.visit-dumfries-and-galloway.co.uk; 64 Whitesands, Dumfries DG1 2RS)

Fife Tourist Board (☎ 01334-472021; www.standrews .com/fife; 70 Market St, St Andrews KY16 9NU)

Greater Glasgow & Clyde Valley Tourist Board (☎ 0141-204 4480; www.seeglasgow.com; 11 George Sq, Glasgow G2 1DY)

Perthshire Tourist Board (☎ 01738-627958; www.perthshire.co.uk; West Mill St, Perth, PH1 5QP)

Highlands of Scotland Tourist Board (☎ 01997-421160; www.highlandfreedom.com; Peffrey House, Strathpeffer IV14 9HA)

Orkney Tourist Board (☎ 01856-872856; www.visitorkney.com; 6 Broad St Kirkwall KW15 1NX)

Shetland Islands Tourism (☎ 01595-693434; www.visitshetland.com; Market Cross, Lerwick ZE1 0LU)

Western Isles Tourist Board (☎ 01851-703088; www.witb.co.uk; 26 Cromwell St, Stornoway, Lewis HS1 2DD)

TOURS

There are plenty of companies in Scotland offering all kinds of tours including, historical, activity-based and backpacker tours. It's a question of choosing the tour that suits your requirements and budget. More tour companies are listed in the individual destination chapters under Tours headings.

Heart of Scotland Tours (☎ 558 8855; www.heart ofscotlandtours.co.uk) Recommended day tour operator specialising in central Scotland and the Highlands.

Mountain Innovations (☎ 01479-831331; www.scotmountain.co.uk; Fraoch Lodge, Deshar Rd, Boat of Garten PH24 3BN) Good-value activity holidays in the Highlands, including walking, mountain biking, kayaking, skiing and horse-riding.

Rabbie's Trail Burners (☎ 0131-226 3133; www.rabbies.com; 207 High St, Edinburgh) One- to five-day tours of the Highlands in 16-seat minibuses.

Saltire Tours (☎ 0131-448 7374; www.saltiretours .co.uk; Suite 130, 12 South Bridge, Edinburgh EH1 1DD) Small company providing a wide range of imaginative tours from art and architecture to Sir Walter Scott.

Scot-Trek (☎ 0141-334 9232; www.scot-trek.co.uk; 9 Lawrence St, Glasgow G11 5HH) Guided walks for all levels, specialising in historical treks.

USEFUL ORGANISATIONS

Membership of Historic Scotland (HS) and the National Trust for Scotland (NTS) is worth considering, especially if you're going to be in Scotland for a while. Both are nonprofit organisations dedicated to the preservation of the environment, and both care for hundreds of spectacular sites.

Historic Scotland (☎ 0131-668 8600; www.historic -scotland.net; Longmore House, Salisbury Place, Edinburgh EH9 1SH) A year's membership costs £30/23 for an adult/child or student, and gives free entry to HS sites (half-price entry to sites in England and Wales). Also offers short-term 'Explorer' membership – three/seven/ 10 days for £15/20/23. Standard HS property opening times are 9.30am to 6.30pm daily April to September, closing two hours earlier (opening at 2pm on Sunday) October to March.

National Trust for Scotland (☎ 0131-243 9300; www.nts.org.uk; 28 Charlotte Sq, Edinburgh EH2 4ET) A year's membership of the NTS costing £32 (£12 for those aged under 25, £23 for seniors) offers free access to all NTS and NT properties (in the rest of the UK).

VISAS

Currently, if you're a citizen of Australia, Canada, New Zealand, South Africa or the USA, you're permitted to stay for up to six months (no visa required), but are prohibited from working. The Working Holidaymaker scheme, for Commonwealth citizens aged 17 to 27 inclusive, allows visits of up to two years but arrangements must be made in advance through a British embassy.

EU citizens can live and work in Britain free of immigration control and don't need a visa to enter the country.

All other nationalities should contact their nearest British diplomatic mission to obtain a visa. Standard/one year multiple-entry visas cost from £36/60.

No visas are required for Scotland if you arrive from England or Northern Ireland. For more information, see www.ukvisas.gov.uk or the Lonely Planet website at www.lonely planet.com.au.

Visa Extensions

To extend your stay in the UK contact the **Home Office, Immigration & Nationality Directorate** (☎ 0870 606 7766; Lunar House, 40 Wellesley Rd, Croydon, London CR9 2BY) *before* your existing

permit expires. You'll need to send your passport with your application.

WOMEN TRAVELLERS

Women are unlikely to have any problems in Scotland, although common-sense caution should be observed, especially in towns and cities. Women can enter most pubs alone, but there are still a few places where this may attract undesirable attention. Cosmopolitan city pubs and most rural pubs are fine – you'll get a pretty good idea as soon as you enter. Sticking to pubs frequented by tourists is always a safe bet.

Many parts of central Edinburgh and Glasgow are best avoided late at night. Be aware of red-light districts in both cities – Coburg St (Leith, Edinburgh) and Anderston/Blythswood Square (Glasgow).

The **Rape & Abuse Line** (☎ 0808 800 0123) can be contacted toll-free any evening.

For general advice on health issues, contraception and pregnancy, visit a Well Woman clinic – ask at local libraries or doctors' surgeries for the details. In Edinburgh, contact **Well Woman Services** (☎ 0131 332 7941; 18 Dean Tce, Stockbridge).

WORK

Hostel noticeboards sometimes advertise casual work. Without skills, it's difficult to find a job that pays well enough to save money. Pick up a copy of the free *TNT* magazine (www.tntmagazine.co.uk), found in the larger cities – it lists jobs and employment agencies aimed at travellers.

EU citizens don't need a work permit – see also Visas earlier for details about the Working Holidaymaker scheme for Commonwealth citizens.

Students from the USA who are at least 18 years old and studying full time at a college or university can get a Blue Card permit allowing them to work for six months in the UK. It's available through the British Universities North America Club (BUNAC). The club also runs programmes for Australians, Canadians and New Zealanders. For more details, check out www.bunac.org.uk.

Transport

CONTENTS

GETTING THERE & AWAY

AIR

There are direct flights to Scottish airports from England, Wales, Ireland, the USA, Canada, Scandinavia and several countries in Western and Central Europe.

From the rest of the world you will probably have to fly into a major European hub and catch a connecting flight to a Scottish airport – London, Amsterdam, Frankfurt and Paris have the best connections with Scotland.

Airports & Airlines

Scotland has four main international airports of its own; London is the main UK gateway for long-haul flights:

Aberdeen (ABZ; ☎ 01224-722331; www.baa.co.uk/aberdeen)
Edinburgh (EDI; ☎ 0131-333 1000; www.baa.co.uk/edinburgh)
Glasgow (GLA; ☎ 0141-887 1111; www.baa.co.uk/glasgow)
Glasgow Prestwick (PIK; ☎ 01292-511211; www.gpia.co.uk)
London Gatwick (LGW; ☎ 0870 000 2468; www.baa.co.uk/gatwick)
London Heathrow (LHR; ☎ 0870 000 0123; www.baa.co.uk/heathrow)

> **THINGS CHANGE...**
>
> The information in this chapter is particularly vulnerable to change. Check directly with the airline or a travel agent to make sure you understand how a fare (and ticket you may buy) works and be aware of the security requirements for international travel. Shop carefully. The details given in this chapter should be regarded as pointers and are not a substitute for your own careful, up-to-date research.

A few short-haul international flights land at **Dundee** (DND; ☎ 01382-643242), **Inverness** (INV; ☎ 01463-232471, www.hial.co.uk) and **Lerwick** (LSI; ☎ 01950-60654, www.hial.co.uk).

There are many airlines serving Scottish airports. The main ones are:
Aer Lingus (☎ 0845 973 7747; www.aerlingus.com)
Air Canada (☎ 0870 524 7226; www.aircanada.ca)
Air France (☎ 0845 084 5111; www.airfrance.com)
Air Malta (☎ 0141-847 1111; www.airmalta.com)
Air Scotland (☎ 0141-848 4990; www.air-scotland.com)
Air Transat (☎ 0870 556 1522; www.airtransat.com)
American Airlines (☎ 0845 778 9789; www.aa.com)
Atlantic Airways (☎ 0845 6072 7727; www.atlantic.fo)
British Midland (bmi; ☎ 0870 607 0555; www.flybmi.com)
Braathens (☎ 0191-214 0991; www.braathens.no)
British Airways (☎ 0845 773 3377; www.britishairways.co.uk)
British European (☎ 0870 567 6676; www.flybe.com)
Continental Airlines (☎ 0800 776464; www.continental.com)
Czech Airlines (☎ 0870 4443 747; www.czechairlines.co.uk)
duo (☎ 0871 700 0700; www.duo.com)
Eastern Airways (☎ 01652-680600; www.easternairways.com)
easyJet (☎ 0870 600 0000; www.easyjet.com)
Globespan (☎ 0870 556 1522; www.flyglobespan.com)
Icelandair (☎ 0845 758 1111; www.icelandair.com)
KLM UK (☎ 0870 507 4074; www.klmuk.com)
Lufthansa (☎ 0845 773 7747; www.lufthansa.com)
Ryanair (☎ 0870 156 9569; www.ryanair.com)
Scandinavian Airlines (SAS; ☎ 0845 6072 7727; www.scandinavian.net)
ScotAirways (☎ 0870 606 0707; www.scotairways.co.uk)

From Australia & New Zealand

Many airlines compete on flights between Australia and New Zealand and the UK and there is a wide range of fares. Round-the-World (RTW) tickets are often real bargains and can sometimes work out cheaper than a straightforward return ticket.

Expect to pay anything from A$1800 to A$3000. Adding a connecting flight from London to Edinburgh should only add around A$100 to the cost of the ticket.

STA Travel (☎ 03-8417 6911; www.statravel.com.au) has offices in all major cities and on many university campuses. **Flight Centre** (☎ 131 133 Australiawide, 09-309 6171 in Auckland; www.flight centre.com.au) has dozens of offices throughout Australia and New Zealand.

From Canada

Air Canada has daily flights from Toronto to Glasgow. Return fares from Toronto start at around C$700.

The charter operator Air Transat has one direct flight a week from Toronto to Edinburgh (May to October), Glasgow (April to October) and Aberdeen (June to September). It also offers weekly flights to Glasgow from Calgary and Vancouver (May to October).

Travel CUTS (☎ 866 246 9762; www.travelcuts.com) is Canada's national student travel agency and has offices in all major cities.

From Continental Europe

Major airlines operate several direct flights a day into Edinburgh from Amsterdam, Brussels, Frankfurt, Madrid, Paris and Prague.

Budget airlines offer direct flights to Glasgow and/or Edinburgh from Alicante, Barcelona, Cologne-Bonn, Fuerteventura, Geneva, Milan, Nice, Oslo, Rome and Zurich.

From England & Wales

There are more than a hundred flights a day between London and Edinburgh and Glasgow, and several daily from other UK airports. BA has flights to Glasgow and Edinburgh from London, Bristol, Birmingham, Cardiff, Manchester, Plymouth and Southampton, and to Aberdeen and Inverness from London.

EasyJet flies from London to Edinburgh, Glasgow, Inverness and Aberdeen. ScotAir-

ways flies from London City to Edinburgh and Dundee; bmibaby has flights from East Midlands and Cardiff to Edinburgh and Glasgow. Eastern Airways flies from Norwich to Edinburgh, and from various English airports to Aberdeen.

Prices vary enormously. A standard economy return ticket from London to Edinburgh or Glasgow costs around £250, while budget airlines offer flights for as little as £20 one way, travelling mid-week and booking a month or two in advance.

Dependable travel agencies in Scotland include **STA Travel** (☎ 0131-226 7747; www.statravel.co.uk) and **Trailfinders** (☎ 0141-353 2224; www.trailfinders.com).

From Ireland

BA flies from Belfast and Londonderry to Glasgow, and from Belfast to Aberdeen and Edinburgh. EasyJet has direct flights from Belfast to Glasgow and Edinburgh.

There are daily flights from Dublin to Edinburgh and Glasgow with Aer Lingus and BA. Ryanair flies from Dublin to Glasgow Prestwick, Edinburgh and Aberdeen. British European flies from Cork and Shannon airports to Glasgow and Edinburgh via Birmingham.

The Irish youth and student travel agency **usitNOW** (☎ 01-602 1600; www.usitnow.ie) has offices in most major cities in Ireland.

From Scandinavia

British Midland and SAS fly from Copenhagen to Edinburgh and Glasgow, and Braathens has flights to Aberdeen from Bergen, Stavanger and Malmo. Ryanair flies from Oslo and Stockholm to Glasgow Prestwick

Icelandair has daily flights between Reykjavik and Glasgow, while Atlantic Airways links the Faroe Islands to Aberdeen and Glasgow.

From the USA

Continental flies daily from New York (Newark) to Glasgow and Edinburgh. American Airlines flies from Chicago to Glasgow (May to September only). Flight time from New York to Glasgow is around 7½ hours, and return fares range from around US$400 to US$700.

STA Travel (☎ 800 781 4040; www.statravel.com) has offices in Boston, Chicago, Miami,

New York, Philadelphia, San Francisco and other major cities.

LAND
Bus

Long-distance buses are usually the cheapest method of getting to Scotland from other parts of the UK. The main operators are **National Express** (☎ 0870 580 8080; www.gobycoach.com) and its subsidiary **Scottish Citylink** (☎ 0870 550 5050; www.citylink.co.uk), with regular services from London and other cities in England, Wales and Northern Ireland (see Getting There & Away for Edinburgh, p98, and Glasgow, p127).

The cheapest London to Glasgow/ Edinburgh coach is the daily overnight service operated by **Silver Choice Travel** (☎ 0141-333 1400, www.silverchoicetravel.co.uk), which charges £24 for an Apex return. For information on bus passes and discount cards, see p420.

Scottish Citylink runs a daily bus service to Edinburgh from Belfast (£35 return, 7½ hours) and Dublin (£45 return, 10½ hours).

BACKPACKERS BUSES

Various backpacker buses offer hop-on hop-off bus services between London and Scotland, visiting places of interest en route:

Celtic Connection (☎ 0131-225 3330; www.celtic connection.freeserve.co.uk)

Haggis Backpackers (☎ 0131-557 9393; www .haggisadventures.com)

Slowcoach (☎ 020-7373 7737; www.straytravel.com)

Wild in Scotland (☎ 0131-478 6500; www.wild-in-scotland.com)

Car & Motorcycle

Drivers of EU-registered vehicles will find bringing a car or motorcycle into Scotland fairly straightforward. The vehicle must have registration papers and a nationality plate, and the driver must have insurance.

Although the International Insurance Certificate (Green Card) is no longer compulsory, it remains excellent proof that you are covered.

Driving to Scotland from mainland Europe via the Channel Tunnel or ferry ports, head for London and follow the busy M25 orbital road to the M1 motorway, then follow the M1 and M6 north.

Train

Travelling to Scotland by train is usually faster and more comfortable, but more expensive, than taking the bus. Taking into account check-ins and the travel time between city centre and airport, the train offers a competitive alternative to air travel on the London to Edinburgh route. You can get timetable and fares information for all UK trains from the **National Rail Enquiry Service** (☎ 0845 748 4950; www.railtrack.co.uk).

FROM CONTINENTAL EUROPE

You can travel from Paris or Brussels to London Waterloo on the **Eurostar** (☎ 08705 186 186 in the UK, ☎ 0892 35 35 39 in France; www.euro star.com) service, but to reach Scotland you'll have to take the tube from Waterloo to Kings Cross or Euston stations to connect with the Edinburgh or Glasgow train. The total journey time from Paris is about eight hours.

FROM THE UK

GNER (☎ 0845 722 5225; www.gner.co.uk) operates a fast and frequent rail service between London Kings Cross and Edinburgh (four hours). A standard return costs around £85 but special offers sometimes have fares as low as £39. The **Virgin Trains** (☎ 0845 722 2333; www.virgintrains.co.uk) service between London Euston and Glasgow is slower at 5½ hours.

ScotRail (☎ 0845 755 0033; www.scotrail.co.uk) operates the Caledonian Sleeper service connecting Edinburgh, Glasgow, Stirling, Perth, Dundee, Aberdeen, Fort William and Inverness with London Euston. A standard sleeper (sharing a twin cabin) from London to Edinburgh is £89/129 single/return, and to Inverness, Aberdeen or Fort William £109/149.

Services to Edinburgh from other parts of England and Wales usually require changing trains at some point.

ScotRail offers various Rail & Sail deals between Edinburgh and Glasgow and Belfast via the ferry crossings at Stranraer and Troon.

SEA
From Continental Europe

Superfast Ferries (☎ 0870 410 6040; www.superfast .com) operates a car ferry between Rosyth, 12 miles northwest of Edinburgh, and Zeebrugge in Belgium (17½ hours, one daily).

Return passenger fares in high season (July and August) range from €160 in an aircraft-style seat to €700 in a luxury cabin. A car costs €230 return.

From Northern Ireland

Car ferry links between Northern Ireland and Scotland are operated by **Stena Line** (☎ 08705 707070; www.stenaline.com), **P&O Irish Sea** (☎ 08702 424777; www.poirishsea.com) and **SeaCat** (☎ 08705 523523; www.seacat.co.uk). There are standard and high-speed ferries on the Stranraer and Cairnryan routes, high-speed only on the Troon crossing.

The example prices given are open return fares for a foot passenger/car with driver in high season.

Crossing	Operator	Duration (hrs)	Frequency	Fare (£)
Belfast–Stranraer	Stena	3¼	2-4 daily	40/240
Belfast–Stranraer	Stena	1¾	4 daily	48/280
Belfast–Troon	SeaCat	2½	2-3 daily (Mar–Sep)	60/240
Larne–Cairnryan	P&O Irish Sea	1¾	2 daily	60/290
Larne–Cairnryan	P&O Irish Sea	1	5 daily	75/355

From Scandinavia

From May to early September, **Smyril Line** (☎ 01595-690845; www.smyril-line.com) operates a weekly car ferry between Shetland (Lerwick), the Faroe Islands (Torshavn), Iceland (Seydisfjordur), Norway (Bergen) and Denmark (Hantsholm). It leaves from Lerwick on Mondays for Bergen, and on Wednesdays for Torshavn and Seydisfjordur.

The Lerwick to Bergen crossing takes 13½ hours, Lerwick to Torshavn is 13 hours, and Torshavn to Seydisfjordur is 15 hours.

GETTING AROUND

Public transport in Scotland is generally good, but it can be expensive compared to other European countries. Buses are usually the cheapest way to get around, but also the slowest. With a discount pass, trains can be competitive; they're also quicker and often take you through beautiful scenery.

Traveline (☎ 0870 608 2608; www.travelinescotland.com) provides timetable information for all public transport services in Scotland, but can't provide fare information or book tickets.

AIR

Most domestic air services in Scotland are geared to business needs, or are lifelines for remote island communities. Flying is a pricey way to cover relatively short distances, and only worth considering if you're short of time and want to visit the Outer Hebrides, Orkney or Shetland.

Airlines in Scotland

British Airways/Loganair (☎ 0870 850 9850; www.loganair.co.uk)
British Midland (bmi; ☎ 0870 607 0555; www.flybmi.com)
Eastern Airways (☎ 01652-680600; www.easternairways.com)
Highland Airways (☎ 01851-701282; www.highlandairways.co.uk)

British Airways/Loganair is the main domestic airline in Scotland, with flights from Glasgow to Barra, Benbecula, Campbeltown, Inverness, Islay, Kirkwall, Sumburgh, Stornoway and Tiree; from Edinburgh to Kirkwall, Sumburgh, Stornoway and Wick; and from Aberdeen and Inverness to Kirkwall and Sumburgh. They also operate inter-island flights in Orkney and Shetland.

British Midland flies from Edinburgh to Stornoway, and Eastern Airways from Aberdeen to Wick. Highland Airways has flights from Inverness to Sumburgh and Stornoway.

Sample return fares are: Glasgow–Kirkwall £150, Edinburgh–Sumburgh £150, Edinburgh–Stornoway £112, Kirkwall–Sumburgh £60 and Inverness–Stornoway £130.

BOAT

The main ferry operators are **Caledonian MacBrayne** (CalMac; ☎ 0870 565 0000; www.calmac.co.uk) for the west coast and islands, and **Northlink Ferries** (☎ 0845 6000 449; www.northlinkferries.co.uk) for Orkney and Shetland.

CalMac's Island Rover ticket gives unlimited travel on its ferry services, and costs £46.50/67 for a foot passenger for eight/15 days, plus £222/332 for a car, or £111/166 for a motorbike. Bicycles travel free. There are also more than two dozen Island Hop-scotch tickets, which give lower fares for various combinations of crossings.

Northlink ferries sail from Aberdeen and Scrabster (near Thurso) to Orkney, from Orkney to Shetland and from Aberdeen to Shetland.

See the relevant chapters for full details of ferry services and fares.

BUS

Scotland's national bus network is operated by **Scottish Citylink** (☎ 08705 50 50 50; www.citylink.co.uk), with comfortable, reliable buses serving all the main towns in the country. To get off the main roads, though, you'll have to switch to local services.

Before planning a journey off the main routes it's advisable to phone **Traveline** (☎ 0870 608 2608) for up-to-date timetable information.

Many remote villages can only be reached using **Royal Mail postbuses** (☎ 08457 740 740; www.postbus.royalmail.com). These are minibuses, or sometimes just four-seater cars, driven by postal workers delivering and collecting the mail. They follow circuitous routes through some of the most beautiful areas of Scotland, and are particularly useful for walkers – there are no official stops, and you can hail a postbus anywhere on its route. Fares are typically £2 to £5 for a one-way journey.

Haggis Backpackers (☎ 0131-557 9393; www.haggis adventures.com) and **Macbackpackers** (☎ 0131-558 9900; www.macbackpackers.com) offer various jump-on, jump-off minibus services, running from Edinburgh to Inverness, Ullapool, Skye, Fort William, Glen Coe, Oban and Glasgow. A ticket, valid for up to three months, costs about £70.

Bus Passes

The Scottish Citylink Explorer Pass can be bought in the UK by both UK and overseas citizens. It offers unlimited travel on all Citylink services within Scotland for three consecutive days (£39), for any five days out of 10 (£59), or any eight days out of 16 (£85). It also gives discounts on various regional bus services and on Northlink ferries. It is not valid on National Express coaches.

Citylink also offers discounts to holders of the Euro/26 card, and the **Young Scot card** (☎ 0870 513 4936; www.youngscot.org), which provides discounts all over Scotland and Europe. There are no discount bus passes for seniors.

CAR & MOTORCYCLE

Travelling by car or motorcycle allows you to get to remote places, and to travel quickly, independently and flexibly. Unfortunately, the independence you enjoy tends to isolate you, and cars are nearly always inconvenient in city centres. Scotland's roads are generally good and far less busy than in England, so driving is more enjoyable.

Motorways (designated 'M') are toll-free dual carriageways; they are limited mainly to central Scotland. Main roads (designated 'A') are dual or single carriageways and are sometimes clogged with slow-moving trucks or caravans; the A9 from Perth to Inverness is notoriously busy.

Life on the road is more relaxed and interesting on the secondary roads (designated 'B') and minor roads (undesignated). These wind through the countryside from village to village. You can't travel fast, but you won't want to.

In many country areas, and especially in the Highlands and islands, roads are only single track with passing places. Remember that passing places are not only for allowing oncoming traffic to pass, but also for overtaking – check your rear-view mirror frequently, and pull over to allow faster vehicles to pass if necessary. It's illegal to park in passing places.

In the Highlands and islands there's the added hazard of suicidal sheep wandering onto the road (be particularly wary of lambs in spring).

At around 80p per litre (equivalent to US$4.80 for a US gallon), petrol is expensive by American or Australian standards, and diesel is only a few pence cheaper. Distances, however, aren't as great. Petrol prices also tend to rise as you get farther from main population centres, and more than 10% higher in the Outer Hebrides. In remote areas petrol stations are few and far between and sometimes closed on Sunday.

Driving Licence

A foreign driving licence is valid in Britain for up to 12 months from the time of your entry into the country. If you're bringing a car from Europe make sure you're adequately insured.

Hire

Car rental is relatively expensive and often you'll be better off making arrangements in your home country for a fly/drive deal. The big international rental companies charge from around £120 a week for a small car (Ford Fiesta, Peugeot 106); rates offered by local companies, such as **Arnold Clark** (☎ 0131-228 4747) in Edinburgh, start at around £18 a day or £90 a week.

The reservations numbers for the main international companies are as follows:

Avis (☎ 0870 606 0100; www.avis.co.uk)
Budget (☎ 0845 606 6669; www.budget.co.uk)
Europcar (☎ 0870 607 5000; www.europcar.co.uk)
Hertz (☎ 0870 844 8844; www.hertz.co.uk)
Thrifty Car Rental (☎ 0870 066 0514; www.thrifty .co.uk)

TICs have lists of local car-hire companies.

To rent a car, drivers must usually be between 23 and 65 years of age – outside these limits special conditions or insurance requirements may apply.

If you are planning on visiting the Outer Hebrides, Orkney or Shetland, it will often prove cheaper to hire a car on the islands, rather than pay to take a rental car across on the ferry.

Road Rules

Anyone using the roads a lot should get hold of the *Highway Code*, which is widely available in bookshops. Vehicles drive on the left-hand side of the road; front-seat belts are compulsory and if belts are fitted in the back seat then they must be worn; the speed limit is 30mph (48km/h) in built-up areas, 60mph (96km/h) on single carriageways and 70mph (112km/h) on dual carriageways; you give way to your right at roundabouts (traffic already on the roundabout has the right of way). Motorcyclists must wear helmets.

See also p411 for information on drinking and driving and other legal matters.

HITCHING

Hitching is never entirely safe in any country and we don't recommend it. Travellers who decide to hitch are taking a small but potentially serious risk. However, many people choose to hitch, and the advice that follows should help to make their journeys as fast and safe as possible.

Hitching is reasonably easy in Scotland, except around the big cities and built-up areas, where you'll need to use public transport. Although the northwest is more difficult because there's less traffic, waits of over two hours are unusual (except on Sunday in 'Sabbath' areas). On some Scottish islands, where public transport is infrequent, hitching is so much a part of getting around that local drivers may stop and offer you lifts without you even asking.

It's against the law to hitch on motorways or their immediate slip roads; make a sign and use approach roads, nearby roundabouts or the service stations.

ROAD DISTANCES (MILES)

	Aberdeen	Dundee	Edinburgh	Fort William	Glasgow	Inverness	Kyle of Lochalsh	Mallaig	Oban	Scrabster	Stranraer
Dundee	70										
Edinburgh	129	62									
Fort William	165	121	146								
Glasgow	145	84	42	104							
Inverness	105	131	155	66	166						
Kyle of Lochalsh	188	177	206	76	181	82					
Mallaig	189	161	180	44	150	106	34				
Oban	180	118	123	45	94	110	120	85			
Scrabster	218	250	279	185	286	119	214	238	230		
Stranraer	233	171	120	184	80	250	265	232	178	374	
Ullapool	150	189	215	90	225	135	88	166	161	125	158

TRAIN

Scotland's rail network extends to all major cities and towns, but the railway map has a lot of large, blank areas in the Highlands and the Southern Uplands where you'll need to switch to bus or hire car. The West Highland line from Glasgow to Fort William and Mallaig, and the Inverness to Kyle of Lochalsh line are two of the most scenic train journeys in the world.

For information on train timetables call the **National Rail Enquiry Service** (☎ 0845 748 4950) or check the online timetables at www.scotrail.co.uk.

Bicycles are carried free on all ScotRail trains, but space is sometimes limited. Reservations are compulsory on certain rail routes, including the Glasgow–Oban–Fort-William–Mallaig line and the Inverness–Kyle of Lochalsh line; they are recommended on many others. You can make reservations for your bicycle from eight weeks to two hours in advance at main train stations, or when buying tickets by phone.

Classes

There are two classes of train travel: first and standard. First class costs 30% to 50% more than standard but, except on very crowded trains, isn't really worth the extra money.

Costs

Rail travel is more expensive than the bus: a standard return ticket from Edinburgh to Inverness costs around £65 compared to around £28 on the bus.

TRAIN PASSES

ScotRail offers a range of good-value passes for train travel in Scotland. You can buy them at BritRail outlets in the USA, Canada and Europe, at the British Travel Centre in Regent St, London, at train stations throughout Britain, at certain UK travel agents and from **ScotRail Telesales** (☎ 0845 755 0033).

The Freedom of Scotland Travelpass gives unlimited travel on all ScotRail and Strathclyde Passenger Transport trains, all CalMac ferry services, and on certain Scottish Citylink coach services (on routes not covered by rail). It is available for four days' travel out of eight (£89) or eight days' travel out of 15 (£119).

The Highland Rover pass allows travel from Glasgow to Oban, Fort William and Mallaig, and from Inverness to Kyle of Lochalsh, Aviemore, Aberdeen and Thurso; it also gives free travel on the Oban/Fort William to Inverness bus, and a discount on ferries to Mull and Skye. It is only available for four days travel out of eight (£59).

The Central Scotland Rover covers train travel between Glasgow, Edinburgh, North Berwick, Stirling and Fife. It costs £29 for three days' travel out of seven.

Note that Travelpass and Rover tickets are not valid for travel on certain (mainly commuter) services before 9.15am Monday to Friday.

DISCOUNT CARDS

Discount **railcards** (www.railcard.co.uk) are available for people aged 60 and over, for people aged 16 to 25 (or mature full-time students), and for those with a disability (☎ 0191-218 8103 or ☎ 0191-269 0304 for those with hearing impairment). The Seniors Railcard (£18), Young Persons Railcard (£18) and Disabled Persons Railcard (£14) are each valid for one year and give a one-third discount on most train fares in Scotland, England and Wales. Fill in an application form at any major train station. You'll need proof of age (birth certificate, passport or driving licence) for the Young Persons and Seniors railcards (proof of enrolment for mature-age students), and proof of entitlement for the Disabled Persons Railcard.

Reservations

ScotRail (☎ 0845 755 0033 for ticket sales and reservations; www.scotrail.co.uk) operates most train services in Scotland. Reservations are recommended for intercity trips, especially on Fridays and public holidays; for shorter journeys, just buy a ticket at the station before you go. On certain routes, including the Glasgow–Edinburgh express, and in places where there's no ticket office at the station, you can buy tickets on the train.

Children under five years old travel free; those aged five to 15 are charged half-price for most tickets. At the weekend on certain intercity routes you can upgrade a standard-class ticket to first class for only £3 per single journey – just ask the conductor on the train.

There is a bewildering variety of ticket types on offer.

Single Valid for a single (ie one-way) journey at any time on the particular day specified; expensive.

Day Return Valid for a return journey at any time on the particular day specified; relatively expensive.

Cheap Day Return Valid for a return journey on the day specified on the ticket, but there are time restrictions (you're not usually allowed to travel on a train that leaves before 9.15am); relatively cheap.

Open Return For outward travel on a stated day and return on any day within a month.

Apex One of the cheapest return fares; standard class only; reservations compulsory and you must travel on the booked services; you must book at least 48 hours in advance, but seats are limited so book as soon as possible (up to eight weeks in advance).

SuperSaver The cheapest ticket where advance purchase isn't necessary; can't be used on Friday after 2.30pm, Saturday in July and August or on bank holidays, or on days after these before 2.30pm. The return journey must be within one calendar month.

Saver Higher priced than the SuperSaver, but can be used any day and there are fewer time restrictions.

SuperAdvance Similarly priced to the SuperSaver but with fewer time/day restrictions; however, tickets must be bought before 6pm on the day before travel and both the outward and return journey times must be specified; limited availability so book early.

Health

CONTENTS

BEFORE YOU GO

While Scotland has excellent health care, prevention is the key to staying healthy while travelling in the country. A little planning before departure, particularly for pre-existing illnesses, will save trouble later. Bring medications in their original, clearly labelled containers. A signed and dated letter from your physician describing your medical conditions and medications, including generic names, is also a good idea. If carrying syringes or needles, be sure to have a physician's letter documenting their medical necessity. Carry a spare pair of contact lenses and glasses, and take your optical prescription with you.

INSURANCE

If you're an EU citizen, an E111 form, available from health centres or, in the UK, post offices, covers you for most medical care. E111 will not cover you for non-emergencies, or emergency repatriation. Citizens from non-EU countries should find out if there is a reciprocal arrangement for free medical care between their country and the UK. If you do need health insurance, make sure you get a policy that covers you for the worst possible case, such as an accident requiring an emergency flight home. Find out in advance if your insurance plan will make payments directly to providers or reimburse you later for overseas health expenditures.

RECOMMENDED VACCINATIONS

No jabs are required to travel to Scotland. The World Health Organization, however, recommends that all travellers should be covered for diphtheria, tetanus, measles, mumps, rubella, polio and hepatitis B, regardless of their destination.

IN TRANSIT
DEEP VEIN THROMBOSIS (DVT)

Blood clots may form in the legs during plane flights, chiefly because of prolonged immobility. The longer the flight, the greater the risk. The chief symptom of deep vein thrombosis is swelling or pain of the foot, ankle or calf, usually but not always on just one side. When a blood clot travels to the lungs, it may cause chest pain and difficulty breathing. Travellers with any of these symptoms should immediately seek medical attention.

To prevent the development of DVT on long flights you should walk about the cabin, contract the leg muscles while sitting, drink plenty of fluids and avoid alcohol and tobacco.

JET LAG & MOTION SICKNESS

To avoid jet lag (common when crossing more than five time zones) try drinking plenty of nonalcoholic fluids and eating light meals. Upon arrival, get exposure to natural sunlight and readjust your schedule (for meals, sleep etc) as soon as possible.

Antihistamines such as dimenhydrinate (Dramamine) and meclizine (Antivert, Bonine) are usually the first choice for treating motion sickness. A herbal alternative is ginger.

IN SCOTLAND
Availability & Cost of Health Care

Excellent health care is readily available and for minor illnesses pharmacists can give valuable advice and sell over-the-counter medication. They can also advise when more specialised help is required and point you in the right direction.

Travellers' Diarrhoea

If you develop diarrhoea, be sure to drink plenty of fluids, preferably in the form of an oral rehydration solution such as dioralyte. If diarrhoea is bloody, persists for more than 72 hours or is accompanied by fever, shaking, chills or severe abdominal pain you should seek medical attention.

Environmental Hazards & Treatment

HEAT ILLNESS

Heat exhaustion (yes, it can happen!) occurs following excessive fluid loss with inadequate replacement of fluids and salt. Symptoms include headache, dizziness and tiredness. Dehydration is already happening by the time you feel thirsty – aim to drink sufficient water to produce pale, diluted urine. To treat heat exhaustion drink water and/or fruit juice, and cool the body with cold water and fans.

COLD ILLNESS

Hypothermia occurs when the body loses heat faster than it can produce it. As ever, proper preparation will reduce the risks of getting it. Even on a hot day in the mountains, the weather can change rapidly, so carry waterproof garments, warm layers and a hat and inform others of your route.

Hypothermia starts with shivering, loss of judgment and clumsiness. Unless rewarming occurs, the sufferer deteriorates into apathy, confusion and coma. Prevent further heat loss by seeking shelter, warm dry clothing, hot sweet drinks and shared bodily warmth.

Travelling with Children

Make sure the children are up to date with routine vaccinations, and discuss possible travel vaccines well before departure as some vaccines are not suitable for children under a year. See also Lonely Planet's *Travelling with Children* by Cathy Lanigan.

TIME

Scotland follows Greenwich Mean Time (GMT) in winter and British Summer Time (BST) in summer. BST is GMT plus one hour – the clocks go forward at 2am on the last Sunday in March, and back again at 2am on the last Sunday in October.

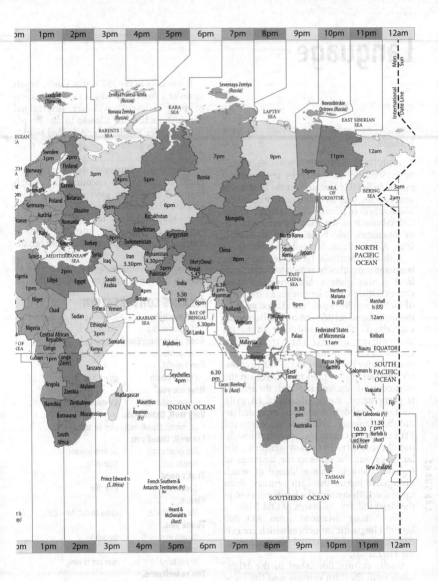

When it's noon in Edinburgh in summer, it's 4am in Los Angeles, 7am in New York, 1pm in Paris (and the rest of Europe), 1pm in Johannesburg, 8pm in Tokyo, 9pm in Sydney and 11pm in Auckland.

Language

CONTENTS

Scottish Gaelic (*Gàidhlig* – pronounced *gallic* in Scotland) is spoken by about 80,000 people in Scotland, mainly in the Highlands and islands, and by many native speakers and learners overseas. It is a member of the Celtic branch of the Indo-European family of languages, which has given us Gaelic, Irish, Manx, Welsh, Cornish and Breton.

Although Scottish Gaelic is the Celtic language most closely associated with Scotland it was quite a latecomer to those shores. Other Celtic languages in the form of Pictish and Brittonic had existed prior to the arrival and settlement by Gaelic-speaking Celts (Gaels) from Ireland from the 4th to the 6th centuries AD. These Irish settlers, known to the Romans as Scotti, were eventually to give their name to the entire country. Initially they settled in the area on the west coast of Scotland in which their name is perpetuated, Earra Ghaidheal (Argyll). As their territorial influence extended so did their language and from the 9th to the 11th centuries Gaelic was spoken throughout the country. For many centuries the language was the same as the language of Ireland; there is little evidence of much divergence before the 13th century. Even up to the 18th century the bards adhered to the strict literary standards of Old Irish.

The Viking invasions from AD 800 brought linguistic influences which are evident in many of the coastal place names of the Highlands.

Gaelic culture flourished in the Highlands until the 18th century and the Jacobite rebellions. After the Battle of Culloden in 1746 many Gaelic speakers were forced from their ancestral lands; this 'ethnic cleansing' by landlords and governments culminated in the Highland Clearances of the 19th century. Although still studied at academic level, the spoken language declined, being regarded as a mere 'peasant' language of no modern significance.

It was only in the 1970s that Gaelic began to make a comeback with a new generation of young enthusiasts who were determined that it should not be allowed to die. People from all over Scotland, and indeed worldwide, are beginning to appreciate their Gaelic heritage.

After two centuries of decline, the language is now being encouraged through financial help from government agencies and the EU. Gaelic education is flourishing from playgroups to tertiary levels. This renaissance flows out into the field of music, literature, cultural events and broadcasting.

The Gaelic language has a vital role to play in the life of modern Scotland.

MAKING CONVERSATION

Good morning.
Madainn mhath. madding va
Good afternoon/Good evening.
Feasgar math. fesskurr ma
Good night.
Oidhche mhath. uh eech uh va
How are you?
Ciamar a tha thu? kimmer uh ha oo?
Very well, thank you.
Glè mhath, tapadh leat. gley va, tappuh let
I'm well, thank you.
Tha mi gu math, ha mee goo ma,
tapadh leat. tappuh let
That's good.
'S math sin. sma shin
Please.
Mas e do thoil e. mahs eh doh hawl eh
Thank you.
Tapadh leat. tappuh let
Many thanks.
Mòran taing. moe ran ta eeng
You're welcome.
'Se do bheatha. sheh doh veh huh
I beg your pardon.
B'àill leibh. baaluv
Excuse me.
Gabh mo leisgeul. gav mo lishk yal
I'm sorry.
Tha mi duilich. ha mee dooleech
Do you speak (have) Gaelic?
A bheil Gàidhlig agad? uh vil ga lick ackut?

Yes, a little.
   Tha, beagan.   ha, beg an
Not much.
   Chan eil mòran.   chan yil moe ran
What's your name?
   De an t ainm a tha ort?   jae an tannam uh ha orsht?
I'm ...
   Is mise ...   is meeshuh ...
Good health/Cheers!
   Slàinte mhath!   slahntchuh va!
Goodbye. (lit: Blessings go with you)
   Beannachd leat.   b yan achd let
Goodbye. (The same with you)
   Mar sin leat.   mar shin let

FOOD & DRINK

I'm hungry.
   Tha an t-acras orm.   ha an tac russ orrom
I'm thirsty.
   Tha am pathadh orm.   ha am pah ugh orrom
I'd like ...
   Bu toigh leam ...   boo tawl lehum
I don't like ...
   Cha toigh leam ...   chah tawl lehum
That was good.
   Bha siud math.   va shood ma
Very good.
   Glè mhath.   gley va

a biscuit	*brioscaid*	briskatch
bread	*aran*	aran
broth/soup	*brot*	broht
butter	*ìm*	eem
cheese	*càise*	kashuh
cream	*bàrr*	baahrr
dessert	*mìlsean*	meehlshuhn
fish	*iasg*	eeusk
meat	*feòil*	fehyawl
oatcakes	*aran coirce*	aran korkuh
peas	*peasair*	pessir
porridge	*lite*	chuh
potatoes	*buntàta*	boontahtuh
salmon	*bradan*	brahdan
vegetables	*glasraich*	glasreech

a cup of coffee	*cupa cofaidh*	coopa cawfee
a cup of tea	*cupa tì*	coopa tee
black coffee	*cofaidh dubh*	cawfee dooh
black tea	*tì dhubh*	tee dhooh
with milk	*le bainne*	leh bahnyuh
with sugar	*leh le siùcar*	shooh car
a glass of water	*glainne uisge*	glahnyuh ooshkuy
a glass of wine	*glainne fìon*	glahnyuh feeuhn
beer	*leann*	lyawn
red wine	*fìon dearg*	feeuhn jerrack
white wine	*fìon geal*	feeuhn gyahl
whisky	*uisge beatha*	ooshkuy beh huh

Glossary

A

AA – Automobile Association
abhainn – river
ABTA – Association of British Travel Agents
aye – yes/always

B

BABA – book-a-bed-ahead scheme
bag – reach the top of (as in to 'bag a couple of peaks' or 'Munro bagging')
bailey – the space enclosed by castle walls
bairn – child
ben – mountain
blackhouse – low-walled stone cottage with thatch or turf roof and earth floors; shared by both humans and cattle and typical of the Outer Hebrides until early 20th century
böd – originally a simple trading booth used by fishing communities, today it refers to basic accommodation for walkers etc
bothy – hut or mountain shelter
brae – hill
broch – defensive tower
BT – British Telecom
BTA – British Tourist Authority
burgh – town
burn – stream

C

cairn – pile of stones to mark path or junction, also peak
carry-out – takeaway food
ceilidh – pronounced *kay*-lay, informal entertainment and dance
Celtic High Cross – a large, elaborately carved stone cross decorated with biblical scenes and Celtic interlace designs dating from the eighth to tenth centuries
close – entrance to an alley
corrie – circular hollow on a hillside
craic – from Irish Gaelic, conversation, gossip, fun, good times, also written as 'crack'
craig – exposed rock

D

dene – valley
dirk – dagger
doocot – dovecote
dram – whisky measure
dun – fort

F

firth – estuary

G

glen – valley

H

haar – fog off the North Sea
Hogmanay – New Year's Eve
howff – pub or shelter
HS – Historic Scotland

K

ken – know
kirk – church
kyle – narrow strait of water

L

law – round hill
laird – estate owner
land – tenement
links – golf course
linn – waterfall
lochan – small loch

M

machair – grass and wildflower-covered dunes
MBA – Mountain Bothies Association
Mercat Cross – a symbol of the trading rights of a market town or village, usually found in the centre of town and usually a focal point for the community
merse – saltmarsh
motte – early Norman fortification consisting of a raised, flattened mound with a keep on top; when attached to a bailey it is known as a motte-and-bailey
MCS – Mountaineering Council of Scotland
muckle – big
Munro – mountain of 3000 feet (914m) or higher
Munro bagger – a hill walker who tries to climb all the Munros in Scotland

N

ness – headland
NNR – National Nature Reserve, managed by the SNH
NTS – National Trust for Scotland

O

OS – Ordnance Survey

P

pap – breast-shaped hill

pend – arched gateway

Picts – early inhabitants of north and east Scotland (from the Latin pictus, meaning 'painted', after their body paint decorations)

provost – mayor

R

RAC – Royal Automobile Association

reiver – raider

rhinn or **rhin** – headland

rood – an old Scots word for a cross

RNLI – Royal National Lifeboat Institute

RSA – Royal Scottish Academy

RSPB – Royal Society for the Protection of Birds

S

Sassenach – from Gaelic Sasannach, meaning anyone who is not a Highlander (including Lowland Scots)

sett – tartan pattern, or cobble stone

SMC – Scottish Mountaineering Club

SNH – Scottish Natural Heritage, a government organisation directly responsible for safeguarding and improving Scotland's natural heritage

sporran – purse worn around waist with the kilt

SRWS – Scottish Rights of Way and Access Society

SSSI – Site of Special Scientific Interest

STB – Scottish Tourist Board

strath – valley

SYHA – Scottish Youth Hostel Association

T

TIC – Tourist Information Centre

tor – bare, rocky hill, or outcrop of granite

tron – public weighbridge

trows – mythical little people (Shetland)

twitcher – bird-watcher

U

uisge-beatha – whisky (literally, 'water of life')

V

vennel – narrow street

voe – inlet (Shetland)

W

way – walking trail

wean – child

wynd – lane

GLOSSARY

Behind the Scenes

THIS BOOK

This is the 3rd edition of Lonely Planet's *Scotland*. The 1st edition was written by Tom Smallman and Graeme Cornwallis. Neil Wilson coordinated the 2nd edition, with contribution from Graeme Cornwallis. Neil Wilson returned to Scotland to coordinate this new edition, with fellow author Alan Murphy.

THANKS FROM THE AUTHORS

Neil Wilson Many thanks to all the helpful and enthusiastic staff at Tourist Information Centres throughout the country, to the travellers I met who chipped in with recommendations, and to Drew at Ardbeg for fixing my bike while I toured the distillery. Thanks also to Carol Downie for help and advice on restaurants and shopping, and to Ruth Jessop for her helpful suggestions. Finally, thanks to co-author Alan (that was some hangover, by the way!).

Alan Murphy Firstly I would like to thank my partner, Justine Vaisutis, and my family for their support. Thanks also to Bryan McRitchie and Andrew Stechmann for their friendship and assistance. All the Tourist Information Centres were a welcoming fountain of information, particularly in Glasgow (Tom Rice and Moira Dyer), Anstruther, Dunkeld, Stirling and St Andrews. Thanks to Cheryl and Nicola at First for their help with bus timetables. Lastly thanks to all those I met along the way for the friendly patter and for making Scotland the very special place it is.

CREDITS

This title was commissioned and developed in Lonely Planet's London office by Amanda Canning. Cartography for this guide was developed by Mark Griffiths. Overseeing production were Ray Thomson (Project Manager) and Kyla Gillzan (Editorial House Style Coordinator). Thanks to the cartographic team, Joelene Kowalski (Coordinator), Simon Tillema, Chris Tsismetzis and Piotr Czajkowski; to the editors and proof-readers who helped EdInk, including Miriam Cannell, Alexandra Payne, Kate Church, Ann Philpott and Liz Calthorpe; and to Max McMaster for creating the index. Quentin Frayne prepared the language chapter. James Hardy designed the cover. Thanks to P.A.G.E. people, Jenni Quinn and Peter Dyson, who laid the book out and made everything fit on the page.

Thanks also to Adriana Mammarella, Jennifer Garrett, Meredith Mail, Bridget Blair, Charlotte Keown, Stephanie Pearson, Helen Christinis, Yvonne Bischofberger, Geoff Stringer, Huw Fowles, Michelle Lewis, Glenn van der Knijff, Michelle Glynn, Andrew Tudor, Ben Handicott, David Burnett and Mark Germanchis for their contributions to the title.

Last but not least, thanks to the authors – for all your hard work and patience along the way.

Series Publishing Manager Virginia Maxwell oversaw the redevelopment of the country guides series with help from Maria Donohoe. Regional Publishing Manager Katrina Browning steered the development of this title. The series was designed by James Hardy, with mapping development by Paul Piaia. The series development team included Shahara Ahmed, Susie Ashworth,

---

THE LONELY PLANET STORY

The story begins with a classic travel adventure: Tony and Maureen Wheeler's 1972 journey across Europe and Asia to Australia. There was no useful information about the overland trail then, so Tony and Maureen published the first Lonely Planet guidebook to meet a growing need.

From a kitchen table, Lonely Planet has grown to become the largest independent travel publisher in the world, with offices in Melbourne (Australia), Oakland (USA), London (UK) and Paris (France).

Today Lonely Planet guidebooks cover the globe. There is an ever-growing list of books and information in a variety of media. Some things haven't changed. The main aim is still to make it possible for adventurous travellers to get out there – to explore and better understand the world.

At Lonely Planet we believe travellers can make a positive contribution to the countries they visit – if they respect their host communities and spend their money wisely.

Gerilyn Attebery, Jenny Blake, Anna Bolger, Verity Campbell, Erin Corrigan, Nadine Fogale, Dave McClymont, Leonie Mugavin, Rachel Peart, Lynne Preston and Howard Ralley.

THANKS FROM LONELY PLANET

Many thanks to the travellers who used the last edition and wrote to us with helpful hints, useful advice and interesting anecdotes:

A Christopher Abbott, Rato Allenspach, Florin Amzica, Alison Armstrong, Barry & Tricia Arnold **B** Mauro Barbero, Paul Barbour, Mathias Berenger Barbara Bodnar, Holly & Rob Borham, Dr Thomas Braeuniger, A Bregman, Mike Breslin, Ken Bunt, Estelle Burgunder, Damon Burn, Christian Byhahn **C** Christopher Calvert, Julie Carroll, Steve Charlton, Yee Cheng, Hilary Clements, Keith Cocks, Diane Collins, Pete Connors, Cathleen Conway, M Cooper, W B Cooper, Lynda Cotton, Marlene Crivello, Joanne Cumine, Pam Currie **D** Ella Delderfield, Barbara Dijke, Fred Dobbin **E** Dr Ilya V Eigenbrot, Renee & John Elliott, Franklin Engel, Svend Erik Steenfeldt **F** Kevin Farrell, Christopher Farmer, Ian Fleming, Carol Forsyth, Simon Francis, Carl Franks, Bjorn Fuchtenkord, Sheryl Fullner **G** Sylvie Gagnon, Michael Gdak, Don Gibson, Betty Giraud, Ingvar Grans, Emily Greenman, Rebecca Griffey, Rachael Griggs, David Gyger **H** Thera Hamel, Carla Hanson, Ian Harrison, Dorsey & Hal Holappa, Nevil Hopley, Joanne Horvath, Matt Hoskins, Andreas Huber **I** Andrew Inglis, Susan Irwin, Jodie Ivers **J** Agnes Jackson, Jennifer Jameson, Kerry Jamieson, Merel Janssens, N Johnson **K** Pako Karabetyan, Mattias Karlsson, Catherine Kinghorn, Jenny Kohn **L** Sean Laing, Terry C Lansdown, Raelene Leach, Thomas Lehmann, Carol Lewis, Jenee Libby, Chris Little, Heather & Denis Liuzzi, Bill Loftus, Sarah Luchansky **M** Liz Macleod, Tara MacMillan, Ross Marlay, Jayne Marshall, Charlotte Martensson, Ben Medley, Patricia Mastrobuono, Phillip Mattle, Barbero Mauro, Laura McLean, M McColl, Helene Mercier, Martin Miller, D W Moore, Heather Moore, Jean Morton, Lisa Munroe, Roberta Murray, Thomas Murray, Gabe Murtagh **N** Stan Nelissen **P** Shaun Paisley, Lucy Parr, Antoine Pécard, Marco Perezzani, Sonya Polis, Stephanie Potts, Jan Purdy **R** Alison Rae, Andy & Philippa Rands, Viola Retzlaff, Sally T Ringe, Andy Robinson, Fernando Rocco, Marjan Romeijn, Jenny Ross, Adam Rudes, Cassie Ryalls **S** Ian Sandles, Gisela Schmitt, Jolanda Schmutz, Katie M Schroeder, A Schneeberger, W Schuurman, Ron Schweikert, George Scott,

Dawn Severnuk, Tiana Sidey, Ruth Spellman, Richard Spencer, Ursula Spitzbart, Mr & Mrs Stanley, Craig Stephen, Dave Stewart, Rebecca Stewart, Tracy Stewart, Jamie Strachan, Vanessa Stubbs, Skye Suttie **T** Kris Tay, Marina Taylor Hehn, Christine Teelken, Gordon & Deborah Trousdale, Michele Tulino **V** Marc Van Opstal, Andrew Veech, Jacques Vejux **W** Mary Beth Walker, Pat Waugh, M Webb, John Wendt, Elena Wiens, Brandyn Wilimovsky, Heather Williams, J T Williams, Scott Williamson, Sally Wingate, Mr T Witney, Sjoerd Wolbertus **Y** D Yudhope, Raymond Yung

ACKNOWLEDGMENTS

Many thanks to the following for the use of their content:
Mountain High Maps® Copyright © 1993 Digital Wisdom, Inc.

SEND US YOUR FEEDBACK

We love to hear from travellers – your comments keep us on our toes and help make our books better. Our well-travelled team reads every word on what you loved or loathed about this book. Although we cannot reply individually to postal submissions, we always guarantee that your feedback goes straight to the appropriate authors, in time for the next edition. Each person who sends us information is thanked in the next edition – and the most useful submissions are rewarded with a free book.

To send us your updates – and find out about LP events, newsletters and travel news – visit our award-winning website: **www.lonelyplanet.com**.

Note: We may edit, reproduce and incorporate your comments in Lonely Planet products such as guidebooks, websites and digital products, so let us know if you don't want your comments reproduced or your name acknowledged. For a copy of our privacy policy visit www.lonelyplanet.com/privacy.

434

Index

000 Map pages
000 Location of colour photographs

INDEX

000 Map pages
000 Location of colour photographs

000 Map pages
000 Location of colour photographs

INDEX

000 Map pages
000 Location of colour photographs

444

MAP LEGEND

ROUTES

	Tollway		One-Way Street
	Freeway		Unsealed Road
	Primary Road		Street Mall/Steps
	Secondary Road		Tunnel
	Tertiary Road		Walking Tour
	Lane		Walking Tour Detour
	Under Construction		Walking Trail
	Track		Walking Path

TRANSPORT

	Ferry		Rail
	Metro		Cable Car, Funicular
	Bus Route		

HYDROGRAPHY

	River, Creek		Water
	Canal		

BOUNDARIES

	International		Regional, Suburb
	State, Provincial		

AREA FEATURES

	Beach, Desert		Land
	Building		Mall
	Campus		Park
	Cemetery, Christian		Sports
	Forest		Urban

POPULATION

◎	CAPITAL (NATIONAL)	◉	CAPITAL (STATE)
●	Large City	●	Medium City
●	Small City	○	Town, Village

SYMBOLS

Sights/Activities
- Beach
- Castle, Fortress
- Christian
- Diving, Snorkeling
- Monument
- Museum, Gallery
- Point of Interest
- Pool
- Ruin
- Skiing
- Zoo, Bird Sanctuary

Eating
- Eating

Drinking
- Drinking

Entertainment
- Entertainment

Shopping
- Shopping

Sleeping
- Sleeping
- Camping

Transport
- Airport, Airfield
- Bus Station
- Taxi Rank

Information
- Bank, ATM
- Embassy/Consulate
- Hospital, Medical
- Information
- Internet Facilities
- Parking Area
- Police Station
- Post Office, GPO
- Telephone

Geographic
- Lighthouse
- Lookout
- Mountain, Volcano
- National Park
- Pass, Canyon
- River Flow

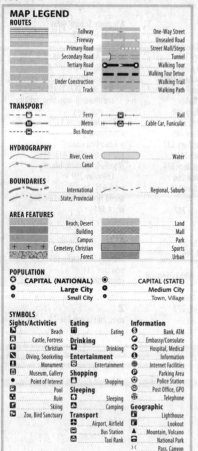

LONELY PLANET OFFICES

Australia
Head Office
Locked Bag 1, Footscray, Victoria 3011
☎ 03 8379 8000, fax 03 8379 8111
talk2us@lonelyplanet.com.au

USA
150 Linden St, Oakland, CA 94607
☎ 510 893 8555, toll free 800 275 8555
fax 510 893 8572, info@lonelyplanet.com

UK
72–82 Rosebery Ave,
Clerkenwell, London EC1R 4RW
☎ 020 7841 9000, fax 020 7841 9001
go@lonelyplanet.co.uk

France
1 rue du Dahomey, 75011 Paris
☎ 01 55 25 33 00, fax 01 55 25 33 01
bip@lonelyplanet.fr, www.lonelyplanet.fr

Published by Lonely Planet Publications Pty Ltd
ABN 36 005 607 983

© Lonely Planet 2004

© photographers as indicated 2004

Cover photographs by Lonely Planet Images: The Braemar Highland Gathering: Kilts, the Stewart tartan, Scotland, Jonathan Smith (front); The remains of Urquhart Castle on the shores of Loch Ness, Highland, Dennis Johnson (back). Many of the images in this guide are available for licensing from Lonely Planet Images: www.lonelyplanetimages.com.

All rights reserved. No part of this publication may be copied, stored in a retrieval system, or transmitted in any form by any means, electronic, mechanical, recording or otherwise, except brief extracts for the purpose of review, and no part of this publication may be sold or hired, without the written permission of the publisher.

Printed through Colorcraft Ltd, Hong Kong.
Printed in China

Lonely Planet and the Lonely Planet logo are trademarks of Lonely Planet and are registered in the US Patent and Trademark Office and in other countries.

Lonely Planet does not allow its name or logo to be appropriated by commercial establishments, such as retailers, restaurants or hotels. Please let us know of any misuses: www.lonelyplanet.com/ip.

Although the authors and Lonely Planet have taken all reasonable care in preparing this book, we make no warranty about the accuracy or completeness of its content and, to the maximum extent permitted, disclaim all liability arising from its use.